ABOUT THE AU

George Edmunds has been looking for treasure since he was a teenager, and he has been diving off coasts around the world for decades. His fascination with buried treasure and shipwrecks led him to publish two books on the subject - *The Gower Coast* (1979-89, Regional Publications, hardback and paperback, three editions, 2,000 copies sold) and *Kidd, the Search for His Treasure* (1996, Pentland Press, hardback, 1,100 copies sold worldwide). His second book is recognised as the definitive work on the Captain Kidd treasure charts found before World War Two. Email feedback shows that the English edition has been sold around the world and is still sought after as a reference work. *Anson's Gold* is his third book. He has a loyal readership and is an expert on the infamous pirate Captain Kidd and his treasure charts.

BY THE SAME AUTHOR

The Gower Coast (Three editions),
Regional Publications, 1979

KIDD: the search for his treasure,
Pentland Press, 1996

FROM AN ENGRAVING ON THE LICHFIELD ESTATE
CAPTION; *The Right Honourable George Lord Anson Baron of Soberton, one of the Lords of His Majesty's Most Honourable Privy Council, Vice Admiral of Great Britain, Admiral of the Blue Squadron of His Majesty's Fleet, and first Lord Commissioner of the Admiralty.*
With thanks to Lord Lichfield

For John.
Regards
George Edmunds
Aug 2016

ANSON'S GOLD

and the Secret to
Captain Kidd's Charts

by George Edmunds

Published by
Filament Publishing Ltd
16, Croydon Road, Waddon, Croydon,
Surrey, CR0 4PA, United Kingdom
Telephone +44 (0)20 8688 2598
Fax +44 (0)20 7183 7186
info@filamentpublishing.com
www.filamentpublishing.com

ISBN - 978-1-910125-38-0

Printed by IngramSpark

For my mother, Mary;
a treasure always there for me.

ANSON'S GOLD
and the secret to Captain Kidd's Charts

CHAPTER LIST

PART 4

PART 5

PART 6

PART 7

PART 10

FOREWORD

Strange, you may think, that I couldn't think of anyone of note within the treasure hunting fraternity (or outside it!) who would have the knowledge or experience to write a foreword for this book. The problem is that with this book, we are treading new ground. There just is not anyone out there who has encompassed this story before in its entirety and can therefore judge it. Not only that, embodied within this story are revelations never before made public. Unsolved mysteries are solved, undeciphered codes are deciphered, but these are mysteries and codes not revealed as such before.

Anyone reading the manuscript then as a precursor to writing a foreword has to be aware that he is probably learning from it. Yes, there are so-called experts – and I say that in not a derogatory way whatsoever. There will be people who think they have the authority to write on subjects covered in the coming pages, for example Rennes-le-Château, Oak Island, Cocos Island, the Juan Fernandez Island treasure hunt and Captain Kidd's charts, to name but a few. I agree that a lot of these authors will be very knowledgeable about their chosen subject. But some are 'cocooned' within that subject, they cannot or will not look outside that world and therefore do not recognise very real outside influences that could make them stop and re-evaluate their train of thought.

The only researcher/author/investigator qualified to write a foreword for this book would be someone who has recognised already that regarding the subjects above everything is not as it seems and one must not believe everything that is read. Not only that, he would have to know that the subjects mentioned, with others, are all connected in some way like a big jigsaw. You may appreciate then why it is I who is writing this!

I want to include a statement here made by one of our early admirals. You will see from it that he at least would have understood this book. His story follows later in the book and here he writes after a failed attempt at looking for a buried treasure after leaving the Navy.

'It seems clear to me that some traditional bits of "my" story had taken root, such as the exact sum of two million pounds, the dead body, and one survivor to the pirates. One can recognize, also, fragments of "Black Beard," "Captain Kidd," "Percival Keene" (a title character from one of Captain Marryat's books. GE) *und others with a superstructure of invention; but thus it is in all history, truth and falsehood are mingled together in one gorgeous and brittle mass.'*

From *Sea Drift* by Rear-Admiral Hercules Robinson. Published 1858

You will appreciate the statement... *truth and falsehood are mingled together...* as you read the coming pages.

George Edmunds, Dorset, 2014

Since writing the above, the content of which is broadly true, I was embarrassed a little by the encomiast aspect of it and I should really try and get an outside opinion of the book. In one of my rare inspirational moments it came to me – what about Lord Lichfield? A direct descendant of Lord Anson and the current Earl of Lichfield. Would he be interested in looking at the MS? I quickly realised his input could be invaluable to the project. When I approached the Earl (he said to call him Tom!) with a précis of the book he was most enthusiastic about my work and graciously agreed to write his thoughts and memories as follows:

'As a boy my head was full of stories of the high seas, crashing waves, huge thunderstorms, shipwrecks, washed-up sailors on small deserted islands, pirates and of course...treasure. My father had told me of treasure and mysteries surrounding its wherabouts but it was never clear what this 'treasure' was or where it was, I just remember treasure being mentioned. He was a wonderful raconteur but did exaggerate frequently so I grew up having my suspicions about the validity of it all. Growing up at Shugborough was a paradise for a small child with a vivid imagination and a tendency to daydream. From gazing at the charts to sitting on the cannons from the 'Centurion'.

Once I had grown up my father revealed to me about the huge numbers of 'nutty letters' he used to receive at Shugborough, many were anonymous and often filled with nothing other than a code of some form but there were themes running through them: et in Arcadia, Poussin, Knights Templar, Free Masons and most mentioned it was all relevant to the/a treasure.

I had always had a fascination with one of my ancestors...Admiral George Anson. Incredible leadership, enduring loyalty, lifelong friendship, murder, betrayal, mutiny and the endless endurance required for such expeditions all fed my thirst for adventure and to some extent still does to this day. (Indeed, Tom has his own extreme fishing adventure company trecking to some of the remotest parts of the world, GE). All of this, combined with an inverted Poussin relief in the grounds of Shugborough, un-deciphered code and stories of lost treasure really did get me hooked. Centuries have now passed, the questions remain unanswered and still no hidden treasure found to this day. This may all be about to change with the publication of this book which quite literally blows the lid off previous theories. George Edmunds has once again produced a beguiling book that will quite literally change the course of history. A renowned author, maritime scholar, a forte for solving treasure mysteries and now it seems a code breaker too. Besides telling my ancestors secret history, this is a thrilling and fascinating book of real events, real people and real treasure mysteries explained and solved. Forget 'Treasure Island', this is the real thing!

Thomas, Earl of Lichfield, 2015

A note regarding the picture and diagram reproductions in this book. The original manuscript contained - for clarity - many illustrations and photographs in colour. For financial and reproduction reasons, the international version of this book could only be presented in black and white. Apologies therefore for any confusion where there is a text reference to colour and where dark shades of grey detract from the clarity and colour of the original. The eBook version is in colour.

INTRODUCTION

In 1996, my second book *KIDD. the search for his treasure* was published. Years earlier, as a teenager, I had first read about the mysterious treasure charts of Captain William Kidd. An article had appeared about them in a now defunct magazine called *The Wide World*. That was the start of my fascination with pirate buried treasure. A fascination that has taken me on a literary journey to many islands and stories of treasure around the world.

How then did *this* particular journey begin? My Kidd book had aroused a lot of interest, because for the first time the complete and true story of Kidd's treasure charts found in the years leading up to WW2 was told. I had also provided the solution as to where the traditional spot marked 'X' was. Nobody had deciphered the clues on the charts before. Whilst the mystery of the treasure location was solved, I was not totally convinced as to the island location, or by the claims of others. One, of course, is no good without the other. I was 99% certain as to the accuracy of my work about the history of the charts, and the stories surrounding them. The remaining 1% of uncertainty was due to some aspects of cartography and questions regarding the British Museum's involvement in the charts authentication.

The breakthrough about the island's identity came about a year after the book's publication. A reader of the book, Robin C of Birmingham, notified me of his discovery of a rather interestingly shaped island just off Hong Kong, an area I had indicated as a possibility. After research, investigation and a visit by both of us, this island so well fitted all my findings and deductions, it suppressed the remaining 1% of my uncertainty. The decoding of the clues also pinpointed this island exactly; it looked like the island of the charts really existed.

So my final run-in with Kidd would possibly be getting another book out of that story. That was to be the end of my involvement with Captain William Kidd and I could move on to other projects. The sun was shining and as far as I could see ahead, it was plain sailing all the way there.

How wrong can one be? Life always comes up with the unexpected. Sometimes it is not what is ahead of you but what is behind you that you have to look for.

In 2003/4, I received a tap on the shoulder in the form of two emails from one Mike Neon (not his real name) - this is the name he chooses to use on the Internet (MN in text that follows) - who resides in Sydney, Australia. They were about a year apart and I cannot remember why I did not respond to the first one. However, his second email caught my eye because of the statement, "Would you be interested to know that the Kidd charts are fake?" Well, of course I would! Who does this guy think he is? Challenging **my** authority on Kidd's charts! I may have had my own suspicions about the charts but hey, this guy is lecturing me, and I am supposed to be the expert!

It turned out that he had a copy of my book he was using as a research tool for a project he was working on. He therefore knew that a small percentage of me had always been a bit suspicious of the charts. But at that time (pre-1996) there had been more going *for* the charts than against them. My research was rather confined to within the Kidd circle looking at the story and history of the charts with no real reason for going outside the loop looking at any tenuous links.

To cut a long story short (the long one comes later), over the next few months I was presented with information that made me doubt the veracity of a lot of what I believed about the Kidd charts. The pressure was increased by telling me he had evidence the charts were a hoax. I counteracted by sending him my proof, an annotated chart disclosing the name and location of the Hong Kong island together with explanations and the coded calculations confirming that it was the right place. These figures couldn't be refuted. "How could it be a hoax?" I exclaimed. I couldn't get my head around that. "For what purpose? It is too complex with no sensible reasoning and therefore not plausible to be a hoax, and anyway as pointed out, the decoded figures fit our island!" Also I pointed out, if a hoax, someone had to benefit and someone had to be fooled; there were no beneficiaries here and who could the victim be? "Where's the proof?" I demanded.

An image of an early 20th century chart of Juan Fernandez Island arrived, its 25 cent price proclaiming its age and commercial origin. I had to admit, that when inverted the chart was worryingly similar in appearance to Kidd's Island.

"What about Latcham and the Herradura story?" I was asked. These are in the public domain! Well in my defence I had to say, that was well outside my research circle, with no direct links at all to Kidd, and being in Spanish I doubt if I would have ever heard of this story. That the JF chart was similar to the Kidd charts could be just an interesting coincidence. However, I realised that whilst fighting in my corner, I was slowly sinking to the floor under the weight of the attack. Eventually, after investigation, I had to succumb. The old 25 cent chart of JF Island was the turning point, and as it turns out, indeed the key to the hoax.

It was also the turning point about any doubts I had regarding the genuineness of what I was being confronted with; a unique and untold treasure hunting story that went well beyond the Kidd charts embroiling one of our most famous admirals. A story was unfolding that convinced me he was onto something special and intriguing. I was impressed by the tenacity and thoroughness with which he tackled his research. I admired his self-belief and you just couldn't argue with a lot he was coming up with.

My interest in the Kidd Charts as I knew of them originally, diminished as the reality became evident. I have tried to suggest and direct others who contact me about the Kidd Charts that perhaps things are not what they think they are, but little heed is taken. I comment more on that later in the book.

MN, not being a writer, had decided to seek out someone who would be interested in writing a book about what the research was discovering, but would also be intelligent enough to work on what was proving to be some highly intellectual concepts. Many questions remained to be answered and a lot of research remained to be done. He started by contacting experts in various areas encompassed by his overall work. Some didn't want to know anything outside their world view because as far as they were concerned, they knew it all. Others, when confronted by something that contradicted their work, just petulantly stopped communicating.

MN had used my Kidd book as part of his research and, studying my work, decided that I was a likely candidate. My research and solutions he could see were close to what should have been worked out by someone following the clues within the Kidd charts. The exact solution he could see was missing not due to any defect in my reasoning but due to a lack of certain knowledge outside my circle of research. There was also a 1% window of uncertainty to work on, more than enough for him to drive a tank into! So one day, he sent out an email to me. Thus started a collaboration and partnership[1] aimed at telling the complete and true story of the search for a fabulous treasure that I believe still lies buried on a lonely island. Whilst the treasure is nothing to do with Captain Kidd, this book lays to rest the mystery and enigma of the Kidd charts and shows how a secret expedition by our Admiral Lord George Anson was the reason for them.

A truly fascinating, incredible, sometimes unbelievable but intriguing true story. Everything you need to know about this treasure and its location is to be found in this book. One of the biggest surprises was how research linked us to Jerusalem, the 'Holy Grail', the Freemasons and the Templars. We also lay open the 'religious' treasure mystery of Rennes-le-Château. This led, as you will see, to Nicholas Poussin's intriguing painting The Shepherds of Arcadia and an enigmatic coded monument in the grounds of Shugborough Hall, Lord George Anson's family seat. All these things we discovered were connected in some way.

A lot of famous and traditional buried treasure stories had to be looked at, from the Atlantic Ocean to the South Pacific Ocean, including Cocos Island, the infamous 'Money Pit' on Oak Island and the 'Loot of Lima'. These all appear to be individual treasure stories, but, through research and investigations, I can show they nearly all in fact, have a common DNA. They are nearly all linked to one real event in history.

An exciting journey and I like to think that between us, we have cleared up a few mysteries on the way. As MN said, somewhat tongue in cheek, "Bletchley Park – bloody amateurs!"[2]

It is a complex story and took forever trying to present it in a coherent, logical, interesting way. One of the problems was that in a conventional treasure-hunting story, you have a beginning, middle and end. For example, treasure map found – decode and work out where island is, who, what and why, go to island and dig up treasure! In our case, we knew where the island was, that came early on in the research. We had to work out who buried what, when and why and unravel many stories of deceit on the way. A lot of it achieved by what one calls 'Reverse Engineering'. It has not been easy. You need your wits about you, as there is a lot of detail and mystery to absorb and understand, with intricate stories and a number of false trails, all interconnected. Add a mix of fascinating stories of murder, conflict, treasure looting, code-breaking, history and recovery attempts and you have an idea of what to expect in the coming pages.

I frequently use the term 'treasure' or 'lost treasure' in the text. This refers always to the story object or subject quest, and no other treasure.

I can only hope that the above gives you the impetus to turn the pages and encourage you to absorb more.

To the best of my belief, the information contained within this book was correct at the time of writing.

I started this introduction with mention of my Kidd book. Readers of *that* book reading this will be pleased to know that within the coming pages is the sequel to the Kidd book. The enigma and mystery of those beguiling 'treasure' charts is finally wrapped up and laid to rest.

A word about the (my) writing style in this book. I am not a university graduate with a degree in English literature. So do not expect grand or delicate prose. My motto when writing has always been 'Write a book the way you like to read a book.' This book then is aimed mainly at the quintessential buried treasure hunter, including those actively searching and those searching for answers to long standing mysteries relating to buried treasures, charts and codes. So the coming pages are full of facts, stories, information and items of interest surrounding the book quest, all blended together in what is hopefully an enjoyable read. At the same time the book will provide most – if not all – the answers to the readers questions mentioned above.

You will find some things repeated. This to emphasize and remind you of something important. Also, with a book this size, it is unlikely to be read in one go and could be days or weeks before you pick it up again. A reminder saves you asking 'Now where did that come from?'

Where you think I may be 'waffling' on a bit, it is to make sure you are taking on board what I am trying to get over. You will also notice I am straight to the point, no messing around. I will have my say about something I feel strongly about, where necessary. After all, as the author, my book is the platform for me to say – within reason – what I want to say.

[1] Unfortunately, after a few years of working together, creating the manuscript, exchanging views and research etc. with the inevitable clashes of personality and differing opinions, MN abandoned the project, he said he was 'canning it', i.e. no more work. He had lost patience with certain aspects and didn't have the fortitude to carry on. I declared my belief in the book and would carry on and finish it. I had

spent too many years writing and was not going to abandon the work and research effort I had put in. I was later to learn he had created another manuscript (unpublished as far as I know). He knew I had fully solved the Shugborough code years ago (January 2005 for the record) so clearly my intellectual property yet his 'new' work was void of any recognition of my input and research contribution carried out over several years. This was a surprise to me, naturally having treated all our work with high confidentiality. Not the actions one would expect of a newly qualified solicitor! His deceit did nothing to further our relationship which for me terminated at that point. Regardless of this, where I use the term 'we' in the book, it is in recognition of the early part he played in the context it is used.

[2] Of WW2 Enigma Code fame. Shugborough Hall had organised a competition and invited the world's best code-breakers to decipher the letters on Lord Anson's *The Shepherd's Monument*. All had differing and unsatisfactory solutions. I was successful here because of a totally different approach. The 'monumental' (excuse the pun) discovery of the solution is revealed for the first time in this book.

Follow your star to the bitter end no
matter what the hazards or the perils;
no matter even if the star proves to be
a false guide and you die in the attempt.
You will have lived life to the full, you
will have enjoyed yourself and even if
you leave behind no material treasure,
you will leave riches in the hearts of
those who have drawn strength from
your strength and who will cherish
your memory until their day is done.

Mitchell Hedges

ANSON'S GOLD
Kidd's Charts

PART 1

CHAPTER 1

"But how do you know there's treasure on that island?" I was asked by an interested colleague.

"Because," I replied, "ten years of extensive research by myself and a colleague at the opposite end of the globe has confirmed it!"

"OK, but how do you know it's still there?" he responded.

"Because we unearthed evidence suggesting that about 90 years ago, it was still there. Expeditions prior to WW2 didn't find it, and besides that, the location is very remote; you could get a major airline to within maybe 600 miles, and then it is island hopping and boat charter. For these and other reasons that will become clear, I am confident it is still there."

Where to Start?

This is the story of the trail leading to a real treasure, not one of fiction, myth or imagination. It is a trail with many twists and turns. It is a trail that has many stories attributed to it. Each story is a building block to complete the bigger picture. Each could be said to be part of a complex jigsaw, and whilst many of these pieces are individual treasure stories which have been accepted in their own right, only by assembling the jigsaw can we begin to understand how and why these stories came about. A quandary then for me with this wealth of historical treasure stories to tell; where to start? There were several options;

    a) My Kidd book, for without it MN would have missed the important part the Kidd charts played, he would never have contacted me and therefore there would be no book.

    b) Four men who in the early nineteenth century found the location of this treasure; whether it was by design or luck, I am not too sure. The only survivor created a trail of deceit to lure investors that would enable him to get back to the island. The story he told was enough to finance a few major expeditions, before and after his death.

c) A Spanish Captain General, who loath to let this treasure fall into the wrong hands, was the one who originally buried it on a lone and desolate island.

d) Admiral Lord George Anson who searched for this treasure. Without his expedition and subsequent correspondence, there would be no story to tell.

e) The Templars, who kept a treasure hidden for centuries until finally removed by the Spanish nobleman.

f) Solomon and the Temple of Jerusalem treasure. A vast legendary treasure, looted several times over the centuries, the remnants taken to Spain and hidden by the Templars for safekeeping.

Without any of these options, there would be no book.

Historically speaking, Solomon would be the starting point. The Bible tells of the vast treasure once held within the magnificent portals of his Temple. Whether or not part of our treasure is linked to Solomon remains to be seen. But the treasures of Solomon and the Templars, whilst ingrained in history, are tantalising in that the legend makes us want to believe they existed. According to some historians, they did and we have descriptions of treasure including the fabled *Menorah* triumphantly paraded through Rome by Titus after one of the many lootings of Jerusalem and its Temple. More recently, documents have been unearthed in the same area where the *Dead Sea Scrolls* were discovered. These documents in the form of a rolled copper plate tell of treasures and where they are hidden. These are legendary treasures, ours is real.

It makes sense then that we start with documents of history and stories that prove the existence of *our* treasure; maybe we can then add any links, tenuous or otherwise, to a treasure of antiquity.

The hard evidence of historical documents associated with our quest should be the place to start. So let us begin with our own Lord George Anson, famous for his circumnavigation of the world in the early 1740s and for his capture of a great Spanish galleon. Later, as First Lord of the Admiralty, Anson sent a secret expedition to find a hidden treasure, believed to be of some great importance to the Royal Society and the State. Lord Anson's story provides the genesis treasure hunt. Besides giving mine the required credibility, it will also give a flavour of what is to come. There are many similar tales of the search for a fabulous buried treasure in the coming pages. With their stories of trials, hardships and disappointment, I show how they all relate to our quest. Anson's expedition was one of great secrecy, which explains why official documents are not available. The documents that *do* disclose this venture are in the form of private letters sent to Lord Anson by his lieutenant, who was dispatched to recover the treasure. These vital letters found their way into the archives and were, we believe, discovered accidentally before WW2. They were surreptitiously removed and found their way to Juan Fernandez Island off the coast of Chile in the mid 20th century, instigating a search there. This then will be the story I tell first, of Lord Anson and the ongoing treasure hunt on Juan Fernandez Island. It will take us on further to interwoven themes of murder, piracy, treasure expeditions old and new, ciphers, star-codes, the Freemasons and a monument bearing an unsolved cipher, situated in the grounds of Lord Anson's ancestral home.

The Story Begins

Early research provided me with solid links between Lord Anson and Juan Fernandez Island. We were brought here also by revelations found investigating the Kidd charts mystery; that story is covered in full in a later chapter. Research brought to light a book whose title is *El Tesoro de Lord Anson* by Anthony Westcott. This book published in Chile in 1999 is in Spanish which helps to explain why this story is little known. It tells the history and story of an ongoing hunt for buried treasure on Juan Fernandez Island, better known as the island made famous by Daniel Defoe in his book *Robinson Crusoe*. I will get to this important and very interesting book in due course. For the origins of our treasure, that which Anson searched for and that which is our ultimate goal, we first have to go back in time to the Manilla treasure galleons of Spain.

Ubilla's Legacy and Treachery

Towards the end of 1712, a fleet of five ships was assembled at Veracruz under the command of Captain General Juan Estaban Ubilla. At about the same time, the Tierra Firma fleet under the command of General Echeverz y Zubiro[1] arrived at Cartagena. These fleets, or *flotas*, were an integral part of an economic system that had developed early in the three centuries of Spanish rule in the New World. Convoys such as this had plied their trade since the late 16th century. Delayed, waiting for convoys, mule trains and loading, meant that this particular fleet would be nearly three years before they could leave their ports and the two fleets could converge in Havana, as was the custom. By July 1715, the combined fleet was ready to sail. This tremendous fleet, laden with 2,300 chests of newly minted coin, silver bars, gold pieces and exquisite Chinese porcelain, headed north along the Florida peninsula before heading east across the Atlantic to Spain. Florida's coast was as far as they got because less than a week after sailing, disaster struck when the fleet was devastated by a severe hurricane. Of the eleven ships which formed the convoy, ten were smashed into the Florida reefs and over a thousand men perished. Ubilla drowned with his fleet. He was last seen on the poop deck, dressed in silk, his hand resting on his sword. He was thrown into the sea with several hundred of his crewmen when his galleon struck a reef and disintegrated.

Ubilla's ship was most likely the *Capitana* and flagship of the fleet. Evidence suggests she was the old *Hampton Court*, a third-rate British man-of-war built in 1678, captured by the French in 1707 and subsequently handed over to Spain.

It was to be 250 years before Kip Wagner located the coral graves of these galleons. He recovered a fortune in Pieces of Eight, gold and artefacts. But this book is not to tell the story of that disaster and the subsequent recovery of the treasure. It is well documented elsewhere, particularly in Kip Wagner's book *Pieces of Eight* (New York, Dutton, 1967). Our interest lies in the story of a treasure buried on an island by Captain General Ubilla, before he sailed with the fleet and drowned. This is our 'lost treasure' and our link to Lord Anson.

A Dispute of Empires

Why would Ubilla want to hide his 'treasure' – whatever it was and in doing so deprive his country and crown of their due wealth? (Tho King demanded his 'Royal Quinto' or one fifth of the value of any treasure landed in Spain). During this period the dynasties of the Bourbon's and Hapsburgs disputed their rights to the throne of Spain. This, because the Habsburg dynasty in Spain had ended with the death of Charles 11 in 1700. Unable to have children he willed the Spanish crown to the Bourbon's of France through his grand-nephew Philip of Anjou. The rest of Europe including England was not happy with this proposed union of France and Spain and so started the Spanish War of Succession which didn't end until 1714. With Ubilla supporting the Habsburg's he was loath to see any of his and Spain's wealth fall into the hands of the French. So he decided that his particular very important cargo of treasure would not end up there – at least not until the political situation had been resolved. One story has it that Ubilla dispatched a galleon to Spain with a small quantity of treasure. This ship was sunk and we surmise this was intentional as Ubilla wanted the authorities to think the entire treasure due back in Spain had been lost.

Prior to the possible scenario outlined above, Ubilla would have been in the South Pacific off the West coast of South America. His hold probably full of gold and silver from the Potosi and Lima mints. His destination would have been Veracruz, the holding port for the South Pacific fleets. We are then led to believe that during the two-year wait here for convoys and ships to arrive, Ubilla left the port and disappeared with his galleon full of treasure. He was absent apparently for about 18 months. Nobody knows where he went.

The other scenario is that he diverted to a lonely island on the way back. At some time during (or after) this period he, or an emissary was in contact with the English – the enemy of the Burbon's. This may have happened even after Ubilla's death in 1715, we don't know. Years later the secret of this communication fell into the hands of Admiral Lord Anson.

Another story has it that Ubilla was a privateer in the service of Charles11 and had amassed a huge treasure in the South Pacific by fair means and foul. Due to the political situation created by his Kings death, he was at a dilemma with what to do with it. So until the situation was resolved and also fearing possible attacks by pirates, the treasure was buried far from prying eyes.

The Spanish War of Succession in effect ended in 1713 with the signing of the Treaty of Utrech. The French speaking Philip became the first King of the Bourbon dynasty in Spain with the title Philip V. One of the conditions of this ascendancy was he had to give up his rights to the throne of France.

One of the sources of information regarding Ubilla's movements *is* from Bernard Keiser. This is because our main source for this information is Bernard Keiser, a searcher on Juan Fernandez Island, who says he uncovered this evidence in the *Archivo de Indias*. This remains unverified but the link seems to make sense of what was to come. An approach to him suggesting that we had information that could be of mutual benefit went unanswered. We have had to rely therefore on Mr Keiser's research for this part of the story and Ubilla's actions. If Mr Keiser's research is correct, it explains the connection between an enigmatic monument in an English country estate and a desolate island the opposite side of the world. Fortunately for us, we also have the all-important evidence of the letters between Lord Anson and his lieutenant sent to recover the treasure. So, whether or not there is a factual link between a treasure that Lord Anson searched for and Captain General Juan Estaban Ubilla's hiding of his treasure, the fact remains that a very important treasure *was* searched for by our Admiral Lord Anson. It is this same Spanish treasure we shall be searching for in the coming pages.

Ubilla's galleon was seemingly sent on a secret mission – officially or unofficially, we do not know. The information that Lord Anson ultimately came into possession of, however, was considered of such vital importance that he sent a secret naval expedition to recover this hidden Spanish 'treasure'. The evidence of secret messages and possible secret meetings between the *Royal Society* and a high ranking Spanish naval officer or his emissary, implies something other than gold and silver may have been hidden. Whisperings of religious relics and the Templars have inevitably led to speculation that the *Holy Grail* might lie buried somewhere on a lonely island. Whatever it is that lies buried, this book tells the story of the intricate trail of confirmation of the treasure and the island where I know it to be buried.

So our trail begins and we must now begin to examine the stories around the island made famous in Daniel Defoe's *Robinson Crusoe.* It is here, on Juan Fernandez Island, that many believe Ubilla buried his King's gold. It is here, due to misinterpreted evidence and belief in the legend, the early searchers (pre-Keiser) believed Anson buried a treasure. Keiser's research and continuing activities promote the legend which lives on, despite nothing being found.

[1]Commanders of Spanish fleets were always military men, Generals in the case of Ubilla and Echeverz.

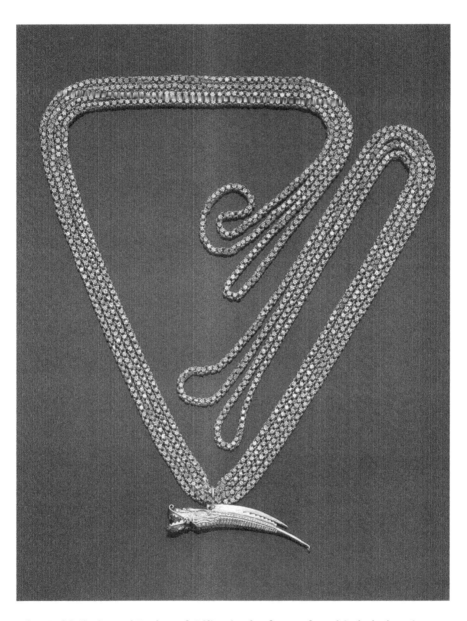

The Gold Chain and Badge of Office in the form of a whistle belonging to the commander of the fleet, Captain General Juan Esteban Ubilla. Found on the beach near Sebastian Inlet, East Florida in 1962, it came from the 'Cabin Wreck' located south of Sebastian Inlet.

CHAPTER 2

JUAN FERNANDEZ ISLAND AND THE MISNAMED TREASURE OF LORD ANSON

Juan Fernandez Island lies at latitude 33º 37′ South, longitude 78º 50′ West. It is some 360n.m. off the coast of Chile. On old maps it shows as 'Más a Tierra' (closer to the land). Soon, the name Juan Fernandez (the pilot who discovered it in 1574) will be confined to history, as in order to capitalise on the tourist appeal, the Chilean Government changed the name to 'Robinson Crusoe Island'. Also one of the nearer islands was changed to 'Alejandro Selkirk Island', the name of the real-life Robinson Crusoe abandoned on the island. The only town is San Juan Bautista in Cumberland Bay, founded in 1750 soon after the Spanish took official possession in 1742.

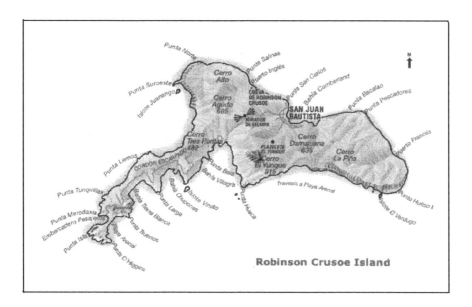

Robinson Crusoe Island

Buccaneers and pirates frequently made JFI their rendezvous and there are tales of treasure buried here. Many famous adventurers and travellers have over the centuries called here. Our interest lies with Anson; we know he stayed here for R & R in 1741 with his ship

Centurion whilst on his voyage around the world. Whilst no treasure was hidden by Anson here, nevertheless a legend lives on.

The story of the search here for Lord Anson's fabled treasure is, like most things, clouded by time but seems to have started in the early 1950s. An Italian yachtsman, Jorge di Giorgio landed at Cumberland Bay and heard about the legend of the treasure.

The following story is taken in part from *El Tesoro de Lord Anson* by Anthony Westcott:

Wanting to know more, he (Giorgio) contacted a Chilean friend living in England, this was Tita Diaz, who became Lady Inverchapel because of her marriage to Sir Archibald Kerr, who became Lord Inverchapel after a distinguished diplomatic career. She therefore had important contacts at a high level in British society.

Exhaustive enquiries into Lord Anson's career in the Navy revealed nothing of interest. Giorgio insisted there must be something somewhere as there is always an element of truth in a legend. Tita Diaz arranged to visit the Anson family home in Staffordshire, this is now called Shugborough Hall and open to the public. (The family of Lord Lichfield (now deceased), photographer of Royalty and descendant of Lord Anson, still had private rooms here up until 2010. GE)

However, in the post-war period the home was still a private residence and not open to visitors, except maybe to those with very good contacts.

Old Letters in Cypher

The story goes that in an old writing desk Tita Diaz found some old letters written in cipher and was allowed to take these away. Giorgio, on seeing them did not see how they could shed any light on his investigation, but his mother, Angelica Lyon just happened to be an expert in cryptograms and puzzles. By association of ideas and some knowledge she interpreted the letters thus:

THE HORSESHOE EXPEDITION (EXPEDICION HERRADURA)

Sent by Lord Anson to the South Seas in 1760
First document from the Castle of Lady Rock Savage (property of [owned by] Lord Anson)

"Orders executed, adverse circumstances forced me to bury the property of the crown in a new place and to blow up the ship. I await orders."

On a piece of paper attached to this letter is written: "This document arrived from Chile six months after my Lord passed away."

Second document in the same place: The map of a bay "Pascoy" with many lines; one indicating a point on the coast where the answer can be found. And written in a corner, as in the first document: "This map arrived from Chile fifteen months after my Lord passed away".

There is a third document which says: Altitude Schuba I Depth Yellow Stone I

Giorgio guessed that 'a point on the coast where the answer can be found' indicated the hiding place of the instructions for finding the treasure. He started a search by land and sea for a bay whose form resembled the map of 'Pascoy Bay', reaching the conclusion that it was Horcón to the north of Quintero. Realizing that this venture required more capitol than he had available, he formed a Company with his friend Louis Cousino. The two had met through high society social circles, Cousino belonged to a well-known and aristocratic family and it is believed Giorgio, who was Italian, was of noble ancestry.

Cousino began to go out at night, so as not to be seen, to search the beaches of Horcon. Guided by the old map, after a time of tracking he managed to locate a box that contained an envelope and, within it, a letter written in the same key as the documents sent previously from England.

Angelica Lyon, now an expert in the key, deciphered it obtaining the following text:

"I, Cornelius Patrick Webb, Captain of His Majesty's Navy and master of the UNICORN, only survivor of the Horseshoe Expedition, leave this account to my Lord George Anson, First Lord of the Admiralty, with all courtesy as I fear that the illness that affects me will not allow me to wait. The UNICORN weighed anchor on the nineteenth of June, rounded Cape Horn on the sixth of December; arrived at the position Latitude thirty degrees and eight minutes on the thirteenth of January; opened the Royal Orders, located the secret entrance, inventoried the Crown Properties and loaded 864 bags of gold, 200 bars of gold, 21 barrels of precious stones and jewels, a gilded trunk containing a rose of gold and emeralds two feet high and 160 chests of gold and silver coins.

On the twenty-fourth of January destroyed the fortress. When returning the twenty-eight of January before a violent storm, the ship suffered serious damage and lost a mast. We were forced to shelter on an island; the third of February found us at Longitude...... Latitude.....and it was impossible to carry out repairs for the safe transportation of the treasure; transferred to new hiding place valley of Anson a cable length from the observation point in direction great yellow stone depth fifteen feet. UNICORN repaired for emergency crossing course Valparaiso; informed of plans for mutiny while ship was becalmed to the West of Valparaiso I made use of the auxiliary boat (Pinnace); UNICORN blown up by me with all on-board; six loyal men sacrificed for the cause of the Crown; I arrived at Valparaiso 1761."

Two others joined the Company, Peter Scotti, a navigational friend of Giorgio's and Ricardo Lyon. They formed a secret society to organize an expedition to search for the treasure, swearing not to say a single word to third parties about their plans.

Cousino prepared the necessary tents, food and essentials. Accompanied by his wife and son Matias he transferred to JF. Most important was the inclusion of coalminers who he obtained through his family contacts in Lota. Good for work with shovel and pick, they were ideal for the excavations that were to come.

Peter Scotti was the most important member of the group, being an expert in the use of the sextant and measuring the height of the sun and stars. His task was to measure the exact altitude of the star

SCHUBA in the constellation Scorpio. This would serve to determine the place of the burial, but not its present position, but where it was in 1761. This was quite a complex mathematical and trigonometrical operation. Scotti and Louis Cousino, keen astronomers, worked together on this task.

Matias Cousino asserts that, in addition, the aid of several university astronomers was enlisted; nevertheless the doubts that must have assailed them are demonstrated in a document that turned up in the trunk of the Cousino family. First appear calculations of altitude, typical of those used in navigation, nowadays almost obsolete as a result of the use of modern satellite systems; then a concise historical recounting of the astral measurements, starting off at Hipparchus in the year 130 BC, then Ptolemy in 137 AD, the Arab Oulog-Bay in 1437, and then in the 18th century Flamstead and Lacaille. It is not necessary to stress how important it was to verify the location at sea at that time. It is evident that the modern planner/calculator has great doubts with respect to the system used by the British Navy in 1760. In addition, there is enough certainty that at least the measurements of SCHUBA would contain various errors.

Matias explains how the exact point of the excavation was determined, between the angle of SCHUBA, the yellow stone that cost much to find and the 'Observation Point'. This consisted of monoliths that permit the visiting ships to establish their coordinates; but of all those they found they could not recognize anything like Captain Webb's. They decided then to try to establish the line that passed through the angle of SCHUBA in 1761 (which was something utopian): then the yellow stone, of which several exist on JFI, and finally the Observation Point with its monoliths difficult to identify. Only an exaggerated optimism could give a foundation upon which to start excavating.

It is known that the expedition members, being highly influential people sought aid at the highest level of Government, to the effect that the Commander-in-Chief of the Chilean Navy sent ships to patrol around the island in case the coveted treasure turned up.

The exact place that was determined to excavate, was in what is today the Calle La Polvora in San Juan Bautista (Cumberland Bay). They installed a camp and set up tents that permitted excavation under their eaves in an effort (useless in so small a place) to avoid possible suspicion. The absolute silence with respect to the operations remained, which did not prevent the noise of banging and crashing of rocks scattered over the island unleashing the fertile imagination of the inhabitants themselves. Excavations to more than thirty meters in depth are spoken of, as it was very likely that later floods following the deposit had increased the fifteen feet depth mentioned by Webb. From a vertical pit they excavated in a horizontal direction, all this lit by candles. Matias Cousino remembers having traveled by these underground passages, where in the end he experienced acute claustrophobia and the candles illuminated less due to the lack of oxygen.

What frustrated them enormously was finding arrows made with pistol balls that seemed to indicate the exact direction to follow, but which never led them anywhere.

After several months of unfruitful search, Cousino's expedition began to be discouraged. All the calculations were reviewed and the various angles and information obtained, which gave rise to the hypothesis that the treasure could be under the sea in Cumberland Bay and they were not prepared for an underwater operation. Saddened and disheartened, the expedition group disbanded and returned to the mainland.

The question of a possible deceit was raised; the possibility that Giorgio invented the entire story and the find at Horcon was an invention. But who could have produced Webb's message in cypher, in 18th century language style and on original paper of the time?

Later investigations have established that Captain Webb and the ship 'UNICORN' really existed, then it is very probably that knowing himself ill and being in Valparaiso he would manage to leave information about the treasure, hidden at Horcon in the hope that his letters to England were received.

What is moderately clear now is that Anson knew of the existence of the treasure when he had reached the highest ranks of the British Navy, that is to say 'First Lord of the Admiralty', long after his voyage to JFI in 1741. It could be that his position allowed him access to trustworthy and confidential information in the archives. Attention is drawn to the reference to 'Royal Orders' and 'Properties of the Crown'.

Another possibility is that in one of the Spanish ships captured by Anson in the course of his voyage around the world, information *existed on hidden treasures that years later, only he had opportunity to act upon, when the responsibilities of his position allowed him to put together a voyage of recovery.*

It comes powerfully to the attention that Webb opened his instructions at latitude 30º 8´ South, being near enough to Guayacan (the question is; why was it called 'Horseshoe Expedition' if it were not La Herradura – The Horsehoe?). Most probable it is the same treasure that many have searched for, (more about this later. GE) but which Webb had already removed in 1761. This theory seems more feasible than the one that maintains the treasure has been dug up and was then reburied on JFI.

This is the end of Anson's treasure story, more or less how Anthony Westcott tells it. He (Westcott) also adds that the greatest doubts he has relates to the island itself, as he says, according to several trustworthy historians, the island was fortified in 1749 with a garrison of Spanish soldiers, so obviously it would be impossible to bury a treasure here under their noses. The fact is, because of Spain's fear of British incursions and occupation in the South Pacific, (this in the main due to Anson's expedition calling here in the early 1740's) the Spanish King directed the Viceroy of Peru to commence occupation of the Archipelago. This commenced in about 1749. In 1751 at least one fort named Santa Barbara had been built with nine cannon in place. To carry out this work, 62 soldiers, 171 colonists and 22 male convicts were landed. When all this finished, efforts were underway to extend other forts to overlook the anchorages.

The first Governor Juan Nevarro Santaella baptised the settlement as 'Santa Bautista' and by 1779 forty houses made up the settlement.'

In 1766 the British expedition of Philip Carteret, commander of the Royal Navy Sloop 'Swallow' noticed there was a fort on Mas a'Tierra and proceeded on.

It is important to remember then that Juan Fernandez Island was occupied by the Spanish from 1749 to at least 1766.

With the demise of the Giorgio/Cousino expedition and its return to the mainland in 1952, the island returned to its previous calm with the activities of fishing and lobster catching.

To bring us up to date to more recent times, Matias Cousino, only son of Luis Cousino, married Maria Eugenia Beeche who lived on the island. She remains enthusiastic about the treasure and knows the full history and story of the search. Indeed, she managed to keep the old papers of Webb, but these are the translated interpretations of Giorgio's mother. Sadly for us, the original papers in cipher from England seem to have disappeared. According to María Eugenia, they were removed from Cousino's house by a son of the 'Count', whoever he was.

ORIGINAL TRANSLATED INTERPRETATION OF ONE OF WEBB'S LETTERS

Juan Fernandez Island remained tranquil for over 40 years, and then another treasure hunt started. Which is another reason for introducing this JFI/Anson treasure story now, for it is not readily apparent why this story known as 'Anson's treasure' had anything really to do with the lost treasure we were looking for. For us, at this stage of our research, it was just another treasure story.

Further mention of *La Herradura* (The Horseshoe) comes later in the very important work by one Richard Latham on the Guayacan pirate's treasure.

In about 1996, a wealthy American industrialist named Bernard Keiser arrived on the island searching for a treasure hidden by a Spanish nobleman, the same treasure known as Anson's treasure. Here to come was the first hint of what was on *our* real treasure island.

Keiser's Crusade

Bernard Keiser's story starts in the early 1990s when a Discovery Channel television crew arrived at Juan Fernandez Island to do a documentary on the island. Hampered by bad weather preventing them filming, the crew were relaxing in Maria Eugenia's hotel when she told them the tale of the treasure and the search carried out by her former father-in-law Luis Cousino. She also showed them the Webb documents still in her possession.

This story was subsequently transmitted and watched by Mr Keiser in the States. It aroused so much interest in him, particularly the Webb translations, that he decided to visit JF Island.

On viewing Maria Eugenia's documents, he realised that being of authentic historical background, there had to be more to the Webb/Anson story. He formed a partnership with Maria Eugenia and started some serious research. There passed several years of research work and visits to the island culminating in his declaration to begin the search in 1998. His research brought to light one of the key aspects of this story for us, confirmation that the treasure was not of pirate origin but Spanish, and seems to confirm earlier stories we had researched. Keiser's research took him to England for several months; the time was spent researching the Webb letters in libraries, museums, maritime logs, public records and archives. It was time well spent, for it was here that he discovered that the *Unicorn* was a merchant ship out of the port of Liverpool and operated with Letters of Marque under the orders of Anson who was now Lord of the Admiralty. She sailed from England in 1760 under the command of Cornelius Patrick Webb. He appears to have been a London accountant by profession and for this trip, to establish authority, obviously given a commission by Anson.

Keiser's important find came during research in Seville, Spain, in the *Archivo de Indias*: that in approximately 1715, a Spanish nobleman, who belonged to the Order of Santiago, Juan Esteban Ubilla y Echeverria, commanded to be buried in 'Más a Tierra' (Old name for JFI) a valuable treasure that the Viceroy of Mexico should have sent to Spain. Ubilla apparently confessed the truth to an intimate friend in Seville, and Keiser found this documentation in the archives.

We have already told Ubilla's story at the beginning of the book so no need to repeat it here. Suffice to say that as the date's tie in, we are almost certainly talking about one and the same thing. That Keiser has identified the treasure on JFI as being of Spanish origin had great ramifications for us as will be seen.

Misnamed Titles

The Spanish title mentioned above i.e. Juan Esteban Ubilla y Echeverria appears quite often in accounts but is not strictly correct. It could be mistaken as one person's name and title to those with no knowledge of Spanish but the 'y' translation indicates we are talking about Ubilla *and* Echeverria. But two noblemen did not bury the treasure. The explanation is thus:

Captain General Don Juan Esteban de Ubilla was commander of the Nueva España merchant convoy (or flota) and this consisted of five ships. This convoy was joined by the six ships of the Tierra Firme fleet returning from South America under General Don Antonio de Echeverez y Zubiza.

Two different people, the mistake is usually due to repetitive copying.

Back to Bernard Keiser;

He had in the meanwhile of course obtained the necessary permits to search and dig from the appropriate government departments. An agreement was signed in which they allowed him to excavate without trouble in exchange for a quarter of the 'booty' and of the commercial rights over what was written or filmed with respect to this subject. But it wasn't to be that easy; searching was only allowed October to March and no mechanical equipment was to be used - hand tools only.

As can be imagined, Keiser's expedition caused great excitement when it arrived on the island. The first in protesting energetically about what was happening was the mayor, as "nobody had said anything to him!" He called numerous council sessions and gave press conferences to the bustle of journalists and cameramen that had begun to arrive.

Then a major press release subdued things a little, which I quote:

'BURIED TREASURE DIG ON ROBINSON CRUSOE DELAYED

Robinson Crusoe Island authorities said Sunday that work to unearth buried treasure discovered using satellite technology (?? GE) has been delayed, due to a rock wall in the zone where digging is necessary. Authorities also want the dig to be as slow and careful as possible, so as not to damage any possible archeological artifacts. The treasure seems to consist of 800 barrels of 17th century gold ingots worth $10 billion, or one-third of Chile's foreign debt.

The work is led by historian and political scientist (?? GE) Bernard Keiser and supervised by experts from the National Monuments Council.

Keiser said the gold was buried by a Spanish nobleman, Juan Uribe y Echeverria, who did not want to pay the Consejo de las Indias the full tribute his vice royalty owed when the Hasburgs took over the Bourbon throne. Uribe finally sent half of what he owed, but the ship carrying the gold sunk, and he was able to make the Spanish throne believe that all of the tribute owed went down with the ship. Uribe would never return to unearth his gold as he died in a hurricane on his way to Spain.

Louis Bork, the Governor of Valparaiso, Region V, arrived at the site to review the progress of the dig. Representatives of the History and Geography Society, and the Historical Commemoration Institute will also be present and will verify the value and veracity of the treasure.

Bork said that according to official documents from the National Monuments Commission, 75 percent of the treasure's value would stay in the hands of the Chilean Government, while 25 percent would be taken by the discoverers.'

It would seem that the Chilean authorities and their representatives had great expectations of Keiser and they were perhaps expecting him to unearth the treasure during the first dig. They were all there and you can imagine them all crowding around watching and waiting to see the glint of gold. I wonder if any of them are still there!

The years passed with Keiser quietly digging away with no luck, then, in 2005, headlines splashed around the world:

'600 Barrels of Loot Found on Crusoe Island', 'The Biggest Treasure in History has been located', '$10 Billion Treasure Found by Hi-tech Robot'.

Followed by:
'All of Chile is celebrating and the islanders have already spent the cash on a new school and hospital. The mayor also wants each islander to have a share.'

I do not know the effect all this was having on Keiser but apparently, with everyone laughing at him because his treasure has been stolen by a little four-wheeled robot named Arturito, he started smoking again!

The media fell in love with the cute little robot with a flashing red light on top that claimed the gold for Chile. Keiser was news no more. Newspapers poked fun at him, calling him 'Gringo Loco' and 'The Great Loser'. All this without any gold actually coming to light!

The robot was nicknamed 'Arturito after the *Star Wars* R2D2. The Chilean company that owned it, Wagner Securities, made amazing claims about its performance; its ground-penetrating sensors were supposed to be able to identify buried metals down to 50 meters due to its 'anti plasma reactor' and 'atomic gamma rays'.

Science fiction? It would appear so, for its inventor, who gave a speech to a physics class in Valparaiso, couldn't even explain how it worked, much to the declared amusement and criticism of the students. Within a couple of weeks, and no evidence of treasure, Arturito was shamed into oblivion.

"It was ridiculous," Keiser says of the episode, arguing that if it was that good, why weren't all the major mining companies in the world after it?

And so, once again, the island turned back to its leisurely pace and Keiser carried on with his digging. But today, with R2D2 a smiley memory, Anson's treasure has still not been found. I have good reason to know why, of course.

Reports indicate Keiser is pretty philosophical about it all and still believes the treasure is there. The Chilean press has moved on to other stories, the locals still talk and smile about Arturito and the silly claims, and the Mayor has now decided diplomatically that the island's greatest treasure is 'its people'.

To the sceptics, Keiser points out that Mel Fisher searched for 14 years before he found the *Atocha* gold off Key West. Keiser's self-belief is admirable. I believe Keiser is failing because he has taken the Webb translations literally, despite the evidence in front of him. The Yellow Stone and Scorpii/Schuba he relates to geographical peculiarities i.e. yellow rocks and formations that maybe look like a scorpion.

It is also noticeable that Keiser is not searching the area in which the Giorgio/Cousino group concentrated their efforts. He is working in the Selkirk Cave area which is a few miles further up the coast at Puerto Inglés (English Port). It is better known as the site of Robinson's Cave. There are a few old cannon scattered around here. The fact they are here, also 'red' earth, are probably influencing Keiser's choice of site. But if the cannon are there because they were to protect the treasure landing site, as some believe, you wouldn't leave them there as a marker, would you? This site is also looked at as the 'observation point' mentioned in the Webb letter, with the hiding place being a 'cable length' from here.

Reports filter back occasionally from visiting archaeologists. For example,

'We saw Keiser and his group excavating a particular spot which with some imagination was supposed to look like a scorpion. It was called 'La Cueva del Escorpion' (The Cave of the Scorpion). Some accounts call it 'Boca del Escorpion' (Mouth of the Scorpion). Apparently the early documents/letters describe the burying place as 'a place of the scorpion'.

We wrote to Mr. Keiser in 2004 and 2005 offering to exchange information. Although we already knew that the treasure was not on JFI, it would have been nice to see some confirmation of Ubilla's part in this. His reply was as follows:

'I received your e-mail via my archaeologist today. I have been working on the archival materials for about seven years, and have found many documents on Juan Estaban de Ubilla y Echeverrez in the archives of the Indies, in Seville and in other archives in Spain. At this time I would not be willing to share any of my research materials as I am also writing a book, which does correct the history about the unknown

BERNARD KEISER POINTING OUT AN 'S' DESIGN ON WALL IN SELKIRK'S CAVE, DEPICTING HE BELIEVES HORSHOES(S) AND POSSIBLY INSCRIBED BY WEBB

SELKIRK'S CAVE WITH CANNON IN FOREGROUND

exploits of Ubilla and the 1715 plate fleet. I can assure you that what I did find in the seven year investigation does change everything that the historians have written. I am certain that you can understand my reluctance to give out any information about my research at this particular time.

Hopefully you will have much success in your project

Respectfully,

Bernard Keiser.'

We had already hinted to Mr. Keiser some crucial information in a previous letter. Quote, in part:

'I (MN) am quite prepared to show you all the information and maps for they are going to be published with a full explanation anyway.

For example, the original directions were in Latin and a fundamental translation error has seen you looking for a 'yellow rock' when this direction really identifies a star in the constellation of the Charioteer for the second bearing.'

Crucial information as we say, that if acted on may have changed his tactics but despite this, we never had any further contact. I have seen this reaction before; a steadfast refusal of help. Hints given that maybe you (the treasure hunter who believes his is the only solution) should be looking at... But the person is so wrapped up in their work and total self-belief that *they* possess all that is required to find the treasure. They exist in a world where their 'tunnel vision' is focused only on what work they have done so far and will not permit themselves to look 'outside the boundary', because they do not believe there is anything else to find. These people are – still looking!

To some degree, you could say I was guilty of it myself years ago when researching my Kidd book. If I had looked *outside* the 'circle' of the charts, I would eventually have been led to JF Island. As my focus was on the charts themselves, their inherent stories and the various expeditions they create, not primarily the solution, I had no need to go outside the confines of Captain Kidd and the charts research circle. All I wanted was within it.

They (the treasure hunters) could also be worried, of course, that maybe any outside interference or communication was a precursor to possible rivals trying to 'elbow' their way into the dig with confidentialities and information perhaps being binding, meaning that any future positive developments would mean a share of any findings going to them. This was never the case – or reason, of course, for our enquiry being already aware that a future share of nothing would not have been worth very much to us!

So for Mr. Keiser, I believe the years will come and go and still no treasure believed to be that of Lord Anson and/or Ubilla will ever be found on JF Island. A bold statement to make but justified in the coming chapters.

I do not know what the situation is today on JF Island. A couple of years ago (2010/11), Keiser was requesting permission from the authorities for a fifth try at locating the gold, this at a cost of another $100,000. Money well spent if he recovers the treasure he estimates is valued at $10 billion. This latest effort will be using highly sophisticated mining video technology. Alas, it would seem Keiser is still looking. Another telling statement is: *'Since 1998, Keiser has been excavating caves all over the island'.* An indication then that the information he possesses is not pinpointing where to look!

However, on a bright note for us, it can be seen that due to Keiser's research, Anson's treasure is really that of a Spanish nobleman.

It will also be seen in the coming pages the treasure's location is really a long way from here. The Webb letters have been totally misinterpreted, which explains why this treasure will never be found on JFI. I reveal the secret of the Webb letters in the investigative part of the book and there is a lot more to say about Juan Fernandez Island and Lord Anson.

Unfortunately, websites and newspaper articles still get the story wrong, usually due to repetitive copying and the lack of proper research. A typical example is:

'....when the treasure was on route to Spain the navigator in charge of the ship landed on Robinson Crusoe Island and buried his cargo. Before he could return to unearth the booty, an English pirate named Cornelius Webb uncovered the Incan treasure and reburied it elsewhere on the island....'

For now, to continue with the background and beginnings of our story, it is time to introduce four characters who changed the course of pirate treasure history.

CHAPTER 3

THE TREASURE OF THE TUAMOTUS

In our continuing quest for the lost treasure and its location, we now introduce one of the books that featured in our original research. It is titled *The Treasure of the Tuamotus,* written by George Hamilton and published in 1939.

I am very familiar with this story. It features in my Captain Kidd book as one of the great buried treasure stories. So let me retell this fascinating tale of treasure, murder and intrigue. Space, of course, limits me to telling you only that which is necessary and important to *our* story, because important it is, being one of the foundation stories for this book. Take in carefully events and facts; why will become very clear later on.

The Shrivelled Old Man

Charles Edward Howe lived near Christchurch, New Zealand. One dark and stormy night in 1910, there was a knock at the door of his shack. Standing soaked and shivering in the rain was a shrivelled old man, ragged, unkempt and dirty with a big bushy beard. The stranger wanted to know how far it was to Christchurch, and, as Howe could see the man was exhausted, he invited him in. He gave the man some dry clothes and a place to wash. The difference when he returned was a surprise to Howe. It was not difficult for him to realise that this old tramp had at some time been a fine and powerful fellow. Later on, after food and whiskey had loosened the old man's tongue, Howe learned something of his past. He had been in gaol for 20 years for manslaughter, and after his release had become a vagrant.

Before the old man left into a now dry and clear night, he turned and said to Howe, "Ye'd think it funny now if, because of what ye've done for me this night I made ye a millionaire, would ye not?"

"I would that," grinned Howe as he watched him until the darkness hid his bent and shrunken form.

Several weeks later, Howe had an urgent request to go to a Convent Hospital. Someone old and very ill going by the name Killorain wanted to see him urgently. Howe did not know who this was and somewhat reluctantly made the journey. He hardly recognised the old Irish tramp that had enjoyed his hospitality weeks earlier. The old man was clearly dying and after the priest and nurse had left, he instructed Howe to get his jacket under the bed, "Now take yer knife and rip up along the lining of the right sleeve, will ye?"

From its hiding place, Howe retrieved a worn greasy sheet of paper gummed to a strip of linen to prevent it being torn. "Now have a look at that!" whispered Killorain. Howe did so and could see that it appeared to be the chart of an island indicating a particular spot, where he assumed something had been concealed. Killorain went on to tell Howe that a treasure was buried there by himself and some pals and the chart was drawn by one of them – a Spaniard named Alvarez. He explained he was giving the chart to Howe because he had done him a good turn and been kind to him when others would only shun him. The treasure, he said, included 14 tons of gold ingots, a chest of doubloons, necklaces of diamonds, golden candlesticks and 'lashins' of other stuff.

"I tell e mister," he said, "that chart as yer holdin is worth not a stiver less than three millions of English pounds, an' it's all yours, if yer like to go an' get it!"

Despite Howe's reluctance to believe such a yarn, he had heard such buried treasure stories before, he was impressed by the Irishman's manner and sincerity. So much so that when Killorain pleaded, "D'ye believe me?" How replied, "Yes, I believe you."

"Listen then," he said, "an' I'll tell ye the whole story. It's as well ye should know it."

This then is the story – albeit a condensed version. The author George Hamilton admits that he had to embroider a little the story as told by Killorain to Howe. His reconstruction, he says, was based upon careful inquiry and research and all the basic facts are correct. Alas not quite, as we shall see.

Killorain's Story

He was, he said, born in County Clare in 1826. He left home for the sea, and by the time he was 24, had sailed into most of the world's major ports. It was in Shanghai 'between ships' that he ran into a 'Yankee' named Arthur Brown, a seaman like himself and about a year older. They shared some adventures and with their similar backgrounds, they soon realised they were birds of a feather. They decided from then on that come what may, they would stick together. As Shanghai was getting too 'warm' for them, they decided to get out on the first available ship in the morning. That night, whilst having a meal in their lodgings, two men interrupted them. One was a tall, dark fellow, with a decidedly foreign look about him. His appearance accentuated by a long thin scar from his left ear down to his chin, cutting across his lip, and eyes that seemed set too close together, with a slight cast in one of them. His companion, shorter and stouter, bore all the hallmarks of a hardened sailor. The two men thought they had recognised Killorain and Brown as old shipmates and offered to buy them a drink. The evening wore on with Brown and Killorain getting pretty drunk – due, in the main to the 'special' rums that the 'tall fellow' was putting on the table for them. They discovered his name was Diego Alvarez, a Spaniard by birth and, as Killorain thought, a bos'n. His mate was an Englishman by the name of Luke Barrett. Killorain passed out for a while. On coming round, he noticed Brown sprawled out across the table whilst neither Alvarez nor Barrett seemed to be drunk at all. As if from a distance, he heard Alvarez say, "They're ok, too much rum. I'll send for the boat and we'll get them back to the ship." In that moment, Killorain realised something was wrong. He staggered to his feet and made to remonstrate with Alvarez but not before a fist that seemed as big as the whole world crashed into his face.

And so began the association of four men who were to leave their mark on the treasure hunting world. Killorain and Brown had, of course, been shanghaied and found themselves on the *Sweet Alice* bound for Buenos Aires.

Alvarez, the bos'n, more or less ran the ship as the captain was drunk all the time and rarely seen. Killorain grew to hate the Spaniard as he observed the inhuman treatment meted out daily by him. He looked for any opportunity to kill him. It came one night when a heavy sea mist was clinging everywhere. Alvarez was on watch. Killorain was about to bring a heavy wooden pin crashing down on the bos'n's head when Alvarez turned and fought him off. Killorain was no match for Alvarez and suffered for over a week from the violent kicks he received in the ribs and stomach. To his surprise, after that, Alvarez left him alone, along with his partner Brown. But Alvarez made up for it by picking on another member of the crew, a Brazilian named Juan Damerion who suffered heavily at Alvarez's hands. After one particular beating, Juan collapsed into unconsciousness. On coming around, he became delirious and started jabbering away in Spanish, none of which Killorain could understand. But Alvarez could and he was staring at Juan. He came over to him and tried to calm him down. To Killorain's surprise, the bos'n tried to ease the man's torment and make him comfortable, speaking to him in soothing words in his own language. Juan quietened down and Alvarez started to ask questions, some of which Juan answered. After a while, Alvarez got up from where he had been kneeling beside the Brazilian and left. He soon returned with a drink that he gave Juan, and stayed beside him until he was asleep.

In his delirium, Juan had revealed a secret to the bos'n. Before he left, Alvarez asked Killorain if he had understood the lingo and seemed relieved when Killorain replied that he did not understand Spanish. Killorain had in fact recognised odd words like 'Church', 'Money' and 'Pisco' but the rest had meant nothing to him.

The crew, having heard of the bos'n's unbelievable caring treatment of Juan, agreed that Alvarez must have got hold of some sort of secret off Juan. That secret was obviously worth more than life itself, for the next night, having sent the crew on watch forward, the bos'n dropped the drugged body of Juan overboard, confident he had not been seen. Killorain, feigning sleep, had witnessed the whole episode. Next morning, after a search of the ship, it was decided that Juan, in delirium, must have gone on deck and fallen overboard.

Killorain was determined that he would denounce Alvarez as a murderer in the next port of call but an incident up in the rigging, during a storm a few days later, made him rethink his decision. In the fierce wind and rain, Killorain lost his grip only to be saved in the nick of time by Alvarez. Later, when Killorain thanked him for saving his life, the bos'n suggested that he might have a use for him in the future. That the Spaniard had something in mind became clear when, standing off port waiting to enter Buenos Aires, he approached Killorain asking if he was willing to let bygones be bygones. As he had saved his life, Killorain agreed. Alvarez continued asking him if he wanted to make money, a lot of money. "Who wouldn't?" was Killorain's reply. With that, a meeting was arranged ashore between the four: Alvarez, Killorain, Brown and Barrett. Alvarez swore them all to a solemn oath before telling them that a secret treasure was hidden in the vaults of a certain church in a certain town. It consisted of gold from the Incas, Spanish Doubloons, gold ingots, church ornaments, jewels, necklaces, all accumulated over many years. Only a few priests who guard it know of it, Alvarez continued, but it is there, of that he was assured. Value was originally estimated at 3 to 4 million pounds. Killorain asked him how he had heard all this, although he had an idea. "From one who was at some time a priest there," Alvarez replied. "That is all I will say for now!"

The year was now 1849 and having deserted the *Sweet Alice*, they joined a mule train across the country to Valparaiso. From there, they took a ship along the Chilean coast to Pisco.

A lot of time was spent investigating and making enquiries. Nothing definite could be found out about the treasure. Alvarez and Killorain became devout Catholics and regular churchgoers to establish confidence and trust of the priests. They discovered that four priests kept some sort of night vigil in the church and guessed this could be because of the treasure. They also learned of Father Matteo, who they recognised as their old shipmate Juan Damerion - befriended then slung overboard by Alvarez. Matteo was a recreant monk who fell in love with a pretty señorita who made him her confessor. He stole a small part of the treasure and they fled together to Buenos Aires. When his stolen wealth came to an end, she left him. Matteo, knowing he could never go back to the church, became a sailor. Alvarez pointed out to his companions that the good fathers assumed that Matteo was still alive somewhere.

Alvarez's plan for establishing the authenticity of the treasure was ingenious. He sought an interview with Father Benito, the senior of the priests. He told him that on a recent trip to Santiago, he had heard from an old sailor acquaintance of his named Juan Damerion of a plan to rob the church. Damerion told Alvarez that at one time he had been a priest. Alvarez described the man and Father Benito, shocked at what he was hearing, recognised him as Father Matteo. Alvarez described how Matteo told him he had stolen some treasure and fled with his lover. He now wanted his help to steal the rest of the treasure. When Matteo told him it was in the church at Pisco, Alvarez knew he had to inform his good friends in the church. At this, Father Benito admitted there was a treasure but kept in a place from which it would be very difficult to steal. Alvarez told him the rest of the plot, that

Matteo had a ruthless gang of desperadoes who, under the guise of an anti-religious demonstration, would rush into the church, murder all who would try to stop them and blow open the doors to the crypt.

Father Benito, now desperately agitated, asked Alvarez what he could do to save the treasure. Alvarez, who had of course previously worked it all out, suggested sending the treasure by ship to the sister church in Callao. Father Benito quickly got the approval of the other senior priests and asked Alvarez for help in finding a suitable vessel. Nothing could be found until Alvarez heard that an American schooner was due in a few days that would suit their purpose. Whilst they waited, the treasure was secured in packing cases and moved at night to a warehouse owned by a trusted member of the church. Alvarez and his gang all helped with the packing, having been introduced as trusted friends. It helped that the fathers knew some of them as regular churchgoers.

Killorain was fascinated by the security surrounding the treasure, realising they could never have taken it on their own. He described it thus: a narrow doorway behind the altar led down some steps, through an iron gate, then along a narrow sloping passage formed out of large stone blocks. The final doors to the vault-like chamber were of oak, three inches thick, covered in steel plate, three-quarters of an inch thick. He knew that trying to blow those doors would have destroyed the place, and possibly the church.

It took two days and nights to pack and move the crates. Their total weight was about 16 tons. Killorain made a secret inventory of the treasure whilst guarding it in the warehouse and listed it as follows:

14 tons gold ingots
7 golden candlesticks, encrusted with jewels
38 long diamond necklaces
A quantity of jewelled rings
A quantity of jewelled crucifixes
A quantity of jewelled bracelets
1 chest of Spanish doubloons
1 chest of uncut stones
Various other jewels and ornaments

Value was estimated at about £4,000,000 sterling.

Three days later, *The Bos'n Bird* arrived. The skipper's name was Thompson. The cargo was put on board as quickly as possible with Alvarez and his gang helping. Alvarez had a plan to commandeer the ship and soon put it into action. He sent the crew ashore to celebrate a win by Killorain and Brown on the local lottery. Left on board were the two crew members on watch, as well as Thompson, Alvarez, Barrett and four priests who were to guard the treasure. The conspirators had pre-arranged that the crew celebrating on shore would be drugged and disposed of. A later search of the Taverns drew blank and Thompson, having to sail on the morning tide and five crew members short, was persuaded to take on Alvarez and his gang. Alvarez was signed on as Bos'n, that being his rating.

Father Benito, full of gratitude to Alvarez for his help and greatly relieved at the safe loading of the treasure, gave a final blessing and went ashore.

The voyage to Callao was along the coast and just a few days sailing, so Alvarez had little time to plan and carry out the murder of the crew and guards. The four of them had already agreed that this was the only way they could take the treasure - no witnesses. A severe storm forced the skipper to head out to sea and by the time it had blown out, they were hundreds of miles off course. This suited Alvarez. He planned that he would kill the priests; Killorain would kill the captain while the other two conspirators were to dispatch the remainder. On the pre-arranged signal, the grisly business was carried out. The bodies were weighed down with iron bars and dumped overboard.

The conspirators had a Council of War. What were they to do now they had the treasure? How could they explain it if they were caught? And what of a schooner that did not belong to them? Ideas were discussed but as usual Alvarez came up with the only sensible plan. Find a lonely uninhabited island, bury the treasure, mark the spot and make a chart. Finally, they would scuttle the schooner near a coast somewhere and go ashore in one of the boats as shipwrecked men. There would be no need to lie. They could tell the authorities they were the only survivors of the *Bos'n Bird* caught in a gale whilst bound from Pisco to Callao. They gave Alvarez due credit; it was a clever plan. They decided to head for the South Sea Islands, and after burying the treasure, they would scuttle the ship near the coast of Australia. A long journey found them off Tahiti in December 1850. They did not risk going ashore. They claimed they had yellow fever aboard and so had a boat sent out to them with provisions. They cruised out into the vast Archipelago for a while until they found the ideal place - a lonely little island, or atoll to be more correct. It was of coral origin, small, deserted and with scant vegetation. They later learned they were in the Tuamotu Group of islands.

It took over four weeks to land the treasure in the ship's boat, mainly because of the surf and shallow reefs. The treasure was buried in a hollow not too far from the sea. During this time, they had to make trips to neighbouring islands for food and water and became friendly with the natives. When they had finished, a chart was carefully drawn by Alvarez - the very one given to Howe. When he finished this, they realised they did not know the name of the island. For the voyage to Australia, they needed stores so went back to one of the islands where they could get provisions and also discover the name. Alvarez questioned a young chief he had befriended about the island. He soon recognised it and gave its name. Alvarez, because of the strange dialect of the Polynesian language, asked him to repeat it several times and carefully wrote it down letter by letter as the chief had said it. Alvarez then did something that so shocked and astounded Killorain that he was momentarily struck dumb. As the chief was walking back to his canoe, Alvarez took out his revolver and shot him in the back of the head! Killorain remonstrated with Alvarez and told him it was a vile and treacherous act considering the friendliness and hospitality of the natives. Once again, Alvarez had an answer ready, that as soon as they were gone, the natives would have gone to the island and possibly found the treasure. At the sound of the shot and soon realising what had happened, the natives ran for their weapons and hurriedly got their canoes ready. On their boat, Alvarez and his gang were lucky to get the sails set quickly and with a decent breeze blowing, they soon out-distanced the chasing canoes. Although grudgingly they had to admit Alvarez's reasoning was probably correct, things were never quite the same between them and their leader again.

They set the compass west and headed for Australia. Everything worked according to plan. They scuttled the ship and landed near what is now Port Darwin. The authorities believed their story. They had brought with them some of the treasure that could easily be disposed of and went to Cooktown, where they squandered the proceeds.

They showed several well-placed people the chart and told a story about an old pirate found dying in Pisco who had disclosed the secret to them. But apparently, such rumours were common along the coast so nobody was interested in kitting out an expedition.

When their money ran out, they went to the Parma gold fields to search for gold but did not have much luck there. One day, Alvarez and Barrett went off into the bush. It was not known what sort of trouble they got into with the natives but their bodies were found later. Killorain said that from the look on their faces, they did not die easily or prettily. He managed to retrieve the chart off Alvarez's body and he and Brown took off again, hoping to find someone they could interest in their treasure. It was not to be. One night, three drunken men were shot dead. Killorain and Brown were charged with murder, later reduced to manslaughter. They both got 20 years in prison. Brown served 15 years before he died. Five years later, Killorain was released and had wandered the country more or less penniless ever since.

Killorain, now on his deathbed, shrugged, sighed, turned to Howe and managed to smile saying, "Funny really, ain't it, when I'm the sole owner of a treasure worth 5 million." It was in December 1910 that Killorain died. Unlike the others, he died peacefully soon after telling Howe his story. Howe was the only mourner at his funeral.

And so ends the *Bos'n Bird* story, within it lays the accepted traditional 'Loot of Lima' story. Later on, I will show there is more than one version of this story and show why you should not necessarily believe any of them!

For now, we continue with Howe's story and his search for Killorain's treasure, which eventually led to collaboration with another group. These are the core stories of great importance to us in following the trail to our treasure.

PISCO CHURCH

Howe's Quest for Gold

Howe's quest for the treasure did not start until over a year later. He had put the old chart away, not really convinced by the old man's story, and forgotten all about it. Looking for something else one day, he came across it again and could not help being drawn to it this time. He recalled with some sadness the memory of the old man sick in bed. Although knowing he was dying, he had told his story for a final time full of enthusiasm.

As time went by, the old man's story kept coming back to him, increasingly filling his thoughts. It got to the stage where he could not sleep properly, his mind and thoughts tormenting him. Could this ridiculous story really be true? Was there a five million pound hoard still buried on a South Sea island?' In the end, it all got the better of him and he made the decision to find out one way or the other. He decided the job had to be done properly and started to make cautious enquiries. Eventually, he found conclusive proof that in February 1850, four shipwrecked sailors had landed near Port Darwin. Their ship, the *Bos'n Bird*, had sunk in a severe storm. Later from Peru came the news that a treasure had been stolen from Pisco in 1849[1] This was enough to convince Howe. In 1912, when he was 42, deciding to go it alone, he started his voyage to Tahiti. Whilst in Tahiti, arranging his trip to the far reaches of the Tuamotus Group of islands, Howe kept a low profile hoping not to arouse suspicion. This had the opposite effect; people were curious and wanted to know why he was there. His second mistake, although not really his, was his intended destination.

Alvarez had written the island's name, as spelled out phonetically by the young chief. It just so happened that, in the language of the islands, 'p' and 't' sound almost exactly alike and are even interchangeable. So what Alvarez had written down should have been something else, similar sounding but different enough to indicate a totally different island. It was, of course, sheer bad luck that there happened to exist an island with that name on the map, a long way from the real treasure island. Howe was ignorant of all this and after looking at many islands, all similar, the captain of the schooner he was on pointed out an atoll he assured Howe was the one (Papee) named on the map. Howe was landed on it and left to his own devices. Strangely, although he could not recognise any important landmarks, he nevertheless decided this was the right island.

A few days later, a schooner appeared and from it landed a Government official accompanied by two gendarmes. The conversation that followed resulted in Howe being marched off the island and taken back to Tahiti. The reason for this was that he would not give an explanation as to why he was on the island, and also the fact that he had already aroused suspicion when previously in Tahiti. Howe's outraged and aggressive attitude did not help either. Back in Tahiti, he was interviewed by a senior official, who informed him that unless he disclosed his purpose for being on the island, he would be deported. Outraged as he was, after all he had not broken any laws, Howe nevertheless knew that if he wanted to see his plans through, he would have to give in and explain himself. So he admitted he was there in search of treasure. He was questioned about where and how but told them only that the story and directions had come from an old Irishman he had done a good turn to and that man was now dead. Howe also admitted that although the old man's story had checked out, he didn't know if the treasure was still there. Although the official stated that anything found on the islands would be the property of the French Government, a permit to search was granted.

So Howe's honesty went in his favour and soon just about everybody knew what he was up to and he became something of a local celebrity.

He had to wait some time for a suitable schooner but eventually landed on 'Papee' with considerable stores and tools. He explored the atoll. which was about four miles long, and two and a half miles wide at the widest point. A typical coral atoll, roughly ring-shaped, enclosing a lagoon. He had no success in finding the landmarks clearly indicated on the chart, only likely indications, and decided that time, weather and nature had probably taken its toll and changed the landscape.

Howe remained on Papee for 12 years, criss-crossing the island with trenches. It had never occurred to him that he might have been on the wrong island. After Howe had spent seven years on the island, in 1919, Charles Nordhoff, a well-known American writer, visited Tahiti, where he learned of the lonely treasure seeker and went to see him. Once Howe was certain Nordhoff was not interested in acquiring the treasure, he told him the story. Nordhoff repeated it in his book *Faery Lands of the South Seas* (published 1921). This account appears later.

Eventually it dawned on Howe that Papee might not after all be the right island. He made some enquiries when next in Tahiti. It was then for the first time he learned of the existence of another atoll with the name 'Tatee'. He wasted no time in going back to Papee and whilst the schooner waited, collected all his stores, tools and belongings.

Remarkably, within a couple of hours of landing on his new atoll, Howe found some of the landmarks left by Alvarez and his gang. Just four days later, he found the first chest packed with jewellery. Three days after that, in the same vicinity, he found the second chest packed full with Spanish doubloons. What he found in the first chest he transferred to copra sacks and re-buried in a different place. He destroyed all evidence of the chests. It is not clear if the coins were hidden the same way. The search for the location of the ingots took another couple of days. The chart described it as being in a 'basin'. Howe found a pool fed from the lagoon. After several days of searching by probing the bottom of the pool with a long metal pipe, he eventually found the evidence he wanted. Stuck to the bottom of the pipe was a sliver of rotten oak[2]. He estimated the depth of water to be about 18ft with maybe 2ft of sand covering the chests[3].

Nothing could therefore be recovered without the aid of a diver so Howe, concluding that his long search was over and headed back to Tahiti on the next passing schooner. The captain of the schooner, a friend of his, questioned him about the treasure. Howe denied that he had found anything and was finally giving up the search. The captain said that the authorities believed that Howe *had* found something. His friend continued by warning him that *if* he had found anything and *if* he had taken some as evidence, the authorities were likely to look for it. Apparently, somehow, the captain said the authorities had got wind that Howe had found something. Impossible, of course, and maybe supposition, but Howe was secretly relieved at this news because he had indeed retained some specimens of the treasure. These were quietly dropped overboard one night without the captain knowing anything about it. The captain's warning proved true enough. The schooner was met off Tahiti. Howe was put under arrest, 'for his own safety' he was told. He was meticulously searched, as was the schooner. Men who had leant him money over the years were in uproar saying they had been duped into giving money under false pretences. A court hearing followed and eventually Howe was sentenced to be deported back to Australia as an undesirable alien.

[1]How did the authorities know it had been stolen, not lost at sea as reported? *GE*
[2]Why no gold evidence? *GE*
[3]How did Alvarez expect to retrieve 16tons of gold from this depth? No commercial hard-hat divers available in those days. *GE*

The Hamilton Quest

Four years in the wilderness followed. Nobody believed his story so Howe was unable to raise the necessary capital to return and 'lift' his treasure. Then in 1930, he was introduced to a Mr William Edwardes, a well-known Australian journalist. Edwardes, whilst initially doubting Howe's tale, decided to try and verify it himself. After seven months, he concluded that Howe's story was indeed genuine. He approached the Samson brothers, well-known Sydney engineers, got them interested, and arranged a meeting. They agreed that a visit to Tahiti was necessary before they could proceed further. A visit to Papeete where they talked with many people who were acquainted with Howe, further convinced the prospective backers that Howe's story was genuine. Edwardes was sent to Paris to obtain the necessary search permit and, whilst in Europe, to try and raise more capital.

Howe, restless and frustrated by the continual waiting, decided to go on a prospecting expedition with an old pal he met in Sydney. He promised to keep in touch with his partners whom he did but his third, and as it turned out, last letter, stated that he was ill. After that, silence.

Meanwhile, preparation for the recovery expedition went ahead. Every effort was made to trace Howe. That was 1932 and nothing was ever heard of him again.

George Hamilton, author of the book about the venture, became involved as an investor and diver, having responded to an advertisement in *The Times*. He and Mr and Mrs Edwardes left London in September 1933 and sailed for Australia. It was, however, to be another four months before the expedition party eventually arrived at Tahiti and another month after that, 25th February 1934, before they actually sailed for the island on the chartered schooner, *Guisborne*.

The shareholders in the party, as well as Hamilton, were Harold Sampson, William Edwardes, George Curtler, Michael Leacovsky and George Farwell. Also on the expedition were two French gendarmes, eight labourers, the ship's captain and the crew.

It is important to mention here, it will be obvious why later, that whilst waiting in Tahiti, Hamilton met a Mr Bunkerly. He said a man named Brown had turned up some 30 years before claiming to be a descendant of the American member of the Alvarez crew. He had other men with him and a boat fitted out for treasure recovery.

That expedition failed due to quarrelling. Brown sold the boat and departed. Six years later, he turned up again with a different name and altered appearance. Bunkerly, however, recognised him and when challenged, Brown flew into a rage and left on the same ship he had arrived on. He was never seen again. This, however, was not some unique anecdote regarding the name Brown. Howe himself had related that when travelling to Tahiti, he thought he was being followed by 'an evil-looking fellow' that was also named Brown. Bunkerly also knew Howe and was quite sure he had never found anything at all.

Three days after leaving Papeete (Port of Tahiti), they had the tantalising experience of passing the island of 'Tatee', but they had to go on to Makemo to see to some affairs and buy provisions before they could return and land there. The next day, they arrived at the atoll. A search along the reef located a pass that was too narrow to let the schooner through. To reach the atoll, they first landed on the reef and re-launched the ship's boat on the other side, which was very difficult in the thundering surf. Once on the atoll, they set off eagerly to find the landmarks given by Howe, one of note being a pinnacle of coral on the western side. However, no trace of any landmarks could be found. The island was bare with just some scrub and a few trees. A thorough exploration was unsuccessful; furthermore the island corresponded to the description given by Howe only in a general way. But it was with some encouragement that they also came across evidence that at some time in the past the ground had been dug up.

After a discussion, they agreed that either they or Howe had made a mistake, as they could not believe that every landmark could have vanished. However, some small South Pacific atolls look very similar to each other. The next day, they decided to sail around and check out some nearby atolls. This time, they did spot a conical column of coral but on the east side of one of the islands. They landed and verified some more of the landmarks but not the seven blocks of coral set at certain distances apart. It was with some encouragement that they also came across evidence that at some time in the past, the ground had been dug up. Realising that without all the landmarks it was going to be difficult to locate the jewels, they decided to leave them for later and concentrate on the gold. According to Howe, this lay at the bottom of a pear-shaped pool. Another thorough search revealed every shape of pool, except pear-shaped.

Their distinct lack of success so far had them all thinking that Howe had deliberately misled them. They compared maps and charts to the original made by Alvarez and had to agree that even the contour was not the same. After a discussion, they agreed that either they or Howe had made a mistake as they could not believe that every landmark could have vanished. The captain came up with what proved to be the right answer. He suggested that as there were several more atolls around, all very similar, why not take a look and see if there were any with a coral pinnacle on the *east* side? They eagerly agreed to this logical suggestion, which raised their spirits. The next morning, they collected their equipment and headed off to the next group of islands. The third island examined produced the right result; there was a coral pinnacle on the east side. Howe's description dictated a pass into the lagoon to the left of the pinnacle and sure enough, it was there. It took three hours of searching before they found the pool. It was perfectly pear-shaped with walls of coral. Hamilton dived in and found the pool to be about 12 ft deep with sand and broken coral on the bottom. It was only when he got out and was dressing that Hamilton said he noticed with great relief the seven large blocks of coral set at even distances apart. Hamilton now knew he was at the right place and that within a short distance, the jewels were also buried.

As keen as they were to get started, they were short of fresh water and had to go to Makemo first to stock up again.

Back on the island, most of the party were suffering from coral poisoning caused by cuts from scrambling over the coral. Hamilton, not suffering as badly as some of the others, got on with the work of bringing the equipment ashore. A renewed search was made for the jewels. Measurements were made from the pinnacle, according to Howe's figures: 84 feet E. by N., and 75 feet N. by E. They got to work and dug a trench about 12 feet by 4 feet but found no sign of the jewels. The next day, because of the surf on the reef, they had to use the pass and walk some three miles overland to the pool; not an easy task with their injuries and heavy equipment, which all had to be carried.

First, large lumps of coral had to be moved out of the pool. Drilling tests into the bottom were at first unsuccessful, and then on the sixth attempt Hamilton was sure the drill came into contact with something

of interest, probably a foreign substance. Further attempts convinced him it was neither rock nor sand and could only be the gold.
(Once again, at this point I am wondering why there was no evidence of gold on the drill bit. GE)

The gold, if that is what it was, was supposed to lay a further six feet down and because the coral-sand refilled the hole as soon as it was removed, they realised a coffer-dam was required to hold it back. This was constructed from corrugated iron sheets purchased on Makemo.

The pool was tidal with an underwater inlet through which the seawater came in and with it unwelcome visitors from the deep. Whilst sinking the coffer-dam, Hamilton was attacked by a large octopus and only got away by using his diver's knife to good effect. After that, one of the native labourers who used to be a pearl diver accompanied him but that didn't stop them being attacked again by a huge moray eel. Just as the eel launched its attack, Hamilton was able to thrust his spear into it, and the ensuring maelstrom enabled them to escape to the surface. Work within the coffer-dam continued but it was slow and laborious. They all took turns with the drill and agreed 'something else' was down there. When the captain announced that stores had to be replenished, they were all glad of the opportunity to rest. They had to go to an island called Katieu this time and whilst there, Hamilton got talking to one of the old islanders. He said that the young chief murdered by Alvarez came from his island and the story was still handed down through the generations.

Returning to their island, they were horrified to find that at the pool, the coral-sand had filled the hole to the top of the coffer-dam. All of Hamilton's work was in vain. The group decided that a proper pump and better-constructed coffer-dam was the only way ahead. So they decided to go back to Tahiti and send an explanatory cable to London asking for more money to be sent out. They were quite happy to return to civilisation for a while. They set sail convinced that they would soon be back to conclude their treasure hunt and recover the 14 tons of gold.

Alas, they would never see their island again! Claims were made in London by bogus prospective investors that the hunt was a scam. The story made the papers and being totally untrue a writ for libel was issued. Hubbard, the gentleman in charge of their London offices, sent the party a cable;

'Impossible to raise further capital owing to libellous publicity, will write.'

This was the end of their adventure. The members of the expedition had no idea or details of what the libel action was about, but realised it would take some time to settle. They decided to disband for a time. Sampson went back to Australia to make an intensive search for Howe. Hamilton went back to London where his first-hand evidence might be needed. The immediate problem for them all was one of finance. They divided what money was left between them and each went their separate way. Hamilton eventually reached London practically penniless. Eventually, the newspaper concerned decided to settle the matter out of court and paid all costs, damages and published an apology, but the damage was already done. The original libellous action and resulting publicity ruined further attempts to raise capital to fit out another expedition. The London office was shut down and they abandoned further attempts to recover the treasure. All attempts to trace Howe had failed and to them, his disappearance remained a complete mystery. That was the state of affairs then, in 1939.

Hamilton never recovered financially from the expedition and his reputation suffered. Fate dealt another blow when in WW2 the Luftwaffe bombed his house. The resulting fire destroyed most of his possessions and documents he held from the expedition. He died in the 1970s ruing his involvement with it all. The surviving members of his family want nothing more to do with the story as they blame the expedition for the family's penury.

An uncorroborated report on the internet says that in 1994, a descendant of Hamilton's made an attempt to recover the treasure. He charted the *Sea Belle* from Fakarava to Tepoto where he believed the treasure had been relocated. Soon after his arrival at Tepoto, the weather turned foul and, narrowly escaping with his life, he abandoned the search.

A similar attempt to recover the treasure by the Discovery Channel was abandoned before it commenced.

Today, local legend claims that several years ago, the islanders of the region, not wanting further publicity or foreign visitors/intruders, believing the gold cursed, recovered it and dumped it at sea. Is anybody going to believe that? If I had, I wouldn't have written this book!

There is more than one version of this 'Treasure of the Tuamotus', or 'Loot of Lima' story. To further our investigation, they all need to be looked at; we do so in the following chapters 4, 5 and 6.

Newspaper Reports of the Time

The following report (too long and narrow to reprint) appeared in a Hawaiian newspaper on April 12, 1934, quote:

'FOUND NEAR PAPEETE, Will Salvage 45 Million in Buried Ingots. Huge Treasure Located in 18 Feet of Water Near Uninhabited Island. French Government Watches Operations; Will Claim Half of Cache. – Buried pirate treasure, 25 tons of ancient Peruvian gold ingots worth $45,000,000, is reported to have been found in the Tuamotu Islands. Treasure seekers who sailed from Papeete last month returned from the Tuamotus claiming they had located the cache at an uninhabited island which they declined to name. The French Government ready to enforce its right of salvage, is watching to claim half the treasure, if recovered. The leader of the expedition from here said the gold lies under 18 feet of sand and water. He said borings brought up samples of the gold. His party plans to return to the island carrying materials to erect a coffer dam and machinery to pump out sand and water. The expedition leader said his research in Peru verified tales of the taking of the treasure, its amount and marks stamped on the ingots. He said it appeared that the treasure originated in Inca times in Peru and was first buried on the island of Hiti, in the Tuamotus, then removed to this nearby island.'

The claims we know were nonsense. The leader (Hamilton?) never went to Peru. That the gold is of Inca origin is mere supposition based on what Howe had told them and there were never any samples of gold. Hiti and the relocation statement is of more interest to us. Prospective searchers are also reminded that the islands belong to the French Government and a deal must be negotiated with them for any treasure recovery.

BURIED TREASURE

AN EXPEDITION TO TAHITI

(From Our Correspondent)

LONDON. Oct. 19 — An expedition has been organised in London by Mr. P. W. B. Wood, of Melbourne, with the object of searching on Makatea Island, French Oceania, in the Pacific Ocean, for a quantity of treasure trove which history proves to have been buried there. The expedition is the result of three years' investigations. The treasure consists mainly of gold bullion. Records show the value to be about £4,000,000. The leader of the expedition will be Captain B. J. Bentley, of London, formerly aide-de-camp to the late Lord Kitchener, and the leader of several South African expeditions. Other members of the expedition will be Mr. W. Edwards, of London, and Messrs. Sampson Bros., of Sydney.

A permit has been obtained from the French Government to allow the expedition to operate on the island, and a French official has already left Paris in advance of the main expedition to confirm this arrangement with the Tahitian Government, which is placing an armed schooner at the disposal of the expedition on arrival at Tahiti.

The treasure, history relates, was originally stolen from Lima, in Peru, by four sailors during the revolution in Peru in 1849. These men afterward stole a ship, loaded the loot, and sailed for the low Archipelago, where they buried the loot on the island. An old original map is in the possession of a member of the expedition, and it shows the situation of the treasure. A start will be made from Sydney in December or January next. During the visit of the American Fleet to Australia in 1926, Mr. Wood discovered and salved the seaplane which was lost in Port Phillip Bay during manoeuvres by the cruiser Pennsylvania. Mr. Herbert Weld, of Lulworth Castle, England, who has carried out research work in Egypt, is assisting with the financial side of the undertaking.

PIRATE GOLD

DISCOVERY IN PACIFIC

MILLIONS ALREADY RECOVERED

Report From Tahiti

NEW YORK. April 11

An Associated Press dispatch from Tahiti states that a group of treasure-hunters have traced a reputedly enormous cache of pirate gold through researches in Sydney. They have already discovered more than £10,000,000 worth of the metal on an island in the Tuamotu Archipelago, under 18ft. of sand and water. The French Government is reported to have placed a guard over the spot.

The finders are now organising an engineering expedition in the hope of lifting to the surface 25 tons of wedge-shaped gold ingots dating back to the Inca times in Peru.

(The Tuamotu (or Paumotu) group consists of 80 low coral reefs in the South Pacific, where the principal occupation is pearl-fishing.)

The above are Australian newspaper reports of the time: The first in October 1933 tells of early preparations for Hamilton's expedition. Makatea is named as *the* island and the treasure was stolen from Lima in 1849.

The second in April 1934 states 'They have already discovered more than £10,000,000 worth of metal......25 tons of wedge-shaped gold ingots dating back to Inca times in Peru'.

CHAPTER 4

FURTHER ACCOUNTS OF THE FATEFUL FOUR

Before we look more closely at the Killorain/Howe story and to complete this aspect of our investigation, it is necessary to look at other accounts, particularly that of the aforementioned journalist who visited Howe on his island. Besides being another version from the same source, it was the first time that the Killorain/Howe story had appeared in print, long before Hamilton's version.

The Charles Nordhoff Account

Faery Lands of the South Seas was published in 1921 and written by Charles Nordhoff, an American writer. On a homeward voyage to Papeete, he was becalmed off one of the tiny atolls. This one, according to his chart was named Pinaki; just another atoll amongst the hundreds that dotted this region. Drifting slowly along the north-westerly side of the island, one of the crew called out to Nordhoff, "You see him? What he do there?" Nordhoff, using his binoculars, could see a man, arms folded, leaning against a tree and looking at them. Nordhoff could see that although his skin seemed as dark as a native, he was unmistakably white. He too wondered what a white man could be doing on an uninhabited island. His native crewman said he knew nothing about the atoll, except that it was supposed to be uninhabited and belonged to the natives of Nukatavake, which lay about nine miles to the north-west.

Nordhoff went ashore and found the solitary resident frying fish before a small hut built in the native fashion. He described him as any age between thirty-five and forty-five, powerfully built, with a body as finely proportioned as a Polynesian. He made Nordhoff welcome and invited him to stay for a couple of days whilst they were becalmed. Nordhoff guessed his host was English by his accent. Their talk was general: about the island and natives, how he preferred to be alone and that the natives, who used to come over, didn't bother him anymore. He spoke freely of his earlier adventures and gold prospecting in northern Australia. For three days, there was not a hint of a breeze, the sea as calm as the lagoon. Nordhoff remained the Englishman's guest and was beside himself with curiosity. What under the sun was the man doing here? All he had gotten out of the man so far was that he was fond of fishing! There were no books or writing paper; just a chest, fishing gear, picks and shovels. How had he kept sane for seven years?

On the morning of the third day on the atoll, an incident occurred that made the situation clear. Howe was already up and out. After breakfast, Nordhoff decided to go for a walk around the atoll, estimating it should take about an hour. He found Howe on the opposite side of the lagoon diving with a steel-tipped rod. When he finished, he nodded to Nordhoff and looking up the beach (it was sloping down to the lagoon here) and said, "You can see I've been doing a bit of digging here." Nordhoff had not noticed the trenches before that were higher up the beach and was amazed at the work that had been done. They inspected the trenches; three were at least a quarter of a mile long and three to four feet deep. They were parallel and about four paces apart. Fifteen to twenty shorter trenches cut through them at right angles. They sat down in the shade, and after a few moments silence, Howe said, "I suppose you know what I'm doing here? If you have been in Papeete, you must have heard. There is no secret about it. At least, not any longer."

Nordhoff said that he had been in Papeete only a short time and didn't remember having heard of Pinaki.

"I thought you must have known. The fact is, I'm looking for treasure. Would you care to hear the story?"

"Very much, if it won't bore you to tell it."

"On the contrary," said Howe. "It will be something of a relief. Seven years of digging, with nothing to show for it, must strike an outsider as a mad business. It seems only yesterday that I came here. As you see for yourself, it's not much of an island. And to know that there is a treasure of more than three million pounds buried somewhere in this tiny circle of scrub and palm..."

"But do you know it?" Nordhoff asked.

"I am as sure of it as that I am smoking your tobacco. That is, I am sure it was buried here. Whether it has been moved since, I cannot say, of course. The natives at Nukatavake remember a white man whom they called Luta, who came here about twenty years ago and remained for something over a month. One of the four men who stole the gold and brought it to Pinaki was a man named Luke Barrett and it may have been he who came back, although he was supposed to have been killed in Australia forty years ago," he rose suddenly "If you don't mind a short walk, I will show you something rather interesting."

They went along the lagoon beach for several hundred yards and then crossed towards the ocean side. Near the centre of the island, they came upon an immense block of coral broken from the reef and carried there by some great storm of the past. Cut deeply into the face of the rock, Nordhoff saw a curious design, three marks side by side. The first was a feathered arrow pointing up, next to that was an upside-down 'L', then looking like a magnifying glass with a handle was a vertical line supporting a circle with a dot in its centre.

Nordoff asked him what it meant. "Man, if I knew that! I believe it's the key, and I can't master it, but we may as well sit down and I'll tell you the story from the beginning."

The Treasure Tale as Given to Nordhoff
[Edited but retaining the parts of importance to us.]
'Four men (Howe started off) had a hand in the business: a Spaniard named Alvarez; an Irishman named Killorain; and two others of uncertain nationality: Luke Barrett, whom I spoke of a moment ago, and Archer Brown.

They were a thieving murdering lot by all accounts - adventurers of the worst sort who, in the hope of plunder, I suppose, had joined the Peruvian Army during the war with Chile in 1859-1860. Their hopes were realised beyond all expectations. They got wind of some gold buried under the floor of a church, and the strange thing was that the gold was there and they found it. It was in thirty-kilo ingots, contained in seven chests, the whole lot worth in the neighbourhood of three and a half million pounds. How they managed to get away with it, I don't know, but I have investigated the business pretty thoroughly and I have every reason to believe that they did. They buried it again in the vicinity of Pisco and then set out in search of a vessel. Alvarez was the only one of the four who had any education. They had all followed the sea at one time or another, but he alone knew how to navigate. The others could hardly write their own names. At Panama, they signed on as members of the crew of a small schooner, and as soon as they had put to sea, knocked the captain and the two other sailors on the head and chucked them overboard. They returned to Pisco, loaded the gold and started for Puamotus.

This was in the autumn of 1859. In the December following, they landed at Pinaki, where they buried the treasure. The island was uninhabited then, as now, and they crossed to Nukatavake to learn the name of it. The natives were shy, but they persuaded one man to approach, and when they had the information they wanted, shot him and rowed out to their boat. If you should go to Nukatavake, you will find two old men there who still remember the incident.

Then they went to Australia, scuttled their vessel not far from Cooktown and went ashore with a story of shipwreck. They had some of the gold with them; enough to keep them in comfort for the rest of their lives, but it soon went. The four were next heard of at the Palmer gold fields. Alvarez and Barrett were both supposed to have been killed there in a fight with some blacks. Killorain and Brown had not mended their ways to any extent and both were finally jerked up for manslaughter and sentenced to twenty years penal servitude. Brown died in prison, but Killorain served out his term and finally died in Sydney hospital in 1912.

Most of these facts, if they are facts, [Howe continued] I had from Killorain himself the night before he died. I met him in a most curious way. I had been recommended to Australia to convalesce after having been wounded in New Guinea. I had very little gold dust left when I reached Sydney so was compelled to put up at a cheap boarding house in a poor quarter of the town. One evening, I was waiting for supper when someone rapped on the door. Before I could get to it, the door opened and an old man came stumbling in asking for something to eat. I thought he was drunk and was about to hustle him back the way he came when I noticed he was wet through; it was a cold, rainy night. I could see he was really suffering from exposure and lack of food. I made him remove his coat - he had nothing on under it - but not without a great deal of trouble, and he insisted on drying it across his knees. He was a 'wizened little ape of an Irishman', about five feet three or four in height with deep-set blue eyes, bushy eyebrows, a heavy discoloured moustache and a thick shock of white hair, altogether the most frightful looking little dwarf that ever escaped out of a picture book. He was tattooed all over the arms and chest with 'Hands across the Sea', the Union Jack, a naked woman, and several other designs common in waterfront tattooing parlours. His body was as shrivelled as a withered apple and he looked a hundred years old. In fact, he told me he was 87 and that is about all he did toll me. I made him stay until the worst of the weather was over; he said he had a job as a night watchman at Rushcutters Bay. I went with him some of the way and gave him a couple of shillings, as a loan, I said. Just before I left him, he asked for my name and address, mumbling something about doing me a bit of a good one of these days.

He didn't come back. That was in May 1912 and I heard nothing more of him until September. An attendant at the Sydney hospital called at the boarding house to say that a patient by the name of Killorain was about to die and would not give them any peace until I was brought to see him. The name meant nothing to me and I could not imagine who it could be. It was getting on toward midnight when we reached the hospital. The old man was in one of the public wards. I recognised him at once; although he had shrivelled away to nothing at all, it was impossible to forget his eyes once you had seen them.

When everyone was out of the room and earshot, he motioned me closer and asked me to hand him the coat lying across the foot of the bed. It was the same coat he had been wearing in May, when he came to the boarding house. He asked me to rip open the lining of the right sleeve and to give him the paper I would find there. It was a soiled, greasy sheet of foolscap, pasted on a sheet of cloth. "Once," he said, "you gave me two shillings for car fare to Rushcutters Bay. It probably wasn't any hardship on you, but never mind about that. You said I could pay it back if I'd a mind to. Well, I'm going to pay it back with a bit of interest. I'm going to give you this bit of paper, and it's as good as three million pound notes of the Bank of England."

He gave me a circumstantial account of the whole affair, which I have already outlined to you and I came to the conclusion he was perfectly sane and was telling the truth. He went over the chart with me saying it had been made by Alvarez, the scholar of the party. Before I left him, he made me promise that I would go to Pinaki. He wouldn't rest easy in his grave, he said, unless he knew that I was looking for the treasure, and it ain't likely I'd lie to you on my deathbed! I asked him why he hadn't gone back for it himself. He told me that of the 53 years since it had been buried, he had spent 40 in prisons and the rest of the time he was trying to earn or steal the money to buy a schooner. I told him I would come back to see him the following day. "You needn't bother," he said. "I'm finished." And it was true. He died three hours later.

I tried to forget the incident, but it was one of those things which refuse to be forgotten. It was always in the back of my head. I decided to check up Killorain's story where I could. I made enquiries in Peru and found that the gold had actually been stolen. The dates and circumstances coincided with his account. A friend in the Customs at Cooktown confirmed for me the story of four shipwrecked sailors who landed in February 1860 from a ship called the *Bosun Bird*. I decided I had to go for it and, with the money realised from a small property sale, I took passage for Tahiti on my way to Pinaki. In February 1913, I was put ashore from a small cutter, not 400 yards from where we are sitting and started the search immediately. For two months, I slept in the open - had no time to build a house - and ate tinned food which I had brought with me. Killorain's chart was of but little use. It made reference to trees which had long since rotted away or had been cut down by the natives of Nukatavake. The marks, which I found, corresponded precisely with those on the chart, but several of the most important ones were missing. That's the end of the story, you know the rest.'

Thus ended Howe's account of how he came to be on the atoll.

After these revelations, Nordhoff was hoping for a week of calm to learn more, but later that night a message from his skipper requested he come back on board as the weather was about to turn. He wanted to get away at once. Their farewells were brief.

"When shall you come to Tahiti?" Nordhoff asked.

"Not until I have found what I'm looking for."

"Well," Nordhoff said, "I hope that will be soon."

So, two versions of the same story, both from Howe but 11 years apart, Hamilton's being the second and later published version.

We continue with another variation on a theme.

The Third (Farwell) Account of the Story

George Farwell was one of the members of the failed Hamilton Expedition. In 1937, some three years after the demise of that expedition and two years before Hamilton published, he told the treasure story to *The Queenslander*, an Australian newspaper.

It is considered by those not in a position to know otherwise that Hamilton's account is the first and only published account of this affair. We can now see that in fact, it was the third published account.

It is interesting to recount Farwell's version here because it is not *quite* the same story. He starts off by making the following statement:

'In April 1934, it was erroneously reported that the Tuamotu Treasure had been discovered by a British Expedition, I was a member of this expedition, but actually we located nothing.
The incidents related here are historically accurate: The disappearance of the Bosun Bird and its valuable cargo have been confirmed in Lima: the wreck of the schooner and the landing of the four ship-wrecked sailors in Cooktown have also been confirmed: Killorain died in the Sydney Hospital in 1912, passing on the chart and the story to a man who had once done him a good turn: and the story of the treasure has become a legend in Tahiti. Several other expeditions with the sanction of the French Government have made a fruitless search for the treasure.'

I will pick up Farwell's story in Callao - his account of the dying old man in a Sydney hospital is told more or less as we know it. Farwell continues as follows.

'In the year 1849, a strange procession might have been seen threading the deserted midnight streets of Lima. Two carts drawn by oxen rumbled slowly over the cobblestones. On each side paced a file of monks, their cowled figures casting weird shadows in the light of the torches; the monks of the church of San Marco. Preceded by the tall sombre figure of the Abbot, they made their way silently down to the docks of Callao. Moored to one of the quays was a small two-masted schooner. In the dim light the lettering on her counter could be distinguished; *BOSUN BIRD. CALLAO*. A lean, swarthy man paced up and down the poop, Alvarez, the captain. The crew stood or sat about the fo'c'stle head; a polyglot collection of whites, half-castes and Creoles. At last the monks appeared on the stone quay. The only three white members of the crew leant curiously over the port rail; Killorain, a young Irishman, Brown, a hard-bitten American shellback and Barrett, an English subject. The carts drew up alongside the vessel. Alvarez shouted an order. The crew sprang into action; the monks girded up their habits. Within a short while the objects on the carts were stowed in the forward hatch—nine, surprisingly heavy casks and two brass-bound chests scarcely less heavy.

"By'r lady!" exclaimed Killorain. "There be a deal of weight to them casks!"

"Yeah!" said Brown. "I'm figgurin' that's a might queer cargo. What do you reckon it is, huh?"

They were given little time to speculate. As soon as the hatch was closed, Alvarez gave orders to sail. Seven of the monks took up their quarters in the half-deck, their sandalled feet shuffling softly over the decks. The remainder melted away into the night. One hour later the *Bosun Bird* was at sea, rolling in the long Pacific swell. The dim coastline of Peru faded rapidly into obscurity.

In the fo'c'stle the three white sailors discussed the turn of events. What was the meaning of this escort of monks? What was this cargo they were carrying? They become suspicious of this surreptitious landing and their midnight departure. They knew too, that many curious things were being smuggled out of Peru at the time. Valuable possessions the out-cast Spaniards had been forced to leave behind during the recent revolution, silver, jewels, and gold.

The history of Peru during the early part of the nineteenth century is one of violence and disorder. The birth pangs of a republic. After many attempts the Spanish oppressors had been finally driven out of the country. Many of them had been lucky to escape with their lives. But, now that comparative peace had settled over Peru, they were recalling to Spain the treasures they had been forced to leave behind them. Killorain and his companions knew this. They decided to investigate. Without doubt that freight must be of great value. Those monks were armed. That was sufficient evidence. They wasted no time. Shortly before dawn they waylaid one of the monks. They dragged him into the fo'c'stle and threatened to kill him, if he did not give them the required information. Their victim, evidently not prepared for a journey into the next world, readily told them everything.

The nine casks contained gold ingots and the two chests of specie - gold ornaments, jewels and coin. They were the property of a Spanish Grandee and for years had been concealed in the vault of the church of San Marco. It is sufficient to say that they were his by right of conquest. In a vanquished country the Spaniards of that period had few scruples. They were to be taken to a pre-arranged spot on the Isthmus of Panama, thence to be transported overland to the Atlantic coast and re-shipped to Spain. To avoid as much risk as possible, the Abbot had given Alvarez sealed orders - orders that were not to be opened until well out to sea.

Next, the three men demanded an interview with the captain. Well, perhaps interview is hardly the word, for they had pistols in their hands when they entered his cabin. They found him sitting at his table examining a sealed packet. He scrambled to his feet.

"All right, cap'n," said Killorain smoothly. "We'll not be troublin' ye, that's if ye'll listen to reason. Please be seated."

Alvarez sat down. "What d'you want?" he demanded, his dark face flushed with anger.

"We've a likin' to discuss plans with ye."

"Plans! Pon my oath! Who's captain of this ship? I'll not…"

The sight of those pistols and the three ruthless faces behind them silenced him

"Ye'll have orders from the Holy Abbot? Where are they?" Alvarez indicated the package in his hands, the seals still unbroken. Killorain snatched it from him. The three men sat down. Briefly they outlined their proposition. They offered him one of two alternatives. Either he must fall in with their plans, or else… it did not need much intelligence to realise what that meant.

The sun was above the horizon when the men emerged from the cabin. Fresh orders were issued. The schooner, which had been heading north-west, altered course for Australia. The mutineers had decided on Australia as being a country sufficiently distant to avoid detection. Also, by putting the coast of South America farther behind them each day, they would be in less danger of pursuit should their disappearance be discovered. Alvarez had no option but to fall in with their plans. Pistols can be very persuasive.

The red-sealed package containing the orders was thrown overboard. The following night, the bodies of the guards followed too. Monks are not the best guardians for anything so valuable as gold ingots. They were swiftly dispatched to a less avaricious world. Alvarez, now that his hand was forced, determined to make the best of his position. Having been driven to piracy, he intended to be a successful pirate. He was a type frequently to be met with in South American ports of that time, fearless, unscrupulous and cunning. He proposed a different plan. He warned the others that they were unlikely to cross the Pacific without sighting another ship. At that period, the ocean was not as peaceful as its name implied. The Californian gold rush was at its height and many were the ships from Australian waters making for San Francisco. There was a number of ships too, roaming about the South Seas with an eye open for just such a cargo as theirs. Suppose they encountered a vessel better manned and better armed than they? Suppose even, they were merely sighted and a description of the *Bosun Bird* reached Peru? No, they could not afford to take such risks.

And so, he suggested they plant the treasure on the first convenient island they came across. Later, when their disappearance was forgotten, they could return for it at their leisure. In the meantime, they could keep sufficient to provide for their immediate needs.

Rather unexpectedly, they fell in with his plans. Alvarez was a clever man. Probably he had ends of his own in view; plans in which the rest of the crew had no part. He understood human nature. He realised that with such men on his ship the voyage could only end in disaster. Already they were suspicious of each other. If the treasure remained on board, they would be at each others' throats night and day. They would kill each other through greed and jealousy. And, probably, he himself would be the first to be killed.

Two months after leaving Callao, they reached the Tuamoto Archipelago. These islands are strung out in a long arc to the east and south-east of Tahiti; a chain of low-lying atolls, many of them uninhabited. Just the place to conceal their valuable cargo, it would be safe there till the end of the world (and to their credit, it must be said that the treasure has yet to be located).

The schooner bore down on the very island for their purpose. They sighted it a bare nine miles off. All that was visible was a long line of foam and the dark jungle of vegetation beyond. It was a typical coral atoll, a narrow ring of land encircling a lagoon, barren of all but coconuts and scrub. The *Bosun Bird* hove to. Alvarez took a party ashore to investigate. They found no pass deep enough to admit the schooner. Consequently, they had to take the casks ashore one by one in the longboat, row through the pass into the lagoon and land them on the sand cay they had selected. An arduous task, after 28 days, for they only dared work in calm weather - the risky job was completed.

The treasure was buried, the position marked, and a plan of the island drawn. Alvarez was responsible for the chart; he was the only one who could read or write. A definite advantage, as later expeditions found to their cost. For apparently he had distorted the directions. Without him, the plans were practically useless. The next step was to discover the name of the island. With this object in mind, they called at a neighbouring atoll. They landed at a point distant from the native village and were lucky enough to come across one of the inhabitants by himself. Having learnt from him the required name, one of the sailors drew his pistol and shot him dead. This was their first mistake. For another native had witnessed the scene; he escaped before they could reach him.

In Tahiti to day there is a descendant of this native, who remembered being told of the incident by the native himself.

The *Bosun Bird* sailed on. The coast of Australia was sighted without further incident. Here, Alvarez, to destroy all evidence, decided to wreck the schooner. They landed close to Cooktown under the guise of shipwrecked sailors. And in the official records, there is a mention of four men who were brought ashore from the wreck of a schooner, the *Bosun Bird*, about this time. At Cooktown, where they apparently aroused no suspicion, the four survivors decided to split into two parties. They arranged to meet at a specific time in Sydney. Alvarez and Brown set off together into the bush and were never heard of again. They are believed to have been killed by aborigines. The other two remained for a while in Cooktown. Finally, Killorain, alone, reached Sydney. What happened to his companion, he never revealed. It is possible, however, to hazard a guess, knowing the qualities of the Irishman.

From the time of the wreck, Killorain never again left Australia. There were several reasons for his not doing so. The principal one was because out of the 50 years of life that remained to him, 40 of them were spent in gaol. His life was a tale of constant violence; robbery, murder, piracy. And for the murder of a digger at Ballarat he received a 20-year sentence. The other ten years were passed in fruitless attempts to interest people in his story. He could find no one to believe him.

'Buried treasure. An old sailor with a chart.' " Ah Yes!" they would say. They'd heard that tale before, they laughed at him.

With his money long gone, Killorain worked desperately in Sydney, on the gold fields, and in the bush. But never could he make enough to take him back to that island. His final, almost inaudible words, as he lay on his deathbed were;

"There's a curse on that damned treasure! Too much blood spilt over it. T'is cursed, I'll swear!" He did not speak again.'

This is the end of Farwell's account.

Different Tales

Three different versions but all from the same source i.e. Killorain via Howe. Some major differences as well and one wonders how could the original story change so much in just 29 years, from when Killorain knocked on Howe's door in 1910, to Hamilton publishing in 1939. It also leaves one to speculate how much could such a story change in, say, 100 to 200 years? The answer to that comes later.

Some examples of the changes to Killorain's story:

HAMILTON: Howe lived in Christchurch, New Zealand. Killorain died here.
NORDHOFF: Howe lived in Sydney, Australia. Killorain died here.
HAMILTON: Killorain and Brown shanghaied by Alvarez and Barrett to serve on the *Sweet Alice*.
NORDHOFF: All four were adventurers together and in the Peruvian Army.
FARWELL: Three were crew on the *Bosun Bird*. Alvarez was captain.
HAMILTON: Treasure was secured in special vault under church in Pisco.
NORDHOFF: Buried under floor of a church.

FARWELL:	Church of San Marco in Lima.
HAMILTON:	(1849) Inventory of treasure: 14 tons of gold ingots, 7 golden candlesticks, jewels, rings, bracelets etc 1 chest Spanish doubloons, 1 chest uncut stones.
NORDHOFF:	(1859-60) 7 chests containing gold in 30 kilo ingots.
FARWELL:	(1849) 9 heavy casks. 2 brass-bound chests.
HAMILTON:	*Sweet Alice* deserted by the four, taken on as crew at Pisco by Thompson, captain of the *Bosun Bird*.
NORDHOFF:	Stolen gold re-buried in Pisco, signed on as crew on boat at Panama, Murdered crew, retrieved gold at Pisco.
FARWELL:	*Bosun Bird* in docks at Callao, Alvarez Captain.
HAMILTON:	The four go ashore at Darwin.
NORDHOFF:	The four go ashore at Cooktown.
FARWELL:	The four go ashore at Cooktown.
HAMILTON:	Parma gold fields. Alvarez and Brown killed in bush.
NORDHOFF:	Palmer gold fields. Alvarez and Barrett killed in bush.
FARWELL:	Alvarez and Brown killed in bush.

So, some major differences, even a 10-year gap in relation to when it happened. Why? Killorain told one specific story to Howe. So, for whatever reason, Howe gave misinformation to Hamilton's party; also Nordhoff. But the big question in all of this is; how true was the story Killorain gave to Howe?

One of the things questionable about the story is regarding where the four went ashore: Darwin/Cooktown circa 1859. One would think Cooktown, as this is on the east coast where one would expect a landfall to be from the Tuamotus. They stayed in Cooktown then two of them went to the Palmer gold fields. But, Cooktown wasn't founded until 1873 when the gold rush started!

All this should be preparing you for what is to come. If somebody tells you something is true, do you just accept that it is? Many, to their cost, did just that. Hamilton himself admits (as Howe had disappeared) that he had to reconstruct the story to a certain extent in certain places and to embroider a little the story as told by Killorain to Howe. He said his reconstruction had been based on careful enquiry and research and certainly all the basic facts were definitely correct.

We will see how factual and correct later!

Treasure Found!

Shortly after the failed Hamilton expedition had returned to Tahiti, the press got hold of the story (leaked by one of the party) and the finding of the treasure was big news.

Whilst in New York on his way home to England, Hamilton was shown a cutting from a Canadian newspaper which gave an account of the finding of $50,000,000 worth of gold ingots in the Tuamotus group by an expedition which had returned to Ireland to get further equipment.

We have seen in an earlier chapter that at about the same time (April 1934), newspaper headlines led us to believe gold had been found but as we have seen, Farwell later admits they found nothing!

Back to Charles Howe, he declares his discovery of the gold in a letter dated 1920 to the Minister of the Colonies. It is in French and the important selected parts read:

"......having found on the bottom of the sea, in the lagoon of Pinaki Island (Tuamotus Archipelago) by 142 degrees 11 long west and 20 degrees latitude south some quantity of gold ingots representing a value of 86 million francs......"

"......I would like to ask you the authorization of getting the gold and to keep 2/3 for me as finders rights......"

"......the boxes containing the gold are completely rotten. That proves they are in the water a long time......"

Howe writes officially to the Minister, so what he is saying must be true - of course it is! Or is it another little untruth by Howe? Besides that, the coordinates quoted are for an empty space in the ocean, nowhere near Pinaki!

Whilst on the subject of letters to Officials, just a year later in April 1921, the French Ambassador in Washington D.C. received from an Attorney in New York the following letter, which I quote in part:

'Your Excellency will recall that at the conclusion of the interview you kindly granted to me at the Embassy on Saturday, you suggested that I embody the substance of my moral statements in a written communication which you would forward to the French Government and I am accordingly sending you this letter.

A client of this firm, M. Mark I. Adams, knows the name and location of an island included among the French Colonial possessions in the Pacific Ocean upon which he has reason to believe that there is now buried a large quantity of gold, silver and precious stones of the approximate value of $60,000,000. This treasure is said to have been taken by an American Captain from Spanish vessels off the coast of Peru in 1820 after the Spaniards had been raiding Peruvian cities and it was buried at a certain place from where it was later removed to the island where it can now be found. Its identity as the hiding place of the old Spanish-Peruvian treasure is known not only to our client but also to a group, which is now taking active steps to secretly remove the treasure. This piratical project may be successful because of the distance of the island from any European settlement.

Could you please arrange for a compensation for disclosing the location of the treasure to the French Government upon a contingent basis: M. Adams to receive nothing unless the treasure is found and it is a percentage thereof.

The island moreover has been located upon a chart and story has been corroborated in many details so that our firm has no hesitancy in stating its belief that there is such a treasure and that Mr Adams can locate it.'

You don't need to understand French to pick out what the Ambassador thought of this, in a letter to his head of department.
"Treasure Island" de Robert Louis Stevenson, -- 'de la lettre du Moderne Aladin' 'Lampe Marveillause.'

What we can see in the story detailed by Adams is in fact a somewhat mix-up of two other stories and one real event, the Loot of Lima, the *'Black Witch'* and the *'Aruacano'.* But more of those later.

Howe's Deceit

In 1921, Howe was working in a curio store in Papeete to gain finances for provisions etc. Two locals walked in offering help in the search. They were brothers named Juventin. Howe told them to search in a hole in the lagoon on Pinaki and described the location. A mistranslation in the French obviously occurred because after following Howe's directions, they were shocked to find what they had understood to be a shallow pit in the lagoon was in fact a deep hole. They returned to Papeete and angrily confronted Howe who looked at them impassively. As far as he was concerned, he had told them where it was; it was their fault if they could not do anything about it!

According to Hamilton, it was in 1920 that Howe was supposed to have abandoned Pinaki and travelled to the other island and located the gold there. So Howe was claiming to two different parties he had found the gold on two different islands. Neither, as we know, has yielded any gold.

Research, in the meanwhile, had discovered that William Edwardes, whom Howe first made contact with, was really William Edward Graham, a Barrister, admitted to the bar in Queensland in 1904. It is obvious now that Edwardes the Barrister had made Howe enter into a formal legal agreement to guarantee his participation and performance in the expedition. For Howe, this was no mere pair of local brothers who vented their anger on him. This was a fully-fledged expedition that was expending considerable amounts of money. Howe knew he would be sued by the expedition when they failed to find the gold he was claiming was on two different islands. With a contract comes liability if the contract is not fulfilled. He did the only thing possible; he went missing and stayed missing.

Edwardes, using his legal know-how and to prevent Howe leaving the country, had a letter written in May 1933 to Customs and Excise. This is what it said:

MEMORANDUM:

Charles Edward Howe

I should be glad of the Collector's advice should one, Charles Edward Howe, apply for passport facilities.

Enquiry respecting Mr Howe has been made by the legal representative of persons with whom he had entered into a contract and who stated that he had not fulfilled the terms of such contract.

Mr Howe, until recently resided at 207 Victoria Road, Darlinghurst, Sydney. He is a prospector by occupation and was born at South Stoneham, England, on the 25th May 1875. He arrived in Australia *from the United Kingdom about the year 1910 and proceeded to New Zealand the same year. He last returned to Australia from New Zealand by the S.S. "Ulinaroa" arriving at Sydney during August 1930. He is 5 ft. 7 Ins. in height with blue eyes and brown hair.*

As we know, searches by the police and private detectives failed to find him. MN's experience told him that Howe was actively hiding rather than just being missing. His last known location was in Armidale, New South Wales from where he sent a letter claiming he was ill. MN, ever investigating, in a search of record of deaths, found an entry of a death of a male named Charles Edward Howe. It was registered in 1945 in the small New South Wales coastal port of Bellingen, which is near Armidale. So Howe had gone into hiding and successfully evaded those who sought him.

Should you have read Hamilton's book and it is the only version of this story you have seen, you would be forgiven for declaring it 'A real good pirate buried treasure read'. You would probably accept it as written with no reason to question any of it. You can now see, however, that many questions need to be asked about this story.

Whilst we are at this point a long way from Lord Anson and JF Island, we can only close the loop by continuing to examine buried treasure stories of the time. It is only by studying them that ultimately we will be led to the man who is the architect behind the stories covered so far. Even more so, he also created one of the most traditional buried treasure hunting stories still alive and circulating to this day! Part 2 explores the myth behind this legendary story; our current trail eventually takes us there.

CHAPTER 5

THE SEARCH FOR KILLORAIN'S REAL IDENTITY

You may argue at this stage that the stories and 'facts' so far presented establish Killorain as a real person involved in the taking of a real treasure. Hamilton and co. had no doubt he existed. So why should we doubt the veracity of what has been told so far? Well we have seen that there are two locations given for Killorain's demise: Sydney, Australia and Christchurch, New Zealand. This anomaly had to be checked out and who better than by MN using his investigative skills as a policeman. He discovered that having checked the records of deaths at both places, there was no record of anyone registered at either place with that name. Conclusion - Killorain did not exist!

But, we have a story of a dying sailor, whatever his name is, with a treasure map. Knowing that Howe obtained his story from someone, somewhere, a comprehensive investigation started for any reports of a person who matched the description of Killorain who may have talked to Howe in Sydney around 1910. Were there any other reports of a sailor, even dying, trying to sell or tell a story of a fabulous treasure?

A Living Breed of Dying Pirates

So, we have a story of a dying sailor with a treasure map. Those familiar with pirate buried treasure stories will be thinking, 'That's familiar, haven't I read that in a story somewhere before?' Far from being a unique event, reports about a dying seaman telling the tale, or passing on a map to a treasure island, were to be found in locations all over the world. The circumstances and character of the dying pirate are a lot more familiar to people than they generally realise. So let us look at some of these stories; it is surprising what can be gleaned from them. In fact, the dying pirate has been a perennial character in fiction and familiar to most schoolboys since he most notably appeared in a fictional story written in 1883. Robert Louis Stevenson's *Treasure Island* begins with a mysterious pirate who dies leaving a map to the young Jim Hawkins.

In fact, there is an earlier story, overshadowed by Stevenson's. In 1849, James Cooper (Last of the Mohicans) wrote *Sea Lions*. Briefly, it tells of one Tom Daggett who whilst in gaol is befriended by a pirate about to be hanged. He gives Daggett a map to where he cached his ill-gotten gains on an island in the Bahamas. Old age overtakes him before he can get it and dying, he passes the secret on to one Deacon Pratt.

A point of interest here is that Stevenson's *Treasure Island* map has, at the bottom, 'Capt. Kidd's Anchorage' and 'Skeleton Island'. The author H.T. Wilkins used this in the title for one of his books, *Captain Kidd and his Skeleton Island.* For these and other reasons, we will be looking at this story again later on.

In 1888, a book was published in New York called *Captain Kidd's Gold*, a supposedly true story. It tells the story of the search for treasure buried in the Bahamas by one of Kidd's crew. A dying sailor who had come into possession of the secret from another old sailor, who had died in Greenwich Hospital, he had passed the written directions (not a map) to his son. Notice the similarity in this story to the Sea Lions story above?

The directions from *Captain Kidd's Gold*;

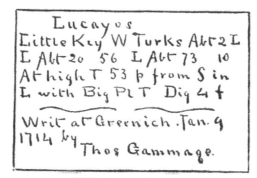

THE PARCHMENT

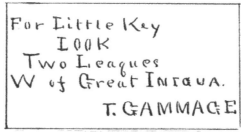

IN INVISIBLE INK, ON THE BACK

It is worth comparing this with the suspiciously similar looking Kidd/Palmer 'Yunnan' parchment that will be shown in a later chapter.

Trinity Land

Same decade again, in 1897 a book with the title *Captain Kid's Millions* was published. The story relates how a sailor named Kid, in 1695 called in at Madeira, where he was recognised by a very old man who said he had been keeping a packet of papers for him. Kid did not know what he was talking about but the old man insisted the papers were his. Amongst them was a paper in Spanish, the end of which was in some secret cipher. Other papers told of the burying of a treasure 'in a bay in the Magellan Strait'.

Kid was eventually cast away upon an island in the South Atlantic called 'Trinidada'.

He spent a lot of time trying to solve the secret of the code and eventually decoded it as follows:

'Taken to △ land 20 ½ South Pan de Azucar noon
March equin Brazil 600'

The interpretation was thus; he was at about that latitude namely 20 degrees and a half south of the line and Brazil was some 600 miles away.

The triangle symbol caused him a lot of thought but eventually he realised it signified the ancient symbol of the holy mystery and therefore meant 'Trinity Land'. i.e. 'Trinidade'.

Those conversant with Spanish waters will know that whenever the Spanish find a conical rock or mount, they name it 'Sugar Loaf' (Pan de Azucar) and there was such a rock near the south point. The noon of the March equinox he guessed related to the shadow cast by this rock. He, however, found the treasure by chance after a tidal wave, caused by a minor earthquake hitting the island. The beach changed totally, clearing a huge amount of sand off the beach. A large flat stone was exposed that drew his attention. On it was an ancient Egyptian symbol, that of the Ankh. Beneath the stone, he found the treasure in an iron-bound chest. After having taken some of the treasure, he re-buried the chest at another place. He marked where it was buried on a chart he made of the island.

The story continues into the late nineteenth century and tells of the adventures of a descendant of William Kid, one Richard Kedde. It tells of how Kid's papers eventually came to him and of his efforts to solve the chart instructions. The chart appears on the opposite page. The solution is not important to us but as you will probably want to know it anyway, it is to do with the dog Latin, or bad Latin, around the border and the key is the letters that come after the 'a's. It deciphers out to 'Cave under fall' and is at the place marked 'D' on the chart.

Of further interest is the unmistakable similarity between the layout of this chart and the Kidd/Palmer Key chart you will be made familiar with in a later chapter. You might be wondering why Kidd's name had come to be associated with all these places, as he had nothing to do with them. There is a reason, but this will come in due course.

The first map shown of 'Trinity Land' is from *Captain Kid's Millions*. Note the alchemic symbols on the map, and also the fact that it is very unusual to have an Egyptian symbol on a chart.

The second map of 'Trinidad Island' is from E. F. Knight's book *Cruise of the Alerte*, published in 1899.

Both maps are obviously of the same island and published just two years apart.

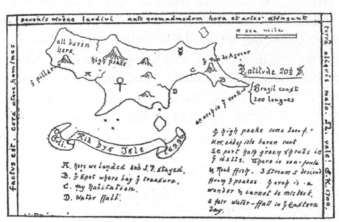

CAPTAIN KID'S CHART OF TRINITY LAND.

Drawn by himself in the years 1699-1700, A.D.

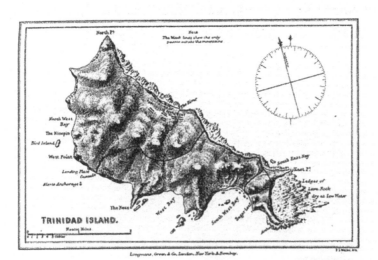

Trinidade and a Closer Link

In the latter part of the nineteenth century, there was living not far from Newcastle (England), a retired sea captain, Captain Peters. He was in command of an East Indiaman engaged in the opium trade in the years 1848 to 1850. At that time, the China seas were infested with pirates, so his vessel carried a few guns, and a larger crew than was usual in those days. He had four quartermasters, one of whom was a foreigner. The captain was not sure of his nationality, but thought he was a Russian Finn. On board the vessel, the man went under the name of 'the pirate', on account of a deep scar across his cheek, which gave him a somewhat sinister appearance. He was a reserved man, better educated than the ordinary sailor and possessing a good knowledge of navigation.

The captain took a liking to him, and showed him kindness on various occasions. The Finn was attacked by dysentery on the voyage from China to Bombay, and by the time the vessel reached Bombay he was so ill, and despite the captain's nursing he had to be taken to the hospital. He gradually sank, and when he found that he was dying, he told the captain, who frequently visited him, that he felt very grateful for the kind treatment he had received at the captain's hands, and that he would prove his gratitude by revealing a secret to him that might make him one of the richest men in England. Insisting on the door of the ward being closed, he then asked the captain to go to his chest and take out from it a parcel. The parcel contained a piece of old tarpaulin with a plan of the island of Trinidad[1] on it. The Finn gave him the chart and told him that at the place indicated on it - that is, under the mountain known as the Sugarloaf - there is an immense treasure buried, consisting principally of gold and silver plate and ornaments, the plunder of Peruvian churches which certain pirates had concealed there in the year 1821. Much of this plate, he said, came from the cathedral of Lima, having been carried away from there during the war of independence when the Spaniards were escaping the country and that among other riches there were several massive golden candlesticks. (I hope you recognise the similarity here to the Hamilton story. GE)

The Finn further stated that he was the only survivor of the pirates, as all the others had been captured by the Spaniards and executed in Cuba some years before, and consequently it was probable that no one but himself knew of this secret. He gave the captain instructions as to the exact position of the treasure in the bay under the Sugarloaf and died shortly afterwards.

To cut a long story short, on returning to England, the captain told the story to a lot of people but nothing was done until 1880. He persuaded a shipping firm at Newcastle to allow one of their vessels to visit the island. The captain's son would go ashore to identify and report on the location site. He found that a great landslide of red debris had fallen at the site but the place tallied with the pirate's instructions.

Captain Peters finally managed to interest a group from South Shields in his map and they departed the Tyne in 1885 on the barque *Aurea* led by a Mr Aem. The expedition was unsuccessful due in the main because for the fourteen days they were on the island, the eight seamen were so exhausted with the want of water, provisions, and the scorching heat, that in the end they had to be carried back on board. Two of them died.

Three years later, Mr E.F. Knight, a journalist/correspondent, did a deal with Mr Aem who handed over details of the treasure location. And so it was, that in August 1889, Knight, with four crew and seven 'gentlemen adventurers', sailed out of Southampton in the cutter-yacht *Alerte*. About three months later, they arrived at Trinidad, having stopped off on the way at the Salvage Islands. Knight had been told of another treasure here.

On Trinidade, Knight sought out a gulley 'where the pirate and his men had erected 3 cairns, which should serve as landmarks to those who had the clue, and point the way to the treasure'. Unfortunately, only traces of these cairns could be found as Mr Aem had obliterated them previously with gunpowder. What followed was three months of digging and clearing the landslip to seek the treasure buried under a hollow (this probably was meant to read 'hollow under rock') rock. They never found anything!

Knight wrote a book of the adventure called *The Cruise of the Alerte*, published in 1889.

[1]Also known as Trindade or Trinidade Island.

The Salvages

The Salvages, or Salvage Islands (there are three) in the Atlantic, were the scene of another treasure hunt spawned by a dying seaman in 1813. This one had the sanction of the Admiralty! Rear Admiral Hercules Robinson told the story of the expedition, in his book *Sea Drift*, published in 1858. The (shortened) story goes like this:

In 1813, a 'respectable looking foreign seaman', after an interview with the Secretary of the Admiralty in Portsmouth, was granted an audience with the Admiral. The outcome was that a fortnight later, Robinson was sent for by the Commander-in-Chief Sir Richard Bickerton. He was given some papers and a letter from the Secretary. The letter said:

'The enclosed, which are left open for perusal, will explain to you the purpose of sending the man to Madeira. I believe there is not the least truth in the story, and that the treasure, island and all, are visionary. But Lord Liverpool and Mr Vansittart think it worth while to make a trial of the thing, as it can be done without any great inconvenience; will you therefore have the goodness to let the man be sent in the first King's ship likely to touch at Madeira'.

Robinson was introduced to the foreign seaman whose name was Christian Cruise. He took occasion to examine and cross-question the seaman during the passage, and compare his verbal with his written testimony. The substance of both was that some years before, he had been sent to the hospital of Santa Cruz, with yellow fever, along with a Spanish sailor, who had served for three or four voyages in the Dutch merchant ship in which Cruise was employed. He was in a raging fever, but notwithstanding recovered. The Spaniard, though less violently ill, sank under a gradual decay, in which medical aid was unavailing. The Spaniard moreover, had a 'mind diseased', and told Cruise he had something to disclose which troubled him and which accordingly a few days before his death he related as follows:

He said that in 1804, he was returning in a Spanish ship from South America to Cadiz, with a cargo of produce and about two millions of dollars in chests, that when within a few days' sail of Cadiz they boarded a neutral, who told them that their four galleons had been taken by a Squadron of English frigates - war being declared and that a cordon of cruisers from Trafalgar to Cape Finnistere would make it impossible for any vessel to reach Cadiz or any other Spanish port. What was to be done? Returning to South America was out of the question, and they (or rather the captain) resolved to try back for the West Indies, run for the north part of the Spanish Main or some neutral island, and have a chance thus of saving at least the treasure with which he was entrusted. Keeping out of the probable track of cruisers, they reached a few degrees to the southward of Madeira, where they hoped to meet the trade winds. They eventually found themselves close off a cluster of small uninhabited islands, fifty leagues to the southward of Madeira, and nearly in its longitude, the name of which they did not know. The centre island, about three miles round, was high, flat, and green at top, but clearly uninhabited; the temptation was irresistible, here was a place where anything might be hidden; why run risks to avoid the English in order to benefit their captain and their owners? Why not serve themselves? (The crew were mutinous, having preferred running the risk of attempting Cadiz.)

The captain was accordingly knocked on the head or stabbed with their ready knives and carried below, and the ship hauled in to what appeared the anchorage, on the south side of the island. There they found a snug little bay in which they brought up, landed the chests of dollars, and cut a deep trench in the white sand above high water mark, buried the treasure and covered it over, and some feet above the chests, they deposited in a box the body of their murdered captain. They then put to sea, resolving to keep well to the southward, and try to make the Spanish Main or a neutral island, run the ship on shore and set her on fire, agree on some plausible lie, and with the portion of money they resolved to retain on their persons, they were to purchase a small vessel, and under English or other colours, to revisit their hoard and carry it off at once or in portions. (Again, do you recognise anything familiar with this story? GE)

They passed Tobago and due to their clumsy ignorant navigation, with it blowing hard, ran over an uninhabited cay. The ship went to pieces, and only two lives were saved. The story of one of those survivors is now being related.

Robinson in particular questioned Cruise about the murder and burial of the captain. Regarding the murder, well, that was a way of life for a lot of the crews looking to make easy money. Burying a body over the treasure is straight from the tales of pirates and buccaneers. The pirate Blackbeard, for example, considered it expedient when he buried any treasure, to cut the throat of a Spaniard and place the body over the deposit, that the ghost might guard it. Robinson pressed this point and was relieved when Cruise said that he understood the object was, that in case any person should find the marks of their proceedings and dig to discover what they had been about, they might come to the body and go no further.

When they arrived at the sandy bay with the white beach and level spot above high water mark, Cruise confirmed it was the place. Robinson entrusted the officers with the story and the men were told they were looking for the body of a sailor. To encourage them, they were told that the discoverer of the coffin would have a reward of $100. Fifty of the crew were landed armed with shovels and pikes for probing. They dug for several hours but found nothing.

Robinson resolved to go back one day and persuaded his officers to keep the secret. However, it was not until he was out of the service in 1856 that he found himself back there, on board the yacht *Dream*. This was, of course, a private venture, with two colleagues and a crew of six. Bad weather prevented them landing, so they decided to weather out the storm in Tenerife. Here they heard a story of how years ago, a pirate ship was sunk by an English man-of-war. One man only was saved, who was treated so kindly by the captain that he told him where a treasure was hid and gave him the marks on the rock to find it. The story somehow or other got to Liverpool and the *John Wesley* came out to search the Great Salvage. After two or three months digging, they found nothing and went to Tenerife for water. They returned to the island and a report was received later that an amount of money had been found. Nobody on Tenerife knew if this was true or false. Some time later, some sailors turned up at Tenerife saying they had belonged to a ship which fitted out at Liverpool *after* the *John Wesley*'s return. They were in a sorry state, thin and starved. Two millions sterling were supposed to be hidden. They had come out to the Salvages in good earnest, with wooden houses, miners, tools and six months' provisions. They had dug, dug, and dug, even down to the bare rock. All they found was a body buried under the sand,[1] a few boards and a copper coin - a penny piece of the reign of George III. The coin had been marked with a sort of index on the back, and on the face, the four points of the compass with the letter N at every point. The landlord who was narrating this story to Robinson said that he tried to buy the coin but the sailor said he would not take £100 for it, as he thought it pointed out something, if only he could find out what. (Haven't we heard that before somewhere? GE)

Robinson's expedition returned to the Salvages but weather conditions were still not suitable for landing everything. They realised that even if some of the treasure had been found, their yacht was not a suitable transport for the many tons of silver Robinson estimated was there. Reluctantly, they returned home and endeavoured to find out the truth regarding the *John Wesley* and if they had found anything. They all, however, went their ways and nothing more was done.

Robinson, after his first venture to the island with the Admiralty, had, save for his officers, kept the treasure story to himself. He relates in his book how, after a lapse of many years, he mentioned the story as a fireside gossip. He heard a similar tale back but said that the facts had been woven inaccurately into one of our thousand and one nautical narratives, and later on he says:

'It seems clear to me that some traditional bits of my story had taken root, such as the exact sum of two million pounds, the dead body, and one survivor of the pirates. One can recognise also, fragments of Blackbeard, Captain Kidd, and others with a superstructure of invention; but thus it is all in history, truth and falsehood are mingled together in one gorgeous and brittle mass.'

With that observation, Rear Admiral Robinson could have written the Foreword to this book, which is why the above quote was included in the Foreword.

For some reason, Captain Kidd has been linked to the Salvage Islands treasure. What follows is a newspaper article from *The Canberra Times*, dated 20 May 1936:

'PIRATE SHIP----MAY SEEK KIDD'S TREASURE....Vessel Seen at Salvage Islands....CAPTAIN HAS "TREASURE" CHART....LONDON, Monday.

The British steamer Avoceta advised Lloyds to-day that passing Salvage Islands, 180 miles south of Madeira yesterday, the watch saw anchored a fishing vessel answering to the description of the pirate trawler, Girl Pat, which has disappeared.

Several boats were working close in shore and another was ashore.

The islands are a small rocky group and are dependencies of Madeira, used mainly as fishing bases. It is suggested that the Girl Pat's crew is searching for Captain Kidd's pirate treasure, which is reputed to be hoarded on the Salvage Islands.

A resident of Grimsby, who once participated in the search for Kidd's treasure, says that the Master of the Girl Pat, George Black Osborne, was in possession of rough treasure charts. Osborne, he added, often questioned him regarding the treasure and hinted that he intended making a search for it.

The British Government sent an expedition in 1930, but the treasure was not found.

All the above stories you can see are linked in some way. DNA features very much in this book. Later, we give you a full introduction to it but one example is already very apparent; the dying sailor. We do not finish with these stories here; they will feature again later where we show some of the inherent clues and more DNA relating to the lost treasure.

In our continuing search for the real identity of Killorain and the source of Howe's story, we introduce to you in the next chapter to Captain Brown, a key player in our story.

[1]Remember the earlier Christian Cruise story? They should have dug deeper below the body!

CHAPTER 6

THE HERMAN EXPEDITION - EVER CLOSER TO KILLORAIN

Looking for what could be the source of Howe's story and the identity of Killorain, extensive research finally paid off. Two books were found; *The Voyage of the Herman* and *Our Search for the Missing Millions*. Between them, they helped to finally solve this mystery. Both books tell the story, albeit 64 years apart, of an expedition to search for the treasure of the Tuamotus.

Our Search for the Missing Millions was published a year after the demise of the expedition. It was written by J.C. Wood (nom de plume of John Chetwood), one of the participants, and published by The South Sea Bubble Company. He followed the title with *Being an Account of a Curious Cruise, and a More than Curious Character*. It is a rather self-deprecating narrative of the trials and tribulations of the expedition but nevertheless corroborated more or less the account in *The Voyage of the Herman*.

The Voyage of the Herman was published in 1966. It tells in detail of the expedition that set out in 1902 to search for the treasure. This, you will note, is 10 years before Howe starts his search, and 32 years before the Hamilton expedition. The story was culled from the records of one Captain George Sutton of New York, who for reasons to be shown, took over command of the expedition. Captain Sutton kept these records of the expedition with almost fanatical detail, and not only of the voyage itself but for years afterwards, anything to do with it; letters, newspaper cuttings, diaries, the log and charts etc. Everything was assembled in a massive scrapbook. Captain Sutton died in 1934, unable to complete his classification of the work to tell the complete story. He left everything to his son, George Sutton Jnr. who left them for years buried amongst his father's effects. He eventually started to assemble everything together to finish his fathers work, but he died in 1958, the work unfinished. We have his widow, Ione Ulrich Sutton, to thank for making the story available to the public. She corroborated with the writer Theon Wright in putting together the whole fantastic story.

The story I present is culled in part from both books and as with Hamilton's story, space permits me to present only a condensed version and parts that are of essential interest to us.

Captain Brown's Story

The 'Ecclesiastical Treasure of Lima' as it was then known, gives us our first link to another - if not *the* most famous Treasure Island - Cocos Island. This treasure, we are led to believe, was once buried there! According to Captain James Brown, an old mariner who arrived in San Francisco at the turn of the 20th century, he helped dig up this enormous hoard on Cocos and re-bury it on a remote island in the South Pacific Ocean. Cocos Island and its treasure legends will be looked at in more detail later in this book, but for now, let us tell the captain's story:

Captain Brown was an imposing character; big, striking, domineering and with a thick bushy beard, giving him the appearance of an old Viking. At over six feet in height, in his younger days he would have been a formidable opponent in any fight. In 1901, he was living in a small hotel and appeared to spend his time talking only to men of wealth, leisure and a sense of adventure. He said he was the only possessor of the secret of a fabulous treasure, having once been a pirate himself. He was treated with curiosity and sometimes some interest but could get nobody interested in a venture. Stories of hidden treasure were rife along the waterfront in those days, along with the perennial old pirate or sailor touting his worn and weathered map, which led to a fortune in gold.

Brown usually had himself to blame; his temper, mistrust and ingrained suspicion of everyone did not win him any friends or potential partners. Dr. Luce, another resident of the hotel, had made the acquaintance of Brown and one day, learning that Brown was desperately ill of recurrent malaria and slowly sinking, went up to Brown's room. Over a period of weeks, Dr. Luce nursed him back to health. During this time, Brown, in a detached, vague sort of way, started to mention things about an immense church treasure, Lima, burial, re-burial and a lonely island in the Pacific. All were mentioned in a confusing rambling story to Dr. Luce, but as Brown got better, the story became clearer. During this time, they discovered they were brother Masons and under that Order's oath, Brown said to him, "I am the only man alive today who knows where lies the thirty million worth of jewellery, coin, plate and bullion that Captain Schmidt carried away with him from South America so many years ago". To back his story up, Brown showed Dr. Luce a number of coins, English and Spanish, minted between 1750 and 1790. These and many more, he said, he had brought back from the island where the treasure lay. "There's millions more where that came from," he said. "We dug it up on Cocos and I'm the only man left alive who knows the island where we buried it. That is the reason why all the searchers on the island since '51 have failed. We dug it up and carried it off".

In 1850, some 31 years had elapsed since the disappearance of this famous treasure and the original freebooter and his companions had never lifted it from its hiding place. This was probably owing to there having been shadowed too closely by the owners or their emissaries. Between 1821 and 1850, this lost treasure undoubtedly lay buried on Cocos Island. Captain Schmidt and his comrades found no opportunity to retake it. They gradually died off leaving the secret of the location to their heirs.

Whilst dining with friends one night, Dr. Luce decided to mention the old Captain's tale to them. He had more or less put all the pieces together and wanted to know what they thought. The friends, John Chetwood, Donzel Stoney and Frank Green, were familiar enough with Cocos' treasure stories. A lot of expeditions had been fitted out over the years but in spite of the seemingly authentic reports of treasure(s) having been buried there, nothing was ever found; not reported anyway. Captain Brown's story, they realised, was a possible reason for this treasure not being found; he said he had removed it! So they were intrigued enough to find out more and decided they should meet with Brown. But Brown had gone back to Providence. He had, however, left a letter for them suggesting that if they were interested in the venture to contact him. This is how Captain Sutton became involved. Frank Green had an old friend in New York, a lawyer, Arthur Waldradt; he asked him to investigate Brown. Waldradt, needing the opinion of someone familiar with things of this nature, contacted his friend Captain George Sutton, who was Commodore of the New Rochelle Yacht Club. A meeting was eventually set up with Sutton travelling to Brown's home near Providence, R.I. Sutton's first impression was again of the old man's size; big, broad and weather-beaten, with remarkable eyes.

Brown started his story with his early days at sea and how he met the instigator of his future life as a pirate adventurer. He witnessed a young fellow being beaten up by a gang of roughs in Kingston Harbour, Jamaica. He stepped in to help him and, as he said, "They all ran like rats." They became close friends after that and Brown discovered that his name was Henry Schmidt, from New Bedford, near Providence. It turned out that Schmidt was fitting out a vessel for a trip around Cape Horn to the West Coast. The name of the vessel was the *Sea Foam*, with a crew of 52. With an invite, Brown signed on as a junior officer. Not only was his curiosity aroused by the size of the crew - a dozen could normally handle a brigantine - but it carried almost no cargo. Captain Schmidt set sail with the announced intention to engage in pearl fishing in the Pacific. Out at sea, Schmidt confided in Brown as to the real purpose of the trip. He had charts and maps given to him by his father, who had also been a captain. The charts gave the location of a treasure buried on an island 'off the coast of South America.' Brown went on to tell Sutton that about a hundred years ago, a lot of gold and silver had been buried on Cocos. The crew of a ship called the *'Black Witch'* buried one of the hoards. The young Schmidt's father was master. The loot consisted mainly of church treasures out of the Spanish colonies. Sutton recognised this part of history. He had done his research, ready for his confrontation with Brown. A huge treasure had disappeared from Callao in the early 1820s. It consisted of church relics, coin, and gold and silver ornaments. Sutton discovered that to safeguard it for the authorities, a Captain Henry Smith had loaded the treasure aboard an American Schooner called the *Black Witch* when the Spanish rebels were marching in the city and it was under the threat of bombardment by a Spanish fleet.

The young Schmidt told Brown that his father was supposed to have sailed out of Callao and cruised around until the insurrection was put down. His Peruvian employers were unaware that in his youth he had engaged in 'piratical enterprises'. Temptation got the better of him and they sailed instead to Cocos Island.

Brown showed Sutton the map of Cocos with the treasure directions saying, "Don't mind showing ye this now. Won't do ye any good, cap'n. The gold ain't there any more."

Trouble apparently developed amongst the crew of the *Black Witch* when they discovered the nature of the cargo. They insisted on a 'division of spoils' in accordance with the code of pirates and privateers. Captain Schmidt would have none of it and mutiny broke out. It was vigorously put down with half the crew shot and the remainder flogged. After leaving Cocos, the *Black Witch* ran into foul weather off the coast of South America. With the depleted crew unable to keep control, she was driven ashore and most of the crew lost. Captain Smith somehow survived and eventually made it back to New York. Before he died, he confided the story of buried treasure to his son.

Brown continued the story of the *Sea Foam*. She had put in at Juan Fernandez Island on the way up the West Coast and later in Chincha, avoiding any of the major ports. (Later research by Sutton's group, showed that a vessel named the *Sea Foam* had been off Callao for several days in 1851, presumably on a pearl fishing expedition to the Bay of Dulce). On reaching Cocos, Schmidt went ashore in one of the longboats leaving Brown in charge. He watched him follow the directions on the map left by his father, and then disappear from view. That night, Schmidt, having confirmed the directions, burnt the map. He feared that suspicious crew members might attack him that night. The map directions led to a sealed cave and the next day, the face of the cliff was blasted out to reveal the cave. Wasting no time, they started to move the casks and chests down to the shore. It took two days and thirty trips in the longboats. Finally, with its immense load, the *Sea Foam* headed westward into the Pacific.

The Tuamotu Archipelago is, as it says, a sea abounding in islands. The area is also known as French Polynesia and comprises the Marquesas Islands, Society Islands, Tubuai Islands and Gambier Islands. They stretch east to west for about 1,000 nautical miles. Centre is about 140 degrees west and 17 degrees south. Tahiti lies at the western extreme. The *Sea Foam* had to sail something like 4,000 nautical miles from Cocos to reach here, which they did sometime in late January 1852. As an aside, you may recall that the famous adventurer Thor Heyerdahl in the *Kon-Tiki* did approximately the same distance, to the same islands - Callao to Tuamotus group in 100 days in a traditional Polynesian craft.

The *Sea Foam* sailed down amongst the islands and eventually anchored off one that Brown said was 'well out of the way of trading routes.' The island was about three miles long and maybe one mile wide, a typical coral atoll. There were two entrances to the lagoon;

both were too dangerous for their ship to enter so they hove to in the channel, outside two points of land. The beach was reached in the longboat. Brown, in describing the island, said there were cliffs of limestone facing the lagoon and the open sea, and behind that an irregular ridge, which was probably volcanic. There was a cave in the cliff facing the lagoon, ideal for their purpose. The treasure was ferried ashore in longboats and carried to the cave.

"How did you hide the treasure?" Sutton asked.

"Blasted the cliff down!" Brown said.

During this part of Brown's account, Sutton was puzzled by the choice of island. Brown said it was not likely to be visited by wandering ships, since there was no easily accessible landing area. Yet he said that there was a "large plant of oysters in the lagoon." Now pearl fishing was a pursuit of the South Sea Islanders, so the island therefore was likely to be visited by them.

Brown did not elaborate too much on what happened after the treasure was hidden but it appears this immense wealth only seemed to whet their appetites more. They made for Australia, lured there by the reports of fabulous amounts of precious metal that was being taken from the Australian placers. A lot of this bullion was sent to England and they discovered in some cases the treasure ships had no convoy protection. Having found the date set for the sailing of two of these ships, they managed to get aboard each vessel some of their own crew. This accomplished, they had little difficulty in stopping and capturing these vessels when they were far out in the vastness of the South Pacific Ocean. It appears that after this lucrative trip, a huge fight broke out. A celebratory generous supply of rum had been given out and a lot of the crew became ill. Accusations were shouted at the captain of putting poison in the rum, but warning shots subdued them. During the night, a few of the crew died and in the morning, the remainder, in an ugly mood, advanced on the quarterdeck. When the shooting was over, only three were left: Brown, Schmidt and the cook. An earlier comment by Brown that 'Too many people knew about the gold,' might explain the outcome of the fight!

Realising that just three of them could not sail the ship, they rigged out a longboat and loaded some of the kept treasure aboard. The *Sea Foam* was sunk. They headed west on the long journey to the Australian coast. The cook became ill and died; his body was dumped overboard. Things became very uneasy between the two after that with weeks of watching each other, the blazing sun, dwindling water and food supplies. There was only one gun between them and Schmidt had that. "Men don't think straight in times like that," Brown said. One night, he heard Schmidt moving towards him so jumped him first and wrestled the gun off him. Moving back to his place in the bow, Brown waited for first light. "I knew he'd gone crazy. When it was light enough to see, I shot him!"

Brown eventually made it to Australia safely and converted enough of the treasure into English currency to buy a sheep station. After a few years, he said he returned to his 'Treasure Island' to replenish his money supply. He later travelled to England where he married and settled down. Eventually he moved back to America and bought the house he now lived in near Providence, Rhode Island. Money was invested in a shipping business in Philadelphia, which turned out to be running guns into Cuba. Caught out by a naval patrol, his two vessels were seized and confiscated. Brown reckoned he lost "several hundred thousand dollars." Even so, he was comfortably off and although his wife, who knew the secret, wanted him to go back for more, he didn't feel the need to at that time. However, at over 70 years old, he was now getting on in years, and decided he needed to enlist the help of partners to get the rest of the treasure, which is why he had gone to San Francisco and where he had met Dr. Luce.

During a tea interlude, Brown having gone indoors, Mrs Brown said of her husband, "He is greatly concerned about this and thinks of nothing else. He knows where the island is, I am sure of that. He will do anything to get it back and is very determined."

Stormy Seas

On his return to New York, Sutton presented to Waldradt a favourable report of the whole matter. The upshot was that the San Francisco group agreed to the venture. One of the reasons they were convinced of the veracity of Brown's story was the evidence of cancelled cheques, old money receipts and cheque book stubs. These all showed that at times between 1850 and 1860, Brown had over $200,000 in London banks. Here at least was evidence that he had in his youth acquired, and very suddenly acquired from some mysterious source, what amounted at the time to a considerable fortune.

Sutton, Captain Brown and Waldradt travelled to the West Coast to organise an expedition. Sutton was by now a major shareholder. Brown was left to find a suitable boat for charter and found the *Herman*, a 90ft schooner with a crew of ten, two officers, a cook and steward.

To learn of the rows, dissent, suspicions and distrust that took place, leading up to their departure, all of which was accompanied by the rumour mongering of the press, I suggest you read Wright and Sutton's aforementioned book. So much was the speculation about where the expedition was headed that August Gissler himself, the self-imposed 'Governor of Cocos Island', turned up at the docks to lecture the crowd that had gathered on how he would put a stop to the expedition to Cocos with Government gunboats!

The *Herman* finally left San Francisco in July 1902. The expedition was to be long and troubled and to last 14 months. There were many trials and tribulations, all can be said due to Brown's surly outspoken attitude and keeping much to himself. With his history of piracy, murder and domineering manner - 'I am captain of this ship and will tolerate no insolence' - it concerned Sutton and the others. They had many confrontations over the coming months, libels for unpaid bills, demands for money from Brown. Sutton and co. also learned things about Brown during their stop-offs down through the Pacific. For example, they learned during a reception party in Honolulu something of his activities. A princess (daughter of a chief) told them that her grandmother came from a group of islands called Paumoto. She told her that, when a girl, a ship came and took some of the young men away to work on the ship. Some of the men were killed in fights with other ships. Those that came back told that they took a lot of money in chests and then sank the other ships. Later, the 'big ship' was for many months at an island west of the place where her grandmother lived. She didn't know what it is called now but then it was called the 'Island of Smoke' because of a small volcano now dead. This seemed to confirm to Sutton that after burying the treasure, Brown and Schmidt had attacked the ships carrying gold to England from the Australian gold fields. Later in the voyage, during a conversation Brown confirmed to Sutton that they took natives when their own sailors died or got killed in the fights.

Delays in Sydney, repairs and waiting for the weather all added to the tension on board. At one point during the voyage, Brown attempted to abandon the expedition wanting to go to Tahiti in another boat. Brown's authority was withdrawn and he was threatened with an Admiralty Court and served with a Court Restraining Order. This only compounded the problem, of course; no Brown, no treasure! Faced with possible jail, broke and unable to return home, Brown reluctantly signed on as 'supercargo' to 'protect his seaman's rights'. This also protected the expedition against his last-minute desertion. Despite this setback, he quickly assumed his old dictatorial air of authority with the crew but Sutton had now taken over the role as Master of the Herman. This didn't make things any easier!

They continued east from Sydney, past the 180th meridian, then due south of Tubuai, the largest of the Austral islands. Brown had given no indication yet where his treasure island was, although he had agreed 'on his Masonic Oath' to lead them to it. This only added to the mistrust that already existed and didn't improve when a loaded pistol was found under Brown's pillow.

Some 1,000 miles south of Tahiti, they veered north-east on a course that would take them east of that island. Brown was even more annoyed when Sutton refused to call in at Tahiti. Sutton explained that the notoriety of events so far would have alerted the French authorities and everyone else. They couldn't risk anyone following them. Brown's protests were such that he threatened not to take them to his island. A stand-off ensued with Sutton ordering him out of his cabin and meals were refused to him at the captain's table; he had to wait until all had finished. An order to work his passage seemed to bring Brown to his senses. He promised to take them to the island but first he had to go ashore to rest-up and get rid of the fevers.

They sighted Maitea (Mehetia?) south-east of Tahiti, one of the outposts of the Tuamotus archipelago. Next Makatea, 124 nm NNE of Tahiti. This is one of only four islands amongst the islands of the archipelago that does not take the form of a true atoll i.e. no central lagoon. Surrounded by cliffs some 200 feet high, the centre was once a solid mass of phosphate that was mined by the French and British until 1966. You may recall from the Hamilton chapter that this island was mentioned in a newspaper report as being where the treasure was buried. Continuing north, they went to Tikihau then Matahiva. To relive Brown of his illness, they went to Penrhyn Island (now known as Tongareva Island) which was some 600 miles northwest of Tahiti.

You can see on a map in the next chapter this was taking them even further away from Pinaki.

The *Herman* worked its way back south-east. Brown was aboard but under protest. He had declared himself too ill to sail and wanted to stay on Penryhn but Sutton would have none of it. They continued on a 130 degree heading calling at Matahiva then Makatea again, hoping to get Brown talking about the island. Sutton had his suspicions that as Brown and Schmid must have had a base to work from, it could well have been Makatea. It was whilst Sutton and Chetwood were exploring Makatea that Brown attempted to take over the *Herman*. He was overpowered but declared he just wanted to shoot birds. He still refused to give his island location so they sailed back to Penrhyn. He was put under surveillance the whole trip with a crewman on guard outside his door. The Resident Agent advised them that Brown could not be held on Penrhyn, so they decided to proceed to Papeete and from there determine the future of the expedition. Whilst there, in the American Consul's office, the Consul admitted that they knew about the expedition, so he said did the British Consul, and also the French Government representatives. Asking about the British interest, they learned that *they* were interested because it was suspected the *Sea Foam* was responsible for the attacks on the Australian specie ships that disappeared back in the middle of the nineteenth century.

Sutton, in a later conversation with the Mayor, asked him what he knew about Makatea Island. He said its official name is Aurore and many years ago it was known as Moku-iti. Asking what that meant, the Mayor told him 'Little Smoke Island'. He also said there were once pirates in the area. This convinced Sutton that Makatea must have once been the base of the *Sea Foam*. This, besides Brown declaring to Sutton, "I ain't ever been on that island!" It was now useless information, of course; they still did not know where Brown's Treasure Island was.

Brown, because he had no money, stayed aboard the *Herman*. Sutton found him in his cabin, lying on his bed, still and lifeless, and for an instant he thought he was dead, but he turned his head and glared at Sutton. "It ain't no use for us to talk anymore, Cap'n. The spirits won't let us go back (Brown had talked of the ghosts of the treasure many times before), unless you let me take over this ship, Cap'n."

"I'm not likely to," Sutton replied.

From this book's point of view, that is the end of the story of the Herman Expedition. The ship was sold for $8,250, a month after they arrived in Papeete. Brown, a sullen and unwilling companion, left with the group for San Francisco on the *SS Mariposa*, arriving there September 13th 1903.

Fourteen months of futile wandering across the great South Pacific Ocean thus ended, never getting anywhere near 'treasure island'. One wonders why they wandered aimlessly around the western end of the Tuamotus group. Brown was the only one who knew where the island was. Almost before the expedition had began, he became disillusioned, having to give up his role as captain of the *Herman* and leader of the expedition. As you can see from the account, there was too much mistrust and dissent. His recurring malaria and old age didn't help either. At an early stage, he had given up on this expedition, he would only do it on his terms and had secretly decided he would wait for another time.

CAPTAIN JAMES BROWN IN STUDIO POSE

Killorain Unmasked

Some 9 years after the 'Herman' group parted company in San Francisco, Sutton unexpectedly received a letter from Brown. Dated March 19th 1912, it briefly mentioned another failed expedition organised by him three years previous; a typhoon blew them ashore on New Caledonian Island, and so they did not get very far.

Of far more interest to us is that contained in the explanation for writing to Sutton. Brown said he had been contacted by a 'party' interested in outfitting an expedition *'but they wanted to go by themselves'*. Brown obviously wasn't too keen on this as he asked Sutton to go in his place, as his representative. Sutton declined.

Note the year—1912. When did Charles Howe leave for Tahiti? 1912. If you have not worked it out by now...

...Killorain was none other than Captain James Brown! And everybody, including other researchers and authors, have failed to make the connection.

As we have seen, Brown had held back the vital information needed to find the island from two of the principle parties i.e. Howe and Sutton. Hamilton's party, as we know, used Howe's information and a study of the facts indicate that Hamilton and the rest of his expedition were truly unaware that Howe's source of information was Brown. So, three major expeditions so far, all yielding precisely nothing, with nobody any the wiser as to where the island was, except that it was supposed to be in the Tuamotus Archipelago. What is also interesting is that Howe seemed to be totally unaware of Brown's involvement in the earlier Herman expedition.

What we do know is that Brown, unwittingly gives up different and sometimes additional information to the different groups/personnel he is in league with. What is interesting is that 18 or 19 years after the demise of the Herman expedition, he must have given Charles Howe previously undisclosed information because it would seem Howe got closer to the treasure than anyone else as we will see. These snippets of information are the pieces of jigsaw that will complete the puzzle; or at least give us a damned good idea where his island is and what it looks like. So these clues, gleaned by the observer who knows what he's looking for, are vital pieces of the jigsaw. Each account has some of these pieces, if you can recognise them, so all accounts must be looked at, to see how much of the jigsaw we can complete.

The 'Gennessee' Expedition

Captain Brown, if nothing else, was a determined man. That the/a treasure existed is in no doubt. He made numerous efforts to get it, and except for his own lone (we assume) trips sometime in the mid 1800s or thereabouts, every expedition was met with failure.

His last effort was in 1919. He set up a company called the Brown Exploring Company. Sadly, the old man died, aged 89, in his home in Augusta, Maine, a couple of months before the start of the expedition, which nevertheless went ahead. They were obviously confident in the information given. The expedition was organised by a Captain James T Houghton of New York. The schooner *Gennessee* had a complement of 35 when she sailed, first to Cocos and then to the Low Archipelago. The large complement of men was due to the South Pacific Films Company on board. These 20 men had been hired believing that they were to participate in the shooting of a film but the trip to Cocos was but a ruse to put people off their real purpose.

Once on the atoll of Tupai, (in some accounts it is Tubuai to further confuse) the open-air temple called the Grand Marae was located. The treasure was believed to be buried under here. After three weeks of digging, all they uncovered were the skeletons of a dozen men!

A brief report of the expedition by one of its members appeared in *The New York Sun*.

'On February 27 (1920) we sailed out of Tahiti for an island in the Tubuai group. We left our craft outside the harbor of a beautiful island and went ashore. Excitement ran high as news of the search spread among the crew. Captain Crowley, (of Boston) was armed with maps and charts. The point we sought was inland, and we found a mound where the treasure should have been. We began digging and continued to dig for three weeks, uncovering a huge area. But we found only the bones and we finally gave up the task.

Though this report says the island is in the 'Tubuai group', 'Tubuai' is an island in the Austral Group. It is really referring to 'Tupai', which is in the Society group of islands. 'Tupai' was sometimes spelt 'Tubai' and due to the involvement of a real pirate ship we will read about shortly, associated with both 'Tupai' and 'Tubuai', this mix-up often occurred. In one of the author's H.T. Wilkins books, it is even referred to as 'Zubai' and if you were observant, you will have noticed it spelt 'Zubia' in the earlier *New York Herald* article. Another account says that around the end of the nineteenth century, a British subject named Blackett, living on Tupai, found the treasure. He employed 12 Polynesians on his coconut plantation and to ensure there would be no witnesses to his find, he killed them all. Their graves were subsequently discovered near the path linking the western path with the little village. The Queen of Bora Bora had Blackett arrested, and loath to execute a British subject, she forced him to disappear at sea in a small boat. Blackett never returned to recover the treasure and was never seen again.

There is a promotional booklet in colour titled *Tupai Island–L'île au trésor* (*Treasure Island*). Besides explaining the geology and history of the island (it was discovered by Captain Cook aboard the *Endeavour* in 1769), its history of buried treasure is also recounted, that being the *Araucano* tale, which follows in a later chapter. It goes on to say that around 60 years after the *Araucano* incident, two Belgian brothers arrived in Tahiti where they chartered a schooner. Almost to the point of committing murder, they took full possession of the ship which they took by force. They were eventually condemned to death by the courts of Papeete, a sentence that was never carried out. However, concerning their diggings on 'Tupai', they were all in vain, even though they excavated without restraint nearly everywhere. They kept their crewmen working under threat of death. The same narrative goes on to tell the story of the 'Genese' expedition (the incorrect date of 1932 is also given). I quote, in part:

'...after having confirmed, both in London and Sydney, the veracity of information imparted by an old seafarer who was apparently in on the secret, a Captain Brown. The archives consulted in both cities were categorical; the existence of the treasure could not be doubted. Once on the atoll, the grand marae, the open air temple under which the treasure was believed to be buried, was located, and the edifice was dug up and turned over from one end to the other. However, once again, the adventurers wasted time and money, for nothing was brought to light but some old bones.'

His Bloody Island

Brown, as we have seen, was determined to get back to his island. Prior to the final Gennessee Expedition, he made two other attempts. In 1909, he persuaded a syndicate in Boston to finance an expedition. Sailing from San Francisco for Australia on February 9th, he intended to charter a small steamer in Sydney but instead he obtained a sailing vessel. Brown, armed with a suitcase full of maps and sailing directions, left Sydney with his party on March 3rd for the mysterious 'treasure island'. They got as far as the Tonga Islands where Brown said he sighted 'his bloody island', but just then a storm broke out and drove him back on the New Caledonian reefs.

(Must have been one hell of a storm to blow him back over 1000 nautical miles! GE)

They got ashore at a place called 'Nouma' and a French man of war picked them up. Later that year, Brown secured the backing of another group in Boston and New York. A steamer, the *Ethelwold*, was chartered, but after some mysterious events aboard ship, Internal Revenue agents seized it. The expedition never got beyond New York Harbour.

Newspaper Reports of the Time

IN SEARCH OF TREASURE

CAPTAIN BROWN'S STORY

A REMARKABLE NARRATIVE

SYDNEY, April 22

These were the headlines of an article that appeared in 1903. The article itself would reprint too small for these pages so I quote it as follows:

'In connection with the Cocos Island treasure, Captain Brown, who is to command the schooner Herman, which has been equipped for a search expedition, and which is now lying in Port Jackson, awaiting

the conclusion of a Supreme Court case, was interviewed to-day. He said; "The treasure was said to be worth 50 million dollars. Captain Smith, of the American schooner Black Witch, sailed with it from Callco, when, in 1822, there was trouble between the Spaniards and the Peruvians, and brought it to Cocos Island. Then trouble arose amongst the Black Witch's crew, and heavy weather was experienced. The upshot was that Captain Smith and another man were the only persons to return to the mainland. The captain made his way home to Salem, and related his experience to his son."

And how did you become connected with the matter?

"In the latter part of 1849 I was mate of a New York ship lying at Kingston, Jamaica, in the West Indies, which was the most approved rendeavous for pirates in those parts. I made the acquaintance of Captain Smith's son, who was master of a fine big schooner, which he was fitting out ostensibly for pearl-fishing."

Why ostensibly?

"As a blind to the Custom-House officers. He was really going for the Cocos treasure. At that time I was only a youngster and fit for anything, and he had little difficulty in inducing me to join him. He sailed as master, and I as mate. We arrived at Cocos Island and had no trouble in finding the treasure, which we quickly transferred to the schooner. Then we set sail for a certain island in the Tahitian group. There we excavated a cave, and planted the treasure, together with some more which we had added to it. Well after that I came away in a small yacht."

And what about the master and the crew of the schooner?

"They died, and the schooner was burned."

Why was she burned?

"Well" - with a significant shrug of the shoulders - "the captain knew - but he's dead."

And where did you go to?

"I came across to Australia, and landed at Guichen Bay, near the mouth of the Murray. I brought with me £100,000 of treasure, but, as a blind, I first went on the gold diggings. Subsequently I took up a cattle and sheep ranch at Mount Gambier, and later on I went to England. I remained in London about ten years as a ship-broker. Then I went to America, and have since then been carrying on a business as a 'wrecker' and ship-broker in Providence City, Rhode Island. Later on *this syndicate was formed by Dr Lewis, and the schooner Herman was bought in San Francisco for the purpose of this expedition."*

And why didn't you go direct to the treasure island, instead of coming from San Francisco to Sydney?

"Because we could not get down to the islands in time to escape the 'hurricane season' but I am ready to start now if this legal trouble was only over."

A classic case of Brown spinning his yarn to anyone who would listen.

HIDDEN TREASURE

THE QUEST ABANDONED

SYDNEY, September 7

This report, five months after the one above, is poor in reproduction so is quoted as follows:

'The last has probably been heard of the search for hidden treasure of untold value in the islands of the South Seas in connection with which the schooner Herman started out from San Francisco in July of last year. A cable message from Auckland states:- "News from Papeete had been received that the schooner Herman has been sold there, the search for hidden treasure having been abandoned. The party searched about twenty islands without success and the man who confessed to know where the treasure was hidden then confessed he could not place it, and the crew, realising that they were on a wild goose chase, refused to continue the search.

The Herman, it will be remembered lay for some months in Sydney Harbour, differences having arisen between Captain Brown, who was in charge, and the members of the syndicate, who had organised the expedition, litigation ensued. Captain Brown, who is over 70 years of age, claimed to be the only living soul who knew where the treasure was buried. According to his story, during the Spanish-Peruvian war in 1822, the whole of the Peruvian national funds, consisting of silver dollars, silver and gold plate, and jewellery, valued at 50,000,000 dollars, were shipped in a schooner called the Black Witch, which was wrecked at the islands, and the treasure went down with her. The only survivor

114

told the story to his son, who years afterwards took with him, amongst others, Captain Brown to where the treasure lay, and recovered it and buried it on the island. Some of it was afterwards dug up by the adventurers, and Captain Brown alone spent over a million pounds.

After being in various businesses Captain Brown took command of the Herman to, as he said, recover the remainder of the treasure. The Herman sailed out of Sydney Harbour on May 20 last, and with it went Captain Brown, but only as a passenger, who was to guide those on board to the spot where the treasure was to be unearthed.'

Another variation then, which tells that the *'Black Witch'* was wrecked on the island.

TREASURE HUNTERS

IN QUEST OF THE PIRATES' GOLD

These headlines appeared in a Tasmania newspaper 13th Feburary 1905. Again, the copy is too poor to reproduce so I quote as follows:
'Occasionally the spirits which once drove men into almshouses and asylums after vainly endeavouring to find Captain Kidd's hidden treasure is revived in a new generation. Several years ago a number of apparently hard-headed men of business listened to a tale of buried pirate gold which a certain Captain Brown, who claimed to have seen the treasure, told, and after investigating his story, they set out in a schooner to find it in Cocos Island, a dot on the map of the Pacific about 480 miles south-west from Panama. It is needless to say they came home empty-handed. It appears, however, that there was more than ordinary reason to accept this tale. In which 60,000,000 dol of treasure figured. A gang of pirates in 1822, so the story goes, looted a number of rich churches and residences in Peru. Their plunder was loaded on the schooner Black Witch, which sailed for Cocos Island. Here they buried their treasure, and sailed forth on another piratical raid. A storm arose, the ship was wrecked, and only a few of the pirates, the captain among them, escaped. The captain before he died is said to have told his son the location of the treasure. About 50 years ago this young worthy set out to find it. And Captain Brown, then a lad of 19, fell in with the man and went along.

£10,000,000 Worth of Plunder.

Brown asserts that they found £10,000,000 worth of the plunder just as the old pirate chief had directed. This they loaded on their vessel, and sailed to an uninhabited island. Pirate treasure is always buried in uninhabited islands – in fact, the difficulty must be to keep up the supply of islands. Having hidden this vast wealth, according to Brown, the expedition, not intent with so neat a sum, decided to hoist the black flag at the foremost of their ship and gather in the gold dust then being brought from Australia. Three golden vessels, it is claimed, were captured, yielding £2,000,000 in bullion. This was then taken to the unknown island, and hidden with the other spoils. Another bagatelle of £1,000,000 was taken from another ship, and during the jubilation which followed someone put poison in the rum. The pirates who did not succumb to the rum and poison started a mutiny, in the course of which the ship was fired, and the next morning there were three survivors in a small boat making for Australia. Brown was one, the captain another, and the third was the mate. Only Brown reached Australia. He told a terrible tale of hunger, thirst, fatigue, and murder. The captain stabbed the mate, and in defending himself Brown states he shot the captain. It was to find this uninhabited island and its hidden treasure that an expedition set out from San Francisco two years ago. Brown was in command, but neither threat nor entreaty could make him disclose the location of the treasure. He said he was suspicious, although a full quarter share was to be his, and the expense borne by the syndicate. The party went to Honolulu and to Australia, where it was agreed to return without ever casting a glance on the great hidden store of gold.'

This report, a variation on a theme, is nevertheless interesting because it tells that Brown took three bullion ships that were on their way to England, and also another ship. If true, it confirms the reason the British were interested in his movements and corroborates the earlier story that treasure was added at a later date to the original cache.

What I find quite amazing is that with the abundance of newspaper reports appearing over the time the expeditions were news, why was Hamilton and his syndicate seemingly unaware of the Herman Expedition some 30 years before? If so, it is obvious diligent research had not been carried out. There is no mention of Captain Brown or the *Herman* in Hamilton's book.

No Gold Raised, But Suspicions Are!

That a treasure is still on Brown's island is highly probable. That this is one of the church treasures of Peru - fact! Err, no! That it was once buried on Cocos and relocated elsewhere – fact! Again, no! "But the stories all say so!" you exclaim. They do - Howe, Hamilton, Nordhoff, Sutton - they all tell of a Church treasure of Callao, Pisco or Lima stolen, buried on Cocos, retrieved and reburied on an island in the middle of the South Pacific Ocean. Many people spent thousands of pounds and dollars, all believing this story, all wanting to follow the dream and it is a very good, very plausible story. But where did it originate? Where is the source? Why was it believed?

Think back over the previous chapters; the source is, of course, our Captain James Brown. Later on, Howe tells the same story, as told to him by Killorain,whom **we** know was really Brown. Hamilton retells Howe's story and, as we know, not quite the same. "But Sutton and others corroborated the facts," you say. Some of the facts were established but if for any reason you wanted to tell or sell a (fake) story as being true, the tried and true method is to make it half-fake and half-truth, because the half-truth part gives it credibility. You will see this occurring all the way through. Everybody says, "I heard that before so it must be true!" Brown used this method to very great effect. You can also see we are getting mixed up versions of the story. Howe, in retelling his, is also trying to hide the origin and identity of his source. You may have noticed also that Brown did not give the Cocos relocation detail to Howe, or maybe he did and Howe didn't mention it to Hamilton. Hamilton himself admits that he had to reconstruct the story to a certain extent and to embroider a little the story as told by Killorain. He also tries to put followers off the scent by describing Howe's island as being about 4 miles by 2½ miles (this, we know, would be Tupai Atoll), whereas Nordhoff identifies it as Pinaki, which is only just over a mile in diameter.

So we have secrets, lies, rumours and deliberate confusion. Why? What is really behind all of this? Students of Pacific Ocean pirates and treasure may have noticed that there are bits of just about every known treasure story thrown in, also some little known. But the Bosun Bird story is truly artifice. It is brilliant when you understand it. Someone had researched, knew of and understood real events from the 1820s, then mutated and rolled them into each other.

I have now nearly completed the telling of the stories that are the background to the burying of a treasure on a lone Pacific island. In Part 2, we conduct a methodical examination of Captain Brown's story comparing it with real known events, showing how this carefully crafted story mixed in these events with parts of popular treasure legend. But first, we finish this Part 1 with a look at the geographical trail of deception that Captain Brown took his investors on in the South Pacific Ocean. At the same time, we look at the many islands and atolls that play a part in this story. Yet only one is important, the island of the lost treasure. Earlier we mentioned a pattern of islands as being important. The geography and shape of the atolls is equally important, as you will see.

CHARTS OFFERED TO SEARCH FOR $60,000,000 TREASURE

Augusta Man Willing to Obtain Maps if Prof. Dill of Iowa Will Seek Buried Plunder From Peru Revolt While on Cruise in South Seas.

IOWA CITY, Iowa, Feb. 25.—Since it was announced a short time ago that Prof. Homer R. Dill of the University of Iowa is to cruise the South Seas next year in search of museum material, he has received a letter from Frederick Mason of Augusta, Me., offering to obtain for him the maps and charts of a certain island where treasure worth $60,000,000 is buried.

The treasure, according to Mr. Mason, is part of the plunder from the insurrection in Peru in the early part of the eighteenth century.

AUGUSTA, Me., Feb. 25.—Maps and charts of an isolated island in the South Seas on which treasure worth $60,000,000 is said to have been buried in 1820, are in the possession of Mrs. James Brown, widow of an aged retired sea captain who died here three years ago. These are the papers which Frederick Mason, a newspaper correspondent of this city, has offered to obtain for Prof. Homer R. Dill of the University of Iowa, who is to cruise the South Seas next year in search of museum material.

Capt. Brown said he was the only man in the world who held the key to the location of the treasure. He said he helped transfer it in 1850 from the island on which it originally was hidden to another island where it was again buried. Cocos Island, about 350 miles southwest of Panama, is said to

have been the original location of the hoard.

Several companies have been formed in the last five years in different parts of the world to recover the gold, silver, jewels, diamonds and other precious stones. One or two expeditions are said to have found the island, but to have had no success in the search for treasure.

Capt. Brown was mate of the schooner Seafoam, in which Capt. Henry Smith of Salem, Mass., set out from Kingston, Jamaica, in 1850, to recover the fortune. Capt. Smith told his mate it was loot obtained during the Peruvian insurrection in 1820, and that his father, master of the schooner Black Witch of Salem, had buried it on Cocos Island.

The expedition, Capt. Brown told his friends, found the treasure and moved it to another island. There all the crew died except the captain, steward and himself. They started in the ship's long boat for Australia, taking about $1,000,000, but on the passage the other two died. He arrived at Cochin Bay, West Australia, and was sure he was the only person who knew where the treasure was buried.

The Brown Exploring Company about two years ago, with the yacht Gennessee, made an investigation on Cocos Island, also on Zubia, a reef ring in the Society group, but did not locate the plunder.

Mr. Mason said to-night he never had seen the maps and charts.

The above is a newspaper report that appeared in *The New York Herald* in 1922, three years after Captain Brown's death.

CHAPTER 7

THE ISLAND TRAIL AND TRINITY DNA

Extending into the massive Pacific Ocean north and east of Australia and New Zealand are the thousands of islands that make up greater Oceana. A glance at a map shows the vastness of it, approximately 10,000 miles wide east to west at its widest point and approximately 8,000 miles north to south. As you know, we are interested in the islands south of the equator. It is into this vast area our searchers had to navigate, from San Francisco in the north, Sydney to the west and Lima to the east.

The Tuamotus, (Tuamoto means 'islands on the oceans back'), known as 'Tahiti's Strand of Pearls', is the largest of the Polynesian archipelago, including 76 low islands and atolls spread out over more than 7,500 square miles.

Pinaki, the atoll on which Nordhoff found Howe, belongs to the commune of Nukutavake, and the Englishman Samuel Wallis was the first recorded European to visit Pinaki Atoll on June 6th, 1767 while searching for the 'Southern Continent'. He named the atoll 'Whitsunday'. Frederick Beechey found Pinaki uninhabited in 1826 but observed that there were huts on the island as well as small reservoirs cut in the coral rock for the collection and preservation of fresh water.

As you know, there is just one 'lost treasure' island. It will be interesting to follow the trail where we can, of the expeditions we know about and where they went. It will show you that with the exception of Howe, they went nowhere near *the* island. It is also a demonstration of how effective our Captain Brown was with his tales of deception.

Island Trail of the Expeditions

The important expeditions and the islands visited. The map that follows gives an idea of the vastness of the area searched.

The Herman Expedition

Leaves San Francisco July 20th 1902 - Hawaii - Apia - Sydney (start of expedition proper)

Maitea (Mehetia)

Makatia -	Went ashore, abandoned native village here.
Tikihau -	Went ashore.
Matahiva -	Went ashore.
Penrhyn -	(Tongareva) Spent time here with Agent and family.

Matahiva

Makatea -	(Aurora, Little Smoke Isle)

Penrhyn

Papeete -	(Tahiti) Brown steadfastly refused to identify the correct island.

The Howe (Lone) Expedition

Pinaki -	1912. Thirteen years searching here. (Named as 'Papee' by Hamilton). Claims to have found the treasure here. Visited by Nordhoff in 1919.
Tuanake -	Although not specified, research indicates this island was visited.
Hiti -	Named as 'Tatee' by Hamilton. Claims to have found the treasure here also.
Tahiti -	Deported back to Australia

The Gennessee Expedition

Tupai -	1922

The Hamilton Expedition

Sydney to Tahiti -	December 1933.

Maihitia (Mehetia)

Mototunga (Motu Tunga)

Makemo -	Passed 'their' island 'Tatee' on way to here.

Hiti. (Tatee)-	Search starts on this island, finds conical column of coral on *east* side also evidence of digging in past. Sailed around this (Raeviski) group after abandoning Hiti.
Tepoto -	Whilst not specified, I would suspect this atoll was visited as it has a pass on the eastern side. Not only that, but a cairn, (survey/navigational marker) north of the pass I would have thought this small atoll worthy of more attention!
Relocates to:	
Tuanake -	Coral pinnacle on east side, pass into lagoon to left of pinnacle. Find pool.
Makemo -	For supplies.
Tuanake	
Makemo -	Coffer-dam materials.
Tuanake	
Katieu -	More supplies.
Tuanake -	Coffer-dam flooded.
Tahiti -	Expedition abandoned (*'Impossible raise further capitol owing to libelous Publicity—writing....'*)

The list of different islands above, begs the question; why were so many different islands/atolls searched up to 600 miles apart, as surely, if you have a map, you go to just one place? Well we have seen that Brown, the only possessor of the map, was playing games with his expeditions but to help you answer that question, all you need to do is reconstruct the map.

TUAMOTO ARCHIPELAGO (Shaded area)

CONSISTING OF OVER 70 ATOLLS AND ISLANDS, PRINCIPLE ATOLLS AND ISLANDS ONLY SHOWN TO GIVE AN IDEA OF THE VAST DISTANCES INVOLVED AND TRAVELLED BY DIFFERENT EXPEDITIONS

15 S
20 S
140 W
145 W
150 W
155 W

PENRHYN
TUPAI
MATAHIVA
MAKATEA
HITI
TAHITI
PINAKI
MURUROA
TUBUAI

PENRHYN TO MATAHIVA 650 N.M.
630 NM TAHITI TO PINAKI
SYDNEY TO TAHITI 3,300 N.M.

123

Reconstructing the Map

Though sounding a bit daunting, this is much easier than it appears. The first task was to work out how Howe had come to know of the second 'three-island' group containing Hiti, because it was the explanation as to why he originally thought he was on the wrong island (Pinaki) and was able to convince the Hamilton expedition that Hiti atoll is where to look. This was able to be deduced by examining the events that had occurred in the 1920s involving Howe and Brown.

In 1921, Howe had sent the Juventin brothers to a 'deep pool' on Pinaki to search for the gold. In 1922, the Brown Exploring Company, aboard the yacht *Gennessee* went and searched Tupai (on some charts Tubai) for Brown's piratical treasure. It is easy to deduce then that Howe had learned of the Gennessee Expedition and must have considered he had in some way been misled by Brown. But as the Gennessee Expedition had not found the gold either, Howe had then commenced a search for another 'three-island' group, thereby discovering the Hiti group, at the same southerly latitude of the Tupai 'three-island' group i.e. 16º30′ and at approximately 144º30′ West longitude. This was taking him further east, back towards Pinaki. Measuring the relationship of the islands in each of the three groups (Pinaki, Hiti, and Tupai) revealed that the Pinaki and Tupai groups were very similar to each other in relation to distance and angular divergence between the islands. The Hiti group was half the size with different angular divergence but nevertheless a small group of three islands or atolls. So the map was therefore known to show the position of three islands a certain distance apart and with an angular relationship in the form of a triangle (Trinity).[1] Also, the triangular layout would be very similar to that of the Pinaki and Tupai 'Triangular' groups.

A second task was to examine what Hamilton wrote in his description of the map and how they were using it. As Howe had believed for many years that Pinaki was the correct place, it is obvious then that Pinaki must also match in a predominant way with what is depicted on the map. Hamilton's narrative is of them arriving at 'Tatee' (Hiti) and discovering nothing matched what they were told they would find.

---

[1] I define this term in a chapter to come shortly.

He describes how they examine the map and all have to agree that the contour of the island is not the same as shown on the map. Hiti and Pinaki are similar only by their general shape, which accounts for this discrepancy but that was not the only problem. Howe had said they would encounter a series of directional landmarks, the first of which was a 'pinnacle of coral' on the west side, to the left of which was a pass through the coral reef. Next was that the correct location for the gold was a 'pear-shaped pool', near which seven blocks of coral were set even distances apart. None of these landmarks could be found on Hiti.

Howe had also said that after finding some chests buried on the island, he had reburied the treasure at a new position: '84ft. E. by N. and 75ft. N. by E.' from the pinnacle.

We know a lot of what was said by Brown, Howe and Hamilton were lies and that each had also withheld certain information from the next. This resulted in a progressive loss of understanding and distortion as to what was the landmark and what was the target the landmark led to. For example, Howe had searched the land, the shore and the lagoon at a *particular* location on Pinaki, after following incomplete clues he was fed by Brown. It was to a pool at this particular location that he directed the Juventine brothers (note pool).

This (incomplete) background information was not passed to Hamilton who, as you can see, changed the focus and merrily searched every island he landed on, until he found a 'pear-shaped pool' which he then asserted, in a backwards sort of way, was the proof he had found the correct location. A desperation trip around the Hiti (Triangular) group, searching for an island with the sailing mark of a pinnacle on the west side, to mark the pass through the reef was unrewarding. The confusion felt by the group is palpable to this day in Hamilton's book. We have seen in the earlier *Treasure of the Tuamotus* chapter how Hamilton then decides, in a moment that one cannot describe as inspirational, that Howe had reversed his directions, so that the pinnacle was really to be found on the east side of the (correct) island. Abandoning Hiti, Tuanaki is finally decided upon as being the correct island, as Hamilton said they located a pinnacle of coral on the east side of that island together with a pass. A picture appears in Hamilton's book of him excavating near this pinnacle but nothing was found. About 60 years later, a private French expedition found no pinnacle on this island, or seven blocks of coral! One of the partners said they could not identify anything specific on Tuanaki they could call a 'pinnacle' to say this is the place to dig.

A glance at the map of Tuanaki also shows that the (major) passes are to the south and west of that Island! Critically, Tuanaki is not the shape of Pinaki either (you will see later the importance of *our* atoll's profile) but this did not stop Hamilton claiming (out of self-delusion) this was the correct island and the pool he found was the correct pool. It appears that frustration was causing Hamilton to grasp at shapes that seemed to match the clues. Hamilton's own confusion is very evident in his book. I quote from page 215:

'I set off eagerly to find the landmarks enumerated by Howe – notably a pinnacle of coral on the western seaboard'.

Page 220. Hamilton is explaining his thoughts on the problem to the group and says that he (Howe) 'probably thought that someone may do the dirty on him in some way, so he's deliberately *reversed his bearings.* He says the conical pillar of coral is on the east-side. It isn't, it's on the west!'

Page 221. Even the skipper of the schooner gets taken in by the confusion;

'There are several more atolls around here, as like this one almost as two peas in a pod. If we could only pick up one with a coral pinnacle on the east side....!'

Further confusion, or misleading information, is evident in the book where Hamilton says that Howe landed on an atoll about four miles long, by two and a half wide at the widest spot (he is describing Tupai). This is where Hamilton says Nordhoff found him seven years later. We know, of course, that Nordhoff found him on Pinaki which is more or less circular and about a mile diameter.

I think I said earlier, you need to keep your wits about you with many parts of this story! I say, "Take the hint, don't look at just that page, look at the rest of the silly mistakes, gaffes, fabrications and wrong conclusions Hamilton comes up with including Howe's reversed directions." He got himself confused again when he wrote his book and reversed his already reversed directions! Hamilton, aware of the Trinity clue as given by Howe, attempted to hide this by making up the Tatee/Papee (dialect) fabrication. This does not even survive to the end of his book, as he contradicts it himself by eliminating the first island they were directed to (Hiti), which was supposed to be the island upon which Howe had discovered the gold.

As Hamilton's narrative indicated they were able to assess that the shape of Hiti did not match what was on the map, it was therefore a safe assumption that the map, apart from showing a Trinity, also showed the shape of the island, which logic said was something akin to the shape of Pinaki. But there was also a major anomaly between where Howe and the Gennessee Expedition had searched. Each Trinity group (with the exception of Hiti) was made up of three islands in a repetitive pattern; two islands adjacent on the eastern side, one above the other and the remaining island further out to the west. Howe had searched Pinaki, the lower of the eastern islands in that triangle, with the Gennessee Expedition searching Tupai, the upper eastern island in that triangle. Though this provided the reason as to why Howe had subsequently searched both Hiti and Tuanake (the upper island in that group), it was problematic in that Tupai and Pinaki are two very differently shaped islands.

To identify what particular area Howe was focused on for his search, Howe's movements on Pinaki were plotted from Nordhoff's narrative of their walk on the island and from later French magazine articles. Howe had been exclusively focused on the north-western sector of Pinaki, which was the area reported to have been trenched meticulously by Howe and later excavated by other searchers. The scale of these diggings (which included underwater probing in the lagoon) was described in one French article as *'Grandes excavations de la dimension d'un court de tennis!'*

Examination of a naval chart and a photo of Tupai revealed the north-west sector was almost identical in its shape to Pinaki. Not only that, both had the major pass into the lagoon on the west side. Also, one of the landmarks Howe gave was even printed on the chart. A conspicuous white rock denoted as a 'sailing mark' was on the western beach, to the left of which was the pass through the coral reef. We can see now why Hamilton was doomed to never find the gold; he was never on the right island. Even Howe, the man who was on the right island abandoned it believing he had been misled by Brown.

At this point, I will mention the opinion of another author, Tim Haydock, who wrote *Treasure Trove*, a book that includes the Hamilton/Tuamotus story. In his 'summing up' of this story, he states:

'Pinaki, however, is not the treasure atoll, nor for that matter is Tuanaki, the atoll which Hamilton's party first visited.'
He goes on to declare: *'The correct island will have the following relevant landmarks; 1. a coral pinnacle on the eastern side. 2. a pass just to the left of the pinnacle. 3. a pear-shaped pool, with seven coral blocks nearby, about three miles from the pass.'*

Whilst I would not, of course, ever intentionally demean Mr Haydock, (he did after all mention one of my books in his *Treasure Trove*!), he has written an excellent book and has his own opinions, and it is evident nevertheless he has not carried out the in-depth research required for this intricate story and has accepted the traditional constructed Alvarez/Killorain story. But in his defence, we must say this *is* a very complex story.

By now, research was indicating a fair idea of what had been depicted on the map everyone had been following. Not only did it depict a representation of a Trinity group of islands (without giving any obvious indication where this group was), it also showed some shape that was understood by searchers to be a representation of a portion of one of the islands in the Trinity (without indicating which island it was in that group). This shape was something akin to the north-west sector of the islands of Tupai and Pinaki; almost banana-shape with one end tending to curl back on itself.

It could be seen that by comparing the two islands, the directions and landmarks given to Hamilton by Howe were actually just those Howe had found on Pinaki. In particular, the 'pear-shaped pool' was just the same pool Howe had sent the Juventin brothers to search and was where Nordhoff had seen Howe diving into the lagoon years earlier. In this instance, the pool and lagoon are just one and the same thing. However, Howe had searched the north-west sector of Pinaki whereas the Gennessee Expedition had been sent to search an area on the east side of Tupai.

It was also recognised now that Howe's landmark of the seven blocks of coral near the pool qualitatively matched the location excavated by the Gennessee group, who were following Brown's direction that the treasure was buried under a native altar or marae.

Before we discuss Maraes, I show the principle islands and island groups next.

Main Islands and Island Groups

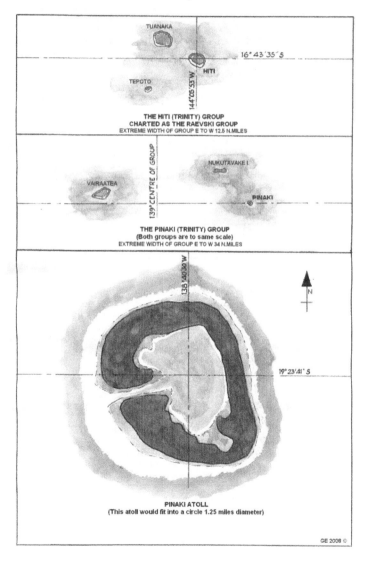

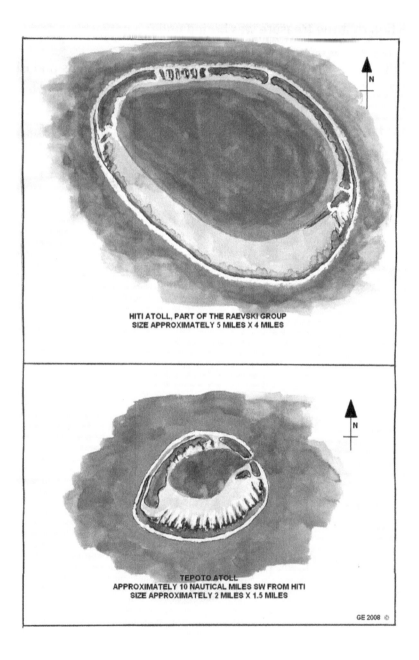

HITI ATOLL, PART OF THE RAEVSKI GROUP
SIZE APPROXIMATELY 5 MILES X 4 MILES

TEPOTO ATOLL
APPROXIMATELY 10 NAUTICAL MILES SW FROM HITI
SIZE APPROXIMATELY 2 MILES X 1.5 MILES

GE 2008 ©

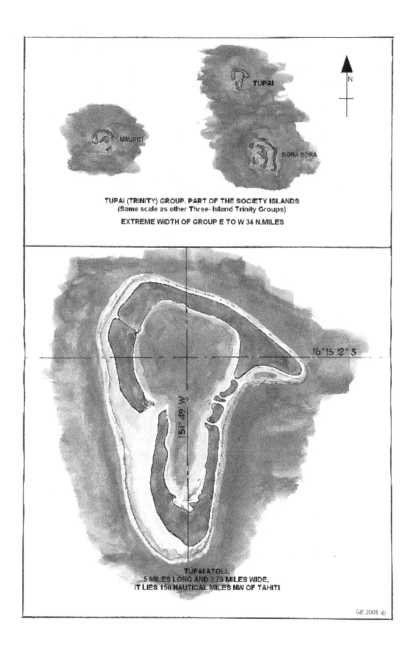

TUPAI (TRINITY) GROUP. PART OF THE SOCIETY ISLANDS
(Same scale as other Three-Island Trinity Groups)

EXTREME WIDTH OF GROUP E TO W 34 N.MILES

TUPAI ATOLL
5 MILES LONG AND 3.75 MILES WIDE,
IT LIES 150 NAUTICAL MILES NW OF TAHITI

GE 2008

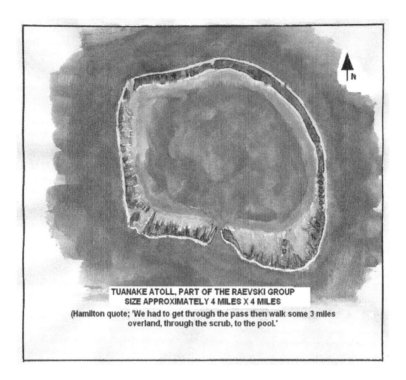

TUANAKE ATOLL, PART OF THE RAEVSKI GROUP
SIZE APPROXIMATELY 4 MILES X 4 MILES
(Hamilton quote; 'We had to get through the pass then walk some 3 miles overland, through the scrub, to the pool.'

Maraes

The term marae (sometimes marai or morai) is given to native temples, altars or sacred sites which were constructed in past ages. These can range in size and complexity from huge pyramid shaped constructs with paved patio areas to simple alignments of stone blocks. In some locations, human sacrifice was practiced and in some places storage receptacles were cut into the bedrock that were known as 'skull pits'. On Tupai itself, there are about 10 sacrificial sites ranging from simple rock alignments to the larger temples. One named 'uira Ta'ata ofai' is merely a limestone slab near the sea but was used for horrific sacrifices where the victim was literally dragged back and forth across the surface grinding them to death.

It was to the marae named Tupaiofai on the eastern side of the island to which the Gennessee group was directed and which they ended up destroying by dynamiting it a number of times. This meant Brown had directed them to a marae specifically on the eastern side of the island. Yet it appears that though Howe was also searching near a marae, it was one he found on the west side of the island! Was this then the correct place to look, near a marae on the east side, and was this a vital direction withheld from Howe by Brown? Brown, of course, was holding an 'ace' card for this island anyway; he knew - and would have made sure the investors knew - that this island (Tupai) had a famous legend of buried treasure (story follows in Part 2), so investors were already half convinced this was the right island.

Another problem for the searcher who has an alignment of stones, rocks or blocks of coral as a clue is; are they sacred maraes or merely remains of traditional house platforms? This is usually very difficult to determine with any accuracy because of the condition of the remains and being completely invaded by the exuberant growth of the native vegetation.

At this point, we remind you of the earlier anomalies and point out that a 'Church Rock' would be better known as a marae in the South Pacific, and although said to be on the western side of the island, Church Rock is actually on the (north) east side!

The Major DNA of the Triangle and Trinity

One of the puzzling aspects that had intrigued us in the first place was the reference to a map that was said to have come from Killorain and which was followed by Hamilton. As this map was now long lost, anyone else would naturally have assumed that whatever it had shown would never be seen again. But events investigated and researched enabled us to eventually reconstruct what it is likely to have shown and identify its actual source.

As a map is a representation of the earth's surface, if you know where an expedition went following a map, you could then 'reverse engineer' what the map depicted by examining the geography of the location visited. In this case, he had not one, but four locations searched following a map or chart provided by Brown: Pinaki, Hiti, Tuanaki and Tupai. Therefore each location must have had geography which was both similar to what the map depicted and to each location. This insight went hand in hand with a crucial detail given by Hamilton as to the identity of the correct island, but which had subsequently exposed itself as a fabrication. Hamilton, you may remember, gave the explanation that due to a mispronunciation of the name of the island by a native, Howe had spent years searching the wrong island 'Papee' instead of the correct island 'Tatee'. As it was now known that Howe had been on Pinaki and that Hamilton's expedition first went to Hiti before settling on Tuanaki, then this explanation was a lie. There must therefore have been some other reason why Howe had abandoned Pinaki after 14 years and moved on to Hiti. Not only that, whatever reason he had come up with had been powerful enough to convince a group of investors a decade later that it was worthwhile funding an expedition (Hamilton's) to the island of Hiti.

The reason lies with one of the secrets of the lost treasure: the 'Trinity/triangle DNA'. The triangle and 'Trinity', in its different forms appears everywhere and is integrated very much into this story. I have to familiarise you with it now because it will help you understand why some of the searchers went where they did. During our research, we finally recognised a recurring theme for what it was; 'Three'. It recurred in several different ways: three peaks, three mountains, three dots, three cairns, three islands. When in 1498 Columbus discovered an island in the West Indies with three tall mountain peaks seen from afar before landing, he called the island 'La Trinidad', the Spanish word for 'The Trinity'. There is also a Masonic link here but that comes later in our story.

This Spanish DNA link was a major breakthrough and explained many of the seemingly obscure and unconnected stories. For example, three small circles in the layout of a triangle on the Kidd 'Key Chart'(mentioned in the Introduction) can now be explained, particularly because we now know that the island on that chart is an inverted, early version of Juan Fernandez Island, which has a strong presence in our story and is told later. Also, the earlier Christian Cruise story (dying pirate) and expeditions to the Salvage group of islands (three), the cruise of the *Alerte* and its expedition to 'Trinidad' Island with its three cairns, and so on. So for our story, I can say that three of anything is another form of DNA that we call 'Trinity'. Likewise, a triangle in its varying forms we can also call 'Trinity DNA'. But, you will not find the word 'Trinity' appearing as a direct clue in any of the most popular stories. An exception could be the cipher given in *Captain Kid's Millions* that began, 'Taken to Trinity land and 20½ South Pan de Azucar....' One might suspect that the word 'Trinity' was being used as some type of directional codeword to identify a group of three islands. Not only that, the 'Pan de Azucar' (Sugarloaf), which was being used as a landmark to find the treasure in the story, was a feature that occurred on both Trinidade and Juan Fernandez Islands. The meaning of this was even clarified in the book immediately after the cipher;

'Now as to the Pan de Azucar - that was plain to one conversant with Spanish waters. Wherever your Spanish findeth a conical rock or mount, he nameth it 'Sugar Loaf'.'

It was becoming ever more apparent that we were looking for three islands and not three markers on an island.

The discovery of directional codewords occurring in another language led us to comprehend the reason why no one else realised that for a number of different locations, searchers were all just following the same directions; the difference between quantitative and qualitative descriptions. This may sound complicated but needs to be explained here, as understanding it will provide the reason why the same treasure was searched for at different locations without anyone realising what was occurring. A quantitative description of something, how, or by what terms its *form* is described, will vary due to language, culture and custom. The qualitative description of the same thing, however, will not vary, as it is its *function* that is now being expressed. In other words, one man's 'Pan de Azucar' was just another man's 'pinnacle' or 'conical rock', because they were all just names for what is known nowadays as a 'Sailing Mark', which is a feature observable from the sea and is used for navigational purposes to verify your position.

More clues in the above narrative; 'Playa Banca', 'Pinnacle' and 'Conical rock' - they are all features that help to build up a picture of 'the' island.

Confirmation of the island 'Trinity' came when nautical charts of the islands of Pinaki, Tupai and Hiti/Tuanaki were scanned to see if any common factor about these islands could be detected. The most cursory glance reveals an aspect so apparent it leaps off the paper to slap you in the face; each of these islands were but one in a triangular shaped cluster of islands of very similar layout.

The answer then to the question asked at the beginning of this chapter; why were the searchers going all over the archipelago? The answer is due to the trinity DNA clue; a group of three islands in a triangular pattern. This then was one of the clues left by Brown, but it left another more important question: which group of islands was the correct one?

A Link to the Kidd Charts?

Because of all the above, it is here I interject with mention of one of the Captain Kidd charts known as the 'Key Chart'.

Though referred to in the stories, examples of *the* lost treasure map was either not shown or copies of them could not be found. It was almost as if the image of them were being actively suppressed. This is understandable, of course; the owners would naturally keep them hidden. But three authentic samples were eventually located and appear later in our story. One set of lost pirate treasure charts were easy to locate and study; those of Captain Kidd. I had conveniently written the full history of them in my book *KIDD, the search for his treasure* (details of these charts follow in Part 3). In particular, one of the three Kidd charts catches your attention, the aforementioned 'Key Chart'. This depicted a banana-shaped island upon which was tantalisingly placed three dots in a rather familiar pattern; a Trinity.

This, of course, was a new set of leads to be followed, for Kidd's name had already been raised once before, laterally, in connection with the treasure upon the Salvage Islands. A quick read of the background story of the charts made suggestions that this map was to be inferred as being implicit to the 'Money Pit' mystery on Oak Island. This comes via our friend Harold T. Wilkins, whose treasure hunting books we had become increasingly reliant upon due to their compendious coverage of lost treasure legends. It was at this stage that we therefore began to massively expand the search to look for matches, not only in the geography of the various locations searched, but also compared the qualitative meaning of features or landmarks given in any directional instructions. This, in an effort to isolate the DNA, the common features in all the stories which could, like a jigsaw puzzle be assembled to show a picture, or in this case, a map with directions. Wherever in the world a treasure story was found that contained a piece of known DNA, this was then added to the database to be analysed to identify new DNA. This led the investigation to places and locations never before suspected by anyone to be merely versions of the grand legend that was the lost treasure.

However, before we expand our searches and research outside the South Pacific, we need to complete the part played by *these* islands and tell something of their geology.

South Sea Island Geology

Occasionally, our Captain Brown gave descriptive clues to his island and these should help us to determine the type of island he is talking about. Unfortunately, as we know, Captain Brown is a mass of contradictions; he gives conflicting descriptions of the island and where the treasure is. The reader should be aware now that some of the descriptions of the island Captain Brown gives come from the related lost treasure stories and are designed to confuse.

In an earlier chapter, we wrote of the types of native altars to be found on the islands. It is prudent therefore to now discuss the types and morphology of the islands to be found in this archipelago, as this will also help to give us a better understanding of what Brown was erroneously describing.

Birth of an Island

The atolls in the South Pacific are between three and four million years old. They were created by a submarine volcano breaking through a thin spot in the Pacific Continental plate. Over time, this volcano transpierced the surface of the ocean three or four thousand meters above. If at this point the magna ceases to flow, then the volcano is condemned to 'die'. Firstly, at the level of its own foundations, its weight will make it sink back into the earth's crust that supported it. Then, in that part projecting into the atmosphere above sea level, erosion starts its slow work. Eventually the volcano finishes up disappearing below the surface. All that remains is a coral barrier which to maintain itself close to the ocean's surface, never stops growing. The volcano continues to sink until one day there is no more volcano; only a simple ring of coral remains as a sign of its passing. This surface coral dies and breaks down to simple limestone. On some atolls, the coral captures sand and this allows vegetation to establish.

Contrary to appearances, water can be found on a lot of the atolls, either fresh or brackish. It is usually located by digging just a bit below ground/sea level. It is this water that feeds the coconut palms. The fact that water can be found is important to us, as in the form of a spring or well, it is an important DNA clue.

The atoll maps plainly show the plan of typical coral atolls. The inner body of water surrounded by the island's landmass is known as the inner lagoon. If outside this main island landmass there is another body of water surrounded by an outer ring of coral, this is known as an outer lagoon. Tepoto and Tupai are examples of this type of island. The strip of land of an atoll is not continuous; it can be intersected by drain channels which allow the exchange of water between lagoon and ocean. In the Polynesian language, these are called 'hoa'. The small strips of land, semblance to small islands the hoa separate are called 'motu'. The atolls can be equipped with a master 'key' (pass or opening) and can be a broad opening of several metres depth allowing boats of a considerable draught to enter the lagoon. In this case, one says that the atoll is open. With no pass, it is a 'closed' atoll. Some atolls have more than one pass. This can define whether or not an atoll is inhabited. Closed and very small atolls are usually uninhabited.

An atoll's shape is dependent on the growth of the coral, and this is dependent on the weather. The outside coral rim is living coral and constantly extending outward. The still water of the inner lagoon is surrounded by dead coral which slowly dissolves, so that the lagoon is slowly but ever increasing in size. The opening, or master key, is usually found opposite the side attacked by the prevailing winds. Because the water has less movement, the coral does not grow so well. Knowledge of this is important if one wants to get onto one of these islands. As the windward side has the coral growth, the leeward side will generally be the place where a pass is located as a gap through the coral reef to get onto the island. If there is an outer ring of coral, then the pass through here is known as the 'outer pass'. The 'inner pass' is the one through to the inner lagoon.

Birth of an Island (2)

The following is included here out of interest as it is to do with our group of islands and what appeared to be a new island/atoll. Take a look at this map, which is centered on Pinaki.

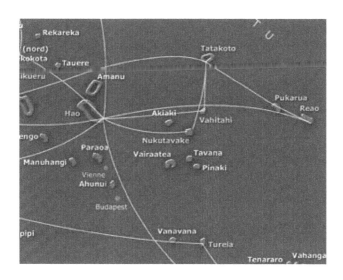

A new atoll has appeared, Tavana, in the same place as Nukutavake is (or was!). There are now six atolls in this group, not five. We have hinted many times so far in this book not to believe that everything you read is true. The main reason I show this map is that it is a classic case of this. What you see is part of a modern flight-connection map to the islands issued by a Tahiti Vacation company. You would be forgiven for believing that as a Tahiti company created it, then indeed Tavana exists where shown, especially if you were not in a position to believe or think otherwise. When I challenged them on this, the reaction was, "It is on the map so must be there!" Further frustrated enquiries eventually landed on the desk of the Deputy Director of Tahiti Tourisme North America who immediately took an interest. He involved the *Stations des Pilotage* in French Polynesia and, of course, there was a quick reaction –"Yes you are right, big mistake! We are advising Air Tahiti, Air Tahiti Nui and all our constituents." I eventually received a thank-you email off Air Tahiti saying it was a 'transcription error' and that Tavana is really the name of the main village on Nukutaraki atoll.

Like I said, a classic case of 'don't believe everything you see and read'. Just because it is written and somebody said so, doesn't mean it is true!

Back to our quest:

Doubtful Descriptions

Captain Brown's tactics of deceit, confusion and deception are plainly evident in his trumped up descriptions of the island given to expedition members. The following quotes from Chetwood's and Sutton's accounts (the Herman Expedition) admirably demonstrate this:

'Brown added that whilst the island was in the hurricane belt the treasure was far above reach of submergence or any tidal wave disturbance, as it was snugly buried about the centre and summit of a high and rocky Isle'

*'Brown requires a launch to get from the ship through the reef to the island, two wheeled trucks, to put the treasure on and wheel it **a mile and a half downhill to the shore of the lagoon**'*

'The island was barren and had practically no vegetation and no water'

'The island was about 3 miles long and maybe a mile wide, there were cliffs of limestone facing the lagoon and open sea'

'He seemed to be describing a low level coral island without much height to the land, and the treasure was buried in a cliff facing the lagoon'

Later, from the information supplied by Brown, Howe went to Pinaki, Hiti and Tuanaki. These are low sand/coral islands. He also sent the Gennessee Expedition to Tupai which is a low sand/coral island. What a chuckle Brown must have been having to himself; Tupai and Pinaki are about 770 nautical miles apart! But at least the searchers were going to the right type of island. Did Brown knowingly give misinformation because he wasn't part of these expeditions?

I asked the question earlier on in this chapter; why were the searchers going all over the archipelago? Knowing it was because of the Trinity DNA led us to the next question; which is the correct group of islands? It has been narrowed down to three groups as we have seen by the searchers themselves, but as they were jumping from island to island, which island is the correct one? For reasons only that Howe spent a long time there, Pinaki is the strongest contender. Even though after 14 years he went to another island in another group, there must have been good reasons for Howe going to Pinaki in the first place. He must have been satisfied that the directions supplied by Brown applied to this island atoll. What was missing for us was the common factor that made Howe and Hamilton say, "Yes, this [place] looks like it!" They were looking for some feature or shape that corresponded to their chart that equated to where they were. Obviously, for them to go to different islands, suggested a common feature on these islands besides the pinnacles and passes. We are aware that the already discovered DNA of a conical rock, pinnacle and maraes in relation to a pass is important in reconstructing the chart, but several island atolls have these features. There needed to be something else to narrow it down.

Following the Hoofprints

Captain James Brown was a cunning intelligent operator who had carefully concealed the secret he was guarding within a confusing mass of different stories spun to each party he had contact with. Though successful at the time, it was this tactic that led ultimately to the cracking of his secret, for Captain Brown would never have imagined that over a 100 years later, someone would be easily able to compile the various reports and books in which he had featured.

As each party was given a slightly different story surrounding a base core, he inadvertently divulged enough clues that were able to be followed, in this instance, one that left a trail as big as a horse. It is sobering to consider that if Brown had stuck to the one story, with the same details given each time instead of trying to confuse all with different versions, his secret may have remained just that. In Brown's version of his story given to the Herman group, he included a unique detail, that the treasure had originally been hidden on Cocos Island and that it had been relocated to another island, which is why no one could find it. Searching all related stories for DNA, one vague version was found which told of the treasure being first taken to Cocos Island then somehow ending up on the Galapagos Islands (about 440n.m. SW of Cocos Island). A search was made in the 1920s by a local 83-year-old named San Christobal, known as 'Johnson from London' but whose real name was Thomas Levick. Allegedly buried on the island of Marchena, the location of the treasure was marked by a chain laid on the beach from the water's edge to a large boulder. Assisted by two personnel from a visiting Norwegian expedition to the islands, Johnson was finally able to sail to Marchena where he surveyed the coast intently for the landmarks. Not finding them, the disappointment was so great it broke his will to live and he died a few days later in his shack

Another version of the Cocos story uncovered contained the unique relocation DNA and even had a map accompanying it. According to this story, Thompson, Captain of the brig *Mary Dear,* who stole the Lima treasure in 1821, had returned to Cocos Island and relocated it to an island closer to the coast of Central America. The map of this island was passed by Thompson on his deathbed (previous DNA) in Guatemala City to a friend.

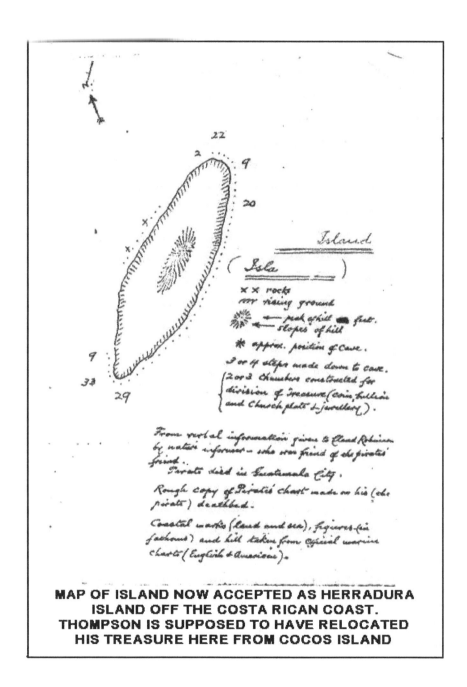

Island

(Isla _____)

x x rocks
꙼꙼ rising ground
☀ ← peak of hill ▬ feet.
← slopes of hill

* approx. position of Cave.

3 or 4 steps made down to cave.
{ 2 or 3 Chambers constructed for
division of treasure (coin, bullion
and Church plate & jewellery).

From verbal information given to Claud Robinson
by native informer — who was friend of the pirates'
friend.
    Pirate died in Guatemala City.
Rough copy of Pirate's chart made on his (the
pirate) deathbed.

Coastal marks (land and sea), figures (in
fathoms) and hill taken from official marine
charts (English & American).

**MAP OF ISLAND NOW ACCEPTED AS HERRADURA
ISLAND OFF THE COSTA RICAN COAST.
THOMPSON IS SUPPOSED TO HAVE RELOCATED
HIS TREASURE HERE FROM COCOS ISLAND**

Referring to the map, for those having difficulty in reading the small handwriting, it reads as follows:

XX rocks
//// rising ground
------ peak of hill   feet
------ slopes of hill
• *approx. position of cave.*
3 or 4 steps made down to cave.
2 or 3 chambers constructed for
division of treasure (coins,bullion
and Church plate & jewellery)

From verbal information given to Claud Robinson
By native informer who was friend of the pirates'
friend.
    Pirate died in Guatemala City.
Rough copy of Pirates' chart made on his (the
pirate) deathbed.
Coastal marks (land and sea), figures (in
fathoms) and hill taken from official marine
charts (English & American).

The island takes its name from an adjacent bay which is in the shape of a horseshoe. In Spanish, 'horseshoe' is 'herradura'. This island is in fact an old pirate haunt. Its shape is not as depicted i.e. a smooth elongated coast but pocketed with small bays and headlands.

Apart from the relocation detail in the story, it is the word 'horseshoe' that catches our attention. This word also appeared in information now streaming out of Juan Fernandez Island in relation to Bernard Keiser and his search for a treasure said to have been 'relocated' to JF Island by something called the 'Horseshoe Expedition'.

Whilst this (Herradura) map did not match a horseshoe island, it did match the shape of an island shown on another treasure map which appeared in Edward Rowe Snow's book *True Tales of Pirates and their Gold*, published in 1953.

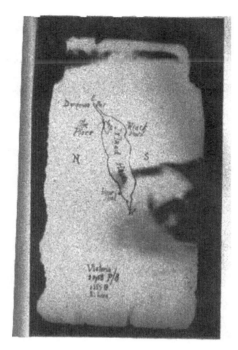

THIS MAP OF HAUTE ISLAND IS SUPPOSED TO HAVE BEEN
CREATED BY THE PIRATE EDWARD LOW

In 1947, the writer Edward Rowe Snow bought a 'pirate treasure map' of Isla Haute (High Island) which is in the Bay of Fundy, Nova Scotia. Apart from being an enthusiastic writer of marine tales, Rowe Snow was also a hunter of pirate's treasure.

Making his way in 1953 to the island, Rowe Snow arranged to stay with the lighthouse keeper John Fullerton and glean whatever intelligence he could about the island and the pirate Edward Low who is supposed to have drawn the map. Keeper Fullerton proved to be a wealth of information about previous searches for treasure on the island, particularly those of the searches conducted by a Dougald Carmichael between 1923 and 1936. Whilst Rowe Snow believed he was looking for the pirate Lowe's treasure, Carmichael was in fact looking for Captain Kidd's treasure. Quoting from a source of the time, his story is as follows:

'Much Sought Treasure Trove Believed Buried in Lake On Island in Bay of Fundy.

Captain Kidd's treasure is now being sought at the Isle o'Haute off Harbourville. The plan is to put in a sluice to drain a small lake on the island so that the supposed wealth of gold and jewels may be recovered. While a vigorous search is being made by a syndicate at Oak Island, Lunenburg Co., for the same treasure, Dougald Carmichael of Advocate, Cumberland Co,. is making plans to prosecute operations at Isle o'Haute. It is reported that a marble slab bearing a chart of the lake and certain specifications are now held by a bank in St John, until a disagreement between Carmichael and a man named McCready is settled.

A well informed and responsible citizen of Harborville declares his faith in the Isle o'Haute project and believed that ere long Kidd's treasures, which he declares total in value several million pounds sterling, will be taken from this lake.

The story as told by Mr. Carmichael is most interesting. The Advocate man is 82 years of age and at one time was station master at Hampton, N. B. He was in the Northwest rebellion and was wounded, and was a visitor to Vancouver when that city was nothing but a camping site. Mr. Carmichael first learned of the alleged Kidd treasure being on Isle o'Haute from ancestors who are said to have secured first hand information from a member of Kidd's crew. The sailor is said to have declared that he saw the gold and jewels landed and placed in the lake, which was then scheduled two fathoms deep. With a man named McCready, Mr. Carmichael started for Isle o'Haute to reclaim the treasure. Their efforts failed because of the water and sand that drifted into the lake and buried the chest of gold and jewels, it is believed. Some of these jewels came from South America, he declares and he refuses to allow a steam shovel to be used to dredge the lake in fear that some of these valuable jewels might be damaged.

Many years ago a builder of the light-house on the island, while walking on the beach, stepped on a marble slab. This attracted his attention and he stopped to turn the slab over. It was cut three-cornered shape and on the reverse side was inscribed in old English letters the words, "R. Kidd 5 fathoms east and two fathoms deep." This slab is shaped exactly like the lake on the island declares Mr. Carmichael. It may be seen by anyone going to the bank of Montreal in Saint John.

The inscription on the slab tallied exactly with the location said to have been told by the member of Kidd's crew to Mr. Carmichael's ancestor. In a few weeks operations are expected to be carried out at this place and Mr. Carmichael believes that the hopes of his whole life time will be realized.'

It is believed Mr. Carmichael recovered some $20,000 in buried treasure from the island between 1923 and 1936 but other accounts differ on this. Apparently in 1929, after a strenuous day's digging, he is said to have appeared at the lighthouse shouting that he had found not only gold but jewels as well. Later that same week, he left the island, never to return, and there are those who say he made an important valuable find on that occasion. But there are others who swear that they were with Carmichael constantly and that he never discovered any treasure at any time! Many people have dug for treasure here, most of them concentrating on two locations on the island. One we know is (or near) the lake at the north-eastern end of the island, the second is in the vicinity of a great rock on the path which winds up to the top of the island. Apparently, on his last visit Carmichael had spent his time digging near this rock. It is also said he attempted to drain the lake but failed. We assume that Edward Rowe Snow searched north of the lake as that was the place indicated on Low's map. Snow found some gold coins and the following account appeared at that time:

'Edward Rowe Snow of Marshfield Mass., a historian whose hobby is treasure hunting, made the find in a brief visit to the island Thursday night. He found the gold with the aid of a metal detector and old charts.
The charts belonged to the late Dougal Carmichael of Vancouver who recovered some $20,000 in buried treasure from the island from 1923 to 1936.
Snow found parts of a skeleton near the gold. It appeared that some of the coins had been clutched in the bones of the hand.
One of the doubloons was dated 1710 (so obviously nothing to do with Kidd as he was hung in 1701. GE) *and all bore the cross of the Holy Roman Empire. Snow said it is unlikely that there is any sizeable cache left on the island.*

Legend has it that the money was buried by the notorious pirate Edward Low, who cut out the tongues of his captives and served them, fried, to his crew.

Legend and charts also indicate that the Isle Haute treasure came from the Spanish galleon 'Senora de Victoria', captured in 1725.'

Having declared the coins (eight) Rowe Snow was granted a licence and allowed to export them from Canada. It is generally accepted now that the coins that Rowe Snow found were those from the wreck of a Spanish galleon, the *Senora de Victoria*, captured in 1725, and not of any pirate named Low or otherwise.

Digging on the island is now outlawed by the 'Nova Scotia Special Places Act' and most of the island is now being taken over by the Canadian Wildlife Service to protect its unique ecosystem. Another feature unique to this place (Bay of Fundy) is that it has the highest tidal range in the world.

What was puzzling was as one layer of the mystery of the lost treasure was peeled off, it merely exposed others. We now had two maps showing a strange lozenge shape, a treasure said to have been relocated from its original hiding place, the word 'Horseshoe', Kidd, and the Kidd/Palmer charts. There was also, of course, a link with Juan Fernandez Island. What possibly could these have to do with a Spanish treasure deliberately hidden in none of these locations?

In-depth research continued.

PART 2

CHAPTER 1

THE 'BOSUN BIRD' AND CONTEMPORARY STORIES - AN EXAMINATION

The stories featured so far (with the exception of Lord Anson) establish the 'Loot of Lima' story with what would appear to be a lot of credibility. Indeed, whilst there are variations on a theme, the basic story has been accepted for going on 200 years. Many books tell it, or should I say 'copy it'. It is the old adage; "It said so in the book, so it must be true!" In the coming chapters, you will see why at this stage I may sound a little sarcastic on this, telling you that maybe you should not believe everything you read. With the tale as told by Killorain, again, we have variations on a theme, and all start with the traditional 'Loot of Lima' story. You may be suspecting by now, I appear to be throwing doubt on this story. That being the case then it also gives us cause to doubt Killorain's story. I have already shown discrepancies in it, so the whole episode needed to be looked at in a lot closer detail, also other contemporary and related pirate/treasure stories. Only this way would it be possible to separate truth from fiction.

Although we concentrate on the craft of Killorain's story next, the 'Loot of Lima' gets our undivided attention further on.

It took several years to research treasure tales and nautical history in the Pacific. They come from local newspaper articles, old books and histories of the islands. MN is to be thanked for unearthing a lot of these. It was fortunate that he lives close to where a lot of the action took place, in particular close to the Pacific Ocean.

An examination and retelling of these stories will show that the Brown/Killorain account is but a very clever mixture of these tales with historical facts thrown in to give that air of credibility. Hamilton, as we know, believed the story told him by Howe, who in turn believed what he was told by Brown. So it is Brown we have to blame, or applaud, for this story. Brown was obviously very well read and far more intelligent than people would have believed. Having spent most of his life in the

Pacific and its adjacent shores, he would have been well acquainted with its history and tales of island folklore. One of the books consulted was *My Adventures and Researches in the Pacific* by Handley Bathurst Sterndale. It is a collection of newspaper and journal articles first published in 1871. One of the stories, titled *The History of Jack Sclute* tells the story of Jack, 'a remarkable beachcomber', from when he left home in England to living amongst the natives of Rakahanga. In short:

In Valparaiso (a port in Chile, blockaded at that time), broke and hungry, a mate persuaded Jack to join him on a ship he'd just found and signed on for a gold dollar. Having signed on out of desperation, he soon realised that he's signed on with a bad lot. He said that during this time, he saw much devilment, wickedness and barbarity. They were eventually taken by a vessel-of-war called the *Aurocano*. The captain, being an Englishman, spared his life and he was allowed to join the crew. The ship, in the pay of the Chilean Navy, took good prize money but with the war coming to an end, the captain invited the crew to 'go on the account' (to go a-pirating), as the saying was. They all agreed and went marauding up and down the west coast of South America, pillaging, looting and sacking ships. They all ended up with chests full of valuables, gold and a lot of money. On Tubuai (an island in the Austral Group), whilst carrying out repairs, they were captured due to the deceit of an acquaintance of the captain. Jack managed to escape and hid on the island until the ships left with the bulk of the treasure. Prior to the attack, as a precaution, Jack and some of the crew had hidden some of their plunder and gold on the island. He never needed it and stayed on the island for several years, and when he did leave, his treasure remained behind, undisturbed.

The remainder of Jack's story is of no interest to us, so let us pick up on the parts that Brown used.

Jack: *I am an Englishman from the County of Kent.*

Brown (Killorain): *Well I was born in County Clare.*

Jack: *My uncle taught me to fight; on one occasion, I knocked him clean overboard.*

Brown: *I was strong and sturdy, took part in a good many wild things.*

Jack: *Weary of brutal ways, I went to Dunkirk.*

Brown: *I got safe over to France.*

Jack: *Stuck in Valparaiso, one of his mates comes up, "Let's go and liquor."*

Brown: *Idle in Shanghai, meets the Yankee Arthur Brown who says, "What about a drink pardner?"*

Jack: *He and his mate go to meet the bosun of a ship in a dive, which was the back room of a hotel. There they meet a yellow-skinned greaser, with rings on his fingers. He was a Spaniard who spoke some English. Jack signed up with him. The Spaniard gave him a doubloon and a glass of pisco (a liquor which got its name from the town in Peru).*

Brown: *Both go to a sailor's dormitory, then to a low underground cellar for supper and a drink where they meet 'a long thin dark fellow of decidedly foreign looks', a Spaniard with the name Diego Alvarez who gives them 'two special rums'.*

Before we further in to Brown's account and how he fabricated his story, it is fitting to stay with the *Aurocano* and identify a real event.

In 1822, the Chilean Navy was under the command of Admiral Cochrane. One of the warships, the *Araucano*, was commanded by Captain Robert Simpson. In that year, she turned pirate and attacked the town of Loreto where Simpson was abandoned before the *Araucano* sailed off into history. It seems that besides the usual victims to their plunder, they targeted in particular the treasures of the Peruvian churches. With enough treasure to satisfy every man on board, they made sail for Honolulu, changing the name of the ship en route to the more tranquil *Providence*. In Hawaii, the authorities became suspicious; this distrust made the captain decide to up-anchor and sail to the south. They eventually arrived at Huahine, in the Society Islands. There again, the ways of the crew created problems; often drunk, they bragged about having a fabulous stolen treasure aboard. The captain, concerned with the need to appear respectable, made every effort to ingratiate himself with the English missionaries working on the island. However, trouble over one of the native women resulted in several men being killed. They sailed east again, towards the Tuamotus and Marquesas. On the way, they stopped at Tupai, then uninhabited, where, according to legend, they buried treasure. This allowed them to now make for Tahiti where they could get rid of the ship which had become a considerable encumbrance. The captain made out they wanted to join a seal hunting expedition and the plan was to seize one of the ships and set sail for Tupai. The plan was thwarted, however, when due to deceit the *Providence* was seized. The surviving mutineers managed to flee, once more to Huahine where they convinced the missionaries that their previous conduct was due in the main to the orders of their officers. Some stayed working on the island for years, whilst others slowly drifted away. As far as is known, none were able to return to Tupai and recover the treasure.

How easy it is for names to become something totally different with time and the re-telling of a story are shown later on in this chapter.

Returning to Brown: being familiar with the 'Bosun Bird' story, you can now see what Brown used to fabricate the beginning of that story. Now let us see what other popular stories and events of the time Brown used.

Robertson and the 'Peruano'

Robertson, a Scot, was at one time in the British Navy. In 1817, he enlisted in the Chilean Navy. He was first lieutenant on the *Congresso* and participated in the siege and capture of Callao in Peru. In 1822, after capturing 60 soldiers of the royalist army of Benavides, he revealed his ferocious nature by ordering all his prisoners hanged. After hostilities had ceased, he retired to Callao, and it was here, in 1826, that he met a rich Spaniard's widow by the name of Teresa Mendez. An ebony-haired beauty of 21, Robertson fell hopelessly in love with her. But she refused his advances, telling him that she would only marry a wealthy and famous man. Some time later, he was visiting the Commandant of Callao Harbour, who, pointing to a ship in the harbour, said, "You'd be more powerful than a squadron leader if you owned that brigantine over there."

"Yes, I know," replied Robertson, who knew of the ship. "They say she's got more than 500,000 gold piastres hidden in her hold."

"A lot more than that!" The commandant replied. "She's called the *Peruano* and carries 2,000,000 piastres in gold from the Government vaults. I oversaw the transshipment."

The desire for Teresa had tormented Robertson for a long time and in the *Peruano* he could see how to fulfil his dreams, how to make Teresa his own. He made his mind up; he would take the ship of gold. He rounded up a band of adventurers in the taverns and that night they captured the brigantine by sudden attack. When dawn came, the *Peruano* was nowhere to be seen, but a dinghy appeared from the open sea carrying members of the crew released by Robertson. Several brigs left in pursuit but Robertson with an unbeatable head start had disappeared to the south-west. At Tahiti they made up for the long journey by spending money as pirates do, in the bars and taverns. To help ease the hardships of the forthcoming lengthy voyage, they took on board 15 pretty native girls. At the next lonely island they stopped at for water, Robertson, who always had it in mind to get rid of his accomplices, abandoned eight of the men, on the pretext of insubordination. Now, with a skeleton crew and the women, the *Peruano* headed for the Mariannes. It is thought they anchored off Grignan, though some say it was Guam Island. The women, now frightened and disillusioned by the behaviour of the crew, tried to swim ashore. Now a hindrance and troublesome witnesses, Robertson and the crew hunted them down and murdered them. They then buried the thousand iron-bound wooden chests containing the gold in an immense trench under two feet of sand.

A year later, the Spanish captured Robertson, who had got rid of his accomplices. Under torture, he admitted his crimes and was made to sail back to his treasure island. After anchoring and disembarking on the ship's boat, knowing all was lost and the lovely Teresa would never be his, he jumped overboard, quickly sinking under the weight of his chains.

Over 600 natives were employed by the Spanish Governor to look for the treasure; nothing was ever found.

The 'Peruvian'

Another account names the ship as the *Peruvian*. In 1821, with revolution in the air, the Spanish Viceroy in Callao arranged to have their gold and valuables loaded on some ships for transportation to other Spanish territories. One such ship, the *Peruvian*, Robinson in command, under orders to sail to Guam, instead sailed for Hawaii. (Long-time treasure hunters in Hawaii believe the *Peruvian* eventually dropped anchor somewhere off Ka'ena Point.)

Robinson and four crewmen (including an officer named Brown!) somehow trapped the rest of the crew below sealed hatches. They unloaded the treasure onto a longboat and sank the *Peruvian* with the men still inside. Once on land, the quartermaster, a man named Monks, was told to stand by the boat while Robinson, Brown and the three crewmen made two trips inland to hide the six chests of gold. Monks would later say that on the last trip he heard gunshots and only Robinson and Brown returned. Some weeks later, Robinson and Brown left for Australia intending to retrieve their gold with another ship at a later date. They left Monks for dead but he survived. He died in Hawaii in 1928, afraid for his life; he never looked for the treasure himself. For whatever reason, Robinson and Brown never made it back.

(This story regarding Monks' participation is a bit suspicious; he would have to have been well over 100 years old when he died to have taken part! GE)

Agrihan Island and the 'Peruano'

Yet another account of this story, considered to be the more accurate and reliable, is that by Gabriel Lafond de Lurcy. He knew Roberton and was present when the conversation took place at Callao Harbour regarding Roberton's predicament with the widow Teresa. One of the officers laughingly remarking that he (Roberton) would have no problems with the lady if only he could take over the *Peruano*.

Lafond de Lurcy's account more or less follows the earlier *Peruano* account but with more detail and some differences. After abandoning his eight crewmen, Roberton does go north-west to Grignan, also known as Grigan or Agrigan but now known as Agrihan. The chests of gold coins were buried at a short distance from the sea in a clearing at the foot of a cliff. Marks were left on the rocks and trees to guide them on their return. Roberton had two trustworthy assistants and conspirators, Irishmen called George and William. Close to the Hawaiian Islands, they scuttled the ship with the crew trapped inside. They rowed ashore at Oahu, one of the islands (close to Pearl Harbour), claiming to have been shipwrecked. They kept 20,000 piastres from the treasure for their own use.

Unknown to them, the *Peruano* failed to sink; it drifted about for some weeks, low in the water. When it was found, three of the eight men had starved to death and another was barely alive. The survivor recounted his story to Lafond de Lurcy in 1828.

As we know, Roberton always intended the treasure was for himself and Teresa and subsequently his gang of three soon became two. George disappeared in Rio de Janeiro and we assume at the hand of his conspirators. In 1827, they are in Hobart, Tasmania, where they persuade an old sailor named Thompson to take them in his schooner back to Agrihan. During the journey, Thompson managed to piece together the real purpose of the voyage from William during his drunken stupors. But William did not know the name of the island where they had buried the treasure. He could only identify it as an island north of Saipan

Thompson awoke one night with a start to hear William's death scream. Very aware he was in the presence of a murderer, he now stayed vigilant at all times. Sleep and exhaustion finally overtook him, however, and Roberton, waiting this moment, pushed him overboard. Miraculously, Thompson managed to stay afloat and was picked up soon after by a Spanish ship, which chased Roberton to Saipan. Not suspecting he was being searched for, he was soon captured and clapped in irons.

Thompson, who was familiar with this part of the Pacific, was certain from William's description that Agrihan, their original destination was Roberton's treasure island. The Spaniards took Roberton there but he revealed nothing. They flogged him over a cannon until he promised to show them the hiding place. Wrapped in chains, with everything to lose and nothing to gain except a noose around his neck, he threw himself over the side as they rowed him ashore.

The *Peruano/Peruvian* story, because of the inconsistencies, is similar in a way to the *Bosun Bird* story. We have three versions of the principle character's name; Robertson, Roberton and Robinson. You can see how easy it was for the name of the commander of the *Aurocano*, Robert Simpson, to get mixed into the story of the *Peruvian* and *Peruano*, to become the 'Robertson' of one of the versions.

There are three possible treasure locations; Oahu Island (one of the Hawaiian Islands), Guam and Agrihan Islands, the latter being some 3,300 nautical miles directly to the west of Honolulu! One thousand chests, or six chests? If the quoted 2,000,000 gold coins are correct, then at 2,000 coins per chest, 1,000 chests are required! If Agrihan is the island, then why hasn't anything been found? Because of the work and weight involved, Robertson wouldn't have carried them very far inland, yet 600 natives excavated tons of earth and sand without finding anything. Added to that, the fact that 1,000 chests of gold is a huge, highly conductive mass of metal, and therefore shouldn't be too difficult to find with today's deep-seeking metal detectors, perhaps Agrihan Island is not the correct island after all.

The basic facts about Robertson and the event of the theft of a ship named the *Peruano* or *Peruvian* are correct. The main source, as we have seen is Lafond de Lurcy, writing in his *Voyages Autour du Monde*. He was around as a first-hand witness when all this was happening and had met Robertson. But it is only Lafond de Lurcy's testimony as to the theft of the ship that can be relied upon. The rest of the account, as any good barrister would no doubt point out, is pure hear'say. Other accounts are only mutated versions of this and likewise are not wholly credible.

To add to this confusion and another 'spanner in the works', in 2006, one Gerald Crowley said he excavated a sunken ship off a small island near Australia. The ship he thought to be either the *Peruvian, Peruana* or *Pervano*. He also said a French LeFaucheux pistol, patented in 1845, was recovered. If the ship is indeed our *Peruano* or the *Peruvian*, then obviously she was lost sometime probably after 1850, nearly 30 years after the hijacking in Callao Harbour. This does not tie-in with any of the above stories.

The above mentioned pistol was said to be x-rayed enabling the serial number to be read, less the last digit. It was said that from the French records, four possible owners could be identified, with the name William Doig suggested as one of them. This name will not mean anything to you now but it features later on.

It is a mystery to me why the purported x-ray is not that at all but in fact a photographic negative!

The Pieces of the Jigsaw

Perhaps you are now beginning to recognise the parts of these stories that Brown used to fabricate his tale that so many believed. For example:

a) The dying pirate (Killorain) with a map is, as we have seen, a common enough story in the 1800s.

b) Killorain's earlier life, as we can see, is embellished from Jack Sclate's story.

c) Regardin 'a glass of pisco' in the dive, Brown was inspired to use that name for the treasure, i.e. the Pisco Treasure.

d) The mule train trip, when Alvarez and the gang of four went across the country, Buenos Aires to Valparaiso, is straight out of the famous cross-country attack by Drake on Nombre de Dios. Hints here also of the infamous attack by the pirate Benito Bonito on the Spanish mule train from Mexico City.

e) Stealing a treasure (Juan Damerion of the *Bosun Bird*) for the love of a pretty señorita is straight out of the Robertson and the 'lovely Teresa' story.

f) The scuttled ship, rowing ashore and claiming to be honest shipwrecked sailors is what Alvarez and his cronies did, landing near Port Darwin.

g) Roberton, waiting his chance and tipping Thompson overboard. Brown used a similar story to get rid of Schmidt when he was alone in the boat with him, and so on.

What's in a Name? An Island!

A little more difficult is, where did Brown get the name of the ship, the *Bosun Bird*? Also the Spaniard's name, Diego Alvarez? To get to the answer, we must look at a third piratical event that took place in the 1820s. Whilst at this stage only part of the story is relevant, it enhances our story to tell more of what happened. Benito de Soto was, in 1827, a crewman on board the slave ship, the *Defensor de Pedro*. Whilst the captain was ashore, Soto and the mate mutinied. Those who did not want any part of it were put off in the longboat. To enforce his own authority, Soto soon shot the mate, who he saw as his rival. Over the next couple of years, they plundered many vessels. The treatment of one, an American brig, typifies the atrocities they revelled in. Having plundered all the valuables they could find, they hatched down all hands to the hold, except a black man, who was allowed to remain on deck. Having then set fire to the ship, they watched with great delight the dance of death as the man tried to escape the flames. He finally fell, screaming into the hold, joining the rest, as they died in the inferno.

A year later in 1828, they are in the Atlantic close to Ascension Island. They turn to chase a vessel, which they discover is a British vessel, the *Morning Star,* on her way home to England from Ceylon. This vessel, besides a valuable cargo, had on board several passengers, consisting of a major and his wife, a surgeon, some civilians, 25 invalid soldiers and several of their wives.

A superior sailor, the *Defensor de Pedro* soon overhauled the hapless unarmed *Morning Star* and fired a round of grapeshot across her decks. What followed was barbarity of the worse kind. Soto shot the captain in the back. The mate met a similar fate. Those left alive after the initial boarding attack were driven below. The women were separated and locked in the roundhouse on deck. Beaten, bleeding and terrified, the men lay huddled together in the hold, while the pirates proceeded in their work of pillage and brutality. It took them two hours to empty the vessel of its valuables, helping themselves to the ships store of liquor at the same time. The women were ordered out and treated with less humanity than the others. All were raped. The screams of the helpless females were heard in the hold by their incarcerated menfolk. Soto, whose orders had been to butcher everyone on board, had remained aboard his own vessel during the vile brutal actions of his crew. Those left alive aboard the *Morning Star* were, however, spared. It is thought that by the time Soto called them back, because they had spent so much time drinking and indulging themselves, they had no time to murder everybody. Instead, they locked the women in the cabin and heaped heavy lumber on the hatches of the hold. Holes were bored in the hull. They hoped for a swift demise of the ship, which they left sinking fast to a certain fate.

Fortunately, the women, with great courage and fortitude, managed to break out of the cabin and they soon managed to free the men in the hold. With renewed energy and all hands at the pumps, they managed to keep the vessel afloat, despite six feet of water in the hold. Good fortune stayed with them, for the next day they were rescued by another vessel that was also going to England, which they reached in safety.

Meanwhile, Soto, having discovered his orders had not been carried out, lost no time in putting about and running back to complete the deed. As far as he was concerned, 'Dead men tell no tales'. But it was too late; no sign of the vessel could be found, so he consoled himself with the belief that she was at the bottom of the sea. The pirates continued on their course of murder and plunder. At Corunna, he disposed of a great part of his booty and obtained false papers. He then set out for Cadiz where he hoped to sell the remainder of his plunder. However, caught in a storm they were wrecked on the coast not far from that city. They presented themselves as honest shipwrecked mariners to the authorities at Cadiz and were met with some sympathy. Soto even managed to get a contract for the sale of the wreck but before the money could be paid, suspicions arose because of the inconsistencies in the pirate's account of themselves. Six of the crew were arrested, six managed to escape to the Carraccas and Soto, with one of his crew, fled to the neutral ground before Gibraltar. He was captured in that fortress after being identified as a suspicious character by a servant girl, who noticed that his clothes were embroidered with different names. He was kept in jail there for 19 months, whilst the evidence was gathered against him. He pleaded his innocence up to the day before his execution but the certainty of his fate at length subdued him and he made an unreserved confession of his guilt. On the gallows, he murmured, "Adios todos" (Farewell all), before he fell.

Before we leave Benito de Soto's story, I trust you have recognised the similarities with part of this story to the previous stories, i.e. Robinson trapped men below and sank the *Peruvian* after unloading the treasure. In the Agrihan/Peruano version, the ship was scuttled with the crew trapped inside, but she failed to sink and drifted about for some weeks.

Just to put yet another 'spanner in the works' as they say, I will recall to you the Salvage Islands story and similar significant events: Rear Admiral <u>Robinson</u>, Christian Cruise, 1804, Spanish ship with *two millions* worth of dollars in chests making for Cadiz, wrecked before they got there! And just to add a little more confusion, later on we will talk about the pirate Benito Bonito!

So how do we link the Benito de Soto story to Brown? One of the obvious links is 'Father Benito' who features in the Hamilton/Howe/Killorain story. The other link is Ascension Island, for located near the east side of this island is - Bosun Bird Island!

And for Diego Alvarez:

There is, in the South Atlantic, an island called 'Gough Island'. There is supposed to be a pirate treasure buried here close to a conspicuous spire or pinnacle of stone known as Church Rock. One Goncalo Alvarez discovered the island in 1505. The island was given his name and on early charts appeared as 'De Isla Goncalo Alvarez'. It was later shortened to 'De I. Go. Alvarez' and then to 'Diego Alvarez Island'. So, Diego Alvarez the island becomes Diego Alvarez, the Spanish Bos'n.

The story of a treasure associated with this island comes from Ralph D Paine's book *The Book of Pirate Treasure*, published in 1911. Could it be that Brown read this book? Another tie-in that seems to confirm it is the fact that Paine describes the place to dig as;

'close to a conspicuous spire or pinnacle of stone on the western end of the island, the name of which natural landmark is set down on the charts as Church Rock.'

But there is more to this than it seems and you would not be aware of it unless you studied the chart. In fact, 'Church Rock' is a sea stack in the water to the *north-east* of the island. Is Paine trying to put people off the scent here? This reveals itself as important not only when you realise that Hamilton was following this exact wording to search for a pinnacle of coral on the *western* side of the atolls they visited but when they changed atolls, assessed that a conical column on the *east* side was really the correct location.

Brown and/or Howe used Paine's (deliberate?) mistake of reversing directions. As we saw, Hamilton and his treasure seekers eventually cottoned on to this and successfully (they thought) located the right island.

Is this island in the Atlantic, Diego Alvarez, via Captain Brown, giving us a clue to the treasure location? This landmark of a 'pinnacle on the west side' or its actual qualitative identity Brown was able to use for more than one island. Later on, you will be made aware of the word association of 'native altar' to 'Church Rock', used in conjunction with this mistaken location for this feature in Paine's book.

We can add that the author H.T. Wilkins, in his book *Treasure Hunting*, mentions Gough Island but not Diego Alvarez. He tells us there is a cache of silver under a rock called 'Church Rock' which lies at the *western* end of the island! Proof then that you cannot always believe what an author says. Wilkins obviously didn't check the chart but copied what Paine had written.

The Loot of Lima, Pisco, Callao or Peru?

You can see that it is the stories so far in the previous chapters that give Brown the basis for his story. He has taken parts of these real events and mixed in tales of his own, again with hints of other stories. But his story is all about the taking of a great treasure, so what real event of stolen treasure did he introduce, or did he just make it up? A good question, or should the question be, "Was there a real event of Spanish treasure stolen?" "Of course there was!" you say. "The books say so!"

I think I have already proven to you that it is folly to believe all you hear and read, as Hamilton, Howe and Sutton did to their cost. Like the treasure stories that change with each telling, so often the book tells the current story, unaware it is but a mutated version of an earlier story, which was itself probably copied from another. And, as previously stated, just because it says so in a book, does not make it correct! Let us elaborate on what it is I am getting at here. One researcher researched the story and checked in the Pisco church. It did not have a crypt! Another researcher and treasure hunter found out that there was no Father Matteo in any of the church records in Pisco, also, the church was poor and never had 14 tons of gold!

Lieutenant Harry E. Rieseberg was famous around the middle of the last century as a hard-hat diver and treasure hunter, and also as a prolific author of treasure hunting books. During his research of the fabled stolen treasure story, he visited the cathedral at Lima and was astounded to discover that at no time had the cathedral ever been plundered. A priest even pointed out the life-size effigy of the Golden Virgin Mary and the twelve Golden Apostles, all supposed to have been stolen by pirates. Also, at no time had there been a war between Chile and Peru. Not quite true. In fact, they were at war, Bolivia included, in the 'War of the Pacific' 1879-1883. But for the part of the century we are interested in, the 1820s, the sabre rattling was for independence from the Spanish, Chile getting hers in 1818 and Peru in 1821. The war continued for a couple more years, during which Lima was for a time reoccupied by the royalists and it was not until the battle of Ayacucho in 1824 that Spanish domination in South America was ended forever.

Fortunately, history does record for us that there *was* a treasure at Callao. Lord Cochrane, formerly of the Royal Navy, was Commander-in-Chief of the Chilean Navy during the time of the Peruvian independence. Much to the chagrin of Lord Cochrane, General San Martin (the liberator) allowed the Spanish to remove their treasure from the fort in Callao three weeks *after* he had claimed the independence of Lima. Writing of the incident in his diary, Lord Cochrane said:

'The Spaniards today (August 19, 1821) relieved and reinforced the fortress of Callao and coolly walked off unmolested with plate and money to the amount of many millions of dollars—in fact, the whole wealth of Lima—which has been said, was deposited in the fort for safety'.

Of great interest to us is the fact that Lord Cochrane makes no mention of any of the Spanish treasure being subsequently stolen by pirates. It is also a fact that no other writer in Peru at that time mentions any Spanish treasure being stolen. But, a Spanish treasure was stolen from Lima. We say Lima because the treasure is traditionally known as 'The Loot of Lima', and Callao, closely associated with our story is the port of Lima, Pisco being some 90 miles or so further down the coast.

How do we know a treasure was stolen? Because all the books tell us so therefore it must be true! (No comment!)

There are many versions of this traditional story. Unfortunately, they all take us to the infamous Cocos Island. Cocos and its stories (because mostly they are stories) is a minefield for the unwary and uninitiated. We have already come across this island. You will recall this is where, in Brown's story as told to Sutton, Captain Henry Smith sailed to in the *Black Witch* and buried his plunder from the churches of Callao.

Now that Cocos Island comes back into the story, I can reveal that at Rieseberg's request, the British Vice-Consul at Lima, A. Stanley Fordham, made further enquiries among people familiar with Peruvian historical records. These included the head of the Peruvian National Library, generally regarded as the best-informed authority on Peruvian history. All those contacted agreed that there appeared to be no connection between Lima and any treasure buried on Cocos Island. That there is a connection we know, albeit a dubious one created by our Captain Brown. So we have to look at the 'Loot of Lima' story and see what, if anything, Brown used to 'pad out' his story to make it believable.

One of the most reliable books for the history of the treasure stories is that titled *The Lost Treasure of Cocos Island* by Ralph Hancock and Julian Weston, published in 1960. The book traces the history of the various treasures, tells how the booty came to the island and the many expeditions that have tried to recover it. This book is comprehensive, which is why I recommend it. There are many others, and hundreds of articles on the subject. Cocos Island is nearly always featured in books of pirate buried treasure. Whilst recommending the Hancock and Weston book because of its content, does not mean that I agree to the veracity of its content regarding the Lima loot. The same misgivings apply to all other narratives of the same story. In a word, they got it wrong! I do not say this just because the evidence of the contemporaneous records show it never happened - Cochrane, Rieseburg, the Peruvian authorities and so on, (although these records on their own are damning evidence) - but because research brought to light the *real* event in history that all these lost treasure stories are more than likely based on. The event already described at the beginning of this book, the clandestine operation carried out by Captain General Juan Esteban Ubilla.

Let us now look at the traditional 'Loot of Lima' story.

CHAPTER 2

THOMPSON, THE 'LOOT OF LIMA' AND COCOS ISLAND

This version of the 'Loot of Lima' story is the one accepted more or less by most researchers of the subject but there are many versions; my account mentions some of the discrepancies. As Hancock and Weston say in their book:

'If all the versions (Thompson) so far written about the Lima treasure on Cocos Island were printed in one book, you couldn't carry it.'

As far as I am concerned, this all goes to show (or prove?) that it is just a traditional story, embellished with time. Had it been a factual event recorded as such in official records of the time, then there would be just one event to speak of, with no variations.

How the Legend Started
We have already seen that because of the political upheaval of the time, the sea routes to Spain were closing down. Unable to ship the King's remit, the Viceroy in Lima had allowed the bullion to build up in the vaults of the fortress of Lima. Commanding authority over a vast area including Peru, the South American Colonies and almost all the Spanish Governors of the continent, the Viceroy never imagined that there could be any threat to Spain's wealth. However, the Chilean Navy under command of the bold Admiral Thomas Cochrane, was slowly sweeping the Spanish flag from the Pacific. The military leader Simón Bolivar and the rebel General San Martin were closing in on Peru and the colonies. Indeed, the Viceroy did not appreciate the threat to Lima until those forces were within 50 miles of the capital. Panic set in amongst the Spanish population; more gold and silver plate of the Grandees were secured in the fortress. As mentioned previously, the value was in millions of dollars. They took every opportunity of escaping to sea in any sort of vessel they could procure and a fugitive fleet of merchantmen steered out of the hostile coast of Peru. They

carried with them all the property they could collect in the hope of reaching the mother country or some neutral port. Besides the holds piled high with gold and silver, the cabins were crammed with officials of the state and church and other residents of rank and station.

It is said that Admiral Cochrane, blockading the port at Callao, through his spyglass was able to witness the movement of the cathedral treasure down to the fort there. Piled high onto oxcarts and wagons were crates, strong boxes and jewelled statues. Also transported down were the contents of the mint at Lima, together with its store of gold and silver. Admiral Cochrane offered to let the Spanish governor depart with two-thirds of his treasure if he would surrender the remainder and give up the fort without a fight. Much to the Admiral's disgust, however, the Peruvian liberator San Martin allowed the garrison to evacuate the place, carrying away the treasure held there.

Many pirates got wind of this fabulous wealth and treasure sent afloat from Lima in all sorts of sailing craft without any proper protection, and there is no doubt that much of it failed to reach Spain due to their activities.

It is estimated that treasure to the value of at least £6,000,000 was held in the fort waiting to reach Spain. It is with this dazzling booty as a backdrop and the Grandee's panic to get out of the country that we are introduced to Captain Thompson.

The only suitable ship to convey such a cargo safely was the Spanish gun ship *Esmeralda* (later captured by Cochrane's forces) but the Viceroy had to hold her there for the possible defence of the port. The only other ship was not even Spanish but the British merchantman, the *Mary Dear* of Bristol (other accounts vary from *Mary Dyer* to *Mary Dier* and *Mary Deer*), with Captain William (or Marion) Thompson, a Scot, in command. (You may recall here that Brown's account names the ship as the *Black Witch*, Captain Henry Smith in command.)

Thompson was known and trusted by the port authorities, having traded for some time up and down the coast there. This stood him in good stead, and for a price, he was persuaded to take on board the church treasures of Lima, including a life-sized statue of the Virgin Mary made of gold and encrusted with jewels. This alone weighed over a ton. Also stowed in the hold were the coins, gold and silver from the mint. The size of the treasure stowed aboard can be gauged from the fact that it took two days to be stowed properly in the hold. Some soldiers and priests were also taken aboard to keep an eye on the fabulous cargo. Thompson's instructions were to cruise off the coast out of danger. Should Lima fall, he was to sail to Panama. Should the rebel forces attack fail, he was to return to Callao forthwith. It is obvious that soon after leaving Callao, Thompson succumbed to the temptation of the vast treasure in the hold. Whether it was his own doing or forced to by the crew is not known. One 'authentic' story has it that it was the mate's idea, one James Alexander Forbes. With the crew on his side, he challenged the captain: "Are you with us, or the sharks?" Thereafter, Thompson was merely a puppet to Forbes. The guards were obviously murdered, as were the priests, no doubt becoming food for the sharks.

They quickly recognised the fact that with such an incriminating cargo, they needed to hide it as soon as possible, for once it was discovered they had disappeared, all hell would break loose and the Peruvian authorities would hunt them down. Thompson knew Cocos Island, remote and uninhabited, not too far up the coast and about 300 miles off the coast of Costa Rica. Ideally situated, they could bury the treasure there without any interference. Anchored off Chatham Bay (or was it Wafer Bay?), it took 11 longboat loads to land all the treasure on the beach. Some of it was shared out amongst the crew. Where it was then buried, nobody knows. Some say in the beach near the high water mark, the exact spot marked by a large boulder. Or was it a cave, the well-hidden entrance covered by a stone slab? Others say it was up a creek at the foot of a hill, or even maybe up the creek and under a coconut tree!

What happened after that is mixed up in the folklore and tales of the event. Some say a Peruvian warship caught up with them after they left the island. Taken back to Callao, eight were shot. Thompson and two others were spared on promising to reveal the hiding place of the treasure. Thompson told them it was hidden on the Galapagos Islands. He escaped, served on a whaler and eventually made it home to Nova Scotia. Another version says they scuttled the ship getting rid of the evidence, then rowed ashore to the mainland and posed as shipwrecked mariners. Others say a Spanish man-of-war that had escaped Admiral Cochrane's squadron caught them. The captain, knowing a deal had been done with the Viceroy, put them all on trial for piracy, murder and theft of the crown property. All were hung except Thompson and the mate; they offered to show them where the treasure was hidden if their lives were spared.

Yet another version says that a Peruvian warship soon caught up with them and all but Thompson were captured on the beach. He escaped into the thick undergrowth and climbed a hill to view the proceedings. He saw the landing party return to the boats without his crew and concluded they had been executed. He was rescued after a week or two by a trading vessel that stopped for water. Put ashore near Panama and with the gold he had taken with him, he purchased a boat. He then sailed north and found a lonely island, and here he fashioned out a cave large enough to take the treasure. A succession of trips to Cocos followed until all of it had been removed to its new hiding place. With enough capital in gold coin, he moved once again north and settled down becoming a much-respected citizen with business enterprises. This relocation aspect of Thompson's story will be looked at in more detail later.

If we stay with the version that Thompson and the mate were captured; they were taken back to Cocos. A pre-arranged plan was put into place that when far up Chatham Creek, they would suddenly dart into the dense undergrowth. This they did and successfully evaded capture. (Why were they not manacled and in chains? GE) For two weeks, they avoided the Spanish (or Peruvian) soldiers, who eventually had to leave due to lack of supplies. Other search parties were sent out but the fugitives were never found. Eventually, a British whaler called at the island for fresh water and rescued them. They were put ashore at Puntarenas where it is believed Forbes died in hospital of yellow fever. We next hear of Thompson about 20 years later in Newfoundland. What he did in the intervening years is not known but he never had the money or opportunity to go back for the treasure, otherwise it would be on record that he had come into unexpected wealth. To further confuse things on this issue, Ralph D. Paine, in his *The Book of Buried Treasure*, says that Thompson was one of only two survivors of Benito Bonito's crew that had been captured and executed.

John Keating

Next on the scene is a sailor named John Keating. Born in 1808 in Harbour Grace (Isle of Newfoundland), he moved to St John's where he worked as a ship's carpenter before becoming a sea captain. No one knows the real circumstances of their meeting but it is said that Keating was in Cuba when Benito Bonito was there. Thompson was there as part of Benito's crew, and he and Thompson became good friends. Keating eventually took him into his own home and treated him like a brother. A version has it that on his deathbed, Thompson confided the secret of Cocos Island to his young friend in gratitude for his care. He gave him a chart and instructions for finding the treasure.

It was to be a year or two later before Keating was able to sail for Cocos Island in the brig *Edgcombe*, with captain Gault or Gould in command, and also on board one Boag (or Bogue, even Boig), ship owner and/or sea captain. He was Keating's partner in the venture.

There are several versions around as to what happened next. Keating and Boag found the treasure as per Thompson's instructions. Boag was murdered by Keating or drowned in the surf, or they both hid on the island to avoid Gault and the crew who they knew would demand a share. They eventually got away from the island in the ship's longboat with what treasure they could carry without causing suspicion. Or did a passing ship eventually pick up Keating alone? Nobody knows exactly how Boag disappears from the scene. We will never know and for us, it does not really matter!

We next hear of Keating back in Newfoundland where he is said to have disposed of some Spanish gold coins, evidence that he had indeed found the treasure. He is believed to have made at least two further trips to Cocos. A Judge Prowse of Newfoundland said, "I have heard persons describe the astonishment of Keating's wife when he threw all the gold and jewels on the bed for her to see." The returns on these trips enabled him to purchase a farm, several commercial properties and a schooner. It was in this ship that Keating was shipwrecked in 1868. He was rescued and cared for by a Nicholas Fitzgerald, and in gratitude Keating invited him on a future expedition to the island. Fitzgerald declined, and in a letter to a friend he said:

'I thought I would be running grave risk of my life to go single-handed with him. The disappearance of Boag was unsatisfactorily explained to me by him...'

Of interest to us is an account that on one of his trips, Keating with the aid of others, moved the treasure, or part of it, to another location on the island. You can see the obvious inference here to the earlier Brown/Schmidt relocation story, and also to an earlier paragraph, where the story relates how Thompson relocates the treasure to another island. Another now forgotten account of Keating gave a detail that echoed an activity Captain Brown had also referred to, for it was said that in 1846, Keating, in company with a man named Bogue, fitted out a small schooner for the ostensible purpose of *pearl-fishing* in the Bay of Dulce.

The Judge Prowse who talked about Keating earlier, also had something to say about Bogue:

'Bogue and his wife I recall very well, they being one of the handsomest couples I have ever seen. They sailed for the North Pacific, ostensibly on a bear-hunting expedition to Dulce Bay, but made an excuse to call at Cocos Island to replenish their water casks....'

This 'Bay of Dulce' has a habit of cropping up!

Keating eventually bequeathed treasure directions to Fitzgerald, his young wife, his son-in-law and a Thomas Hacket. Before he could act on the information, Hacket died and so his brother Fred inherited some of Keating's maps and charts, and he went to the island in 1902. All the beneficiaries apparently had contradictory information, which of course resulted in all the subsequent inevitable expeditions finding nothing.

A final version of the Cocos story is worth mentioning here because it introduces a new name to the mystery.

The Doigs of Scotland

It is in the family history that the brothers John and William Doig moved to Peru where they became merchantmen. In the bid for freedom from Spain, John commanded his own warship and fought alongside Lord Cochrane. He preyed on the commercial shipping and warships of Spain. There is a story in the family that John eventually returned to Scotland with huge wealth from his time in South America. However, to continue with this other version for Cocos:

In around the year 1818, a British pirate Bennet Graham, or Benito Bonito as he preferred to call himself, buried on Cocos Island the loot from Peruvian churches and merchant ships. It is thought fairly certain that more treasure was added at a later date, or dates.

With Benito was one William Thompson who turns up at Cocos again in 1824. The Spanish had managed to get away with much of their treasure from Lima when Peru was in revolt against the rule of Spain. (All this action i.e. the war of independence from Spain, took place in the early 1820s) Lord Cochrane went to the port of Callao where a lot of the treasure had been moved to and demanded two-thirds of it to pay his men. Thompson appears on the scene in command of the trading brig, the *Mary Read*. ('Dear' with front and last letters exchanged.) He arranges to take off some of the Spanish grandees with their enormous fortunes and so avoid the attention of Lord Cochrane. We know that out at sea the Spaniards were killed and Thompson headed for Cocos where he buried the loot.

It was to be many years before he could return, this time with a partner named Doig. He discovered that the treasures that he and Benito had buried remained there undisturbed. They decided that at that time, it would be too risky to remove a lot of it, and anyway, there was far too much to bring away in one go. They returned home and started to make better preparations. Before they could return, Thompson died. Some years later, Doig and his son made the trip. This time they were faced with landslides, which made recovery a serious engineering task. Totally unprepared for this, they had to return home to reconsider plans. The elder Doig died; whether it was John or William, we are not told. His son never had the chance to return to the island. But he left 'clear' directions regarding the location of the hoards. These were of no use to the succession of treasure hunters that followed. A few coins and ornaments were found but treasure seekers have obliterated helpful landmarks, and also storms and natural changes, including earthquakes, have taken their toll over the years.

Many have gone in search of the legendary treasures of Cocos Island. Besides the 'big' ones of Benito and the traditional Lima loot, there is no doubt that many crewmen of these pirate ships have left other smaller caches. It was normal for pirates to quickly spend their booty on wine and women in the next port of call but a lot of them, in these times of easy pickings, had too much. They had to hide it until given the chance to spend it. Yet there is no record, officially anyway, of anything ever being found. OK, we are now aware that the 'Loot of Lima' treasure was a non-event; even so, I would have thought there were more than a few small caches waiting to be found.

Amongst the uncorroborated reports are the following:

'A group of mercenaries fled from Nicaragua in 1856, sailing to Cocos they anchored in Chatham Bay. A scouting party rowing over to Wafer Bay found by accident a huge cave. The tide was low, on exploring they saw a huge bronze chain anchored to the rocky floor and running out into the ocean. It took 10 men to pull the chain in and they found there was a large iron chest bolted to the end. After much effort they got it into their boat, then back to their ship. The story goes that after finally opening the chest they found it full of gold doubloons from Peru. Old letters telling this story seem to confirm it.'

Another one again close to Wafer Bay:

'Two Equadorian soldiers, ordered to blast away the roots of a large tree dislodged a ledge of rock which brought down with it a small heavy chest. It contained a number of gold ornaments rifled by Benito the pirate, from South American Churches. Letters were found in the chest belonging to a Welshman named Evan Jones who appears to have been one of Benito's trusted officers.'

There is also a well-reported story of a Belgian student who is supposed to have found two skeletons and treasure in a cave, again unconfirmed.

As suggested earlier, there were probably more than a few private caches hidden here over the years, by officers and crew of many different pirate ships in the eighteenth and nineteenth centuries. A report from the early 1900s even lists what might be found! A reporter of a London newspaper apparently 'unearthed' an old gentleman living in Essex who showed the reporter a chart of Cocos Island. He stated it was a copy of the chart drawn up by the captain and the chief mate of the *Mary Read* (same letters as Dear again!). The site of the cache was marked on the chart. The old gentleman said that he had fitted out an expedition to hunt the treasure but they were beaten by tropical disease and had to leave the island after just ten days. The treasure, he said, contains a five-foot figure of the Madonna in solid gold - it would take ten men to lift it. It also contains 250 swords studded with jewels, and a vast quantity of church plate, coin, bar-gold and bar silver. He added that an 'Old pirate named Bonito has buried 25 million dollars worth of more treasure on the island. Its location is uncertain, but it seems to be almost in the same spot as the ill-gotten spoil of the *Mary Dyer*. So altogether, 60 million dollars worth of treasure may lie buried in the soil of Cocos Island'.

Even members of Jacques Cousteau's (the famous diver and co-inventor of the aqualung) crew tried their luck with a metal detector during a visit to film the island and its reefs. A modern technology search advantage, but it did not help. Like everybody else, they came away empty handed.

You can make the connection we trust between the name Doig and the Boag who features in the earlier stories. As if to bait us even more, Captain William Thompson of the *Mary Dear* was a Scot. Perhaps his real name therefore was William Doig! To further interest in this proposition, P. E. Cleator's book *Treasure for the Taking* includes an extract, with the assistance of a grandson of Boag, from a work on Newfoundland:

'Arriving in Panama, Captain Boag, second mate (W. Boag Jr.) Keating and Gault went ashore to see the British Consul. A squall upset the boat, and they were thrown into the sea. Keating, Johnny Boag and Gault managed to right the boat and climb into her. Boag Sr. being a good swimmer, swam a mile to the land and to safety. The other three in the upturned boat were rescued by the first mate of the

'Edgecombe', who heard their cries and put off to the rescue from the ship in another boat. Captain Boag was drowned. He is said to have been pushed from the half-submerged boat by Keating and was devoured by sharks.....'

Cleator, the author, goes on to say:

'In other words (and ignoring the question of the identity of the hitherto unmentioned Johnny Boag), after swimming a mile to the Panamanian coast and to safety, Captain Boag was drowned!'

The probable proof that 'Boag' should be 'Doig' lies in the above 'Edgecombe' quote; W. Boag Jr. and Johnny Boag have to be the brothers William and John Doig who emigrated to Peru from Scotland.

You can see what a minefield this whole 'Cocos, Loot of Lima, Thompson' business is. Fortunately, it is not my task to sort it out. My task is to give you as much background as possible to our affair only, to enable you to understand better the role played by our Captain Brown.

The Nautical and Travellers' Club
Many treasure-hunting books have, over the years, made mention of the Nautical and Travellers' Club in Sydney and in particular an item registered number 18,755. This was supposed to be a letter from Fitzgerald containing instructions by Keating, which said;

'At two cables length, south of the last watering place, on three points. The cave is the one which is to be found under the second point. Christie, Ned and Anton have tried but none of the three had returned. Ned on his fourth dive found the entrance at 12 fathoms but did not emerge from his fifth dive.
There are no octopuses but there are sharks.
A path must be opened up to the cave from the west.'

Both MN and I made inquiries in each respective city named 'Sydney' in Australia and Nova Scotia about the Nautical and Travellers' Club. We can find no record of such an organisation. If the club exists/ existed, there must be an awful lot of filing cabinets to hold over 18,000 documents! Therein lies a coded clue given by the author of the book when these details were first published in 1962. More on this later but the book in question is *Treasures of the World* by Robert Charroux. This was not all that appeared in the book relating to the instructions. Another instruction from Keating seemed to identify the Bay of Hope on Cocos Island;

'Disembark in the Bay of Hope between two islets in water five fathoms deep. Walk 350 paces along the course of the stream then turn north north-east for 850 yards. Stake, setting sun, stake, draws the silhouette of an eagle with wings spread. At the extremity of sun and shadow: cave marked with a cross. Here lies the treasure.'

Accompanying these two instructions was Fitzgerald's version of an inventory of the treasure given by Keating. We will further examine the author's coded clue and Keating's legacy later. For now, just compare it with similar instructions given in *Treasure Island* or the *Captain Kid's Millions* book published in 1897 relating to the Trindade treasure. Also, there is a practical point doubting the veracity of some of the instructions; who is going to carry all that booty 1200 yards? Remember, it is the same journey back with it!

Our interest in the Thompson/Cocos/Lima story stops here. It has taken us to a point in the history of this treasure where we can say that this 'Loot of Lima' treasure did exist (in tradition) because Keating, on more than one occasion, came away with a part of the treasure. How else could he have financed the property and businesses he bought? It is consistently reported by neighbours and residents of St John's that Keating always returned with renewed wealth from whatever long sea voyage he undertook.

The other reason our interest stops here is because of the reason for telling this story, which was to answer the question; 'was there a real event of Spanish treasure stolen that Brown could have based his story on?' The answer is quite obviously 'Yes!' How do we know Keating recovered it from Cocos Island? Well, he said so! (Warning bells should be ringing here again!)

There have been many expeditions to Cocos Island since Thompson's time. It is not the intention of this book to tell of them but no 'Loot of Lima' treasure has ever been found. Captain Brown as we know has told us why; he said he moved it to another island!

For a detailed history of treasure hunting on Cocos Island, refer to the aforementioned Hancock and Weston's book; published in 1960, it brings you up to date with all the expeditions to that date.

I do not know why, but the Costa Rican authorities gave the BBC special permission to take an expedition to the island in 1987. They filmed a hunt by the actress Moira Lister who had a map given by a distant uncle who got it in 1926 from (yes, you guessed it) a dying pirate! The map apparently claimed that a fabled hoard looted from *Spanish galleons* is buried on Cocos. Known as the *Lima treasure* (my italics), it is said to include a life-size gold Madonna statue and thousands of Peruvian silver dollars. Nothing was found, of course.

So even in these modern times, it seems that people still cannot get the story right. It is still hopelessly mixed up! The traditional story is still believed and repeated as if it was an actual, real event.

Benito Bonito has been mentioned earlier and he has close associations with Cocos Island. His story gave Brown a lot more fodder for his story, so we now tell Benito's story.

CHAPTER 3

THE PIRATE BENITO BONITO AND COCOS ISLAND

Cocos Island, or 'Isla Del Coco', lies at approximately 5° 33' North and 87° 2' West, or if you prefer, about 1,200 miles NNW of Lima. It belongs to Costa Rica and is a small tropical island about three miles wide and four miles long. Shear vertical cliffs rise out of the sea on three sides. Beyond these, the island is covered with a dense tropical forest with thick undergrowth of vines, bushes and brambles. There are two seasons, rainy and wet! Summer heat is oppressive and the island is, in fact, an inhospitable hellhole. The only place small boats can make a landing is on the northern end; at either Chatham Bay or Wafer Bay, as both have small rocky beaches. A few Costa Rican soldiers used to be garrisoned at Wafer Bay to repel treasure hunters and I understand that the Costa Rican Government will not issue search permits anymore.

Besides those who buried treasure, a German, August Gissler, is the man with more connections with Cocos than any other. We need to start with his story, which will take us to Bonito's involvement with Cocos Island.

August Gissler

August Gissler first arrived on Cocos Island in 1888 after hearing of a treasure there. He spent 17 years on the island with his wife who lived there with him before finally leaving in 1905. He died in New York in 1935. During all that time on the island, he claimed that all he ever found were 33 Spanish gold coins and a gold gauntlet. These were sold in order to obtain provisions etc. He was known as the 'Hermit of Cocos Island' but by formal presidential decree, in 1897, he was appointed the first and only Governor of Cocos Island. You may recall we met him during the Brown/Sutton expedition.

In 1880, Gissler, on route from London to Honolulu, got friendly with a young Portuguese man who had embarked at San Miguel in the Azores. He told him he wanted to find an island called 'La Palma', or 'Los Palmas'. He asked Gissler for help which is how he was able to read a long letter written by the man's grandfather, who was called

Manoel. It turned out to be an extraordinary narrative of the man's life and adventures. Although it took him several days, Gissler was allowed to copy it, including a map of an island, with directions to treasure His young friend told him that his grandfather had bequeathed the documents to him on his deathbed. The grandfather's story:

The family were fishermen. One day in 1812, Manoel, along with five others, were out fishing when a sudden squall broke their mast and took them out to sea. Captured by a French privateer, the *Le Renard*, they were forced to join the crew. They discovered there were 25 prisoners in the hold. Through his duties, Manoel became friendly with a man who appeared to be their leader; his name was Dom Pedro. With help from Manoel and a carefully laid plan, Pedro and the other prisoners managed to take over the ship. The French mate joined forces with them, as did some of the crew. The rest, including the captain, were put ashore at Madeira. Soon at sea again, in a speech to the assembled crew, Dom Pedro informed them that he had been a second Lieutenant in a Portuguese man-of-war when the Frenchman captured them. He was now determined to go privateering on his own account, and that is how the young Manoel became a pirate. For several years, they did well and prospered. They captured a brig, it became Dom Pedro's new command and he renamed it the *Relempago*. Cadouse, the French mate, became captain of the *Renard*. The two ships eventually parted ways, the Frenchman working the Mexican coast whilst the *Relempago* decided to sail into the Pacific.

Off Concepcion, on the south coast of South America, Manoel had been sent ashore with others for provisions. On the beach, they were stopped by a priest, who asked if theirs was the ship that was to take him and his companions to Spain. Manoel was no fool or ignorant seaman; he knew that because of the revolution, priests usually returned to Spain with considerable wealth. A check on the priest's luggage revealed it was unusually heavy. He and the captain hatched a plan. Subsequently, the priests came on board with their luggage. With them safely in their bunks, Manoel and the captain examined the luggage stowed for 'safety' in the captain's cabin. There were several bundles of gold, church vessels, several heavy boxes of jewels, large bags of doubloons and many crucifixes inlaid with precious stones. The captain stowed everything away in his lockers. They made the priests' luggage back up to its original weight and size with any ballast and metal they could find. The next morning, they broke the news to the priests that a mistake had been made; they were on the wrong ship.

The crew weren't too happy at having to take the priests and their luggage back and there was obvious dissent in the ranks. The crew, of course, had no idea about the treasure. Later, some of them mutinied but superior numbers amongst the loyal crew quelled this uprising. The promise of extended shore leave when they reached Valparaiso also calmed things down. Here, 17 of the mutineers sailed for shore and despite his promise to wait three days for them, Dom Pedro ordered all canvas set and he ran before the wind up the coast as soon as they were out of sight. A few weeks later, after a fight, they took the Spanish ship, the *Rosario*. After transferring her bullion and valuables, the *Rosario* was scuttled; the dead and wounded went down with her.

Heading NW for Acapulco, they came across an island previously unknown to any of them. They could see high mountains and a waterfall. A reconnoitre revealed no signs of habitation. A council was held and they agreed this was an ideal place to bury the loot taken from the *Rosario*. This was buried in a small grove of coconut trees. The priests' treasure was buried at a different location. Manoel made a note of both locations.

About ten days later, they found their intended latitude of Acapulco and headed east. Close inshore, they captured a small fishing boat. The two occupants told the captain that two galleons were in the harbour ready to sail for Spain. They were waiting for the remainder of a mule pack train from Mexico City. Manoel and another seaman named Alonzo used the fishermen's boat to sail into Acapulco to find out more about the galleons. In a bar, they got into a fight and both were badly wounded; it was a couple of months before they were able to walk again. In the meantime, they had heard that a foreign vessel had captured the galleons. Also inland, a rich mule train on its way from Mexico City had been captured. They, of course, knew the name of the pirate responsible.

They both worked in the silver mines for a couple of years then headed for Vera Cruz on the east coast. Here, Alonzo died of the fever. Manoel hoped to get word of the *Renard* but never heard anything of her. News of the *Relempago* reached his ears though. She was back in the Caribbean, but it was not long before an English frigate captured her; 81 of the crew were hanged in Jamaica. He never found out if Dom Pedro was amongst them.

Whilst in Acapulco, Manoel had found out that the name of the island they had buried the treasure on was La Palma. He now endeavoured to work his way somehow back to that island and sought work on ships heading for the Pacific. But it was not to be. Manoel eventually got married and moved to San Miguel where his wife had been left a property. When his daughter married, he hoped his son-in-law would complete the quest for the treasure. He proved to be useless for the purpose, so Manoel decided to leave the story and documents to his grandson, in the hope that one day he would retrieve the family fortune.

Whilst the young Manoel earnestly believed his grandfather's story, Gissler, whilst intrigued, was not entirely convinced.

Our link in this story to the pirate Benito Bonito is through the ship the *Relempago*. Most versions of his story give this ship as being his command. So Dom Pedro is really Benito Bonito and it is a mystery how the name Dom Pedro became associated with him, probably somehow through word association. In the earlier Bonito de Soto and 'Morning Star' story, he was on the *Defensor de Pedro*. Another source says that he was Portuguese and his baptismal name was Don Pedro. Again, look at the similarities with this story, Soto and the mate mutiny, those who didn't want to take part put ashore; same as the Dom Pedro story! Confusing? Yes, very much so! All students of this particular part of pirate history agree on one thing; it is a hopeless mix-up of stories. Many doubt if Benito Bonito really existed at all and just to further confuse things, it is agreed by many that the name Benito Bonito was used to disguise the real identity of Captain Bennett Graham. He was a British naval officer sent to the Pacific in command of *H.M.S Devonshire*, to survey the South American coast.

For some years, Gissler worked his way through the islands and on the schooners that plied them. He became friendly with a young farmer and his family. One day, they told Gissler they had sold their ranch and would he be interested in a proposition to help them look for a buried treasure, the location of which was known by his father-in-law. Gissler knew him as 'Old Mac'. And so Gissler started out on the second trail to treasure that was to bind him forever with Cocos Island.

Old Mac's story starts in 1851. With his young wife and family, he left Hawaii and went east to seek an island off the west coast of Central America. For a long time, he had been in possession of a treasure map and was certain he knew the island depicted, and how and where the treasure was buried on the island. (He never explained to his family how he came into possession of the map.)

They got as far as Baja, California when their funds ran out. It was several years before they returned to Hawaii. Another expedition failed before it started; Mac decided not to go when he realised his life could be jeopardy if and when he found the treasure. That was the last time an attempt was made.

The story of the treasure was, Mac told them, that years ago, a Captain he knew by the name of Benito had taken a Spanish galleon off Acapulco and had then sailed to Cocos Island where he buried the plunder. Before they could return and recover it again, they were caught by a British man-of-war. All were hung except two men called Chapelle and Thompson.

Now entrusted with Old Mac's papers, Gissler could see they were very old and written in Spanish. The map showed two bays at the NE and NW of the island. Compass bearings showed an intersection point where the treasure was buried. A latitude and longitude for the island was also given. With this information and description of the island, Gissler was convinced that this was the La Palma Island that the young Manoel was searching for a few years before. He also guessed that Old Mac must have been one of Benito's crew to be in possession of the information given.

In May 1888, with the young farmer and his son, Gissler left Honolulu for San Francisco; here they purchased equipment and then headed down the coast to Costa Rica. In Puntarenas, Gissler got talking to some men from Canada and was shocked to discover they were just back from a failed treasure hunting expedition to Cocos. He learned that the instigator of this expedition, a captain Carr, had pretended to have obtained the information about the treasure from a man by the name of Keating who had been on the island in 1844. At that time, Keating, with a Captain Boag, claimed to have found the treasure and taken away as much as they could conceal and carry safely. During the return journey to their ship, Keating claimed that Boag had fallen overboard and drowned due to the weight of the gold and jewels he had on him.

Gissler, with renewed enthusiasm for the hunt, searched for a suitable boat to take them to Cocos. During this time, his friend's boy became ill with the fever. His father became alarmed and wanted to return home. They agreed on an equal share of the treasure should Gissler find it, and his friend handed over all of old Mac's papers. Gissler never saw or heard from him again. Gissler, however, was doomed not to get to the island this time. Obtaining a lift on a boat as a working hand, they couldn't find the island and so ended up in Valparaiso. After several months, he managed to get a syndicate together. In February of 1889, he and the syndicate of 14 arrived off Cocos. Due to lack of wind, it took several attempts before they were able to land on the island. One of the syndicate, who knew Spanish, was able to translate old Mac's map. Besides giving the latitude and longitude correctly, it said:

'In the year 1821 we buried here a treasure of immense value. After we had buried the treasure we planted a coconut tree on top and took bearings by compass which showed locations to be N.E. by E. ½ E. to the east mountain and N. 10 deg. East to the West Mountain.'

After several weeks of fruitless searching and digging, the majority were ready to give up. It was not only the lack of treasure that was disillusioning them but the constant battle against tropical downpours, the heat and tangled undergrowth. This was Gissler's harsh introduction to a way of life he was to endure for the next 17 years. Despite his determination, he never found any treasure.

It is pretty obvious he had never read *Treasure Island* by Stevenson either. If he had, he might have noticed a disturbing similarity in the bearings he was given by Old Mac and those on Captain Flint's treasure map; 'Tall trees, Spy-glass Shoulder, bearing a point to the N. of N.N.E. Skeleton Island E.S.E and by ten feet'.

An important point to realise before we finish with Gissler is this; you have seen that he spent many years on this island searching for the fabled 'Loot of Lima'. He never found it, despite having all the time in the world. Then there are the countless searchers, all with the enigmatic map detailing where it is. Failure to locate the treasure has been attributed to every conceivable cause except one: that it may not be there to be found!

There are a couple of things to ponder on with the two buried treasure stories. The Dom Pedro story, because of the dates mentioned (1812 and 1821) and the name of' the ship *Relempago*, then we are talking about Benito Bonito and his activities.

Old Mac's story doesn't tell us which Benito he is talking about but he tells us his search started in 1851. If he had served with Benito de Soto, around 1828 and was about 20 years old at that time, then he would have been about 43 years old with a young family when he started his search. Plausible, you can say, making his date of birth around 1808. Not likely then that he would have served with Benito Bonito, he would have been too young! But, the story he gives is that of Benito Bonito, look at the similarity of events; a Spanish galleon taken off Acapulco, captured by a British man-of-war, all hung except two.

Whichever way you look at it, as I have said, both stories relate to Benito Bonito and his activities but there is an obvious mix-up in dates somewhere along the line.

Benito and Australia

Down in the bottom right-hand corner of Australia is Queenscliff, a holiday resort situated near the head of Port Phillip Bay in Victoria state. A signboard erected by the Geelong Regional Tourist Authority, says the following:

'IN 1796, SO LEGEND HAS IT, THE PIRATE BENITO BONITO SAILED THE PACIFIC OCEAN AND PLUNDERED SPANISH VESSELS LADEN WITH TREASURE. THIS INCLUDED GOLD COINS, PRECIOUS STONES AND FOUR LIFE-SIZED GOLD FIGURES ENCRUSTED WITH JEWELS FROM THE CATHEDRAL OF LIMA, PERU. HE THEN SOUGHT A SAFE HIDING PLACE FOR HIS TREASURE. MONTHS LATER, HE ANCHORED HERE IN WHAT IS NOW KNOWN AS SWAN BAY AND WAS HIDING THE PLUNDER IN A CAVE WHEN A BRITISH WARSHIP CAME IN SIGHT. HURRIEDLY SEALING THE CAVE WITH A CHARGE OF GUNPOWDER, HE TRIED TO OUTRUN THE BRITISH SHIP BUT WAS CAUGHT AND EVENTUALLY HANGED. THE ONLY PIRATE TO ESCAPE WAS A CABIN BOY WHO HAD A MAP OF THE TREASURE TATTOOED ON HIS SKIN. HE IS SUPPOSED TO HAVE ESCAPED TO TASMANIA.
IN 1931 A MELBOURNE SYNDICATE OBTAINED A MINING LEASE AND SEARCHED THE SITE. SEVERAL OTHER SYNDICATES AND INDIVIDUALS HAVE SINCE TRIED TO FIND THE TREASURE BUT IT STILL ELUDES THEM.'

Enough said about that version! We include it because it contains some of the DNA of the lost treasure; more of that later.

Captain Bennett Grahame

To complete the chapter on 'Benito', we finish with the aforementioned Captain Grahame with more conflicting stories. Bored with his mundane task of surveying, he turned to piracy. The story goes that those not willing to join him were to be put ashore at Panama, but instead they were taken to Cocos where, having been put ashore, they were murdered by Grahame and his crew. Apparently, many years later, skeletons were found on Cocos but there was no evidence to show who they belonged to.

On one occasion, he is supposed to have engaged five Spanish ships, three of them being men-of-war guarding two treasure ships. He successfully defeated them, capturing the Spanish galleons laden with gold and silver. His ship, the *Devonshire,* was extensively damaged during this engagement so he transferred his command to one of the Spanish ships named *Relampago.* With the treasure captured, he sailed to Cocos and made the island their base, building a small settlement in Wafer Bay. Knowing British ships had been sent in pursuit of them and fearing capture, they melted all the gold down into bricks and hid them in a tunnel 35 feet long. The face of the cliff was blown down with gunpowder to hide the entrance.

Besides plundering Spanish vessels, he went ashore near Acapulco and seized a rich cargo of gold. (No doubt the mule train mentioned in previous stories.) This was also taken to Cocos where it was buried in Wafer Bay.

A British warship was eventually dispatched to deal with him. However, Bonito defeated this ship but was eventually cornered in the Bay of Buena Ventura after his ship had been sunk. Bonito and his crew were taken to England where they were tried, convicted and hanged. One of the crew, a female named Mary Welch, was transported to Tasmania. It is she who claimed that Bonito was really Bennett Grahame. She said he had picked her up in Panama years earlier. It is she who also claimed that they came ashore at Queenscliff, buried their treasure in a cave and dynamited the entrance. Shortly after heading back out to sea, they were challenged by a warship. After a battle in which they were captured, Bonito blew his brains out on deck, rather than face the gallows.

A similar version goes like this:

As a young man, he was one of the crew on a Portuguese trading ship. He had an argument with the captain and murdered him, taking over command of the vessel. He attacked an English sailing vessel, the *Lightning*. Having summarily dealt with the crew, he transferred to that vessel renaming it the Spanish equivalent *Relampugo*. Thompson, an Englishman, and Chapelle, a Frenchman, saved their hides by agreeing to join the crew. There followed a series of raids on coastal towns and shipping up and down the west coast of South America. Around 1821, they dressed as muleteers then attacked and captured the annual gold shipment from Mexico City destined for Acapulco then Spain. This was said to be worth around 11 million dollars. They headed for Cocos where the booty was divided out. Benito secreted his share in a concealed cave; the crew buried theirs in various spots around the island. (One of the reasons why there are so many treasure maps for this island.) Trouble brewed up amongst those not happy with the division of spoils and when the opportunity arose, Benito sailed away when the worst troublemakers were ashore. Amongst those left behind were Thompson and Chapelle who were later released after having been picked up by the Costa Rican authorities. The remainder captured on the island were found guilty of piracy and executed.

Chapelle, last heard of in San Francisco in 1841, was said to have a treasure map of Cocos and often spoke of Benito's exploits. Thompson went on to live on one of the South Sea Islands.

The British warship *H.M.S. Espiegle* eventually cornered Bonito. Outfought, and rather than being hung from the yardarm, he blew his brains out.

So again, contradicting stories but generally the same theme runs through them all. They all seem to agree that Benito Bonito, whoever he was, buried more than one treasure on Cocos Island.

Trinidade Island Link

A reminder here of the tenuous links between Cocos Island, Trindade Island and the 'Loot of Lima'. It can easily be seen that Trindade Island, off the east coast of Brazil and on the homeward route Lima to Spain (Via Cape Horn), could be the hiding place of treasure. Earlier chapters tell of the 'Russian Finn' in the 'Alerte' story who on his deathbed spoke of the immense treasure buried under the mountain known as the Sugarloaf. Much of this plate, he said, came from the cathedral of

Lima during the war of independence, but as can be seen, it is really just the same as given for the 'Loot of Lima' story. Benito de Soto is alleged to have buried loot here; this is plausible when you consider he operated mainly in the Atlantic. His namesake, the legendary treasure pirate Benito Bonito, although harrying the Spanish in the Pacific, a different theatre of operations, nevertheless gets his exploits hopelessly mixed up with Soto. One should also question how much sense it makes that after looting Lima, Benito Bonito should decide to sail around The Horn to bury a treasure on the desolate island of Trindade. The only official record of these characters is that of Soto being hung in Gibraltar, so it would appear that Benito Bonito is really a constructed character made up of the names and events of the disgraced English Captain Bennett Grahame, Benito de Soto and as you will learn, something else completely.

A Geographical Connection?

An important realisation here is that we have now identified three locations for a buried treasure - Queenscliff, Cocos Island and Trindade Island - where the same treasure was said to be buried by the same person. Therefore if searchers are using a map which can align to the geography of these locations - 'the map shows this shape so we must be at the right place' - then the three different places must have the same shaped geography or feature. This feature will be discussed later when we talk more about the DNA of the lost treasure.

CHAPTER 4

SUMMING UP - THE REAL IDENTITY OF THE PIRATES AND STORY DNA

Parts 1 and 2 of this book have so far given you the important stories that are the background to our lost treasure with hints to its location, probably in the South Seas. I have at the same time unravelled the traditional stories surrounding the 'Loot of Lima' legend, and in doing so maybe for the first time, unveiling to the public what really went on. We have established beyond doubt that a Spanish treasure is waiting to be recovered somewhere. It has already been searched for by one of our most senior admirals and Keiser continues to search for it on JF Island. Yet Brown didn't look for anything here. We know he at some time found treasure because as a young man he became very rich. He visited his 'Treasure Island' at least twice, and what about Keating? His name crops up frequently in this saga. Can there be any connection between the two? Did they both find the same treasure? If not, what treasure did Keating find? And what treasure was our Captain Brown looking for? Because as we have seen, there was no singular 'Loot of Lima' treasure recorded as lost or stolen around the 1820s.

Most importantly, we discovered the true identity of Killorain. But what of the other three who were party to the legend; who were they? What happened to them? To answer these and the other questions, we delve once more into Brown and stories of the time.

Brown the Storyteller

As we have seen, all the previous tales of pirates, treasure and events of history have been told to show you how Captain Brown constructed the story he told to Captain Sutton then Charles Howe, who in turn told a variation to Charles Nordoff and a similar story to the Hamilton expedition. George Farwell of the Hamilton expedition tells the familiar story with some slight variations.

In all the versions of the pirates and treasure tales, you can see the parts that Brown selected to create his story. Some we have already covered. Some other examples we can add; Killorain and Brown were shanghaied by Alvarez and put aboard the *Sweet Alice*, an endearing term for a lady, just like *Mary Dear* could have been *Sweet Mary* or *Dear Alice*!

Treasury gold put aboard a ship (the *Peruano*) in Callao Harbour was then hijacked by Robertson - a real event; Brown used this as the basis for his story but uses church gold. Brown uses the same Robertson/Teresa love story with Robertson becoming the young priest Juan Damerion murdered by Alvarez.

The Russian Finn with a scar across his cheek becomes Alvarez with a scar running from his left ear down to his chin.

Farwell's account tells of the procession of oxen drawn carts accompanied by monks making their way silently down to the docks. Brown uses Admiral Cochrane's account here where he says he watched just such a procession with his spyglass.

Brown had obviously read 'Captain Kidd's Gold' published in 1888, I mentioned this book in an earlier chapter. The story of Howe being summoned to a hospital by the dying sailor Killorain is almost the same construct word for word of Captain Garry being summoned to the Greenwich hospital bed of the 'One-Eyed Mate'. And for the same reason and outcome, - a previous kindness resulting in being given details of a buried treasure.

Brown created a glorious cocktail of historical events, stories, folklore and legend, all carefully blended together to produce a story that enthused many who became blinded by the lure of gold. It would be too tedious to reconstruct Brown's story here and it is not necessary. The story told so far tells you what it is anyway. I think you can see now that the story believed by Howe, Hamilton and Sutton is a very clever reconstruction, created by somebody with high intelligence and totally familiar with what was going on in the South Pacific at that time.

Why did he have to create such a story? Because he was getting on in years and knew he could not do it on his own anymore. He had to have a good reason for tempting investors who would pay for him to get to his island. It had to be a big temptation, a big treasure hoard that would be worth the investment and time for anybody with the money and a sense of adventure. So he created this story, which as we have seen, is based on tradition, hearsay, history and fact, sure to get attention when the fabled 'Loot of Lima' was mentioned.

All the elements of pirate treasure stories were used very cleverly and it worked. The potential investors eyes glazed over when they realised they were in the very presence of a real pirate, someone who was there, "Yes, I've heard that," they would say. "It must be true!" Edwardes and Hamilton made the grave error of checking Howe's story but not beyond that. He confirmed that Howe did this and that, but that, of course, did not make the story that Howe was told true! When checking the Loot of Lima story, he confirmed the tradition of it! Everybody said it happened so it did! Sutton made similar mistakes when checking the story Brown told him.

Brown's story that Peruvian church treasures were on a ship in Callao Harbour was so close to the traditional story that it had to be believed. You now know that it never happened. With permission to leave with the contents of the fort, the viceroy had it loaded on numerous ships leaving for Spain. In other words, the treasure was scattered far and wide, some of it possibly succumbing to pirate attack.

We asked a question in the earlier 'Loot of Lima' story, to quote:

'Was there a real event of Spanish treasure stolen that Brown could have based his story on?' The answer is quite obviously, 'Yes!'

The 'real event' is the mix of stories that became the traditional event. People have looked for the fabulous stolen loot of Lima, so it must have existed! Books tell the story, so it must have happened! You have seen that it did not happen. Previous authors have conveniently ignored the evidence that it did not happen because they either believed it, the story is better as it stands, or they did not do the research.

Let us remind ourselves of that evidence:

a) Lord Cochrane stood by helpless as the Spanish were allowed to sail away with the contents of the fort at Callao (Port of Lima).
b) Lord Cochrane makes no mention of any Spanish treasure stolen by pirates.
c) Observers at that time and historians make no mention of any great Spanish treasure stolen during this period.
d) The diver and researcher Harry E. Rieseburg confirmed the above and that Lima Cathedral had never been plundered.
e) The best informed authorities on Peruvian history all agreed that there appeared to be no connection between Lima and any treasure buried on Cocos Island.

f) Despite many 'authentic' treasure maps, and just as many expeditions, no treasure has ever been found on Cocos Island.

g) We can add that Lloyd's Register of Shipping contains no reference to the *Mary Dear*, though there is a mention of a brig called the *Edgecombe*, built at Bristol in 1835 and registered at Liverpool. This brig, you may recall, is the one that is associated with Keating.

Robert Langdon

There have been very few previous authors with the insight to recognise that the 'Loot of Lima' story is but a fabrication of similar stories. One of these was the Australian author Robert Langdon. He was a contributor to the *Pacific Islands Monthly* magazine. Incidentally, an earlier issue of that magazine, published in July 1937, carried an article about the failed Hamilton expedition. To quote (in part):

'The Hiti treasure expedition was hatched in England. The song of the sirens was embodied in an epic written on ancient parchment - an heirloom of an old county family. The story was of a Spanish treasure ship laden with Inca gold; a mutiny; the sailing, again, into the sunset; burial of the treasure on a desert isle, and, of course, a map. The bearings on the map, taken from various small atolls in a compact group in the Tuamoto Archipelago, converged on the island of Hiti.'

You will recognise here, of course, the similarity to the Anson story told in Part 1, yet Hamilton **does not** mention Anson in his book. Something then that Langdon has slipped in, so how does he know of the Anson connection?

Something else of interest in the above quote is the statement that bearings converge on the island of Hiti. This is the same as saying Hiti is where bearings were taken from to neighbouring atolls i.e. to pinpoint Hiti. To know this, Langdon must have been privy to the map or in the confidence of one of the expedition members. *The* map then must have shown bearings. Notice also *'small atolls in a compact group'*. This information easily explains why the Pinaki and Hiti groups became mixed up - you can see why from the following diagram; the angular similarities may have become confused or misinterpreted with time.

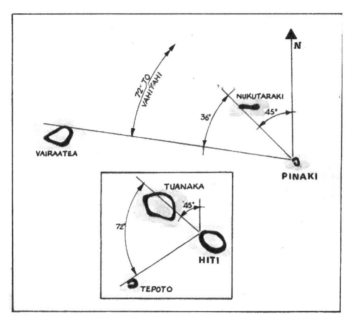

SHOWING THE SIMILAR ANGULAR COMPARISONS
BETWEEN THE TWO GROUPS (TO SCALE)

The original map then may have shown a bearing of 45º NW to a neighbouring atoll with 72º separating it from another atoll. This information, if right, would help in reconstructing the map as talked about in an earlier chapter. One must also not forget that sightings taken at sea level are limited by the curvature of the earth; I doubt if a low atoll 20 miles or more away would be seen unless from the top mast of a ship.

Langdon goes on to recognise that the Spanish wealth stored in the fort at Callao seems to be the starting point for most of the melodramatic stories that have snowballed down the years about buried treasure on islands in the Pacific. He lists the main treasure island story contenders as follows:

a) Pinaki atoll in the Gambiers (135ºW23ºS. GE). He says this is supposed to comprise four tons of gold and a huge quantity of pearls, diamonds and amethysts, all in metal caskets sealed with lead and bearing the face of Father Combes.

b) A Spanish galleon, which is supposed to have left 15 tons of gold bullion in the Tautira district of Tahiti in 1774.

c) A huge hoard of Spanish-American dollars reputedly buried on Suwarrow atoll in the Cook Group.

d) Cocos Island with its legends of Spanish treasure.

e) The age-old tale about a Spanish treasure on an atoll in French Polynesia.

f) An unnamed island near Guam in the Marianas. (The Robertson hijack)

g) Trinidad Island off the coast of Brazil.

h) Hat Island (Vatu Vara) in Fiji.

Langdon was taken to task by a fellow journalist for doubting the authenticity of the Pinaki treasure, among others. As a result, he made a thorough investigation of all the Pacific treasure stories. His conclusion; with the possible exception of the Suwarrow treasure story, (of no real interest to us, so not discussed) none of them is true! He reaches this conclusion for the same basic reasons as us but he takes this insight no further. He points out, as I do, that most of the stories are suspiciously similar and that there appears to be no real evidence that any treasure was stolen from Callao in the 1820s, which is what is alleged in the case of three of the islands above. Also, most of the stories about the various islands are vague but where they contain details that can be checked, the details are almost invariably wrong.

In the July 1962 issue of the magazine, he asks, "Is it mere coincidence that most Pacific buried treasure stories bear a resemblance to R. L. Stevenson's *Treasure Island*?"

It was not even public knowledge that a Spanish treasure had been stolen by pirates until the 1880s when Gissler was making the Cocos treasure connection and Stevenson's book was published capturing the imagination of the world.

The story of the Trinidad Island treasure is, he points out, remarkably similar to that of Cocos Island. It was also first heard of in the 1880s and, according to some versions, it even features one of the same pirates, the Portuguese Benito. His story we covered earlier.

The Spanish Trail

We have finally stopped following Captain Brown! Now we try to find and follow the trail that leads to the treasure that he and maybe Keating had found.

A small clue to the Spanish treasure connection turned up during the investigative research. Small in that it was more or less overlooked by the participant but big ramifications for us in that it put us on the real trail to what was being looked for. The clue turned up during Nordhoff's visit to Howe whilst Howe was searching one of the coral atolls. He took Nordhoff to see 'something interesting'. You may recall this was an immense block of coral broken from the reef and cut deeply into the face of the rock was a curious design. Nordhoff asked him what it meant.

"Man, if I knew that! I believe it's the key, and I can't master it." Howe replied. Howe was right, it was the key! He could not master it because the three symbols were what we know as 'Spanish Signs'. Also known as treasure marks, it is an age-old symbolic code used by the Spanish hierarchy to lead them back to a treasure or mine. The key to what the symbols meant was known only to those in high authority and the padre who accompanied the ship or mining expedition. Quite often, the coded message was based on religion. Howe correctly surmised that these signs were linked somehow to the pirate treasure.

It was at about this juncture in our research it was realised that in reality there *is* a *Spanish* treasure on the island; no pirate or 'Loot of Lima' treasure

Spanish signs have been in use since the 16th century when the Spanish were conquering the Americas. They were used extensively to lead the way to the mines and where they had buried gold and silver for later retrieval. So prolific were the use of these signs that we get from them the well-known phrase always imaginatively associated with treasure maps: 'X marks the spot', as the letter X was carved into rocks by Spanish surveyors as a marker for the inward trail to a mine or cache. Decoding these symbols is something we will look at later but the important thing for us is that when the Spanish retrieved their treasure, **the directional marks or signs are erased**! This is a good indication to us that the treasure is still there. Of course, one has to look at the possibility that the cache could have been found by others, and if by accident then they may not have gone to the trouble of defacing the signs to remove the tell-tale evidence. Same could also apply even if they were aware of the signs! Or maybe the marks were far enough away from the cache site so as not to be noticed anyway.

So the whole thing has been a misrepresentation as to what is actually on the island. No longer are we searching for stories about a huge treasure being pirated from Lima or similar, we now have to look for stories that tell of a lost Spanish treasure in the area. As you can imagine, reports of such events were probably lost to history and it took a lot of dedicated research to find any evidence of any Spanish galleons this far south in the Pacific, a long way off their traditional routes.

One reference was again tracked to the author Sterndale, whose story of Jack Sclate was used in the 'Bosun Bird' tale. Sterndale reported that on the night of 17th August 1867, a 'black brigantine' lay in Port Jackson (Sydney):

'She was said to have a large quantity of arms on board; she was said to carry too many boats and too great a number of hands for her intentions to be altogether honest. Certain well-known speculators were mentioned in connection with her outfitting, various wiseacres when she was spoken of, and pretended to look knowing, but it was mere pretence, they knew nothing in reality, save that she was choke full of valuable trade, including firearms, ammunition and spirits; that she carried an engineer officer and a surgeon, as also divers with armour and apparatus for disentombing the secrets of the sea. Stories were in circulation about sunken wrecks containing specie, mysterious islands for which adventurous captains had made unsuccessful search, but from whence traders had been known to procure enormous pearls, which falling into the hands of Storr and Mortimer, Emanuel (period jewellers) *and others, had been disposed of to crowned heads at fabulous prices.'*

Was this the secret of the treasure, a sunken galleon containing gold and discovered by Brown on the *Sea Foam* whilst pearl fishing in the islands? This may have accounted for the marks on the rock, as it was also practice for Spanish shipwreck survivors to mark the positions of the wreck or cached valuables. But as this meant there were survivors (and high ranking, to know the code) who had time to do so, what happened to them, and why had they not returned to retrieve what they had marked?

Another story was located. This also suggested the treasure was of Spanish origin and was lost due to shipwreck.

Don Bruno and the Palmyra Island Treasure

Contemporary to Sterndale was the Australian author Louis Becke. His *Pacific Tales* was published in 1897. One of the stories was called *The Treasure of Don Bruno.* It told how a rich Spanish merchant with the name Bruno do Bustamente had fallen out with the Governor of the Mexican province he lived in. Deciding to escape with his wealth back to Spain, 90,000 silver coins and 25,000 gold coins were put in bags of bullock-hide, and then secretly stowed aboard his brig, the *Bueno Esperanza*. This ship was sent ahead to Manila with his daughter whilst he cleared up his affairs and followed a month later. Alas, the brig never arrived. It was 10 years before a letter reached Don Bruno telling how an open boat had been found with bodies aboard and a letter in Spanish addressed to him as follows:

'Wrecked on an uninhabited island in lat. 7º 29´N. long 160º 42´E. Six of the crew drowned, also owner's child, Engracia Bustamente, and her nurse. The body of the former was buried at a spot above high-water mark, about 300 yards from a large round knob of rock, covered with vines on the eastern point, and bearing E. by N. from the grave. No provisions were saved except some jerked beef, packed in hide bags. Were four months on the island. Left there July 3rd, in open boat, to try and reach Manila.'

Don Bruno dies a broken man, but leaves the above directions to his son Don Pedro (this name has cropped up before!) who engages a merchant officer named Forrest. Using these directions, the treasure is recovered.

This story is identified nowadays as the 'Palmyra Island Treasure' but the coordinates given are not those of Palmyra Island (5º 52´N162º 05´W) nor does the description of the island given in the text match that of Palmyra.

Our friend, the author H.T. Wilkins, knew about Louis Becke and his stories. In his *Modern Buried Treasure Hunters*, he relates one of Becke's stories about Cocos Island where two rival expeditions fight it out and one of the schooners is blown up. I am not familiar with that story and I think Wilkins deliberately may have mixed things up a little again. He goes on to say that $80,000 worth of silver money and $30,000 worth of gold coins were found. The coins had been found in canvas and *bullock-hide* bags!

The two stories, as you can see, have been mixed up, just like so many others. One of the stories uncovered proved to be very important and contained elements similar to the Don Bruno story. It is a South Pacific native legend and appears below with spelling errors and translation difficulties uncorrected.

Mururoa Atoll Treasure Legend
The Mururoa atoll treasure legend was pounced upon as it was suspected, due to its unembellished form to be a recount of an actual event.

'Once upon a time there was a three masts ship which transported between Peru and Spain, the treasures recovered by the Spanish conquerors. The business was too tempting for the captain to resist so he decided to leave without awaiting his escort. He thus set sail on a beautiful moonless night and sailed towards sparsely settled places where he was less likely to be noticed by corsairs or the King's ship. A combat took place nevertheless against a sloop of which the crew was made prisoner and taken on board. After days on a west cours this three- masted ship reached Moruroa whose lagoon allowed for a safe anchoring, to replenish with water and food. The captain made the decision then to hide in the ground part of his treasure and charged his lieutenant and two men to have the prisoners dig a hole large enough to contain the trunks. During the operation the prisoners revolted and killed the lieutenant and his men. The rebellion was quickly subdued and the furious captain, killed all the prisoners whom he buried with his trunks in the hole that had been prepared. This captain and his ship never had a chance because it sank a little afterwards and nobody til this day has found, on the "Motu Te Papa" the treasure which is hidden within twelve steps to the west from a sign representing a hand.

I don't know if there is any truth to this legend but I wonder whether the atoll would not owe its name to him in which it would be necessary to interpret like that of an island which has it's great secrecy.'

One of the reasons of the importance of this story is the location of the island. Mururoa Island lies approximately 22 degrees south and 139 degrees west. A study of a chart of this part of the Pacific will show you that we are in the Tuamotu Archipelago! Just 3 degrees north and *on the same longitude* is a small group of three islands. One of these islands is Pinaki, the same island identified by Nordhoff when he visited Howe.

What is this legend telling us? It is not telling us that an exploring Spanish galleon was shipwrecked. It is telling us that the captain of a Spanish galleon with intent and for a specific reason took the treasure away and buried it on a remote Pacific island. But which island? For reasons unknown, it was never recovered by them (the Spanish). If a map or directions were left, no one could follow them or they were never found. But intriguingly, included in the story is the detail that the ship sunk afterwards, which was inferred as being the reason why the treasure was never recovered.

It is an accepted fact that behind such legends and folklore, there is, buried in the dim and distant past, an element of truth, or how would such a story originate? Indeed, how did it originate if the reason given for the non-recovery of the treasure was the ship was sunk? Either there was a survivor or this event was known to others external to the occurrence. Maybe not just legend after all! And why were reports of something real proving so elusive amongst the flood of similar lost treasure stories?

I will now quote you the modern version of the Palmyra treasure story so that you can see how the old version and the above Mururoa treasure legend are now mixed together:

'In 1816 the Esperanza, a Spanish pirate ship loaded with gold and silver plunder from the Inca temples in Peru, came under attack from another vessel and a fierce battle ensued. Several crew members who managed to survive the fight sailed off with the treasure only to wreck on a nearby reef. As the ship was sinking they managed to transfer the treasure to an Island located beyond the reef whose name was

Palmyra. Stranded there for a year, they supposedly buried the Inca gold under a tree on Palmyra and then sailed off in rafts they had built. One raft was later rescued by an American whaling ship with only a single survivor left onboard who soon succumbed from exposure and pneumonia. The other raft was never heard from again.'

This is a good example of a story mutation. Don Bruno's brig, the *Bueno Esperanza*, becomes the *Esperanza*, a Spanish pirate ship. The survivors, after four months on the island, leave in an open boat but perish from exposure etc. The battle between the Spanish ship and another vessel is straight out of the Mururoa story.

If you did not know of the existence of the first two stories, you may be forgiven for thinking that this later version is the *real* story! This example also emphasises the importance of stringent research.

A Grandee and Juan Fernandez Island
Further research brought to light a similar story. *Adventures in Peru* by Cecil Prodgers, published in 1925, contained the following item in a chapter on JF Island.

'Buccaneers frequently made Juan Fernandez their rendezvous, and, there seems little doubt, deposited some of their ill-gotten gains there. An old Chilean supplied me with particulars of an incident that supports this view. In 1716, so he said, his grandfather had told him, a barque unloaded several boatloads of treasure there, the operation being superintended by a Spaniard who was reputed to be a grandee. He and a black remained behind to see to its safe disposal. Six months later, the barque brought another cargo of booty. No sailor was permitted to leave the ship, except those who manned the boat or carried the treasure ashore. After the plunder had been shared out, the leader of the buccaneers had it hidden snugly away. At the entrance of the cache, he buried an axe, a cutlass, and a crowbar. Nearby is the grave of his slave companion who died from the effects of a blow sustained during a quarrel with his brother pirates.'

So again, a Spanish Grandee/Nobleman burying a treasure instead of taking it home to Spain. But also again, the same detail of an altercation occurring on the island causing the death of a participant.

Note in particular the date, 1716, close to the time of the gathering together of the great Tierra Firma fleets under Ubilla and Echeverz.

The earlier mentioned author Harold T. Wilkins repeats the above story in his book *Modern Buried Treasure Hunters*, and also *Pirate Treasure*. In the latter, he even publishes a map showing where this treasure is (at the back of Windy Bay) and to further compound how absurd this map is, he adds a cryptic note, *'It waits to be found by a modern treasure hunter'*. Further more, he has the audacity to declare that the chart was made by an English buccaneer, Captain Bartholomew Sharp when it is quite clearly recognisable (by me) as created by Wilkin's own hand but based on the Sharp map.

With this new clue of a Spanish grandee burying a treasure on JF Island, a web search for treasure stories for that location was carried out. It was with a bit of a shock we find there is one Bernard Keiser on JF looking for the treasure of the Spanish nobleman, the same one we are. And he has (allegedly) done the research into the Spanish archives already, finding out that Echeverria was the Spanish nobleman who made off with the Royal Tribute and hid it somewhere. Echeverria, who drowned in the 1715 hurricane.....

We now know who buried the treasure on the island, why it was buried and what was buried there.

All the related famous treasure island stories are linked, they are all twisted versions: direct descendants of the Spanish treasure story but with later parts added. This is confirmed by checking the geography and directions which are repeated, island after island.

I will remind you of the singular clue that we are looking for; a Spanish treasure rather than a Pirate treasure. The Spanish signs shown to Nordhoff, that were obviously made by a person of high-ranking, are the prime evidence. I show them here now:

**THE SIGNS CUT INTO A ROCK
ON PINAKI ATOLL**

We are approaching the end of this part of the book, that is, the influence Captain Brown had on our story. Before I do and as promised, we reveal the identity of the other characters so influential to this story who were with him when the lost treasure was found.

The Crew Identity

You now know that the 'Loot of Lima' story is a mix-up of traditional stories of the time. Similarly, Brown's 'Bosun Bird' story is a clever reconstruction of events to lure investors as a ticket to his island; the stories of pirates burying gold is just a disguise. You can now also see that as there was no great Lima treasure, then Brown must have been trying to recover something else. We now have a good idea what that was; a Spanish treasure purposely concealed. How do we know the treasure is there? We have the evidence of the symbols and of Brown becoming rich as a young man. As he went back a second time, maybe a third, he obviously knows where the island is. More evidence surfaces as the pieces of the story fall into place.

It is highly unlikely that Brown found the treasure on his own. Being young, it is more than probable that he was part of a crew who found this treasure. What of this crew, who were they, why do the stories not tell us their names? And surely, if we can identify one or more, this may lead us on another trail back to the island? Conversely, could the island lead us back to the crew?

At this stage, we need to build up the real picture of Brown's story from the beginning and try and answer the question, 'How did Captain Brown come to know about the treasure?' We cannot, of course, show and repeat in this book all the research material that was used. The picture we build therefore is from all that we know using what appear as disparate clues from numerous sources. A main clue comes from an unexpected source; the author H.T. Wilkins. But it is because the numerous clues *are* from different sources and seem to match each other, a picture slowly builds that has probative force. Let us say also that without the comprehensive research undertaken, it would not have been possible to establish the obscure links that brought the crew together.

I cannot, of course, say with certainty that this story trail is what happened to Brown, but we are pretty sure it is something like that which is proposed here:

There were three other main characters with Brown when they found the treasure, but the circumstances were a lot less exiting than pirates, mule trains, murder or sacrilege of the church. We can assume that James Brown was Scandinavian, as Chetwood tells us he was recognised by a relative and later descriptions of him use the word 'Viking'. As a young lad, about 19 years of age, he runs away to sea and as he says, "Took to it like a duck takes to water." Around 1848, (some reports of the trip set it as early as 1846 and others as late as 1850) finding himself in Jamaica, he intercedes in a waterfront fight to assist another lad, an Irishman of around the same age whose surname is Kelley. Brown is assessed and invited to join the same enterprise as Kelley, a special trip on a ship named the *Sea Foam*. The captain is a Spaniard whose name is similar to 'Diego Alvarez'. The mate is an Englishman whose name is similar in form to Luke Barrett. There may also have been native pearl divers on board.

The *Sea Foam*, far from being a pirate vessel, is a small pearling ship and ostensibly sails for the South Sea Islands where pearls and shells are in abundance. This is the era of the South Seas exploitation. Associates of Captain Sutton verified that the *Sea Foam* was off Callao on a pearling trip in 1851, and this is qualified with the comment in the 'Herman' book that it was 'presumably on a pearl fishing expedition to the Bay of Dulce'. (We can mention here - it is of importance later - we know that some five or six years earlier, around 1846, John Keating went somewhere in the Pacific on a pearl fishing expedition and returned with gold and jewels. Perhaps his directions were the same as those known to Alvarez!)

The *Sea Foam*, following a chart and directions, some in Spanish, some in English, but understood by Alvarez, sails to a three-island group about 139º W and about 19º S. Running low on freshwater and continuing to search for pearls, they land on the small atoll named Pinaki. They observe an abundance of pearls in the lagoon. (Captain Brown, if you recall, makes many references to pearls, suggesting that they abound on *his* island.)

Following the chart directions, the crew are told to seek a water source, near which they will find a large rock or block of coral with carved signs on it. Two of the lads go ashore to search, possibly in the small volcanic craters. (Small water filled craters are something else that Captain Brown makes a point of mentioning in his stories).

As they search, one of them finds a large rock or block of coral with carved signs on it. This is no coincidence, as we know one of the clues is there is a rock (Ebanin) near the source of freshwater/spring/well. The Spanish captain, having been shown the signs, would have understood and recognised them as marker signs to the treasure he was seeking, or maybe he was a Spanish captain from the old days of when the Spanish galleons plied their trade from the Americas and was therefore familiar with this code, or maybe he was just privy to the information he alone possessed.

The map that is shown to Hamilton is somewhat Spanish sounding in its construction and workings. It is made of 'buckskin', as the Spanish made their maps. It shows bare shapes with no scale, bearings or much else. They know where the island is, so as per Spanish maps, they are just a memory aid. We have already heard how the Spanish leave coded, carved, landmark signs to their mines and caches; all location details are not committed to one piece of paper or map.

That a treasure is found is certain. Brown we know returns a rich young man with a healthy bank balance in London, and as he said, he returned later to replenish his money.

By his own admittance, Brown said that for his age, he was a pretty knowledgeable young fellow. He is indeed a somewhat surprising intellectual package and with his wealth is bound to have furthered his education and become literally a man of the world. He studies, reads widely and researches various subjects, one almost certainly the origin and history of the treasure and its story, which he certainly would not have been fully aware of, being a 19-year-old 'runaway'. Knowing now of the importance of what he was involved in, he familiarised himself with the disarray and confusion of buried treasure stories of the time to be able to put that disarray and confusion to good use to conceal the identity and location of the treasure.

Time passes on and Brown loses his fortune when he is caught running guns to Cuba. He has to return to the island but this is somewhat problematic as he has to rely on others to get him there, and he wants to do it without divulging the secret of the source of his treasure due to the very nature of it. Not only that, once he identifies the location to others, the entire thing is given up to everyone and the place will be overrun with treasure hunters. His other fear is, he realises it would be no problem, once the location is out, for him to have an 'accident'. It is an 'all or nothing' situation he is caught in. Nevertheless he has to go ahead and organises expeditions, but using his knowledge of the workings of lost treasure stories, attempts to hide, obscure and disguise the identity and location of the treasure. Any person trying to follow his directions and attempts are caught up in the confusingly related stories and locations. All along he was really trying to engineer the situation so he would get the chance and equipment needed to get to the treasure but without giving up its secret. He nearly got caught out by Charles Howe who, obviously satisfied he had enough information, did a runner without him, but Brown was clever enough to leave some final directional details missing.

It is undoubted that the author H. T. Wilkins knew about Pinaki (even prior to 1934) and its links to the treasure. He also knew a lot about our Captain Brown. His books, in particular the aforementioned *Pirate Treasure* and *Modern Buried Treasure Hunters*, repeat stories and snippets about Brown. For example, on one page he quotes (in part);

'reminiscent of the Marianne treasure story and the yarn of old Captain Brown of Frisco'

On the opposite page, as part of another story, quote (in part);

'a certain James Brown, then aged nineteen, who drifted into the harbour of Kingston, Jamaica'

If you took Wilkins' writings on face value, it would appear he could not make the connection between the two, but do not be fooled by what appear to be just his cranky ramblings! Wilkins continuously relates, and repeats the traditional treasure stories in a clue-like way by grouping them together so that the reader can follow what is a linked story. One story stood out in a grouping because not only did it included what we could call DNA clues of pearls, freshwater and a large amount of gold, but the name of one of the participants - Kelley! The story goes that Roland Kelley of Harvard University was left a large fortune in 1913 by his grandfather on condition that he complied with the testator's wish that he search for a treasure discovered by his grandfather. Before his 21st birthday, Roland Kelley had to find certain pearl fisheries and a treasure on two uncharted islands in the Pacific. The islands, said the will, were found by the old mariner to have a large amount of gold. He lit on them on one of his voyages when he was searching for freshwater. (The same detail of the search for freshwater was also given by Brown.) The pearls were seen on another voyage.

The elder Kelley had made several attempts to organise expeditions to these unknown islands but fate had stepped in and he was never able to return. The young Kelley, of course, abandoned his studies and organised an expedition to follow in his grandfather's footsteps. Unfortunately, we know no more of this venture and can only assume it is just another one on the list of failed attempts.

Is it no mere coincidence then that this story is followed in Wilkins' books by another one concerning our Captain Brown? We will digress to tell it:

There was an aged sea captain who used to haunt a tavern near the docks downtown in New York. He told a story to a party of young Americans who were so taken in by his story that in November 1921, they started a syndicate off on a voyage to the lone isle of Tubai, in the Society group of islands. The ancient mariner said that £20,000,000 worth of pirate loot was buried in Tubai and he mentioned the names of three ships which had vanished. The captain's story was that the gold was originally hidden on the island of Cocos but removed to Tubai by a captain turned pirate who added to his loot by capturing three more ships. They found the altar, under which it was believed the treasure lay but found nothing but bones.

Another one of Wilkins' tales even names the man that befriended the beggar Killrain as being named Thompson *(Modern Buried Treasure Hunters)* and he was accosted in the streets of Sydney, N.S.W. by an elderly beggar. Unfortunately, in the same tale of the treasure, he (Wilkins) also places the Puamotu (Tuamotu archipelago) 300 miles west of Tahiti. The direction should, of course, be east. An unusual mistake by Wilkins.

With our now extensive knowledge of Brown and his stories, we recognise, of course, that he is the 'old mariner' and we are talking about the failed Gennessee Expedition. But there is a lot more to Wilkins in the overall story of the lost treasure than many have ever suspected. He also knew a lot more about our Captain Brown than any other person, including that Brown was actually Howe's source, something only recently discovered. In his book *Treasure Hunting*, Wilkins actually identifies that the story of the 'pirate' (Brown) who buried the treasure on Iupai Is also linked to the 'island of Pinaki' (Howe) and to an island in the 'Paumotus group' (Hamilton). It is only when you are familiar with the history and have an understanding of the 'big' picture, you can make these connections.

To continue with Roland Kelley: Harvard University was contacted to verify that this person existed. They sent a short biography. It said that Roland Paddock Kelley was born 24 May 1894, Brockton Massachusetts, the son of Frank Leslie Kelley. He was at Harvard 1911 to 1915. You notice that his full name is Roland Paddock Kelley, plainly from Irish descent. The name 'Paddock' being a version of an old English name for 'frog', is more usually used as a surname but here as a middle name, so his middle name, Paddock, was most probably that of his grandfather, Paddock Kelley, the same grandfather who in 1913 left to Roland 'a large fortune' on condition Roland search for the treasure discovered by his grandfather. One could describe Captain Brown's age by this date as grandfatherly also, and it can be seen they would have been of similar age.

It is the way the treasure was said to be found and what the treasure is said to be that tells us more than just what was written:

'Roland Kelley had to find certain *pearl fisheries* and a *treasure* on two uncharted islands in the Pacific.' 'The islands, said the will, were found by the old mariner, *to have a large amount of gold.*' 'He lit on them on one of his voyages when he was *searching for freshwater.*'

You can immediately pick up on the similarity here to how it was said Brown and his mates came upon the island, looking for pearls and freshwater they found gold! Recall also the previous 'Spanish Trail' chapter and the 'black brigantine', an expedition kitted out to look for pearls and gold;

'mysterious islands for which adventurous captains had made unsuccessful searches, but from whence traders had been known to procure enormous pearls.'

So it appears 'Killorain' really did exist but not by that name, and was with Brown when they found the treasure. But again, the actual circumstances of how they found the treasure have been obscured. We turn back to when Howe told the tale to Nordhoff:

"Four men", Howe started off, "had a hand in the business, a Spaniard named Alvarez, an Irishman named Killorain and two others of uncertain nationality, Luke Barrett and Archer Brown."

Archer Brown? He's easy. We know it is James Brown but we take heed the name has been changed slightly in a poor attempt to disguise by Howe. How poor can be seen also in the way Howe mixed in real features of Brown into the fake character names; 'Alvarez's' squinted eye and club like fists are actually Brown's features.

Killorain? Part of Brown's description again but this is a name supplied by Brown to Howe. So there would have been Brown and another person whose name had an Irish ring to it, something *like* Killorain. We know from Kelley's will, it has to be him, Paddock Kelley, everything fits and points to him.

Diego Alvarez? Again, a clever pseudonym given by Brown, built around the name for the island of 'Diego Alvarez'. Could the real 'Alvarez' be a Spanish Captain? A Grandee, or descendant of a Spanish nobleman? We suspect, any one of those, but also a member of a particular religious military order. The real identity of Alvarez, at the moment, is a mystery to me. I have not been able to track him down. There was a pirate named Alvarez but he was from a much earlier era. Whoever he was, he was in charge and impressed them enough, maybe even scared them enough so his identity was never mentioned and absolute secrecy about his involvement maintained. Secrecy may have in part come from the honour code between Freemasons. Brown we know was a Freemason, 'Alvarez' for certain was part of an order of similar kind but of higher authority.

We have two options regarding the part he played; either he was Captain of the *Bosun Bird/Sea Foam* and recognising the Spanish markers, found the gold by chance, but the details assembled do not indicate the treasure was merely stumbled upon this way. Alternatively, he knew about the treasure and was actively searching for it. Maybe he was a descendant of one of the Spanish Knights who buried it there.

Let us examine the first option. It is possible that they may have been on a pearling trip but just by chance landed on the correct island, and by chance they just happen to notice marks on a rock, and by chance the captain, who by chance happens to be Spanish, also by chance can interpret the signs that lead them to a treasure. By chance they then make a survey of the near islands which reveal them to be in a particular triangular pattern (the triangle is DNA and its importance has already been explained). Brown, we know, revealed this triangular island feature to Howe.

To hit on this particular island, which is just one of over 70 islands and atolls in this Archipelago alone, was no mere chance. As we know, exactly what chart and directions he was using, including the correct interpretation of the coded information on them, the trip was a planned and clandestinely executed recovery operation of something of great importance.

So we favour the second option, for the reasons not of chance or coincidence. When you examine all the evidence and do the assessment, the crew of four were looking for the treasure, not pearls. There is more evidence to come later showing that one of the crew had the island location details that could only have come from Alvarez, confirming he was actively searching for the island. At present, the actual name of Alvarez is unimportant to us. What is important is that he, as part of this gang of four, found treasure, of that we are sure; the treasure he set out to find. But so far, we have a crew of four with the identity of one missing.

Luke Barrett. Who was he? We have no other name we can equate it too. We only know he was English or English speaking, nothing really positive to go on. So we have to tackle it in a similar way to that which we used to confirm Paddock Kelley as part of the crew: who else is there, who around the 1850s, went on a trip to find the treasure, or Loot of Lima, and came back with gold? Someone we know who went on a ship and therefore must have been with other crew members? When you know the associated stories, it stares out at you... John Keating!

When you know all the other stories associated with the lost treasure, and the way Brown worked, you can see that the 'Luke Barrett' name is a clever derivative to confuse with the similar double-letter names given in all the other stories where a map is left by a dying sailor, e.g.:

- Tom Daggett in *The Sea Lions* (1849, first appearance in a book of a dying sailor leaving a map).
- Tom Gammage in *Captain Kidd's Gold*.
- Tom Sinnott in *Cruise of the Alerte*.
- Another 'built in' reminder, Luke Barrett, 4 and 6 letters.
- John Keating, 4 and 6 letters!

We can say that with the exception of the pseudonym 'Alvarez', we are 99% certain that the names of the crew of four who sought out the lost treasure are:
- Diego Alvarez
- James Brown
- John Keating
- Paddock Kelley

You might be saying now, 'That cannot be, for it's well known that John Keating went to Cocos Island and found the treasure there. All the stories say so!' I agree, all the stories say so. I also suspect that John Keating used the same chart and directions that 'Alvarez' used and these are not for Cocos Island. There are no pearls on Cocos! Keating, whose name is well known to treasure hunters, is well documented as returning with gold and treasure from whatever 'that' trip was he went on. His name is well known to treasure hunters and students of the Cocos treasures, unlike Alvarez and the rest of the crew. In other words, instead of maintaining absolute secrecy about what occurred, he was in fact indiscreet, which, given the identity of the treasure and the warning of secrecy given by 'Alvarez', was unforgivable.

Keating, given the scrutiny he was now under and in order to save himself, never dared attempt any further trips. To throw any seekers off his trail, he actively maintained to all until he died that he had gone to Cocos Island, but the chart and directions he did leave will prove otherwise. Another rather obvious clue to the veracity and claim of that declared above is the simple fact that in the almost 200 year span of treasure hunting on Cocos Island, the 'Loot of Lima' has never been found. You know why, it did not exist and therefore was never there in the first place. That Captain Brown claimed to have relocated it from Cocos; just another deceptive story of his.

A brief change in direction now. I have mentioned common DNA in relation to different treasure stories. I introduce the following chapter now because DNA has already occurred many times and we need to start collating it before it gets 'lost in the crowd'. Also, I will be referring to it at times so you need to be aware of what I am talking about.

Introduction to DNA

A part definition of DNA is 'DNA is self-replicating and is responsible for the transmission of hereditary characteristics'.

I use the term in this book to define the certain characteristics of stories we were investigating that we could see kept occurring. In other words, there are important parts in most of the stories that can be recognised as having occurred before. It could be a name, place, action, direction, or event, but it has been inherited from the past and comes originally from the 'genesis event', the event which is the parent that spawned all the descendant stories and legends. This DNA can be identified in all related descendant stories and can then be tracked backwards to identify the genesis event. Whilst the theory is simple, the practical application of identifying what is genesis event DNA and what is not, is a lot harder and takes understanding of the way humans perceive, describe and communicate their experiences as well as understanding the dilative effects of time and distance: what is a version of the same story and what is not, what is DNA and what is not? What filters do you have to be aware of that might need applying? For example, what can you expect to find when a similar sounding event occurs or what do you do when the local populace of a region has a particular villain or hero they like to add to stories to make the story their own?

An outstanding example of genesis DNA we have already seen many times; the dying sailor who leaves a map to buried treasure. It occurs in the earlier 'Don Bruno' story; a dying sailor leaving directions. 'Trinity' and 'three' you have already seen. Other DNA present is; a Spanish grandee escaping authority with a treasure, relocation of a treasure. Also; a large knob of rock, and the directions 'E. by N.' In particular, you will see N.E. as DNA, with variations of it appearing frequently in this book. A typical example is;

'Keating looked at the chart, and read how the treasure-hunter should proceed to the north-east part of the island.'

Masonic DNA

Besides the prime genesis DNA you can now identify with, we introduce you to another form of DNA that appears in, for example, the earlier JF Island 'Grandee' story. It is what I call 'Masonic DNA', being particular signs and symbols pertaining to Masonic Lore. The example in this story is the phrase 'an axe, a cutlass, and a crowbar'. These are items that would be accepted by most readers as just that - items, for some reason, buried by the pirates. But if a Freemason saw this phrase, it is telling him that this story either contains a secret message or is in someway important as these are Masonic tools and symbols of Freemasonry. Many of the signs and symbols on treasure charts, and phrases in the stories, of no obvious, apparent or particular meaning to the casual reader, are actually devises of important meaning to Freemasons. They are clues if you like for the brotherhood, meant to be recognised by other Freemasons. This symbolic Masonic DNA is scattered throughout the story and takes us to the very heart of it, as you will see. For now, when we say, 'This is DNA' or 'This is Masonic DNA', you will know what we are talking about and will be able to recognise the application.

We have completed our examination of the Killorain/Brown story and now know what we are looking for.

Island maps and charts, as you have seen, play a big part in our story. In relation to buried treasure, there are genuine charts (very few) and very dubious ones (many). We said at the beginning, in the chapter on Juan Fernandez Island, that there would be more to say about this island. We introduce to you now, in the next couple of chapters, some of the more dubious charts playing their part in that story and beyond, not only because their authenticity is somewhat doubtful but because they are important and their originator has played a big part in our research.

So as with DNA, it makes sense to interject here with the part played in our story by the often mentioned H.T. Wilkins, and this by default will also take us on to the previously mentioned Kidd/Palmer charts and explain their importance in our story; future references will then not be a mystery to you.

PART 3

CHAPTER 1

JUAN FERNANDEZ ISLAND AND ITS VARYING ASPECTS OF CARTOGRAPHY

Maps, charts and directions feature in any good buried treasure hunt, certainly in fictitious stories. But there are exceptions - ours!

The original map or directions have yet to come to light due to the secrecy which surrounded the hiding of the treasure by those involved. Even so, there was a lot of circumstantial and 'hidden' evidence created around and about them. You cannot hide something that big and important without someone, somewhere, knowing about it. When you know what you are looking for and are aware of the bigger picture, a lot of it comes together and you can assemble the map and its accompanying direction. Quite a few of the maps, charts and directions in our quest contained 'hidden' directions. Things that one might look at on a map and cause you to stop and think, 'That's strange, why is that there? It doesn't mean anything.' You might just shrug your shoulders at it and leave it for another day. The link to being able to answer those questions is very tenuous and it could be only by chance that you see something else and can say, 'Ah, now I understand'.

Unfortunately, it can be years before you are able to make the link and it could hang on whether or not you just happen to buy a particular book, sometimes down to even a particular edition of a particular book, as I found, when clues in one edition were not to be included in a different edition. This is why in this sort of quest, your research must reach far and wide to gather together anything that might be remotely connected. It has taken ten years to piece this story together, that and a library of at least 100 books on the subject enabled this story to be finally told.

We start with a modern map and profile of Juan Fernandez Island.

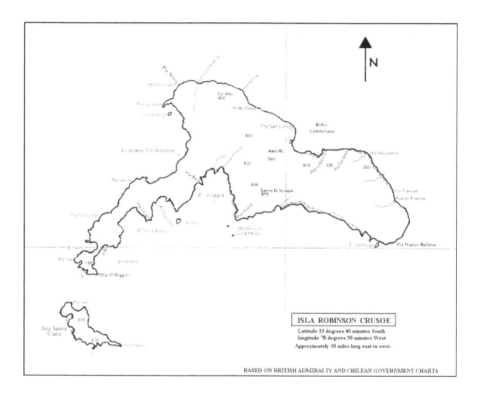

A MODERN RENDITION OF ISLA ROBINSON CRUSOE
(NEW NAME FOR JUAN FERNANDEZ ISLAND)

The above map, being modern, does not feature in our quest for the treasure.

But I show you one now that does. This map, indirectly, caused me many headaches years ago but more on that later.

No.1267

Price 25 cents

GLOSS NO. 176

OLD MAP OF JUAN FERNANDEZ ISLAND FROM A SPANISH SURVEY IN 1795. IMPORTANT BECAUSE THIS IS THE MAP THAT WHEN INVERTED WAS WHAT WAS USED TO CREATE THE INFAMOUS KIDD/PALMER CHARTS

LORD ANSON'S CHART OF JUAN FERNANDEZ ISLAND FROM HIS BOOK
A VOYAGE ROUND THE WORLD, PUBLISHED IN 1748

Whilst not as detailed as the Spanish survey carried out 50 years later, the opposite chart does feature the salient points of interest to us, in particular the extended banana-shape. Note it is unconventional in that it is not drawn on a N.S. axis. Also, as longitude could not be measured with any accuracy, JF's east/west position is given as 110 leagues from 'Chili' i.e. 110x1/20º=330nm. (Actual to land is 360nm.)

H. T. Wilkins, Author Extraordinaire

The Spanish survey chart of 1795 is of particular interest to us as it embodies the features utilised in charts created by the author Harold T. Wilkins. These were to have a big impact on the treasure hunting world. These charts known as the Palmer/Kidd charts we discuss in more detail in the next chapter and show the conspicuous link between them and the Spanish survey chart.

H.T. Wilkins was a prolific writer of pirates and buried treasure stories prior to WW2 and to a lesser degree after. Some of his books have already been mentioned; they are a mine of information with his stories covering the globe. Born in 1891 in Gloucester, England, he was educated at Cambridge University and began his career as a schoolmaster, then went into newspaper journalism rising to assistant editor in Fleet Street. His treasure hunting books started appearing at the end of the 1920s; at least seven were published prior to WW2 with a few more in the 1940s. There were also countless articles in newspapers and magazines. A lot of his tales of treasure are interesting and entertaining. At the time, and even today, many would say they are a very enjoyable read, and what more could an author want? But with hindsight, superior knowledge (from latter day research) and investigation, we are able to show that our Mr Wilkins was not all that he made out to be. By that, we mean that a lot of his material should be treated with suspicion and even a pinch of sea salt!

In keeping with the theme of cartography, we start with one of Wilkins' maps. Although he does not admit it, this is one of his creations depicting JF Island typically flavoured with ambiguous clues meaningless to most.

CHART W1

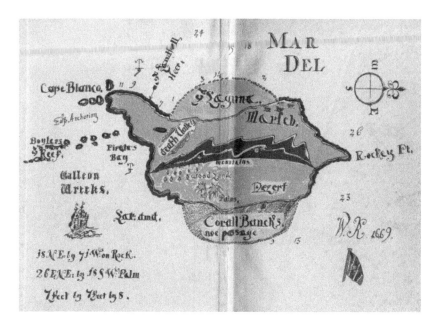

THIS MAP APPEARS ON THE INSIDE FRONT AND REAR COVERS OF H.T. WILKINS' BOOK *CAPTAIN KIDD AND HIS SKELETON ISLAND*

With reference to the above map, there is nothing on it that would make one say, 'Yes, that is Juan Fernandez Island'. One can only make the association knowing the bigger picture and later on we will show you its mistaken similarity to another infamous treasure island.

H.T. WILKINS

The next map shows him once again playing with the reader. It appeared in the same book and obviously depicts the same island.

CHART W2

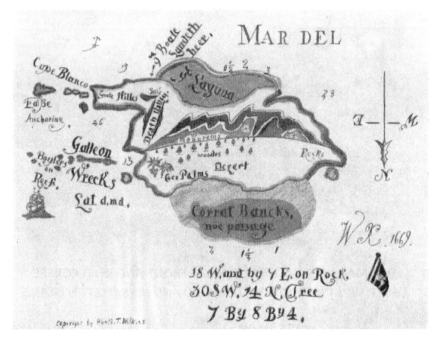

NOTE DIFFERENT DIRECTIONS AND COMPASS NORTH.
FLAG DESIGN BOTTOM RIGHT IS COPIED DIRECTLY OFF ONE OF THE
CHESTS IN HUBERT PALMER'S MUSEUM COLLECTION

Both the above maps show Captain William Kidd's initials and the date 1669, which corresponds with the date on the first Kidd/Palmer map found in 1929. These maps bear no physical resemblance to that map, which also included the location 'CHINA SEA'. Note also 'Laguna' (Lagoon). There is no lagoon associated with JF Island.

We continue with the Wilkins map saga with another one he says is a reproduction of a chart in the log of the English buccaneer Captain Bartholomew Sharp.

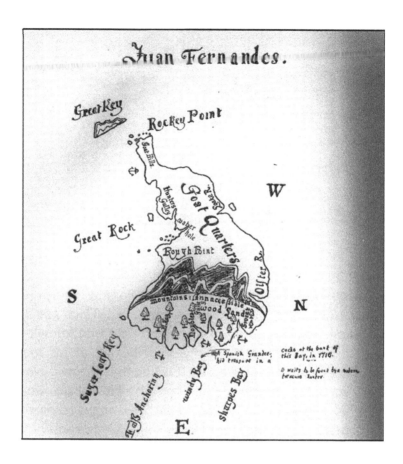

There are more changes to compass north. The small italic writing says, 'A Spanish Grandee hid treasure in a cache at the back of this Bay,(windy Bay) in 1716. It waits to be found by a modern treasure hunter.'

Note also 'Suger loaf key' and 'water hole'. Clues to JF Island lie in the word 'Goat' and 'Suger loaf key', which alludes to 'Sugar-Loaf Bay' on Anson's depiction of the island. Also orientation, N is same as E, (DNA). At least he names the island this time.

The above map is attributed to Bartholomew Sharp (English buccaneer, 1650-1702) but you can see where Wilkins got a lot of his inspiration from for some of his maps. With no knowledge of seventeenth/eighteenth cartography, and looking at his maps on their own, one might be forgiven for thinking that is how it was done 300 years ago, but when you are familiar with all of Wilkins' work, you know it is *his own* work. So where are all these maps leading us to? Besides furthering our quest for more linking DNA and answering the question; which island trinity?

Wilkins, his charts, Kidd and the Kidd/Palmer charts, were also linked to another infamous treasure location. Though the Kidd/Palmer charts depict JF Island, there is actually another island in the world that is similar to the shape of JF as depicted on older charts and in particular charts W1and W2 above, but before we reveal the identity of this other island, we have to look a little deeper into the part Wilkins plays in this story and finally reveal the secret of the Kidd/Palmer charts.

CHAPTER 2

THE WILKINS HIDDEN TRAIL TO CREDIBILITY AND THE KIDD/PALMER CHARTS

It must be understood that at this stage, despite the tenuous clues uncovered, with the exception of there being a Spanish treasure, there was no single line of enquiry that produced a breakthrough in the secret of the lost treasure.

Due to the complexities of what was unfolding in our quest, it makes relating the multiple lines of investigation and discovery impossible to do in a linear fashion. We must therefore interject with an explanatory chapter to show what was occurring and how to follow the clues. By studying the writings of Harold T. Wilkins, we knew that *Wilkins knew.* His writings of ambiguity that could be recognised were suggestive of something, but what it was all about was still a mystery. There was even a type of clue trail left by Wilkins, to be followed in his writings. He grouped related treasure stories, placed obvious attention to drawing mistakes and noticeably remained silent on other aspects. Though a lot easier to follow now with all of Wilkins books on hand and knowing what he was up to, it must be remembered that these clues appeared in books that were published over a ten year period. His first book *Hunting Hidden Treasures* (1929) contain no clues at all. All subsequent books related to treasure hunting up to 1948 carry the clues. As mentioned in the previous chapter, these clues become easier to read over time. Once you realise it is occurring, these clues can be easily interpreted as instructions as plain as 'follow this' or 'look here'. The following examples demonstrate the subtle way his methodology worked.

One clue trail being followed came to an abrupt end with no further explanation or continuation. Told in *Pirate Treasure* (1937) and *Modern Buried Treasure Hunters* (1934), Wilkins relates the story of the 'Hong Kong Pilot' which appears next to stories about our Captain Brown. To alert the reader to the import of the story, Wilkins uses a recognisance technique of deliberately copying another related story, yet this other related story - *we* know he knows about - he deliberately excludes from his books. He begins the 'Hong Kong Pilot' story with:

'In ports all over the Eastern Seas, from Singapore and Manila, to Yokohama to Frisco, you will find today seafarers who are sure they know of caches of immense treasure ashore on lonely beaches and desolate islands, or sunken bullion wrecks in the waters of the South Pacific or off China. They have seen the old charts with the imprints of Mr Bill Bones, master of the Walrus of Savannah, who sailed the seas under captain Flint, or crude sea-stained maps bearing the anchor-his-mark of Israel Hands, who begged his bread in the streets of Old Wapping, what time poor Kidd hung in chains at Execution Dock. Sometimes these yarns have a foundation of fact. The treasure-seekers are not always unscrupulous adventurers or tattoed whisky swallowers. A pilot, well-known in Hong Kong, for his skill and business ability, once possessed a chart of a sunken ship of a most convincing nature.'

'Many hundreds of tales have been written about the discovery of buried treasure, and the wise people of today laugh and shake their heads when some boy, pondering over an exiting treasure story in which doubloons, and pieces of eight, and pirates, and buccaneers inflame his imagination, asks someone "If any part of it all is true." Yet, although ninety-nine out of a hundred of such tales may be, and probably are, purest fiction, treasure has been found, not only in the haunts of the old-time pirates of the Caribbean Sea and the Spanish Main, but in both the North and South Pacific Oceans; and the story of the finding of the treasure of Druno do Bustamente on an island in the North Pacific is true-true in every detail as here narrated, save the name of one of those who found it has been changed. He was an Englishman, and less than thirty years ago was well known in the Southern Colonies as the chief officer of a steamer trading between Sydney, Hobart, and Melbourne.'

The 'Hong Kong Pilot' was.......a strict abstainer and had acquired a considerable fortune by care and good luck. Much of his time was passed pouring over rare and historical and geographical works in several languages, and he was a subscriber to New York and London newspapers.'

This pilot had obtained a small chart of 'a crude' drawing of a coral reef and shoal, north-east of the Philippines where a Spanish galleon on route from Lima to Manila had foundered on a reef late seventeenth century. The chart had come from a Captain Salmon, who had obtained it in the Philippines circa 1850. Dying, (DNA) Captain Salmon gave the chart to his employer. The employer, after wrecking and losing everything, sold the chart for a pittance to the Hong Kong Pilot.

In *Pirate Treasure*, the story includes a footnote which gives one of the three references to George (Lord) Anson made by Wilkins, that being in 1743, Anson looted the Spanish galleon *Nuestra Senora de Covadonga* off Manila. Of the few instances, a reference to Anson appears; this is the only time Anson's name is given in a directly related treasure story, so it must be considered to have been placed there as a clue. Another time Anson is mentioned is merely in context with speaking of the times that saw spectacles such as Anson's wagon loads of captured gold paraded to the treasury in London. A third mention will be detailed shortly in its proper place. Nowhere does Wilkins ever mention Anson in the context of a treasure on Juan Fernandez Island.

The story of the 'Hong Kong Pilot' by Wilkins is to be read as a directional clue that says, 'Look for something to the north-east of the Philippines that you will recognise.'

The Philippines is recognised as important to us because the *Flota de Nova Espana* which served the trade of the Mexico Galleons out of Vera Cruz operated out of here from Manila. This is where the far-east Chinese treasures were loaded aboard the Spanish galleons prior to their long voyage across the Pacific to Mexico. At Acapulco, the treasures were loaded aboard an overland convoy to Vera Cruz, then again aboard the galleons to Havana. From here, the combined fleet sailed to Spain.

The area north-east of the Philippines can be said to be centered approximately around 19º north and 140º east; these bearings are close enough to be immediately recognised as the bearings of the Pinaki Trinity Group of atolls but hemispherically reversed.

After this, no further clues were forthcoming. The Hong Kong Pilot trail ended abruptly. That Wilkins knew something about Pinaki was obvious. What was the reason the clues pointing east, away from Pinaki, suddenly stopped?

Wilkins, Juan Fernandez Island and the Kidd/Palmer Charts

When researching my Kidd book, I had been trying to relate a combination of the Wilkins and Kidd/Palmer chart clues to an actual island. This involved many coordinate combinations based on the lat/long clues and different meridian combinations. MN had not looked at this as it appeared to him to be a completely independent subject to the Wilkins coded clues to the treasure. The situation altered when the Trinity clue was isolated and we were tracking the appearance of three markers in the form of a triangle; these were somehow believed to indicate the treasure's position. Three markers also feature in an earlier chapter about the search for a treasure on 'Trinidade Island'. I quote:

'The pirate had described a small gulley in the middle of this bay, at the foot of which he and his men had erected three cairns, which should serve as landmarks to those who had the clue, and point the way to the treasure.'

'Three' is important DNA and the three 'markers' now catching attention were those on the Kidd/Palmer 'Key' chart which has been seen, was patently depicting JF Island. I need to explain now what the Kidd/Palmer charts are. The full story of them is in my book mentioned in the Introduction but I will explain briefly. In the 1930s, a collector of pirate memorabilia, one Hubert Palmer, found, in items of Captain William Kidd's furniture (chests, bureau, workbox), a series of charts. They were (in order found);

a) A simple, island outline drawing found in a writing bureau with 'X' in the middle, 'CHINA SEA' at top, a signature 'W Ki? (no definite 'd'), a date 1669, a NSEW compass marker and along the bottom 'of me Sarah W'. This discovery started his search for, in particular, anything related to Kidd

b) Second chart found was in a chest reputed to have belonged to Captain Thomas Masterman Hardy (of HMS Victory fame). This was more or less the same as the first chart found, nothing new but no reference to the China Sea.

c) Third chart, known as the Morgan 'Skull chart', was found in a chest that had on its lid a plate engraved with a monogram

'K' and the skull and crossbones. The chart was found hidden behind a mirror hidden behind a false bottom. This chart was a lot more detailed but contained no clue to the identity or location of the island.

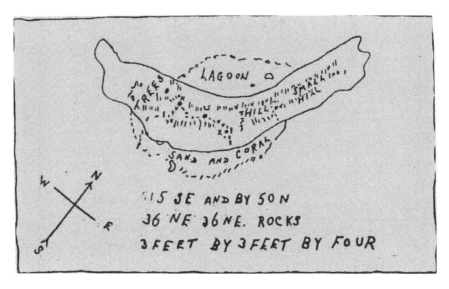

THE 'SKULL' CHART, THIRD CHART FOUND BY PALMER

d) Fourth chart found (in 1934) was in a small box believed to have been Mrs Kidd's workbox. The chart is shown on the following page. I named this the 'Key' chart because it shows a lot more information including a latitude and longitude.

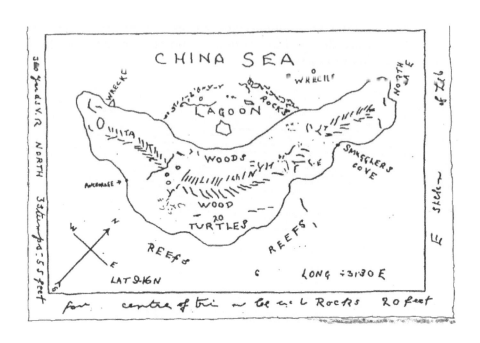

THE KIDD/PALMER 'KEY' CHART. LAST CHART FOUND, HIDDEN IN COMPARTMENT AT BOTTOM OF SARAH KIDD'S WORKBOX

SARAH KIDD'S WORKBOX IN WHICH THE 'KEY' CHART WAS FOUND

224

e) Of further interest, a small document known as the 'Yunnan Parchment' was found some three to four years after the 'Key' chart in a cavity in the back of a mirror frame that had the initials 'WK' carved in it. The parchment contained three lines of treasure recovery information. It is shown further on in 'The Auctioneer's Find' chapter.

PALMER WITH THE 'HARDY' CHEST, HOLDING FALSE BOTTOM

My book shows how I solved the instructions to the treasure location on the island – the 'Key' chart and 'Skull' chart have to be used together. It was not until after my book was published that the island location was discovered. As mentioned in the Introduction, with a colleague who had helped in the discovery, we went there to confirm that it was the island as depicted on the charts. (The solution follows later in this chapter)

The three 'markers' appear as you can see on the 'Key' chart as three tiny circles in the form of a triangle. Where they appear, between two lines, has been named by Wilkins as 'Death Valley' on some of his fanciful charts. By implication only, you might associate '3 stumps' on the left hand side margin with these circles but it is all meant to distract you from the real purpose which is another clue left by Wilkins to show that he knows about Captain Brown and the Trinity.

Copyright G Edmunds 2011

The above photograph shows the 'Skull Chart' chest, false bottom exposed with plaster cast skull and Bible resting on it. Author at right, Anthony Howlett to the left (original researcher into the charts in the 1950s), Mr. Arno, owner of chest, in centre. Sadly, both Mr. Howlett and Mr. Arno have now passed away.

Out of minor interest, I appeared in a Yesterday Channel TV documentary series called *Myth Hunters* in November 2012. In *The Hunt for Pirate Treasure* documentary, I demonstrate how the charts were hidden and how they were discovered.

The Cunning of the Kidd/Wilkins Chart

The chart diagrams that follow demonstrate clearly how the 'Key' chart was based on the early (1795) chart of JF shown in the previous chapter. The word 'TURTLES' was there not as a clue to that amphibian being a resident of the island, but to turn the chart 'turtle' i.e. upside down.

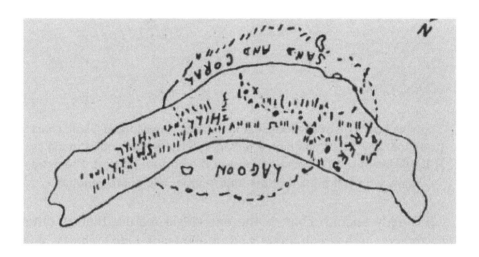

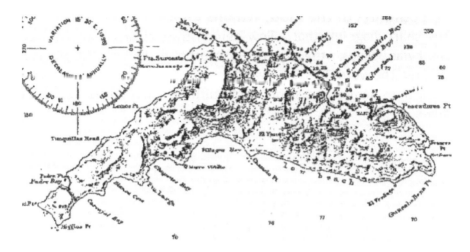

Showing how two of the Kidd/Palmer charts, the Morgan 'Skull' chart (top) and 'Key' chart when inverted are really creative copies made by H.T. Wilkins of the 1795 chart shown at the bottom (above). There are many who still think that the Kidd/Palmer charts are genuine.

This early Spanish chart is the one single feature that all other researchers, treasure hunters and students of Kidd's charts have missed and greatly to the cost of many. Myself included to some extent, of course, although my book was mainly about the history of the charts and the expeditions they created. I would eventually have found the JF Chart but when writing my Kidd book, that particular chart was outside my terms of reference and research. How many, I wonder, of those students, researchers and expedition organisers, old and new, reading this are exclaiming, 'Oh my God!' or similar expletives when taking on board this revelation about the charts? The money wasted, the dreams destroyed. Although I have never been part of an expedition and so have not lost any investment, for research and confirmation purposes as you know, I did go to the island Robin C. and I discovered it was indeed in the South China Seas as declared on two of the charts. But it was not until starting research for this book and the further investigative research undertaken for Anson's treasure that I became aware of this early chart of Juan Fernandez Island. All then became clear, 'I saw the light' as they say, and must admit, greatly admired the subterfuge of Wilkins.

Now take another look at the centre inverted 'Key' chart, as there was a further clever trick about the word 'TURTLES' and the inverted shape of the island. This has been completely overlooked because being so incongruous, the mind refuses to recognise it until it is pointed out. The island actually also embodies a drawing of a turtle. Known as 'trompe l'oeil' (literally, 'to fool the eye'), this was a technique used even by renaissance artists to hide coded clues within their work and toy with the perspective to create optical illusions. To the left of the picture, you can see the turtle's eye and the mouth which is devouring the text 'North SA E', the coastline is the shell and the rocks defining the lagoon are the flippers.

With reference to the above, you can see that Padre Bay (far left) on JF becomes 'Smugglers Cove' on the 'Key' chart and Cumberland Bay (with anchor symbol) becomes the 'Anchorage' on the 'Key' chart. The rocks/islets either side of Villagra Bay have been extended to create the lagoon on the 'Key' chart. Even the small elongated circle at the right hand end of the JF chart is repeated on the 'Key' chart. The exaggerated promontory at the RH end of the charts is copied from the same on the JF chart. Just more proof if you want it that one is copying the other. Going back to the full copy of the 'Key' chart (also two of the other charts), you can see that the unconventional orientation of the compass rose is copied from that on the earlier Anson chart and is in the same lower left-hand corner. This is just another hint by Wilkins that he knows all about the Anson link to JF Island and meant it to be recognised by the few, privileged to be 'in the know'.

Those familiar with *Treasure Island* by R. L Stevenson may recognise the following quote: *"Yes, sir," said he, "this is the spot, to be sure, and very prettily drawed out, who might have done that, I wonder? The pirates were too ignorant I reckon. Aye, here it is: Capt Kidd's Anchorage....."*

You can now see Wilkins got more inspiration from that book by including 'Anchorage' on his 'Kidd' (Key) chart. He also used 'Skeleton Island' from that book in the title of one of his own as you will see in the next paragraph. Wilkins composed the charts somewhat in the same fashion as Captain Brown did with his story. He used bits of information both real and fiction and spread it over four charts. Add all this to the statement Kidd made during his trial: *"I have lodged goods and Treasure to the value of one hundred thousand pounds......."* And the overall impact on the mind of those not intimately familiar with pirates/treasure/islands/charts and Kidd would be; 'These charts must be real and show the way to that treasure.' Many, many people have taken the bait laid down by Wilkins (and Kidd).

The Pacific Link

In his early research, for the above reasons, MN decided to look into Captain William Kidd and these charts a bit more. The most cursory enquiry into the charts kept linking Harold Wilkins' name with them via his book *Captain Kidd and his Skeleton Island*, first published in 1935. The only thing to do, he decided, was to contact the Kidd 'experts' and ask a few questions about the authenticity of the charts and a certain group of three dots appearing on them. Unfortunately, when confronted with some rather probing questions and evidence that didn't fit their Kidd treasure location theory, the experts just petulantly stopped answering! Faced with this, MN decided to obtain what was considered to be *'The Complete and true story of Captain Kidd's Treasure Charts, the problems of identification, the expeditions that followed and where to look.'* That being the sub-title of my book, **KIDD***, THE SEARCH FOR HIS TREASURE*.

Reading it from cover to cover, MN recognised enough in the history of the Kidd charts and Wilkins' involvement to know that something ulterior was occurring contrary to what everyone knew or commonly believed. In his words:

'Apart from raising issue with the authenticity of the charts and Wilkins' part in it all, George himself had attempted to follow what he thought were clues given in Wilkins' Kidd book which seemed to disclose an area in the Pacific where the mysterious island shown on the charts was supposed to be. I smiled to myself when I saw George's results of his combinations of chart clues and meridians relating in particular to the Pacific. This is how they appear in his book:

Island Groups in the West Pacific Ocean

Yap	Approx.	9º 30´ N	138º 20´ E
Ulithi	Approx.	10º 00´ N	139º 30´ E
Fais	Approx.	9º 80´ N	140º 40´ E

You do not need an atlas to work out that these positions are 'northeast of the Philippines'. More importantly, the longitudinal values, standing out like flashing lights are those of the Pinaki Trinity Island group.

Wilkins' clues are such that you need to already know what he is talking about in order to understand them. It is a form of 'reverse engineering' e.g. we know where we are, now we can work back and evaluate how we got here. It seemed to be an additional security measure in his (Wilkins) encoding and included multiple levels of this feature.

Here was an example of this measure which had George looking at the clues for an island in a Trinity group but with all the clues rolled into one confusing mass. This was because the Kidd/Palmer 'Key' chart was commonly believed to give in the legend around the border, a coded latitude and longitude to the island's location, with the triangle of dots marking the treasure location on the island.'

A thorough examination of Wilkins' *Captain Kidd and his Skeleton Island* (1937) revealed on page 390 the single confirmatory sentence given by Wilkins to show he was using the Kidd saga as a carrier of the lost treasure clues:

'In that year a Spanish Naval Captain, bound from Manila to Mexico, sighted three coral-ringed and lofty islas, which were not marked on his charts, and, in fact were not believed to exist.'

My Kidd book shows the history of these 'vanishing' islands. They were positioned by the Spanish Navy (in 1802) at 131º 22´ East. It was this vital clue of the Trinity, placed within Wilkins' book about Kidd, all the experts in the Kidd charts mystery have completely ignored. But like I said, and to be fair to other researchers, you would have to be aware of the importance of the Trinity in its various forms. As Wilkins was now also using Kidd to carry the lost treasure clues, other Wilkins books were scanned to see what was written about Kidd. Mentioned briefly in *Modern Buried Treasure Hunters* (1934), Wilkins relates how 'Old salts in a certain Japanese port used to roar out a thrilling shanty':

> *'Eyeless and hairless, on th' island Pristarius,*
> *Kidd's angels do lie,*
> *They guard the Death Valley,*
> *Through whose narrow alley,*
> *Thee'st pass to the treasure,*
> *Buried near fathom five.'*

This ditty about Kidd is immediately followed by details about the Manila Galleons and the third reference to Lord Anson, and repeats the details of the 1743 capture of the *Nuestra Señora del Covadonga*. I direct your attention to the island's name 'Pristarius' in the shanty. It is being introduced here as it will assume great importance later. Those wishing to look for it now are advised to not bother with consulting an atlas or marine chart but rather a star chart! (Explanation follows later.)

In the previous chapter about the varying aspects of JF's cartography, I mentioned how Wilkins, Kidd, and the Kidd charts are also linked to another infamous treasure location. Although the Kidd/Palmer charts depict JF Island and with an ulterior motive another island as you will see in the South China Sea. This other infamous island in the North Atlantic is similar to the shape of JF island as depicted on the older charts and some of those created by Wilkins. This aspect of similar shape caused Wilkins to view his charts with some incredibility as we will see later. But simply matching an island's shape to a chart does not mean you are on the actual island depicted by that chart (try telling that to some treasure hunters!) as the multitude of unfortunates who poured their money and their lives into a bottomless pit on Oak Island, Nova Scotia are about to discover. But first, a more detailed exposition of the 'Key' chart.

Wilkins, the 'Key' Chart and Solution

This is going to be a long chapter. Besides publishing for the first time the solution to the 'Key' chart (pre-2000), we delve more into the idiosyncrasies of Harold T. Wilkins. As this chapter is revealing the secret of the Kidd/Palmer charts, it is opportune to interject here with some more information of interest, in particular in relation to the previous statement regarding matching an island's shape.

In fact, there *is* irrefutable evidence to put the 'Key' chart island in the China Seas. Two of the charts have on them 'China Sea' and one document the 'Yunnan Island' parchment has on it 'Sh China Sea'. This, of course, on its own is not enough evidence to place the island there. If you are falsifying charts, you can put anything on them! However, as you know, I went to an island in the South China Seas. This matched almost identically to the island shape as depicted on the 'Key' chart. This, as we have said, is not enough to confirm it as 'the' island, but when you know how the simple code works, the latitude and longitude specified on the chart exactly pinpoints this island. Not only that, the size is right (about 1½ miles long), as is the island's compass orientation - very important but conveniently ignored by many.

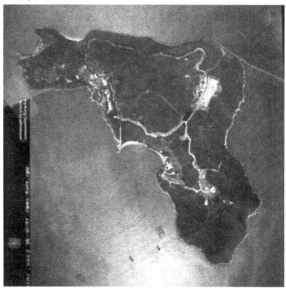

THE ISLAND IN THE SOUTH CHINA SEAS THAT MEETS THE IDENTIFICATION REQUIREMENTS OF THE 'KEY' CHART, INCLUDING THE EXACT (CODED) LATITUDE AND LONGITUDE

The 'Anchorage' and 'Smugglers Cove' are clearly recognised. So if you were not aware of the JF connection and having cracked the code, it is easy to make the obvious assumption *this* China Seas island is Kidd's island, everything points to it. Even the hills and tracks are all there as depicted on the Kidd charts. Another tantalising confirmation clue was that Mrs. Dick (Hubert Palmer's housekeeper and confidant) was quoted as saying that the maps identified an island off Hong Kong. Two of the charts also say 'China Sea'. Don't forget also Wilkins' Hong Kong Pilot clues. A Pilot is a steersman. All along with that tale, this was just another way of 'steering' you to Hong Kong. You can see in the newspaper article that follows (March 1950), that she is confirming that the South China Sea is the area to go. This article also demonstrates how *not* to believe everything you read in a newspaper as Oak Island is definitely not in the Caribbean. Also, Captain Kidd was certainly not a blood-thirsty pirate.

KEY TO PIRATE LOOT OFFERED FOR SALE

Australian Associated Press

LONDON, Mon.—Americans will be offered a chance to bid dollars for maps that are believed to show where Captain Kidd, one of Britain's most blood-thirsty pirates, buried loot worth about £1,000,000.

MRS. ELIZABETH DICK, of Eastbourne, Sussex, who now owns Kidd's maps, said yesterday she would sell them to meet taxes.

The only clue she would give to the whereabouts of the hoard was that it would cost a great deal to equip an expedition "to combat Chinese pirates and Communist armies."

Kidd was sent out in the 17th century to hunt pirates, but he decided that there was more money in pirating.

The last reports of him before he became a pirate were in waters near Madagascar.

When he returned to England he was hanged—and took to the gallows the secret of where he hid doubloons, jewels, and rings from fingers of victims, who, according to tradition, "walked the plank."

For generations the legend was that Oak Island, in the Caribbean Sea, was Kidd's hiding place. Some

believed it was in a cache a few miles out from Nova Scotia.

At least seven syndicates have spent thousands of pounds and dollars searching for the loot.

The previous newspaper article may be difficult to read, so I quote it as follows:

'Australian Associated Press

London, Mon. - Americans will be offered a chance to bid dollars for maps that are believed to show where Captain Kidd, one of Britain's most blood-thirsty pirates, buried loot worth about £1,000,000.

Mrs Elizabeth Dick, of Eastbourne, Sussex, who now owns Kidd's maps, said yesterday she would sell them to meet taxes. The only clue she would give to the whereabouts of the hoard was it would cost a great deal to equip an expedition "to combat Chinese pirates and Communist armies." Kidd was sent out in the 17th century to hunt pirates, but he decided that there was more money in pirating. The last reports of him before he became a pirate were in waters near Madagascar. When he returned to England he was hanged - and took to the gallows the secret of where he hid doubloons, jewels and rings from fingers of victims who, according to tradition 'walked the plank'. For generations the legend was that Oak Island, in the Caribbean Sea, was Kidd's hiding place. Some believed it was in a cache a few miles out from Nova Scotia. At least seven syndicates have spent thousands of pounds and dollars searching for the loot.'

The Solution

It is no good me stating that the 'Key' chart figures decode out to the exact coordinates of this island in the South China Seas without showing you how this is achieved, and a lot of people have been waiting for this even if now redundant information. It is quite simple - as it should be, otherwise easily forgotten with time, but, you do require knowledge of the meridians in use at that time (seventeenth century). To help those without this specialised knowledge, a meridian is a north/south line joining the poles which passes through the measuring datum point. Distances in degrees are measured east/ west from here (the longitude). In conjunction with the horizontal (latitude) line which is measured north/south of the equator, a position anywhere on the earth's surface can be fixed. Today, and since 1884, Greenwich (London) has been internationally adopted as the prime meridian. In the seventeenth century, up to a dozen meridians were in use, some countries using their own capital city as the datum. So any latitude or longitude figures on a seventeenth or eighteenth century chart were not of much use unless you knew where the longitude was measured from. Be aware also that whilst latitude could be measured accurately, until J. Harrison perfected the chronometer in about the middle of the eighteenth century, longitude could not be measured with any accuracy. If shown on early 'treasure' charts with 'minutes' attached, it should therefore be treated with some suspicion.

A clue to the meridian used by the author of the chart appears where it should - in front of the longitude. Only part of the character appears and research indicates it could only have been an 'H'. In other words, 'Hierro' was being used as the meridian. The part-figure could even be an 'F' as Hierro was also known as 'the isle of Fez'. Tenerife, one of the Canary Islands, was a commonly used meridian in those days. The simple code key is 100. Add this to both sets of figures and they become:

109.16 and 131.30
Subtract one from the other to give us:
22.14N (latitude)
Hierro is 17 degrees west of Greenwich
Subtract this from the longitude of 131.30E to give us:
114.30E, today's longitude from Greenwich.

At the positions calculated, 22º14´N and 114º30´E, we have the island shown above. Today it is known as Hei Ling Chau, an island not very far from Hong Kong. Actually, if you are astute, the accuracy with which this island is pinpointed should be another clue to you that the charts are a modern fake. For reasons given above, there is no way a longitude could be measured with this sort of accuracy i.e. 30´ in the seventeenth century.

The Spot Marked 'X' is 'T'

The complete and detailed methodology is shown in my book. I show how the traditional treasure location marked 'X' is in fact the centre 'T' in 'TURTLES'. Basically, the figures on the 'Skull' chart have to be used geometrically and plotted on the 'Key' chart; one is no good without the other. Using the 'Anchorage' as the obvious starting point several lines and arcs bisect exactly this letter. In fact, on the actual island, a very large lone rock stands at this very location, not very far from the water's edge. So;

'This be where it lyes, me lads, oarrgh, oarrgh!'

I discovered that the starting point of the geometrical construction was the two wreck circles; they are exactly horizontally in line and equidistance from the vertical line bisecting 'A' at the top, middle 'T' in Turtles and the 'a' missing from the word 'triangle' bottom border. Like most things, it is all obvious when you know how.

You can now see why Wilkins was pushing 'Hong Kong' a lot in his books; to tempt you in that direction.

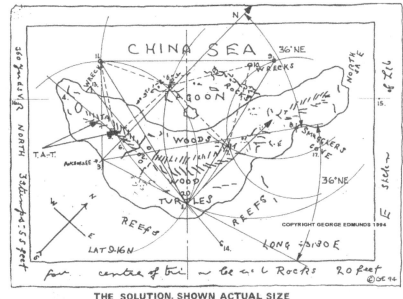

THE SOLUTION. SHOWN ACTUAL SIZE

A note regarding the Kidd/Palmer charts; all the reproductions in this book are not copies of copies. I am fortunate to have in my possession the original negatives of the charts, so what you see is the genuine article, even if their genuineness is suspect!

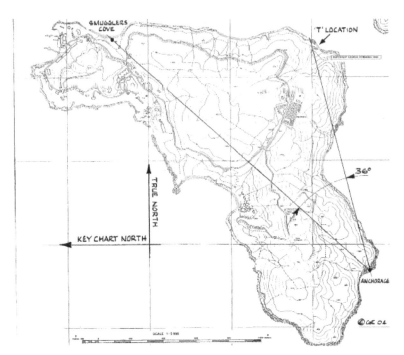

SHOWING HOW THE 36º ANGLE WORKS ON HEI LING CHAU ISLAND EXACTLY AS ON THE 'KEY' CHART. IT COULDN'T HAPPEN ANYWHERE ELSE SO PRECISELY

You can see from the above that the geometry can only work with an island that has the same profile as the Key chart, particularly in relation to the Smugglers Cove, and Anchorage Cove indentations also the prominence of the land mass at the 'T Location'.

No other shape can achieve the requirements of the angular relationship. The overall shape was near enough for the perpetrators and anyway you could not expect a chart drawn in the seventeenth century to accurately determine the profile of an island correctly.

We were prepared to do some metal-detecting and digging on the island at the 'T' location, but a sign not very far away warned the unauthorised off and to keep 100 yards clear of the coast. As the thought of being interred as guests of the Chinese Government for an indefinite time did not appeal to us, and as we could see movement on the island close by, we decided to get permission first. We told them the island but not the treasure location. After years of excuses, they never did grant permission and we suspect they had a look themselves. It turned out the island is Government owned, and hosts a Penal Institution for young offenders.

This island shows the whole saga of the Kidd/Palmer charts is a very clever, complex hoax/subterfuge, and despite the compelling decoding of the charts and identification of the island, it is but a ruse. I have for years now been trying to drop the hint to many of my correspondents, even to the point of telling them they are a hoax. Most reply saying, 'I respect your thoughts/theory (some are not so polite!) but I'm sure I know where the island is,' or words to that effect. (I will shortly mention the more colourful offensive replies that have continued over the years from one particular individual with a seafaring surname who seems determined to be oblivious to the obvious!). It is obvious these searchers have not carried out the required in-depth research and as stated in a previous chapter, their restrictive self-belief will not allow them to look outside their own 'tunnel vision'. They think they know it all so will not look at any other point of view or evidence. It is a point I make more than once in this book. So besides pouring scorn on others, they continue to pour time, energy and money into a bottomless non-existent treasure hole on an island found by supposition/guesswork, manipulation of the figures and stretching history a bit to fit their theory. Also, if the island looks about right, then that has to be the one! Oak Island comes to mind as another major contender! Infamous modern-day searchers who come to mind are Richard Knight, Alan Marshall and the respected author Rupert Furneaux. Their stories are in my Kidd book. Others have contacted me over the years saying they know where the island is. All were/are sadly misguided, which is why nothing was found. One of the reasons for writing the Kidd book was to try and answer the question 'Why are they all going to different islands?' The pointed question I ask of all these people is, 'If you know where it is, show us the treasure'. It is then embarrassed silence or all sorts of excuses why they can't!

Mr B Keiser on JF Island is another example, as we have seen; we offered help but he wasn't interested in talking to us. I wonder if any of the Kidd treasure hunters will admit after reading this and the earlier solution, "Yes, OK, I was wrong!" I somehow doubt it, and if C.F. is reading this, "Don't forget the £1,000 wager, you can contact me through the publishers!"

Many hint they are on the brink of recovering Kidd's treasure. Many make excuses about why they have not - yet! The years roll on and I'm still waiting for the headline breaking news, with books about to be written and promised film documentary of the recovery expedition. Names of big-time operators and investors, colourful websites full of Kidd's history mask the fact they cannot come up with the treasure - nothing new there then! This is happening, that is happening, and in the end, still no treasure!

I am not trying to be smart or smug here, but for years I have been taking flak off certain people ridiculing what I have been trying to tell them. I have known the truth for a long time but unable to divulge it because obviously it had to wait for now and this book. (I also reveal the truth in my updated website www.captainkiddscharts.co.uk This has stirred up antagonism even more in some people!) In particular I will mention Mr P Hawkins of Bristol (he names me on his website!) who appears to take great delight in running me down on his website, for example; (sic) .....his-(me GE) crazy claims to have solved the maps using creative and imaginative arithmetic.....misleading and factually wrong.....ludicrous interpretations.....if only he realised how his pomposity, arrogance and blind belief in his new stupid scenario will shortly come back to haunt him when I publish the FULL solution. This will not be long in coming as I have permission to conduct a full survey and excavation of the island. Unquote.

He also goes on to say; 'My (PH's)discovery which is irrefragable.....' This is just a big word for 'cannot be challenged'. My (not so) big word that comes to mind is 'deluded'.

Quite clearly PH is rattled by my revelations and now has to resort to abuse. Maybe you the reader is asking yourself-as I have- If he has solved the charts as he claims and knows where the island is (Indian Ocean), Why does he have to do a full survey and excavation of the island? As surely, if you've solved the charts you know where to go!! Sounds like Oak Island all over again. He also declares he's been on this island full of riches. If so, why didn't he go to his solved location marked 'X' with a bucket and spade?? He also says on his website (2012) 'I will be making an announcement in the near future'. Well Mr H, we are still waiting for the headline breaking news and pictures of Kidd's gold, also for the 'FULL' solution you promised.

Mr PH and the others who have claimed to have solved the charts are also determined to ignore the advice of respected experts. I would not know if I should consider myself in the latter but even the Curator of Maps at the British Library says the maps are fakes, as do experts in palaeography at the British Map Museum. One only has to look at these maps to be suspicious; they are book-size pages and certainly do not have the cartographic style one would expect of a seventeenth century map or chart!

And four charts found by one man in a six-year period! Stretching the credibility thing a bit far, isn't it? Unless he was 'set up' and coerced into it. There is also the suspicious order in which they were found, starting with the least informative, followed by each one with a bit more information, to the final chart with all the necessary clues required to complete the puzzle. Simple decoding methodology, as utilised above, will be further demonstrated later on in this book where, amongst other revelations, I reveal how the 'Key' chart and JF Island are inexplicably entwined.

Having exposed the charts as fakes (in fact, a deception) and how they relate to two real islands (JF and HLC), neither of which will realise a treasure, whether it be Anson's or Kidd's, there will still be believers out there refusing to accept what is staring them in the face saying, "Look, I've spent all this time and money and convinced myself and my partners so I must be right, I don't care what anybody says!" So if they want more evidence of Wilkins' falsification and fabrication of the Kidd/Palmer charts, look no further.

The Damning Evidence

It appears that Wilkins' papers and research notes were not kept by his family after his death but sold to private collectors and are now scattered far and wide. Found amongst papers taken to the USA after his death is what I call my 'Ace' card, which in reality is a postcard having on it an island sketch done by Wilkins.

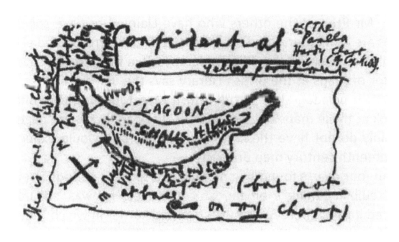

WILKINS' COMPOSITE POSTCARD SKETCH OF 'HIS' ISLAND

As you can see, unmistakably by Wilkins' own hand. Nobody was meant to see this, hence he has headed it 'Confidential'. The writing is easily recognisable now the same as that on the 'Key' chart.

This is the proof that Wilkins had a hand in all the charts and was therefore a major player in the hoax or party to it!

His handwriting style is not easy to read so this is what it says:

Left hand side and corner; *'This is one of four charts identical in shape but not in detail or topography'.*
Top; *'Confidential, The Pamela Hardy Chart (of Cap Kidd), yellow parchment'.*
Bottom; *'Legend at base (but not as on my chart)'.* Note; **my chart.**
On Chart; *'WOODS, LAGOON, SMALL HILLS, Death Valley, coral and sand'. Two 'X's in middle of island.*

Other than the fact this is a Wilkins creation, it is difficult to comment on his notes around the sketch as I do not know at what point during his creation of the charts did he pen this one! For example, he mentions the 'Hardy Chart' which I know had little more than an island outline on it, not legend etc. It was the second chart found by Palmer and had just an island outline with an 'X' in the middle, very similar to the first chart found.

'Death Valley' does not appear on any of the Kidd/Palmer charts, only on the subsequent creations for his book.

So, those of you still actively looking for Kidd's treasure based on the Kidd/Palmer charts, put your buckets and spades away, have a strong cup of tea and quietly thank me for saving you a lot of time, trouble and money! Any monies yet to be invested can be diverted to me c/o the Publishers. The individual mentioned earlier, will, I hope, stop sniping at me now.

I like Ken Kinkor's (of the Whydah Museum in Mass. A trove of pirate lore) quote regarding Kidd's treasure:

'I don't want Kidd's lost treasure. I want all the money that's been spent looking for it!'

Wilkins and the Mystery of the 1947 Book

Having gone silent for the duration of the war to protect the lost treasure, Wilkins recommenced activity in 1947 with the publication of a really strange book titled *New Facts about Mysterious Captain Kidd and his Skeleton Island Chests*. It had a sub-title, *The Strange Story of a Secret Cunningly Hidden for 272 Years and Discovered in 1942.*

There was, however, a change of direction for the clues, the eastern line had been dropped, a combined effect of the war and political instability in the east due to the rise in communism.

This little booklet (only 30 pages) was unknown to me during my Kidd book research so I was intrigued by its title and sub-title; what secret was discovered in 1942? The first two-thirds of the book was taken up with Kidd's story, as known. Wilkins tells it in his usual exaggerated colourful style where in the middle of a particular story he would go off on a tangent with irrelevant ramblings and come back to the main storyline a paragraph or two later! Things start to go wrong when he tells of the discovery of the charts. It is difficult to understand how he gets it so wrong when the collector and finder of the charts, Hubert Palmer, was a personal friend. It begins when he starts talking about the 'Hardy' chest. Now, because as they say, 'I wrote the book,' I knew that the second chart was found in this chest, it being more or less identical to the first chart found. He gets the provenance of the chest right, and also the description of what was engraved on the lid. It all falls apart with the description of the chart. Wilkins describes it as a chart of a coral island in an unnamed sea. Ink used is black and red. It has compass bearings, shows a lagoon and little hills marked with crosses denoting caches. At the bottom a legend directs towards the location of a cache. WRONG!

What Wilkins is describing is in fact the Morgan 'Skull' chart, discovered a year later in 1932. The 'Hardy' chest chart was very basic, showing just an island outline with an 'X' in the middle. I have never seen this chart and don't know anyone living who has. It was discounted by Palmer because it was almost identical to the first chart found in the bureau. The difference was that this first chart included the words 'CHINA SEA', and also a reference to Kidd's wife Sarah and a date, 1669.

The fourth map, which I named the 'Key' chart, he says was found in a brass-bound chest with an engraved plate, 'William and Sarah Kidd. Their Chest'. In fact, it is a box (workbox) no bigger than 12x7x7 inches, and the last part of the engraving on the plate reads 'their box'. The only brass is the engraved plate, hinges and a small brass acorn knob to open the lid. According to Wilkins, the Naval pensioner who offered this box to Palmer had already discovered the hidden map! It had fallen out when he removed some queer-looking nails in the bottom. I will quote from what Wilkins says he wrote in his diary when he examined this chart.

'This chart of Kidd's skeleton island is identical in shape with the other three. It has been carefully drawn by a skilled hand on a piece of musty brown parchment and stuck onto an ancient leather binding which looks as though it had been cut from an old Bible. I pried up the binding carefully and saw that, on the reverse of the parchment, were sentences in the court hand used by legal scriveners in the late 17th century. It is signed 'WK' and dated '1669'! Wrecks, old galleons and briganteens, are marked round the shores of this island, whose waters are clearly reef-sown and dangerous. On two sides of the margin runs a legend in hardly faded black ink. A landing place for a boat is marked. Right through what is called 'DEATH VALLEY' runs a way to a cache in some hills. The marginal directions tell how many feet the hunter must step to reach stakes in a lake. He will find himself amid tropical greenery and palm trees on the sides of a mysterious hill

from where he should hear the roaring of the waves splashing on the beaches of a 'laguna'. No name is given to this skeleton island.'

Well his mind must have been really wandering when he wrote that. Take a look at the actual 'Key' chart found in that box. As you can see, there is no 'DEATH VALLEY', Laguna or Galleons and the 'WK, 1669' comes from the bureau chart. What he is in fact describing is (are) the 'Del Mar' maps (W1 and W2) he created for his book *Captain Kidd and his Skeleton Island*, published in 1935. Even more puzzling is that he wrote the same misleading chart information in that book. It also appears, as we have seen, on his postcard sketch.

I did discover what was important about the year 1942. It was when the document I call the 'Yunnan Parchment' was discovered. I did not know that before, only that it was found some years after the discovery of the 'Key' chart. But he does it again, misleading us with incorrect detail of what was found, yet getting the provenance right. The parchment found, no map this time, it was hidden behind a mirror. It said (according to Wilkins):

"(   ) ISLAND....CHINA SEA. 4th Map. 2 ft Deep. Back of cove in Cliff... under ledge on.....side.

    W. K."

    X.

At this stage, it is easier to show you the actual parchment:

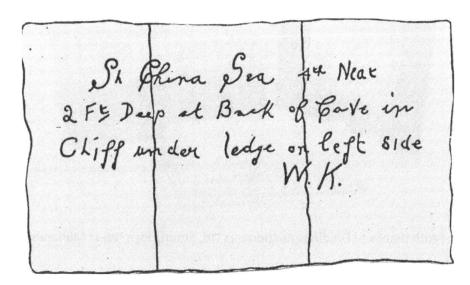

It is called the 'Yunnan Island' parchment because on the back, as if pricked out by a pin, were the words 'YUNNAN ISLAND'. Wilkins mentions none of this. Of puzzling interest is the interpretation of the word 'N?at'. The questionable character I have often thought is a seventeenth century version of the abbreviation for 'and'. So reading 'North and at'. Or is it an 'e'? So reading 'North East at'. Either way, 'Map' it certainly is not! Why does he do it? Beats me! But, of course, it is all irrelevant; you can see that these so-called Kidd/Palmer charts and documents, particularly anything with a reference to the China Sea on it, are all part of a grand strategic deception. The 'China Sea' clue is there to pull you in that direction. When you find HLC Island, you think you've got it, end of quest.

The Auctioneer's Find

An interesting sequel to the above occurred during research for this book. I was contacted by 'Fieldings Auctioneers', who are in the West Midlands. They had three lots coming up for auction believed to have once been the property of Captain William Kidd, they appear below;

(With thanks to Fieldings Auctioneers Ltd, Stourbridge, West Midlands)

I went to the auction in particular to examine the mirror and a (failed) attempt to buy the items. My friend Pat Croce of the Pirate Museum in Florida successfully bid for them. The mirror is the 'Yunnan Island' mirror. You can see crudely inscribed on the top a 'W' and a 'K' with a skull and crossbones symbol in between; these already make the item suspicious. On examination, I could see the mirror was obviously of the right age and period. Above the skull and crossbones was a small arrow, and directly behind this was a hidden compartment. This compartment was covered by parchment (as was all of the back). Marked out by dots as if pricked out by a pin were the words YUNNAN ISLAND, one above the other. The specially constructed compartment was just over two inches square and directly behind the skull, it contained the parchment shown previously that would have been folded three times then in half. Someone has inserted into the space a piece of paper (below).

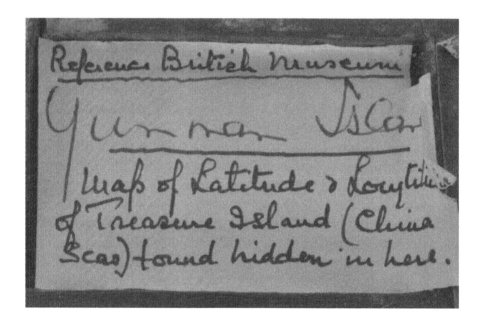

This is wrong information, as we know; the map with the latitude and longitude on was the 'Key' chart found in the workbox. The St James Bible is obviously very old and of the period; marked on the front cover and very faded was, 'Kidd's Family Bible, Pentland Farm, Leith, Edinburgh'. On the back cover, again very faded, was, 'Capt, Wm Kidd, Ship Adventure Galley', all in old English text. But, if you were nominating the Bible as that of the family, wouldn't you start with, 'The Kidd Family Bible....'? The carved oak Bible box has a hinged lid over a carved double lunette front. Below the lock plate, the initials 'WK' are inscribed. Unfortunately the label on the lid is completely faded. All of these items I recognised as coming from the Palmer collection auction sale in 1950. They remained out of the public view until the present-day auctioneers were asked to value the contents of a house in Peterborough; they were found lying under the grand piano! These items do appear to be of the right age and period. The only comment I will make is the same as that to other correspondents regarding the whole Kidd saga and mystery; fakers were very expert at turning any old box or piece of furniture into something the subsequent owner believed it to be. This is not to say, of course, that some items and relics in Palmer's collection may have been the genuine article. Something I found very strange and a little spooky was that Kidd was brought up at Pentland Farm, and the publishers of my Kidd book were Pentland Press! Anyway, back to the topic in hand.

I suspect Wilkins copied the style of the 'Yunnan Parchment' from a similar document in a book mentioned in an earlier chapter; *Captain Kidd's Gold*, published in 1888. I also suspect that the front page title is a mistake and was to have read (in part) ..... 'Skeleton Island Charts' and not 'Skeleton Island Chests'. The remainder of the book is taken up with Kidd related treasure stories, some we know, some new. The only one I want to repeat here is because Spain and the Salvage Islands is the subject and they are part of the treasure story. Wilkins writes (Spelling and grammar are as original. *GE*):

'Kidd's own statement before the "Tabellion notary" in Boston, in 1669, was that he touched at Madeira and two neighbouring islands only on the outward voyage of the "Adventure Galley" and took in salt and fresh water. This has also inspired a story about which I am frequently asked by USA folk, that Kidd cached $3,000,000 in gold in

the Salvage Islands, near Madeira. In May, 1934, there was actually an expedition by an adventurous British naval captain who chartered a steam yacht in London, and, with a dowser and witching wand, set out to find and dig up this Salvage island treasure. Let me say, at once, that, again, Kidd was never ashore in the Salvage Islands, and that this treasure was cached by Spanish mutineers in a much later day when Britain was blockading Spain, to which a gold laden Spanish galleon was bound from Spanish American ports. The British Admiralty actually sent a king's ship to the Salvage Islands, in 1813, but they merely blasted the rocks with gunpowder and sea-faring oaths and sailed away more empty than they come.'

The complete story of the above (1813) treasure hunt involving our Navy is told in my Kidd book. The same applies regarding the stories of the circumstances surrounding the discoveries of all the charts. I end this chapter only by saying, once again "A strange book. Can't figure out why Wilkins wrote it!" –Unless, –maybe he was purposely drawing attention to it! For included within the booklet was the story about marks on a boulder in Nova Scotia. Readers of my book will be familiar with these marks and I show two similar versions but that's another story. However, some of the markings he says read:

EIE KIDD 1670

My problem with this is that this line of characters does not appear as depicted on any of the previously published drawings of the boulder(s). So why has he introduced these characters? Why has he highlighted this group in particular? When you know how Wilkins works, you can guess that something ulterior is going on and anything unusual deserves looking at a little more closely. A code therefore but we have to find out what type of code it is, or more correctly, whose code it is, before we reveal its secret (in Part 9), which is in fact a coded reference to the treasure.

Real Faking

H.T. Wilkins, we have seen, was quite a character; besides writing profusely about treasure stories from around the world, he points the finger where necessary to those who cross his path. Amongst others, these included the Japanese and those who used his charts as a basis for creating their own fake charts. It is amusing to me to read how he admonishes those who fake charts knowing all the time that he was guilty of it himself. He writes about how it was done and condemns those who do it; it is a sort of smokescreen allowing the reader to side with him and so believe that he (Wilkins) would never step *that* low. In his *Panorama of Treasure Hunting*, he writes in particular about the 'Cocos Island crooks' and their chart-faking factory somewhere downtown in New York. The fact is, the 'business' of creating fake treasure charts has been going on for hundreds of years and whilst maybe not so common today, up until modern times i.e. prior to WW2, it was a prolific international business.

The secret to creating a 'genuine' treasure chart is the paper; it must be, or appear to be, of seventeenth or eighteenth century stock. If you couldn't get your hand on some genuine ancient parchment or vellum (fine parchment), the next best was a plain leaf out of the old family Bible. These usually had the brown stains of age on them and about the size one would expect a chart to be. If there were palimpsest marks on the page, better still; it all adds to the intrigue. Today, modern light-shaded brown parchment (or vellum) paper, ripped to create antiquity, soaked and stained here and there with tea and/or coffee of different strengths, buried in the garden for awhile, then folded and crumpled a bit before flattening out, is not a bad substitute for the real thing. Follow this with the line, "Excuse me, Sur! You looks like an intelijeckle (Popeye comes to mind!) kinda man. Looks what I found stuck behind the cuva of an old Bible I found in a junk shop! Any idea if ict's worth anyfink? Give me twenty quid and yuse can ave it. I wouldn't know what to do wiv it." And so, twenty pounds richer, he moves on to the next sucker with another copy.

You would be forgiven for thinking that all this tarradiddle belongs to a time past but no, it was happening at the beginning of this century. Someone in the States had for sale an 'Authentic 1634 Pirate Treasure Map'. He says that when looking through a seventeenth century Dutch Bible, he found that there were hundreds of pieces of old paper placed in almost every page. Upon further examination, he noticed that the front and rear covers were unusually thick. Closer examination of the front cover revealed that a wooden panel could be removed to reveal a secret compartment, and it contained a folded parchment. It was, as he said, 'an actual pirate treasure map signed by the pirate himself'. Photographs were available of the map 'written in an older type of English' and showed Indian villages, harbours, ships, trees and other marks, 'one of which are 3 triangles clustered together'. Written below a symbol of a circle with a cross on it was the word "Booty".

Some things just never change!

I have in my possession a copy of a letter from the Home Office Forensic Science Laboratory, dated August 1951. They were asked to examine and report on the Bureau Chart. I repeat the final concluding paragraph here:

'In view of the forgoing, in my opinion, the only conclusion which is justified on the evidence is that the initials 'W. K.' were not signed by Captain Kidd and that other evidence points to the map being a comparatively recent production on what might very well be an old sheet of parchment.'

The same report makes the point that the characters/writing was not written with any of the coloured inks in use in the 17th century. So it all adds up to more proof of a fraud being perpetrated. Again, does one argue with such a respected establishment?

Having the right paper does not, of course, guarantee a sale. The cartography, calligraphy, detail and style must look right for the period in question. Some can spot a fake a mile away, others wouldn't have a clue; if it looks right, it must be! So, 'caveat ěmptor'. That the paper may test as genuine, as we have seen, does not mean that the chart is! One of the most common mistakes of chart fakers is basing the outline of their island on the current version available, forgetting, or not being aware, that 200 or 300 years ago there was no way one could accurately draw the outline shape of any island. Charts of the time were usually hopelessly inaccurate. Here is an example from fairly modern times.

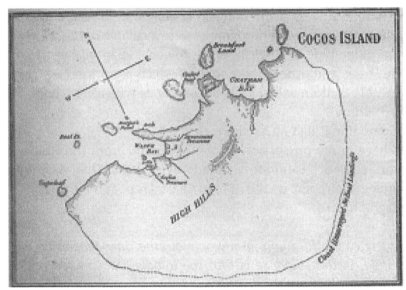

COCOS ISLAND CHART, CIRCA 1902

Compare with the following from a 1942 survey.

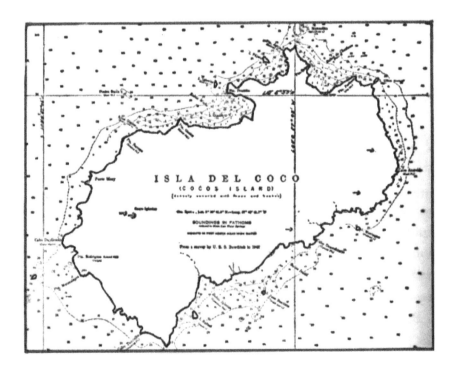

Cocos Island, as you have already read, is probably *the* most famous real treasure island and another device was to slip the 'real, antique genuine chart' into a book published in the early 19th century. The book would have been one that a scholar or educated person might have read. The idea was to create a 'vision', to evoke in the 'victim's' mind that the book owner was of a type not easily fooled, was studious and careful, but ultimately a disappointed man who, armed with his chart, went to Cocos in his day and came back empty-handed. He stuck his chart in a book on his shelf and promptly forgot all about it.

The confidence trickster also plays on the fact that his victim is probably more than half a crook himself, since he knowingly seeks something for nothing. He feels smug about the fact that he has got the better of an exceedingly good-natured old gentleman who may have appeared to be a little defective mentally, but happy to get rid of a chart which was of no use to him anymore.

Wilkins also makes a comment on another fake chart he talks about which is worth noting, for as he says 'brushed' upon it in 'atrocious dog Latin' was:

'Vista Interiora Terra
Rectificando Invenies
Occultum Lapadem (or Lapatem).'

Wilkins translates this as:
'Interior view of the land, For rectification, thou shalt, or wilt find the hidden stone'.
The original phrase, coming to us from the world of Alchemy via the acronym for VITRIOL is:
'Visita Interiora Terrae Rectificando Invenies Occultum Lapidem'.
Which translates to:
'Visit the Interior Parts of the Earth; by Rectification Thou Shalt Find the Hidden Stone'.

The explanation of why this alchemical phrase came to be written on pirate treasure charts is a bit advanced for now. You will just have to wait until we get there.

Confusion and Intrigue - Far East Style

During research for my Kidd book, I was always a little suspicious of the charts for a lot of the reasons previously mentioned, but then, *we find the island* they depict off Hong Kong. What a quandary! But as research continued after the book's publication, it became obvious that the charts are indeed a hoax but via the number code very cleverly based on a real island in the South China Sea. This became difficult to comprehend because as you have seen, the charts when inverted are really based on JF Island. This was a major predicament, two real islands, both meeting the identification requirements of the 'Key' chart. There is no doubt Wilkins, probably in league with another, created the 'Key' chart. You might say that the cartographic style on these charts do not match his earlier JF maps. Well of course not; that would have given the game away immediately.

With research for this book opening up the JF link, my interest in the Kidd/China Sea Island waned. No point in pursuing it; all part of a grand hoax or conspiracy. But then you ask the question - why were these charts created with a China Seas link? To recreate the China Sea Island and its position so accurately with its (coded) coordinates indicated prior knowledge. Where did Wilkins get it from? Was Wilkins' 'Hong Kong Pilot' friend a part of it? And is it just an incredible coincidence that it was so similar to JF Island? Or maybe the Pilot recognised it as a good match for JF and tipped Wilkins off to this fact. (This could be how Mrs. Dick was able to say the island was near Hong Kong.) You could also ask the question, "What if none of the charts had ever been found by Palmer?" Where would we be now? As we have seen, they were, of course, expertly planted in items of Kidd's furniture and knowing the thoroughness with which Palmer searched such items, they were meant to be found. (The stories in my Kidd book, surrounding the circumstances of some of Palmer's purchases, are quite amusing and smack of dialogue straight out of *Treasure Island* - thereby adding further suspicion.)

It seems clear to me now that sometime during the years prior to WW2 and maybe after, Wilkins became aware of important documents/information pointing to a great treasure on JF Island (more on this later). The Kidd/Palmer charts came to light during this period i.e. prior to the war. Palmer was duped. Wilkins had to have them 'discovered' somehow. He created them to lure treasure hunters *away* from JF. He wanted to keep this newly discovered treasure to himself. Why else? It was very cleverly done; a lot of work went into it, but to what purpose other than that suggested? This might sort of wrap the mystery up albeit untidily, otherwise how do you make the connection to this other real island in the China Seas that is an almost perfect fit to the 'Key' chart - and the coded figures confirm it? The trouble is; the 'Key' chart is by subterfuge cleverly depicting JF Island, there is no doubt about that and what with the inclusion of the triangle of circles, Wilkins is showing he knows about the Trinity. (Later on, you will see that these three circles have a dual depiction.) Besides that, I show in a later chapter how he is also hiding a positional reference to the Trinity group in one of the charts. To tantalise the reader and further suggest the China Seas, he wrote an article in the November 1936 issue of *Modern Mechanix Hobbies and Invention.* The article was titled *Maps Spur New Hunt for Kidd Treasure.* It starts off with *'I am laying plans to land on a mysterious island in a far eastern ocean'.* What follows is a misleading story of the charts and how they were found and at the end. I quote:

'All I can say is that even the British Admiralty's Charts do not show this island, which lies in very dangerous waters of which its sailing directions say: Coral reefs abound.....by day and night, navigators must keep a sharp look-out and the lead going. It would be well to give this region a wide berth in foul weather, or in the dark'.

Juan Fernandez Island was known, of course, to our Admiralty so is he trying to throw people off the scent here, or indeed hinting at a South China Seas Island? But then neither of these islands abound with coral reefs, atolls in the South Pacific Ocean do!

Another clue appearing on the Key chart is 'NORTH SA E', i.e. NE, this is reoccurring DNA. In another way, the letters are also saying 'North Same As East'. Many have assumed there is a missing letter 'F' here and it should read 'NORTH SAFE' i.e. indicating a safe anchorage, which would normally make sense and this was obviously the intention. In fact, when you now turn the Key chart through the required 90 degrees (N same as E), its orientation is corrected to exactly that of Hei Ling Chau Island in the South China Sea. More evidence this is indeed the island of the charts you were meant to find to sidetrack you away from JF. You can also see now that the 72NE angle (36NE+36NE) when measured from the 'Anchorage' takes you to the middle of the word 'TURTLES' i.e. highlighting this word, drawing your attention to it. Without the JF connection, you are allowed to think that 'T' (also because of other intersections here) is where the Treasure is. The 'LAGOON' is, of course, hinting at a coral island, more subterfuge by Wilkins.

If it were just these clues, the 'Key' chart, and JF Island, it would all be more or less clear; all part of the trail to a treasure on JFI, end of story! But the glaring anomaly of the evidence of a real South China Seas Island with the accompanying work and detail that went into creating the deceit, throws things a bit. These anomalies tend to put into the shade the brilliancy of the work involved in using Hei Ling Chau Island and its coordinates, and as we will see later, very cleverly using the Key chart figures with those associated with JF Island to pinpoint our real lost treasure island a long way from here. It does not alter the end result and is but a minor quandary in the grand scheme of the lost treasure.

There seems to be no doubt then that prior to the 1940s, Wilkins and others were conducting some ongoing plan to place a series of clues within books and fake maps that led to something important. One level of clues (the Kidd side) had you searching for an island somewhere in the eastern seas which matched the shape of that on the charts. It can therefore be deduced that the shape of the island was somehow the important factor rather than the actual identity of the island: whatever was intended to be given next as a clue was something to be used on an island of the specific shape to match the 1795 chart of JF. It seems the intent was to let the puzzle sort out the wheat from the chaff as Wilkins sat back and watched various groups or individuals expend time and money chasing Kidd's non-existent treasure. At least he included in the puzzle the redeeming feature that if you made it to the correct shaped island, you might just learn something there... if you suddenly woke up to it all (the story of Anson's treasure). For Wilkins' part, it does not seem that malicious glee was the motivation in doing the puzzle this way but a security measure to screen all comers, so only the correct person 'got it' and the rest 'got what they deserved' by their own cupidity.

The trouble is, for whatever theory you want to come up with about this 'Eastern Island', at the same time another deeper level of clues were being hidden in his books that had you searching for clues about a trinity group of islands and something hidden there. To the frustration of followers of the 'Kidd chart line', the trail of clues to the east left by Wilkins ended without any real resolution or reconciliation between the two. Partially, the reason why this side was dropped can be explained by the conflagration that engulfed the globe known as WW2, with the eastern seas falling under the glare of the Rising Sun. This left the locations carefully selected and, planned over the previous ten years, now occupied and unapproachable. But an event during the period leading up to the outbreak of war involving Wilkins and his charts was the main cause.

Wilkins drew two charts loosely depicting JF Island, known as the 'Del Mar' maps (shown previously as Charts W1 and W2). They appeared in his *Captain Kidd and his Skeleton Island* book. One of these maps was stolen from Wilkins in 1938 by 'Japanese fishermen alias secret service men', as Wilkins informs us in his *Panorama of Treasure Hunting*. That map, the author subsequently learnt via a Reuter newspaper telegram from Tokyo, was used by the 'fishermen' on a vain hunt for a treasure island, which it was, alas and vainly, thought to have been in Japanese territorial waters. I find this strange as the chart profile is nothing like that of Japan or any of its islands. It can be said though that the general mainland profile of Japan is very similar to that of the 'Skull Chart'. Not only that, when that map is orientated NS correctly, it corresponds to that of Japan. Another tenuous fact is that the centre of Japan has a longitudinal figure important to us, as you will see. To add to the mystery, there is a treasure legend here known as the Tokugawa Treasure. However, Wilkins finished the chapter in his usual colourful style with this admonition:

'All is not as it seems, my dear negrito Asiatics of chrysanthemum and cherry blossom land, and if, once again, you blandly and honourably plow the author's pastures, you will find that it is for your coulters, rather a sterile soil. We Occidentals, have a proverb: A woman does not tell all she knows of a secret.'

We know what he's getting at; they were way off the mark! This was, however, more than disconcerting for Wilkins, for this map was not merely for Captain Kidd's mythical treasure but actually contained clues integral to the lost treasure, as will be seen later. The stereotypical image portrayed by Wilkins of 1940's Hollywood-style Japanese spies was not accurate either. In fact, the Japanese Kempeitai, a ruthless organisation, was tasked to find something that the Emperor sought and which Wilkins was now known to be publishing coded clues for. It wasn't only the Japanese after the lost treasure either; the Germans, as you will learn, had their own man on the job.

In conclusion regarding all of the above, **nobody will ever find Kidd's treasure based on the Kidd/Palmer charts** and in reality Wilkins and Co could just as easily used any other pirate's name to be associated with them.

I will remind you, Kidd's name was probably used because during his trial, in an attempt to buy himself out, he declared in a letter to the Speaker of the House of Commons, '....*I have lodged goods and Treasure to the value of one hundred thousand pounds......*' The Lords took no notice.

Associating Kidd to the charts was a good ploy; it added to the intrigue making them more plausible. It helps, if you want to convince someone of the veracity of your fake/hoax to introduce a real name and a few facts. Blinded by the vision of a chest full of gold, jewellery and silver, it usually works and is still doing so to this day! We have seen Captain Brown was very good at this form of deceit.

Scrimshaw Maps

There are probably more than a few people out there with scrimshaw showing the Kidd/Palmer charts. As the subject matter is topical, it is opportune to discuss them now.

A couple of years after my Kidd book was published and before my work on this book, I was contacted by a Mr Brian Harris telling me that he had an example of scrimshaw engraved with maps and whilst Kidd wasn't mentioned, the maps looked familiar. For those not familiar with what scrimshaw are, I will explain that it was a pastime of sailors of old to make engravings of a nautical nature on typically a whale's tooth.

I had never heard of or seen this particular scrimshaw and assuming it was an original genuine one-off scrimshaw, wouldn't have expected to. At my request, Mr Harris sent me a drawing of the engraving, I was amazed to see that from the shape of the islands and the attendant information, they were without doubt copies of the Kidd/Palmer charts. OR, was this the original and the charts were copies off it? I was naturally quite excited and wanted to examine this scrimshaw in detail, and in particular to see if I could read more into the longitude shown. Understandingly, Brian wouldn't part with his scrimshaw.

After my appearance in 2000 on ITV's show *Find a Fortune*, Mr Don Arnold of Eastbourne in Sussex contacted me. He said the same as Brian; he had a scrimshaw showing maps that looked the same as those I showed on the TV programme. Alarm bells started to ring. There can't be two scrimshaws showing the same... can there? Unless Kidd, or whoever, purposely made two copies. On questioning Don, he said he had purchased the scrimshaw, together with one or two other pieces at a church bazaar or boot sale about 10 years before. He kindly sent photographs, we eventually did a deal and I bought it off him.

Sadly, I soon discovered it was a reproduction. Brian and Don's examples were identical, even to the palm trees and Indian shown. Whilst the engravings were superbly done with wonderful detail, I could see they were made of polyester resin and marble powder. They *were* difficult to tell from the real thing. What a let down, but the artist must have copied them off the Kidd/Palmer charts or copies of them. Who was he? What did he use as his master? It may have even been a different source; I had to explore the possibility. Fortunately, I was selling a similar product in my shop at that time. To cut a long story short, after much detective work and a lot of phone calls, I finally tracked down the artist. It was John Adams, who lives in Sussex. He sent me a copy of the old Atlas map he copied to create the surrounding/background artwork showing an Indian and palm trees but just could not remember what he used to draw the charts. He said it was done as a private commission years ago. Ah well, that's life.

A bigger surprise was to come. A year or two later, MN told me he possessed two different ones. One the same as I had, the other with an engraving of Kidd and his ship as well as the charts! It looks as if those scrimshaw copies are out there, sprouting up like mushrooms around the world!

ENLARGED DETAIL OF ONE OF THE TUSK SCRIMSHAWS

THIS 'KIDD' SCRIMSHAW PIECE IS APPROXIMATELY 14CM HIGH
ENGRAVING OF KIDD'S SHIP THE 'ADVENTURE GALLEY' IS ON REVERSE

Pirate Captain Kidd's treasure found in Madagascar

The above were the headlines splashed across the world in May 2015. A headline indicating that there is/was a treasure to be found attributed to Kidd and it has now been found. This is further proof of the hint I have been giving throughout this book; just because it says so in a newspaper/book/radio/documentary, doesn't mean it's true!

A silver bar was found by explorer Barry Clifford on a wreck on the island of Sainte Marie, Madagascar, it was presented with great ceremony to the president of Madagascar. The report goes on to say; 'The location of the ship, thought to have sunk in 1698, has been known about for many years but the silver bar was only discovered this week.'

To those 'not in the know', you would be forgiven for thinking Kidd's ship had sunk, the wreck found and this silver bar recovered. Facts are; Kidd, because his ship the Adventure Galley was by this time in no fit state to sail – half full of water and resting on a sand bar, had her stripped and her hull burned for its iron. It raises the obvious question; If Clifford's wreck was Kidd's ship, – would Kidd have left any silver bars on board??

'Since the above report, a team from Unesco, the United Nations cultural body visited the site and in their report said (sic) 'the silver' ingot was just a lead weight/ballast and the supposed shipwreck was old rubble in a bay of Sainte-Marie, a small island east of Madagascar.'

I don't think I'll comment any more on that.

Earlier in the chapter about Wilkins and his '1947' book, we mentioned marks chiselled into boulders on an island in Nova Scotia. This leads us nicely into the next story which is about the 'Money Pit' on the infamous 'treasure island' known as Oak Island, which is at the western end of St Margarets Bay, Nova Scotia. This will take us deeper into related stories which will give us more evidence and testimony to our quest for the treasure. You will see also that we have not finished yet with our Mr Wilkins.

In conclusion regarding this part of the book and the Wilkins/Palmer/Kidd charts saga, they are, as you have seen, a fraud/ruse/deception to take you to HLC island off Hong Kong, away from Wilkins' JF island where the clues to Anson's treasure lay. You would be saying, "Very clever, so this is where we can find the treasure," and unless you were aware of the real story, you would be unloading your pick and shovel here. But it is just a stepping stone in the quest for our treasure. Wilkins knew it; you will see later on how his hidden clues are really pointing to a lonely atoll a long way from here.

CHAPTER 3

OAK ISLAND

You may be querying at this point, 'Why are we going to an Island in the North Atlantic which is nowhere near our apparent theatre of operations i.e. the Pacific Ocean?' The reason is, you will see we come quickly into contact with our Mr Wilkins again, and not only that, there are strong connections here with Captain Kidd. So the stories here have to be examined and explored to see what can be gleaned. If anything, that may add clues and information to our continuing quest.

Located off the south coast of Nova Scotia in Mahone Bay, this island equals Cocos Island with its popularity as the location of buried treasure. A hunt for treasure in the infamous Money Pit has been going on here for over 200 years and carries on to this day.

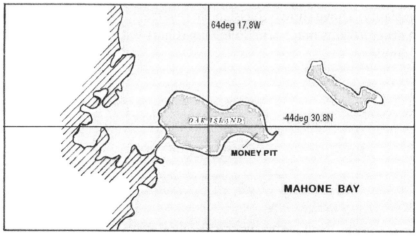

Oak Island, Approx. 0.83Miles long x 0.4Miles at its widest. A modern causeway about 200yds long links it to the mainland.

Oak Island Comparability

If it were possible to 'morph' all the previous JF maps, especially including all the Wilkins versions, with some imagination you could come up with a shape similar to this:

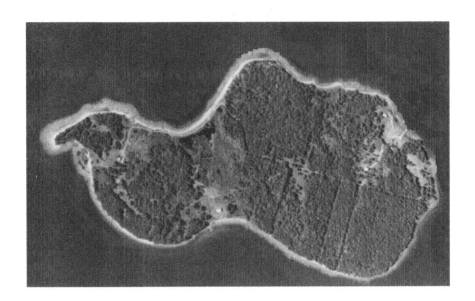

This aerial photograph is, of course, of Oak Island (causeway removed for clarity). I have shown the island in reverse, to show how it is similar to other Wilkins maps. The following (Chart W1) 'Mar Del' map is an example:

Mistaken Identity?

The similarity of the island shapes put Wilkins in something of a quandary. In the 1930s, Gilbert Heddon, one of the searchers on the island was shown a copy of Wilkins' book *Captain Kidd and his Skeleton Island*. He looked at the two maps on the inside covers including that opposite. This together with the various features and similarities, led him to believe they may be of Oak Island. You can see why when looking at the opposite aerial photograph. In particular, he looked at the directions and using them made some discoveries including a triangle of stones not seen for 40 years.

There has always been a legend that Captain Kidd buried his treasure here. These map discoveries, together with the other similarities, convinced Heddon that Kidd must have buried his treasure here. He travelled to England in 1938 and traced Wilkins who was (acted?) dumbfounded when told of the similarities between his chart and Oak Island. He said there could be no possible connection between his charts and an island in Nova Scotia; he had never even seen Oak Island. That last slightly misleading statement by Wilkins may or may not be true but he certainly knew about Oak Island having written about it four years previously. Heddon's interjection could be one of the reasons why in future years, particularly after the war, Wilkins seemed to switch his energies to Oak Island and its treasure mysteries. This was strange when you consider the efforts he had already put into the JF/Kidd maps.

But all was not quite as it seems and true to form, Wilkins was playing with the reader and maintaining the JF link. At the bottom of one of his created maps, he makes the strange statement, 'It waits to be found by a modern treasure hunter.' and the title of his 1948 book? *A Modern Treasure Hunter*! It tells the story of Oak Island focusing in particular on the folk lore, myths, legends and ghost stories. The content regarding the Money Pit itself is merely repeating that found in other books. I have to recount Oak Island's history here in order that you can understand the revelations to come. My version is repeating the traditional story, then trying to authenticate and complement it using contemporary reports and newspaper articles of the time. Some respected works were also consulted. Some of these early reports have been conveniently ignored by some authors and those trying to create 'investment' opportunities. It is much more convincing and exciting to point to the workings and say to the punter, "Look! There's the hole, there's treasure down there somewhere!" For me, it seems to be the old adage; someone's dug a hole here, so there must be something down there!

From the above comments, you may be forgiven for thinking there may be a little sarcasm here (again) and you would be right. Read what follows; it is then up to you, the reader, to make your own mind up.

Oak Island, the Early History

The popular history of Oak Island I have found has its comparisons with the 'Loot of Lima' story. A lot of authors have copied what was written before and because *'someone said'* there was a treasure here, then it is accepted there is! And, as I have said, a lot of authors also seem to conveniently ignore certain worrying aspects, or maybe their research was not diligent enough to start with. Either way, one has to go back as early as possible to try and find out the origins of this story and what has been going on.

The traditional story starts in 1795 and goes like this; a teenager, Daniel McGinnis, out canoeing for the day, landed on the south-eastern shore of Oak Island and went exploring. It is said the first thing he noticed was a semi-submerged boulder into which was fixed a heavy ringbolt. Following an ancient path up from the beach, in the middle of the woods he came across a clearing (the island carried a dense growth of Oak trees). Some old stumps of trees were visible but an ancient gnarled oak tree remained in the centre of the clearing. About 16 feet up, a branch had been lopped short and below that McGinnis noticed a shallow depression in the ground. Another version says that the lopped branch had an old pulley block attached to it and this hung directly above the depression.

I will introduce a sentence here from the *Liverpool Transcript* newspaper in 1862 as it adds some important (and different) information;

'Sometime after the arrival of these persons, a Mr McGinnes went to Oak Island to make a farm, when he discovered the spot in question from its being sunken, and from the position of three oak trees, which stood in a triangular form around the pit.'

A report that appeared just a year later said that just old stumps of oak trees were visible. This possibly is what gave Wilkins the idea to write in the left hand margin of the Kidd/Palmer map '3 Stumps'. On that same map, he shows three small circles in a triangle in a clearing! Note again, the Triangle DNA. To continue with the history:

His curiosity aroused, McGinnis returned the next day with two friends, John Smith aged 20 and Anthony Vaughan aged 13. One of the boys climbed up the tree and pushed the pulley block, it fell to the ground and shattered, suggesting it was already of great age. At this time, they also discovered the remains of an old track running across the middle of the island from east to west. Brought up on a coast the haunt of pirates, with boyish excitement and enthusiasm, they decided either a treasure was buried or was sought here. It had to be investigated. It wasn't long before they were back with picks and spades and started to clear out the loose earth they found in the depression. Eventually, they found themselves in a well-defined circular shaft about 13 feet diameter, hard clay with pick marks defined the walls. Just two feet further down, they struck a layer of flagstones; these were not indigenous to the island and came, they guessed, from a river a couple of miles away. At about ten feet, they found a platform of oak logs. The logs were rotten but the ends were firmly embedded in the pit wall. Having cleared them out, they carried on digging, the subsoil was easily removed with the shovels. Another ten feet down, they came to another platform of oak logs. Beneath this was more soil, which had settled about two feet below the platform. Ten feet further down at the 30 feet level was another log platform but it is not clear if they found this platform at that time.

At this point, they realised the task was too much for them. They covered the pit over and left three stakes to mark the spot. It was to be nine years before they had the backing to resume digging for the treasure they were convinced lay just a few feet further down. To facilitate their search, McGinnis and Smith settled on the island. It is on record that in June 1795, Smith purchased Lot 18, the area that contained the site of the discovery. By 1825, he had acquired lots 16, 17, 19 and 20. You can see from the following plan, this comprised all the land to the east of the discovery and probably because he owned the land, the bay (where McGinnis had landed) became known as 'Smith's Cove'. Rupert Furneaux, in his *Money Pit the Mystery of Oak*

Island (1972) says it was also called 'Smugglers Cove'. This should 'ring a bell', as this also appears on the Kidd/Palmer 'Key' chart.

What is interesting about the survey diagram that follows is having been carried out ten years before McGinnis landed here, **it is obvious this is no deserted, unexplored island**. Being a small island, the early purchasers and/or surveyors would have been well aware of any obvious clearing with an equally obvious depression in the ground, and a singular old oak tree adjacent to it, with a pulley block!

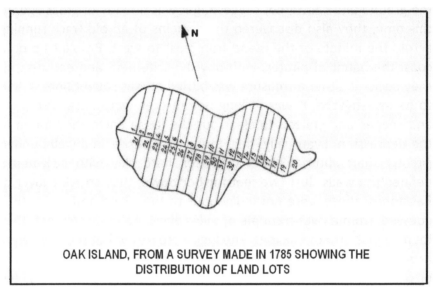

OAK ISLAND, FROM A SURVEY MADE IN 1785 SHOWING THE
DISTRIBUTION OF LAND LOTS

The island was thus well known to the people of Shoreham just across the bay (now Chester), the town having been established some 36 years prior to the pit discovery.

To continue with the traditional story:

In 1804, Vaughan showed Simeon Lynds, a relative of his, their discovery made nine years previously. Lynds immediately took interest and went home to form a company.

The Colonist, 2 January, 1864 records:

'The late Simeon Lynds of Onslow, a man well known in many parts of Colchester County, at the time happened to visit Chester on business. As Lynds' father and Vaughan were related, he called and passed an evening with him. In the course of conversation during the night, Lynds was let into the secret of the 'Pit' on Oak Island, and the opinion

entertained about it by Vaughan and his companions. The next day Vaughan crossed over to the place with Simeon Lynds, in a boat, to let him pass his own judgment upon it. The result of Lynds' visit was that he became of Vaughan's way of thinking.

Lynds was then a young man (about thirty years) and his father (Thomas Lynds) was in comfortable circumstances, and he had a good many well-to-do friends. He concluded to go home, form a company among them, to assist the pioneers in the search after the treasure and to complete it.'

The newly formed Lynds, or Onslow Syndicate, recommenced excavations in 1804. Some books say that oak platforms were found at 10 foot levels all the way down to 90 feet. However, the early accounts make no mention of oak platforms below 30 feet. Ten feet levels do appear to be defined though beyond 30 feet and made up of levels of charcoal, coconut fibre and putty. It is not clear if these materials were combined at each level or separate. Unfortunately, the Onslow Syndicate did not keep any records of their excavations. All we know is that reported in newspaper accounts and journals many years later, and the inevitable discrepancies make it difficult to interpret exactly what went on. For example, one of the searchers who worked on the island in 1863 (after the Onslow Syndicate) states: 'at forty feet a tier of charcoal; at fifty feet a tier of smooth stones from the beach with figures and letters cut on them; at sixty feet a tier of manilla grass and the rind of a coconut; at seventy feet a tier of putty. Another version says that putty was spread over a platform of logs at the forty foot level.'

A major discovery was apparently made at the 90 foot level when a large inscribed flagstone was discovered. The strange characters cut into the face were undecipherable to the finders. Reports vary on the size of this stone but it appears to have been between two and three feet long, 16 inches wide and up to 10 inches thick, so very heavy. The stone was last seen in 1919, left in premises that had closed down; it had been used for beating leather. One wonders why this important discovery was treated with such disregard over the years. After its discovery, the stone was incorporated into the fireplace of Smith's home on the island. In about the mid 1860s, it was taken to Halifax to have the inscription deciphered. James Liechti, a professor of languages, is credited with deciphering the inscription to read; 'Ten feet below two million pounds lie buried'. Another account says it was 'forty feet', not ten. At this time, the inscriptions were almost illegible anyway. For many years after, it was on display in the window of a Halifax bookbinding firm before being put to use by them. Searches in the years since have failed to locate the stone.

Excavation proceeded down to the 93 foot level where the soil was getting very wet and soft. Probing five feet deeper with rods, they encountered resistance which some thought was wood, possibly chests. However, it was Saturday evening and work had to shut down for the night. One can imagine the excitement and speculative chatter about what they hoped to find the next morning. Alas, it was with total disbelief, on returning to the workings they discovered the pit had 60 feet of water in it i.e. to sea level. With their basic equipment, it was impossible to bail out.

Work was suspended for a year and they then decided to dig another pit alongside, about 14 feet south-east, and go down deeper, below the treasure level, and tunnel through to the pit. They almost achieved this without too many problems, other than those involved with digging a new pit. They started the lateral tunnel at about 110 feet and got to within about two feet of the pit but then mud, water and debris burst through. The workers were lucky to escape with their lives and once again, with great disappointment, they watched as their new pit filled with water in a couple of hours to the same level as that in the Money Pit. It was obvious there was somewhere an insurmountable underground link to the pits with the sea. This apparently was not obvious to the diggers at that time.

This was the end of the first attempt at excavating the Money Pit. The Onslow Syndicate abandoned the dig having run out of funds.

This is more or less the traditional story of the early years as handed down and impossible to corroborate, as no proper records were kept.

The Dig Goes On

It was to be over 40 years before another syndicate was formed. Vaughan and Smith were still alive and enthusiastic about the unrecovered treasure. McGinnes had disappeared from the scene. The new venture, known as the Truro Syndicate, started work in 1849. Vaughan had identified the original site for them which was a large caved-in area full of debris, mud, water and timber. The adjacent shaft, over the years appears to have collapsed into the first. It took nearly two weeks to clear the hole out down to 86 feet and the flooding appeared to have subsided. An account of these activities, written in December 1863, appeared in *The Colonist* in 1864 and carries on;

'Sabbath morning came and no sign of water, more than usual appearing in the pit, the men left for church in Chester Village with lighter hearts. At two o'clock they returned from church, and to their great surprise found water standing in the pit, to the depth of sixty feet, being on a level with that in the Bay.'

So they were, in effect, set back to how the workings were left 45 years previous, with nothing new to show for it. Undeterred, they erected a platform in the pit just above water level in order to probe the lower depths with a pod-auger. Five holes, each a few feet apart, were bored down to 106 feet. Jotham McCully, operations manager, in his later report stated:

'We went through the platform at 98 feet originally sounded by the first diggers, this was five inches thick. The auger dropped twelve inches and then went through four inches of oak; then it went through twenty-two inches of metal in pieces; but the auger failed to bring up anything in the nature of treasure, except three links resembling the links of an ancient watch chain. It then went through eight inches of oak, which was thought to be the bottom of the first box and the top of the next; then twenty-two inches of metal, the same as before; then four inches of oak and six inches of spruce, then into clay seven feet without striking anything.'

The other boreholes produced similar results including evidence of a brown fibrous substance. As Rupert Furneaux says in his book, "What did these borings really disclose? Did the chests filled with metal and the piece of gold chain (some say it was copper!) exist other than in the fervid imagination of people to whom the wish was father to the thought? We can conclude only that the 1849 borings disclosed objects at the depth of ninety-eight feet which *may* have been oak chests."

In 1850, a new shaft was started to the north-west of the pit and about 10 feet from it. The intention was again to excavate to below the 98 foot level then tunnel across to below the supposed chests. But exactly the same thing happened as that experienced by their predecessors; the men lucky to escape with their lives, and they watched as once again their new pit slowly filled up. It appears it wasn't until about this time they realised there was a link with the water level in the pit(s) to that of the sea. A thorough search was made of the shoreline which resulted in an amazing discovery at Smith's Cove; they observed water still oozing out of the shingle after the tide had dropped below it. Excavations subsequently discovered an elaborate fan-shaped drainage system converging to a funnel-shaped sump hole above the high water mark. They assumed some sort of flood tunnel linked this hole to the Money Pit. The inference was obvious; to protect whatever was at the bottom of the pit, the originators ensured it was filled with water at each high tide.

I repeat a statement made earlier. The important thing to remember about these early (60) years is that there is no official record of what went on, just the stories handed down.

A Brief History, Pro 1850

It is not the purpose of this chapter to chronicle the history and detail all of the diggings on the island; it is well documented in many books and papers elsewhere. A book I would recommend is *Oak Island and Its lost Treasure* by Graham Harris and Les Macphie (1999). It contains a concise history with some excellent drawings of the numerous diggings. Whilst the content virtually ignores any Masonic connection - which, as you will see, I believe could be important - it nevertheless tells you all you want to know about Oak Island up to 1999, including the author's views and theories on who may have been involved in constructing the pit and how they may have carried it out.

Regarding the digs, suffice to say that since that time (1849) and up to the present day, there have been at least 50 excavation shafts and many more boreholes in and around the area of the Money Pit including several attempts at clearing out the original pit. Six lives have been lost and it is estimated at least $5million has been spent by at least 16 syndicates, organisations and individuals. The exact location of the original pit is unknown because of 200 years of excavations in the area. A lot of irreversible damage was done in 1965 to 1966 when Robert Dunfield excavated a hole over 100 feet wide and conical in shape down to 140 feet. Exploratory drilling went on down to 190 feet. Any evidence of chests etc. would surely have been brought to light during this and subsequent excavations, unless, as some (treasure devotees) have suggested, they have fallen further down into natural subterranean caverns that frequent the structure of the island's geology.

From 1996 to 2008, the exploration work has been carried out by David Tobias and Dan Blankenship. Their company is (or was) called Triton Alliance. They have drilled numerous holes in and around the Money Pit, the most infamous known as 'Borehole 10X' situated about 180 feet NE of the pit. It begs the question, 'If the treasure devotees say the Money Pit is obviously the location of any hidden treasure, why has activity moved to another area?' I have found no logical explanation for this. A lot of time, energy and money has been devoted to 10X. From an original six inch hole to 235 feet depth, it has been enlarged to eight feet in diameter with a steel casing down to 90 feet. Beyond that, it was cased with concrete in the late 1970s down to 126 feet. Ten years later, the casing was continued down to 181 feet! And still no treasure. It appears all this activity was caused by murky TV footage taken in 1971 by an underwater camera lowered into a cavity in the bedrock at the 230 foot level.

The Halifax's *Chronicle Herald* reported on the sensational findings on November 23, 1971 as follows:

'A series of pictures show faint outlines of what project manager Dan Blankenship says he is certain are three chests, one having a handle on the end and a curved top. Besides another of the chests or boxes, he says, is some sort of tool, not unlike a pick-axe.'

A more gruesome revelation by the camera was what appeared to be a severed clenched hand, suspended in the water. At this point, I think a question to be asked is, 'Would anybody (those originally responsible) in their right mind go to the trouble of digging a 200 foot hole to a natural cavern they could never have seen, just to hide three, four or five chests?' We are talking a huge mining project here and yet it is generally accepted that pirate buried treasure was never buried more that 10 feet down!

The floating hand? That would sink, wouldn't it? Even if it could survive over 200 years. However, the management was obviously spurred on by these revelations to spend more money. A couple of weeks later, a diver was sent down. He found nothing but an empty cavern.

Another Map, Another Hole

The map that follows accompanied an article that Wilkins wrote for an American publication in 1940. You should be able to recognise his style instantly by now so you know this is no genuine treasure map. Briefly, the story he tells is of he and a companion searching an old deserted and haunted house (he locates it in Jamaica) where they heard was a mysterious chest. They find it and eventually open the old corroded and battered iron box;

'We peered in at a collection of papers and parchments. Carefully lifting them out for future study we stared at an object in the bottom. It was a small silver casket carved like a Renaissance jewel box. We found in it a stiff, brown parchment, mouldy and stinking – but legible. Drawn in faded black and red ink was the map of an island.'

The island, reproduced below is not shown as an island but details a bay.

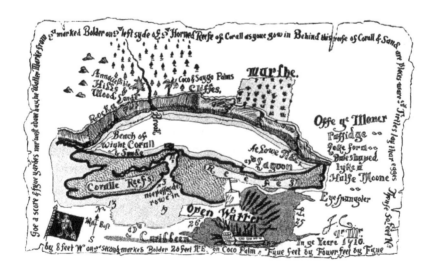

The story continues with them flying to San Domingo to look for the 'halfe moone baie'. Hiring boats and native fishermen, they eventually find the bay; again, one gets the impression this is not an island. They landed and, 'We gazed across the wide beach hemmed in by coral reefs'. Following the directions, they eventually came to where once stood the 'Coco Palm'.

H. P. (Wilkins' companion, the initials probably a corruption of the initials of Hubert Palmer and Patrick Nolan) took out his 'dowser', or divining rod. "If there's anything here, this'll find it," he declared. Slowly walking around, suddenly, his rod violently dipped downward. "Here it is," he roared. They dug down and eventually came across some rotted oak. Below that, they found a layer of compact brown fibre, probably coconut husk, put there to keep the water out. Below that, Wilkins' pick suddenly jarred on something solid, sending a shock through his body. On clearing the sand and enlarging the hole, they could see the top of a chest banded with iron. But the hole was starting to fill with water. They jumped into the hole and grabbed the iron loop handles in the top of the chest. They jerked madly and something gave way beneath their feet. The top of the chest came away, the sides of the hole caved in like a concertina and water welled up in a strong flood. They barely had time to scramble out and a great hole gaped at their feet, the remains of the chest disappearing into utter blackness. They stood like fools, the lid of the chest in their hands. After calming themselves, they dropped a plummet and line in the hole and found no bottom at 250 feet!

There is no mistaking, of course, that with this story, Wilkins is imitating Oak Island's futile quest and inferring the searchers are all fools. Their money has gone into a bottomless hole. In this story, they don't come away empty handed, they find three (note, three!) pieces of eight stuck to the underside of the lid, and also a diamond studded silver crucifix.

There are several items of interest in this story and map, clues abound, and you may be versed enough in our story now to recognise some of them. The map first, which is a mishmash of detail and clues, some unrelated to our lost treasure, frankly makes a mess of the whole thing, and as a result, the map could be said to be laughable!

1. A 'Beach of Wight Corall & Sande' (DNA).
2. 'Noe paffafede rowe in'. i.e. narrow passage.
3. 'At Lowe Tide a Lagoon.'
4, 'Coralle Reefs.'
5. Picture of a ship blowing up. (Webb destroying his ship and DNA.)
6. 'Tirtles lay thar egges.' (Link to the 'Key' chart.)
7. 'Qr Mr' (above 1710, a reference to the *Quedah Merchant* ship taken by Kidd.)
8. Black pirate flag, as used by the pirate Bartholomew Roberts, - totally unrelated.
9. The black outline, pointed each end and looking like a fat eel will mean nothing to you at this stage, but they could be representative of lines on another map you will be acquainted with later.
10. On bottom; 'marks Bolder 20 feet NE' (DNA).

The storyline, created to employ the Oak Island quest (which also proves he knew all about it prior to WW2), includes at the beginning the finding of documents in a chest in an old building. This no doubt alludes to Anson's ancestral home and the finding of the Webb documents. Similar storylines appear elsewhere. Item five is very important as it also proves that Wilkins was familiar with the Webb documents as nowhere else is there any reference to Webb blowing his ship up. For 'Coco Palm', you can read Oak Tree. The rotted oak alludes to the oak platforms in the pit and he hasn't forgotten the layer of coconut husk that alludes to that supposedly covering the oak platforms in the pit. His map is emphasising a coral beach, white sandy bay, reefs and a lagoon with a small entry passage i.e. the island of the lost treasure. The diamond encrusted crucifix was, of course, included so that Wilkins could show he was linking the treasure to the church. NE appears, as does boulder (rock) marks, alluding to the marked rock on Pinaki.

So Wilkins is playing games again, entwining the lost treasure story with Pinaki and Oak Island and because of his extensive pirateology background, is able to create a story which is plausible to the public (much like Brown did), many of whom would have been easily taken in by it. But at the same time, he is telling another exclusive band of people, 'I know the secret as well!'

A Scientific Survey

In 1995, Triton Alliance brought in the Woods Hole Oceanographic Institute, the people behind the discovery of the *Titanic*. Subsequent reports suggest it may have been a private survey *allowed* to take place by Triton. A two or three week scientific survey was carried out. The commissioners of the report are very secretive about the results of the survey. Richard E. Joltes, a contributor to the 'Critical enquiry' website, claims to have had access to some of the findings which as he says "prove much of what we 'know' about the island to be false". For example, no dye was detected anywhere around the island after being introduced into Borehole 10X. Similarly, no indications of any sort of flood tunnel between the pit area and Smith's Cove were found. Freshwater has been found in the pit(s), as well as seawater, indicating a subterranean stream and/or normal filtration of water through the soils. Indeed, a scientist with the Bedford Institute of Oceanography in Dartmouth, Nova Scotia says that the flooding and supposed anomalies can be explained by natural phenomena and natural geology.

The underwater video was examined by the scientists who said they were unable to discern anything resembling the previously observed objects on the video.

The conclusion from the test findings is that none of the numerous theories for the pit hold water (excuse the pun). Then there is the glaring fact that despite deep shafts all over the place, no treasure, or indication of any treasure, has ever been found, especially in the Money Pit or in the immediate area of the Money Pit. Does this not indicate that maybe there is none to be found? If you think about it logically and as stated earlier, don't you think it a bit ridiculous that anybody would dig a hole *that* deep and leave clues in the form of inscribed stones as well?

Triton Alliance seems to have given up the quest some time after the Woods Hole investigation, with no active shaft digging/boring being carried out for over a decade now. The partners fell out years ago over disagreements on how to pursue their goal. Tobias has now sold his share to Michigan Consortium, an Oil and Drilling Company and Blankenship is now working with them. The last I heard from my contact in Canada (2010) was that the Government had revoked the Treasure Trove Licence, so maybe the new owners have had their noses pushed out!

We now look at some compelling reasons for suggesting maybe there are other reasons for all this activity on Oak Island.

Revelations, Triangles and Crosses

We now have to look at other evidence, including that of possible fraudulent activity regarding the Money Pit, and also historical connections and the untold parts possibly played by some of the early main players in this treasure saga. If we try to get to the base roots of the Oak Island treasure story, we go back beyond the time of McGinnes and the finding of the clearing with its oak tree. In *The British Colonist* (1863), an article titled *An Original Sketch – History of the Oak Island Enterprise* begins:

'Better than a century ago an old man died in what was then known as the British Colony of New England. On his death-bed he confessed himself to have been one of the crew of the famous Captain Kidd; (hung in 1701. GE) *and he assured those who witnessed his last moments, that many years past he had assisted that noted pirate and his followers in burying over two million of money beneath the soil of a secluded island, east of Boston.'*

The 'dying pirate' DNA rears itself again.

This confession helped to bolster the many searches along the eastern seaboard for this great treasure, adding to the myth of Kidd and his fabled hidden treasure. Indeed, at the last count I have read of over 30 such stories along the eastern coast of America. But Oak Island could certainly be listed as a 'secluded' island. Another story links Kidd to Oak Island; this one also gives a different account as to how Simeon Lynds (Onslow Syndicate) became involved. The story is also told in William S. Crooker's *Oak Island Gold* (1993) and goes like this:

Somewhere in Virginia, an old man (yes, on his sickbed!) told his son, himself an old man of 70, that in his sea chest he would find, on a piece of paper, details of a treasure buried on an island up north. The old man's father had helped to bury, under the watchful eye of Kidd and an armed guard; a treasure to a great depth on an oak-covered island. When the work was near completion, he and another crew member escaped, fearing they would be killed when the work was finished. Later, he drew a rough map of the island and part of the bay including some particulars pertaining to the burying of the treasure. The grandson found the paper but found little interest in the locals to help him look for the island.

Somehow Lynds heard of the old man's paper and was able to see the drawing of the island. Being familiar with Oak Island and the tales of treasure associated with it, he found the outline in the sketch compared quite favourably with that island.

Kidd has always been associated with Oak Island and if these tales did not start the legend, then they reinforced the legend already there.

Another story of particular interest to us is that of the 'Spanish Sailor'. It comes from Frederick L. Blair who was associated with the Oak Island Treasure Company from 1894 to 1934. He was one of the few who collected old records diligently. The story was told to Blair in 1893 and subsequently appeared in the *Boston Traveller* and in the *Halifax Evening Mail*. His correspondent had been told the story by an elderly relative who had met the sailor in his youth. This would date the tale to about the beginning of the 19th century and it goes like this:

'When a young man of about 20 years of age, I was working in a shipyard when one day a sailor came into the yard. He was evidently from a foreign ship that had arrived to load deal. He was a man of about 50 years of age, large, heavy, dark and swarthy. I entered into conversation with him. He said he was anxious to raise money to get back to Boston and if I could advance him say $20, he in return would give me a valuable secret of where there was an immense amount of money buried. He then told me something of his history. That he had been a pirate, and in later years a privateer, and that now as the latter occupation was about played out, he was getting weary and wanted to get home to his native Spain. He showed me a plan which he said had come into his possession. It was of an island of a certain form, situated on the south-western coast of Nova Scotia, and was once a rendezvous of pirates, and that a large amount of treasure was buried there. On this island was a certain oak tree, from a branch of which hung a large ship's block which was used in sinking a deep shaft, the bottom of which communicated with the sea level by a tunnel. The

shaft had been filled up as being of no use, as the exit for the removal of the treasure would be through the tunnel. But for reasons unknown to him the treasure was never put there, but buried only 20ft from the surface, at a certain distance from the tree, naming the distance, where it would be safer from the inquisitive intruder than if it were at the bottom of the shaft, the most likely place to look for it, and then it may have been the original intention of the depositor that the shaft was intended for a blind, for who would not be deceived under such conditions. When I paid him the money he was to give me the name and directions how to find the island, also to mark on the plan the exact course by compass from the tree that the treasure lay buried.
Yes, of course, I would agree to his offer and the money would be forthcoming next day.'

Alas, the storyteller dallied with indecision how to raise the money, and the story seemed too good to be true. He wavered all day, undecided with what to do. When the next day came, the sailor had disappeared. In later years, he regretted his decision, having heard about the parties digging on Oak Island which he believed corresponded in many points with that described by the sailor.

The correspondent went on to say to Blair that during conversations with his elderly relative, he attributed considerable importance to a large rock as being an important landmark. (We have more DNA, a Spanish sailor and a large rock. Remember also the large rock on Haute Island.) What are we supposed to make of this story? There are two interesting aspects 1) that the treasure is **not** buried in the Money Pit but some distance from it (maybe this is the reason for Borehole 10X?) and 2) the Spanish sailor knew about the so-called 'flood tunnel'. This tells us two things: a) as the 'flood tunnel' was not found or believed to exist until the mid 1800s, then the sailor had prior genuine knowledge of the tunnel, or b) this is a story constructed to help verify and/or justify the work being carried out and therefore maybe bring more investors' money in.

A story in R Furneaux's book mentioned earlier relates how, after pirates had spent considerable time excavating the deep pit and driving long underground tunnels to let in the sea, they were captured by two English frigates which carried them home where they were either hanged or sentenced to gaol. However, one of the crew, a slow-witted man, was spared, and years afterwards while at Bristol gave a sketch of the site to a young sailor who passed it on to a young Halifax pilot. He in turn gave it to his grandson who lived in Boston. I am sure you can see the parallels with this story and the one preceding it.

Preserved amongst Blair's records is an article written by Josephine Fredea of Chester. It appeared in *Collier's Magazine* in 1905:

'With the hope of securing such prizes to inflame their avarice, it is small wonder that a hoard of lawless and adventurous spirits of many nationalities were soon sailing under the black flag. The last Will and Testament of one of these men had been recently discovered by a gentleman prominent in English literary circles.

This gentleman, whose name I am not at liberty to disclose, recently purchased an old manor house located near a certain seaport in England. Rambling over his new property he one day visited a long-unused room, where the dust lay thick on floor and furniture. His attention was attracted to an old oaken chest, covered with quaint carvings. This he opened and discovered within clothing, nautical instruments and a casket containing a considerable sum of money, several old maps or charts and other documents as well as the last will and testament of the owner.

The testator had obviously been a master mariner, presumably the principal in nefarious transactions, since his will began with a lengthy prayer for forgiveness for past mis-deeds, the text of which left little doubt that on his death-bed his conscience was giving him serious trouble.

He proceeded to bequeath to his son 'then on the high seas', all the property and money of which he died possessed including the casket of letters and diagrams containing instructions as to the location of certain hidden property.

The significant fact that the old sea chest had lain there undisturbed for so many years, since the clothing, nautical instruments and money were all of ancient date, induced the finder to sift the matter thoroughly. Investigation shows that about the year 1780 the testator's son was impressed from a merchant ship into the Navy and was killed in action. After further careful and exhaustive enquiry, the present owner came to the conclusion that the information was of great value and was about to embark on a search for the hidden property when he chanced to read the story of Oak Island in 'Collier's Magazine'.

He was immediately struck by its remarkable similarity to a certain island clearly indicated on the chart in his possession. Between this island 'past Sesambre' (now Sambro Island SW of Halifax port. GE) as it is written on the chart, and a certain islet in the West Indies, there is marked a clearly defined track; and although most of the writing thereon is in Spanish and Dutch, yet it is apparent at a glance that there was a well-traveled path between the two islands mentioned.

Other papers show that a removal and subsequent deposit of seven packages took place on certain dates, each package bearing separate symbols and initials.

There is also a diagram of the Cove on Oak Island, in the form of a Dutch tobacco pipe, and to this diagram is attached a paper which has not been easy to decipher.

Members of different companies engaged in excavation work on Oak Island, always believed that documents were in existence which would make plain the mystery of the island, and the discovery of the old sea chest shows that their opinions were correct.'

You will no doubt have noticed the 'old chest in an old manor house' and its similarity to the earlier Wilkins story. Besides that, the 'Master Mariner' can only be Anson. Another link with Kidd to Nova Scotia is that after his execution in 1701, his cabin boy Richard Barlicorn moved here. He said he witnessed Kidd burying a treasure in these parts and described what he saw. It is a story that has been handed down through the generations of the family that took him in and little known until the middle of the last century. However, as the island's location is a long way from Oak Island, this tale is not for our story.

Besides setting down markers for us and our story, the purpose of telling these stories is to show you that Kidd and pirates were associated with Oak Island and Nova Scotia long before McGinnis supposedly discovered the clearing with its oak tree. Also, as with Cocos and other legendary treasure islands, pirate maps abound for Oak Island and the 'dying pirate' story lives on. But the important thing to note here is that the story originally told for Oak Island is of a crew member of Kidd dying and leaving a map i.e. the traditional story. The clues and features documented on these maps have been attached to Oak Island by treasure hunters. This early legend is now conveniently ignored and has been overtaken by the 'three youth's story' which when the historical facts about the island are examined is just too fanciful.

Digging for the Truth

A lot of useful information on the early years of Oak Island is supplied by Judge Mather Des Brisay in his *History of Lunenburg County*, published in 1870. He says the deeds show that several plots were allocated in 1785. Lot 18 (that purchased by John Smith ten years later) was taken up by Caspar Woollenhaupt, a merchant and boat builder of Chester. Another plot was bought by Anthony Vaughan, father of the young Anthony.

McGinnis was apparently one of the first settlers on Oak Island, having purchased Lots 23 and 28 in 1790; poll tax records list him as a farmer on Oak Island.

This early activity on Oak Island must have meant log cabins or some form of habitat being constructed. The above mentioned Woollenhaupt must have had some sort of abode and *if* a tackle block and rope were found, then obviously it was used by him to help move timber for boat building. To suggest that they (particularly the rope) could have survived from a much earlier treasure burial is ludicrous. The extensive timber structure excavated much later (1967) on the shore adjacent to the Money Pit is almost certainly the remains of a slipway constructed by Woolenhaupt. Equally, the pit could have been an attempt at digging a well, or it is a natural sink hole (common in these parts) that over the years has been filled in with all sorts of debris. This filling would be softer than the surrounding ground and give the impression of a previously dug hole. Woollenhaupt could also have had a saw pit here and created a firm base with flagstones, after putting some logs down. Alas, we will never know. It was over 60 years before written accounts appeared of a treasure hunt and nobody really knows what went on during that time, just stories handed down, distorted, embellished and maybe spun to support a good story and encourage interest and maybe investment. The point of the above is to show that the island was used and worked on, not deserted, before the boys made their 'discovery'. This small point tends to be ignored or glossed over when the traditional story is told.

Gilbert Hedden, one of the searchers mentioned earlier, found a stone triangle in 1937, shortly after his visit with Wilkins. It was located about 40 feet from the shoreline, south of the Money Pit. The triangle was rough in appearance and construction and made of large uncut stones. Each side was 10 feet long with an added half circle of stones enclosing the base. A dividing line of rocks forming an 'arrow' passed from the circular base to the apex; this is not at right angles to the base but approximately 7 degrees offset to the left and points directly to the (original) Money Pit area. Frederick Blair had noticed these stones some 40 years earlier and for some reason placed little importance to them. (They had been originally observed in 1897 by a Captain Welling.) Checking the Stone Triangle, a surveyor plotted that the offset gnomon of the triangle pointed to true north. The Stone Triangle and its centre line itself pointed 7 degrees west of true north.

The triangular relationship of the Stone Triangle, westerly stone and easterly stone can be found diagrammatically plotted in Rupert Furneax's book, *The Money Pit Mystery*, which makes it apparent that the drilled rocks and Stone Triangle were part of a systematic survey system that was fixing datum positions with some exactness. It shows that a bearing following the heading of the Stone Triangle's gnomon (true north) passed through the Money Pit to the westerly stone. A bearing then shot to the easterly and another from there to the Stone Triangle completed a triangle. It also showed that following the heading of the Stone Triangle itself (7 degrees west of true north), off this bearing a 90 degree right angle shot a bearing through the westerly stone to the easterly stone. Along this line was the 'Cave In' shaft. From the easterly stone again, a bearing shot back to the Stone Triangle also completed a triangle.

If the intention of the stones was as a 'marker' to the Money Pit, why wasn't it constructed as a right-angled equilateral triangle? The offset triangle then with its semicircular base was indicating something else but nobody has come up with a conclusive answer. One must admit, it is rather strange to add a semicircle of stones to the base. The triangle was later destroyed to make way for other excavations.

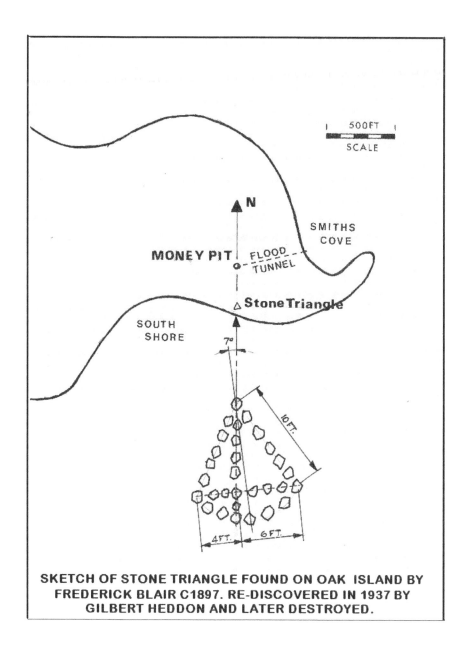

SKETCH OF STONE TRIANGLE FOUND ON OAK ISLAND BY FREDERICK BLAIR C1897. RE-DISCOVERED IN 1937 BY GILBERT HEDDON AND LATER DESTROYED.

In 1981, Fred Nolan, a land owner on the island and one of the searchers, discovered what he says is 'a large cross' outlined by six large boulders. Its dimensions were massive, something like 900 feet long and 800 feet wide. There was a boulder at each point, one at the intersection and another halfway down the main leg. It is situated north-west of the Money Pit with the left-hand boulder on the shoreline. As there is no obvious reference to anything, one wonders; if it is real, is it in fact at all related to the Money Pit? So, is it even an intended cross construction, or maybe a few boulders that just happen to coincidently outline a cross, as most people now believe?

A question of Oak Island I would ask is the following. A pit of this size and depth (150 feet plus) together with a 500 feet tunnel linking it to the eastern shore would have been a huge engineering and mining operation, involving maybe up to 100 miners for many months. Add to this the logistics of the supporting operation, food, tents, supplies, tools and supply ships. In other words, a big commotion and a lot of activity for quite a while, on a little island close to the mainland. The French settled here, even before the English, so why do local records show nothing? How is it that nobody noticed anything? Some of the participants must have said something, even if a long time after the event. Was everybody shot? Why is there absolutely no record of such a big undertaking? Why is there no evidence on the ground, lost possessions, camp remains, artifacts etc.? One author says the labour support force to the work on the island was provided by the men of the 47th of Foot. A whole labour force on the island and no one ever said, heard or remembered anything about it! Surely there would be a record of this activity in the archives. Were they destroyed and they forgot why they were there and what they put there? Also, being a metal detectorist, I know that in particular, all old camp sites, particularly army sites, if the military were involved, *always* produce lost buttons and badges etc. But then it is said the British Army never used military people to excavate tunnels, they always used experienced miners. And where is the excavated earth? There would have been a small mountain of it. Answers on a postcard please!

Hang on! Could it be that maybe there was no such undertaking at all?

Theories

Claims for what lies at the bottom of the Money Pit are many with some far-fetched ideas. The following also include names of those associated with what could be buried there:

- A lost Spanish Galleon's treasure. The treasure of the Knights Templar. The Holy Grail.
- Money hidden by the British Military. A past civilisation, Sir Francis Drake. The Vikings.
- Sir Francis Bacon (Shakespeare's Manuscripts). Captain Kidd and the ill-gotten gains of pirates. The 'Concepción's lost treasure, buried here by Sir William Phips.

My friend, the author Graham Harris, proposed the latter backed by some in-depth research but like all the others, there is no practical sound undeniable evidence at all for any of the theories. When are they all going to see sense? Quite obviously, there is nothing there! It would have been found by now if there was.

We haven't quite finished with Oak Island yet. We have seen that the roots go back to one of Kidd's crew confessing his secret but the real story is conveniently ignored by many, maybe because it just doesn't fit in with a saleable buried treasure story!

The next chapter will show you that the traditional Oak Island story is one with an underlying meaning.

CHAPTER 4

DIGGING DEEPER, FREEMASONRY, MORMANISM AND PLUM ISLAND

In recent years, there has been a lot of speculation and research into possible Masonic origins for the Money Pit legend. It might sound fanciful but there is unmistakable evidence of Masonic involvement with undeniable parallels between the Money Pit story and the Masonic Secret Vault allegory. Indeed, it has been said that the Oak Island mystery is born out of practices developed elsewhere; treasure divination, Freemasonry and Mormonism.

Research by John Bartram (*The Making of the Oak Island Mystery,* 2005) indicates that the Smith family, and also possibly McGinnis and Vaughan, immigrated to here from New England. He states:

'The Joseph Smith family was known and acknowledged to have been a close knitted one, where strong individual affection and loyalty existed between each of the members. It was a Masonic family which lived and practiced the estimable and admirable tenets of Freemasonry. The father, Joseph Smith, Sr was raised to the degree of Master Mason in 1818. An older son Hyrum was also a member.'

There is much more to this family than is commonly known, for a son of Joseph Smith Sr., born in 1805 and known as Joseph Smith Jr., was the founder of Mormonism. It is on record that he accompanied his father on expeditions in search of buried treasure and participated in a 'craze for treasure hunting' as a youth. Smith was paid to act as a 'seer' in attempts to locate lost items and buried treasure. He also made extensive use of divining rods. There are even references to him (Smith Jr.) wanting to find Kidd's treasure. He was so involved in treasure hunting in those days that he even organised crews to dig for him. Another report says that the Smith family belonged to a company of 'money diggers' and it was a fact that in New England and in western New York at that time, digging for treasure was widespread among respected citizens and churchgoers.

Joseph Smith Sr. taught his divination method to his son and they worked together in this, also apparently hunting for Captain Kidd's treasure along the eastern seaboard before they emigrated. A connived practice was not necessarily to find treasure, but to persuade a landowner that they knew where to dig and so receive payment for their labours. The divination element was their means to explain how they 'knew' what was buried. Failing to find the treasure was of, course, the norm. The excuse for the repeated failures became represented by the 'treasure slipping away' imagery, found in Mormon sacred texts.

Many scholars have noted the strong resemblance between the Mormon ordinance and Masonic ritual. Indeed, the early church leaders taught that the Masonic ceremony was a corrupted form of temple rituals that had descended directly from the biblical Solomon and were restored in their true, pristine form by the inspired Joseph Smith.

Joe Nickell in his *The Secrets of Oak Island* (*Skeptical Inquirer Magazine*, 2000) states that the search has been carried out largely by prominent Nova Scotia Freemasons, including Frederick Blair, William Chappell, Gilbert Heddon, and Edwin Hamilton who succeeded him. Heddon even corresponded with Mason King George V1 about developments in 1939, whilst Hamilton corresponded with President Roosevelt, another famous Freemason who actually participated in work on Oak Island in 1909.

Reginald Harris, who wrote the first comprehensive book on Oak Island, was a provincial Grand Master from 1932 to 1935. Whilst not proved, we also have our suspicions that our friend, the author Harold T. Wilkins, was also a Freemason. The freemasonry link is not just the member participants but how it parallels with the earlier mentioned 'Secret Vault' allegory. Freemasonry, its degrees (levels), and there are many initiation ceremonies, what it stands for and symbolism is very complex. I am not going to try and explain it; there are many books available on the subject. It is therefore not a secret society but could be said to be a 'society with secrets'. The latter we will elaborate more on later. For my part, I will show you the allegorical (story symbolising an underlying meaning) connection that parallels the Oak Island story:

The Secret Vault Allegory

One of the essential elements of any true Masonic group is 'a legend or allegory relating to the building of King Solomon's Temple'. And an allegory of the Secret Vault, based on Solomon's fabled depository of certain great secrets is elaborated in the seventh or Royal Arch Degree of Freemasonry: Three sojourners (in our case; Smith, McGinnis and Vaughan) 'successively lowered each other into the dark vertical passage, each reaching farther than the one before him. Finally they reached the 9th apartment where he discovered the treasure left there by Enoch'.

MASONIC MEDALLION SHOWING THE THREE SOJOURNERS' TWO LOWERING THE THIRD INTO THE VAULT

Before we proceed any further, a brief explanation is called for regarding the medallion. You will have noticed that triangles of 'three dots' intersperse the letters. The explanation is that three dots (or three points) were formerly fashionable in Masonic writing instead of the usual periods after initials. The practice was apparently started in France by the non-recognised Grand Orient of France in 1774 and Masons were sometimes called 'Three Point Brothers'. The usage became popular in the United States and is seen today in some Scottish Rite documents. Any significance they had two or three hundred years ago is now long lost.

The letters in the border are; R, S, R, S, T, P, S, R, I, A, J, et S, ANNO ENOCHI 2995.

These stand for; Regnante Solomone, Rege Sapientissimo, Thesaurum Pretiosissimum Sub Ruinis Invenerunt Adonirum, Joabert, et Satolkin ... Anno Enochi 2995.

Translated it reads; 'In the reign of Solomon, wisest of Kings, Adonirum, Joabert and Satolkin found under the ruins the most precious treasure'.

So another example furthering the Masonic legend of a secret treasure. On the reverse side of the medallion is a **triangle** emitting rays. Later on in our story, we will feature another medallion, triangular in shape with an arrow in the centre. To resume with the secret vault allegory:

So regarding the nine layers of oak logs claimed to be at 10 foot levels down to 90 feet, this is Enoch excavating nine vaults below ground, each roofed with an arch. Enoch deposited in the lowest vault a gold plate, inlaid with jewels and containing the secret name of God.

The Money Pit story handed down says that in 1804, the searchers probed the bottom of the pit with a crowbar and struck what they thought was the top of a treasure chest. Their actions recall the Royal Arch Degree in which the secret vault is located by a sounding blow from a crowbar. Regarding the inscribed cipher stone found at the 90 foot level, a description said; 'it was freestone, with the appearance of dark Swedish granite or porphyry'. And according to the teachings; 'Enoch.....concealed the grand secret, engraved on a white oriental porphyry stone, in the bowels of the earth'. Based on the popular drawings of the marks, the inscription on the stone is a simple substitute type cipher familiar to Freemasons since the 18th century. Not only that, the professor who is said to have deciphered the stone to read 'TEN (or forty) FEET BELOW TWO MILLION POUNDS (are buried)' was said to have been an investor in the search himself! So maybe a vested interest and an opportunity to encourage more investor's money.

The Masonic parallels go on and on. For example, the soft stone, charcoal, and clay found in the pit are consistent with the Chalk,

Charcoal and Clay sited in the Masonic Degree of Entered Apprentice as symbolising the virtues of 'freedom, fervency and zeal'.

Even the flood tunnel and drains on the shore don't escape: 'Enoch...and again I raised my eyes to heaven, and saw a high roof, with seven water channels on it, and those channels discharged much water into an enclosure...water began to bubble up, and to rise above the floor...'. There were also examples of Masonic symbolism found but we have to stop somewhere with a final example, or the Oak Island story will overtake our lost treasure story.

Earlier, we showed the triangle of stones found on the south shore, with no explanation of why it had a semicircular base. Knowing how active Freemasons were on this island, I offer an explanation; it is nothing more than Freemasonry symbology:

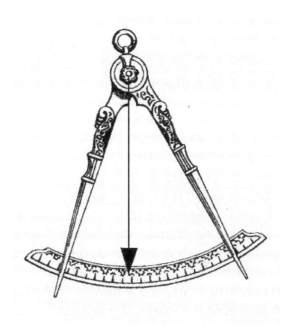

MASONIC SYMBOL FROM THE SCOTTISH RITE DIVIDERS AND PLUMB BOB

The triangle of stones is more than likely representative of the above symbol. More often, the compass is shown with a set square. In this example, it is replaced with a protractor scale, and also a plum (bob) line; all tools of the Masons.

There seems to be little, if anything, about the Oak Island story as relayed to us that does not appear to be in either Mormonism or the Freemasonry's Secret Vault allegory. Bartram goes as far to say:

'This is not a series of miraculous coincidences, but the result of a fraud, the type of which was played out on many occasions, mainly in the United States, but also on occasion in Canada.'

I have never really got my head around the Freemasonry thing as applied here. It consists of a problem with answers that don't make sense. If a fraud for no other reason than to make money, which came first, the pit found or the story created? Were the Masonic elements opportunistically added to an existing treasure quest? It is interesting to note that there appears to be no mention of a Freemasonry connection in the early writings and records. Why not, if Freemasons were actively involved? Were they the creators of a fraud? If so, why put their own money into looking for a non-existent treasure? They wouldn't, would they, so maybe encouraged others to do it for them and so make money? The only other possible answer is that they believed the early stories about the platforms 'discovered' at regular intervals and attached the Masonic allegory. The other aspects of Masonic symbolism discovered over the years convinced them that this must be the location of Freemasonry's 'hidden secret'. The treasure's (or equivalent) of Solomon's Temple must be here. They all got carried away, not by circumstantial evidence (there is none) but by circumstantial stories, myth and legend. It all fitted what they *wanted* to believe. It is an incomparable conundrum.

We know it started with Kidd and/or the dying pirate story but that was (conveniently?) forgotten over time and was replaced by the legend of the three youths finding a pit. This is now suspect as you have seen, and does anybody now after over 200 years of evidence (or lack of it!) really believe a shaft was constructed to hide something, as the legends tell us? Once the Money Pit and the area immediately around it was obliterated (Dunfield) and opened out down to 140 feet, with subsequent shafts and boreholes going on down to over 200 feet with no (positive) result, why do people carry on? Investors don't want the story to be debunked, do they? All that money poured into it! They can't be made to look silly, but insist;

'Look, a long time ago, somebody's dug a hole there (pointing), they said there's a treasure at the bottom. So there must be!'

The treasure story of Oak Island as it is given now cannot satisfactorily provide any logical or verifiable explanation why the location of the Money Pit was excavated in the first place. Too much of the story is false and too many of the real facts have been deliberately excluded as inconvenient truths. There is also the endemic problem of researchers simply repeating earlier information without checking the veracity of it and glossing over details that contradict the accepted storyline. A glaring example is how the island was already subdivided with a shipbuilder owning the Lot where the Money Pit was found, before the pit was found!

The Oak Island story is actually very short on details even for a treasure legend, as the five 'w's, which give it some varnish of believability, are missing; when, who, what, why and where. When boiled down, all the story of Oak Island is; in the year unknown, a person unknown, buried something unknown, for reasons unknown, on the south-east of Oak Island. Even the location on the island itself is not even certain, as things are a bit vague when it comes to explaining why; if the Money Pit was here, why were all those other shafts dug over there?

The story goes on, and carries on, with everyone ignoring the real and obvious starting point of this whole saga; the early stories. These had a dying sailor as the source of the information. This is just one of a number of important clues (DNA) that never made it into the preferred modern version. For us, as with Juan Fernandez Island, Cocos Island and others we have talked about, Oak Island is just another misidentified island on our trail of the lost treasure.

Before leaving the shores of Nova Scotia, we tell the story of the misguided Captain Allen. Some thought he was looking for Oak Island.

Captain Allen's Failed Quest

Who was Captain Allen? A man with a chart!

In about 1870, a man calling himself Captain Allen arrived in Shad Bay, which is about 21nm. east of Oak Island across St Margarets Bay. He was described as 'well to do, was of handsome appearance, dark complexioned and talking with a foreign accent. He asked one of the locals, a man named Silex if he could tell him where Plum Island was. 'No Sir' said Silex, 'I've never heard of it, and my folks have been settled here for many years past.' (It was then known as 'Cochrane's Island' and prior to that 'Redmond's Island'. GE)

It transpired that Allen was a descendant of a pirate who in the early 18th century helped bury a treasure on Plum Island. Allen said the cache consisted of gold in kegs and barrels, wine and brandy (the pirates had hoped to return in a few years), all timbered around and shored with heavy props to support the roof.

Having purchased a small sloop from a man named Ganter, he searched the bays, creeks and coves between Halifax and Lunenburg for two years, always starting out from a position identified as 44º N, and 63º W. This is a long way offshore,about 30 miles, and over 60nm from Oak Island, so these figures are suspect; he would not have seen St Margarets Bay or Mahone Bay from here with any clarity. From here, he took the altitude of the sun, and then sailed shoreward on a compass bearing apparently to the north-west. He checked his course on a chart spread out over the deck but would not permit his crew to examine it and never showed anyone the papers he was working with including an ancient chart believed to be worded in a foreign language. He would sit on the deck of his sloop, sunk in study, hour after hour studying faded documents and charts drawn on aged vellum, elbows propped his chin and his eyes were in a perpetual frown. A boy named Zink one day took a chance and peeped over his shoulder; he said he saw a chart covered with a cobweb outline of ship's bearings, courses, rhumb lines and a criss-cross of other spidery indications. (Remember this map description; it will be important later.)

The course that Allen followed always took him into St Margarets Bay, which is about 10nm east of Mahone Bay. After two years (some say four), he said he'd had enough. He handed his gear and certain information to one Captain Pickles of Mahone Bay, telling him, "What you must look for is an island with three mounds of rock, shaped in triangular form. The island is not large and lies at the head of a bay. A stream flows out of one end, and east of the triangle of stones is a well which is near a wooded gulley. The well is one of the principal clues or markers." With that, Allen left and was never seen again.

Pickles had no more luck than Allen until one day, whilst having lunch with his mate, a fisherman by the name of Billy Baker appeared; he chatted about his quest and outlined the shape of the island he was looking for. The fisherman was certain he recognised it and took Pickles to Redmond's Island in Shad Bay. They landed and looked for the three stone mounds which Pickles found behind a grove of fir trees. Two were cairns of beehive shape, the third, and the largest, in the shape of a pyramid. Some locals soon arrived from the mainland, curious to see what the activity was about. 'Boys,' said Pickles, 'this is the Plum Island Captain Allen was looking for and somewhere near the eastern shore we must look for an old dry stone wall. Close by is a well.' The pyramid, standing on a base of eight feet, was frantically torn down by Pickles looking for clues. They never found anything and eventually gave up. Over 20 years passed before the well was found. Another search had started and Thomas Ganter found the well by chance. It was under a couple of feet of watery moss he was trying to cross in a ravine. They also found the site of the old fireplace where the pirates cooked; it lay under two feet of earth. This treasure hunt was to last, with intermissions, for 43 years. Come 1936, Ganter, now aged 70 with nothing to show except confirmation of Allen's island, had had enough, and so it ended. I have in my possession a detailed handwritten account by Ganter of the history of the dig, their highs and lows and adventures. There is no doubt in my mind that this island, with its well, stream, correct shape, and at the head of a bay, is the island Captain Allen was looking for. Oak Island cannot be said to be at the head of a bay. The other thing that confuses the issue is that the latitude of Cochrane Island, which at 44º 31.8′N, is almost identical to that of Oak Island which is 44º 30.7′N.

The confusion and error on Allen's part has to be down to the original quoted 44N 63W, the point from which he is supposed to have taken bearings. This is ludicrous; if having buried your treasure here (either Oak Island or Plum Island) and wanting to make a record of what bearing to sail on, you would do it from a point where the island or entrance to the bay is visible, not 60nm away! This point then would be on the 64º longitude line which passes through the middle of St Margarets Bay.

So 44N 63W cannot be the starting point but probably an early and/or misread record of the location of Plum Island, now Cochrane

Island, whose position is 44º31.8′N, 63º47.7′W. If one is dealing with just the whole numbers, then its position can be said to be 44N 63W. This would have been good enough for the author of the chart/sailing directions because on returning to that Latitude and Longitude or thereabouts, he knew where he was going to from there by recognition and knowledge!

Westhaver and Smith

Interestingly, we have a link to this island with our friend, the author Harold T. Wilkins. James Patrick Nolan had heard about the treasure hunt and he made an agreement with Ganter to help look for the gold with his 'dowsing rods'. This is the same Nolan about whom Wilkins wrote a book (1948) called *A Modern Treasure Hunter*. Nolan was put in touch with one Herman Westhaver who with a friend, Joseph Smith (also known as Amos Smith), apparently found in 1912 a box containing charts in a cairn of stones on this same (Cochrane) island.

An old local first told Nolan about Westhaver and his story goes something like this:

He said that years ago, before the Great War, one evening, he and Joseph Smith (appears to be a common name in this area!) an old Pilot, followed what they thought was a phantom ship into Shad Bay. It anchored in the lee of Cochrane's Island and they watched as a longboat was lowered with 13 men in it. They landed in a small cove, took something out of the boat, lashed it to the oars and carried it up into the island. They were armed with old flintlocks. A second boat left the ship with three men in it, each with a large basket hilt sword and superior quality clothing to the other men. Their clothing was typical of English noblemen of the 17th century. The three officers went up a gulley followed quietly by Westhaver. They stopped by a large flat stone on the ground and, after a few minutes, they came back. Westhaver walked on to see if he could see the other 13 men but lost his way in the dark. When he found the beach again, he called out to Smith and saw the phantom ship promptly vanish. When he found Smith, who was quaking in his shoes, he persuaded him to go up the gulley with him to where he had seen the three men stop. They found the flat stone which they prized up. On the underside, there were inscriptions in Latin and English, only some of which he could read but appeared to give directions. Excavating the hole, they found a small iron box. Once home and in the presence of friends, they managed to open it. In it was a ship's log and several charts, all in a foreign writing they could not understand. The papers were torn and rotten from the damp and like a jigsaw to put together. Out of it all, they could only recognise some dates (1768, 1798), the name Plum Island, and a name that appeared several times - 'Keede' and 'William Edward Keede'. A pirate by the name of 'Cult' was also mentioned together with a treasure buried in a 'queer island'. They had the charts translated by a Jew in Halifax and destroyed the originals which were too brittle to handle. The charts apparently gave details and directions of other treasures on other islands.

I trust you have noticed the similarity of the above story to Oak Island and Cousino and co. (JF Island) finding a box.

The full story and other similar tales of the area are told in my Kidd book. Suffice to say the information was ultimately of no benefit to any of them, despite Westhaver having men digging for it in 1923. He said, 'The treasure is at this moment, stored in a strong room, in the shape of a subterranean cavity, 18 feet long, the same width, 8 feet deep, from the floor to the roof, which is of heavy oak beams. The sides are strongly walled, and the top of the cave is four feet below the surface of the ground.' He continued, 'Besides the gold bars, gold dust, 'dyamuns' pearls and rubis, there are other articles stored in the cave, or approaches...there are fowling-pieces, old cannon, gun-powder and merchandise of different sorts.' The chamber, with its description of contents, in particular the mention of 'fowling-pieces' is of particular interest, as you will see later.

Westhaver confirmed this story to Nolan and Wilkins when they met him. It comes down, I suppose, to whether or not you believe in ghost stories and there is some interesting detail in this one. Also, as Captain Allen was looking for his elusive Plum Island, the question arises; was he looking for the box they found giving directions, or the treasure buried on the island by the 13 men?

Cult, Kidd, or Keede! (Kidd was pronounced 'Keede' in Boston. GE) It has all passed into folklore now and to this day, Cochrane's Island is still known as a pirate treasure island. It was once known poignantly as Weeping Widows Island. Captain Kidd had 43 men dig two treasure pits here. Once the treasure was buried, he ordered the workers slaughtered and he made off with 43 weeping widows.

I would love to know how such a story started. You might say this Plum Island story could relate to a genuine treasure hunt on Cochrane Island and totally unrelated to our quest. You are right, of course; not every treasure tale and treasure map lead to our treasure island. Behind every myth, legend and folklore story lays a truth somewhere. Cochrane Island then possibly needs more in-depth research. Its location at the end of an inlet to the sea is perfect, making it difficult to be seen from the sea,

But does the story sound any better than the one associated with Oak Island? A flat stone found with inscriptions, translated by a Jew in Halifax.

Islands of Symbols

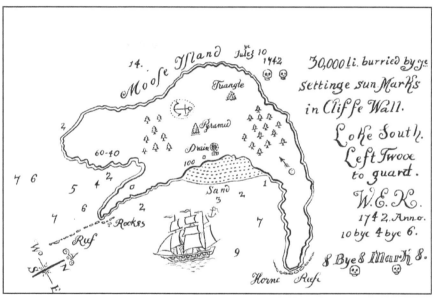

H. T. WILKINS NAMED THIS 'MOOSE ISLAND' AND COPIED THIS OFF A CHART FOUND ON PLUM ISLAND IN 1912 BY SMITH AND WESTHAVER.

A Mr Blake had the same chart as that above, found, it was said, in an old house in England (ring any bells? GE) and signed by Cult and Kidd.

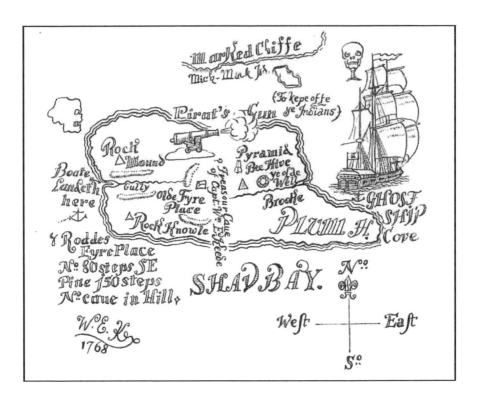

ANOTHER OF THE CHARTS FOUND BY SMITH AND WESTHAVER AND AS COPIED BY WILKINS, WHO HAS ADDED HIS OWN SYMBOLIC CLUES

We have seen that H. T. Wilkins was a prolific creator of old treasure charts, using his imagination to great effect to create a pirate treasure map how he thinks it should look. (And convincing many people along the way the maps are genuine.) In reality, there are very few genuine charts in existence, for obvious reasons. If you are lucky enough to have one, you are not going to go public with it, are you? Embellishments, typical of Wilkins, are evident in the two charts above and by putting them in, he is showing those in Freemasonry that he knows...!

Pre-WW2, Freemasonry was more secretive than it is now and this confirms to us our suspicions that our friend Mr. Wilkins was a Freemason. The thing that stands out on the first chart is the misplaced anchor; it is on the land! This is overlooked by many but it raises the obvious question; why? It is, of course, a Masonic symbol. Its allegorical meaning, *an emblem of well-grounded hope and firmness*, means it can be placed almost anywhere. But this emblem usually appears with an ark or ship. Wilkins, knowing that drawing an ark on the chart would look silly in this context, has it substituted by a ship. So for those who can recognise them, we have a dual emblem with a more esoteric interpretation. To put it simple (not easy in the world of Freemasonry), the ark represents a safe and guarded place, whilst the anchor symbol, which is a development of an ancient symbol of a wand entwined by serpents, was a symbol of power and authority.

The anchor is intended to convey the same meaning in connection with Temple or Lodge convocations. Therefore, in Masonic terms, the dual emblem means:

'The *depository* of the secret and sacred papers *or* jewels of the Temple, and the *power* or *authority* of the assembled body.'

H.T. Wilkins was obviously trying to pass on the esoterical knowledge! From both charts, you can now pick out allegorical symbols, namely:

a) A triangle - four times.

b) Two wells - drawn the same symbolically.

c) A pyramid - twice.

d) A bee-hive - once.

e) A rock knowle and a rock mound.

And the second chart:

a) The Triangle; besides being major DNA for us, geometry and architecture are central to Masonic thinking.

b) The Well; not Masonic but more DNA for us.

c) The Pyramid; typically Masonic. After Napoleon invaded Egypt, an obsession with all things Egyptian soon gripped the nation and the myths and legends were incorporated into contemporary Masonic lore. Freemason's were/are dedicated Egyptophiles. You may also recall in Part 1 we saw the symbol of the Ankh on a flat stone on Trinidade.

d) The Beehive; for Freemasons the bee is a symbol of industry - as busy as a bee - obedience and rebirth. It also represents the Temple. Esoterically, unless you are a bee, you cannot see what is going on (in the beehive), so unless you are a Freemason you cannot see what is going on in the Lodge.

Wilkins is saying, 'You have to be able to see to understand what is going on here'.

e) The Rock; more DNA for us.

Wilkins' 'Plum Island' drawing is representative of Cochirane Island and as I have said, maybe there is something here, but his 'Moose Island' is fictitious. It has an unusual shape, namely the long thin 'arms' or 'horns' that seem to be embracing a sandy beach. This feature is depicted in an exaggerated scale to the rest of the island. On one level, this is in fact is more DNA for us; I am sure you can see the similarity to a coral island which it is meant to represent without giving the game away too much. On another level, it is a recognitive signal. You may have recognised it already from the Trinidade map and story where three cairns (mounds) of rock also mark the treasure. This is Wilkins' way of confirming you are indeed 'seeing' what is going on. Part of that map is now shown:

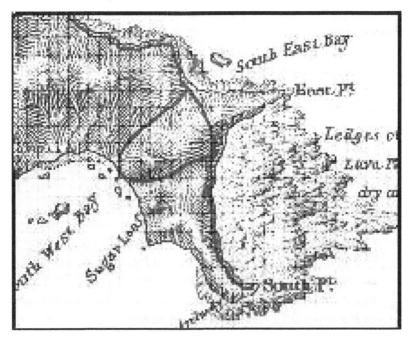

FOR THOSE WHO CANNOT READILY RECALL, THIS MAP FEATURE IS TO BE FOUND ON THE MAP OF TRINIDADE ISLAND (PART 1) WHERE E.F. KNIGHT SOUGHT A TREASURE MARKED BY THREE CAIRNS IN A GULLEY (EARLY DNA)

Wilkins therefore is trying to 'push' the clues to us and they are there but you need to already know the related stories as well as understand the esoteric meanings of coded allegorical symbology. In the end, all this just means that Captain Allen had a map containing DNA of the principle markers to the treasure, being three piles of stones and a well. That he was attempting to locate an island to match what he understood was being portrayed on the map is obvious. The more important clue gleaned from Captain Allen was *how* the map was being used in that the search commenced at a datum point in the ocean before a certain bearing was sailed in the expectation it led to the island.

As you might expect now, there are more revelations and parallels to come with respect to the above stories. When you reach them, you are likely to exclaim, 'Hang on! Haven't I read something like this before somewhere?' They may also make you think, 'So this maybe, is how these (Nova Scotia) stories originated!' However, we continue with more surprising revelations about the role of Freemasonry in our quest.

CHAPTER 5

STORIES FAMOUS, INFAMOUS AND THEIR MASONIC DNA

It is one thing to uncover a minor secret involving a mad sea captain's treasure as well as discovering Wilkins putting clandestine clues to this secret in his books and maps (exactly what secret was still yet to be discovered), but when others were also found to be hiding clues to the same thing meant things then took on a different shade.

In tracking down the various lost treasure stories of a dying person leaving a coded map, others were also found to be placing coded references to the lost treasure within their stories. The problem, though, was identifying the possible link, if any, between disparate persons across the globe to give this finding actual substance. The answer was found in the symbols blatantly given by Wilkins on his illustrations of Moose and Plum islands, which were of the society known as the Freemasons for whom the Temple of Jerusalem (or King Solomon's Temple) forms the template around which they base their lore and teachings. In the previous chapter, it has been identified how the accepted story for the origin of Oak Island's Money Pit is more than likely to be a thinly disguised Masonic tale.

There are many persons who believe the Freemasons are behind some great secret or in control of various aspects of society and Government; there are even whispers of a higher order. The Freemason's themselves continuously attempt to discount these beliefs as fantasy. But proof was slowly being uncovered that there was indeed some coded information about a treasure being transmitted within stories.

This required an intensive course of study of Freemasonry to try and get an insight into what was occurring. Study of Freemasonry is thankfully much easier these days with numerous books or papers on the subject's history, symbols, and codes being readily available, so it was not long before we became familiar with the psychology of using symbols and numbers as (coded) metaphors and allegories for Masonic lore and learned to identify these for what they were when they appeared. There appeared to be two types of stories for this purpose of the transmission of a clue. One type was an obviously fictional story which contained within it definitive Masonic symbology designed to be recognised by other Masons to alert them that the story was saying something important.

The other type was what can be termed a 'hoax/riddle'. These appeared to be a factual report about a 'treasure' which was in reality cunningly constructed hoaxes. These contained within them some riddle or code which was meant to be recognised or solved and passed a hint about a lost treasure. This also served to warn a fellow Freemason that the story was nothing but a hoax, a luxury not given to the many uninitiated who have believed these stories true and have wasted time, effort and sometimes their lives futilely following these stories in the belief they were real. Again, the technique was to mix the real with the fake to give some gloss of reality to the construct. It should also be understood that by the time these books and stories were written, the authors themselves were transmitting what was a distorted and fragmented picture of something they themselves were aware of but did not fully understand. Accordingly these distortions have to be factored for.

Simple Masonic DNA Stories

One of these stories we have already mentioned, *Captain Kid's Millions*, which shows the map of Trindade Island upon which are Masonic and alchemic symbols. Another is the most famous pirate treasure book written, *Treasure Island* by Robert Louis Stevenson. First published in 1881 as a serial in the magazine *Young Folks* then as a book in 1883, it is considered to be a mere children's story supposedly written for Stevenson's young stepson Lloyd, and comes replete with a treasure map. Whilst young Lloyd is said to have drawn a map to occupy his time in the wet Scottish highlands during a holiday there and Stevenson had then invented a story about pirates and a treasure island to accompany the map, a little Masonic insight discloses this story and the map to be something more.

The story starts with the arrival of a mysterious sailor, William Bones, who dies to leave a map to the fabulous treasure island. But as Long John Silver discovers, the map will not lead you to the treasure because it has been relocated. You can now recognise that the basic plot of *Treasure Island* is a repetition of part of the Cornelius Webb/

Anson story. The map that Stevenson (not Lloyd, unless he was a Freemason also) drew for the book was drafted to embody some clues as he dimly understood them; that a triangular plot is made on an island shown on a map left by a dying sailor to find a treasure. The directions given in the text;

'Tall tree, Spy glass shoulder, bearing a point to the N. of NNE. Skeleton island ESE by E. Ten feet', were again degenerate and as we have already seen, a version of these was used by August Gissler on Cocos island.

To ensure that other Freemasons recognised the import of the book, Stevenson twice gave Masonic symbology via literal description. The first occurs when we meet the character Ben Gunn who says, *"As for you Benjamin Gunn, says they, here's a musket they says, and a spade and a pickaxe."* This is Masonic symbology of a Mason's tools and was also used by Prodgers when he spoke of "an axe, a cutlass and a crowbar" for his story about Juan Fernandez.

The second occurs when a description is given of the log house in the stockade built on the island where it is described, *"There was a porch at the door, and under this porch the little spring welled up into an artificial basin of a rather odd kind - no other than a great ship's kettle of iron, with the bottom knocked out, and sunk to her bearings as the captain said among the sand."*

This is a symbolic reference from Masonic lore about the Temple of Solomon where a never-ending spring poured out from under the eastern entrance to the temple. The spring, the endless supply welling up, also has much deeper esoteric meanings.

There are many treatise on Stevenson and *Treasure Island*, yet none of them mention a Masonic connection!

You can see why Wilkins deliberately used the name 'Skeleton Island' from this story, (it appears on the treasure map) when using his book about Kidd to transmit further clues. In addition, Stevenson tells of 'Capt Kidd's Anchorage' adjacent to Skeleton Island. You can now see where Wilkins got the title of his book from i.e. *Captain Kidd and his Skeleton Island*.

An interesting anecdote is that the German author Alex Capus suggests, based on enquiries by the Swiss Walter Hurni, that Stevenson found the 'Loot of Lima' treasure on the island of Tafahi around 1890. This island (approx. 16º S, 174º W) is part of the Tonga Archipelago. Stevenson was staying on Upolu, not far from Tafahi, and seemed to have undertaken 'a few mysterious sailing tours with unknown destinations'. Stevenson became rich and built a large and expensive mansion in Samoa. Stevenson possibly did search for the treasure on Tahafi. It was known about at that time due to the activities of Gissler on Cocos amongst others. Why did he search here? Because at that time, Tahafi was known as 'Coconut Island' or 'Cocos Eylant'.

The Three Peaks

Treasure Island has a Masonic brother, the book called *King Solomon's Mines* by H. Rider Haggard. The book displays an even deeper level of knowledge about esoteric subjects by the author but passes clues to the lost treasure in a more direct form. The story behind the writing of *King Solomon's Mines* goes that after reading *Treasure Island*, Haggard wagered one shilling with his brother that he could write a better story and much quicker. Written over the course of some months, *King Solomon's Mines* was published in 1885. Rather than the popularly accepted version of the one shilling wager, it is apparent now that after reading *Treasure Island* and recognising what Stevenson was doing, Haggard was so unimpressed that he decided to do a much better job of passing the coded clues to the lost treasure and at the same time create a thrilling story.

The story is about three men, Alan Quatermain, Sir Henry Curtis and Captain Good, who venture into darkest Africa to find the lost brother of Sir Henry at the fabulous location of the mines of King Solomon. Battling hardships, warriors and a witch, they enable a usurped king to regain the throne, visit the mines and in the end find Sir Henry's brother.

Thought to be only a boy's own yarn, it displays a remarkable depth of Masonic and esoteric lore ranging through to the Masonic sojourn of three men to King Solomon's realm. To philosophical insights provided by the usurped King Umbopa to a discussion on the various guises of the goddess Astarte which is footnoted with a reference to Milton's gnostic poem *Paradise Lost*! Masonic lessons aside, it is the directions used by the three men to get to the mines which show this story for what it really is.

Quatermain is in possession of a map to the mines which he obtained from a dying Portuguese man named Jose Silvestre. Silvestre was found expiring after trying to follow a map and directions left by his ancestor, also named Jose Da Silvestre, who had achieved the mines in 1590. The dying Silvestre is again replicating the details of Cornelius Webb, but this is the only version that expands the details so that a map has an accompanying directional text. In Haggard's book, the directions are accompanied with the original version in Portuguese as a footnote but the directions given are just imaginary referring to later plot features and persons.

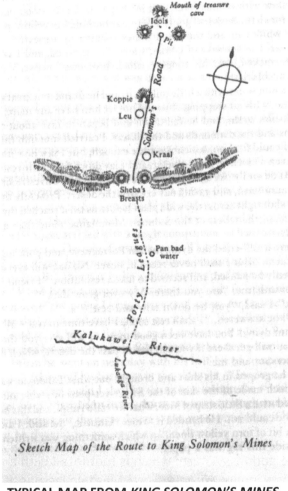

Sketch Map of the Route to King Solomon's Mines

TYPICAL MAP FROM *KING SOLOMON'S MINES*.
NOTE THE THREE PEAKS

The map is more important to us at this stage and some editions will include an illustration of sorts to show how the location of the mines were located at 'the three peaks of the mountain'. A further phrase used by Haggard is that the three peaks are 'in the form of a triangle' which now leads us to an example of a Masonic hoax/riddle type of story known as the *Treasure of the Cerros Llanganati*.

Inca Gold Perhaps

"The ingots WERE moulded by the Incas and actually bore hieroglyphics which proved it: they were wedged shape". So runs the description of the gold given by Charles Howe. We know Howe never found the gold so he was either making it up to create some validity about his story or maybe Brown had hinted to him that Inca gold was part of the treasure. And some related lost treasure stories suggest the identity of the gold is that of Inca origin. Tales of lost Inca hoards arising out of the invasion and eventual conquest of the Incas in South America by the Spanish Conquistador Francisco Pizarro can lead to this belief.   Out of this sad history of the destruction of the Inca nation comes the legend of what was said to be the resting place of the final and greatest part of the ransom which was on its way from Quito to Cajamarca when Atahualpa (the Inca King) was slain by the Spanish. Known today as Valverde's Derrotero (literally a map coarse) of the Llanganati Treasure, the region where this story is set is now modern-day Equador. The legend tells that not many years after Pizarro had subdued the Incas, a poor Spanish soldier by the name Valverde married an Indian girl, said in some versions to be an Incan princess. For some reason, Valverde's father-in-law discloses to Valverde the location of, or takes him to, the treasure cave which is in the Llanganati Mountains. Valverdi, now rich, after many years returns to Spain. On his deathbed, he composes the derrotero and has it passed to the King of Spain. The King sends an expedition to find the treasure but they fail to find it.

Many have searched for this treasure and it is well documented for those who wish to find out more. But what all ignore is the fact that Valverde's derrotero never came out of a Spanish archive which would have provided it with some semblance of authority. The source of this document can actually be found in the pages of an English botanist's notebook. Richard Spruce was tasked by the British Government in

1858 to gather plants of the Chicona tree in Ecuador. As a source of quinine, this plant was vital in the combat of malaria. In one of his notebooks is a copy of the derrotero; he said he had discovered it in the archives of Latacunga (home of the Spanish soldier). This copy of the original, he said, was made in 1827. A prefix to the derrotero text reads:

'Guide, or route, which Valverde left in Spain, when death overtook/ seized him, having gone from the mountains of Llanganati, which he entered many times and carried off a great amount of gold; and the King commanded the Corregidors of Tacunga and Ambato to search for the treasure; which order and guide are preserved in one of the offices of Tacunga'.

The story took to popular imagination only after Spruce died, as it was included in a book published in 1908 entitled *Notes on a Botanist on the Amazon and Andes.* It was a compilation of Spruce's work assembled by a colleague. However, 20 years prior to this, two British naval officers, Blake and Chapman, said to be from Nova Scotia, using Valverde's derrotero penetrated the Llanganati to locate the socabon (cave/tunnel). How these characters came to be in possession of the derrotero is told in true 'treasure island' fashion:

'A house in Maine, New England, was near a small island. Inheriting it from his uncle, a typical old sea captain, the inheritor's husband found a note within a Bible on a bookshelf that said to seek another book named 'Knapsack and Rifle'. This book was found sometime later in the attic and within it another note which said 'All about the Inca treasure in Equador in the hollow tree on the island'. Further, just to make sure everyone got it, it was said that pin-pricks were made under certain letters in the Book of Judges in the Bible. When assembled the letters spelt out 'Atahualpa's gold in the lake of the Marcasitas' also, 'Treasure in dead volcano by extinct lake'. Of course a bottle was located in the tree on the island. It contained letters and maps. These detailed how Blake had heard of the treasure from a young sailor in the Royal Navy who was the nephew of Richard Spruce.'

It was said Blake and Chapman were the only persons since Valverde to have actually found the treasure - as one would expect of characters in any treasure hunting story. The Llanganati Treasure Hunting Fraternity should take heed of the circumstances that brought Valverde's derrotero to light and how it appeared in the same era when other intricately constructed stories that hinted and gave clues about the lost treasure were also circulated. The Llanganati Treasure story sounds authentic because it was based on earlier legends of lost Inca gold and utilised Guzman's map (another map associated with the quest), all of which were further vibrantly enhanced with the author's local knowledge. But sounding authentic and being authentic are two different things. A final fact, either not acknowledged or not wished to be acknowledged by the Llanganati Treasure Hunting Fraternity, is the source of inspiration for the name that was used for the story; the Padre who gave the Bible to Atahualpa, prior to his execution in the square of Cajamarca, was Vincent Valverde.

What better way to pay back the suffering visited upon the Indians than to have those who, like the conquistadors, blindly seek the Inca gold make the repayments?

This beautifully worked hoax is partially the cause of our lost treasure being identified in some instances as being of Inca origin and it is no coincidence that the exact phrase used in Valverde's Derrotero to describe the layout of the three Cerros Llanganati, *"in the form of a triangle"*, was used word for word by L Rider Haggard in King Solomon's Mines for his directional clues. Similarly - and the reason the Valverde story is of interest to us - this is because our Harold Wilkins took an interest. Likewise it was no coincidence that Harold T. Wilkins inserted into his 1945 book, *Mysteries of Ancient South America*, a strange hand-drawn map which he alludes to being the secret of the 'socabones' of the Incas. According to Wilkins, at Ilo in Peru is to be found a **rock marked with hieroglyphs** (DNA) which is the key to 'Ancient Lost World Mysteries & Gold', a door to which is behind one of 'The Three Peaks' (DNA).

DETAIL OF WILKINS' MAP WITH THE THREE PEAKS CLUE

It is because of this 'three peaks' clue that the treasure on Juan Fernandez in some versions became to be identified as being of Inca origin. Said to contain a necklace of Atahualpa's Queen, the Key to the Wall of Sorrow (Muro de Los Lamentos), an inestimable stone known as the Rose of the Winds (Rosa de Los Vientos), and other Incan treasures, Juan Fernandez was (in part) thought to be the hiding place, for in the mountains behind English Bay is the Cerro Tres Puntas, the hill of three peaks (or more correctly the "hill of three points").

The name, Muro de Los Lamentos, was the most perplexing name found associated with the treasure and made no sense as given. Though it needed to be recognised as a clever Masonic allusion to 'the wall of sorrows/lamentation' as in the western wall (or 'wailing' wall) of the Jerusalem Temple, why it was such named could not yet be fathomed, nor why the Freemasons were involved in all this to such an extent.

The Royal Bank of Scotland

Of more importance to us, though, is the strange but true claim made upon the Royal Bank of Scotland in 1965. Sending the Llanganati Treasure Hunting Fraternity into doubt and confusion, the story of a ship named the *El Pensamiento* (The Thought) and it's fantastic cargo gives a fascinating demonstration of how the cross pollination of details can occur from one lost treasure story version to another. However, unlike most associated lost treasure stories where a treasure ship is said to go to some unknown location, this one has a mysterious treasure arriving to a very well-known location.

In 1965, a legal action was raised by Senora Violeta Aguilar de Caceras of Lima, Peru, who claimed from the bank '598 large merchant bags which were dispatched from Lima, Peru, in 1803 by the ship *El Pensamiento* under Captain J Fanning and J Doigg to the Royal Bank of Scotland and delivery entrusted to Castillo de Rosa'.

Another simultaneous claim of the treasure said it had been shipped from Lambayeque, Peru by a corregidor named Antonio Pastor y Marin de Segura, Marques de Llosa. The ship, *El Pensamiento*, was jointly commanded by John Fanning and John Doig (or Doigg). It was the descendants of de Segura, who died in 1804, that were also laying stake to the treasure pursuant to a fifth generation will. Contained in 90 wicker baskets, the treasure was said to be deposited in the bank by a Sir Francis Mollinson (or Mollison).

Royal Bank of Scotland officials had to deal with solicitors, South American banks, the Peruvian consul, the Procurator Fiscal of Edinburgh and tellingly the Masonic Grand Lodge of Scotland, acting for its South American brothers. A search was made of the bank's vault and strongrooms in Edinburgh and Glasgow which, of course, did not turn up the missing treasure, but enabled the bank to say they had checked. Safe custody books were of no use either in settling this strange case as these only went back to 1860. No treasure or settlement was forthcoming and all ended up viewing the incident as an 'experincia simpatico', an interesting shared experience.

De Segur and Fanning are all real personages, and along with Doig (whom you met earlier), were well known seafarers.

Other examples of books, stories, legends and tales which contain coded Masonic DNA we will come across in their due order as we crack the secret of the lost treasure. In all these, you have to know what you are looking for before you can identify when codes and ciphers are given. The above examples were given to show that indeed as all the legends and rumours imply, the Freemasons were the keepers of a secret, withheld from the world and passed amongst themselves. This begs the question, that if the Masons know about a lost treasure, why don't they go and find it? The answer lies in the fact that whilst the Freemasons do know something, they don't know that they know it!

Having made you aware of the complexities of the treasure hunt on Oak Island and shown you how fictional treasure stories contain our treasure DNA, you can see that when you are able to look at it as a whole, and not just the unconnected stories that on their own would be accepted for what they are, then you realise something is going on. It is as if forces far and wide are at work with one goal in mind, but only if you can harness them will you get a result, and that is only achievable if you can recognise them for what they are and therefore *know* how to harness them.

To help resolve the many questions raised, we have to return to JF Island and dig a bit deeper (excuse the pun). Also, using the knowledge we now possess, we can open up a bit more the part Wilkins and co. were playing in this saga.

CHAPTER 6

SUSPICIONS OF IMPROPRIETY AND THE GUAYACAN TREASURE

We are back on JF Island to try and find answers which, knowing the complexity of our subject, will probably result in more questions! We must also not lose sight of the fact we are still trying to answer the question, which island and the importance of the Trinity DNA, i.e. are we looking at three markers/cairns/rocks, three mountains/peaks or three islands?

The chapter that introduced us to JF also introduced us to the source of the lost treasure via Bernard Keiser. Via the efforts of Jorge Di Giorgio and Louis Cousiño, we were introduced to the Webb documents that will ultimately confirm the location of the treasure, but circumstances surrounding the finding of these documents is somewhat dubious and could even be said to be suspicious. So we backtrack now to the story as told by Anthony Westcott, and examine it a bit further.

According to the story, a lady by the name of Tita Diaz was supposed to have located the Anson documents by visiting Anson's castle home, inferred to be Rocksavage Castle. This is impossible as Rocksavage Castle was in ruins as early as the 18th century. Apart from that, a check of the castle's history reveals the name Anson does not have any association with it. (Lord Anson's ancestral home is Shugborough Hall in Staffordshire and is open to the public.) Besides that, it is highly unlikely that anyone would be allowed to rummage around a house belonging to the aristocracy, let alone be allowed to leave with family documents! So this is obviously a fabricated story; these documents then must have come from another source. You will recall that the old (Webb) letters had attached to them a note or were annotated that they had arrived from Chile six months and fifteen months respectively 'after my Lord passed away', i.e. Lord Anson. They were no doubt gathered together by Anson's secretary after Anson's death, filed away and later presented to the British Museum and British State Archives for preservation due to their historical value, as such documents were in those days (the British Museum being the early equivalent of the National Archives). Like most files, it was simply forgotten about, lost amongst the British Museum's vast uncatalogued collection of manuscripts, books, maps, files and letters that had been accruing since the museum's establishment by Act of Parliament in 1753. This collection had grown to such unwieldy proportions that a cataloguing programme commenced In 1898 to identify and give order to the vast holdings, which took until 1922 to complete.

Staying with the British Museum, our friend, the author Mr Wilkins, must have been very familiar with this institution in the decades prior to WW2 as his body of written works show, spending hours going through the pirate and treasure related archives. There is no doubt he had friends there; a Mr R. A. Skelton (Superintendent of the Map Room) comes to mind, who was involved in authenticating one of the Kidd/Palmer charts.

Someone, either Wilkins or a colleague, had come across the Anson file, which would have been in the Naval and/or Maritime History section that Wilkins was most familiar with. Almost certainly it would have been in Latin and it is obvious that Wilkins was a Latin scholar. That this file, or anything remotely resembling the information in this file, is not nowadays recorded at either the British Musem or the (English) National Archives indicates it was held back from the cataloguing and discretely removed from the premises.

The circumstances so far related regarding the finding of the Webb documents is mostly based on Westcott's book with the clearly fabricated Tita Diaz version being the one most promoted. This is understandable as an alternative report in Spanish was discovered which raises unresolved suggestions of impropriety. I quote part of the translated report, the brackets are my inclusion to help you make more sense of it:

'According to Errazuriz Senales, nephew of Eugenia Maria, the letters (of Webb) had been to stop in the hands of its (his) aunt because in the decade of 1940, the father-in-law of it(his), Luis Cousiño, were (was) contacted by an English (man), who had found the manuscripts that spoke of such treasure and it (he) delivered it to them. As it she(Maria) was married to the only son of Cousiño, (she) inherited the documents. In 1950, Cousiño, Peter Scotle, Benjamin leon and Jorge Di Giorgio had initiated the search for the third writing of Webb. In that year, the group found target log book of Webb and the inventory of the treasure.

After traveling (to) London to verify certain data, the adventurers had arrived at an agreement with the authorities of the time to divide what was found in equal parts.

When travelling (to) London in search of more details on the treasure, Cousiño was taken (took) possetion of the letters sent by Webb (found?) in a London museum.'

So Westcott's knowledge of what happened appears to be the result of a smokescreen to what actually did happen. Contact between the group (Cousiño?) and England appears to have been initiated c1940 by an Englishman who we suspect was Wilkins. The above translation also tells us that Cousiño subsequently went to London for more information and no doubt met with Wilkins. Three questions then which naturally arise from the above set of circumstances are; was this group 'fed' the documents via Wilkins? Were they complete? For what reason would Wilkins do this? The first question is answered by examining the photograph of the 'translation' of the Webb report and comparing it with the lettering on the Kidd/Palmer charts (part of the 'Morgan' chart is shown as an example). It becomes obvious that Wilkins did indeed have a hand in all this.

WEBB LETTER WITH INSERT OF (WILKINS') LETTERING FROM PART OF THE MORGAN 'SKULL' CHART

The answer to the second question does preempt a lot more which is yet to come. Our comments on the Webb letter were that it was a crap translation from Latin! Apart from that, it has just been done up to appear old with ye olde words and curlicues on the letters. I am not saying Wilkins invented the text; it looks like he copied whatever suspect English translation was in the Anson file that was probably done by some flunky in 1762. If you think about all the m'luds who got their greedy hands on the file, naturally they would have had the Latin contents translated for themselves. And so, back in the 1760s, with none of Anson's staff being able to understand the complexities of what was coded information contained therein (and it is complex), the documents were bundled up and eventually ended up in a dark and musty file, to be discovered 170 years or so later by the inquisitive eye of Wilkins or one of his colleagues. Perhaps this was the scene: Wilkins at a desk in the British Museum, c1930, poring over papers, approached by an employee:

"Ah. Mr. Wilkins, Sir, (hands rubbing together, sly smile, expectant glint in his eyes that furtively look side to side for anyone who may be in earshot). I think I've found something that may be of interest to you."

Wilkins carefully unrolls the parchments and takes a look. "Ah, yes, very interesting indeed. (Glancing side to side) Meet me in the pub later."

I am not saying, of course, that Wilkins was involved in any impropriety, suffice to say that somehow Giorgio and Cousiño obtained documents or copies of documents from the Anson file. It should also be remembered that though no record of this file exists in the archives, its contents were leaked and copied, as the codes in it can be traced appearing for directions in various locations where the treasure was searched for.

The third question's answer is a lot more complex but has to do with what was going on in total regarding Wilkins and the treasure. It is apparent by now that Wilkins was not working on his own on this. We have seen how he was obviously involved in the Kidd/Palmer charts deception but the whole thing was on too large a scale for him to be the sole instigator. This grand riddle, which was created around the treasure, involved close friends or colleagues who became the means to release the clues. Two of the names of note involved with

Wilkins are Herman Westhaver and Patrick Nolan, who we met when we investigated Oak Island. Contrary to what Wilkins told Gilbert Heddon when Heddon visited him in England, Wilkins *did* know all about Oak Island and he wrote about it in his early 1932 and 1934 books.

Except for a brief mention in the Introduction, you will not have heard of another colleague named Richard Latcham. Wilkins, we know, corresponded with him (he was English and lived in Chile) and in one of his first books, *Modern Buried Treasure Hunters*, published in 1934, he tells of 'The Brethren of the Black Flag' and Latcham's investigation into treasure documents found buried in a pot near the coast. That they knew one another before 1934 is interesting and shows that they were in touch for reasons other than Latcham's book which was not published until 1935. Latcham is the missing connection whereby we join the northern lost treasure (English language) clues to the southern (Spanish language) clues and it is through him Wilkins was able to impose his machinations upon the unsuspecting Cousiño. The formative link between them all has been identified as occurring through Latcham, Nolan and Cecil Prodgers, as they were all in the expatriate mining community (Cousiño's family having large mining concerns). To understand how Latcham was the link and how Cousiño and his group were being used, we need to examine the timeline of events just after WW2 when Wilkins reactivated the clue trail.

Whatever the manner was in which Giorgio took possession of the Anson/Webb documents, it is evident he did not get the Latin originals but a poor English translation. The originals, we suspect, were kept by Wilkins and his group. The earlier comparison of the style of the letters on the translated Webb document with obviously similar type on the Kidd/Palmer charts is confirmation that our friend Mr. Wilkins has been up to his tricks again! We have seen how Wilkins became aware of the Giorgio/Cousiño group. Tita Diaz *may* have been involved; she was Chilean and being married to the British Ambassador to Chile, would have had connections in high places. During her searches, she may have been introduced to Wilkins who would have been 'hovering' in the same halls of information with a reputation as *the* man to talk to about such matters as pirates and buried treasure. The result of a chat between them *may* have resulted in an introduction to the Giorgio/Cousiño group. However plausible this sounds, this high-profile society connection was probably introduced to give the story some credibility.

The most likely way is that previously described- through the aforementioned Richard Latcham. He wrote a book about a treasure hunt along the Chilean coast prior to WW2. Cousiño, a native of those parts, would have known about that. A mutual interest could have brought them together. Latcham would have communicated this to his friend Wilkins, and through that, Cousiño would have been put in touch with Wilkins. However, we will never know the exact circumstances of the transfer of the Webb documents.

Suspicions about this story do not rest with just the circumstances of Giorgio and Cousiño receiving the documents but also the manner in which the last documents were found. We have seen in a previous chapter that Giorgio apparently had information indicating 'a point on the coast where the answer can be found'. The 'point' in this case was on the coast of 'Pascoy Bay' (I have yet to identify 'Pascoy Bay'). After searching the coast of Chile by land and sea in his yacht, he came to the conclusion that it must be Horcón to the north of Quintero. Breaking off the search to form a company with his friend Louis Cousiño, who lived in Quintero (this is taken from the Westcott version), Cousiño resumes the search. We are told that guided by the old map and working at night searching the beaches of Horcón, he finds a box containing the other Webb documents. You may recall to yourselves that you've read that before somewhere, and indeed you have; it is very similar to the Westhaver and Smith story where they find a box of treasure documents on Plum Island. Cousiño is carrying out his search c1950. The Westhaver/Smith story is in Wilkins' *A Modern Treasure Hunter*, published in 1948.

Whilst you ponder on the possible implications of this, we look a bit closer at Horcón.

Horseshoe Bays

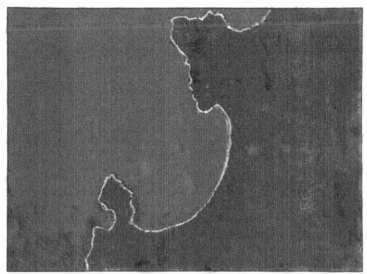

THE BAY AT HORCÓN, APPROXIMATELY 3.5 MILES WIDE AND SITUATED AT 32º 45´ S, 71º 30´ W

The immediate question is, of course, why did Cousiño search this area and not the coast adjacent to JF, which would be about 180 miles north of here? It can only be that the shape on the map was indicative of the shape of the bay at Horcón i.e. a part enclosed semicircular bay. Also, maybe Cousiño assumed (because he recognised it) that this must be the place. It can also be said that if you travel this Chilean coast, you will come across many similar bays. Westcott has this to say about the matter.

'Concerning a possible deceipt, the possibility that Jorge Di Giorgio invented the whole story is quite remote since it would exceed what is known with respect to his intellectual capacity. It is said that the matter of Horcón was an invention. But who could have produced Webb's message in cipher, in 18th century language and on original paper of the time. Later investigations have established that Captain Webb and the ship 'Unicorn' really existed, then it is very probable that knowing himself ill and being in Valparaiso he would manage to leave information about the treasure hidden at Horcón in the hope that his letters to England were received'.

Valparaiso is about 20 miles further south on the coast. We have seen that Anson's expedition was called 'Expedición Herradura', or the 'Horseshoe Expedition'. We have also seen Keiser describing the 'S' in the cave as a double horseshoe but he discards the supposition that the treasure is that of 'La Herradura' at Coquimbo. Once again, this is the treasure spoken about by Richard Latcham, which you will soon be made aware of.

The following map shows the Guayacan/Coquimbo coastline:

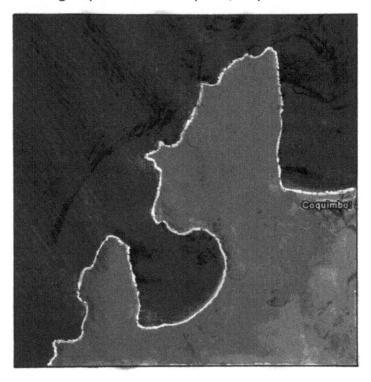

The above map shows the small, almost enclosed Herradura Bay, close to Coquimbo. The bay is approximately 1.5 miles across. You can immediately see that this (Herradura) bay is almost identical in shape to Horcón Bay; also, the contours of the coast to Coquimbo Bay are very similar. One of the reasons for all this interest in this part of the Chilean coast is, of course, the information in the last of Webb's documents to be found i.e. *'arrived at the position Latitude thirty degrees and eight minutes....'* Strange, don't you think, that it is this part of the coast Cousiño is searching where he finds the box on/in the beach containing Webb's letter **that designates this part of**

the coast? In other words, as previously stated, finding the box was rubbish; the group were already aware of this part of the coast and its importance. Let us have a look at it:

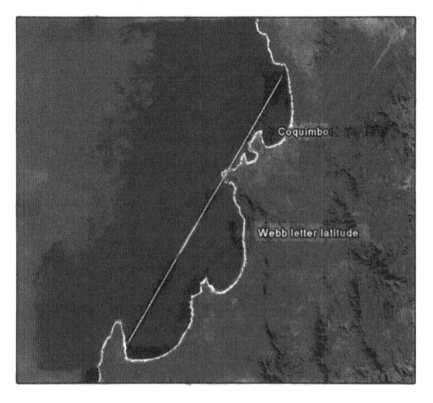

WEST CHILEAN COAST AT WEBB LETTER LATITUDE OF 30º8´S
DISTANCE FROM TOP BAY (YELLOW LINE) TO SOUTH BAY APPROXIMATELY
35 MILES

The thing that immediately strikes you looking at this map is that there are three bays very similar in shape. Add the smaller Herradura Bay just below Coquimbo and you have four almost identical bays. Therein lies the observational and coded clue; La Herradura - The Horseshoe i.e. bays shaped like a horseshoe.

Any map applicable to our quest therefore was showing a horseshoe-shaped bay. (Major DNA)

Though nothing is expressed in the documents you have already read, which suggests a geographic shape for the correct location other than the word Horseshoe in 'Horseshoe Expedition', the map of 'Pascoy Bay' was understood by the searchers to be showing a horseshoe-shaped bay.

The Map in the Watch

This story is appropriate here because of the shape depicted on a hidden map.

Wilkins, in his *Modern Buried Treasure Hunters* (1934), mentions the story of a watchmaker in Toronto who finds a map in a pocket watch. I will mention at this time another of Wilkins' idiosyncrasies; MN had a copy of Wilkins' *Treasure Hunting* (1932), and this same story is told there but, I also have Wilkins' *Treasure Hunting* (1932) and in my edition, this same story is missing; it just does not feature at all! However, the story originally did not interest us because no map was shown by Wilkins. A magazine article by Wilkins was unearthed which did reproduce the map and this can be seen in a copy of the article that follows. (Ignore the scroll-type map, this is just artistic licence!) *Assuming* the map with its accompanying directions are genuine, there are some points of interest to us. First is the obvious DNA, that of the shape of the bay. The similarity to Horcón and Herradura Bays is unmistakable. Second, an important rock is mentioned from which measurements are made. Third, the date, 1827. You may recall it was about this time things were happening at Lima with stories of a boatload of treasure disappearing. Fourth, the newspaper article mentions 'a small uncharted south sea island'.

Normally, one would not take a lot of notice of this sort of find; we have seen in a previous chapter there was an abundance of fake maps around in the 19th century. Indeed, a relative of 'J.L.' came forward to say that the old man was very imaginative and had rather a flair for drawing maps and charts in his declining years. Who knows? But, would a father send a son off on such a merry goose chase? However, you can see why it caught our attention. Isn't it also strange that the word 'Trinidad' appears? On top of that, Wilkins, in his story of the map, says, 'Also, this *derrotero* may be an old shellbacks' fake.....' Why would he introduce a Spanish word for the map?

We have mentioned Richard Latcham several times so far. As with Wilkins, it is now time to look a little deeper into the very important part Latcham plays in this story, for it is through him we will eventually be introduced to the all important ' Trinity Map' - a real treasure map.

"Treasure Map" Discovered in Old Watch

Above is the tarnished old watch inside of which the tiny treasure map, shown at right, and the letter was found.

Above is M. C. Rice, Toronto watchmaker who found the chart, shown at the left, inside an old watch which he was cleaning. The letter accompanying the map told of $250,000 in gold bullion being buried on a small, uncharted South Sea island, and gave specific directions for finding the treasure buried 8 ft. deep.

A CHART and letter giving the position of $250,000 worth of buried treasure on an island in the South Seas was found by M. C. Rice, a Toronto watchmaker, while cleaning a tarnished old watch. He found the yellowed manuscript, protected by a velvet covering, inside a watch which had been given him six years ago by a woman, as payment for a clock repair job.

The treasure map is circular in shape, and cut to fit exactly inside the watch case.

The letter found in the watch is dated 1868, and says: "Paul, my son, I am not long for this world. I fear that I can not bring you this chart as I planned, so the only course left is to hide it in some place and hope you find it. I am the only one surviving with this secret. At the spot shown lies a tidy sum, at least 50,000 pounds *(British)* in gold bars and coin. This island is small, uncharted and far from the main sailing. The rock shown is large, with two small ledges. A line drawn through these bears west, northwest. Lay off 100 fathoms, then bear west, southwest and 100 fathoms more. The chest is buried eight feet. Good luck lad and leave the sea. It is no life for you. J. L. Trinidad."

Rice is now searching for the woman who gave him the watch. He believes the letter is genuine, and plans to organize an expedition to search for the hidden treasure.

CHAPTER 7

INTRODUCTION TO RICHARD LATCHAM

From the previous chapter, we are in part still answering our third question here about why were the documents being fed to the Cousino group by Wilkins, and the answer leads us to Richard Latcham. Unfortunately, Wilkins was using them as mules, mere carriers of the clues. How concerned he was that they would wake up to what was happening is shown by the Webb letter being in the same handwriting style as the Kidd/Palmer charts.

In the timeline of events, it was not until *after* Cousiño obtained the Webb letter that they went to search JF, and this was *after* the search of Horcón.

As the story about obtaining the Anson documents via Tita Diaz was fake, they had to be searching Horcón for some other reason. The reason is quite simple when you know all the players pulling the strings behind the scenes. If you haven't figured it out yet, Cousiño and co. were treasure hunters. They were searching Horcón because it was similar in geography to Guayacan where a local treasure legend said a fabulous treasure was hidden in Horseshoe Bay (Bahia Herradura) but which cannot be found. A treasure for which detailed maps, written directions and an inventory exists, all of which were contained in one referential book. Of course, as part of your search, you would go and speak to the expert on the matter who wrote that book, Richard Latcham, so they must have been searching prior to 1943 as Latcham died that year.

Knowing who was involved in the background of all this, it is no surprise then that this group was rather fortuitously contacted by an 'Englishman' who generously provided the Webb letter which inferred their search should be on JF *('a new hiding place valley of Anson')*. But being given the clues and understanding them are two different matters. It was never intended that Cousiño would ever be able to understand them as the handwriting on the Webb letter, or his story about finding the box on Horcón beach shows. As a convenient cover story to explain the appearance of the documents, it would mean little to him, for us, it is a rather obvious pointer to the box on Plum Island. There were other pointers but you have to know why Richard Latcham and his book were so important.

The name of the Englishman known as Ricardo Latcham is virtually unknown outside the South Americas. This was partly due to his lifelong residence in the country he came to love and partly because, except for a few minor works in the English Journal of the Anthropological Institute, he published his works in Spanish. His biography discloses he was not just a hack writer of treasure tales;

Richard E. Latcham: 1869-1943.

Richard E. Latcham was a self-trained anthropologist. He received his prestige in anthropology on his own accord, through circumstance and perseverance. Born in Bristol, England, on March 5, 1869, he passed away in Santiago de Chile on October 16, 1943. Within these years, he held a number of positions and wrote numerous anthropological publications. After graduation from the Polytechnic Institute of London in 1888 with a degree in civil engineering, he got a job to survey and build roads in Chile, where he lived among the Mapuche Indians. He learned their language, and through established rapport and friendship, obtained knowledge of their culture and manner of living. At his advantage in the anthropological sphere, he had many opportunities for observation along with his devoted intellect and passion for information, which assisted in his subsequent anthropological publications. Following this experience he taught English in Santiago and then in La Serena, where he worked as a mining engineer. One year later, in 1903, his first technical anthropological publication was released. Years later he obtained various positions and received recognition from various locals. In 1927, he was named Professor of Indigenous Art. A year later, he became Director of the National Museum of Natural History. In 1929, he became Dean of the Faculty of Fine Arts at the University of Chile, then in 1935, was appointed the Professor of American Prehistory. Four years later he was given the degree of Doctor Honoris Causa at the University of San Marcos, and the Chilean Government decorated him with the Order of Merit.

Since, his publications and honor has lived on. With a degree in civil engineering, his accomplishments have outnumbered those in the fields of Art and Anthropology. A number of detailed studies of the Atacama region and a similar study on the Diaguitas were published before his death. Other publications include: La Organizacion Social y las Creencias Religiosas de los Antiguos Aracanos, Prehistoria Chilena, and Alfareria Indigena Chilena. Publications such as this keep the memory of him alive today.

El Tesoro de Los Pirates de Guayacan (The Treasure of the Pirates of Guayacan)

Recognised as the pre-eminent expert of native South American anthropology, his book, *El Tesoro de Los Piratas de Guayacan* (The Treasure of the Pirates of Guayacan), published in 1935, is regarded as an academic hiccup. Written in Spanish, lurid illustrations swirled across the pages, tabulated data was interspersed with what looked like maps. Pages of sigils followed pages of hand-drafted lines of text in some strange alphabet. Was that Hebrew? The drafting style looked vaguely familiar. It was enthusiastically read to see if it had anything to do with our treasure, especially why the word 'Herradura' was appearing in it. Once translated, the weird and wonderful three-part story of Richard Latcham and the treasure of the pirates of Guayacan was learned. The first part of the book, *The Discovery of the Documents*, sets out the story:

The bay of Guayacan (see previous chapter) located to the south of the bay of Coquimbo is often called the Bay of the Horseshoe (la bahia de la Herradura) and is considered one of the warmest and safest bays on the coast of Chile. It has a narrow entrance that widens out and the area of interest to us is the north-western corner of the bay. This is an amphitheatre 600 metres in length by about 400 in depth, enclosed to north and east by cliffs, opening onto a small beach which appears white on the account of crushed shells amongst the sand. Treeless, without vegetation, sown with rocks and rocky crags, this small enclosure is usually deserted.

The bay of Guayacan, after being discovered by Sir Francis Drake in 1578, became a refuge and a meeting place for privateers and pirates. Bartholomew Sharpe landed there in 1680, along with Edward Davis in 1693 **and George Anson** in 1744. When Drake landed there, he was attacked by 100 Spanish horseman and 200 Indians on foot, forcing them to return to ship and the following day, weigh anchor. Drake made a sketch of the bay, fixing latitude and longitude. On his return to Europe, he distributed plans of the bay to navigator friends of his. It was known by the name Drake gave it, the Bay of the Horseshoe.

On 25 May 1926, an unidentified ship entered the bay. Boats were loaded with men and boxes which rowed towards the north-west corner of the bay. After unloading on the shore, the boats headed back to the ship which, half an hour later unfurled its sails and headed out to sea. With one man issuing orders, a camp was set of three or four tents. Some with axes went to look for firewood. Curious locals arrived seeking to know what was happening. One of them, Manuel Castro, tried to communicate with the men, but none spoke Spanish. After a while, one man was found who did speak Spanish, Don Jose, but he answered Castro's questions evasively as to what was occurring. A bargain though did ensue as Castro was employed to supply the crew with firewood and water. According to Castro, the crew, 27 in all, was made up of English, French, Germans, Dutch, an American, a Portuguese and a Spaniard.

Utilising a small troop of donkeys, Castro daily supplied the crew with water and firewood. Gaining the confidence of Don Jose, who was the only person who spoke the language, Castro learned the purpose of the expedition. The men were there to find a 17th century pirate treasure and to locate a fabulously wealthy gold mine. To do so, they had a map of the part of the bay of Guayacan where these were supposed to be and which was where they had set up camp. Regarding the mine, they had no further information other than that there was to be found nearby a furnace, seven bushes of 'sumach' and two large rocks lying parallel to each other next to a gorge. The crew, morning to night, set to excavating the beach and surrounding areas. The leader of the group was an Englishman. He and two others rented horses which they used to traverse the region looking for the landmarks, accompanied many a time by Castro, who acted as a guide. Finding nothing and with food in short supply, the crew became disheartened. After 24 days, the ship reappeared, loaded the crew and stores and sailed away.

Castro resolved to continue searching for himself. With the aid of his sister Rita, they used their small savings and inheritance to conduct excavations. These they did at night to prevent them being spied on, with Rita standing watch and Castro working with bar and shovel. The search continued for four years during which Castro dug more than 300 holes. Having spent more than 3,000 pesos, their small resources were exhausted. Mortgaging their last piece of property for 2,000 pesos, the search continued when at the beginning of 1930, Castro found a large clay pot buried two metres underground. Within the pot was a mass of rotted leathers. These were wrapped around a heavy copper plate. When the plate was cleaned, what could be made out was the depictions of a caravel, a cannon and a rose and on both side were symbols taken to be lettering. Castro was both excited and despairing, as having found the plate he couldn't read what it had to say. Taking the plate to Rita, she viewed it from many different angles but to no avail, she couldn't understand it either.

Not trusting any close friends and relatives, Castro and Rita decided the best course of action would be to show the plate to a foreign gentleman with whom Castro had some dealings and had appeared to be well educated. Castro, with the plate wrapped in paper, shortly called at the residence of Mr X. After much circumlocution, Castro explained the reason for his visit and produced the plate. Mr X examined the plate but could not decipher it either. Mr X had a compatriot in Buenos Aires, who was well versed in modern and ancient languages. He offered that if Castro wished to form a partnership, then Mr X would see to it the plate was translated. Castro demurred saying he had to consult his sister first. After consulting with Rita, it was decided to go into partnership with Mr X. who took a tracing of the plate and sent it to Buenos Aires as well as instructing Castro to continue excavating where the jar was found as there might be other objects nearby.

The next day, Castro located an amphora buried three or four metres west of where the first jar was found. Breaking it open, it exuded a thick and fetid liquid which made Castro sick for half an hour. Within the amphora was a roll of skins made into parchments and covered with the same lettering as the copper plate. Informing Mr X what had occurred, he was advised to soak the skins in benzine to dissolve the oils and act as a deodorant. Whilst the skins were soaking, Castro continued to excavate, turning up a small plate of gold shaped like a bag closed at the mouth. About a week later, Castro unearthed a gold virgin, 30 centimetres tall and weighing 10 or 12 kilograms which bore the date MDC. This was with two Spanish knives, a star of lead with six points with the now familiar lettering, a coin from the time of Pericles, a small gold idol and a triangular piece of copper called (by the Buenos Aires translator) an "A of Charlemagne". With these was another clay jar. Castro threw rocks from a distance to break this jar. It also contained oil soaked skins of a different type to the amphora but with the same lettering. In all, between the two jars, Castro had a total of about 70 skins. Castro placed all these in a cloth bag and at dusk returned home via a path that did not pass through town. Fixing up a type of altar, he placed the gold virgin and other objects on it where he photographed them.

When one of the children in the house became ill, Castro, who was superstitious, packed all the found items into a box and gave the box to a friend for safekeeping. Two or three days later, the child recovered, reinforcing Castro's superstitious convictions. The friend disappeared along with the box, leaving Castro in a quandary, for he could not report it to the police without having to explain the source of the treasure. In the meantime, some translations had arrived from Buenos Aires; the delay was caused due to the difficulty in discovering the key which was made up of letters from archaic eastern languages. The copper plate read:

Aqui hay un tesoro. A la distancia de 90 metro(s). Dejo estop or haber perdido mi galleon. Hay 80 zurrones lleno de oro y 90 de plata.
Ano 1640. Deul.
(Here there is a treasure. At a distance of 90 metres(s). I leave this due to having lost my galleon. There are 80 zurrones full of gold and 90 of silver.
Anno 1640   Deul)

Castro was ecstatic and his beliefs were now vindicated. If each zurrone (leather bag) contained 50 kilograms of gold, that was four tons of gold at 5,000 pesos per kilogram. He even had a place to look, 'At 90 metres', which he took as to be from the place where the copper plate was found.

With more parchments sent to Buenos Aires for translation, Castro excavated a zone 90 metres from the original hole but no treasure was forthcoming. Beginning to lose confidence about the translations and mistrusting Mr X, Castro went to visit another friend, Dr Cohe, who was a professor in eastern languages in Santiago. With Dr Cohe also translating the documents, these were compared with the translations from Benos Aires and were found to match. Running out of money, Castro sold the small plaque of gold to a jewellery shop for 180 pesos Leaving his suitcase with the copper plate at an inn in lien of his debt, Castro went home to be met with more translations from Buenos Aires. These concerned a confederation of pirates and a fortress established in the bay of Guayacan.

Castro had a few more adventures, seeking out the mine and treasure until further translations arrived. According to them, a community of pirates operated around the year 1600 with their headquarters at the bay of Guayacan, exactly where the crew from the ship in 1926 searched. There was a great 'subterraneo' (underground chamber) which was a combined storehouse, powder magazine and treasure repository. A list of the treasure was included along with references to ship's names, tonnage, crews, armament etc., and references were also made to the mine, but no specific directions. What was not sent to Buenos Aires were maps, topographic plans, a plan of the 'subterraneo' and one of the mine. But none of these had a point of reference by which they could be oriented. Though measurements and angles appeared in the documents, there was no point of reference from where they were to be taken or directions to which they were to be shot. Castro continued to haphazardly search as more translations arrived. This is where Ricardo Latcham comes into the story.

The second part of his book, *The Author's Investigations*, introduces us to Latcham's involvement in the matter. In September 1930, Latcham was summoned to the office of the Director General of the Department of Libraries, Archives and Museums. The Director had received a visit from a Mr Arthur Cohe, a 'doctor in philology'. Dr Cohe was seeking support via facilities and funds to conduct further investigation into a treasure hidden by 17th century pirates in the vicinity of Coquimbo. This treasure had come to light after the discovery of a plate of copper, a small plaque of gold and other parchments, all covered with obscure lettering. In a later meeting with Dr Cohe, he produced the small plaque of gold and Latcham was also shown;

'.....a tracing of both of sides of the copper plate, on which could be distinguished, in addition to the writing, the drawings of a caravel, a great cannon and a rose. The photographs were of a plane or topographic map, another plan that claimed to be an underground chamber (subterráneo) where the pirates had hidden their treasure, and one document full of letters, sentences and drawings, that he assumed referred to the map of the subterráneo.'

Reporting this to the Director, Latcham was given permission to conduct an investigation into the matter and in October 1930, in company of Dr Cohe, Latcham arrived at La Serena. From here on, Latcham relates his interactions with Dr Cohe, Castro and Mr X and his own searches of the location. The story continues on with Latcham's narrative and searches the nominated locations.

The third part, *The Documents*, has illustrations of various maps, said to be topographic maps depicting Guayacan and drawings of the documents accompanied by the translations. Latcham informs us that in relating all these to us, he did not see all the documents or translations; that some were fragmentary and also he did not know in what order they were to be assembled. This was further hampered by the translations themselves as these were not literal translations but seemed to contain comments and observations of the translator as well.

Here we learn the story of the pirates as is translated from the documents;

'At the end of 1599 or at the beginning of 1600 there arrived in the Bay of Guayacán two pirate ships whose captains were called, respectively, Subatol Deul and Ruhual Dayo. Deul was Hebrew and Dayo Norman or Flemish. Enchanted with the security of the anchorage, safe from all winds, and of the seclusion and solitarily of the place, they resolved to establish their headquarters there. They spent some months with nothing occurring to bother them. They sallied out, but always returned to their favourite harbour. At the end of May, on their return

from an excursion to the north, they found another ship anchored there, which, when seeing them enter, raised the English flag. The ships of Dayo and Deul immediately raised the black flag of piracy. The strange ship thereupon struck the English flag and also raised the black flag.

Once anchored both pirate ships, with their canons directed towards the intruding ship and with all their crew in position, armed for combat, they signalled to the other to give itself up. In answer this one dropped a boat in the water, in which some men embarked, going to Deul's ship. One of them went on board, the others remaining in the boat. This individual turned out to be Henry Drake, son of the famous Sir Francis Drake. He was well received by Deul, and later by Dayo. That night the three met and as a result of this meeting the three privateers or pirates resolved to form a league and to invite all the pirates who operated in the Pacific to join it. It would be called The Brotherhood of the Black Flag, and its main seat for supply and rendezvous would be that bay, which they called The Refuge.'

More translations, tables and maps follow in Latcham's book. We learn about the Rose:

'Also here was the Turkish navigator Sumastage and the Egyptian Madel Saden, a prisoner. The Rosa de Francia (Rose of France) brought by the Egyptian. He was respected and was revered by generations and ended up deposited in the gorge. Madel Saden was a fisico (naturalist) and spoke several languages. Sumastage is the second Turkish pirate we find associated with the League. Madel Saden, the Egyptian, was also a privateer or pirate, taken prisoner by Sumastage, who burned his contender's ship after sacking it. Madel Saden had taken the Rosa de Francia from a Portuguese ship on the coast of Africa. The Rosa de Francia, whose image is recorded on the copper plate, was a miraculous rose, held in great esteem by all pirates and guarded carefully in the treasure chamber.'

And the treasure in the subterraneo,

EN EL SUBTERRÁNEO CHAMBER	IN THE UNDERGROUND
MCC (1,200) baras de oro.	bars of gold
DC (600) baras de oro.	bars of gold
DC (600) surones de oro en polbo.	bags of gold dust
XX.(20) ollas llenas de oro.	pots full of gold
DCLXXX (680) baras de plata.	bars of silver
(10) tinajas de joyas.	jars of jewels

MDCXXIV (1634) *Dayo.*

Latcham continues on, interspersing details about the pirates with images of the documents and their translation until he ends with the cryptic line,

'And now, readers, we leave it to your talent to unweave the threads of this mystery, wishing you better luck than that which has touched us in our investigation of the subject.'

One of the illustrations (Fig 17) in the book:

Fig. 17. Descripción del subterráneo.

The illustrations get increasingly more outlandish (and wobbly in execution) the further you go through the book. It all gives the appearance that our man in Chile was in the habit of taking the Beefeater before the sun passed over the yardarm when he wrote a quaint book in Spanish about the treasure of Guayacan. One item of interest in the above illustration is the 'fowling piece' at the top. An earlier chapter tells of Westhaver's description of what was in the chamber including '......there are fowling pieces, old cannon...,'. Look at the lower left; see the cannon as well? So there is a missing link here between Westhaver (Oak Island) and Latcham's book in Spanish! That missing link can only be H.T. Wilkins.

This book needed closer studying because appearance is one thing, meaning is quite another, for the book was written with two languages in mind. In Spanish, this is simply an eccentric book written for the locals by one of their leading academic lights about the treasure of Guayacan. But the book was not written for the Spanish locals. A message in English cant placed by Latcham in the Spanish text tells you something else. We say 'placed' as Latcham placed a number of things in the book that were not hidden at all. As the saying goes, the best place to hide something is in plain sight because nobody is looking there, especially if you are told you are looking at Guayacan. What's in the name Subatol?

The story of the treasure of Guayacan brings us to the end of the first part of this book, which was to give you the background and the stories which are the foundations of the lost treasure story.

From now on, we investigate, scrutinise, question, expose and give you more revelations taking us ever closer to the treasure. We also take you to unexpected places new on this ever-more fascinating trail to treasure.

PART 4

CHAPTER 1

LATCHAM, THE TRINITY MAP AND GUAYACAN

In the first part of this book, I covered the informative stories as known to us that relate to our quest. I am not claiming mine is a definitive work on the stories that are the background to the lost treasure, because, of course, there may have been undercover secret expeditions never revealed to the public, although it has to be said it is very difficult to keep such undertakings totally secret. With time, somebody usually lets slip that something has been going on. I am very confident therefore that the disclosures made and revelations to come will not be overshadowed by any other work, learned or otherwise. The exception I have to say could be anything my ex-colleague MN may 'put out there'. After declaring 'no more interest' in the project, I heard he was trying to get something published!

However, I have, as they say, "had my ears to the ground", that, coupled with years of extensive research, have given me the confidence to declare this story unique. All these buried treasure stories have a common DNA, all are spawned from one event in history. All are in this book. I know of no other publication that tells the same story.

We are still only part way there with the revelations. We have already exposed some of the false trails and untruths created to deceive the unwary but which at the same time hide a trail to real treasure, comprehensible only to those with the intellect and insight that something subtle was going on behind the façade. I did say at the beginning this is a complex story and it takes us back to our friend Richard Latcham, whose story is not all that it seems.

Latcham Exposed

Perhaps the (previous) story about Guayacan might contain unmutated or distorted DNA that could yield up some directional clues. The book already contained the Horseshoe codeword and talked about what could be one of the treasure objects; the Rose that was mentioned in the Webb report.

One of the maps in the book stood out from the others, named 'Fig 25, Mapa de los contournos de las bahias de Coquimbo y de Guayca'. In the lower left corner was a complicated triangle which obviously had *meaning*.

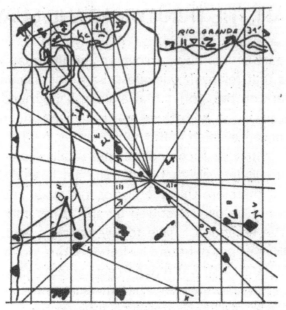

Fig. 25. Mapa de los contornos de las bahías de Coquimbo y de Guayacán.

THE TRINITY MAP

Obviously drawn by someone of intelligence and with a style different to the others, this map was somehow vitally important to the whole mystery. If his book contained undistorted DNA, then this could prove to be a close but misidentified copy of the actual lost treasure map. I have called this map the **'Trinity Map'**. What exactly it was showing and how you were to interpret it would have to be worked out.

It was also quite obvious that there was a bit more to it all than Latcham would have you believe. Photographs existed of the 'Placa De Cobre' found by Castro and this displayed an image of a gun whose design was closer to the year 1900 than to 1600. Indeed, it is very indicative of the type of gun to be found on the German battleship 'Dresden', sunk in 1915 during WW1 in Cumberland Bay, JF Island. So for this plate to be real, it was probably created after 1915! It could be, of course, that Castro *did* find the plate in the circumstances described but it was never part of the scattered hoard he found later indicative of a 17th century burial. The 'modern' gun is an obvious giveaway and it sounds like the plate was planted there as part of a hoax and nobody had benefited from whatever message the indecipherable letters gave.

We must also remember, we only have Latcham's word that things happened as he described them in his book. That he liked to have a bit of fun will be demonstrated.

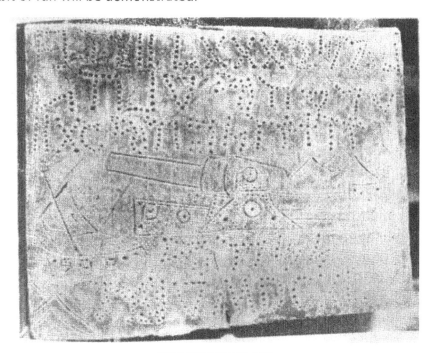

THE COPPER PLATE

This is what Harold T. Wilkins writes of Latcham in his book, *Modern Buried Treasure Hunters* (1934):

'From Santiago Chile, comes a story which if correctly presented, would appear to suggest that there are aspects of the history of piracy in the Spanish Main, or what used to be called the 'South Sea' (the South Pacific) which have been unsuspected by those who have concerned themselves in this byway of history or marine folklore.

The director of the Natural History Museum of Santiago is Richard Latcham, a native of Bristol, England, who migrated to Chile in 1888 and led a romantic life among the brave and intractable Araucanian Indians who made the Conquistador, Pedro de Valdivia, bite the dust in the age of Pizarro and the conquest of Chile.'

Wilkins then informs us how faded and musty documents in a sort of code turned up about the 'Brethren of the Black Flag'. He continues:

'Mr Latcham, who is an authority on the folklore and archaeology of Chile, says this picturesque company of pirates comprised Moors, Egyptians and Jews who "operated in the Spanish Main" between 1600 and 1650, contemporary with true buccaneers. "Their base" he says, has been determined to have been on the North Chilean Coast, and they used their five different languages to maintain secrecy about their movements.
What interests Mr Latcham is the archaeological side of the hunt, in which he is stated to have made subterranean discoveries in the Atacama desert; but the heart of the Chilean Government is in finding the hidden loot, which is the way of all or most treasure-hunters, even those who involve goblin aid.'

We have already seen previously Wilkins must have been speaking to Latcham prior to WW2, for he wrote this prior to 1934 when his book was published and Latcham's book about Guayacan was not published until 1935! This was all a bit strange, Wilkins writing this way about a friend who he was complicit in this story with.

MN had thought he recognised Latcham's drafting and lettering style used elsewhere, particularly the squiggles and disconnected letter or symbols dropped into the maps. He trawled through the lettering in the illustrations in Latcham's book until he found a definitive match; a tiny 'R' in Fig 17 was the same 'R' used in marginal lettering in the Kidd 'Key' Chart.

Fig 17

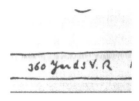

Key Chart

Other matches quickly followed:

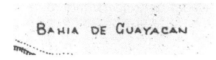

Fig 7

C H I N A   S E A

Key Chart

But not all lettering on the key chart was Latcham's. Some appeared to have been done in the hand that had drawn the other Kidd charts. There was a strange mix of the two hands, even occurring in the same word. This other lettering matched that of Wilkins as it appeared on a rough diagram, known as the 'John S' map appearing in *Kidd, His Skeleton Island*, and also the 'damning' postcard showing the 'treasure island' that exposes his deceit.

So much for infamous Kidd treasure maps! Latcham and Wilkins were in cahoots alright, but in cahoots about what? This wasn't a hoax but a real chase to find something, as this pair both knew about the lost treasure. Assuming he was looking at another complicated Masonic hoax/riddle again about the treasure, we set out to discover what were the real clues to be found in this strange book by Latcham.

Attacking the Manuscripts

Because of the bizarre nature of the book, with its numerous hand-drawn copies of the claimed maps and manuscripts, it would be easy to hide some tip-off that this was a hoax/riddle. MN decided to check if the translations of the manuscripts given by Latcham actually matched what was shown on them. This required drafting a table of the manuscript lettering (said to be ancient Hebrew) to match each with a modern letter. In doing this, the first major hint that this was a hoax/riddle was found; the manuscripts translated letter for letter into a message that was in modern Spanish!

Checking the manuscript text to each translation given was a laborious task as some of the 'Hebrew' letters were similar in appearance, so when loosely drawn, 'c' could be mistaken for 'r,' or 'd' for 'm' etc. In checking one such manuscript and translation, just such an error appeared to be made by Latcham when he wrote:

'It now only remains to present those documents that we have been unable to translate, or whose sense we do not understand. In most of them we have been able to decipher 14 letters, but we have not always been able to combine them in a way that forms intelligible words. In the hope that some reader has better luck we reproduce copies and the translation of the letters, as much as we have been able to decipher them.'

Figure 30 in the book follows:

Fig. 30. Documento.

Latcham's translation we can see was:
De ir e k a h de m.
Estas cosas estan en el camino.
Al mui p en d el.
Si   en S ai indio en el
creo es
tiera nueba
De la son kro
ha he a ola fna le
ke se saca la que da.
Checking the lettering, it was found the last line should really be:
ke se sara la de da.

Looking at the whole translation now, it was apparent that rather than being an ancient text whose meaning was undecipherable, it was a message in a type of pig Spanish based on English cant:

De ir e k a h de m.	Dear Richard
Estas cosas estan en el camino.	The coast is the way
Al mar p en d el.	A map of it
Si en S ai indio en el	Has an indian in it
creo es	He is black
tiera nueba	New tip
De la son kro	He is the son of a crow
ha he a ola fna le	Ha he oh hello here is the end
ke se sara la de da.	Ke se sara (what will be) la de da

Perhaps there were more of these hidden messages to be found. Fig. 26 managed to stand out even amongst the other bizarre images. Not only was the 'translation' incomprehensible, the 'Hebrew' lettering was also different.

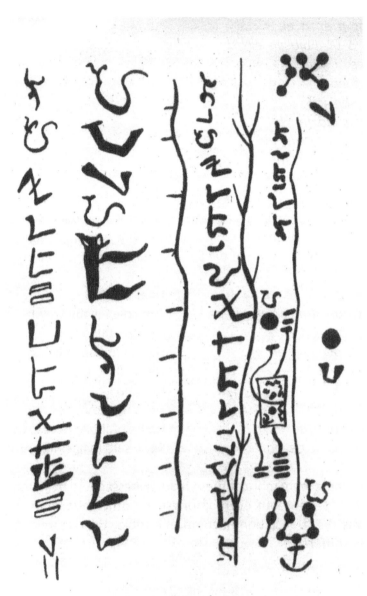

Fig. 26. Documento.

Latcham had this to say about it:

'It is one of those documents that we have been able to understand only by halves, because while it is certain that the letters can be deciphered, these have no meaning. But such as we deciphered we give here:

A sur ei (hay) ke (que) uterin.	*To the south ei (there is) ke (that) uterin.*
S. P. N. AMERO.	*S. P. N. AMERO*
Al sur el sutern N. P. E. A.	*To the south the sutern N. P. E. A.*
a la ida	*to the going*

The translator from Buenos Aires could also not decipher the sense of this document, but he says the following with respect to the lower part:

"Chain and anchor indicate the base of the refuge or that is strategic: Seven planets correspond to the North Pole, which are the seven of the Great Bear and seven correspond to the South Pole, which are the seven of the Little Bear. It is not known if they are planets or stars, but are shown as stars and the two crosses of the navigator, a name given them by Dayo and Deul, belonging the one to the east and the other to the west.'

'Line T. with vertical rays, two small rivers [rivulets, brooks].
Line U. with arrows, the path from the coast to the furnace and the mine and the probable ground [land, plot].
Line F. with anchor, navigational route and island."'

The reason why the 'Hebrew' lettering was different was that the whole image had been mirror reversed. When the image was reversed and the lettering checked, apart from requiring some corrections it was found that there was extra lettering in the text not appearing in Latcham's version.

The text now read:

ASUREIPEUTERIN
SPNSEAMERD
ANSURENSUTERNNSEA
ALAIDA

Recognising that 'ANSURE' and 'SUTERN' was cant for 'answer' and 'southern', the real message was assembled:

ASUReiPeuteRln
spnSEamerd
ANSURENnSUTERNnSEA
ALAIDA

'A surprise answer, southern sea, on the island'

MN pondered the now rather obvious meaning of one of the pirates names, Subatol (Sub-atoll) Deul, having now confirmed this was indeed some complicated riddle. The base story was checked to identify any directional codewords being given. The word Herradura had already been isolated and this applied to the shape of the bay, which when viewed on a modern nautical chart, disclosed an overall shape disturbingly similar to the island of Pinaki and its inner lagoon.

The treasure was said to be found at the Playa Blanca, the White Beach (DNA). This was another codeword as Guayacan was not the only location where a white beach was searched for the treasure. The 1813 expedition of the *Prometheus* commanded by Rear Admiral Robinson was said to have searched on a white beach in a group of three islands: the Salvages. (Robinson revisits these islands in 1856 after retiring from the Navy.) We now knew why they did so. Written in faded ink in the margin of MN's old copy of *The Cruise of the "Alerte"*, at the part dealing with Robertson's search of the Salvages, the book's original owner had penned the island's latitude, 30' 8". This matched the detail given on the Webb report where it had said, '...*arrived at the position Latitude thirty degrees and eight minutes on the thirteenth of January'*.

This latitude is confirmed further on in the book where the writer specifies the latitude and longitude of the 'Great Salvage', one of the three islands searched by Robinson. Strangely enough, in my copy of *Sea Drift* written by Robinson and published in 1858, someone has also written 30' 8" in the margin opposite a reference to the Salvages. For the Admiralty to have been following this detail in 1813, it showed the Webb report was no mere modern treasure tale after all and confirmed **the Admiralty was using the Webb document.**

A strange adjunct to this had been provided quite unknowingly by some earlier (modern) treasure hunters. As part of their hobby-like interest, they decided to have a look at the Salvage Island story for a possible jaunt. Obtaining the details from *The Cruise of the Alerte*, they had hired a light plane and overflown Grand Salvage Island to identify the white beach searched by Robinson. Taking photos of each aspect of this high and desolate island, they were puzzled to discover that no such white beach existed as the island's cliff ringed boundary merely stooped to the water via a series of rocky bays. Time has obviously changed the topography here, as Admiral Robinson in his report said.

'the white sand extended around the bay, and an area of many acres intervened between the high-water mark and the foot of the cliff.'

Another codeword was given as 'aguada', which was for the landmark of a water source. Captain Brown had made comment that the water sources on the island were the small volcanic craters. It was a well that was said to be a landmark for the treasure in *A Modern Buried Treasure Hunter* (1948). This landmark, though, would naturally appear on any treasure map based on an old chart of Juan Fernandez. Villagra Bay was historically marked on Juan Fernandez as being a source of water. A roughly walled embankment had been built there by early seafarers to trap water flowing downhill into the bay. The last codeword isolated by Latcham was 'ebanin' (DNA) when he talked of the inscribed rocks in Guayacan which directed one to the treasure. He suggested this was an ancient Iberian term. As good a name as any for the marked rock seen by Nordhoff on Pinaki. It was worked out that there was indeed a set of directional codewords or phrases given in Spanish that could lead to a particular island. This made sense as they could be used to accompany a map that did not identify the actual area being depicted, as a lost treasure map was known to do. It was also a clever security feature as both were needed, map and directional codewords/phrases, as one without the other was useless.

Shades of the Kidd/Palmer charts are seen here where the 'Key' chart had to be used in conjunction with the 'Skull' chart.

In descending order of scale, by matching what was known for Pinaki to the codewords/phrases, the coded directions appeared to be:

Trinidad	A three island group
Herradura	A horseshoe shaped island
Pan de Azucar	The sailing mark of the pinnacle to identify the pass
Playa Blanca	The white beach
Aguada	The water source
Ebanin	The rock with directional symbols to the treasure

One landmark, previously isolated elsewhere and given by Latcham though, did not fit: 'Cerro de Tres Puntas'. This was the 'hill of three points, taken to be 'hill of three peaks'. This seemed to directly relate to the mountain known as the 'Cerro Tres Puntas' on Juan Fernandez Island, which after all was just one of a three island group. How to reconcile this code phrase with the low sand atoll Captain Brown had pointed to? Was it all really saying that Juan Fernandez was the correct place to look after all? An answer had to be found. Continuing on, a comment by Latcham on the 'Trinity Map' says;

'It is curious to note the direction of the cardinal points, as much on the map as on the plan. On the map, north gives the direction that is truly the east[1] and on the plan, north points towards the southwest. At the entrance of the Bay of Guayacán a galleon has been drawn, which is about to enter the bay.'

Finally, Latcham describes the fourth map;

'The fourth map seems to indicate the area containing the underground chamber. It covers approximately the same region as that of the previous one, but is divided into a series of rectangles that represent degrees of latitude and longitude. In the middle there is a more or less quadrangular block, in whose centre a point has been marked from which fifteen lines spread out, forming diverse angles and which extend to the edge of the map. On one side of the square there is a number II and on the other the number IV. In the peninsula of Cicop we find the letters C. I. Spread over the region are numerous rocky

crags, united by triangles, and each one with a letter, but they do not correspond to those written down in the sheets of measurements. The Coquimbo River has also been drawn on this map, which takes the name of Rio Grande. In the lower part is featured el cerro de tres puntas [the hill with three points], and in the upper part a ship in front of the entrance to the Bay of Guayacán; and on the side beyond the point an anchor is seen.'

Latcham is obviously describing the map numbered Fig 25 shown at the beginning of this chapter (the Trinity Map) which carried the caption, "I Mapa de la contornos de las bahías de Coquimbo y de Guayacán" (Map of the contours of the bays of Coquimbo and Guayacan). He informs us that the complicated triangle in the lower left of the map is to be taken as the hill of three points.

Deciphering the Maps

We had been uncovering and assembling the clues and hints carefully planted by Wilkins and what must have been a small clique of knowledgeable associates in the various books and writings, published in the period which spanned the 1930s to the late 1940s. As no further clues were forthcoming after Wilkins' 1948 book, *A Modern Buried Treasure Hunter*, we concluded that whatever clues or instructions necessary to uncover this mystery had now been completely given by them. The only thing to do was work it all out starting with the Trinity Map. It was studied in an attempt to deduce what it was actually showing, which was certain not to be the Bay of Guayacan. It was in all probability the same map Westcott, in his book, described as having been in the Anson file but for which no image was to be found:

'The map of a bay "Pascoy" **with many lines;** *one indicating a point on the coast where the answer can be found. And written in a corner, as in the first document: "This map arrived from Chile fifteen months after my Lord passed away.'*

To see if I could learn anything from the radial lines radiating from the centre, I decided to measure their angular relationship, and also their values from what pictorially should be north. After progressively working around the map a number of times and determining the angles between the radiating lines, nothing was revealed that meant anything. The map below shows the only lines that at this point in the investigation 'stood out'. '90' appears because it was the only right angle created. The '117' line is shown (measured from the arbitrary N?) because it passes through a triangle that Latcham says is to be taken as 'the hill of three points' and therefore could be important.

There is a lot more to say about these lines further on in this book.

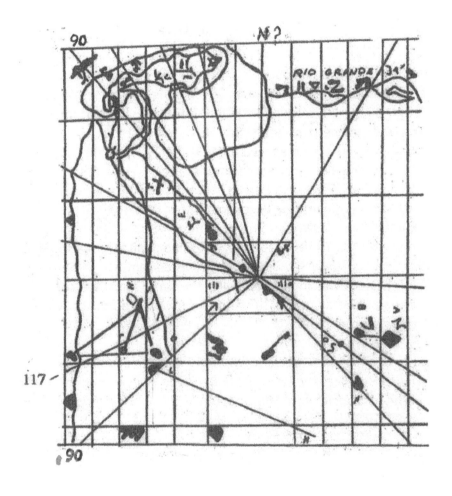

As mentioned previously, of particular interest is the right angle (90/90) as it is the only one there and you have to ask the question, 'Why is it there?'

Having uncovered the truth behind the world's most misunderstood lost treasure story involving the longest and most convoluted hoax/ riddle ever devised (the Kidd maps), it all just pointed you to Anson's lost treasure somewhere near the Cerro Tres Puntas on JF. Some things are not to be though, and finishing here at JF is one of them. Loose ends flapped around JF like a torn sail in a storm for if Wilkins had supplied Cousino the information required to find the treasure (the Anson file), why had neither he nor Bernard Keiser done so?

So all this means is that if the maps are not to be used this way, they are used some other way, so I had to find out how we *do* use the maps and the information they contain. One thing clear from these last couple of chapters is the significance of the word 'Herradura' as it appears in the Herradura Bay name and also Anson's Herradura Expedition (Webb letters). It is defining to us a specific shape i.e. horseshoe or enclosed bay as opposed to an open bay. Sounds like it could even be describing a certain shape of atoll! So where have we got to so far? We seem to have five theatres of operations:

1. An island and/or a group of islands in the Tuamotus Archipelago in the South Pacific Ocean.
2. Juan Fernandez Island off the coast of Chile.
3. Herradura Bay near Coquimbo, Chile.
4. Trinidade Island off the coast of Brazil.
5. The Salvage Islands in the Atlantic Ocean.

They are listed in order of importance and all can be said to be linked through DNA, historical evidence and circumstance. So let us recap with a few pointers to our island before we look at defining its location. Remember also that Captain Brown, for all the trouble and expeditions he was responsible for, never actually named his island to anyone. JF Island, as we know, features very strongly because of the Anson/Ubilla link, yet there is no evidence that Brown searched here. The only time he ever called here, he tells us, was as a young man with Schmidt on the *Sea Foam* on the way up the west coast. We are left then with a lot of descriptive features.

A previous chapter via Latcham gave us, 'A surprise answer, southern sea, on the island'. Coded directions give us via 'Trinity' a three island group. Three being a recurring theme also gives us three markers/cairns/rocks/mountains/peaks. Also remember there are three islands in the JF Island group. A significant clue was, of course, in the Webb letters that mentions the expedition; sent by Lord Anson to the **South Seas.** This secret information cannot be ignored and everything, it must be said, is pointing to an island somewhere in the Tuamotus Archipelago. Brown, as we know, had a lot of people running around here.

The JF link then has so far provided us with Westcott's story of a search by Anson's Captain Webb for a treasure believed to have been located here by the Spanish nobleman Captain General Don Juan Esteban de Ubilla. Although we suspect Alvarez as being somehow connected with Ubilla, we have not yet got a positive connection with him, Brown and JF Island. But as ever, our friend Mr Wilkins helps out. He mentions Pinaki Atoll just a few times in his books and attaches no story of substance to it, yet he hides clues to Pinaki all over the place as we will see later when we expose them.

To get to the formula or 'key' used by those who set the codes i.e. Anson, Webb, Latcham and Wilkins, we need to take a harder look at the Webb letters to Anson. You may question this as Keiser has spent a lot of time and money working to them and hasn't moved from JF Island. This is because it looks like he is using the information given at face value, applying some of his own interpretations... and he hasn't found anything! He, as we know, is misinterpreting the clues, despite hints from us.

Cousino and co. employed experts in astronavigation believing the secret lay here somewhere. Latcham hints at celestial groups in his book and, of course, in Anson's day, positions were fixed using the stars. So it makes sense that if you are coding an island's position a long way from any land mass, it would have to be by utilising the stars. Accurate positioning using latitude and longitude did not come into it until the perfection of the marine chronometer by John Harrison in the latter half of the 18th century and the establishment of the Greenwich Meridian as standard in 1884.

CHAPTER 2

THE MISREAD ANSON-WEBB LETTERS

If this story about Webb was no latter day invention, then perhaps it held cogent information about the lost treasure. However, the information as it appeared seemed to be directly indicating the island of Juan Fernandez was the place to look. Was Cousino deliberately given wrong information or did he just misunderstand it? That Cousino searched Cumberland Bay but Keiser was now searching English Bay indicated that the information was open to varying interpretation. This would then require that the Webb report and the Anson file be completely disassembled to understand what it was really about and what it was really saying.

As the 'Horseshoe Expedition' had been on a naval ship, then this was either a highly secretive official tasking or it was some unofficial affair which privately borrowed the use of naval resources. The notations reported by Westcott in the Anson file e.g., *'This map arrived from Chile fifteen months after my Lord passed away,'* suggested that others were enquiring into the matter as they were not sure of the expedition's status either. These notations were just the type a servant would make on a file's components for someone else who was trying to establish what it was all about. The Admiralty tasked 1813 expedition to the Salvages under the command of Rear Admiral Hercules Robinson suggested that this event was indeed some official state secret, but the information as to the directions to find the treasure in the report was either wrong or had been misinterpreted. As the Webb report appeared to be in fairly plain English, something had gone wrong either through the loss of vital information or some misunderstanding of what the message was actually saying. A clue to this was found in the description of the text of the file's third document:

Altitude Schuba I Depth Yellow Stone I

You have already read how Cousino's group had taken this to be some direction involving the height of a star Dschubba and the depth from a yellow stone but you have to agree, even on face value this direction appears quite insensible. What is known now is that a mistake occurred between the Latin name for the constellation of the Charioteer, Aurigae, and the Latin word for gold bearing, auriger. The Latin word for gold is aurum and it is from here we get the chemical notation for gold, AU. Though aurigae and auriger appear to come from the same root 'au', they are in fact not related at all. This mix-up occurred in part due to the simple mistranslation which changed 'charioteer' into 'yellow stone' but this mistranslation was also helped along by a parallel code which associated the constellation of Aurigae with the colour yellow. The uncovering of this complex colour code will be made as it is met in due course. For now, we need to concentrate on the relatively simple matter of mistranslated Latin. As the phrase 'great yellow stone' also appeared in the Webb report, then this showed that the report had once been in Latin also, with what we were now reading being again an imperfect translation.

It could now be deduced that the Anson documents, all in Latin, had been translated into English when they were discovered after his death in an effort to determine what they were about. It was to these English copies that the notations were made explaining each one's history. No doubt when the file was discovered in the British Museum, Wilkins was able to translate the Latin originals correctly to get the true meaning. It was merely his own copies of the early imperfect translations found in the file which Wilkins more than likely supplied to Cousino.

A Lesson in Latin
It was decided that the English version of Webb's letter should be professionally translated back into Latin. MN, with the help of a Latin teacher, did a good job on what follows in this chapter. Webb's report now appeared thus:

'Ego, Cornelius Patrick Webb, navarchus classis regalis magisterque Unicorn superstes solus Expeditionis Soleanae haec verba equiti George Anson domino primo navali maxima cum concordi relinquo timens morbus qui me affligit prohibeat ne maneam Unicorn 19 June navem solvit circumnavigavit Cape Horn 6 Decemeber ad situm advenit latitude 30' 8" 13 January iussa regalia aperivit introitum celatum locavit tabulas con fecit et oneravit 864 saccos aureos 200 *nummos aureos 21 dolia gemmarum cistam auream in qua rosa aurea et smaragdi alti duos pedes evant et 160 cistas nummorum aureorum et argenteorum 24 January castellum detrui maris rediens 28 January in tempestate maxime laesa est malumque perdidit in insulam perfugere coacti sumus 3 February eramus longitudo.....latitudo..... neque res sarcire poteramus ita ut gazam salve transportaremus eam as nova latebras transtulimus vallem Anson funis longitudi a loco contemplationis ad saxum magnum flavumque alto quindecim pedes Unicorn refecta est ad transportandum inexpectandum Valparaiso certior facta est consilliori seditionis dum navis in litor manet usus sum nave auxiliari Unicorn a me fracta est omnibu nautis inentibus sex vivi fidi Regis causa mortui sunt ad Valparaiso ad veni 1761'*

A notation was added regarding the translation of the reference 'Altitude Schuba I Depth Yellow Stone I', which said, 'The word for depth and height are the same in Latin being 'altitudo''.

You need to note that this translation back into Latin was created using the English translation of Westcott's Spanish version as it appeared in his book. Even so, the interesting point is, the translation does not have any punctuation. So what was the sentence structure of Latin? How did you tell where a sentence began or ended? Was it possible that a person in translating this message from Latin also did not understand the sentence construction and so had incorrectly joined sentences and left others incomplete? With a Latin dictionary, it was now decided to re-translate Webb's report back into English, but this time, if a Latin word is found to have more than one meaning, then try these other meanings as well. Likewise, a Latin word of similar meaning would also be substituted and the different meanings and its use produced also examined. This exercise would also include replacing the words for 'great yellow rock' (in the translation 'saxum magnum flavumque') with Charioteer (Aurigae) after the constellation of that name.

An explanation is required here why we have two versions of the Webb letter. Westcott's version when talking about position reads (in part) as follows; '...arrived at the position Latitude thirty degrees and eight minutes on.......'

Careful examination of the photograph of the translated copy (to be found in Part 1) reads; '....LAT THIRTY D EIGHT M....'

This copy, almost certainly provided by Wilkins shows his translation from the original he found in Anson's papers.

Westcott, or whoever provided him with his version assumed that D stood for 'degrees' and M stood for 'minutes'

The Webb report was first examined to see if there were any obvious anomalies that would indicate a translation error had occurred. The following version is an amalgam of Westcott's version and Wilkins' version as it appears in the photo (spelling mistakes included):

'I, Cornelius Patrick Webb, Captain of his Majesty's Navy, Master of the Unicorn, only survivor of the Horseshoe Expedition depute this account to my Lord George Anson First Lord of the Admiralty (courtisually) because I judgeth malady which ailleth me will not permit to wait. Departure Unicorn June nineteen crossed Cap Horn December six arrived at position lat thirty D eight M. January thirteenth opened royal orders, located secret entrance, translated Crown's belongins, loaded eight hundred sixty four bags gold. Two hundred bars gold, twenty one barrels precious stones and jewellery one golden trunk containing rose of gold and emeralds, two foot high, one hundred and sixty chests with gold and silver coins. January twenty four fortress destroyed. When returning the twenty-eight of January before a violent storm, the ship suffered serious damage and lost a mast. We were forced to shelter on an island; the third of February found us at Longitude ... Latitude... and it was impossible to carry out repairs for the safe transportation of the treasure; transferred to a new hiding place valley of Anson a cable length from the observation point in direction great yellow stone depth fifteen feet. Unicorn repaired for emergency crossing course Valparaiso; informed of plans for mutiny while the ship was becalmed to the West of Valparaiso I made use of the auxiliary boat (Pinnace). Unicorn blown up by me with all on board, six loyal men sacrificed for the cause of the Crown, I arrived at Valparaiso. 1761'

You will realise that the meanings assigned to the directions given towards the end of the passage do not make any logical or practical sense.

This has not stopped Cousino and Keiser from interpreting it all to mean the treasure was originally hidden on JF by Ubilla and it was merely relocated to a new place on the island. This interpretation produces a noticeable inconsistency in that by giving the name of the new location for the treasure on the island, 'valley of Anson', there was no need then for Webb to have written earlier '.....found us at Longitude ... Latitude...' as 'valley of Anson' immediately identifies the island. Apart from that, as you now know, by 1761 JF had long been garrisoned and therefore it was impossible for the described activity of an English ship hiding a treasure in Cumberland Bay to have occurred unnoticed. What this particular phrase with its rather too obvious omissions, '.....found us at Longitude ... Latitude...' did tell was that the locational bearings was not missing at all as the blatant ruse was a signal that they were to be found somewhere else in the report, most likely in code.

The text, when examined to identify any anomalous details, appears straightforward until the sentence 'January twenty four fortress destroyed' is reached. This appears immediately after Webb talks about loading the ship and one wonders how a 'fortress' came to be on a deserted island or why it needed to be destroyed. Experimenting with Latin words;

Destroyed:
Delere: destroy
Evertere: turnout, eject, overturn, ruin destroy
Dirimere: part, divide, interrupt, break off
Fortress:
Arx: figuratively a bulwark, also a citadel or refuge
Castellum: castle, fortress

'Arx' for a bulwark in this passage is literally describing a fortified earthwork which would equate to us as being a strengthened and lined underground chamber. This does fit the Spanish methodology of undertaking detailed constructive work to protect and hide significant caches and would be found at the depths relating to the doctrinal intervals of a 'Estado' (about 5 and a half Spanish feet). A hint to this chamber or vault is given as a clue by Wilkins and Latcham, though in a somewhat exaggerated way, in their stories when they describe the underground fortress, the 'subterraneo'. Some of the linked lost treasure stories do also give the details that the treasure was in an elaborate excavated chamber (Oak Island or Herradura Island) or a rock lined or rock topped cave (Bonito Benito).

It was the directional details that seemed to be the heart of the matter;

'.....and it was impossible to carry out repairs for the safe transportation of the treasure; transferred to a new hiding place valley of Anson a cable length from the observation point in direction great yellow stone depth fifteen feet.'

What follows gets a bit intricate due to the way the words changed the meaning of the whole passage;

Transferred:
Translatio (property): also note that though Westcott earlier uses the word 'inventoried' on Wilkins' version, the word used is 'translated' which means the treasure was 'transferred and loaded' rather than 'inventoried and loaded'.
Traducerre (troops): bring across, lead over, transport across, transfer.
Hiding place:
Latebra: hiding place, retreat
Cable:
Funis: rope, rigging

The phrase, *'saxum magnum flavumque alto quindecim pedes'* for 'great yellow stone depth fifteen feet', now gets corrected to 'Great Charioteer depth 15 degrees'. By applying the alternate meanings and with some judicial punctuation, even though still padded out into full English, a somewhat different message was read;

'I, Cornelius Patrick Webb, Captain of his Majesty's Navy, Master of the Unicorn, only survivor of the Horseshoe Expedition depute this account to my Lord George Anson First Lord of the Admiralty (courtisually) because I judgeth malady which ailleth me will not permit to wait. Departure Unicorn June nineteen crossed Cap Horn December six arrived at position lat thirty D eight M. January thirteenth opened royal orders, located secret entrance, transferred Crown's belongins, loaded eight hundred sixty four bags gold, two hundred bars gold,

twenty one barrels precious stones and jewellery one golden trunk containing rose of gold and emeralds two foot high, one hundred and sixty chests with gold and silver coins. January twenty four bulwark (strongroom) broken (into?). When returning the twenty-eight of January before a violent storm, the ship suffered serious damage and lost a mast. We were forced to shelter on island; the third of February found us at Longitude ... Latitude... and it was impossible to carry out repairs for the safe transportation of the treasure. We transferred to a new retreat, valley of Anson, for rigging. Longitude for the observation point (place to look) is direction Great Charioteer depth fifteen degrees. UNICORN repaired for emergency crossing course Valparaiso; informed of plans for mutiny while the ship was becalmed to the West of Valparaiso. I made use of the auxiliary boat (Pinnace); UNICORN blown up by me with all on board; six loyal men sacrificed for the cause of the Crown; I arrived at Valparaiso. 1761.'

It could be reasonably suspected that the details of events following the loading of the treasure lost some of the flow when translated from the Latin original in that it was really trying to say that the ship had been prepared for the return journey but an intervening storm damaged it. This would then match the consequence of the storm given in Latin *'in insulam perfugere coacti sumus'*, which was literally 'on island refuge forced to be'. The inclusion of the word 'an' in the padded out English translation of 'we were forced to shelter on an island' made the report sound as if the ship had sailed with the treasure to shelter on an entirely new island prior to sailing to JF. The report also made a whole lot more sense now with the ship sailing to what was an inhabited location to seek replacement rigging.

Though it was now understood a basic error in translation had caused the message to be misinterpreted, there was still the issue of the missing directional bearings that could identify the location with certainty. No doubt the phrase, *'Longitude for the observation point (place to look) is direction Great Charioteer depth fifteen degrees'* was some type of code that gave this, but its meaning at this stage could not be fathomed. Was it a code known only to Webb and Anson, the key to which was lost when they both died?

Before we take a closer look at star codes, we need to look at Masonic and alchemic influences used within them. You may consider that what follows is somewhat tedious as here we are far removed from what you may expect in a treasure hunt story i.e. following the clues on a map to find an island then locating the treasure. But those hiding a great treasure would not have made it easy for an 'outsider' to find it, so you should bear with me whilst we look at some of the devious ways clues were hidden. You can, of course, skip the 'heavy' chapter on Alchemy and Masonic influences used in astronomy but you may be left wondering at a later stage why certain techniques were employed in the decoding process.

CHAPTER 3

THE STAR CODE, ALCHEMY AND MASONIC INFLUENCES

Two coded phrases that when properly translated from Latin were now understood to refer to stars in two constellations are as follows. The first was 'Altitude Schuba I and Depth Aurigae I'. The second phrase was 'Longitude for the observation point (place to look) is direction Great Charioteer depth fifteen degrees'. If the key to the code these phrases were using was only known to Webb and Anson, then its loss meant their meaning would never be deciphered. Where do you start?

You start with the proposition that if the correct island is Pinaki, then these coded phrases must produce bearings for that location. In other words, it should be simple to work out the 'key', for this would just be the mathematical formula which converts the references to stars (the factors) into the bearings for Pinaki (the answer). You need to do quite a bit of preparatory study to obtain enough knowledge to do this though. Firstly, you need to obtain a book on astronomy to learn how the designations Schuba I, Aurigae I and Great Charioteer can be rendered into numeric form. Next is to obtain a good understanding of the interrelation between the Zodiac, Masonic Astronomic Theology and the ancient esoteric import of stars known as the Tetramorphs. Lastly, you will need to make yourself familiar with that most incomprehensible of studies, the Royal Art of Alchemy.

This led to many hours of brain wracking work carried out by both of us. The mathematical side of the formula, the second key, is relatively easy; the hard part is getting your mind around the esoteric lore that is used as the first key. To do so, we will work backwards (reverse engineering) from the 'answer' of the bearings for the Pinaki Trinity to learn not only the workings of the code but the profound minds of those fluent with its use. In doing so, we will also learn of a separate parallel code based on the same keys but which used colours rather than the names of the stars.

Masonic Astronomic Theology

Because of the use of stars in the code used by Anson and Webb and the fact the Masons were, if not directly involved in the hiding of the treasure, aware of it, it was considered prudent to investigate the little known subject of Masonic Astronomic Theology. It was becoming more and more apparent that the Masons did have, to some extent, knowledge of the treasure and parts of code could be found in their lore and stories. The Masonic degree or teaching called the 'Royal Arch' you have been introduced to already due to the thinly disguised allusions to it in the stories surrounding Oak Island or in other Masonic influenced stories where three sojourners discover the hidden arched vault containing the lost treasure. Apart from the 'base' level of Royal Arch teachings, there is a 'mystic' level which relates to stars and the zodiac. An investigation of this arcane subject found it to directly relate to the formulaic (second) key to the star codes. Perhaps if one could understand *what* was being said in the Masonic lore to produce its use as the formulaic (second) key, may identify what the first key was.

The (Prime) star Antares features strongly in the code as you will see. It is part of the Constellation Scorpius. The Scorpion also features as a possible clue. However, both, due to an ancient esoteric tradition, are represented symbolically by an eagle. It does not mean you associate the constellation of Scorpius to the constellation of the Eagle (Aquila), but just know that Antares is represented by the symbol of an eagle. For Fomalhaut, its symbol came about by associating it with the 'man' in the nearby constellation of Aquarius (The Water Bearer). Again, it does not mean you directly associate the constellation of Piscis Austrinus with the constellation of Aquarius, only understand Fomalhaut is represented by the symbol of a man.

**MASONIC ASTRONOMIC ROYAL ARCH WITH SHIELD OF THE ANCIENT
ORDER OF FREEMASONS**

In the above diagram, you can see the two most popular symbols of Freemasonry; 'G' and the compass and square. There is also a Masonic symbol (not shown above) replicated as a jewel which stands for the Royal Arch Order, the 'Triple Tau', named after the three T(au)s it is made up from, Tau being the Greek letter for T and the last letter of the Hebrew alphabet.

The Masonic Latin catechism which accompanies the jewel is 'Nil nisi clavis deest', which means 'Nothing is wanting but the key'. The Triple Tau also has a mystical astronomic meaning.

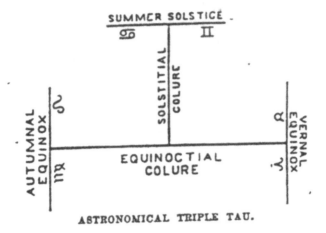

ASTRONOMICAL TRIPLE TAU.

A further explanatory catechism expands that the Triple Tau is,

Templum Heirusolyma
Clavis ad Thesaurum
Theca ubi pretiosa deponitur

which is,

Temple of Jersusalem
Key to the Treasure
A place where a precious thing is concealed

The Freemasons like to say about all this "Si talia jungere possis sit tibi scire satis", which means "If thou can'st comprehend these things then thou knowest enough". If you are starting to have a feeling that perhaps these Masonic teachings might not be allegorical after all but actual directions to find a treasure, please hold that thought for later.

That Royal Star lore was part of the first key requires understanding how the stars Antares and Capella are part of it. This had to do with the hint Wilkins had given via the Kidd key chart riddle that required working in and with opposites as part of a mathematical formula. You will see this replicated in the workings of the star code (to follow) which required the addition of the 'opposites' of the latitude and longitude to produce the answer. It also requires an ability to recognise the meaning of symbols as part of the code.

The star Antares marks the Autumnal equinox; it is opposite in all senses being that of Aldebaran in Taurus which marks the Spring equinox. Next to Taurus is the constellation Aurigae. Capella was used by Webb as it was 'opposite' to Antares and had the needed numeric values produced by the equatorial coordinate system to give the correct answer when decoded. One of the stars used in the codes though was El Nath and this is a white star. That this star was used by Anson and that its colour also had a coded meaning was to be found in the discovery of the first key which was the workings of Alchemy!

Alchemy is a difficult subject, totally alien to the traditional search for a pirate treasure. It is not a subject you would expect to be confronted with, It is complex and difficult, so I am going to treat it very briefly with just enough to show you some of the basic workings. There are plenty of publications out there if you want to delve more into the subject.

I mentioned in an earlier chapter how Wilkins made a point of mentioning the acronym VITRIOL. It had appeared on a map he was sent. This was just Wilkins doing his usual thing of dropping clues all over the place. This one can be explained in the following diagram;

'VITRIOL' CAN BE SPELT OUT UTILISING THE CAPITAL LETTERS

In the emblem above 'VITRIOL' can be made out of the phrase 'Visita Interiora Terrae Rectificando Invenies Occultum Lapidem' in the circular border. The key to the code is in the emblem; the sun and moon pouring their essence into a grail and becoming one. You can also see some of the alchemic symbols that mysteriously make their way onto maps.

So we are looking at the attraction of opposites for e.g.; Sun/moon, black/white, male/female, latitude/longitude. This showed the key to the code used by Anson and Webb was Alchemy, or more correctly knowledge of the workings of Alchemy. Out of all this comes the encoding formula for the star codes (and certain other numerical calculations) – the addition of the opposites, which is a stage in the alchemic process known as the 'coniuncto' (conjunction).

MASONIC SCOTTISH RITE 6TH DEGREE JEWEL WITH ALCHEMIC SYMBOLS FOR MERCURY, MOON AND SUN

In the lore of Alchemy, it is actually the colours red and white which are considered the opposites, red for male and white for female. This is why the stars Antares (red star) and El Nath (white star) were used by Anson to give the bearings via the star codes to achieve the treasure. You have to know the alchemic import of the symbolism being used here because the star El Nath in the constellation of Aurigae is also one of the stars that make up the constellation of Taurus! Webb, for his coded message, utilised Capella, a yellow star in Aurigae. From all this knowledge, we now get the first hints of a parallel code in operation based on the same lore and operating in colours. The star Antares gets it name from Greek as being a *red* star it was named for being the 'rival of mars', Capella is a *yellow star*

Keiser on JF Island is searching the *red* earth near the Cave of the Scorpion and hoping to discover the treasure at a depth from a *yellow* rock. It is this colour code that Keating followed in part to find the treasure and a reference to it is to be found in a garbled document accredited to him where it was written;

'We have buried at a depth of four feet in the red earth...
...28 feet to the north-east, at a depth of 8 feet in the yellow sand'

That the stars could be used for terrestrial navigation to find the lost treasure was itself just another use of the Alchemy as a code. The statement in the Emerald Tablet, 'Whatever is below is similar to that which is above' has been loosely shortened to in contemporary versions to 'As Above, so Below'. In other words, 'What is in the heavens is replicated on earth' (i.e. star position transposed to terrestrial lat/long position). It was now obvious that Anson and Webb were adepts of Alchemy. Their common knowledge of the working of the Royal Art enabled the dying Webb to write his coded report safe in the knowledge that Anson already held the key.

Even with what is yet to come, the extent that Anson and Webb transposed alchemical lore into directional instructions remains unclear. It is suspected though that *if* you can comprehend and have a working knowledge of the Royal Art *and* understand how it can be used as directional instructions, you will then possess enough information to find the treasure. We need to point out something further about the use of this colour code and its appearance in the garbled document accredited to Keating, '*......in* the *red earth......in the yellow sand'*. Nowhere does the mention of the word 'red' appear in what has been related to us about the Anson file or Webb's letter, it is only by virtue of you now knowing the existence of the code that you can recognise Keating was privy to it. The use of 'yellow' can be understood in part as a bad Latin translation of Aurigae but does suggest that it was known that the word 'yellow' was the directional codeword to be preferred rather than what this mistranslation should produce which is the word 'golden'.

As Keating did have the alchemy/star/colour codes and did locate the treasure, then his source of coded directional instructions was not that of Anson and Webb for whilst they used the same codes, they did not use them in that entire form.

What needs to be identified is that there are two sources for the coded directional clues of different nationalities; Ubilla (Spanish) and Anson/Webb (English). Ubilla was the source of the Spanish codewords/phrases as well as the alchemy/star/colour codes. However, the Spanish codeword/phrases became separated from the overall story as Anson and Webb only used the alchemy/star/colour codes in their communications. The form of the alchemy/star/colour codes disclosed by Keating, not coming from the Anson/Webb (English) source could only therefore have come from someone privy to the Spanish source; in other words, a Spaniard.

One can only speculate the purpose of the Spanish Captain's (Alvarez) mission, for what else could it be but a mission if you had the key to the codes, and his command that filled Keating, Kelley and even Brown himself with such fear they never dared mention his name again!

The content of this chapter I can appreciate will be daunting to many but do not get bogged down in it. It all 'thins' out later on in the book and becomes easier to understand, even to the extent that some of it can be ignored. For now, it is all part of the study of the search for our treasure; every element has to be looked at and researched. It is also so that I can say to you, the reader, "I think I've covered everything."

More brainstorming I'm afraid now, as armed with all this alchemic background information, it is onto the stars themselves to discover the island's location hidden within them.

CHAPTER 4

CELESTIAL NAVIGATION, AN EXPOSITION

Each star in the heaven can be plotted and rendered into numeric by using what is known as the equatorial coordinate system. This follows the geographic coordinate system which enables any location on earth to be specified in terms of latitude and longitude. A quick reminder; latitude is the angle between a point on the earth's surface and the equatorial plane (0º), the north pole being 90º North, the south pole being 90º South. Longitude is the angle east or west of a fixed point known as the prime meridian. It is an arbitrary line between the north and south poles through the designated location. There have been different prime meridians over time as each country reached navigational ascendancy and set their own prime meridians such as Hierro, Del Corvo or Paris etc., as seen in the Kidd charts chapter. Today, terrestrial and oceanic navigators worldwide use the Greenwich (London) Meridian.

To help you better understand what is to follow, you need to understand the basics of celestial navigation, basics only, as it is a complex subject and almost made redundant today by satellites and GPS (Global Positioning Systems) now used for ocean and terrestrial navigation. The depositors of the lost treasure utilised constellations in their code so only by getting some understanding of the subject can you hope to understand how they did it.

The Celestial Sphere

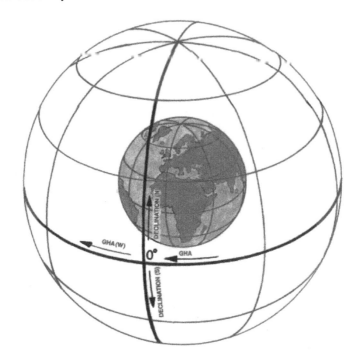

Imagine the earth completely enclosed within a glass globe on which is drawn a projection of the earth's latitude and longitude grid. Instead of land masses all the constellations and heavenly bodies are located on the inside of the globe in their respective positions in the sky.

In normal terrestrial or coastal navigation, if not using GPS, bearings are taken of known land or shore objects in known positions, from these accurate cross bearing fixes, and your own position is determined. In much the same way, the ocean navigator will take sights of three or four stars to ensure the most accurate cross fix is taken.

From the above diagram, you can see that latitude on the celestial sphere is now termed 'declination'. It is laid out in an identical manner to that on earth and has parallels that run north (+) and south (-) from 0º at the celestial equator to 90º at the celestial poles.

Longitude, on the other hand, is termed GHA (Greenwich Hour Angle) on the celestial sphere and unlike earth longitude where it is measured east and west 180º either side of the meridian, it starts at the same Greenwich meridian and runs continuously around the world in a westerly direction for the full 360º. An explanation is required as to why the measurement is in degrees yet includes 'Hour Angle' in its title.

The sun crosses the Greenwich Meridian at noon (12.00 hrs) each day during the earths 24 hour one-revolution journey around its polar axis. Longitude as GHAs also starts at Greenwich on its 360º journey around the world. You can now see how the two equate. The sun moves (appears to) westward covering 15º of longitude every hour. So, for example, 20 hours GMT (8hrs+12) equates to 300ºwest (20hrsx15) GHA.

The GHA of all the bodies in our solar system (sun, moon and planets) commence at the Greenwich Meridian. Stars, because they are outside our solar system, have a different starting point because the earth rotates with respect to the celestial sphere. We cannot therefore simply use the GM as 0º RA (Right Ascension). The starting point used coincides with the Vernal Equinox as shown in the diagram below and is known as 'The First Point of Aries'. It is an angular distance from Greenwich at a particular time and varies slightly hour for hour each day. RA is measured from this point easterly (right) when viewed from outside the sphere.

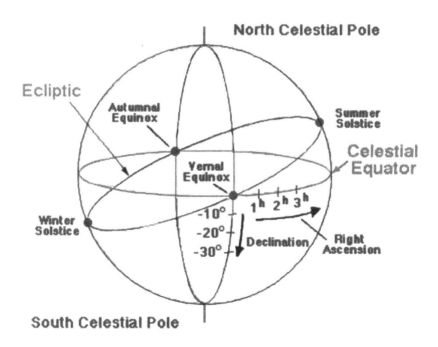

In the above diagram, again imagine the earth as a tiny dot in the centre of the sphere with the poles in line with the celestial poles. Declination, as you can see, is measured the same i.e. north (+) and south (-) of the celestial equator but the celestial equivalent of longitude is now called Right Ascension (RA). It is measured in time (hours, minutes and seconds) but is easily converted to degrees as previously seen by measuring one hour of right ascension as equating to 15 degrees of (apparent) sky rotation. One minute of Right Ascension would then equate to .25 of a degree.

It is important to appreciate perspectives here. Viewing from outside the sphere, direction is to the right, whereas actual view from earth is to the left.

This starting meridian (vernal equinox) is generally known as 'Aries' and is the point reached by the sun in about March 21st as it traverses from south to north intersecting the celestial and ecliptic equators.

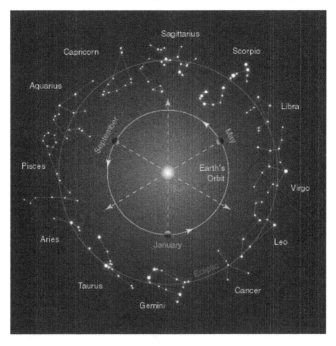

SHOWING HOW THE CONSTELLATIONS CHANGE WHEN VIEWED FROM EARTH

You can see from the above constellation picture it is around January when the sun is in Sagittarius, and in the evening we will see Cancer,

Taurus and Gemini. For us in the northern hemisphere, we would call these Winter Constellations; similarly, we would associate other constellations with other seasons. For our brethren in the antipodes, our northern hemisphere association of particular constellations to a season have no practical relevancy; our winter is their summer. The point being made is that when working with any codes, hints or clues which involves the lore or customs of stars or constellations, you must do so from a northern hemisphere perspective.

Solving the Star Code

What follows, by the very nature of its subject, will for a lot of readers not be simple and straightforward to follow. But follow these basics of astronavigation where you can, as it leads you to how Anson and Webb communicated the location of Pinaki utilising star codes.

The phrase, 'Altitude Schuba I Depth Aurigae I' (from the Webb third document, *Altitude Schuba 1, Depth Yellow Stone 1*) appeared to be nominating the star of Graffias Dschubba in the constellation Scorpius but then only referring to the entire constellation of the Charioteer (Aurigae). What did the Roman numeral of 'I' in the phrase mean?

Each constellation can be identified by what is termed its Prime Star, the star most prominent for that constellation. By convention, this star appears first in the list of stars for each constellation and is designated 'Alpha'.

In an earlier chapter about the author H.T. Wilkins, we showed a shanty he had included which alluded to the treasure's location. It started with the line:

'Eyeless and hairless, on th' island Pristarius'

I had hinted then this was not the name of a real island. Knowing what we know now, this name has a familiar ring to it: **PRI**me **STAR** Scorp**IUS**. Antares is the Prime Star in the constellation Scorpius. So another one of Wilkins' coded clues is laid to rest - and more proof that he knew of the Anson documents and the code they used.

'Depth Aurigae I', however, was not referring to the prime star of Capella for the Charioteer. It was referring to a star called El Nath, which was Gamma Aurigae. But to know this required knowledge of the first key, Alchemy.

We could have used the word 'simple' and its designated meaning when talking about the keys and cracking the codes, not the word 'easy'. To quantify this, they are simple because simple additions and subtractions are involved i.e. nothing complex. They are not easy because to know you have to do this requires 'the knowledge' which includes Alchemy. Only then can you understand what the simple code process is.

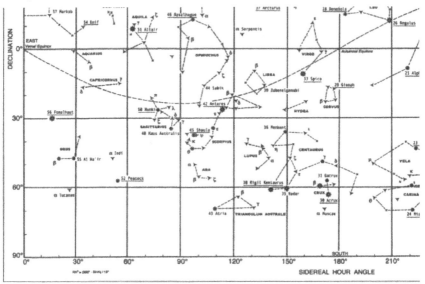

The diagram above is half of a Star Chart. The full chart extends 360º to the right and declination extends + 90º.

An example of the methodology on how to code a position using stars can be given utilising the star chart above. Say, for example, you wanted to give the position of JF Island as a star code; you look for figures in the star almanac that match the latitude and longitude of JF, which is approximately 79º W, 34º S. To make the code more difficult to decipher, you choose two stars; one to give latitude and one to give longitude.

Picking Prime Stars which are easily identified, Scorpius at 108º 34º gives a figure of 34 which is the same as JF's latitude of 34. Looking for a star to give us 79, we find (off the chart) Capella in the Aurigae constellation. This gives us 79º 20º (RA) out of 360–280.40, (SHA).

A code then, however, disguised would identify 'Scorpius' and 'Capella'. Maybe something like 'The scorpion has declined the right to guard Cape Lla'. The recipient, by pre-arrangement, would know how to manipulate the figures but the words 'declined' and 'right' give the clue to those in the know. Stick the above phrase/sentence in the middle of a paragraph containing some genuine looking mumbo jumbo and you would be scratching your head if 'not in the know'.

The Nautical Almanac Table below shows in table format the GHA and Dec (declination +or-) for Aries, sun, moon and planets, and also SHA (sidereal hour angle) and Dec. for stars.

Sidereal Hour Angle is the hour angle of a star measured westwards from Aries on the celestial sphere. It equates to 360º minus stars angular value for RA. GHA of a star is therefore found by adding Aries GHA to star SHA.

2008 January 21, 22, 23 (Mon, Tue, Wed)

GMT	ARIES GHA	VENUS -4.0 GHA	Dec	MARS -0.9 GHA	Dec	JUPITER -1.8 GHA	Dec	SATURN +0.4 GHA	Dec	STARS Name	SHA	Dec
21 00	119°44.7	214°09.9	22°06.5S	35°36.1	26°50.9N	201°33.4	23°06.2S	319°45.7	10°20.3N	Acamar	315°21.2	40°16.5S
01	134°47.2	229°09.0	06.7	50°41.9	50.9	216°35.3	06.2	334°48.3	20.3	Achernar	335°29.6	57°12.0S
02	149°49.6	244°08.2	06.9	65°44.8	50.9	231°37.2	05.1	349°50.9	20.4	Acrux	173°14.0	63°08.5S
03	164°52.1	259°07.4	07.1	80°47.6	50.8	246°39.0	05.1	4°53.5	20.4	Adhara	255°15.4	28°58.0S
M 04	179°54.6	274°06.5	07.3	95°50.4	50.8	261°40.9	05.1	19°56.1	20.5	Aldebaran	290°53.9	18°31.6N
o 05	194°57.0	289°05.7	07.5	110°53.2	50.8	276°42.8	05.1	34°58.7	20.6			
n 06	209°59.5	304°04.8	07.7	125°56.1	50.7	291°44.6	05.0	50°01.3	20.6	Alioth	166°23.8	55°54.6N
d 07	225°01.9	319°04.0	07.9	140°58.9	50.7	306°46.5	05.0	65°03.9	20.7	Alkaid	153°01.9	49°16.0N
a 08	240°04.4	334°03.2	08.1	156°01.7	50.6	321°48.4	05.0	80°06.5	20.7	Alnair	27°49.0	46°56.5S
y 09	255°06.9	349°02.3	08.3	171°04.5	50.6	336°50.2	05.0	95°09.1	20.8	Alnilam	275°50.2	1°11.8S
10	270°09.3	4°01.5	08.5	186°07.3	50.6	351°52.1	04.9	110°11.6	20.8	Alphard	217°59.8	8°41.7S
11	285°11.8	19°00.6	08.7	201°10.1	50.5	6°54.0	04.9	125°14.2	20.9			
12	300°14.3	33°59.8	22°08.9S	216°12.9	26°50.5N	21°55.8	23°04.9S	140°16.8	10°21.0N	Alphecca	126°14.6	26°40.9N
13	315°16.7	48°59.0	09.1	231°15.8	50.4	36°57.7	04.8	155°19.4	21.0	Alpheratz	357°48.0	29°08.2N
14	330°19.2	63°58.1	09.3	246°18.6	50.4	51°59.6	04.8	170°22.0	21.1	Altair	62°12.6	8°53.3N
15	345°21.7	78°57.3	09.5	261°21.4	50.4	67°01.4	04.8	185°24.6	21.1	Ankaa	353°19.7	42°15.9S
16	0°24.1	93°56.4	09.7	276°24.2	50.3	82°03.3	04.8	200°27.2	21.2	Antares	112°31.5	26°27.0S
17	15°26.6	108°55.6	09.9	291°27.0	50.3	97°05.2	04.7	215°29.8	21.3			
18	30°29.0	123°54.8	10.1	306°29.8	50.2	112°07.0	04.7	230°32.4	21.3	Arcturus	145°59.4	19°08.1N
19	45°31.5	138°53.9	10.2	321°32.6	50.2	127°08.9	04.7	245°35.0	21.4	Atria	107°37.6	69°02.4S
20	60°34.0	153°53.1	10.4	336°35.4	50.2	142°10.8	04.6	260°37.6	21.5	Avior	234°19.2	59°32.1S
21	75°36.4	168°52.2	10.6	351°38.2	50.1	157°12.6	04.6	275°40.2	21.5	Bellatrix	278°36.1	6°21.5N
22	90°38.9	183°51.4	10.8	6°41.0	50.1	172°14.5	04.6	290°42.8	21.6	Betelgeuse	271°05.4	7°24.6N
23	105°41.4	198°50.5	11.0	21°43.8	50.0	187°16.4	04.6	306°45.4	21.6			

PART OF A TYPICAL STAR ALMANAC TABLE

Consulting the above table (for January 2008) will produce the following star data:

Antares = Alpha star in Scorpius Constellation has a SHA of 112º 31'.5 and Declination of 26º 27'.0 S(-).

This means that RA has already been converted to an equivalent measurement west from Aries.

El Nath = Beta Tauri star in Aurigae Constellation, a continuation of the table above (not shown for limitation of room), gives a SHA of 278º 17'.5 and Declination of 28º37' .0 N.

To give an example of the calculations involved to obtain a particular star's GHA, I have attempted to simplify it in diagrammatic form. The following diagram shows those involved for Elnath;

The value for Aries (GHA) taken from the table at 12 noon is 300º 14'.3 (west of Greenwich):

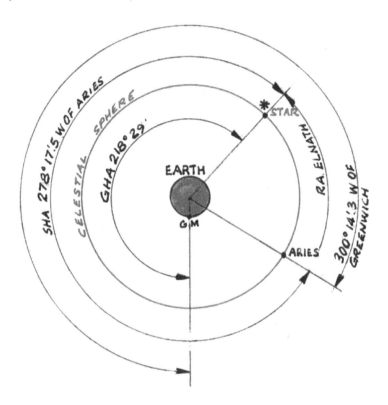

**DIAGRAMATIC VIEW OF GHA, SHA AND RA FOR ELNATH
IN JANUARY 2008**

Star GHA=RA(SHA)+Aries SHA

278º 17'.5 + 300º 14'.3 = 578º 31'
578º 31' − 360º = 218º31' GHA
This equates to;
360º - 218º 31' = 141º 29' East.

BUT this is for midday January 21ˢᵗ 2008, not January 1761. The value for Aries changes with each hour and a star sighting would have been taken at dusk/evening, and also over hundreds of years, the stars' positions change.

You will also notice that the prime meridian being used is that of Greenwich. This, as you know, was not adopted as the prime meridian for world navigation until 1884 but had been used by British navigators since Charles II established the Royal Observatory at Greenwich in 1775. Prior to this, London (centre) was used. That Greenwich was being specifically used mid-eighteenth century was verified by checking the log of a naval ship contemporaneous to the time, that of *HMS Endeavour*, dispatched by the King in 1768 for the Royal Society's scientific mission to the South Seas. *HMS Endeavour* was commanded by the master navigator Lieutenant James Cook and he frequently referred to Greenwich as he logged the Endeavour's course. He was then tasked to seek out someplace called Terra Australis Incognito.

(For a bit of a surprise as to where he went in the South Seas, check Cook's Log for April 1769[1] at the end of this chapter.)

Certainly there would have been no need to identify to someone like Anson which meridian was being used (more on this in 'The Gathering of the Clues' chapter) but in Webb's report, there is a strange reference to the 'rose of gold and emeralds, two foot high'. In Latin, this is 'rosa aurea et smaragdi alti duos pedes' but you need to note the word 'alti' is used which can mean both height and depth. It immediately suggests the phrase to be some coded reference of a two degree reconciliation for some navigational calculation. It is most probably a coded reference (with the clue given by the alchemic colours of gold and emerald) to the magnetic variation to be applied to the (compass) Rose. The magnetic variation for the area would need to be included for any instructions that required a ship to sail on a certain bearing in search of an island.

I have two theories regarding the Latin phrase. My first theory is that it's a rather clever reference to another prime meridian known as the 'Roseline', which is a brass strip running through a church in Paris. The Roseline is two degrees east of Greenwich. A British Navy navigator would have been using London anyway at this time i.e. prior to 1775. I would guess therefore that Webb's strange reference, if containing a hidden code, is to add or subtract two degrees but to what? And theory two is it's the key to a code that Webb used in his letter (More on this in the 'Gathering of the Clues' in a later chapter).

The Star Code, Practical Calculations

The first part of this chapter shows what is considered to be the basics for studying astronavigation. You can see it can be complex and somewhat mathematical but as with Alchemy, I recognise that not everybody will have the need, patience or interest in ploughing through figures. The methodology is therefore shown at the end of this book in Addendum 1. It shows the solving of the star codes and how they worked. The result of that work produced the following figures by calculation and reasoning:

138º 58' 5
138º
19º 21
138
139.5º
18 75º
138º

You can see that by different methods we are always getting figures that are representative of the Pinaki group of atolls. Also, although we said at the beginning of this chapter we can 'reverse engineer' from the known location of Pinaki to establish and prove which stars were used, we didn't have to do this.

Given the stars and knowing the code, we were able to confirm the Pinaki group as *the* location.

Harold T. Wilkins was the one to give the clues that enabled the codes to be worked out. Apart from the hint given by the imaginative name 'Pristarius', the lesson given by the instructive Key Chart/ Guayacan riddle and Alchemy treatise was the requirement that to solve its code it was necessary to **add** the latitudes and longitudes on two specific charts together to obtain the coordinates for Pinaki. But also to add the **opposites** i.e. latitude to longitude as will be demonstrated in a forthcoming chapter.

What needs to be noted is though the same code is being used, Anson's application produces 19°lat, 139°long whereas Webb's produces 138° longitude. Webb's reason for giving 138° was discovered later but Anson's reason for giving 139° was able to be worked out after Wilkins gave another clue. This clue also solved the question about what appeared to be the same Spanish directional codewords of 'trinity' and 'cerro tres puntas' appearing in the stories

To conclude then with star codes, it answers the question 'which theatre of operations?' Most certainly, it is the south-eastern corner of the Tuamotus Archipelago. Not only do the Webb letters show this but it establishes the link to our Captain Brown as this is where his island is and where he ultimately wanted to be.

Another positive link to this area via Lord Anson will be revealed later when we show the solution to a cipher on an enigmatic sculpture known as the Shepherd's Monument in the grounds of his stately home.

So Juan Fernandez Island, it is not. Those looking for Anson's treasure here will be looking for a long time.

What can be gleaned from everything shown in this part of our book? It is that, regardless of whether or not I have applied the codes correctly and similarly, whether or not any other interpretation is correct utilising Alchemy etc., does not really matter. Whichever way you look at it practically and theoretically, the figures 138, 139 and 19 keep repeating themselves, even allowing for inaccuracies in 18th century measurement taking.

As there is only one Trinity group of islands that could conform location-wise with these figures, regardless of how you manipulate them, there is no mistaking; **all roads, ships, codes and directions lead to the Pinaki group of atolls.**

Next, we answer the 'Trinity' question; three what?

[1]Cook's Log:
> Some, at first alarming circumstances, became suggestive when Lieutenant Cook's great voyage was studied. Tasked to sail to King George's Island (Tahiti) on the instigation of the Royal Society to record the transit of Venus in 1769, Cook actually navigated through the Tuamotus Group of islands including our target location. Quote:

'Tuesday 4th. A steady fresh Trade and clear weather. At ½ past 10 a.m. saw land bearing south, distance 3 or 4 leagues. Haul'd up for it, and soon found it to be an island of about 2 leagues in Circuit and of an Oval form, with a lagoon in the Middle, for which I named it Laqoon Island. The border of land Circumscribing this Lagoon is in many places very low and narrow, particularly on the south side, where it is mostly a Beach or Reef of rocks; it is the same on the North side in 3 places, and these disjoins the firm land and make it appear like so many islands covered with wood. On the West end of the island is a large Tree which looks like a large Tower, and about the Middle of the island are two Cocoa Nutt Trees that appears above all the other wood, which as we approached the island looked very much like a flag. We approached the north side of this island within a Mile, and found no Bottom with 130 fathoms of line, nor did there appear to be Anchorage about it. We saw several of the inhabitants, the most of them men, and these Marched along the shore abreast of the Ships with long Clubs in their hands as tho' they meant to oppose our landing. They were all naked except their Privy parts, and were of a Dark Copper Colour with long black Hair, but upon our leaving the island some of them were seen to put on a Covering, and one or two we saw in the Skirts of the Wood was Cloathed in White; these we supposed to be Women. This island lies in the Latitude of 18 degrees 47 minutes and Longitude 139 degrees 28 minutes West from the Meridian of Greenwich. Variation 2 degrees 54 minutes East.'

You can see from the latitude and longitude above that Cook was uncomfortably close to Pinaki but it must be a coincidence. Sailing from Cape Horn to Tahiti, he was bound to be on a track for the Tuamotus Group of Islands. Cook also explored the islands to the north-west of Tahiti which make up the Tupai Trinity (we looked at these in detail in a previous chapter). As close scrutiny of *HMS Endeavour's* log and Joseph Bank's (a wealthy participant) diary revealed no hint of extracurricular activities suggestive of a search for a certain treasure by the Royal Society, thankfully we were able to eliminate Cook's mission from the story of the treasure. This is not to say others did. The Tupai Trinity is remarkably similar in size and layout to the Pinaki Trinity but is found at 16ºS,152ºW which in no way fits any permutations of the star code. It may have been the suggestive circumstances of Cook's voyage that led searchers of the Lost Treasure to follow his course and identify the Tupai Trinity.

Then there is the search for the treasure in an obscure south-east corner of Terra Australis Incognito, known as Queenscliff. We covered this earlier in the chapter on Benito and Australia.

CHAPTER 5

THE ETYMOLOGY OF NOTHING (ZERO) AND A HILL

In earlier chapters, we were pondering about the question as to where the trinity clues were leading us i.e. three markers/mountains/islands etc. We have seen Wilkins highlighting within a map 'Los Tres Picos' (The Three Peaks) and with it 'La Puerta Secreta del SOCABON' (The door/way to the secret of the Socabon).

'Cerro Tres Puntas' i.e. a hill with three peaks, also features on JF. Where I am taking you with this is to show how two similar sounding words with almost identical spelling means two totally different things. They are the Spanish words 'Cero' and 'Cerro'. One means 'zero', and the other, as we know, means 'hill'. But, hundreds of years ago, 'Cero' also meant 'Cipher', or code.

Wilkins, for all his questionable and dubious writings, was also very competent at various aspects of language. He demonstrates this whilst translating a Spanish galleon's sailing directions from an archival manuscript. When speaking about Anson's raid on the Manila galleon in 1734 in his book *Modern Buried Treasure Hunters*, he makes reference to a manuscript in the British Museum. Wilkins describes the sailing directions given by a Spanish navigator to identify the island of San Bernadino and its dangers to the Manila galleons on their voyage to the Philippines.

I quote, in part (the word 'cypher' in brackets is Wilkins' own inclusion):

'The island of San Bernadino is a high, bare, uninhabited rock in 12º45´ N. lat., and in the Cero (cypher) of longitude, according to these charts, by which I regulate my calculations...'

Without Wilkins' insight, the manuscript's sentence reads this way;

'The island of San Bernadino is a high bare uninhabited rock in 12º45´ N. lat. and in the zero of longitude......'

With Wilkins now showing the subjective meaning, when the word 'Cero' is used by Spanish navigators, the sentence reads thus;

'The island of San Bernadino is a high bare uninhabited rock in 12º45´ N. lat., and in the cipher of longitude (the coded number to be used as longitude) according to......'

Cero is the Spanish word for zero. The words zero and cipher are interchangeable as they both share the same common roots of language. Whilst fourteenth century French sited *cyfre*, it ultimately came from the Arabic *sifr*. The Arabs had developed mathematics and they required a symbol for the value of nothing, the cipher or zero. Today, we more likely use the word zero when speaking about the number zero and the word cipher when talking about a code (as in a code where a symbol or group of letters has a meaning).

To add to the problem, the almost identical Spanish word 'Cerro' means something totally different (Hill). One needs little imagination to realise now how the original Spanish code phrase of 'CERO TRES PUNTAS' (the coded number to be used as the longitude of the three points) was misheard as 'CERRO TRES PUNTAS', (the hill of three peaks). Due to the similarity in pronounciation therefore, the true meaning was lost.

If you are astute, you can see the Masonic connection of 'three points' in the code phrase. In other words, there is a coded number that leads you the way (to the secret) which is not three hills.

The replication of this directional phrase as a clue to the treasure by the Masons either symbolically as 'the three points' or as a phrase for a treasure location involving a 'three peaked hill' proves this. Our other code word and major DNA 'Trinity' we already know refers to a group of three 'things' so it is not necessary to double up with 'Cerro Tres Puntas' which shows it must be a mistake.

We now change course dramatically to the opposite side of the world and take to dry land to show that the mystery of an enigmatic lost religious treasure in France will ultimately take us back to Lord Anson to further our quest.

We will come back to the 'Trinity' later to explore the important geometrical relationship of the islands in the Pinaki Group.

PART 5

CHAPTER 1

THE TRAIL LEADS TO RENNES-LE-CHÂTEAU

It is from this point that things will now catastrophically fall apart for many experts of some very large lost treasure mysteries. It had been recognised that Admiral George Anson, coded directions and a lost church treasure were also part of another famous lost treasure location, one completely unassociated with treasure islands. Not recognised as being linked by any other person's until now, these details occur within the infamous history of the enigma known as the treasure of Rennes-le-Château. This place, a tiny hamlet in the bottom south-east corner of France, became the subject of much hype and speculation in the mid 1900s, continuing to this day.

Theories from the whole host of self-proclaimed experts that endlessly circle Rennes-le-Château include that the treasure is the tomb of Jesus Christ, the Gospel of (actually written by) Jesus, Mary Magdalene's tomb is supposed to be here, also, the Holy Grail, some type of proof that Jesus married Mary Magdalene and produced offspring, some other type of proof that Mary should be worshipped instead of Jesus, a hoard of Merovingian gold, and the lost treasure of the Temple of Solomon. Anyone wishing to explore this subject today is faced with reports about religious fanatics, shadowy political groups, intelligence agencies, fraudsters (titular and monetary), treasure hunters and various assorted nuts that have taken the mythos of the lost treasure of Rennes-le-Château and transformed it into a high farce cult. The point to note about all this is that again, even with an apparent wealth of information, no one can find this treasure, whatever it may be.

The fact that the directions being used to try to find the treasure at Rennes-le-Château are actually just instructions for something else in another location entirely seems to have been missed by all (but we are now getting ahead of ourselves).

As the fanciful nature of most contemporaneous information and writings about Rennes-le-Château render them worthless, they will not be included in this examination. In exposing the mystery here, I will only refer to the salient points necessary to understand this historical mistake and those few books which contain information of any real import. Any reader wishing to further their understanding of the subject can avail themselves via the many books and websites with the caveat to grade them on the scale of good, bad and fruitcake. As an interesting aside, one of the silliest sounding anecdotes regarding Rennes-le-Château was assessed as being probably true. It was reported that Michael Bentine, ex-intelligence officer and he of the famous BBC Radio *The Goon Show* (there is a thought provoking combination) stated he had seen a room dedicated to Rennes-le-Château at MI6 headquarters, the inference being the SIS (Secret Intelligence Service) was trying to find the treasure! If one knows the role of the SIS, it is quite obvious that Michael Bentine had seen the French Desk where intelligence about French politics was being collated. When some of the desk's political targets (e.g. Pierre Plantard) kept having their names associated with an obscure hamlet named Rennes-le-Château, it would have been routine to find out why.

The crucial clue linking George Anson to Rennes-le-Château was found by scanning a 1996 version of the 1982 book *The Holy Blood and the Holy Grail* by Michael Baigent, Richard Leigh and Henry Lincoln. Credited with bringing to worldwide awareness the mystery of Rennes-le-Château, this book proposes the theory that Mary Magdalen, carrying Jesus' child, escaped to France. Her issue of true royal lineage became the Merovingian Kings. The proof of this church destroying secret is the treasure hidden at Rennes-le-Château. Within a section in the book covering three pages about 'Grand Masters', 'Scottish Masonry' and 'Masonic Sources' was mention of a sculpture known as 'The Shepherd's Monument', commissioned by the Anson family at Shugborough Hall, the Anson family seat.

THE SHEPHERD'S MONUMENT, SHUGBOROUGH HALL, ENGLAND

The enclosed sculpture is a marble relief based on a painting by Poussin. Included underneath the sculpture was the undeciphered cryptic inscription:

O ·U ·O ·S ·V ·A ·V ·V

D·   M·

Not knowing what it meant, it seemed the authors had just included this detail about Anson and his monument because of a Masonic connection and to heighten the mystery of it all, a tactic they used repeatedly throughout the book.

No different for any other location where the lost treasure had sprouted a localised version, and already armed with the knowledge of the underlying source of this version, we firstly had to isolate the information that was being interpreted to indicate that Rennes-le-Château was the correct area to search and then understand how this interpretation came about. The mythos of Rennes-le-Château, its history and accompanying directional clues were found to have come to light only as recently as the 1950s. What appears to be an incomprehensible mess was slowly sorted out and for anyone unaware of this legend, the most common version of the Rennes-le-Château tale will be told here:

In 1891, Abbé Francois Berenger Sauniere began to restore the church of Sainte Madeleine, Rennes-le-Château which had fallen into disrepair. In a hollowed column used to support the altar slab were discovered four ancient parchments, two of which were recognised as being coded. After taking the parchments to Paris to be decoded, it is assumed Sauniere returned to Rennes-le-Château with copies of three paintings, named as being Nicholas Poussin's *The Shepherd's of Arcadia,* David Teniers the Younger's, *The Temptation of St Anthony,* and a portrait by an unspecified artist of Pope St Celestine V.

Clues gleaned from the parchments, paintings and some other coded instructions inscribed on the headstone of a Marie Haupoul in the church's graveyard, and also on the engraved tombstone, enabled Sauniere (it is said) to locate 'Le Tresor Maudit' (The Accursed Treasure). To ensure no one else would be able to follow him, he destroyed the gravestones of Marie Hautpoul to hide the coded message. From then on, the wealthy Abbé lived a veritable life of an ecclesiastical Reilly, spending lavish amounts on his residence, the Villa Bethania, and hosting parties frequented by the social elite of the day. Dying in 1917, Abbe Berenger Sauniere took the secret of the treasure with him, be it to heaven or hell.

Fortunately for all, images said to depict Marie Haupoul's headstone before it was destroyed, along with a drawing of the tombstone, appeared in a book of the time so these details were preserved, as were the coded documents (or copies of the documents or images of copies of the documents; it gets a bit vague on this detail).

To begin with, we decided to concentrate on the source of the clues, which were not from the Abbe Sauniere in the 19th century but a group of four persons in the late 1950s. The bare details of the history of the popular version indicated there was deliberate subterfuge going on to manufacture what sounded like an actual history. The telltale sign of this was the standard methodology of mixing details of real personages, dates and events within a web of fabrication to give the overall construct the appearance of factuality(very much in the same manner as our Captain Brown). Taking the benefit also of the many researchers who have done detailed study of the clues in this story, we were quickly able to determine what had really been going on. It begins in 1955 when Noel Corbu opens the Hotel du Tour in Sauniere's ex residence, the Villa Bethania in Rennes-le-Château. In January 1956, Corbu told the story of Sauniere finding gold, to the paper *La Depeche du Midi*.

FIRST APPEARANCE OF THE MODERN STORY OF RENNES-LE-CHÂTEAU INCLUDING INCORRECT PICTURE OF ALFRED SAUNIERE, BROTHER OF FRANCOIS

The Creation of the Myth

It is apparent that Corbu had been prepared with this story to lay the groundwork for the next stage by three others; Gerard de Sede, Pierre Plantard and Philippe de Cherisey.

Pierre Plantard himself proved to be a rather interesting character. A supporter of the Vichy Government in World War Two, he published French nationalist magazines during this period with the approval of the German occupiers. In the 1950s, he was convicted of fraud. Managing to always be peripherally associated with whatever Government was in power at the time, he had all the hallmarks of the typical fraudster. The three went on to expand on the fabricated myth by producing and planting a number of self-supporting documents and books. Around 1965, the tactic employed was to doctor up some pamphlet or booklet and anonymously submit the result to the Bibliothèque nationale de France in the hope cataloguing would somehow impart authenticity to the information.

Pierre Plantard and Philippe de Cherisey even produced some fake genealogies that made Plantard a direct descendant of a Merovingian king, Dagobert 2. In 1967, De Sede published the book *L'or de Rennes ou la vie insolite de Berenger Sauniere, Cure de rennes le Chatea.* Shortened now to *Le Tresor Maudit de Rennes le Chateau* (*The Accursed Treasure of Rennes-le-Château*), this is the book where the full fabricated myth for Rennes-le-Château, including clues to the alleged treasure, were published. What is important to note is that the treasure is identified specifically as being that of the Temple of Solomon. The clues given by de Sede as we have seen consisted firstly of a reference to Sauniere obtaining reproductions of the paintings *The Arcadian Shepherd* by Poussin, the *Hermit Saint Anthony* by David Teniers, and a portrait of Pope Saint Celestine V from some unknown source (strangely, these paintings are not small and wouldn't go unnoticed, yet there is no evidence at all of these paintings having existed at Rennes!). Next came a diagram of Marie Haupoul's headstone, and also the tombstone, said to have come from a pamphlet titled *Engraved Stones of Languedoc* by Eugene Stublein. A signature for that name appears on the slab.

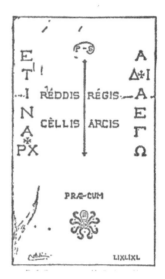

DRAWINGS OF MARIE HAUPOUL'S GRAVESTONE AND THE SLAB WITH STUBLEIN'S SIGNATURE, FROM GERARD DE SEDE'S BOOK

Thirdly, an image of copies of the parchments said to be found in the pillar by Saunierer. The parchments, one large, one small, were biblical tracts in Latin and scribed using medieval and Merovingian style uncials:

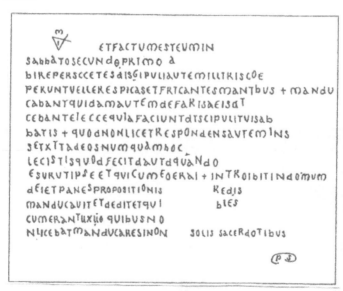

PARCHMENT 1

The location of the originals of both parchments is a mystery having not been seen by any modern-day researchers. Reproductions appear to be of those in Gerard de Sede's book. Actual size is a mystery but they appear to be in the ratio and similar in size A6 to A5.

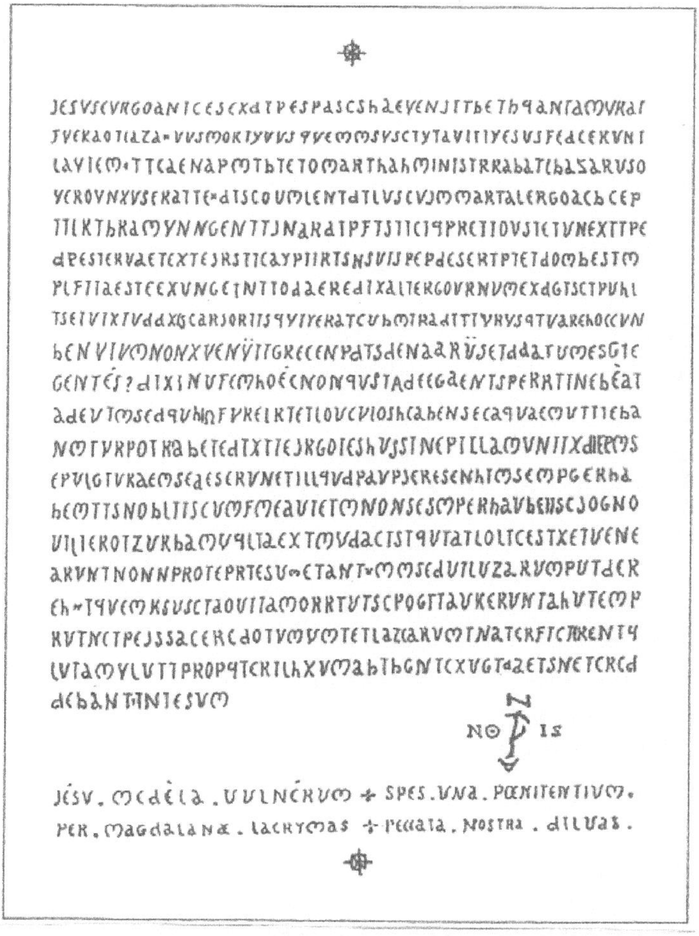

JESVS(VRGOANICESCXATPESPASCSH2EVENJITHETH9ANIAMVRAI
JVEKAOTIAZA•VVSMOKIYVVJ9VEMMSVSCTYTAVITIVESVJFEdCEKVNI
LAVIEM•TTCAENAPMTbTCTOMARTHAHMINISTRRAbATIbA SARVSO
YCROVNXVSEKATTE=dISCOUMLENTATLVSCVJMMARTALERGOA(bCEP
TILKTbKAMYNNGENTTJNAKATPFTJTIC19PRCTIOVSICTVNEXTTPE
dPESIEKVAETCXTEJKJTICAYPIIRTSHJVIJPCPdCSCKTPTETdOMbESTM
PLFTIAEJTCEXVNGCINTTOd2EREdIXALTERGOVRNVMEXdGTSCTPVhI
TSEIVIXIVddXGCAKJORIIJ9VIYEKATCVbMIRAdTTIVRVS9TVAREhO(CVN
bENVIVMNONXVENYITGRECCENPdTSdEN22RVJCTddATVMESGIC
GENTÉJ?dIXINVF(MhOÉCNON9VJTAdEGG2ENTJPEKATINEbÉAT
2dEVImSCd9VhINFVKELKTCTLOVCVIOShCAbENJECA9VAEMVTTIEbA
NMTVRPOTKAbCTEdTXTIEJKGOIESHVJSINCPILLAMVNIIXdIEEMS
EPVlGTVKAEMSEAESCKVNETILL9VdPAVPJEKESENhTMSCMPGEKhA
hEMTTSNObLIISCVMFMEAVIETMNONSCSMPERhaVbEIISCJOGNO
VIIIEKOTZVKbAMV9LIAEXTMVdaCIST9VTaTLOLICESTXETVENE
aKVNTNONNPROTEPRTESV•CTANT•MMSEdVILVZaRVMPUTdER
Eh•T9VEMKSVSCTaOVIIaMOKKTVTSCPOGITAVKERVNTAhVTEMP
KVTN(TPEJSSaCERCdOTVMVMTETLaZCaKVMTNaTCKFIC7AKENT4
lVTaMYLVTTPROP9TCKILhXVM2bThGNTCXVGTa2ETSNETCKCd
dCb2NTHNIESVM

NO �
IS

JÉSV.MCdÉLa.UVLNÉKVM + SPES.VNa.PŒNITENTIVM.
PEK.MaGdaLaNa.LaCKYMaS + PECCaIa.NOSTKa.dILVaS.

PARCHMENT 2. THE LARGER OF THE TWO PARCHMENTS

Finally, De Sede made a reference to a book titled *La Vraie Langue Celtique et Le Cromleck de Rennes-les-Bains* (*The True Celtic Language and the Cromlech of Rennes-les-Bains*), published by Abbé Henri Boudet in 1886. He was curé of the nearby Rennes-le-Bains during Saurnier's priesthood and some say the supreme machinator behind the scenes of the enigma. He died in 1915.

It was Henry Lincoln, later to be one of the authors of *Holy Blood, Holy Grail*, who was first to rise to the fly when he picked up a copy of De Sede's *Le Tresor Maudit de Rennes-le-Château* during a visit to France in 1969, previously published as *L'Or de Rennes, ou la vie insolite de Berenger Saunier* (*The Gold of Rennes, or the strange Life of Berenger Saunier*).

Noticing some of the letters in Parchment 1 were slightly raised to the others, he picked these out to assemble the following messages:

A DAGOBERT II ROI ET A SION EST CE TRESOR ET IL EST LA MORT.

This could be translated as;

TO KING DAGOBERT II AND TO SION DOES THIS TREASURE BELONG AND HE IS THERE DEAD (or AND IT IS DEATH)

You may also notice that the right-hand end letters of the bottom four lines when read top to bottom spell out 'SION'.

De Sede, after hooking Lincoln, landed him quickly by providing him with the 'decoding' of the larger of the parchments (2). This by a fiendishly complex decoding process known as a Vigenére Square; a key word is required and letters are place-shifted. Finally, via a tortuous method called a 'Knights Tour' which is based on the movement of the knight on a chessboard, De Sede said the large parchment gave the following message:

BERGERE PAS DE TENTATION QUE POUSSIN TENIERS GARDENT LA CLEF PAX DCLXXXI PAR LA CROIX ET CE CHEVAL DE DIEU J'ACHEVE CE DAEMON DE GARDIEN A MIDI POMMES BLEUES

Taken to be in English: SHEPHERDESS NO TEMPTATION THAT POUSSIN TENIERS HOLD THE KEY PEACE 681 BY THE CROSS AND THIS HORSE OF GOD I COMPLETE (or I DESTROY) THIS DAEMON GUARDIAN AT MIDDAY BLUE APPLES.

It was inferred also that this message, to be decoded, required the letters PS PRAECUM from the Haupoul tombstone and 119 letters from the headstone. Combined (128) they created a keyword.

This was not all. Other words could be extracted from the parchment text using letters smaller than the rest and off-line. From these we get; REX MUNDI and AD GENESARETH intended to confuse.

(For those students requiring a detailed solution to the ciphers, I would recommend Bill Putnam and John Edwin Wood's book *The Treasure of Rennes-le-Château,* Sutton Publishing Ltd, 2003. It has a sub-title *A Mystery Solved.* They haven't solved it, of course, the real solution being Anson's monument intended to confuse, but they approach the mystery logically and with common sense. They come to the correct conclusion that four men came together and produced *'......one of the most famous historical puzzles of the century.'* But like every one else, they have missed the real clues within the puzzle.)

Some of the facts you need to know in regards to all this:

1. There really was a Marie de Negri d'Ables Haupoul, Dame d'Haupoul de Blanchefort, who appears to have died in 1681. She was buried by an Abbé Bigou. The epitaph on her headstone was recorded in a pamphlet published in 1906 by the Society for Scientific Study of the Aude and said (in English),

    'Here lies the noble Marie de Nègre D'Arles, La Dame d'Haupoul de Blanchefort, aged sixty seven, died 17 January 1681, May she rest in peace'

    It is said she was the trustee of a great secret and is alleged to have confided it to Father Antoine Bigou. He moved to Rennes-le-Château in 1774 to replace his uncle as parish priest. The secret included documents and because of the political unrest in France at that time, Bigou is supposed to have hid them in a cavity within one of the Visigothic pillars supporting the altar in the church. He then had a large slab of stone placed flat atop the tomb of Marie Haupoul and engraved on it several inscriptions in Latin and Greek. It appears Bigou was also responsible for the upright stone containing the epitaph. Eugene Stublein, whose pamphlet reproduced the engraved gravestones, was a real astronomer and meteorologist who had a history of publishing minor works of history and antiquity. It is no surprise that the only copy to exist of the pamphlet, *Engraved Stones of Languedoc*, was found at the Bibliothèque nationale de France in 1966. Included was a note from an Abbé Joseph Courtaly of Villarzel-du-Razès (near Rennes-le-Château) dated 1962 which informed all:

'The book by Eugene Stublein, edition of Limoux 1884, having become very rare, and being perhaps one of the rare owners to have it in his library, I owe it to myself to satisfy the numerous requests of researchers to make a reproduction of the plates of the book, no. XVI to XXIII on the countryside of RENNES-LES-BAINS, RENNES-LE-CHÂTEAU and ALET'.

Unfortunately or fortunately (depending if you are Abbé Courtaly, de Sede, de Cherisey or Plantard) Abbé Courtaly died in 1964 making verification of his magnanimity impossible. It is not even an avenue worth pursuing because Stublein's real signature bears no resemblance to the one appearing in this book.

2. The source of the biblical tracts used in the parchments have been identified, and unsurprisingly, they are not of medieval origin. The large parchment is of John, Chapter 12, as it appears in a 19th century version of the *Novum Testamentum Domini Nostri Iesu Christi latine secundum sancti Hieronymi* by John Wordsworth and Henry White. The bottom two lines of text are taken from the foot of the altar in the church of Rennes-le-Château before someone stole it.

The smaller parchment is of Luke, Chapter 6, from the Codex Bezae which appeared in the *Dictionnaire de la Bible* by Fulcran Vigouroux published by Letouzey et Ané, Paris around the turn of the 20th century. To make the texts appear authentic medieval French, the letter W was removed, as W was a later inclusion to the French alphabet. The ploy backfired because the removal of the letter W from the texts was so noticeable, it tipped researchers off that the texts must have been taken from a modern source to require the removal of W. This is not the only example of sloppy attention to detail by the fabricators. Researchers who had painstakingly checked the texts and followed the decoding methods have found a number of spelling and transcription errors made by the author.

This shows that the primary concern of the author was the transmission of a message which had to include the word 'shepherdess' (BERGERE) and the clue 'Poussin holds the key'. The window dressing of decoding an ancient parchment was of secondary concern and suffered accordingly in attention to detail. Some researchers suggest that one of the parchment clues 'AD GENESARETH' is to be used in the middle of the 'Bergere' message above and then inserted into the large parchment message, which makes the whole thing even more ridiculously complicated. The fact that the parchments are fake to start with seems to have been missed by a lot of 'learned' people. Anyone wishing to get an understanding of the level ability of these fraudsters (assessed as low to medium proficiency) are directed to the book, *The Messianic Legacy* (1986), also by Baigent Leigh and Lincoln, described on its cover as 'The controversial sequel to the bestselling *The Holy Blood and The Holy Grail.* With Pierre Plantard deciding to well and truly gild the Rennes-le-Château lily, part three of that book, titled *The Cabal*, is one of the most unintentionally humorous pieces you will read as the authors, treating this subject with gravity, try to work through the maze of obviously fake documents and stories that Plantard was feeding them.

PIERRE PLANTARD AND PHILIPPE DE CHERISAY

In 1983, Plantard had shown them what appeared to be notarised documents dated 1955. The documents included an application for permission by a Viscount Leathers, a Major Clowes and a Captain Nutting to the French consulate in London to export parchments from France. Another had a Lord Selbourne declaring that the parchments were now with the International League of Antiquarian Booksellers, 39 Great Russell Street, London, and would shortly be moved to the business of Lloyds Bank Europe Limited. It should be said here that notarisation of a document is a tactic used in frauds as it gives the document a dressing of legality. In reality, notarising a document merely provides a dating mechanism for the document and does not confer validity to what is contained within it. These didn't even have the benefit of this slight glossing as the notarising itself was fraudulently commandeered from elsewhere.

The documents were inferring the answer to the question everyone was by now asking; as images of Sauniere's parchments exist, where are the originals? Though asked (naturally) by Plantard not to discuss these documents or reproduce them, the authors to their credit set about checking all the details, including tracking down the notary Patrick J Freeman, whose name and seal appeared upon them. He at least was able to confirm he had undertaken notarial duties for the names which appeared on the documents in the 1950s. This was to do with certifying signatures for registration as French law required this to be done for anyone conducting insurance work in France. All the names involved were found to be connected to the Guardian Assurance Company so it doesn't take a brain surgeon to work out how Plantard in France could have come up with the names, details and signatures on the fake documents. Met with the typical dead ends and dead signatories, the authors resignedly had to declare the documents to be fakes. When confronted with the author's findings, "M. Plantard looked genuinely distressed," (I'll bet he did). But after successfully untying all these knots, the authors retied them back up again, declaring Pierre Plantard was also a victim of the faked documents, for the conclusion was reached that due to all the machinations, there must have been some shadowy cabal in operation monitoring enquiries into Rennes-le-Château. In the mess that the myth of Rennes-le-Château has become, one could dismiss the whole thing as a fraud perpetrated by a group of French associates in the 1950s for their own gain. Plantard even later supplied the parchments to a French writer and journalist Jean Lac Chaumeil; on one was a notation that de Cherisay was their creator! In fact, there is also a letter dated 29 January 1974 to the author Pierre Jarnac and signed by Cherisey where he states (translated):

'P.S. Do you know that the famous manuscripts supposedly discovered by the Abbé Sauniere were composed in 1965? And that I took responsibility for being the author?'

Another author and researcher says that a parchment was found by Antoine Captier, the carillonneur (bell-ringer) of the church in 1887. He found a small tube with a rolled-up parchment in it in a wooden baluster that was being moved in the church. He gave it to Sauniere. Captier didn't witness the contents of the parchment but it is after this event that Saunier's life takes a different path. Captier's grandson still has the baluster and can show the hiding place of the glass tube. So something was indeed found, but what? Apparently, the small parchment was signed by Jean Bigou, uncle of the Abbé Antoine Bigou, and it contained a clue which led Sauniere to the Visigothic pillar and/or a tomb. Details of this episode are not clear; stories are confused as to what actually happened and in what order.

Why are there so-called 'learned' people out there who still refuse to believe these parchments are fake? Cherisey makes several admissions over the years that he faked the parchments. But at the bottom of Parchment 2 is a strange character symbol:

By inverting this symbol, a certain English Admiral's name appeared!

Everyone sees 'SION' because it is recognised as part of the saga here. Heads nod, 'Ah yes,' and nobody looks beyond that. But what you are really being shown is 'ANSON'.

Note also that the 'O' had a dot in the middle, creating a symbol for gold, but also as we shall see there are Masonic connections between this symbol and Sauniere.

Whilst on the subject of symbols, you may be puzzled by the octopus/spider on the bottom of the gravestone shown earlier. It appears that Pierre Plantard was a great admirer of Paul Lecour (1871-1954) and was inspired by his esoteric works. In 1926, Lecour organised the Society for Atlantean Studies. He wrote *The Age of Aquarius* in 1937, and in it, he quotes from a 1926 work on Atlantis......*the book contained a drawing of an octopus 'une symbole de la tradition primitive: le poulpe' (a symbol of the primitive tradition: the octopus).*

According to Lecour (a Priory of Sion member), the octopus was a solar symbol used in Atlantis. It also contains the same symbolism of a Arachne, the spider goddess in regards to the number eight and the chessboard. So links here to the 'Knights Tour' and chessboard moves. One must also ask the allowing question: 'What is a 1926 symbol doing on a 17th century gravestone?' Maybe an answer to this last question lies in a report that the earlier mentioned baluster containing the glass tube had on it what appeared to be a carving of a spider or octopus!

CHAPTER 2

THE SEARCHERS OF RENNES-LE-CHÂTEAU

What was Plantard and the Rennes-le-Château gang doing? It wasn't all a fraud, as we could see there was a code being given on the fabricated diagram of Marie Haupoul's upright tombstone and there was a disguised reference to Anson's name on one of the parchments. As there was no mention of a dying sailor, or a map, or directions to be used for a map, how was it this landlocked hamlet came to be a lost treasure version? Though we had recognized things needing decoding to be understood. Likewise, the message given by the parchments was most likely insensible because it also still had to be decoded. This was indicative that Plantard and the gang had conducted an elaborate ruse by placing lost treasure codes into the fake parchments and stones to allow them to be found. For some reason, the clues as they had understood them had identified Rennes-le-Château as being correct, but the rest of the clues' meanings remained beyond them. In what must have been a gambit borne out of frustration, they concocted a way to release the clues without fully disclosing what they were about in the hope someone would be able to understand and fully decode them. This proved to be rather a successful tactic in one sense, for the number of persons who to this day continue to devote time and effort to solve the mystery of Rennes-le-Château are legion. This is in part confirmed by Plantard himself, who, though being implicit in this fabrication, was constant in maintaining throughout it all that what is taken to be the parchments found by Sauniere were actually modern-day constructs by de Cherisey that were based on something else.

The area did have a history of mystery, being associated with the reign of the Merovingian Kings and the heresy of the Cathars whose last stand against besieging papal forces transpired at the castle of Montsegur. Plus there is the little known story of a certain German, Otto Rahn, employed by the SS, who also sought out a treasure in the 1930s around Montsegur. Perhaps they were related.

Researchers have also studied the works of Jules Verne and identified cryptographic word plays within. One of his works, *Clovis*

Dardentor, takes its name from a Merovingian King Clovis and the words 'dardent or' meaning ardent gold. D'ardent was a title given to a descendant of Dagobert 2, who allegedly sought refuge at Rennes-le-Château. Pierre Plantard himself had even claimed the title of 'rejeton ardent' (ardent offshoot).

The clues had certainly been installed as a play on the layout of the wording of Marie Haupoul's epitaph, but this could not have been done by the Plantard gang who were ignorant of the meaning and merely knew of its importance in the altered form. It must have been done by the person who buried Marie Haupoul in 1781 (not 1681, as implied on the gravestone) the Abbé Antoine Bigou, Cure of Rennes-le-Château and chaplain to the Haupoul's. Abbé Bigou fled to Spain after interring Marie Haupoul to escape the impending turmoil of the French revolution, where he died shortly afterwards. However, the secret he possessed he passed to another exiled priest, the Abbé Cauneille. He in turn communicated it to two other priests; Abbé Jean Vié, the parish priest of Rennes-le-Bains from 1840 to 1870, and Abbé Emile Vayron. The successor to Vié was the Abbé Henri Boudet, who we know was friendly with Sauniere.

It appears the knowledge these priests possessed was that a great treasure lay somewhere in the area, the key to which the Abbé Bigou had concealed within Marie Haupoul's engraved gravestones.

A further clue to Saunierer's real involvement in all this can be found in his adopted bookplate.

Taken from the title page of Heinrich Madathanus' 1625 book, *Golden Age Revived*, it is the shape caused by the occlusion of the triangle by the smaller circle that gives the game away, the Masonic Royal Arch keystone complete with circle and dot. Whilst Sauniere's involvement in all this could easily be surmised as that of a cure conducting his own low level search for the local lost treasure, the reports of financial transactions with and visitations by Archduke Johann von Habsburg do indicate a higher level of involvement with others privy to a Masonic insider's knowledge of the lost treasure. It seems the Archduke was there at

Rennes-le-Château sniffing around in the hope of finding the missing family fortune which was spirited from their grasp by Uhilla all those years ago. He gave Sauniere the then huge sum of 3,000 francs in return for looking for any documents hidden in the church. Far from being the person who discovered the treasure, Suaniere's wealth was a combination of the financial support he received from the Archduke and the income he received from his acts of Simony, that being the advertising and selling of masses. What's more, it seems the other family involved, the Bourbons, were also on the case! The website of the 'Societe Perillos' references a 1970 article by an A. M. F. Guy appearing in a 1970 publication named *'l'Intermédiaire des Chercheurs et Curieux*. I quote:

'Here is a fact about which I was recently informed and which I give for what it is worth. It appears that the case of Father Saunière has aroused, after the death of the priest, the curiosity of certain high-placed people in Spanish society. As they could not openly make enquiries in our country [France], they progressed with great caution via intermediaries and those that were not compromised. These events have remained shrouded in absolute secrecy. They go back forty years. Remains to be explained how the history of the treasure of Rennes - for it is of course about that which this is all about - could have created interest in a foreign country more than a half century ago, father Saunière having died, I believed, around 1920.'

This is then linked to a similar article in *"L'independent'* on the 22 March 1980 which is said to basically repeat the above story but adds that a report of matter had been commissioned but was never forwarded to the principals due to the collapse of the Spanish monarchy in 1931. This report was brought to France by refugees of the Spanish civil war and though the treasure was searched for by the Germans during WW2, it has never been found. Nevertheless, Sauniere and his search was the factual skeleton upon which Plantard sewed the skin of the modern Rennes-le-Château myth. Our next story tells of one of the searchers from a darker side of history.

Otto Rahn and the Lost Candlesticks

Anyone enquiring into the mystery of Rennes-le-Château will nowadays come across the name Otto Rahn. Rahn's story, which has been mainly confined to the German media as being of a strange Nazi treasure hunt, has only relatively recently been made accessible to a greater audience via English publications. Rahn is inextricably linked with that of Rennes-le-Château as he searched for the same treasure in the same region, though the source of information he followed led him to believe it was located in a ruined mountain fortress called Montsegur.

As his story only laterally supplied a clue pertaining to the identity of our lost treasure, we will give only a brief outline of his quest. Those wishing to learn more are directed to two books, *Otto Rahn & The Quest for the Holy Grail, The Amazing Life of the Real Indiana Jones* by Nigel Graddon and *Emerald Cup-Ark of Gold, The Quest of SS Lt. Otto Rahn of the Third Reich* by Colonel Howard Buechner.

In the early 1930s, a young philology graduate and historian named Otto Rahn, had, through his study of ancient manuscripts and the story 'Parzival' by Wolfram von Eschenbach, become convinced that a fabulous lost treasure was to be found in the grottoes and caves

of the French Pyrenees. His book published in 1933, *Kreuzzug geggen den Grail* (Crusade Against the Grail), sets out his findings. Unfortunately, the artistically inclined Rahn fell in with the Nazis who in those times supported various studies into arcane history that might support the National Socialist world view of history. There is some controversy whether Rahn fully embraced Nazi ideals or whether he sided with the devil out of necessity, artistic types tending to starve on the streets in those days. One way or the other, Rahn ended up as an SS Lieutenant working under the direct command of no less than Reichsfuhrer Heinrich Himmler himself. This was certainly not a good move, for Der Reichsfuhrer's preferred image was that of his SS men hand in hand with Aryan maidens, whereas Rahn's preferred image was that of himself hand in hand with other men. Indiscretions of this sort resulted in him being disciplined with punishment tours of duty at Auschwitz concentration camp. Even though this was before Auschwitz descended into the worst excesses of Nazi hell, what Rahn witnessed there made him realise he had sold his soul and was now wearing the mark of the Beast. In the middle of March 1939, Rahn went to Soll, in the Tyrolean Mountains. After walking along an Alpen track alone, he ingested sleeping pills before he froze to death in the snow.

The important detail for the present is that through his study of the medieval romance *Parzival*, Rahn became convinced that Eschenbach's book was no mere work of fiction and that Eschenbach was referring to a real treasure to be found at a real location and giving you clues to find it. In Wolfram's book, the knight Parzival sought the 'Gral' said to be a Stone, the 'Lapsit exillis' at 'Munsalvaesche' (Wild Mountain). This was guarded by war-like knights, the 'Templeisen', which through Wolfram's allusions to the colours black and white at the commencement of his story, can be taken to be the Templars whose battle standard, the beaucent, was a simple partition of equal black and white. Rahn suspected that 'Munsalvaesche' was most likely the mountain citadel of Montsegur in the French Pyrenees. In 1234, Montsegur was the last stronghold of the Cathars who, after a 34-year crusade started in 1209 by King Louis IX on order of Pope Innocent III, ran from the citadel into the waiting pyres to take their lives as free men rather than surrender to the besieging forces. Monstsegur had a traditional history which told that the night before this mass suicide, four knights had escaped carrying the Cathar treasure, inferred as being the Holy Grail.

In Rahn's view of history, the hoard was 'Solomon's Treasure', the vast riches looted from the Temple of Jerusalem in 70AD by the victorious Roman Legions at the bloody conclusion to a Jewish insurrection which ultimately destroyed their nation. In turn, this treasure was looted from Rome by the Visigothic King Alaric around 410AD during the last gasps of the expiring Roman Empire. Alaric was supposed to have hid it somewhere in the region that encompasses what is now known as the south of France and the north of Spain. It is the same treasure with this unique Jewish/Roman/Visigothic line of succession that de Sede identified as being 'Le Tresor Maudit' for Rennes-le-Château.

A strange addendum to all this is the story regarding the Reichsfuhrer's excursion to Montserrat Abbey during a visit to fascist Spain in October of 1940. According to Andreu Ripol Noble, a German-speaking monk at the time, Himmler was seeking the Holy Grail. Visiting other castles in the area, a picture exists of Himmler standing outside a castle at Quermanco, holding a copy of Rahn's book. The circumstances of these inspections are not suggestive of a concerted search effort being mounted by the Reichsfuhrer for the Third Reich; more like Himmler was taking a jaunt to satisfy his own curiosity of the subject raised by Rahn.

Colonel Howard Buechner was a medical officer in 45th Infantry Division in World War Two and was the first American physician to enter Dachau Concentration camp on 29th April 1945. It seems that after witnessing the vast amounts of looted works of antiquities hoarded by the Nazis (and no doubt access to intriguing documents when cleaning up the wreckage of the Nazi regime), he became interested in the subject of Otto Rahn and his treasure hunt. Buechner's book, whose title is given above, sets out his findings and beliefs in the subject, one of which was that Rahn had located the 'Treasure of Solomon and the Emerald Cup' (the Emerald Cup being some ancient grail like object originating from Abraham's first temple at Ur). This fabulous treasure of antiquity had ended up stockpiled with other Nazi loot at a salt mine in Merkers but was slowly dispersed prior to the arrival of the US 3rd Army under Patton who captured the mine and its contents intact.

The treasure list makes interesting reading.

The Treasure Confirmed

What was most distracting in Buechner's book was a descriptive list of this 'Treasure of the Ages':
The treasure consisted of items in six categories:

1. Thousands upon thousands of gold coins, some of which dated back to the early days of the Roman Empire.
2. Items which were believed to have come from the Temple of Solomon, which included the gold plates and fragments of wood that had once made up the Ark of Moses. Identification of the object was somewhat uncertain because most of the

wooden parts had rotted away as the centuries took their toll. However, the accompanying items lent strong evidence that the partially decomposed relic was indeed the Ark of the Covenant There was a gold-plated table, a candelabra with seven branches, a golden urn, a staff, a harp, a sword, innumerable golden plates and vessels, many small bells of gold and a number of previous jewels and onyx stones, some which bore inscriptions. And, of course, there were other less well-known objects too numerous to be mentioned in this account.

3. Twelve stone tablets bearing pre-runic inscriptions which none of the experts were able to read. These items comprised the stone Grail of the Germans and of Otto Rahn.
4. A beautiful silvery Cup with an emerald-like base made of what appeared to be jasper. Three gold plaques on the Cup were inscribed with cuneiform script in an ancient language.
5. A large number of religious objects of various types which were unidentifiable as to time and significance. However, there were many crosses from different periods which were of gold or silver and adorned with pearls and previous stones.
6. Precious stones in abundance in all sizes and shapes.

This was compared with an inventory said by the author Charroux to be left by Fitzgerald from Keating. This inventory was the one which contained the colour code of red and yellow.

"We have buried at a depth of four feet in the red earth:
1 chest: altar trimmings of cloth of gold, with baldachins, monstrances, chalices comprising 1,244 stones.
1 chest: 2 gold reliquaries weighing 120 pounds, with 624 topazes, cornelian and emeralds, 12 diamonds.
1 chest: 3 reliquaries of cast metal weighing 160 pounds, with 860 rubies and various stones, 19 diamonds.
1 chest: 4,000 doubloons of Spain marked 8. 5,000 crowns of Mexico. 124 swords, 64 dirks, 120 shoulder belts. 28 rondaches.
1 chest: 8 caskets of cedar-wood and silver, with 3,840 cut stones, rings patens and 4,265 uncut stones.
28 feet to the north-east, at a depth of 8 feet in the yellow sand: 7

chests with 22 candelabra in gold and silver weighing 250 pounds, and 164 rubies a foot.

12 armspans west, at a depth of 10 feet in the red earth: the seven-foot Virgin of gold, with the Child Jesus and her crown and pectoral of 780 pounds, rolled in her gold chasuble on which are 1,684 jewels. Three of these are 4-inch emeralds on the pectoral and 6 and 6-inch topazes on the crown. The seven crosses are of diamonds."

That was then compared with the list given by Hamilton from Brown via Howe:

14 tons gold ingots
7 golden candlesticks, encrusted with jewels
38 long diamond necklaces
A quantity of jewelled rings
A quantity of jewelled crucifixes
A quantity of jewelled bracelets
1 chest of Spanish doubloons
1 chest of uncut stones
Various other jewels and ornaments

This great treasure suddenly announced its name: 'The Lost Treasure of the Temple of Jerusalem', the fate of which was the world's biggest historical mystery! Apart from the overall similarity in the inventories, you will notice how in the different treasure stories, a particular item is consistently identified as being part of the treasure; the candlesticks or candelabras. E.F. Knight for Trinidade says, "........ *and among other riches there were several massive gold candlesticks.*"

This is another example of how the translation of a word from one language to another, the quantity/quality problem, caused it to lose both its and the entire treasure's identity. Though the English Bible uses the word 'candlestick' for a particular item of the Temple of Jerusalem's furniture, the correct word is 'Menorah'.

What was worse, an even greater translation/identification error became evident, one with far-reaching consequences.

As Wolfram's story is taken to be now just one of a number of what are termed 'Grail Quest' romances which all appeared around the same time, it was decided to check out the other Holy Grail stories to see if there was any other medieval scuttlebutt about a certain missing treasure. Checking Chretien de Troye's Grail romance *Conte de Graal*, the following description was given of the items said to make up this most sought of treasures,

> "Two more attendants then entered, bearing in their hands candelabra of fine gold inlaid with niello. Handsome indeed were the attendants carrying the candelabra. On each candelabrum then candles, at the very least, were burning. Accompanying the attendants was a beautiful, gracious, and elegantly attired young lady holding between her two hands a graal. When she entered holding the graal, such brilliant illumination appeared that the candles lost their brightness just as the stars and the moon do with the appearance of the sun. Following her was another young lady holding a silver carving platter. The graal, which came first, was of fine pure gold, adorned with many kinds of precious jewels, the richest and most costly found on sea or land, those on the graal undoubtedly more valuable than any others. Exactly as the lance had done, the graal and the platter passed in front of the bed and went from one room into another."

You need to take heed of the word 'graal' and what this actually is as it appears in company with the 'silver carving platter'. The word 'graal' is a medieval term for a sort of deep dish affair or serving bowl. It is not the same word or object that most persons now use and identify these stories with, a quest to find the 'Holy Grail' being a chalice or goblet used by Christ at the Last Supper and which caught his blood during the crucifixion. What was being described here was matching more of the Temple's equipment, for along with the menorah, an ornate bowl used to carry sacrificial blood and a platter to present the sacrifice were rather standard fixtures.

It looked as though we (MN's opinion, not mine. GE) could be well and truly along that ultimate of sojourns, the Quest for the Holy Grail (make that Graal) and the 'Quest' was for something very real indeed.

One of the best depictions of a menorah from the Temple is

sculpted into the Arch of Titus in Rome. This depicts scenes of the triumphant parade of the treasure through Rome by the conquering Roman General Titus after he crushed the Jewish nation's insurrection in AD 70 and razed the Temple in the process.

There are not many people who can say they had to set aside what was the real Quest to find the Holy Graal because they had more important things to do, but between the Temple's treasure appearing on Titus' Arch, Lord Anson, the Treasure of the Temple of Jerusalem, a Spanish Admiral, a strange map, and with the Graal now being one of the items of the overall cache, its story just had to wait. Too many things are piling up and we haven't even finished with Rennes-le-Château yet.

CHAPTER 3

THE RULE OF 42

In a book titled *Sacred Sites of the Templar Knights,* the author, John K. Young, identified that at 42 degrees north latitude, a 72 degree angle occurred between the sun and moon at the solstice making the event observable from Rennes-le-Château and Compostella, as both were at this latitude! With the probability that Ubilla had been a Knight of Santiago, a religious military order that was associated with Compostella, this immediately suggested there was some known link between the treasure and this number.

If you know the Coniunctio (2nd) key, 138 as longitude can be readily worked out as the opposite in sense to 42 as latitude (180-42=138 long). As an important clue to locate the treasure, the number 42 is to be found hidden in or associated with the stories. Though it could be traced in a wide variety of applications where searchers for the treasure struggled to divine its navigational meaning, many applications suggest it was known to be a latitudinal value. This number would have been a recognitive signal to those steeped in alchemy, and anyone who recognised it also knew that the number 6 was to be taken as its prime factor. Alchemy lore taught that the godfather of alchemy, Hermes Trismegistus, wrote 42 books of arcane knowledge known as the Hermatic Mysteries. These were divided into 6 categories, education of the priesthood, rituals for the temple, geographic knowledge, hymns in honour of the gods as well as royal deportment and lastly wisdom. With 6 as a factor of 42, the other factor 7 then was already well known to alchemists as it had numerous arcane applications and meanings.

An example of how this clue was transmitted occurs in Charroux's book when he related details about Cocos Island. Within the details of how the invented 'Nautical and Traveller's Club' held a letter by Fitzgerald 'registered number 18,755', is a Masonic number riddle and requires dividing the second number (755) by the first (18) to obtain the value of 41.9 (possibly, 755 due to a typing error, should have read 756, and on division we then get 42 exactly). This letter purports to give Keating's 'instructions' (shown below) and it sounds as if the three points talked about are headlands of an island. You should now be able to recognise and understand the true meanings of the terms being used to enable you to work through the garbling;

'At two cable's length (similar term in Webb document), south of the last watering place (well/water source), on three points (tres puntas). The cave is the one which is to be found under the second point (identification of which island in trinity).'

The number 42 for latitude will be found for lost treasure stories including those which featured Kidd on the east coast of America, but in a lot of locations, 42 became blurred through 43 to 44 for no other reason than to make it latitudinally match the treasure's supposed location in whatever local version of the story was being told. An example of this via a Masonic number riddle is given in my Kidd book. It is the 1894 *'Olmstead story'*, a purely fictional tale designed to sound real. In this, Kidd is supposed to have passed a card to his wife in Newgate Prison (she stayed in America. GE), upon which were the numbers 44106818. The story then identifies this to be Deer Island at 44º10´ latitude 68º13´ longitude where a treasure chest was found. The variation from the figures of 44106818 to 44106813 is explained in the story as an allowable navigational variation. The Masonic trick in this one is to know that the author is drawing your attention to what the number should be 44106813 and is giving the number 44 as a clue with the next numbers to be recognised as part of Phi (or better known as the Golden Mean, 1.61803).

For those of you a bit more advanced into how numbers were used to hide others via formulaic codings should note for Oak Island's lat and long; 64+44= 108. Add this to the longitude of 138, i.e. the Pinaki area identified by Wilkins and you get 246 being the bearing for Scorpius. In the end though, after discovering via Rennes-le-Château the number 42 was known to be important and could be used in the alchemic code, it was not known why it was used other than it was suggesting some important link between the latitude of Compostella and Ubilla as a Knight of Santiago.

Back to Rennes and what it all means for us.

CHAPTER 4

RENNES-LE-CHÂTEAU GIVES UP ITS CLUES

Turning back to the Haupoul clues, the original French words for 'aged sixty seven' were being spaced on the headstone diagram to indicate a bearing, as 'agee' was short for 'apogee' alluding to height or latitude with 'ante' (as before) alluding to depth or longitude. Part of the reason why Rennes-le-Château was then thought to be the correct location was that someone must have also suspected that a number code was being used; a multiplication of 6 with 7 to arrive at 42, the latitude where Rennes-le-Château sat. Plantard and the gang got this far at least into the codes but no further.

The accompanying engraved slab image was merely a fabrication to include the words 'PS PRAECUM', the letters of which were necessary to be used with the headstone words to anagram the 'Bergere' (shepherd) message. Other letters on the slab (ETINA*PX AΔ*IAEΓΩ) are a transcription into Greek from the Latin thematic saying made famous by a succession of artists and the myth of Rennes-le-Château itself: 'ET IN ARCADIA EGO'. These words appeared on the lavish painting, *The Shepherds of Arcadia* by Poussin, which was referred to as a clue in the message but are also replicated on the Shepherd's Monument at Shugborough Hall, Lord Anson's ancestral home.

As it was specifically given 6 then 7, this meant that 67 was a key number to be used for decoding (one number following the other).

MDCOLXXXI on the gravestone taken as 16081 (see explanation later) was recognisable as a permutation on the golden section 1.618. But as it was specifically given this way again, it meant it was to be used as a key number.

Running down the encoding permutations from the numbers:

180 degrees-42 = 138 degrees ante (long)
42+67= 109, 109-90degrees = 19 degrees agee (lat)
16081 ÷ 67= 240 + 6 (first number) = 246 (Prime star Scorpio).

Why was Scorpio's number being repeated? That could wait for later.

Firstly, the 'decoded' message from the large parchment and slab needed to be examined. Beginning with the word 'SHEPHERDESS', the message was already taken by many to be some reference to the image of the Poussin painting but what else it meant was uncertain.

You may ponder over the meaning of the bizarre words that this message in English finishes with, 'BLUE APPLES', as many do for they are nonsensical. Of course these are the English words for 'POMMES BLUES" because we have to translate it from French which literally is "APPLES BLUE". But it's not the translation from French that makes the words nonsensical for in French it still just means blue apples. As the French words were still nonsensical, MN suspected that again he was perhaps just looking at the garbled mistranslation from Latin of a set of original directional clues as there was a Latin word, 'DAEMON' which appeared in both the French and English versions. But this was not the only problem as some French words also had different meanings as the words 'PAS DE TENTATION' in French could mean either 'NO TEMPTATION' or 'ON THE THRESHOLD', 'MIDI' could mean either 'MIDDAY' or 'SOUTH' and 'J'ACHEVE" could mean 'I COMPLETE' or 'I DESTROY'.

Things get further complicated if you used phrases that have meaning in one language but cannot be directly translated to another. For example, an English speaker can understand that the phrase 'fruit of the sea' means an island. But when the Latin word for the colour 'blue' can also mean the 'sea' and the word 'apples' is the same word for 'fruit', then there is no way 'fruit of the sea' was ever going to survive from English into Latin then to French and finally back into English again.

SHEPHERDESS NO TEMPTATION/ON THE THRESHOLD THAT POUSSIN TENIERS HOLD THE KEY PEACE 681 BY THE CROSS AND THIS HORSE OF GOD I COMPLETE/I DESTROY THIS DAEMON GUARDIAN AT MIDDAY/ SOUTH APPLES BLUE.

MN thought the message, though still garbled, originally went something like this:

SHEPHERDESS ON THE THRESHOLD THAT POUSSIN & TENIERS HOLD THE KEY TO PEACE, 681. BY THE CROSS AND THIS HORSE OF GOD I COMPLETE/DESTROY (solve) THIS DAEMON GUARDIAN FOR THE SOUTH SEA FRUIT (south sea island).

This just seemed to be a message to look to the paintings to solve something about them which led to an island (this, of course, is the real intent). Another school of thought suggests the reference to 'POMMES BLEUES' relates to a stained-glass window that used to be in the Church of Saint Sulpice in Paris, which keeps popping up in this whole mythos/mystery surrounding Rennes. The link to this church and Rennes we show later.

For now, let us take a look at the paintings.

The Paintings

The first painting, most famously known now due its association with Rennes-le-Château, is Nicholas Poussin's *The Shepherds of Arcadia* (Les Bergers de Arcadie).

There are two paintings of this theme completed by Poussin and it is the later version we are interested in. Executed around 1640 when Cardinal Rospigliosi commissioned Poussin to complete a series of four works, two of these paintings, *The Rest on the Flight into Egypt* and *Time Saving Truth from Envy and Discord'* are now lost. Of the two paintings that survived, *A Dance to the Music of Time* and *Happiness Subdued by Death*, it is the latter we are interested in being known now as *The Shepherds of Arcadia II.*

THE SHEPHERDS OF ARCADIA II

Lord Anson's own version of *The Shepherds of Arcadia II* is a bas-relief sculpture of the painting's scene and is known as 'the Shepherd's Monument' at his ancestral home in Staffordshire. We show it next with the enigmatic cipher underneath, the whole surrounded by an arbour.

A Bas-Relief Sculpture

THE SHEPHERD'S MONUMENT

You would think that maybe the Shugborough Estate would/should have the original painting by Poussin hanging from its walls somewhere but no, the original is in the Louvre, Paris. However, interestingly, Lord Lichfield does have in his possession a sketch of the shepherd's of Arcadia (1) probably by Poussin that he may have done prior to the first painting in 1627. It is the same subject but viewed from the side rather than full on, as is the painting (11) that followed ten years later.

The other painting given as a clue is variously identified as being a David Teniers the Younger's illustration of the temptation of St Anthony. This was problematic as there were a number of versions of this subject executed by Teniers. A link though was identified to Anson by two researchers into the Rennes mystery, Richard Andrew and Paul Schellenberger, in their book *The Tomb of God*. Though it was common knowledge already that Anson had the Shepherd's Monument, they had discovered that a portrait existed of Anson's wife discretely pointing to what is thought to be a drawn version of *The Shepherds of Arcadia* she was holding. This painting was an earlier version of the Poussin painting above.

A Bear-Faced Painting

They had also discovered a Teniers' painting *St Anthony and St Paul* existed in England. The telling clue was the small mention by them that a copy of this obscure painting could be found at Shugborough Hall. The copy had been executed by Ann Margaret Coke; an accomplished artist in her own right, she had married Lord Thomas Anson in 1794.

As Teniers had the habit of painting a number of variations of the same theme, this forgotten version in England was compared with another of Teniers; though nearly identical in layout, there were some obvious additions.

ST ANTHONY AND ST PAUL BY TENIERS. ENGLISH VERSION USED AS PART OF THE TREASURE CODE

So far, all the images associated with the treasure code depicted persons pointing; either the shepherds pointing at a tomb, or Lady Anson pointing discretely at the drawing she was holding, or St Paul pointing skywards. What were you being told to look at? A not so close examination of the English version above disclosed a clever 'trompe l'oeil' by Teniers of a large animal head. If you follow to where St Paul is pointing, it is not towards the raven delivering the bread, it is actually to the head of a rather large bear hidden within the foliage at the top. This was rather interesting as the bear and the constellation of Ursa is the esoteric symbol for the mythical Arcadians. Known as the Bear Race, they were guardians of the Ark of the Covenant. Latcham was making a reference to this in his comment about his Figure 26:

'Seven planets correspond to the North Pole, which are the seven of the Great Bear and seven correspond to the South Pole, which are the seven of the Little Bear.'

St Anthony appears with a white Tau painted on his shoulder. On paintings this is not unusual as it was a convention amongst artists to add this as an identifying mark so you knew you were looking at St Anthony the Great. It is used here though as a clue and directly relates to the Masonic Triple Tau which was known to be a key to find the treasure. There is also a date (XVII JANVIER) identified on Marie Haupoul's gravestone which gets raised in most stories about Rennes-le-Château as somehow being vital to find the treasure. This is January 17th and that happens to be St Anthony's Day. It is also one of the days Cornelius Webb was on the island locating the treasure. Given all the codes relate to astronomic positions, one might suspect then perhaps this day is when a certain heavenly alignment takes place that may help point you to the treasure?

In fact, this exposed the reason why the whole set of clues given in the story of Rennes–le-Château could not be made to give up any real sense in the form of actual directions to apply to the landscape there; they were not for there at all!

The paintings associated with Rennes-le-Château are of persons pointing and these are indeed clues telling you to look at something. The problem is, over the short time the story of Rennes-le-Château has been with us, the focus has been concentrated on the *The*

Shepherds of Arcadia II somewhat in isolation to Teniers' painting so the messages given by these two paintings together has been missed. The first message is given by the Teniers' painting via St Anthony who is telling you to look at the Stone Arcadians by pointing to the Stone Bear. The Stone Arcadians are the four shepherds sculpted on the Shepherd's Monument at Shugborough Hall. They in turn are pointing to something in their scene. The clue trail therefore becomes obvious: Teniers' painting→ stone bear→ stone arcadians→ shepherd's monument→ Anson. Also, as pointed out earlier, Latcham places a depiction of the constellation of the Great Bear in one of his ciphers in his book.

Abbé Henri Boudet, who was believed to be a carrier of the secret and friend of Sauniere, wrote that the key to the secret is in the interpretation of a word composed in a foreign language. To the French, English was a foreign language, so that word was more than likely 'shepherdess'.

We also have to give you a bit of a prompt here because in the mass of detail, it tends to get missed. If you recall, mention was made of the colour code in operation paralleling the star code. The colours given in this code were red and yellow so please go back and look at *The Shepherds of Arcadia II*, in particular the colours of the robes of the shepherdess and the shepherd whose shoulder she has her hand upon; red and yellow, but of course this could also be a coincidence.

CHAPTER 5

A BRIEF SUMMARY OF THE RENNES MYSTERY

From the previous chapters, you can see that the enigma and mystery surrounding Rennes is one of some complexity requiring at times a certain level of intellect. I can quite understand a reader's frustration at having to take on board religion, a wayward priest, sculptures, paintings, dodgy coded parchments and so on, when you might have been expecting a code with directions to the traditional spot marked 'X'. The trail to our treasure *could* have been that simple. I could have said at the beginning;

"Look, forget all about the religious treasure/mystery that has taken hold here. It is all rubbish. Those involved just haven't got a clue (excuse the pun) as to what is really going on here. The clues are for a painting that will lead you to a monument that will lead you to the location of a treasure, nothing else."

In reality, quite simple. But I don't think that statement would have satisfied most readers. You would have wanted to know how I am able to make such a defining statement which in effect is a damnation on what everybody else has written about this subject. What is going to be the reaction of these authors? There are a multitude of books out there on Rennes by reputable and respected authors. I have mentioned the more important books. All I can say, with respect to my fellow authors, is *"Prove me wrong!"* It is going to be difficult because one just cannot deny the link between Rennes-le-Château and Lord Anson. But I hope common sense will prevail and they will realise that in trying to solve the mystery and/or find their 'treasure', whatever it is, they have followed the wrong trail.

A big industry has built up around the mystery and mythos that is indelibly ingrained here in this remote small hamlet. It has its devotees and believers and will no doubt continue to do so because for many, they just *want* to believe that there is a religious treasure mystery here, regardless of the truth.

In recent years, the whole Rennes saga has been compounded (again) by the release of television documentaries including one titled *Bloodline* that deals with the controversial subject that Jesus was married to Mary Magdalene and they had children. They (or Mary only) had somehow made their way to France and Rennes-le-Château is where she was buried. It is just the most recent rehashing of the rather recently invented Jesus and Mary secret liaison theory. The so-called 'evidence' this time was supplied by one Ben Hammott (an anagram of The Tomb Man), real name Bill Wilkinson. He says he followed clues found in the church at Rennes that led to hidden bottles containing parchments that led to a chest, pottery, coins, bottles with more parchments and subsequently to a tomb. The contents of this tomb could only be viewed by pushing a camcorder through a narrow hole. What it revealed was an open box containing artifacts (chalice, goblets etc.) and on a raised plinth, a white shroud with a red-cross covering; it was supposedly a body. In the best interests of controlled and scientific archaeology(?), Hammott (filming himself in secret - the location is known only to him) somehow manages to manipulate the long camera-carrying probe to remove the shroud and reveal a mummified body.

Whilst the French Government is inferred to be involved now, there are a lot of questions that need to be asked about what Hammott was doing. The documentary is also suggestive of the fact that the Priory of Sion is a real and on-going organisation that is somehow a protective custodian of the Magdalene myth - whispers of persons getting too close being murdered etc.

That the 'tomb' *could* be a rather ordinary film prop is suggested by what *could* be expanded foam filler holding rocks together in the access hole; when pushing the camera 'down', no rocks or rubble were seen to be falling into the tomb. This can only be explained by the 'hole' being horizontal - much easier to film! We know from the 'Indiana Jones' type movies that it is very easy to create realistic mummies etc. Golden goblets shine nicely from their open cask. The white shroud also appeared white, looking fresh and not disintegrated after 2,000 years with no layer of dust, dirt or grime! As mentioned above, where are the rubble and stones that would have fallen down on to the artifacts when enlarging the access hole? One wonders if the directors/producers of this film were taken in, or were they party to it? "Hey, who's gonna notice?"

If a set-up, well I suppose it does make good television for the uninitiated. Maybe Hammott really has found a hidden tomb of some sort, but if it is *the* great religious treasure with an equally great religious 'body', why haven't we seen the worldwide headlines announcing it?

I do not want to dwell too much on this; the Mary Magdalene variation is for us a very recent mutation of the original quest, the 'treasure' in this case now being identified as the earthly remains of a religious figure waiting to be found within a tomb and not the traditional gold and silver one would expect. Rennes-le-Château is, after all, just another place, one of a number of similar places, where a fake story was concocted that carried real clues to the lost treasure of Ubilla. These clues and codes are not even unique, having been found in use elsewhere. Like the other locations that had a fake story containing real codes, the persons promoting the story neither understood nor could decode the ciphers themselves. The story that has grown up around Rennes is only some 50 to 60 years old but the codes and clues implanted in it can be traced as appearing some two centuries earlier. These codes, like the other locations they appear in, are just of the standard format, and just use a common encryption method, so one key fits all. They all relate to and can be traced to Anson. They were designed to give navigational information sufficient for a ship to find an island using the lost map.

Some important points:

1. The 'treasure' for the story for Rennes is that for the Temple of Jerusalem, nothing else. It is identified in the book *Le Tresor Maudit* but has been lost due to Baigent, Lincoln's and Leigh's *The Holy Blood and The Holy Grail* leading the reader astray or sidetracking him, if you like. So in the short 60 years this story has been made public, the identity of the treasure has been changed into some myth about Jesus' bloodline.

2. The traditional story 'window dresses' up the real codes which are then 'found' by decoding the fake parchments etc. The trouble is, the 'decoded' message found in the fake parchment is still in code; it is not decoded at all. Planchard, de Cherrisey etc. got as far as working out the number 42

from the code (from Haupoul's age on the gravestone i.e. 67) which is the latitude Rennes lies on but got no further. The most cursory view of the 'clues' reveals 'Agee soix', 'Ante sopt' quite plainly in Latin, 'Apogee' (for latitude) and 'Ante' (for longitude). It might not be obvious why the Plantard gang took the latitudinal coordinate to be 42 degrees (latitude for Rennes is closer to 43 degrees) and then assign the prime meridian (longitudal co-odinate) as Paris i.e. 00 degrees but there is a simple reason. I mentioned in a previous chapter that the Church of the Saint Sulpice in Paris has the famous 'Roseline' brass meridian strip running through it at 2º15′E (of Greenwich) which just happens to be the same longitude as Rennes. The Chapelle-de-Agnes in St Sulpice once had a stained glass window which depicted Adam and Eve being expelled from Eden, carrying a blue apple (the image was not replaced after the window was broken in 1900). For the Plantard gang (through de Cherisey's research), this matched the 'blue apples' code clue and confirmed in their minds they were correctly interpreting the coded instructions to use this as the longitudinal meridian.

Because they can't see or work out what the rest of the numbers are giving, they don't go any further than the accepted story, but that's Rennes all over!

3. The clues are indeed real and there to first locate the Shepherd's Monument and then the coded navigational directions (the monument cipher). This is, of course, entirely removed from what the so-called 'experts' would have you believe for Rennes.

Where did the clues originally come from? You could say it's not important because they were there and they are real. But it is possible to trace their origin and it more than likely goes like this: Saunier was a Freemason, that has been traced and identified, and rather a worldly priest. He did like money, luxury and sensuality, which proved to be his downfall; he was charged with simony, the trafficking of masses for money to keep his lifestyle going. Was he just 'local colour' included in a fake story to make it sound real? No. All evidence and information suggests he had the codes, Masonic codes that is, for that is what they are, and searched for the treasure himself. He never found anything. Another reason for his high lifestyle was, as stated previously, his financial dealings with the Archduke Habsburg who had the same interests.

Where did the codes come from? Evidence and information suggests they *were* actually on the Marie Haupoul gravestones which Sauniere is said to have destroyed to hide them from others. He was aware of what they were but, of course, not what they meant, nor how to decode them. Freemasons of that era would have been able to recognise when coded details were being revealed about their 'lost treasure'. We have seen enough examples of this sneaky passing of coded references appearing in contemporary books and stories. They (modern Freemasons) do not seem to be able to recognise them anymore. Did Sauniere just happen to notice these irregularities in the text one day and say to himself "Mon Dieu! Here are some codes for our lost tresor. I will use them to find le tresor and keep it for myself." Well no, Masons don't operate alone. There would have been Masonic knowledge passed to a brother mason of Masonic history like; "Hey! You know that gravestone in your cemetery, the one with the crazy badly spelt message? That looks like it's got the codes for our lost tresor. Pass the baguette."

The person who put the gravestone there and allowed them to be inscribed 'badly' is actually identified; he was a predecessor of Sauniere, a priest called Abbé Bigou (1719-1794). He being the family priest ministered to Marie-de-Haupoul and buried her when she died 17th January 1681[1]. Rumour has it she was the source of the clues and was the local nobility; apparently the Haupoul Chateau still stands today. Bigou with the Haupoul secret fled to Spain in 1792 due to the French Revolution, because Holy places of worship and priests were not excluded from the murderous rampaging of the new Republic. The new order dictated that the clergy were to be made employees of the State. All priests and Bishops had to swear an allegiance to this order under threat of dismissal, deportation or death. Bigou, who had no wish to become part of this new Republic, knew if he stayed he would not remain unscathed. He had no option but to flee the country. In 1792, aged 73, he fled to Sabadell in Spain, where he died aged 75 having never returned to Rennes-le-Château.

It was only the upright Haupoul headstone that had the real clues. As was found by researchers, the 'shepherdess' message can be anagrammed from the headstone text by utilising its 119 letters, plus 9 letters from the tombstone. These extra letters required for the anagram ACEMPPRSU, or as arranged in their suggested form PS PRAECUM, to give a hint towards the mythical Priory of Sion. The central vertical arrows pointing to these letters indicate they are to be used together.

Whilst on the subject of the gravestones, the (fraudulent) mystery is further compounded by the discrepancy in the spelling of the name of the deceased. What we show here is an enlargement of part of the text, taken from plate XXI of the forged 'Stublein' pamphlet *Pierres Gravées du Languedoc* (1962). This publication you will recall also shows the slab or flagstone. Quite clearly you can see that a 'T' has been crudely inserted as an afterthought between the U and P.

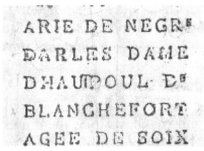

ENLARGED PART OF HEADSTONE DIAGRAM
FROM THE FAKE STUBLEIN PAMPHLET

Hautpoul is also the name of a place not very far from Rennes and as well as not being uncommon as a persons name in France, shown here it is undoubtly how it should be spelt. This no doubt its where the family chateau is located that goes back beyond the sixteenth century. Many publications about the mystery of Rennes can't seem to make their minds up about what the spelling should be. The problem is compounded by the French convention of accepting both Haupoul and Hautpoul. This is a leftover from the days when a scribe, listening to an oral deposition, transcribed the name as they heard it being pronounced. Both forms then, Hautpoul and Haupoul, could refer to the same person.

This confusion was then built upon by what was shown by De Sede in *The Accursed Treasure* which was the image of the upright headstone from the Society for Scientific Study of the Aude's pamphlet and the slab image from the forged Stublein pamphlet. Henry Lincoln's book *The Holy Place* added to the confusion by showing the world the upright and slab images taken from *The Accursed Treasure*, but removing from the slab image the fake Stublein signature and the letters LIXLIXL on the bottom.

Very few of the images of the upright shown in the various recounts of the story use the 'Stublein' version that includes the 'T'; a lot just show the two images from Lincoln's book with the slab sans the fake Stublein signature. Nobody seems to have picked up on this before, or if they do they just ignore it because it cannot be explained. I have in this chapter shown it without the 'T' because that has been the accepted way it has been shown. However, the 'correct' spelling poses a problem because with the inclusion of the 'T', the total number of characters is now **120+9**! This doesn't fit in, of course, with the earlier mentioned chessboard solution. This is more proof that something ulterior is going on because any French headstone engraver would have spelt the name correctly i.e. with the 'T', unless they were uneducated or on the vino! But the French convention of accepting either form Haupoul/Hauptpoul does allow it to slip in without too much notice. The 'T' version for Hautpoul does not then get used in *The Accursed Treasure* because it didn't then fit with the elaborate decoding methodology as part of the constructed story. Likewise, though the name 'Abbe Joseph Courtaly' appears on the fake Stublein pamphlet as its beneficent donator, it seems to be generally accepted that this is the same as 'Abbe Joseph Courtauly'. It's not as if the gang was unaware of what the spelling should be. References to 'Courtauly' first appeared in a tricked up pamphlet titled *Un Tresor Merovingian a Rennes le Chateau* which turned up before the fake Stublein one. *The Accursed Treasure* even has the following dedication, 'To the memory of Abbe Joseph Courtauly'.

Un Tresor Merovingian a Rennes le Chateau appeared to be a preparatory work which simply copied the story, unreferenced, straight out of Robert Charroux's book *Treasures of the World*. Images of the upright (the DHAUPOUL version) and the slab without the fake Stublein signature, as well as Merovingian genealogical tables, were added as part of the overall package. Side notations for the images of the D'HAUTPOUL (sic) stones infer they are from Stublein's pamphlet via 'Abbe Joseph Courtauly'. Prominently on the genealogical tables, side notes again identify their source as 'Abbe Joseph Courtauly'. An interesting twist for those who can remember that far back, *Treasures of the World* is the book where Charroux hid a treasure cipher, the number 18,755 in the story for Cocos Island and is the source of the Keating documents' text. For Charroux, the story of Rennes-le-Chateâu had nothing to do with the lost treasure which he inferred was the mystery behind Cocos Island. Here was the Plantard gang even using Charroux's book but missing the treasure cipher Charroux was giving, as Rennes-le-Château for them had nothing to do with Cocos Island!

To cap it all, (again, excuse the pun), the slab or flagstone drawing (plate XXII) after being devised was included in the fake pamphlet in order to give it some credibility, because the all-important letters PS etc. were essential to the encryption. Amongst the other illustrations, it was hoped that it would be accepted as genuine. Overall, de Cherisey, who is the acknowledged artisan behind all these "confections" as Plantard called them, did some pretty inspired work with a somewhat mischievous bent designed to distract. Anyone researching the story and coming across the tiny but obvious 'mistakes', e.g. a missing 'T' or 'U' in a character's name, tends to concentrate on them to discover what such a mistake could mean rather than examining the story as a whole.

A brief explanation may be called for here regarding the earlier mentioned 'Knights Tour' decoding method used to create the important Shepherdess/Poussin message. The letters utilised (9+119) to extract the message from the fake parchment required the use of two chessboards, i.e. 128 squares made up of 64 squares (letters) on each board. The Knights tour chosen is known as 'cyclic' where you move (the Knight) around the board following successive numbers i.e. 1 to 3 to 4 and so on to 64. Each square, of course, relates to a letter. You don't have to start at 1; the idea is to link the ending and starting squares to close the path making it cyclic.

Our knowledge dictates we can try to date the clues given in the story because <u>they must at least be post-1748</u> when the Shepherd's Monument was constructed/started because that is what they relate to; they give clues to find the monument and use it as a map utilising, as we will see, coded navigational instructions. They are probably <u>post-1762,</u> after Anson's death and, given the date they were permanently recorded on the gravestone stone (1781), had their origin in this twenty-year period. There would be no need for codes to find the map and directions whilst Anson was still alive as he was the keeper of them. They are, though, very early and original, containing not only coded navigational instructions as we have seen but also clues to find the map (the monument). This is the only version where the link to the map is not lost. By the 19th century, the link was lost. Its line of clues is somewhat unique in that it gives (when you bundle the numbers) 4216081 which means, in a sort of code, at cipher 42 find the golden section, which is pretty direct if you know the cipher for 42 and what the golden section means in regards to the treasure (this comes shortly but is to do with the Trinity islands). This is not unique in form because if you recall from an earlier chapter, the number group in the Kidd/Olmstead story became 44106813. You were meant to recognise Phi, the golden mean i.e. 1.6183.

It is quite evident from the level of the headstone's codes that the person who put them there (Bigou?) knew what they were about; he was not just repeating them unaware of what they were but what they mean, translated garbling included.

In case you missed it, I will also mention the blatant inclusion of the 'P-S' emblem on two of the 'essential' items, namely the slab and Parchment 1. The characters appear enclosed by a curved line. This to make sure you recognise that the slab and parchments are somehow linked. Devious sleight of hand here, Parchment 1 does nothing for us in regard to solving the mystery. It is there to confuse, waste your time and make you believe it has relevance that can maybe only be through the words 'Tresor' (Treasure) and 'Mort' (Death/Tomb).

What you might not have picked up due to the sleight of hand which occurred in the overall story is this; how do you know which of Poussin's or Teniers' painting to look at? Extra information was available to the Plantard gang that identified that the correct paintings to look at were *The Shepherds of Arcadia II* and Teniers' painting whose subject is St Anthony. This extra information is only supplied to you through the *narrative* of the popular Rennes story. Likewise, the 'shepherdess' message is not *decoded* from the Haupoul headstone, but it is *anagrammed* from it only and to do so required the supply of the extra 9 letters, ACEMPPRSU. These were supplied by the inclusion of the fake slab image to suggest the above letters in the form PS PRAECUM and as well as the phrase 'ET IN ARCADIA EGO' in Greek/Roman style letters to suggest to you further the painting *The Shepherds of Arcadia*. (This phrase occurs on the tomb in the painting.) The story then suggests that the parchments are decoded to produce the 'shepherdess' message. Only via the narrative again is it then further identified which of Poussin's two executions of the subject is to be utilised; *The Shepherds of Arcadia II*.

The 'shepherdess' message is a version of some prior knowledge clues which were given in phrase form and accompanied the Haupoul headstone, somewhat like the Spanish code phrases are meant to accompany a map. These clue-like phrases were what the Plantard gang were aware of. They have been released in the fabricated story of Rennes-le-Château for two reasons; the first is that these are the clues they <u>cannot</u> understand the meaning of. The clues that they thought they understood are not being given again in the coded 'Bergere' message e.g. the identification that Teniers' painting has St Anthony as a subject. They have released these phrases, with a cover story, in the hope you, or the legion of followers of Rennes, can solve them without tipping you off what it is really for.

The whole thing via the paintings, gravestones and clues is just "Look to Anson and the monument copy of the painting", but this step was lost. **Everyone, because the clues were found at Rennes, assumed they must be for there!**

In the end, the trouble is we are but dealing with a shadow of the real codes and clues, the original information Bigou left, Suaniere used and that which Plantard and co. admitted basing their fakes upon. What we have is only what Plantard and co. deigned to release, chosen by them after assessing it to be sufficient information for others to use to hopefully solve the code's meaning but not then be able to identify what they were really about. As the manifest clues to Anson in the fabricated versions they chose to release went right over their heads, one can only wonder how much detailed coded information it was that they were keeping to themselves.

So, real codes hidden in fake documents and artifacts. The perpetrators knew they had something, but not what exactly. They didn't understand them at all; if they did, they would have been skulking around Shugborough Hall, Anson's ancestral home, instead of haunting Rennes-le-Château!

Saurniere thought he was onto something, which is why he bought Poussin's painting but couldn't get any further with it. Some have made the link to Shugborough (even the producers of *Bloodline*) but none have made the direct link to Lord Anson. Some have even denied there are any links.

Threads of Freemasonry, as we know, run through the whole mythos that is Rennes. Patrick Byrne, a Freemason, upon reading about the mystery of Rennes-le-Château intuited that Masonic ritual is linked to the findings of a real lost treasure there. In his book *Templar Gold*, he lays out his suspicions and sets about translating his knowledge into actual directions to locate the Temple treasure. I quote:

'At an early stage my research was providing evidence that beneath this Masonic ritual encoding of geographic landmarks identifying Pech Cardou (Mountain in France. GE), there appeared to be something else equally intriguing. It appears that **particular lines of longitude** *may have been allocated to mark the resting place of something of immense importance on its journey from East to the West.'* (My highlighting in bold. GE).

His book is intriguing as it gives an insight into the actual working methodology of a Freemason attempting to follow the implanted directions to find a treasure here, religious or otherwise. In particular, he identifies the Holy Royal Arch as being the important key. We have already identified the Royal Arch keystone on Sauniere's bookplate acknowledging his involvement in the world of Freemasonry. But look how close Byrne was in identifying *particular lines of longitude.*

Students of Rennes, who with nothing better to do, indulge and revel in its mystery and mythos, may at this point be asking, 'Why didn't I include this story aspect or that story, or those documents, or explain this coded solution or that...?' and so on. Well, why should I? I will remind you that at the beginning of this chapter, I said we would refer to the salient points necessary to understand this historical mistake. There are many books and websites deep into Rennes If you want to indulge in the waffle! As with our Captain Brown and his concocted story, we are in effect giving the background only necessary to present the real story, not to probe in detail every aspect of Rennes, but it has at the same time given me the opportunity to cover a few anomalies that others have avoided.

I am really only interested in the story pre-Sauniere back to the construction of the monument at Anson's home. Somehow the main 'ET IN ARCADIA EGO' clue found its way from England to this small remote village in southern France shortly after the monument's construction, but how? What is the connection between the two? The only plausible answer I can find (so far) is that provided by the author Shannon Dorey in a website article (2005) titled *Shugborough is Associated with the Ancient African Dogon Religion through the Merovingians.* (And no, I've never heard of the African Dogon Religion either!). She says that a Operative Masonic Society associated with the monument was a secret underground political group involving the exiled Stuarts. Shugborough was a meeting place for this group. Since most of the Stuarts were exiled in France, another meeting place for this group existed at Rennes-le-Château. Maybe what they knew about the monument was passed to the Hautpouls. Who knows!

The only other possible French connection I could find that fits in with the period is through a French Jesuit priest by the name of Abbé Augustin Barruel. You will see in a later chapter he wrote a book that included a code used by Anson.

The sometimes suspect and questionable involvement of the Habsburgs didn't die with Sauniere. It appears that in 1975, Archduke Rudolph of Habsburg visited Rennes. The locals who spoke with him noted he appeared very knowledgeable about the mystery. He also spoke with priests who were very versed in the enigma; all agreed he took a more than usual interest. Maybe the Habsburgs are still trying to track down their long lost treasure.

Just as the Kidd/Palmer charts are nothing to do with Kidd but ultimately guide you to a real treasure, the clues at Rennes are nothing to do with a treasure here but are guiding/pointing you to the same real treasure via the monument at Anson's ancestral home. The previously mentioned author Robert Charroux (real name Robert Grugeau, died 1978) took an active interest in Rennes-Le-Château after hearing Monsieur Noel Corbu's story. In his *Treasures of the World,* he finishes his chapter on Rennes as follows:

'One day an inhabitant of Rennes-Le-Château who may know more than he says, said to a member of the Treasure-Seekers' Club (Founded by Charroux. GE); "The secret of the millionaire priest lies at the bottom of a tomb. It is simply a question of finding out which...."'

Whoever made this statement is, of course, believing that an actual tomb holds the secret, and why not? Tombs and gravestones is what Rennes is all about.

I hope you, the reader, is versed enough in this story now to appreciate the real meaning of the words ....*lies at the bottom of a tomb.* They are, of course, inferring to the tomb in the sculpture of Poussin's painting at Shugborough, Anson's ancestral home, at the bottom of which lies...the cipher! Unfortunately, as with a multitude of others, the clues have been totally misunderstood. That statement was made in the 1950s, so closer to the truth and not distorted. The person who made it was privy to the truth without realising it. It is a pity we do not know who that person was and how and where he got his information from. One can speculate that maybe Wilkins travelled to France and planted the Anson seed, but there is no evidence for that. Anyway, how would Wilkins have known about the gravestone clues? The only evidence was in rare French documents.

Charroux, by utilising the 18,755 number cipher, knew that 42 was important. How did he know? Maybe from the same person who made the above statement, or from 'insider' knowledge.

Amongst the millions of words in books and in documentaries, films and websites dealing with the mystery of/that is Rennes-le-Château, you will find the following subjects covered:

Encryptions and solutions thereof, History, legends, alignments of churches/places/objects, lines, lay lines, geometry, Golden section, pentacles, pentagons, triangles, archaeology, geology, Christianity, genealogies, secret societies, languages, translations, conspiracies, mapping, landmarks, peaks, geography, Grandmasters, Freemasons and so on

You need to be a university graduate to understand a lot of the above but my point is, within that list, ninety percent is irrelevant and not required! So much unnecessary work! The mystery is relatively simple and solved by basically deciphering the clues on the gravestone and tombstone of Marie Haupol. When you know what you are looking at, the Poussin inscription ET IN ARCADIA EGO is recognisable in its Greek letters form on the tombstone. Indeed, the very first time I saw it, I recognised it straight away with only a limited knowledge of Greek and Latin. But then I have to say, I was already familiar with the inscription. The giveaway are the characters E, T, I and N. Immediately, we have the connection to Poussin's painting and by rote the marble relief copy of it as part of the monument. Lord Anson's name again stands out when the symbol on one of the parchments is turned upside down.

The paintings play a part but only to push you towards Anson via the inscription clue; they play no other part in this mystery. The message in Parchment 2 is again there only to give the Poussin clue *('Poussin and Teniers hold the key')* and also via the word BERGERE, (shepherdess). On the face of it, it couldn't be any plainer, could it? Unfortunately, a lot of people have been set off on a wild goose chase assuming the paintings themselves hold the key. They look for hidden secrets and reveal geometry that was previously unnoticed that, at the end of the day, doesn't help them at all in their quest.

As previously mentioned, the only mystery left, as far as I am concerned, is who had the knowledge of Anson's monument and the Poussin paintings link to plant them as clues in Rennes-le-Château in the first place?

The only thing to do now then is to leave Rennes-le-Château and go and have a look at what everyone is pointing to; Lord Anson and his enigmatic monument in the grounds of the ancestral home at Shugborough Hall, England. Having said that, I can't help but to finish this chapter by quoting a sentence from a popular book on the treasure of Rennes-Le-Château:

'As the Poussin painting has nothing in reality to do with Rennes-le-Château, the Shugborough monument is equally irrelevant.'

No, comment! And forgive me for having a last dig.

[1]You may, or may not, have spotted the deliberate mistake here. How could Bigou have buried Haupoul in 1681? Look at the date on the gravestone; MDCOLXXX1. This reads; 1600(O)81. There is no 'O' in Roman numerals. Originally it probably was MDCCLXXX1 i.e. 1781 but later altered, easy enough to turn a 'C' to 'O' The reason? More that likely to bring your attention to the figures 1681. You should recognise them now, those of the golden mean (ratio). This anomaly also helped to highlight 'o' as a necessary letter in a key word (MORTEPEE) used as part of the decoding process.

PART 6

CHAPTER 1

LORD ANSON, SHUGBOROUGH AND ITS ENIGMATIC MONUMENT

Very little has so far been mentioned of Lord Anson. We told in Part 1 of his association with a treasure on Juan Fernandez Island and other than that, his name has cropped up just a couple of times in the Rennes story. To the reader therefore it may appear that so far he is someone who is part of the story but maybe of not particular importance. Well we can put you straight on that one, as he is as important to this story as our Captain Brown, perhaps even more so, and the reason his name is in the title of this book. He can be said to be the architect of our treasure story in as much as had he not dispatched Webb to recover the treasure, there would be no story. We know Anson therefore had knowledge of this treasure and its location; information he became privy to on reaching the highest ranks in the Royal Navy and because of his membership of the Royal Society. So we tell his story here first and how his capture of a rich Spanish Galleon helped create one of the finest estates in the country.

Admiral Lord Anson

A short biography concentrating mainly on the important aspects of his life and rise to fame:

George Anson, younger brother of Thomas, was born at Shugborough on 23rd February 1697. Though George Anson is forever associated with Shugborough, he only spent his early years there and never owned the estate. It was his subsequent illustrious career and good fortune that transformed the estate from the mid 1700s. Destined for the sea at an early age, he first joined as a volunteer aboard the *Ruby* in 1712, aged just 14. This was the start of a career that spanned some 49 years. Five years later, whilst serving in the frigate *Hampshire*, he received an acting order as a lieutenant. By the time he was 21, he had seen active service in the Mediterranean and took part in the Battle of Passaro against the Spanish. His first command was a sloop, the *Weasel* in 1722, used to suppress smuggling in the North Sea and along the English Channel. Advanced to the rank of Captain and appointed to the *Scarborough*, for the next 13 years he served on and off at the South Carolina station combating piracy against English merchant shipping. George Anson proved to be popular with his men also socially - 'modest, good sense, good natured, polite, well-bred and generous'. The latter proved when a later engagement saw him forgoing, as captain, his share of prize money for the benefit of his crew.

In 1739, when war broke out again against Spain, the Government decided to dispatch a naval expedition against the most distance Spanish possessions to try and cut off supplies of treasure from the New World. The annual treasure ships from the Spanish Americas to Spain were known as 'the plate fleet' or 'plata flota'. In Spanish, the word *plata* means silver. These tremendously rich fleets were the most sought after prizes for pirates and the enemies of Spain but many of these grand galleons were also lost to shipwreck, coral reefs and hurricanes, as we have already seen with Ubilla's fleet. An example of the riches to be found in the hold of one of these ships is that of the *Jesus Maria de la Limpia Concepcion*, more widely known as the Capitana of the Armada del Mar del Sur, (the regular Pacific fleet from Peru to Panama). She sank off Ecuador in 1654 apparently due to a navigational error. Her holds contained some 216 chests and 2,212 bars of silver.

George Anson, now Captain, with Captain Vernon was put in charge of this ambitious and dangerous undertaking against the Spanish. In December 1739, in command of the *Centurion*, a ship of 60 guns and 400 men, Anson set out with five other ships. The expedition lasted nearly four years to 1744 and proved to be remarkably successful in terms of treasure taken. A history of this eventful voyage, which took him around the world, was published in 1748 by Anson's chaplain of the *Centurion*, Richard Walter. The book proved very popular and went through 15 editions.

Anson journeyed down to Cape Horn via Madeira, stopping on the way at Santa Caterina Island on the south Brazilian coast to re-fit and obtain fresh food. A Spanish force sent to intercept Anson's squadron failed to find them due to them being scattered whilst rounding the

Cape. Eventually rounding the Cape, Anson's ships suffered the same fate as the Spanish, as he found himself alone in May 1741 at the agreed rendezvous at Socotro. He was unaware that one of his ships, the *Wager*, was totally lost whilst battling the elements around the Cape. He decided to proceed north to Juan Fernandez Island and wait there. By this time, his crew was once again in dire need of fresh fruit and food; the sick were taken ashore to recover. The *Tryal* and *Gloucester* eventually turned up, their crews suffering the same as the *Centurion*. Now reduced to three ships, this did not deter Anson's resolve in seeking out the enemy. After the stop at Juan Fernandez, several small Spanish ships were captured, and one was taken over by the crew of the *Tryal* after they were forced to scuttle their ship due to its dire condition.

The town of Paita on the coast of Santa Fe (north Peru) was sacked and burnt after a ransom was refused; treasure taken here amounted to £30,000. Another Spanish ship taken had treasure worth £12,000 in her holds.

Anson decided to cross the Pacific to China. He did this in the *Centurion* which alone made the journey after scuttling the Spanish ships and putting the prisoners ashore, all of whom had been treated fair and humanely. The *Gloucester* suffered the same fate as the *Tryal*, the crew having to transfer to Anson's ship. October 1742 sees them off Macao (near Hong Kong). In need of provisions, he sends a deputation to the viceroy at Canton, and his request was granted. The *Centurion* was the first British man-o'-war to visit China and created great excitement.

MODEL OF HMS CENTURION, 60 GUNS, 4TH RATE SHIP OF THE LINE. BUILT AT PORTSMOUTH DOCKYARD, LAUNCHED 1732. BROKEN UP 1769.

In June 1743, Anson made his most notable success in intercepting the Spanish treasure galleon *Nuestra Senora de Covadonga* enroute from Acapulco to Manilla. This ship was vastly superior in number of men to the *Centurion* and this was the Spanish Captain's undoing, thinking that with his much larger crew he could out-fight the *Centurion*. Nevertheless, after a fierce skirmish lasting half an hour, Anson, in the *Centurion,* captured the galleon. Whilst the English suffered only three fatal casualties, the Spanish lost 67 men killed and 84 wounded; not surprising since they were up against a well-rehearsed formidable British naval man-of-war. Anson, anticipating the battle to come, had trained his men for weeks, especially sharp-shooters up in the rigging. The galleon was a tremendously rich prize and one of the largest prizes ever taken at sea by an English captain. The treasure in her holds included 1,313,843 pieces of eight and 35,000 ounces of silver. The value of the treasure taken amounted to over £400,000 and Anson's prize share as Captain was over £90,000. This with the £719 he earned as Captain of the 3year-9month voyage, made his fortune. By comparison, a seaman would have earned about £300, equivalent to 20 years wages.

None of these successes were, of course, without sacrifice. Many men died of scurvy and dysentery during the voyage. In April during the second year, 45 men died on the *Centurion*, in May, 80, and in June, another 70. Scurvy, as we now know, is a disease caused by the lack of vitamin C. It wasn't until he stopped off at Juan Fernandez Island that his men were able to recover. Two of the other ships in the expedition turned up with crews even more depleted by death and sickness than the *Centurion*. When they finally left Juan Fernandez with men nursed back to health, the three ships sailed with 335 men; this in contrast to 961 when they left England. Scurvy was responsible for more deaths than any sea battle. Other hardships they had to endure was the weather; it took three months to round Cape Horn, with the ships being continually knocked off course by severe gales and storms, and as a result the squadron was scattered far and wide. The *Wager* was lost and two of the ships gave up the attempt. Subsequently, the squadron was never reunited as a whole.

Another unexpected prize during this expedition came after he sailed into Macao again, with the captured Spanish treasure galleon in tow. He sold this for $6,000. Whilst he was in Canton visiting the viceroy, a serious fire broke out in the town, and the crew of the *Centurion* were able to bring this under control. As a reward of gratitude, Anson was given a magnificent Chinese porcelain dinner service of which there are 208 pieces. This, together with many other treasures, can be seen in the ancestral home at Shugborough.

With his mission accomplished, Anson resolved to return to England round the Cape of Good Hope and set sail in December 1743. After resting at the Cape, they reached the English Channel in June 1744. Fortune favoured Anson to the last, as when he came into the Channel, a thick fog hid him from the French fleet, so he sailed through unrecognised.

The *Centurion* anchored safely at Spithead on 15th June.

The treasure that he brought home amounted to about £500,000 and included 1,000kg of silver and over one million pieces of eight (silver coins shown below). This was all landed at Portsmouth then sent to London. It was paraded in triumph through the city in a procession of 32 wagons, the ship's company marching with colours flying and a band playing.

The above photographs show the obverse and reverse of the famous 'Piece of Eight' (8 reales) pillar dollar silver coin. Mexico mint, Philip V, also known as 'Dos Mundos' (Two Hemispheres), approximately the size of the old English Crown and approximately 26 grams in weight. Values vary with condition and the specimen shown would be worth at least £200 at todays (2015) prices.

Anson's Rise to the Highest Echelons of the Navy

In recognition of his glorious and triumphant service, Anson was quickly promoted, and on 19th June 1744 he became Rear-Admiral of the Blue.

He returned his commission after a dispute with the admiralty.

In December, he joined the Admiralty Board.

April 1745 saw him re-promoted to flag rank as Vice-Admiral of the White.

From 1745 to 1747, he was M.P. for Hedon, Yorkshire.

In August 1746, now Vice-Admiral of the Blue, he hoists his flag on the *Yarmouth*, taking command of the Channel fleet.

In May 1747, he defeats the French fleet (Battle of Cape Finisterre). £300,000 in specie (coined money) is carried through London in triumph.

June 1747 sees him raised to the peerage as Baron Anson of Soberton.

In July 1747, he becomes Vice-Admiral of the Red.

He married Lady Elizabeth Yorke, eldest daughter of the Lord Chancellor, on 25th April 1748. Besides spending time with his brother at Shugborough, from now on he spends greatest part of his life at his town house in St James Square, and also his villa in Carshalton, near London. He acquires his own enormous country house at Moor Park in Middlesex.

From March 1750, he become a member of the Privy Council.

In June 1751, he was promoted to First Lord of the Admiralty and Master of Trinity House, 1752 to 1756.

Court martial of Admiral Byng (in due course, shot on his own quarter-deck) brings down the Ministry, and with it, Anson's removal from the Admiralty in November 1756.

In July 1757, he was back in office (different administration) as First Lord of the Admiralty, a post he holds until his death.

1758 sees Anson commanding the main fleet blockading Brest; this is his last war-related service at sea.

His last sea-service is in July 1761 in command of a squadron of yachts bringing Princess Charlotte of Mecklenburg-Strelitz to marry King George 111.

In the same year, 1761, he was created Admiral and Commander-in-Chief of the fleet.

Anson died suddenly 6th June 1762 whilst walking in his garden at Moor Park. He was at this time a widower, his wife having died two years previously.

In his will, Anson left all his estate to his brother Thomas, who used some of this fortune to develop Shugborough and acquire more land; he died in 1773. Neither brothers had children. Eventually, George Adams, son of Lord Anson's sister Janette, inherited both of his uncles' fortunes. He took the name Anson and his son Thomas was created Viscount Anson. (At the time of the death of Lord Anson, a patent was being prepared to create him a Viscount.)

Lord Anson's great-great nephew was created Earl of Lichfield in 1831, a title that is still in existence today. The estate is now owned by the National Trust but still partially occupied by Anson's descendants.

Anson is best known for his voyage around the world (the second Englishman to achieve this fete after Sir Francis Drake) and the fortune he brought home with him, but behind the scenes in his later career he was responsible for many changes in the Navy reassuring its standing as the leading naval power. He created a standard uniform for officers and put new energy into the administration. The dockyards were inspected. The Marines were transferred from Army to Navy authority, old admirals were superannuated and new Articles of War drawn up. Many young officers who trained under him in the *Centurion* rose to become commanders of distinction and genius. Peter Warren was second-in-command to Anson at the victory over the French at the Battle of Cape Finisterre; his conduct in the battle earned him a promotion to Vice-Admiral of the Red. He said of Anson: "I never wish to serve under a better chief."

As an aside, regarding Navy ranks, those amongst you with a keen interest may be wondering why Anson was not promoted to Admiral of the Red (one assumes this would be the highest flag rank), so it may help to explain the promotion system. In the 17th and 18th centuries, the fleet was divided into three squadrons to make the fleet more manageable. The Admiral's squadron wore a Red flag, the Vice-Admiral's wore a white flag and the Rear-Admiral's a Blue. Lowest flag rank was Rear Admiral of the Blue, next promotion would be Rear Admiral of the White followed by Rear Admiral of the Red. Next appointment would be Vice Admiral of the Blue followed by Vice

Admiral of the White then Vice-Admiral of the Red. Next promotion would be Admiral of the Blue followed by Admiral of the White, highest flag rank at that time.

There was no Admiral of the Red since this would be deemed as being in overall command of the fleet. This changed after the battle of Trafalgar (1805); the rank of Admiral of the Red was introduced to reward the most successful admirals. Coloured squadrons were discarded in 1864, mainly because they had no relevance in the coming age of the Industrial Revolution and steamships. The Red Ensign was allocated to the merchant Navy, the Royal Navy adopted the White Ensign, and the Blue Ensign was used by the naval auxiliary vessels.

The above charts Anson's naval and political career. What is less known, and for some reason seems to remain shrouded, is the fact that Anson was inducted into the Royal Society in 1745. He follows in the footsteps of his elder brother, who was made a Fellow in 1730. A handwritten Certificate of Election and Canditature states:

'George Anson Esqr. Rear Admiral of the White, and one of the Lords Commissioners of the Admiralty, desires to offer himself a Candidate for Election into the Royal Society: We do accordingly upon our personal knowledge of him and his great merit propose him to the Same, and hereby recommend him as every way qualified to be a most valuable member hereof'
London May 29. 1745

There followed a list of 10 recommending members.

By virtue of his entry into the Royal Society, he became privy to that Society's archives and therefore by his standing in the Navy made aware of Ubilla's secret papers.

The Shugborough Estate
The Shugborough Estate in Staffordshire, England, the principal seat of the Anson family since the 17th century is vast; you can get an idea from the fact that the entrance on the main road is three-quarters of a mile from the house. At its height in the 19th century, the Anson household employed over 100 servants based at Shugborough. These included 37 indoor household and personal servants, 17 hunt and

keepering staff, and 28 gardeners. The estate at this time covered over 2,000 acres.

By 1842, fortunes had changed and many of the contents had to be sold when the 1st Earl of Lichfield faced financial difficulties. In 1960, on the death of the 4th Earl, the estate was offered in part payment of death duties to the National Trust. Staffordshire County Council agreed to accept the lease of Shugborough and continue to finance and administer the estate. Open to the public since 1966, Shugborough is the UK's only complete working historic estate and a world-class visitor attraction.

Thomas, the current 6th Earl of Lichfield was kind enough to write a foreword for this book. With his family he occupied private apartments in the hall up until 2010. These are now open to the public for the first time. In 2009 he married Lady Henrietta Conyngham, now the Countess of Lichfield. They have two boys; Thomas (known by his second name Ossian) and the latest arrival Finnian. The names reflect the Irish and Gaelic heritage and connections through marriage.

Patrick Lichfield, the 5th Earl, father of Thomas and famous photographer of royalty and high society died in 2005. He is survived by his widow Leonora Countess of Lichfield.

So how did this once small country manor become a grander setting for such a magnificent residence and estate? A brief look at the history of the Anson family helps to explain.

SHUGBOROUGH HALL

The Anson Family, A Brief History

In 1624, the land formed part of the estates of the Bishop of Lichfield. William Anson, a local lawyer, purchased, for the princely sum of £1,000, 80 acres of land together with a manor house. Seventy years later, his grandson, also named William, demolished the manor house and built a three-storey house; this forms the centre of the house we see today. The transformation into the magnificent mansion was carried out between 1745 and 1748 by the architect Thomas Wright. Later works in the 1760s were carried out by James 'Athenian' Stuart.

Once the new house was built in 1695, the Ansons began to expand their holdings of the surrounding countryside, gradually buying up land and demolishing cottages, then rebuilding them for the workers but clear of what was to become parkland. Thomas, the elder brother of George, had inherited the estate and was responsible for its expansion and mostly responsible for the land and property acquisition. Most of this activity was taking place in the 1730s and 1740s, and by the time of his death in 1773, the Anson family controlled virtually the whole of what was Shugborough village plus about 1,000 acres of Cannock Chase.

The estate is also renowned for its neo-classical monuments mostly designed by James 'Athenian' Stuart. To understand these more ostentatious developments at Shugborough, we have to look overseas. Thomas travelled abroad regularly, on his grand tour, passing through Alexandria, Cairo and Aleppo. He was greatly inspired by ancient Rome and Greece. These influences can be seen throughout the estate in the monuments about which the guide book says:

'Finding structures more suitable for the classical world in a park in rural Staffordshire is a delight for any visitor.'

A brief description follows therefore of some of the magnificent monuments to be seen around the estate, some of which may be more correctly termed a 'folly', given their inspiration. However, no matter how weird the whole effect appears nowadays, it must be understood that this was all completed during the rise of Freemasonry in the 18th century. It was quite common for these large landscaped gardens to embody Masonic principles as part of the overall design. Known as 'Gardens of Allusion', they were carefully laid out to evoke the idea of Elysium, the mythical land where innocent shepherds skipped without a care in the world. Indeed, it is said that Anson's wife liked to dress up as a shepherdess.

However, you will also see that one of the monuments in particular that embodies shepherds is of more than a casual interest to us.

The Monuments

There are eight monuments of national historic importance. We start with what is probably the grandest, but for us, not the most important.

The Triumphal Arch

Modelled on the Arch of Hadrian in Athens, it is set on the highest point of the parkland and dominates its surroundings. It also serves as a memorial to George and Elizabeth Anson whose busts are featured on either side of the central aplustra (martial trophy) which represents the bow of a ship and some spoils of war.

The Tower of the Winds

A replica of the Horlogium (water clock) of Andronikos Cyrrhestes in Athens. Originally standing on the edge of a lake (now drained), it faced the Palladian Bridge and the Chinese Pagoda. It was once used as a dairy and a gambling den (upstairs).

The Doric Temple

Based on the Temple of Hephaistos, this hexastyle portico (six columns) was conceived as the entrance to the kitchen garden. It is now isolated due to the demolition of the old walled garden in 1805.

The Chinese House

Probably the first of Thomas Anson's garden buildings, the design was based on pencil sketches of Sir Percy Brett, Admiral Anson's second-in-command on the *Centurion.* The house was built on an island in an artificial canal, with a boathouse attached and reached by a pair of bridges of Chinese design.

The Cat's Monument
Situated on an island accessed by the bridge besides the Chinese House, it probably commemorates a Persian cat kept by Thomas Anson. But some believe the monument was a dedication to a cat that travelled the world with Admiral Anson on the *Centurion.* Thomas Anson also kept a herd of Corsican goats, which figure around the base of the monument.

The Ruin
Situated behind the house, the Ruin was composed of parts of the old house and fragments of the former palace of the Bishops of Lichfield. Originally, the Ruin was more extensive and included a Gothic pigeon house. Seated on a rubble crag are the remains of a Druid, made from Coade stone, the whole monument is now sympathetically restored to how it looked in the 18th century.

The Lanthorn of Demosthenes
Situated on a knoll overlooking the River Sow, this is a copy of the Choragic Monument of Lysicrates in Athens, erected in the fourth century BC to support a tripodic trophy. It has been known by its present name since the 18th century.

Finally, we come to what is for us the most important and enigmatic monument at Shugborough; The Shepherd's Monument.

The Enigmatic Shepherd's Monument
I quote in part from the estate guide which unfortunately gives a rather misguided view of the monument and its subject theme:

'The most puzzling of all is the Shepherd's Monument. Originally conceived in wood, the unusual swirling carving on the curved arch reflects this intention. It was designed to be 'well backed with wood, of the hardy forest growth, and the more retired the better, as in a Saloon or Lawnet, being chiefly designed for the Enjoyment of Objects near the Eye'. This monument takes its name from the marble relief depicting two lovers listening to an ancient shepherd. The marble relief is based on a painting by Nicholas Poussin and was carved by the Dutch artist, Scheemakers. It includes a cryptic inscription which has defied interpretation.'

THE SHEPHERD'S MONUMENT IN THE GROUNDS OF SHUGBOROUGH HALL

The history of the monument is somewhat clouded with no records existing as to specific dates of construction. Due to its unusual subject nature and overall design, it has been the focus of many learned writings as academics have sought to interpret its true meaning. The mystery has been exacerbated by the inscription it bears made up of two lines of capital letters in the classic Roman style which could not be deciphered:

For clarity:

O·U·O·S·V·A·V·V

D·   M·

I had to take issue with the Shugborough Estate during my research, as their website section *Grail Seekers and Codebreakers* contained a glaring error regarding this cipher. They had published what looked like a photograph of it, similar to mine above but, the 'dots' were in line with the bottom level of the characters and the 'D' and 'M' shown almost underneath their respective top-line end characters. Something they had created then, only vaguely similar to the real thing. This could have had serious consequences for codebreakers, if the layout as designed is important. Regarding the layout, it is interesting in that it looks as if space was left for another line of characters. More on that later.

The general position is that Thomas Wright and James 'Athenian' Stuart built the monument c.1748-50 but this has been due to those researchers who assumed the elements that now make up the collective structure were all created at the same time. This is not so. It should be noted that when we refer to the monument, we are only talking about the central marble sculpture that resembles an upright tombstone. The surrounding arbour is of no importance to us.

In a position of knowing what the monument actually is and who was involved in both the foreground and background during its creation, we are now able to set out its history with some degree of confidence i.e. what we are saying is pretty close to the mark. Please keep in mind that George Anson had been inducted into the Royal Society in 1745.

THE AUTHOR POINTING TO THE CIPHER.
THIS PICTURE DEMONSTRATES THE SIZE OF THE SCULPTURE.

Thomas Wright, James Stuart and the Royal Society

The monument was designed by Thomas Wright and executed by the Dutch sculptor Peter Scheemakers. The whole thing was probably sculpted, erected and completed during the years 1748-1758. You can see by its design it was not intended to be a free-standing piece of art; it would be far too fragile if placed that way. It is obvious that it was intended to be affixed to a backing of some sort. It appears it was originally designed to be an over-mantel; that is, it was to sit on a mantelpiece and grace the wall above a large fireplace of the type you would find in these country estates. For some reason, it ended up being affixed to the outside of the old kitchen garden's wall.

Thomas Wright of Durham (1711-1786) was an astronomer who maintained himself by designing the gardens of the gentry or providing tutoring to their family. His astronomical work was of such a scale it saw him, aged 22, being introduced to the Royal Society in 1733. Some type of communications between Wright and the Royal Society were extant during these early years as they ordered a 'Pannauticon' from him which was some astronomic device made of copper disks that predicted moon/tidal movements and other lunar phenomena.

In 1735, he was nominated for fellowship but the reply came back: "Mr Thomas Wright, being put to the ballot for election and not having two thirds of the votes, The Society expressed their desire of being further acquainted with that Gentleman." Wright is not recorded as a Fellow but there are a few communications in the Royal Society's archives between them of an astronomic nature, one of them titled for example, 'Variation of the polar star determined in observing the hour of the night; or, the nocturnal rectified, assigned as a great help to put in practice the theory of the longitude.' Though brilliant in designing astronomic instruments and tables for their use, his cosmology was that of a philosophy which combined the scientific, the divine and the moral into the universe. In other words, alchemic. Stars, longitude and alchemy, just the person needed to design the monument.

In 1755, Thomas Wright's book *Universal Architecture* contained an image of his design for an 'Arbour of the Cave or Cabin Kind'. No doubt you can see the surrounding arbour of the Shepherd's Monument was made following this idea. This design may have dated from 1750 when it was originally proposed for the Duke of Beaufort's estate but never executed. The addition to the arbour of a Doric aedicule with two columns is ascribed to James 'Athenian' Stuart.

PLATE A
UNIVERSAL ARCHITECTURE, BOOK 1. SIX ORIGINAL DESIGNS
OR ARBOURS, 1755

James 'Athenian' Stuart got his name due to his studies into the ancient world. His studies were compiled into his 1762 book *The Antiquities of Athens and Other Monuments of Greece*. An artist, archeologist and architect, he was inducted as a fellow of the Royal Society in 1758, and in the 1760s was working on building the structures at Shugborough Hall when George Anson died in 1762.

As the monument (the sculpture) was originally backed onto the kitchen garden's wall and the arbour/enclosure was not completed until at least a decade later when James 'Athenian' Stuart was at Shugborough, something must have occurred for a decision to be made to build the arbour and move the monument into it. Due to the persons involved, the dates pertaining to and the importance of the monument, we are able to deduce that upon Anson's death a decision was made to ensure the longevity of it by providing it with a protective enclosure. This was executed by James 'Athenian' Stuart building a free-standing structure which followed Wright's design for an arbour supported by his (Stuart's) Doric aedicule. Stuart and Wright may have both collaborated on this protective enclosure into which the monument was moved and has remained within to this day.

Sculpture, Theme and intent

You will recognise the subject theme of the monument is a version of Poussin's *The Shepherds of Arcadia II* whose image and history you were introduced to in the chapter about Rennes-le-Château. You need to compare the two so the differences can be isolated and identified.

The most obvious difference is that the image is the reverse of Poussin's painting. In itself, not much can be readily made of this as it was common in these times for sculptured reproductions to be in reverse of the original. This was because the sculpture had to use for his template a facsimile of the master painting (the master being located elsewhere in a collection) and the period method for producing a facsimile was to make an engraving. Engravings, due to the manufacture and printing process, produced the final image in reverse so the sculpture was also in reverse. Apart from the reversed shepherds being in the same relative positions, it cannot be said the image's proportions are those of the original. The height is increased, making it taller and thinner. The extra space created by the heightening of the overall image has been filled in with the addition of a pyramid lidded ossuary added to the top of the tomb. The proportions including the cipher tablet are now of the Golden Ratio, but more of that in a later chapter.

The famous inscription on the tomb, 'ET IN ARCADIA EGO', reads as 'I too lived in Arcadia', and is now understood to mean 'Even in Arcadia, I, Death exists' (remember Poussin's original title for this painting). Arcadia is a district in Greece 'an ancient realm of perfect joy'. You will recall there is a transcription into Greek of this inscription on the Rennes engraved slab image.

There is a variation in the spacing of the phrase's lettering with the original being;

ET IN ARCADIA
EGO

and the monument,

ET IN ARCADIA
EGO

In the painting, the Red (cloaked) Shepherd is pointing generally at the phrase/tomb as he looks back at the 'Yellow' Shepherdess. The Kneeling Shepherd is pointing to the R in ARCADIA and his thumb is near N in IN. On the monument, the pointing fingers have been broken off but their remnants make it possible to determine where they were. The 'Red' Shepherd continues to generally point at the phrase/tomb. The Kneeling Shepherd is now pointing to N in IN. Look at the unnatural position of his thumb, the tip of which is placed on the R in ARCADIA.

All in all, even allowing for the reversal, the monument's image can only be said to amount to an artistic interpretation of Poussin's theme rather than an accurate reproduction. If the monument was some cheap knock-off churned out in an Italian statuary workshop for touring punters to fill their gardens with back home, this might be understandable, but it was designed for and by the likes of Royal Society members. In other words, it was intended to be that way. Another obvious observation is that the sculptor and/or designer placed a sarcophagus on top of the tomb. This ossuary or bone container has an Egyptian pyramid for its lid. A laurel wreath is sculptured on the front.

What is the reason for this addition/composition? Maybe it makes this now vertical composition more pleasing to the eye?

I have a theory about it, which will be shown in a later chapter where we show the cipher solution.

The Cipher and Some Contemporary Theories of Meaning

Such is the mystery of the cipher under the sculpture that even experts from the Second World War codebreaking establishment at Bletchley Park were asked in, but even they were not able to come up with a satisfactory solution.

It has been suggested that the initials D and M are for the Latin 'Dis Manibus'. These initials were commonly found on Roman tombs and was a dedication to the Gods (Dis) of the departed souls (Manes). By association, the word "Dis" came to be used as a metaphor for the underworld. This seemed to suggest for the inscription that any meaning likewise should be sought using Latin as the language. Indeed, one of the teams offering a solution in a competition organised by the Shugborough Estate in 2004, said the eight letters represent a Latin poem to a departed loved one which goes:

'Optima Uxoris Optima Sororis Viduus Amantissimus Vovit Virtibus'

This translates as:
'Best Wife, Best Sister, Widower Most Loving Vows Virtuously'

Even MN favoured this solution due to the letters D and M being suggestively spaced to imply Dis Manibus before the real meaning of the inscription was cracked.

A ROMAN TOMBSTONE

Staying with Latin solutions, Stuart Nettleton in his *The Alchemy Key* supplies a solution based on computer searches of classic Latin sources and obscure associated religious writings. Linking all this with biblical prophecy (Genesis 50) and a St Andrew's cross, he comes up with;

'Deus visitabit vos asportate vobiscum sancta ossa upilio occulto maneo'

Which means:

'God will surely come to your aid, and then you must carry away the shepherd's holy bones to remain concealed.'

Nettleton's interpretation of this is that the inscription implies that Lord Anson knew the Knights Templar found Joseph's mummy under the temple in Jerusalem. They removed it to a shrine in Mount Cardou. This is what Poussin's painting is depicting.

The competition held by the Shugborough Estate in 2004 to try to get a solution to the cipher attracted more than 130 respondents from around the world. It is whispered that even GCHQ, the Government signals intelligence centre in Cheltenham, has contributed but as we have seen, no satisfactory solution has been seen from any contributor or group. One such professional codebreaker argues that the inscription points to the hiding place of a stone tablet handed down from the Old Testament prophet Jacob, which was a talisman for a secret society known as the Priory of Sion. He says Anson was a member of the priory, and he captured the tablet from a French ship then buried it on an island off the coast of Nova Scotia. (Shadoc of Oak Island here.) Two Bletchley Park codebreakers claim the code is a message from an 18th century Christian Sect. Furthering their work, another codebreaker believes the Holy Grail was captured in France and brought back to Shugborough in 1746 by Lord Anson. He says the code is a secret message that the Holy Grail is buried nearby. Charles Darwin is also said to have had a go at decoding the inscription, as has Charles Dickens and Josiah Wedgwood.

So, a lot of solutions to the inscription based on classic Latin and it is interesting also that a lot of the theories as to the monument's meaning is that it gives the location of something hidden that has religious and Knights Templar connections. The presumption that Latin was the language to be used when dealing with the monument is correct but using this presumption to conclude the inscription must be a phrase in Latin is not.

You may be asking, "If all these illustrious and learned people much cleverer than you couldn't solve it, how could you?" Well, it is back to what I call 'reverse engineering' mixed in with standard codebreaking practice, common sense and research. I knew that the monument was something to do with the location of the lost treasure and there are two distinct parts to it: an image that has been specially modified from the original and an accompanying encoded inscription.

You have already learnt how the Spanish codewords worked to help identify the location. So could the inscription be something similar in Latin? Looking at the letters on the monument, D OUOSVAVV M, you can see that with the letters O repeated twice and V repeated thrice, it is not likely that these were the first letters of words in any language that could produce directions of sufficient precision to find an island somewhere in the Pacific Ocean. As any sailor will tell you, from First Admiral Anson down, to find an island you need latitude and longitude. Even the Spanish codewords were to be accompanied by the star code to give the 'cero tres puntas', the coded longitude of the three points. It could work the other way around though, if the inscription was giving latitude and/or longitude and the monument was in some way giving directions.

The repetition of the letters in the inscription did seem to suggest it might be some form of alphanumeric code; the letters were simply replacing a numeral. But with 10 letters/numerals and some odd spacing, this meant that there was also an encoding formula needed to covert them into latitude/longitude. As over 250 years had passed since the inscription was first chiselled, then the key was probably long lost!

The knowledge that Latin could be used for the monument does help if you can recall a certain alchemic phrase (that produces an acronym) which is associated with latter lost treasure maps. Wilkins commented on it appearing on a map he was sent in 'atrocious dog Latin'. The phrase is not the key to the inscription but it does tell you how to rectify the components. One of the words in the phrase begins with the letter R and it was the instruction about and for the monument.

Visita Interiora Terrae Rectificando Invennies Occultum Lapidem

or:

V.I.T.R.I.O.L.[1]

This translates as:
Visit the Interior of the Earth; by Rectification Thou Shalt Find the Hidden Stone.

How did you know what to do with the Trinity Map and the monument if you just had one of the later copies of the Trinity Map? D and M was possibly spaced that way on the monument's inscription to be recognised as the dedication Dis Manibus. Being told to visit the interior of the earth, you would go to the underworld where the Manes (Spirits of the dead) are; in other words, go to where you find D & M.

'by Rectification Thou Shalt Find the Hidden Stone':

It is telling you to rectify the components, add the map to the monument to find the lost treasure. Maybe overlay the map using R as your point of rectification.

The previous couple of chapters took us on a necessary diversionary tour to England and France. In the chapter about Rennes-le-Château, it contained many hidden clues to the treasure revealed in this book for the first time.

That there is a link to Lord Anson is obvious through JF Island, the Kidd/Wilkins saga and the Webb letters. Webb aside, the most important link to Lord Anson though as has been hinted at many times, is the Shepherdess monument. That the sculpture of Poussin's painting and the monument itself is of great importance is obvious from the clues given in the Rennes mystery. I am amazed that other researchers have not made the positive connection between Rennes and Shugborough. That aside, regarding the monument, of far greater importance as you will see is the cipher under the painting sculpture.

VITRIOL is telling us; 'Go to where you find D and M.' Those letters are part of the cipher!

We will come to this cipher and its solution later in the *The Gathering of the Clues...* chapter but before that, we must look at more pieces of the jigsaw; the Trinity Map and its geometric connections with the sculpture.

[1]Surprisingly, sailors of Anson's era were actually rather familiar with this word as they could expect to be given a dose of 'Elixor of Vitriol', a herbal concoction based on Sulphuric acid (Oil of Vitriol) which was thought to combat scurvy.

PART 7

CHAPTER 1

TRINITY MAP, ANGLES, RATIOS AND TRIANGLES

Map: a representation in outline of the surface features of the earth's surface, drawn to scale showing natural and artificial features. (For the fastidious, a chart is a marine or hydrographical map).

So what was the Trinity Map representing? What was its scale? How did you even read it? Wilkins, Latcham and the other confederates had put together some grand riddle, the Kidd/Palmer charts hoax, which when solved seemed to show how the Trinity Map was to be read and applied, maybe as follows:

   a. The centre of the map was a datum position on a coastline
   b. Bearings sets shot from this datum position went to landmark
   c. These bearings were 36, 50, 72, 115 and 210
   d. There was a triangle marked on the map which was inferred to be three hills which was the treasure location.

All 'smoke and mirrors' to mislead. This had all been some type of security feature devised by them; if perchance you accidentally stumbled across the Kidd chart clues, the Juan Fernandez '25 cent' map and made the Latcham/Guayacan connection, Wilkins and Latcham then carefully led you through all this so you thought you were making some great discovery about the Trinity Map and how you should interpret it to locate a point on a coastline somewhere. That was if you accidentally came across the parts of this. If you were in the know, you found Wilkins had left a carefully placed pointer, the latitude and longitude on the Kidd Key chart, which was a coded reference, which used a very special formula that gave a location near the Pinaki Trinity. Even though the riddle was designed to deflect the unwary into wrongly applying the Kidd chart, it was also designed to make them cognisant of certain aspects of it all through the intense study of it required when trying to figure out what was going on. This was the numbers produced by the bearings set as these were clues to the next stage.

Up until now, MN had been aware that the Golden Section (or Golden Mean) was mixed up with the treasure as numeric expositions of it were to be found in linked stories. Unfortunately, what exactly the Golden Section was and how to use it remained a bit vague to him. He discovered that it could be expressed in the form $b^2 = a(a+b)$, or a ratio 1:61803, or it had something to do with the angles 36 and 72 so you could draw a pentagram and that renaissance artists used it to layout their paintings. This had all been learnt relatively lately as it was in various texts about Rennes-le-Château; also, the Golden Section had been raised as Poussin's painting and various angles of it were sought in the region's surrounding geography. What he did not equate, the Golden Section too was a triangle and this was the answer needed to reconcile what appeared to be an impossible contradiction; the Trinity was a triangular group of three islands represented by three dots, yet the Trinity Map had a triangle with four points marked, a dot/blob for each apex with another on a line adjacent to the lower RH dot!

It was decided to learn how searchers may have been using the Trinity Map triangle to plot a position on an island. Though no mention is nowadays made of a triangle being a locational clue for Oak Island, the fact that someone once pointed to ground there and said, "Here is where the treasure is," meant they had a plotting of sorts. Strangely enough, it was Gilbert Heddon who solved the mystery. Gilbert Heddon was, as you know, the searcher who in 1937 noticed a similarity in Wilkins' maps (W1 and W2) in his book *Captain Kidd and his Skeleton Island*, with a map of Oak Island. Searching 50 feet north of the Money Pit, he located a large granite stone (westerly stone) which had been drilled. Another drilled stone was located to the east (easterly stone). A further search, which employed a surveyor and used the bearings on Wilkins' map for a guide, saw the rediscovery of the Stone Triangle (mentioned in the chapter about Oak Island).

Even though these triangles were distorted, it did show that they could indeed have been based on the Trinity Map triangle. The Money Pit/shaft plotted along one of the sides between the apexes were what made up the fourth point.

MN decided it was necessary to re-draw the Trinity Map triangle to determine the exact angular make-up of it and what was the relationship between it and the bearing set numbers Wilkins had implanted in his memory. He did so and produced this, though he was still unaware of what it was:

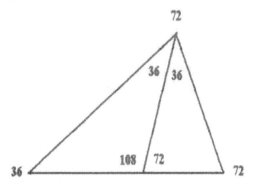

Another minor problem was that his knowledge and experience was that of terrestrial navigation acquired during his service with the Australian Army. This type of navigation which required matching the geography to a map or vice versa to locate your position or determine a route was based on visual, comparative and interpretive methodology. So though he was able to interpret just about any land based map or diagram, any chart by Ubilla would naturally be for marine navigation, and navigation methodology is a bit different when working at sea. Using his methodology, he could not discover how the Pinaki Trinity could match what was being depicted on the Trinity Map. I, however, being a boating person, am familiar with marine navigation and the use of transits, so worked on this problem to see what I could discover. I plotted the islands around Pinaki and the resultant transit lines displayed an interesting relationship. The spiral is there to show you it can be created out of a Golden Ratio Triangle, so it was put in here to see if it had any meaning. Clearly it did not in this plotting, but some interesting possibilities come out later.

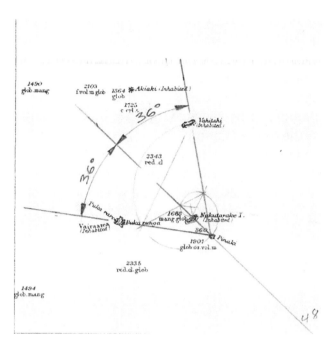

**EARLY PLOTTING OF THE ISLANDS THAT ESTABLISHED
THE 72 DEGREE ANGULAR RELATIONSHIP**

We have talked about the Golden Section/Ratio/Triangle, so it may help to explain to the reader and those with a mathematical interest what it is. It is also important in understanding the trigonometry of the Trinity Map.

The Golden Ratio

It has a big influence in mathematics and the construction of geometric figures. It is also said that a lot of the Renaissance painters utilised 'sacred geometry's' Golden Mean Ratio in their work, appearing as a rectangle with sides or a ratio equal to 1 and 0.618. These are the proportions of a rectangle considered most pleasing to the eye. The ratio is formed out of:

$$\frac{b}{d} = \frac{a}{a+b}$$

This is also expressed as a mathematical constant = 1.618(03), also known as φ (phi).

Where a=1 and b=0.618, it is the only ratio where a+b = a ÷ b.

Expressed another way, Ratio: .618:1:1.618

In a rectangle, any length × 0.618 gives the short side length to create a Golden Proportion Rectangle. (The length of the long side to the short side is the Golden Ratio.)

If mathematics isn't your thing, you may understand the following: if you divide a line into two parts such that the longer part divided by the smaller part is also equal to the whole length divided by the longer part.

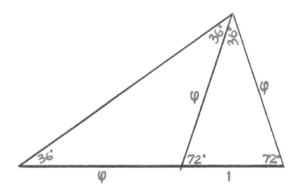

THE GOLDEN RATIO TRIANGLE DEFINED

You can see the Golden Triangle is constructed out of a base of 1 and sides 1.618. Angular construction is always of 36 and 72 degrees. (You should be recalling at this point the Kidd 'Skull' chart where Wilkins is hinting at this triangular construction with '36NE 36NE'.)

Robert Charroux, in his *Treasures of the World* lists some Templar Key Signs. I show them as follows:

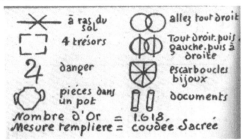

Quite plain to see is our 'golden number' (Nombre d' Or) = 1.618. This is further proof of the relevance and importance of these numbers in our quest.

Sculpture Geometry

I had several goes at plotting relevant geometry on the monument, using all that was known about Masonic symbols, Golden Section triangles and whatever I could think of with regards to the marine bearing transits. This is one of several attempts at trying to find something geometric within the sculpture that satisfied what I was looking for.

This is just one example to show you how I played with it. The geometric profile of the islands created the Freemason's compass symbol. It did seem to fit but I was not convinced the monument showed a map this way. My reasoning firstly was that finding these geometric patterns and angular relationships on the monument/image is nothing unusual. Renaissance artists were well aware of the Golden Section and used it to layout paintings, as such these shapes could be found occurring in other paintings and appear to fit there. Also, the fact that the kneeling shepherds crook just happens to accurately create one side of a pentagon. Secondly, how could you tell the map had to be plotted using that particular orientation? A number of orientations could be made for a map and also appear to fit. You would have to know already the shepherd's knee equates to Pinaki or his left ear equated to Vahitahi as there is nothing definitive to indicate orientation. If you knew their positions well enough to enable you to plot them on the monument, you could draw your own map anyway. Basically it was rubbish because I was using prior knowledge and making things fit rather than discovering how they fitted. There is nothing within that sculpture that could show the island's layout. It was decided to plot the Trinity Map in scale on the photo of the monument as an experiment. Before doing so, mindful of the alchemic code and that the monument was in reverse of Poussin's original, the image of the monument and the Trinity Map were reversed. Then for the plot, the kneeling shepherd's thumb on the R was used as the centre point for the Trinity Map. As the bearing sets and the four-point triangle were plotted on the image, their positioning brought forth a familiar shape, the outline of which had previously been hidden in the robes of the shepherdess. The outline of the shape was delineated; we were amazed by what was discovered.

On the following page is a picture of this work. Though it is not perfectly exact, you will nevertheless recognise its import.

Here was what looked like an old map of Juan Fernandez Island with the plotting of the location for the treasure on it. Or was it Oak Island and the triangle marked the treasure there? Maybe it was Isle Haute, as the triangle marked the position of the boulder and site near the lake also? Then again, couldn't it also be the coastline of Catham and Wafer Bays on Cocos Island? Actually, if you reverse a map of Cocos Island, the backward shape of the island now matched Trinidade Island! This could be why the three cairns were plotting a triangle for there.

This discovery provided a possible answer as to why various locations for pits/shafts were excavated on Oak Island. Even with the surveying and fixing of positions to plot the Trinity Map triangle there, which of the four dots then marked the treasure? That was even if you had a fairly accurate copy of this overlaid monument map to start with. The triangles that Heddon's survey on Oak Island revealed bore only a visual resemblance to the Trinity Map triangle. By the time he came along, over a century of the distortive effects of time had been operating on the maps and copies of maps used by the searchers. How far this outline and its plotting was distorted can be shown by a leather map used by James Forbes IV for his fruitless search upon Cocos Island in the 1940s. It had been passed down from James Forbes I through the generations and was believed to reveal the location of the Loot of Lima. Its authenticity was undoubted by the family, for the map and accompanying documents giving the accompanying story had been notarised in the 19th century, which though going someway to prove their age and lineage, as you now know doesn't authenticate the story in the documents at all. This leather map was indeed just a descendant of the lost treasure map, the bearings N20W and N63E having come straight from the monument map. This was MN's conclusion and maybe right, but I have my doubts as the 63/20 angular relationship is only similar to corresponding lines on the Trinity Map. There are none that match exactly. As an aside, the problem I have with this Forbes map is that the line N 63ºE actually measures more like 73º from north!

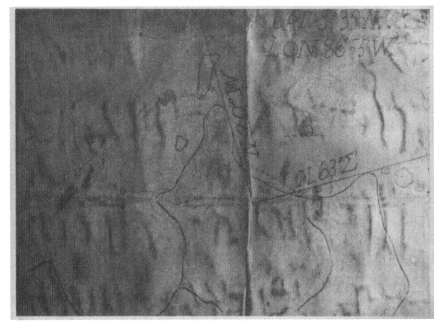

JAMES FORBES IV REMNANT TREASURE MAP THOUGHT TO BE FOR COCOS ISLAND

If any searchers had the insight and prior knowledge to use the monument this way, maybe they took the shape from the shepherdess' robe to be depicting an entire island upon which the Trinity Map triangle was plotted to locate the position of the treasure. For example, Oak Island. For Juan Fernandez Island, you can see one apex dot is suggestive that Bahia Cumberland is the location to search, while another apex dot suggests it is Bahia English.

Superimposing the Trinity Map onto the Shepherd's Monument was possibly the correct application, even if it did produce wrong interpretations of it. Partly, the use of this map to match different locations that varied widely in size can be explained from the fact that without an indication of scale, you didn't know if you were looking at a one or 10 kilometre stretch of coastline.

If the map was really showing the Trinity, where did the idea come from that the Trinity Map triangle plotted the location on land or that this shape of the shepherdess' robe was a land map? Whilst any of the above is a possibility, I have my doubts. I don't see how anybody (outside Anson's closed circle) in the 18th or 19th centuries could have associated this monument with a remote island in the South Pacific. There is no written evidence anywhere of an overlay map being used as described on the monument.

Applying the Figures

Interesting as this discovery about the monument had been, the question of Trinity and how the island could relate to a Golden Section triangle had to be resolved. Reversing the entire monument map image, it was decided to number the Trinity Map lines, which radiated from the centre, in degrees from north, in particular to learn the value of the line which shot through the Trinity Map triangle. Using the central upright line on the map as north, this other line, when accurately measured, came out as 243º30 degrees from north. But you will notice on the map, this upright line and the line to its left, are not perpendicular to the central horizontal line. A true grid north meant a correction of 1 degree anticlockwise and that meant the bearing from the centre to the triangle was 244º30 degrees. The Right Ascension (RA) value for Antares expressed in degrees is 246.

The island Trinity is at 139, which is given by the Anson documents, but 138 was the bearing given by Webb in his report (and Wilkins in the key chart/JF map riddle, as you will see later). You know it relates to the Trinity but 138º is a point in the ocean out to the east of the islands; there is nothing there! And that, according to MN, was the answer. The Trinity is a group of islands whose centre is at approximately 139º, 138º is a datum point for a map. A fantastic, secret map for a great treasure made up of the combination of the Trinity Map, the Shepherd's Monument, knowledge of the Alchemy, the Zodiac and the prime star of the constellation Scorpius.

From the datum point at lat. 19S, long. 138W, you sailed on a bearing of 246º (this is how MN measured it and it fits in with his Antares theory) to the Trinity (Pinaki). Maybe the above was MN's reasoning; it fits in with his theories but the 246º (or 244º30) bearing from a point in the ocean gets more practical discussion later. You can see that from the datum point at lat 19S, long 138 west, you sailed on a compass bearing to the Trinity and this produced a sailing track close to Pinaki. Wilkins also gave a possible clue to this by the notation '?15SE' on the Kidd/Palmer 'Skull' Chart which refers to the Trinity Map bearing of 116º30 (115º as measured by MN; he was adamant on this but I have always thought the mark before 15 is either another 5 or S).

So what did the Golden Section triangle have to do with it? You will see later that the Trinity group of three islands are part of a larger Golden Section Triangle, which was plotted when Ubilla surveyed and charted the region.

What follows is how I played around with it using my own logical thinking and background as an former draughtsman. It was a case of just trying to sort out Latcham's nonsense from fact. The only thing we *may* be missing in Latcham's charade of confusedness is the treasure location on the island, that is if he knew it.

Trinity Map, The Hidden Geometry Revealed

GR. LAYOUT 1.

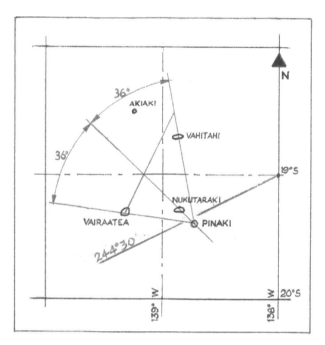

A GOLDEN RATIO TRIANGLE APPLIED TO ATOLL GROUP (TO SCALE)
INCORPORATING ATOLLS ON 36º TRANSITS MAKING UP THE TRINITY

You can see immediately that the islands in the Pinaki group are separated by 36º and *could* form a Golden Ratio Triangle as drawn. Connecting Vairaatea to Vahitahi would not create a perfect GR triangle but maybe 300 years ago the surveyors thought it did. However, this is the only geometric layout that provides (or confirms) an exact 36º angular divergence between the atolls.

From the above diagram, you can now see the possible explanation for two decoded longitudes. 139ºW is the approximate centre of the island group, whilst 138ºW is from where a possible transit bearing of 244º30 is taken that takes you between the islands. It could, of course, be that the early navigator(s) meant this bearing to indicate the island of Pinaki. Looking at the above, I will say any nautical people will tell you this is not practical or maybe not even possible because of the distance from the 138º position to the centre of the group at the 139º position i.e. 1º. This represents 57nm or 65 miles (not 60nm which is what 1º represents on the vertical latitude scale and is why all measurements are taken from this scale i.e.1nm=1minute, tho longitude scale/distance is smaller because the vertical meridian lines converge at the north and south poles, i.e. get closer. In an earlier chapter, we mentioned the problem of sight at sea due to the curvature of the earth. In a sentence, unless you were high up, you wouldn't see Pinaki from out here, it would be 44nm away! (51miles.) More about this in a later chapter.

We now take a closer look at the Trinity Map.

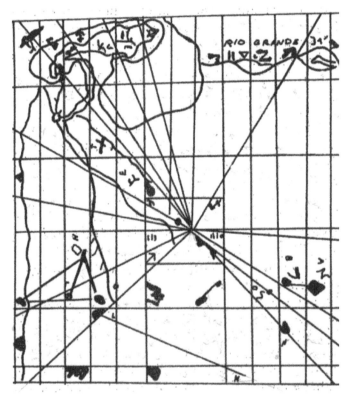

TRINITY MAP

Unless one is familiar with trigonometry, you would not recognise the triangle construction on the left hand side of the map as being of a particular form, but the fact it is there should have immediately alerted you to say, "Why is it there and what is it?" When you know what you are looking for, it is, of course, a major clue i.e. a golden ratio triangle (you can now recognise it for what it is) constructed out of black blobs that probably represent a group of islands (four), on lines radiating from an apex point possibly representing Pinaki. We can see how from the previous GR. Layout 1.

A radial line 116º30 (244º30 reciprocal when corrected by 1º) is shown passing between two islands but in fact was maybe originally meant to take you to Pinaki.

But is this radial line as important as previously theorised, or is it just another line that happens to pass through the GR triangle? And is the position of the GR triangle important relative to the rest of the map as previously suggested? It is shown with the baseline perfectly horizontal but the middle (atoll?) blob is shown intentionally offset to the baseline. Let us look at the practical possibilities of this when the atolls are shown accurately plotted.

GR. LAYOUT 2.

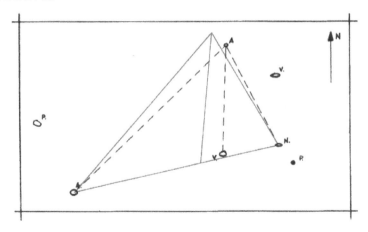

This is the closest we are going to get to the layout of the Trinity Map GR triangle, and it's the Golden Section Triangle referred to earlier, **if** that layout **is** plotting the atolls in the Pinaki group. The baseline connecting Ahunui out to the west to Nukutavake at the east does show Vairaatea just above it, but when plotted accurately (red solid line) the apex does not intersect at Akiaki at the top. The Trinity Map layout shown could be, of course, how the Spanish surveyed this group but then you ask the question, "How could they? Ahunui is that far out to the west they wouldn't be able to see it from the Pinaki group!" It could only be that from individual surveying of the atolls utilising the basic measuring equipment they had, when plotted on a chart they discovered that the four atolls near enough formed a GR. triangle as shown by the blue dash-line.

GR. LAYOUT 3.

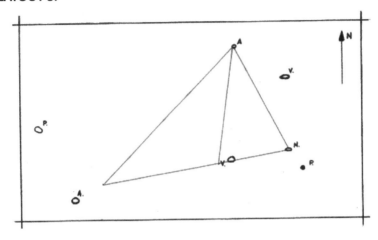

GR. LAYOUT 4.

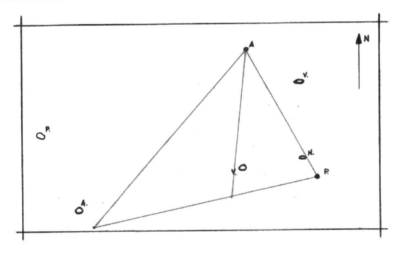

Layouts 3 and 4 are just variations on a theme **not** using the baseline as a starting point. None of them are horizontal and only the layout (1) at the beginning of the chapter shows 36º between atolls centred on Pinaki.

GR. LAYOUT 5.

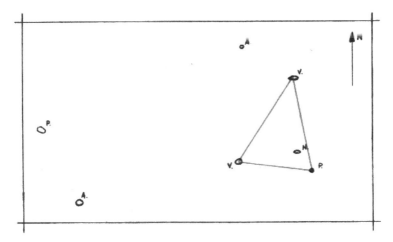

The only 'proper' triangle layout in the group is that shown above. Whilst not a perfect Isosceles triangle, we know from Layout 1 that the angle VPV is 72º. This can obviously be described as a triangle and is no doubt our 'Trinity' triangle as Ubilla surveyed it. It makes sense as P (Pinaki) is the focal point in more ways than one, and as we know, there are 2x36º bearings going to the other atolls that make it up.

GR. LAYOUT 6.

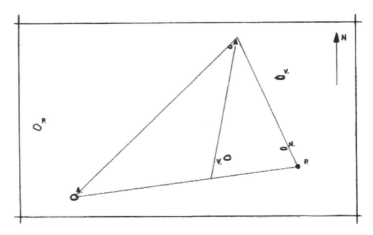

The final GR. LAYOUT 6 above completes the practical application of the GR Triangle to the Pinaki Group of Atolls. You can now draw (excuse the pun) your own conclusions from them but Layout 2 best fits the Trinity Map.

Nautical Spirals

I was puzzled for a long time by the line on the Trinity Map at approximately 21º to the bottom horizontal bisecting a line from the lower left-hand corner with a blob and 'L' in the middle of it and 'X'(or N?) at its right-hand end. It stands out as 'odd', in relation to the other lines, because it is the only line not radiating from the centre, so again begging the question, "Why is it there?" At the back of my mind, there was *something* familiar about it but I couldn't fathom out what; that is, until doing a refresher course on the Golden Ratio, when a diagram of the construction of the Nautilus Spiral jumped out at me. To confirm what I suspected, I first had to see if there was Golden Ratio Rectangle at that place in the Trinity Map.

The following diagram shows that there is, represented by the shaded area:

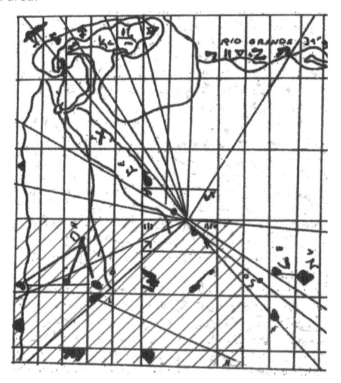

**SHOWING HOW THE GOLDEN RATIO RECTANGLE IS A
INTEGRAL PART OF THE TRINITY MAP**

The sides of the shaded rectangle are as the Golden Ratio i.e. 1:1.618. The angular line in question can be part of a *triangular* construction of a nautical spiral (you will see later on in this book that its purpose is probably something else entirely). But there is more than one way to construct a spiral. The more accurate and pleasing way, and the one that fits in with my theory, is to utilise the G.R. (shaded) rectangle and construct within it a spiral, as shown below.

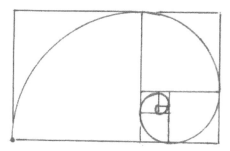

A square is added to the long side of a G.R. Rectangle each time to create the spiral. This is all very good and clever, "But so what?" you are saying. Well a spiral has a starting and finishing point, so you ask yourself, *"Is the author/creator of this map trying to take us somewhere?"* If one makes a natural assumption that the centre of the map is the starting point, we have an interesting revelation. You can see in the following diagram how the finishing point takes us exactly to what could be depicting the 'landing place' of the galleon/ boat depicted on the Trinity Map. What appear to be sailing tracks are taking you to this point.

You will see in a later chapter that the radial line (long side of the rectangle) passing through the pass(?), ship and what could be a filled-in outline of an atoll has other important connotations, especially as its 90º right-angle counterpart has another 'blob' (Pinaki?) on it close to 'L'. To show it here would only add to the complexity of the geometry, and anyway, it is more to do with the 'Key' chart and not the Trinity Map. However, to continue with the theory:

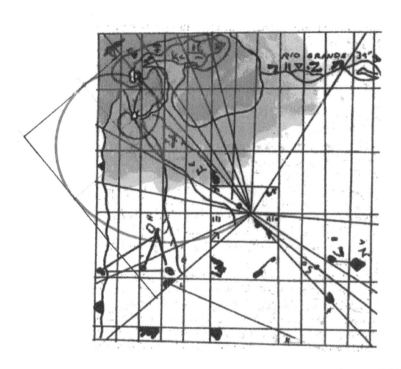

SHOWING HOW THE G.R. SPIRAL RECTANGLE FITS IN THE ONLY RADIAL LINES THAT CREATE A RIGHT ANGLE, TO HIGHLIGHT THEORY OF 'STARTING' OR 'LANDING PLACE'.

That this could be the purpose of the spiral i.e. highlighting the landing place of the treasure is, as we have seen, shown by the fact that when orientating the rectangle (and starting point) around the centre point of the map, the spiral end sits perfectly on the small circle on the map but only when the G.R. Rectangle is positioned on the only 90º angle radial lines created on the Trinity Map. It is my opinion the author of this map was telling you where to position the rectangular box containing the spiral; it will not go anywhere else! Can this be coincidence? Knowing the complexity of trigonometry, I doubt it. MN, forever challenging my theories on this, considered it to be fantasy and nothing to do with the Trinity Map. Maybe, but the 'odd' line L-N (or X) on the Trinity Map above fits the trigonometry almost perfectly; otherwise, why is it there unless as a clue to a GR rectangle? If I had ignored it, I'm sure there are many readers out there who would have spotted it and asked the question, "Why didn't you show that? It's obvious!"

It is difficult to accept the above as coincidence, although one has to accept the possibility. Of all the radial lines on the map, only two are exactly at right angles; if this 'anomaly' amongst the other lines didn't exist, then there is nowhere for a rectangular box to fit. That a spiral box fits, with the spiral ending exactly at the 'landing place', is extraordinary, if a coincidence. The problem with having an engineering/design background is that you are always looking at how and why things work. It is the same with the Trinity Map, which is full of questions; I am merely looking for answers, right or wrong. There has to be a reason for just two lines exactly at right angles.

Was this therefore a dual map? On the one hand, via the G.R. Triangle, is it confirming that two islands lie on the centre line and other islands lie on transits 36º either side of this line? The previous Layout 1. of the Trinity Island Group appears to confirm this. Is it also confirming that via the spiral created through the inherent G.R. trigonometry, you are looking at a possible landing (or starting) place of a ship or boat in a horseshoe (herradura) shaped bay? For Pinaki there is no navigable pass for a boat into the inner lagoon. A natural bar precludes this as a logistical route. Old pictures and modern satellite images show that though the main pass into the inner lagoon is wide, the channel is shallow where it crosses the exposed bedrock (degraded coral) of the atoll's rim. Island geology is such that it is only in the future, as this exposed bedrock erodes away, will you then be able to row into the inner lagoon without taking the bottom out of your boat.

PASS TO INNER LAGOON ON PINAKI, CIRCA 1900

Further, the realities are that access to the island itself is through a small pass in the outer reef located at the north side of the island adjacent to the native village, not something navigable by a large sailing ship. Anyone wanting to access any part of the island after rowing through the reefs in a boat would simply continue to row around the island in the outer lagoon before landing. In other words (MN said), "No one in their right mind would unload a boat, drag it into the inner lagoon, load it up and row a short distance to unload it again". (Maybe, but I show a photograph later on taken in 1899 showing rowboats on the lagoon, so someone did go to the trouble!)

The explanation would be then that Latcham or whoever, when executing their idea of what the map should show, was not familiar with the actual geography of the atoll and had *assumed* a boat could enter the lagoon via the pass as shown on maps. All the maps suggest this. Either way, for some reason they are highlighting a particular part of a lagoon or bay with a small circle. This is problematic in that if this is a copy of a real Spanish map drafted by Ubilla or some close lieutenant showing the island of Pinaki, then it would not show a boat or ship doing this because practically it cannot be done! Only explanation again is that the sailing tracks were added at a later date by someone assuming you could sail or row into the lagoon.

If the map's author is highlighting a particular part of a lagoon or bay with a small circle, but you cannot row a boat through the pass to get there, then what is being marked? MN attempts to offer a solution here to try and untie the knot: "If it is a galleon or ship shown on the map as Latcham suggests, its position would conform to the position of the pass through the outer reef for Pinaki. As you cannot row a boat from the galleon to 'land' at the position, (nor am I going to drag the boat and treasure overland just to do that either) it would not then be a 'landing point' but it might be a 'starting point', a datum position from which you then follow further directional instructions."

You will note on the above Trinity Map that I have highlighted the sea (top left) and land, an obvious assumption to make, I think you will agree. This was also to make it clearer to you that the coastline shown is that of Herradura Bay, also the bay at Coquimbo (see map in Part 3). By rote, you are meant to recognise that the horseshoe is really depicting Pinaki lagoon.

Whilst the G.R. geometry is quite clear cut in its purpose and has been around for a long time, it is evident from the preciseness of it all that this was not done by a pirate sat on a beach 300 or more years ago. Stories of smelly maps found in a mucky pot and found by Castro are therefore extremely suspicious. To determine the position of the islands, some serious surveying and charting of large swathes of ocean had taken place.

If the map is a relatively modern creation, then by whom? It can only be our Richard Latcham, as already suspected. He had, if you recall, a degree in civil engineering and would therefore have been very familiar with trigonometry and the Golden Ratio. We have seen from some aspects of the text in his book that he is playing games with the reader, so what is he doing here? Like Wilkins and Brown, is he mixing fact with fiction? Did he indeed come across a genuine map *('with many lines')*? More than likely he was sent a copy of the one mentioned as being in the Anson file by our friend Mr Wilkins and decided to enhance it with their combined knowledge. As all the clues in the fabulous riddle they both put together show, he/they knew all along that Pinaki is *the* island, but did he decided to then maybe add some more clues?

There is also, of course, 'RIO GRANDE' written in modern capitals on the map, not ancient Spanish. But look carefully and you will see below this notation there are also Hebrew letters. That this is just another code is shown in the later *The Gathering of the Clues...* chapter. Aspects of the Trinity Map by the type of cartography employed does suggest that part of it is old, contrasting with obvious modern draughting techniques also employed. It has to be said then that as this map is so uncharacteristic of the other drawings in his book, it is an addition and obviously supplied by Wilkins. I did say in Part 4 that with a style totally different to the other drawings, it had to be done by someone with intelligence.

Could it be that when *this* map was overlaid on the Shepherd's Monument, it produced a composite image that was immediately recognised as being the map which had driven all those historic searches for the treasure across the world? So what they were/are looking at is not a modern creation, but a modern *copy*.

As a 'by the way' and forever challenging MN's theories and thoughts, and in particular taking the part of the reader, I decided to take issue with him on the above theory of overlaying the map on the monument. So it is prudent to include it here. The following is how our email exchange went:

(GE) 'You insist that the Shepherd's Monument was used as an underlay for the 'real' map. As there were no photographs of it on general availability to the public in the 18th/19th centuries, how could it be utilised by adventurers/pirates/whoever etc. the other side of the world? And more importantly, I doubt if anybody outside the Anson family and their close circle of friends were aware the monument existed in those days. Certainly Joe Public, if even aware of its existence, would not have been allowed to prowl the grounds taking measurements. Only a few of the local (British) VIPs had a look, as we know, to ponder over the cipher. You had to be royalty or similar to get invited to Shugborough and you'd need a bloody big sheet of tracing paper to cover the sculpture!

The sensible/astute reader will be aware of the above, so how do you convince him you are right?'

(MN) 'That had me wondering also, but as I was reading the question, the answer suddenly became apparent. You do need both and it is apparent you need both: the plotting of the cairns on Trinidade or the Money Pit on Oak shows it is done this way.

It is quite simple when you think about it. Substantially they are both the same. The Trinity Map is the original Spanish Map done by Ubilla or whoever then.

The monument is the later version which, by manipulation and stretching of an artistic image (The Shepherds of Arcadia), captures some of the shapes from the Trinity Map.

OK, you have two versions of the same map. But you do not have the same amount of information on each. Think what is on one that is not on the other. One has the position of the Golden Section/Trinity Group of islands: the Trinity Map (but it does look like it did have a code on it RIOGA to indicate the datum point). The other has the datum position for the centre of the map: the monuments code is the later 'Illuminated Ones' code of Anson's time, but even if you knew it produced 19-138, AND you happened to know the 246 bearing, there is nothing on the monument to show the golden section/trinity group.

The map of the Herradura island is the remnant of the shepherdess shape without the triangle on it: so the shepherdess was known to be important if you only had the monument.

At some stage then, at some point, someone, well, I'll put it this way:

It's 1762 and Master MN of the English Confidential Service, standing in frock coat and wig with hose, has been handed Anson's file to 'look into'. So naturally I start investigating Anson and all about him to try and learn what is going on. Off I carriage to Shugborough and speak to all the staff to get the inside gossip.

"Pray, my good man, did Lord Anson do anything of note or unusual that he kept silent to others about? Perchance he had a place he spent most time or a library he allowed no one in?"

"Oy yar (this is the simple gardener), he did all like strange monuments and things. They used to dance around in shepherds' outfits and he had built these like statues with writings we know not what."

So off I head, walking stick in hand and the gardener carrying my port, to poke around Anson's library and desks and check out the statues. Now, of course, when I get to the Shepherd's Monument, I can see there is a CODE on it

"What is the meaning of this?"

"Oy yar, no one knows, was the Lord's secret."

"Ahem," says I, "just hand me my port and turn your back a minute, my good fellow. Crown's business and all that."

So I take out the map that was in the file and look at the map and I look at the monument. And as I am looking, I begin to see that the shape down the left of the map is anthropomorphically suggestive of the carving of the shepherdess I am looking at.

"By Adam's beard! Quick, get me an artist. I want a drawing of this monument!"

You'd get the gossip, you'd be poking around Shugborough Hall. Who were his associates? You'd check out the portrait of Lady Anson pointing at the Poussin image. In the end, you'd just say, "I better have a look at this monument thing with a code on it," and you find out it was done by other people who were involved with the Royal Society.

Basically it's not that hard, even the first question is, "Is there any secret or strange thing around here?" and everyone starts pointing at the Shepherd's Monument. (None of the other monuments, just this one.) Everyone still says it to this day, "It's a mystery, something to do with hiding the Holy Grail etc. etc."

Apart from that, OK, I get the gardener to get me a draughtsman who does me a copy of the monument. So I now sit down and overlay one over the other, and I've got something.

What do you think my next step would be? Well knowing that the Webb letter mentions Valley of Anson, and having done *my background check of Anson anyway, I know he went to JF. and he wrote a book, and he drew the maps in the book (the old banana-shaped JF). So I would just look at his book and go, "Hey! That shape I saw (on the Trinity Map), which is this shepherdess! Well the shepherdess' robe is just like the shape of JF!"*

In the end, it's not that hard for anyone doing half a decent enquiry to find it all. I just read about it (the Anson connection) in 'The Holy Blood and Holy Grail' and on that bare mention decided it needed a look.....

The moral of the story is: if I thought to do it 250 years later, somebody thought to do it 250 years ago.'

Thus endeth MN's lesson. Whilst this is a serious book, that doesn't mean to say we can't inject a little humour now and then. But from a practical point of view, and as said earlier, I still have my doubts that any treasure hunter 200 years or more ago would have been aware of this monument and its connection to a treasure. Only Anson knew its secret; in other words, the above scenario never happened.

That a document and picture have to be used in a similar way is hinted at in Wilkins' *A Modern Treasure Hunter* as follows, (in part):

".....According to Westhaver (his informant in Nova Scotia. GE) the 'right person' has to furnish, as credentials, a peculiar, or symbolical picture which dovetails, like an old-fashioned apprentice's indenture, into another portion of a document relating to this mysterious treasure island...."

Are we talking about the Trinity Map and the Monument here, Kidd's charts, Oak Island documents, or something else? Who knows!

Back to the subject in hand:

The Spiral and Other Applications

At this point, we can have a look at another of Latcham's strange drawings, namely his Fig. 24, because what looks like the symbol for a G.R. i.e. φ or Φ, appears in it. Is this the author of the map saying 'Use the G.R. Triangle'? You can see from the diagram below (Map 1.) that it is possible to utilise the G.R. Triangle and its Spiral, which takes you again to a specific point. The shading is there to highlight what *could* be the profile of a lagoon.

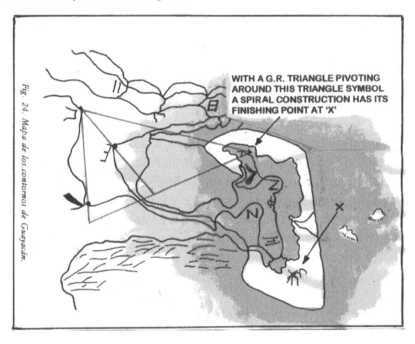

MAP 1. SHOWING HOW THIS MAP COULD BE INDICATING A CORAL ISLAND AND A POSSIBLE TREASURE LOCATION. G.R. SPIRAL REMOVED FOR CLARITY

You can see from the above map that if I have identified the lines as tracks, sailing or otherwise, into a lagoon, then their 'landing' or 'starting' point coincides with similar tracks on the Trinity Map.

With both 'arms' of the headlands adjacent to the pass hooking back in on themselves, diagrammatically we have an outline remarkably similar to Pinaki.

I could see another possible option with this map and it appears as follows:

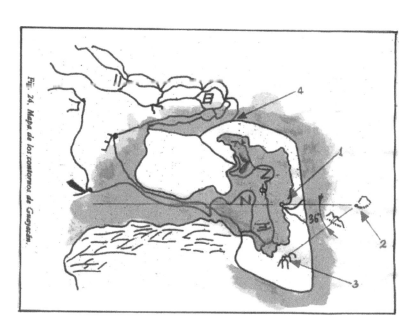

Fig. 24. Mapa de los contornos de Guayacán.

MAP 2. A VARIATION ON A THEME HIGHLIGHTING OTHER ASPECTS OF INTEREST AND GEOMETRY

Map 2 highlights three little circles, numbered 1, 2 and 3, created for a reason that must be important; also, they just happen to create the all-important 36º angle between them. An extension of points 2 and 1 takes you through the middle of what could be the pass into a lagoon. What is suggestive of a long pass is corroborated when you look at the plan of Pinaki Atoll that appears in Map 3. opposite. The pass, as you can see, is long (about a quarter of a mile) when compared with the atoll's size.

What is interesting, referring back to the Fig 24 'Variation on a Theme', and Map 2 above, is that the circle (3) on a rock mound (?) is adjacent to the previously shown possible 'landing' or 'starting' place depicted by a small circle on the Trinity Map. Also, the small circle highlighted by arrow 1, which appears to be on a sort of promontory, roughly corresponds to the same on the atoll, highlighted (1) on the plan on the opposite page.

Disguised sailing tracks (if that is what they are) converge on the arrow point (4), which corresponds to where on Pinaki the current pass and landing place is through the outer lagoon. Is this all just coincidence? Grabbing at straws? Maybe, maybe not, who knows until we get there. Of course, as we know where our treasure island is, we needn't have bothered with any of the attempted explanations above. But one way or another, I am just trying to make sense of aspects of Latcham's whacky diagrams on the assumption they relate to Pinaki, at the same time opening up to you, the readers, the possibilities inherent within them. (And also answering any possible questions - why didn't I try this or that!)

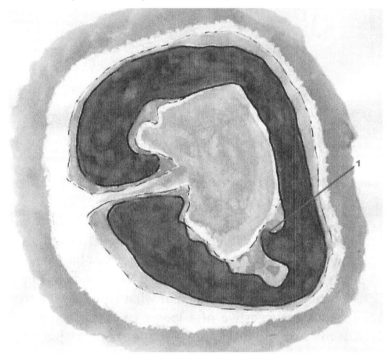

MAP 3. A PLAN, TO SCALE OF PINAKI ATOL (APPROXIMATELY 1 MILE ACROSS) IT SHOWS THAT THE PASS IS APPROXIMATELY ¼ MILE LONG

The above work on nautical spirals contributed to a major disagreement and fall out between MN and myself. He would not and could not take any of it on board saying, "It's bunkum and a con job by addition of your own material you need to get your finding." I know we've had our differences, but this was, to me, a puzzling statement to make. Several times, I have pointed out to him (and you) that I am merely trying to cover all the possible options available. MN, for some reason, was ignoring the geometry that is there. I am not adding any new material or trying to con anyone, just trying to be practical with the geometry to make some sense out of it. I am not saying, "This is how it is and therefore must be the solution!" I am sure if I had not introduced the spiral geometry here, a reader or two would have recognised that it is applicable within the geometry presented and questioned why I didn't show it.

He also questioned the maps, saying, "Colouring in the maps to show a bay that's not there is a con job by omission." Maybe and maybe bunkum, but colouring highlights aspects of diagrams that are a confusion of lines hopefully makes them clearer to understand. I don't see the problem with this. I believe that anything that improves awareness and understanding of something for the reader's sake is allowable. We have seen on an earlier coloured Trinity Map how it clarified Herradura and Coquimbo bays. Again, it is to cover all possible options and try to make sense of what Latcham is up to. None of it is dictorial but is included to open up avenues of investigation for you, the reader.

This is a democratic book. MN had his say on things I don't necessarily agree with, and I have mine!

Directions and Interpretations

It has been suggested that with no navigable pass for a boat into the inner lagoon, you would just row in the outer lagoon until you got to the same area. OK, but if it was me, having to move boatloads of treasure then carry the boat and launch it when you reach the deeper water of the lagoon?? (We know it is deep as Howe was diving in it.) The next photograph proves my point. I would probably have gone southeasterly from there to the promontory (1) as previous - as far away as possible from the pass and any obvious/easy areas. After all, those burying the treasure had all the time in the world and would have taken that time, to make sure their hiding place was secure, even if it did mean going a bit further. Also, the promontory is the only feature that differs from the regular shape or profile of the atoll. Being different, I would have thought makes it a good and easily recognisable starting point, you can go to it straight away and take your directions from here.

However, as far as the marked coral block goes, evidence suggests it was on the north side of the island (probably north-east as DNA suggests). Following the movements of Nordhoff, it was able to be deduced that Howe's camp was on the north to north-west part of the island. (Nordhoff was drifting along the north-western side of the island when they spotted Howe.) Logic tells you that Howe's camp would have been near the island's source of freshwater, most probably the same one that would have serviced the villagers that called there. When Nordhoff awoke after staying in Howe's camp, he had observed Howe diving into the water *on the opposite side of the lagoon* to probe its bottom, so somewhere off the inner lagoon's beach. When Howe took Nordhoff to look at the coral block with the signs, 'they went several hundred yards back along the beach before crossing to the ocean side'. This puts the location of the block to be on the north side of the island and is confirmed by Howe's comment to Nordhoff that he was 'put ashore from a small cutter, not four hundred yards from where we are sitting', meaning he went through the pass in the coral reef to land on the beach at the sparse native village.

ROWBOATS ON PINAKI LAGOON 1899. THIS SHOWS THE LAGOON IS BIGGER THAN IT LOOKS (and possible to launch boats here).
(H.C. Fasset and the Smithsonian Institute)

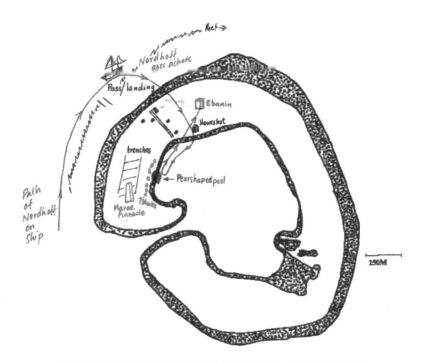

Reef→
Nordhoff
goes ashore
Pass/landing
Ebanin
Howeshut
Path of Nordhoff on ship
trenches
Pearshaped pool
Marae Pinnacle
Tracks
250M

A SKETCH OF NORDHOFF'S POSSIBLE MOVEMENTS

The above is MN's interpretation of where they walked to get to the coral block (ebanin), and he could well be right, but to me it is not all that clear cut and depends on how you interpret what is being said by Nordhoff. It is a moot point but when Nordhoff says, *'Near the centre of the island we came upon an immense block of coral…..',* is he referring to the geographical island centre i.e. approximately opposite the pass, or the centre of the land mass when crossing from the inner lagoon to the outer? Probably the latter, but it could be important when trying to locate the coral block. The same applies when Nordhoff says he saw Howe diving *'on the opposite side of the lagoon'.* Does that mean opposite south-west towards the pass as MN indicates, or does he mean opposite across the lagoon i.e. southeasterly towards the geographical centre? To me, *'opposite side'* would indicate to me 'across the lagoon to the other side', not opposite further down the beach.

PINAKI LAGOON ENTRANCE, 1900. YOU CAN SEE THE SURF ON THE OUTSIDE REEF. THIS PHOTOGRAPH ALSO DEMONSTRATES HOW LOW A PROFILE THIS ATOLL HAS.
(Charles Haskins Townsend and Mr. Minton)

It makes sense to include next a diagram of the island that appeared in a French article from the second half of the last century by Bernard Villaret titled *Le vieux "Charley" a-t-l retrouvé le trésor des flibustiers?* (Did old Charley find the treasure of the pirates?) as this shows where all the action was occurring. The article tells the base story that Howe got his information from an ancient sailor 'Kilrain', which was confirmed by a certain 'Brown, captain of the (ship) Black Sheep'. Villaret goes on to speculate that perhaps Howe really found the treasure on an atoll called Anuanuaro, which is some 350 nm from Pinaki, as a 'troubling document'[1] in the French archives dated 1915 reported that 'upon a large rock there was observed the inscription JAT along with a piece of a wooden box found in an empty hole upon which were the characters FICXXXVIII'. The article included a rather distorted map which marked the locations of interest on Pinaki. (That the last eight characters represent 138 must bo coincidence, as F is the old Roman medieval character for 41 so therefore is not representative of a latitude in this case, but take 41 from 180 and we get 139! Again, coincidence?)

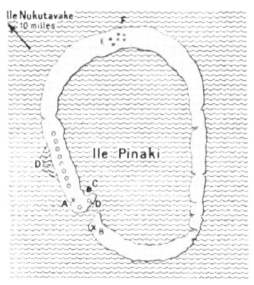

Although the profile is hopelessly inaccurate, this map is important because of what it marks:

A. Skeletons of natives of Nukatavake
B. Six skeletons of blacks with shots to the head
C. Underwater excavations by compressed air
D. Excavations in the ground
E. Paekire village
F. Landing point

The identification that the skeletons of the 'natives of Nukutavake' were (found) in the same area that Howe was excavating is indicative of a marae of some sort being there, probably an upright stone that Howe took to be the pinnacle/sailing mark as well as the seven blocks of coral near the pool he was probing. Howe did not seem to be aware that a marae or native temple was a clue, other than there was one in the area he was excavating, the observation of which, in form but *not* function, he repeated to the Hamilton expedition: that near the pear-shaped pool are seven blocks of coral set at even distances apart.

Item B is interesting for two reasons. The first is, how do you know the skeletons were of local natives?

The second reason is that they were shot, which could suggest a pirate execution and/or they were executed after being used to bury the treasure. At that time, being coloured and therefore slaves would have meant nothing to whoever was in charge. Who knows? *If* part of the treasure burial party, the fact that they are buried on the southern part of the atoll makes sense if the 'starting/landing' point is here also. For all these reasons, I keep being drawn to the promonotory 1 on Map 3. At this point, I am merely backing up my theories that the south-eastern part of the atoll would be a good place to start searching should modern detecting technology and investigation not produce any results at the north-east part of the atoll.

It would appear Howe didn't dig any trenches down the south-eastern end; maybe that is why he did not find anything! There is further discussion on this in the *On Treasure Island* chapter at the end of the book.

Something else worth noting is a squiggly line on the Trinity Map that extends from the 'landing place' all the way into the centre rectangle. If this rectangle is indeed representative of a subterranean vault, it is indicative that the 'landing/starting place' is maybe just that.

The key to it all, of course, is the coral block with the signs that Howe himself said, "I believe it's the key, and I can't master it!"

So let us look at these strange signs and see if **we** can master them.

[1] A 'troubling document' indeed! Including the DNA of both 138 and 'inscription on a large rock'. You may not associate the 'JAT' with our Spanish signs, so where does it come from? They are probably one and the same. Due to morphallax, distortion with time, false repetition by word of mouth, inaccurate copying with the scribe adding his own interpretation etc. With some imagination and all that just described, the arrow could have become 'A'. The upside down L easily becomes 'T' and the line with a circle or curve, must be a 'J'!
On the other hand, they could be just somebody's initials!

CHAPTER 2

SPANISH SIGNS AND SYMBOLS

A reminder of those at the centre of our quest:

**THE SYMBOLS AS RECORDED BY CHARLES NORDHOFF.
FOUND ON A CORAL BLOCK ON PINAKI ATOL.**

How many people know that the traditional treasure location sign or symbol '**X**' is almost certainly derived from the Spanish code of signs? It is one of the basic symbols but as is the case with many of them, it has more than one meaning. For this one, they are:

1. Here, this place.
2. On line to mine or treasure.
3. To break; to divide.
4. Change in course.
5. Landmark.
6. 10.

You can see the problems that treasure hunters have in following this sign. Very often, the meaning will depend on signs that appear with it. In an earlier chapter, we mentioned the origins of 'X marks the spot' but when talking about Spanish trails, 'X' does **not** mark the spot. The signs and symbols *lead* the way to the location; you have to interpret where the 'spot' is. 'X', if it does appear, will appear close to the location and probably with a distance and measurement sign accompanying it. Another important thing to be aware of is that when the Spanish retrieved their treasure, the directional marks and/ or signs are erased. So it is promising for us in that the marks were still on the island 100 years ago.

You may ask the question, "Why is there no 'X' with our signs?" That is because the Spanish had several ways of giving you the same information, and also, when discussing Spanish trail signs, 99% of the time we are talking land-based trails and expeditions. Our signs, as you know, we believe were placed there by a seagoing captain general. Whilst the Spanish regime had a standardised system, the nautical guys may have applied them differently.

The size of the treasure site also influences the location information to be revealed. A Spanish trail in the Americas could be hundreds of miles long, beginning with a mountain symbol drawing showing the mountain/hill in the distance, which is where to look for the next marker. There was a requirement that on a long trail, a marker was to be placed about every quarter of a mile. The closer you got to the site, the more specific the signs become. Our site is only a mile across, so no marker trail is necessary, as it's easy enough to find the main marker (rock/ebanin/block) with maybe some other signs in the area.

How and why did this code start? Five hundred years ago, the Kings of Spain sent out many explorers, their mission to bring back anything of value, and they were driven by Gold, Glory and God. They were told to document ('under pain of Spain') the places of importance such as mines, to this end surveyor/mapmakers were attached to every expedition. The King decreed that of whatever was found, he was to have the 'Royal Quinto' or fifth, and to make sure everyone was working 'to the same book', the signs, symbols and coded messages were standardised. That way, future expeditions would be able to find the sealed up mine or buried treasure even if the original expedition met with disaster with no survivors. This does not mean that everyone was privy to the code's workings on an expedition. To ensure security, knowledge of the code's workings was reserved for the officer class only, such as the commander, his executive officers, surveyors and the padre.

Besides South America, these Spanish adventurers went further than you may think. Starting in Mexico, they went north into Arizona,

New Mexico, Utah, Colorado, California, Nevada and Texas. Even as far as Massachusetts, I have a colleague there who some years ago contacted me via my Kidd book. He sent photographs of strange signs he had found carved on rocks and asked if they could be Kidd related. I recognised some of them as old Spanish signs (and also Masonic!). Knowing now what he was looking at, he has followed these signs and found the hidden cave they lead to, but that's another story!

The signs are also very often carved on trees but of course are now distorted due to the growth and age of the tree making them even more difficult to read. The Mexicans that came in after the Spanish left, altered some of the symbols; they also get disfigured by those not appreciating what they are, adding to the problems of deciphering.

So let us delve a little deeper into this code as it is as fascinating as it is complex. The uninitiated should not attempt to follow a Spanish code trail; it is fraught with danger, deviation, deception and trickery. By danger, I mean exactly that; many places of importance were/are protected by 'Death Traps'. These traps were meant to last a lifetime and are still active today. They include boulders poised to crush, floor traps, water traps and poison. They may be old but being boulders/rocks balanced, incorporating the principle of applied mechanics, they will still work. Disturbed (running) sand was also used as a means of triggering boulder movement. Are there warnings of these traps? Yes, usually in the form of a 'heart' and/or 'lightning bolt'. Whilst the 'heart' symbol can mean gold to a Spaniard, they would modify it in some way to change the overall meaning. The 'lightning bolt' symbol is important in that it tells that this site is where large quantities of treasure are stored but there are death traps too.

You may be interested to know how the 'heart' symbol came to represent gold. It came from the age-old Spanish desire for gold: 'My soul may yearn for God, but my **heart** forever yearns for gold'. Cortez also is reputed to have said, "We Spaniards have a disease of the **heart** which can only be cured by gold".

The Code

I cannot give you the complete code as there are hundreds of signs and symbols and a lot of skills to be mastered, but I can give you the basics and some of the rules you should apply. The Spanish Code System consisted of three major parts: first, a code of several hundred signs or symbols; second, a code based on the Castilian Alphabet; and third, a Bible code that employed numerous passages in both the Old and New Testaments. Important to note here, Spain being a Catholic country logically used the Catholic version and not the King James version, and it has to be an *Old* Catholic version.

First, we start with:

Units of Measurement;
American inches are quoted as the Americas are where most of the action took place.

Pulgada - Spanish inch	=	0.914 of an American inch
Coto - 4.1 inches	=	3.8 American inches
Geme - 6.0 inches	=	5.5 American inches
Palmo - 8.2 inches	=	7.5 American inches
Pie - Spanish foot, 11 inches	=	10 American inches
Codo - 16.4 inches	=	15 American inches
Vara - 32.8 inches	=	30 American inches (= 2ft 6ins USA/UK)

Another important old Spanish measurement was the 'Estado' set at 5' 7". This was the minimum depth that items of importance were to be buried by the Jesuits or Catholic priests. Another was the 'Braza', the Spanish fathom, and again 5' 7". This was used mostly by pirates and sailors.

The Spanish code says to use varas all the time unless specifically told to use some other measurement by reference to a special sign. The Spanish vara was approximately 32 inches, which was the normal stride of a Spanish soldier. The standard Spanish vara is 33 *Spanish* inches long. 'Spanish' is emphasised because it is not 33 American inches long; you can see the equivalent American distance is 30 inches. This disparity is the reason many treasure hunters have missed the treasure. For example, if you figured out a coded stone said 'Go West 300 Varas' and being in America, you went 300 x 33 = 825ft converted, you would not find the correct place which would really be at 300 x 30 = 750ft west, i.e. 75ft shorter! Important to remember then, a Spanish inch is shorter than its American counterpart, and therefore the bigger the distance, the bigger the discrepancy. Important to note also, that the Spanish do not give distances in oddball numbers like 86 or 102 etc. They always have to reflect one of their units of measurement i.e. Coto, Palmo etc. A Palmo is 8.2 inches (spread hand, thumb tip to pinky tip) and each inch represents 10 varas so you have 82 varas. 82 could become 820 but they would have to give you a sign saying to multiply by 100 instead of ten. 82 varas and north-east are one of the Spanish favourites so they use it a lot.

Marks usually represent a distance and are just units meant to be added together. Also, the marks are not necessarily straight.

A unit of measurement not mentioned so far is the league, or legua. Its Spanish code symbol is diamond shaped, either outline or filled in. There are two 'leagues', Statute or land league and Nautical. **The Spanish league** was originally set as a fixed distance of 5,000 varas and believed to have been derived from the distance covered on foot in one hour. It equates to between 2.54 and 2.6 miles, often referred to as 3 miles.

A nautical league, however, is something different being 3 nautical miles. The nautical mile is defined as: the average length of minute of latitude corresponding to 45º i.e. 6076.12 feet. A nautical league is 1/20º i.e. 3minutes or 3x6076 feet or 3.45 statute miles.

The difference then, almost half a mile or more, between nautical and statute leagues Important then to know which one is being referred to. The league was common in Europe and South America but is no longer an official unit in any nation.

The Spanish Alphabet Code

I am indebted to Lou Layton (Omaha, USA) for permission to present this code here. He has published a book called *The Spanish Code to Treasure*. No Spanish trail treasure hunter should be without it as it is one of the more comprehensive and sensible works on the subject.

LETTER	NUMBER VALUE	LETTER	NUMBER VALUE
A	1	M	15
B	2	N	16
C	3	Ñ	17
CH	Not used	O	18
D	5	P	19
E	6	Q	20
F	7	R	21
G	8	S	22
H	9	T	23
I	1 or 2	U	24
J	11	V	5
K	12	X	10
L	13	Y	27
LL	Not used	Z	28

Note there is no 'W' in the Spanish Alphabet. What looks like a 'W' would be two upside down V's connected together to look like an 'M'. This code has several rules that apply that have the ability to change a message. Check out Lou's book to see them all, but as an example, if a letter is separated or broken, the value of that letter is to be doubled.

You may see a letter 'N' that is broken i.e. a gap between one of the uprights. The value then becomes 16 plus 16 = 32.

Another trick used is where the first vertical line of 'N' is slightly separated but still looks like 'N', when in fact it is 'I' plus 'V' giving a total of 6 and 6 is the letter E. So IV turns out to also say N plus E or Noreste (North-east and DNA).

Deception all the way, so you must know the rules.

The Bible Code

Not easy to cover in a paragraph or two, so I won't attempt to! But I will try to give an idea of what it is all about.

We start with Matthew, Mark, Luke and John; each is associated with a different symbol. For example, John's was an eagle or bird, and carvings of wings would be carved along with other signs, letters and numbers. A real example gave seven and three. Going to Chapter 7

Verse 3, it read, 'Lets leave here and go into Judea'. Doesn't tell you much, you may think, but when the Apostle spoke these words, they were in Galilee, which is in the north of Israel. To go to Judea, they would have to travel south. This is what the coded Bible passage was saying: 'Go south'. But how far? Amongst other signs was a single carved straight line measuring 7½ inches, this converts to 8.2 Spanish inches, on going 82 (1 inch is 10 varas) varas south. Nothing there, but digging down, another stone was discovered with more signs. Satisfying proof that the Bible code works.

Another example is that the Spanish very often use the letter 'T' as a cross† and the † as a 'T'. They do this as it facilitates their referring to the Book of Tobias and verses that conform to coded numbers given. There are many such examples. Another thing to remember is that the Spanish repeat their messages 99% of the time so what sometimes looks like a complicated message is merely disguising the fact it is the same message using different letters or signs. For example, as well as saying 'D' for 5, they could put 'BC' i.e. 2 plus 3. They could then add a 'V' which is also 5.

From the above use of biblical passages, you can see one of the reasons a padre accompanied every expedition. These expeditions could be quite large - 300 mules and 400 horses - and well organised. One translated document quotes:

'In the first place the location was selected and subsequently surveyed, also with great care, and the rocks and markings placed in proper place by men who had no other purpose or responsibility. There were ten men whose only responsibility was to mark the rocks with extreme care and place them in their proper place. Fifty men were officers, who directed the work, a number of surveyors, blacksmiths and botanists'.

It is worthwhile then to try and discover the religious influences or doctrine operating upon a particular group. Each Order, for example the Franciscans or the Jesuits etc. have their own favourite saint and so prefer that saint's teachings. Likewise, an expedition commander may have his own patron saint or had been schooled by a particular Order. This knowledge would then provide us a clue as to which book of the Bible may have been used for the code and how the teachings within that book were interpreted. Our knowledge that Ubilla was a

Knight of St James suggests then we should look towards the teachings of St James. Likewise as St Anthony's name has popped up in relation to the lost treasure, we perhaps should look towards that saint also.

The Signs and Symbols

We have already mentioned some of them; the heart, cross, lightning and Apostle symbols. Before we show more, just a fraction of those known, something else you should know and how it could be important in *our* quest: how they indicated a change in the value from varas. If the signs are carved on the side of a stone or rock, making them vertical to the ground, then the distance they relate to are in feet. If on top of the rock horizontal or parallel to the ground, then the distance is in varas. **And**, just to compound the deception and trickery, if the distance line is carved on a convex or concave place i.e. mound or depression on the stone, then the distance ratio is changed regardless if it is vertical or horizontal to the ground.

You can see big mistakes can be made if you do not know the rules.

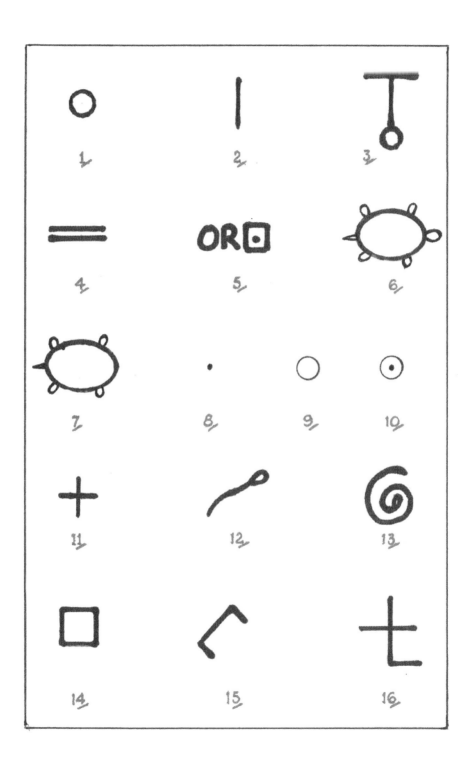

INTERPRETATIONS 1. TO 16.:

1. a) 1 Vara
   b) Cave
2. 1 Vara
3. Treasure buried below, deep.
4. a) Two Varas
   b) Double the distance
5. Gold buried in box or chest
6. Follow head to trail or treasure
7. Treasure removed
8. One
9. Two (if small)
10. a) Three
    b) Gold
11. a) Two
    b) Change direction
12. Measure tip to tip (snake)
13. Double the distance
14. If small 90degrees or East
15. Way to enter
16. Southeast

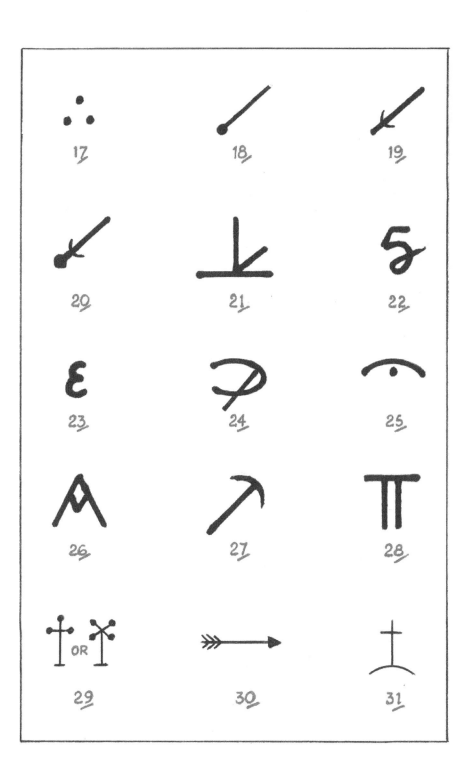

INTERPRETATIONS 17. TO 31.:

17. a) 3 Varas
   h) 9 (3x3)
18. Feet
19. 100
20. 1000 feet
21. 45 degrees
22. Five varas in direction of point
23. Turn to right
24. Down slope
25. a) Treasure under this marker
   b) Treasure under hill/crest
26. Straight ahead 1 legua
27. a) Mine
   b) Follow in direction of pick head
28. Treasure in tunnel or shaft
29. Church objects buried here
30. Travel this direction and/or count flights for distance
31. Silver

One of the problems we have when it comes to deciphering our signs is we do not know how accurately Nordhoff copied them. Was he precise? If the number of strokes of the pen were not exactly those of the original, then the outcome could be very different from what was intended.

Having made a study of these Spanish signs, it is now logical to apply our newfound knowledge and attempt to decipher what is marked on our coral block.

The Signs to Treasure

We have to make some assumptions here that a) they were copied as they appear and b) the surface they are on is vertical. Not until we are on-site can we confirm and, if necessary, make appropriate adjustments.

The Arrow Symbol: 'Go in this direction?'. Cannot go up, so it means something else. The feathers would be the clue, 5 a side, at an angle, so travel 10 varas. Or because it is 5 repeated, then the rule says to double, so 20 varas. Five is also the number for gold.

Upright with Bar Symbol: 'Go north-east?' Or measure vertical line in inches, convert to feet and go north-east or maybe east, Or is it '7' reversed?

Circle with dot over line Symbol: Circle with dot is '3' but sometimes also used for 'Gold'. Vertical bar = 1 vara or 1 Estoda deep? A circle can also mean 'cave'.

So as a possibility, the signs could be saying: 20 varas (20 x 33 inches) NE (or east) gold is buried 5ft 7inches deep. Maybe, but it did not seem right to me somehow as the interpretation gives measurements or distances for each symbol. Logically the combined signs would be giving a distance and direction. But, this was an initial interpretation trying to use logic and an engineer's common sense. That plainly doesn't work with Spanish signs! A more concentrated effort was required using Spanish logic. It became apparent I had made an oversight with the above, and this emphasises how one must be careful and totally familiar with every aspect of Spanish signs to hope to decipher them correctly. Getting '10' for the feathers had to be correct but what about the arrow head? I had totally overlooked that. It is, of course, an upside down 'V' giving another 5: total is now 15. I was kicking myself also for not initially realising the second symbol is, of course, an upside down broken 'L'. The rule for this is to double, so 13, the value for 'L' becomes 26.

Third symbol is 3 as I said **but** plus 1 for the 'handle', total 4.

Add them all up to give us 45.

The sign maker is telling us to go 45 degrees i.e. north-east. (Where have we seen that before? It is, of course, important DNA.)

So what about "How far from the rock?" Look at the above symbol 18. Line with filled-in circle is sign for feet, indicating this is the distance sign. Line with open circle i.e. our symbol means the same. When giving distance measurements 1 inch is 10 feet (unless another sign says to change this), you measure the vertical line in the last symbol in inches and convert accordingly. Be aware then that this sign has two meanings in one; 4 and a distance!

Fitzgerald's Feet

At this point, we can employ some realistic mathematics and reverse engineering to see if a quoted distance is realistic in terms of Spanish measurements. You may recall that Nicholas Fitzgerald (given treasure location by Keating) had left an inventory of treasure that included what sounded like directional instructions i.e. '28 feet to the north-east, at a depth of 8 feet in the red earth' and '12 arm-spans west, at a depth of 10 feet in the yellow sand'.

We know the colours being spoken of are remnants of the colour code. The directions do seem to have some coordinating sound to them, each one suggestive of a longitudinal (east or west) and latitudinal (depth) component. But as we know the colours were a code for the star which gave the coordinates, this makes no sense as these other directions then would be a redundancy. Nor, taken as latitude and longitude, do they have any meaning. They are calculations for something, but for what?

For us 'north-east', of course, stands out being part of our Spanish code solution and does appear regularly as DNA in linked stories. Perhaps from this information, can we get a realistic length for the vertical bar in the last symbol? Using the given '28 feet', we could do it as follows: We assume at the start that Keating was referring to Imperial feet.

This gives us; 28x12=336 imperial or American inches.

From the code, we know that 10 American inches = 1 Spanish foot or 11 Spanish inches.

Therefore 336 ÷ 10 = 33.6 Spanish feet.

The code also tells us that for this sign, 1 Spanish inch = 10 Spanish feet.

Therefore 33.6 ÷ 10 = 3.36 Spanish inches, the length of the vertical bar.

As one American inch equates to 33 ÷ 30 = 1.1 Spanish inches, the length of the bar in imperial inches is 3.36 ÷ 1.1 = 3.05 inches. Seems a bit short to me, but as we have no sense of scale of the symbols, I could be wrong.

To cover another possible option, in the Bible Code chapter earlier, a straight line measuring 7½ inches was used. This makes sense as this is equivalent to the Palmo i.e. 8.2 Spanish inches, and they liked to use units of their measurements. The code is telling us that 1 inch equates to 10 feet (Spanish) and therefore the distance is 82 Spanish feet or 75 imperial feet.

Applying the same mathematics, the '12 arm-spans' (12 x 6 = 72 feet) calculates out to 7.85 Imperial inches. This is maybe a little more realistic and almost equates to the 75 feet quoted.

A distance you may not be familiar with is 'a cable'. The mistranslated Webb report had first appeared with the word 'Cable' being used instead of 'rigging', but 'cable' appears again in the Keating document;

'At two cables length, south of the last watering place, on three points. The cave is the one which is to be found under the second point.'

Perhaps there was some cross contamination, but just in case this is referring to an actual measurement given by Keating, the old 'cable' measurement is 1/10 of a nautical mile. You already know a nautical mile is 6,076 feet. A cable therefore is 607.6 feet and two cables is 1,215 feet.

The trouble is the narratives of the Keating documents are quite obviously garbled and just read as if they are the notes of a person struggling to recall something they had heard.

This brings us to the fact that there are no signs (as far as I know) that tell us how deep to dig. Common sense then tells us it must have been something standardised and therefore 5ft 6/7 inches or 11 feet or 16ft 6 inches. Based on the Estado or Braza, a unit used for centuries and based on the height of a man. It would seem that by mandate of the King when burying treasure, it was to be buried in increments of Estado's.

The signs then tell us where to dig but not how deep to dig except that you have to go down a minimum of 5ft 6 inches. The above two examples both exceed this depth. The clues so far also suggest that as the Spanish buried this treasure, and being methodical, then they constructed a proper stone lined vault, possibly with a capstone, rather than the traditional 'hole in the ground' covered over. Certainly a lot of the related stories describe the treasure to be in a 'rock topped cave' or similar.

Staying with Fitzgerald for a moment, he said you need both the map and directions. He was, without knowing it, talking about the Trinity Map and Webb letter. The story so far, combined with the geometrical clues, have confirmed the island (Trinity) group to us, that and the fact that the signs on Pinaki are, of course, indicative that Pinaki is where a treasure is buried. All the clues so far centre on this very small atoll in the great South Pacific Ocean. We would expect Anson's monument cipher to be somehow linked and there are other clues left by Wilkins yet to be solved that will confirm this atoll. That will all come later. That **there is a treasure** is without doubt, so let us now try and discover what this treasure may be.

PART 8

A TEMPLE TREASURE?

We have surmised it is possible the treasure *could* have connections to the treasure of Solomon and by reasoning the Templars. It was MN's view there is a good argument for this. I am not so sure. Captain Brown never mentioned or hinted at any fabulous religious artefacts or ornaments. That there is a treasure of immense value waiting for discovery is evident, as to what it is...we will just have to wait and see. It is, however, useful to try and follow briefly the treasure trail from Jerusalem and see if there could be any possible connection with Ubilla. I use the term 'briefly' because a detailed account, not necessary here, would cover many volumes.

For our purposes, the term 'temple treasure' denotes the collective group of the valuable furnishings, fittings and gold objects that were made off with during the eras of the temple's occupancy, there being more than one of these looting events.

Because any possible link to Ubilla is via the Templars, we delve back prior to their occupation of Jerusalem just enough to get a hint of what the treasure could consist of. The early history of the temple includes destruction and rebuilding more than once. The Bible gives many descriptions of the treasure looted, and sometimes returned over the centuries. For example:

'He (King Cyrus of Persia) returned the vessels which Nebuchadnezzar had looted but these only amounted to; fifty chargers of gold and five hundred of silver, forty Thericlean cups of gold, and five hundred of silver, fifty basins of gold, and five hundred of silver, thirty vessels for pouring and three hundred of silver, thirty vials of gold and two thousand four hundred of silver, with a thousand other vessels.'

Other descriptions include a solid gold table, golden candlesticks and precious stones. The original 'treasure' then was huge in its quantity and value. Whilst the amount varied over the centuries, it is just about impossible to imagine that such a vast store of treasure similar in any way to that described could be left hidden somewhere under the sacred mount. Indeed, the Arch of Titus in Rome records the temple's items being paraded through that city after the sacking of Jerusalem by Titus' Legions. The spoils included the table of gold and golden candlesticks (menorah) The Arch showing the victory procession still stands; I showed it in the earlier chapter on Rennes-le-Château.

The Templars

In the early twelfth century, Hugues de Payens, with eight others, approached King Baldwin II of Jerusalem to create a monastic Order for the protection of pilgrims to Jerusalem. With de Payens as first Grand Master, they created the Order of the Poor Knights of Christ. They then assumed the name Knights of the Temple of Jerusalem, known thereafter as the Templars. The temple was entrusted to the Templars' care who had their headquarters in a wing of the Royal Palace on the temple mount.

Soon the Order was officially blessed by the church and then the Pope. Over the next couple of hundred years, the Order became a huge organisation with castles and interests all over Europe. Whilst primarily a Military Order, it had a huge wealthy financial infrastructure and is said to have created the origins of our banking system. Indeed, by 1307, King Philip IV of France was heavily in debt to them. The Templars' existence was tied closely to the Crusades; when the Holy Land was lost, support for the Order faded. Rumours about the Templars' secret initiation ceremony created mistrust and the King seeing this as a way of freeing himself of his debts, pressurised the Church and ultimately the Pope to take action against the Order. In 1307, many of the Order's members in France were arrested, tortured into giving false confessions and then burned at the stake. A Papal Bul issued by the Pope instructed that all Christian monarchs in Europe were to arrest all Templars and seize their assets. And so by 1311, this once tremendously powerful organisation ceased to exist and was subsequently dissolved by the Pope.

It is said some Templars took refuge in Scotland. That their descendants had anything to do with Rosslyn Chapel is open to conjecture but in later years the chapel has featured in speculative theories regarding Freemasonry and the Knights Templar. In Spain, the Templars were well established. Santiago de Compostela, the capital of the autonomous community of Galicia in NW Spain, was under their protection. They were charged with the protection of pilgrims travelling to St James' tomb. During the Dissolution, most Templars in Spain escaped persecution and were subsumed into existing military orders.

Their presence in Spain gives rise to the theory that Temple Mount treasures may eventually have found their way here. This is another tale passed down through the ages. We have already seen how the Roman Emperor Titus sacked Jerusalem. These spoils from the temple were subsequently seized by the Visigoths when they sacked Rome. It is said that the temple treasure then found its way to the Languedoc area of France in the fifth century. Rennes-le-Château we know is in this region. From here, the treasure is supposed to have been moved to Spain for safekeeping by the Templars. Unfortunately, we have no historical records to back any of this up. But who can say it didn't happen? I find it unlikely, as treasures such as those previously described would have been melted down and scattered far and wide over the centuries. I have to remind you also that Webb when listing the inventory of treasure made no mention of any religious items that could be said to have originated from the temple. That the Templars searched the mount during their occupation is certain. Some artefacts may have come to light and there is evidence that the Knights were in possession of religious relics. However, during the Inquisition of the Templars and throughout their torture and trial, there was never any mention of a treasure. Rumours persist, however, and the legend of the Holy Grail or Graal and its association with the Templars is with us still today.

That Ubilla was privy to a great secret is conjecture. That he had contacts in high places is certain. He was possibly a Knight of Santiago charged with the protection of the treasure and keepers of the secret - that maybe a great treasure was hidden in Ponferreda Castle; the Castle the Knights built on the Way of St James. This was the headquarters of the Templars' Grand Master of Castille. The locals have a legend that this was the hiding place of the Holy Grail.

Then there is the question that if Ubilla had a secret treasure which he removed from Spain, how could he have transported it undetected, thousands of miles to the South Pacific Ocean? MN, whilst backing his temple treasure theory, doesn't appear to have put too much thought to this. The problem is, and one only has to look at an atlas for this, there is a great chunk of land called Mexico separating the West Indies and Caribbean Sea from the Pacific Ocean. There was no Panama Canal in those days.

There were two main treasure fleets that left Spain for the New World; the first, the Esquadron de Terra Firme (also known as Los Galeones), made its way to Cartagena and Porto Bello on the top NW coast of South America, while the second, known as the Flota de Nova Espana (Nueva Espana flota), made its way to Vera Cruz. These Fleets were serviced by three other Fleets; The Honduras Fleet, from Trujillo (Caribbean Sea), The South Seas Fleet, from west coast South America (Peru and Equador) and the Manila Galleons Fleet which sailed the immense distance from Manila in the Phillippines. Due to this trade over something like 200 years, Spain became the richest country in Europe if not the world.

The Manila galleons trade brought back from Asia, (probably in exchange for silver minted in Mexico) once landed in Acapulco had to be carried by mule train overland to Vera Cruz. The South Seas Fleet carried silver and gold from South America to Panama. It is worth mentioning here that the 'Cerro Rico' mine (rich mountain) in modern day Bolivia, was for the Spanish, the richest mine of them all. From the mid 1500's in a 200 year period it produced something like 45,000 tons of silver. In Potosi and Lima the silver was turned into reales of different denominations, first as cobs (sheared off a bar) then later milled coinage. Gold was turned into escudos of one, two, four and eight escudos (a doubloon was 2 escudos or 32 reales). Having arrived at Panama, once again it had to be transported by mule train overland to Portobello. To ready themselves for the voyage home, the combined fleets met in Havana then travelled in convoy to Spain. As we have seen, many were lost to storm and hurricanes.

For Ubilla to have sailed to the Pinaki group meant his galleon must have already been in the Pacific Ocean and therefore as part of the South Seas Fleet. This causes something of a problem because If he had a 'religious treasure' secreted from Spain as MN proposes, having landed at Portobello he would have had to transport it across the Panama isthmus and re-loaded onto another galleon. He then went 'sail-about' and was missing for 18 months! Is this all feasible? I don't think so. There are two other more practical scenarios to consider;

1) For the political reasons already mentioned, Ubilla (or another) was captain of one of the galleons travelling from Callao (port of Lima) fully laden with gold and silver coins minted in Potosi and Lima. He made an unofficial detour to the Tuamotus group of islands, settled on Pinaki as an ideal place to bury most of his cargo then headed back to Panama. The distances involved here, at least 8000 nautical miles would explain a long absence. I say most of his cargo as how would he explain an empty ship in Panama? He could also of course have falsified the ships manifest as a cover up.

2) The only other way of explaining a long absence is that Ubilla sailed from the Caribbean down the east coast of South America, around Cape Horn, then back up the west coast of South America calling in at Calleo on the way. He would then have travelled on to Panama or Acapulco. This is the route favoured by the Beeche family (of JF Island) after research carried out by Marc G Errazuriz Beeche. It would be very convenient to call in at JFI on the way to Panama and bury his treasure. But we know that Ubilla (or someone) crossed the Pacific to the Tuamotus group before heading for home. The distance travelled here in total from the Caribbean would amount to something like 14,000 nm and could easily take a year. It is interesting that Mr Beeche says that Ubilla was a Spanish privateer in the service of the Spanish Habsburg Crown. He had travelled almost all the coasts of the Spanish and Portuguese Colonies in the New World pillaging everything in his path. After sailing aimlessly around the South Pacific for two years and with a boat full of treasure he decided to take his large booty back to Spain. However, due to the political upheaval of the time and not wanting to run the risk of attack by other pirates or privateer's, he decided to bury his treasure on the uninhabited island of Juan Fernandez.

The evidence for Ubilla going to Pinaki is the coral block with the Spanish signs. It had to be somebody of high office to have knowledge of the signs. Did he bury a temple treasure here? No, unless something small kept in Ubilla's personal chests and therefore unnoticed by anyone. So I am pretty confident no Holy Grail or golden candlesticks from the temple will be found here. The same applies, of course, to the myth surrounding Rennes-le-Château. You now know the legendary 'religious' treasure here is that to be found by following the clues to Anson's monument.

MN is convinced the 'Holy Grail', whatever that is, and the temple treasures will be found following the clues here. He seems obsessed by them. Indeed he has been calling himself *'The Holy Graal Finder General'* and goes by the name Czar Mike Neon. I think I'm relieved we parted company! But why does he want to hide his identity? I am happy to put my name on the cover of this book.

However, having said all that, it concerns me somewhat that there appears to be a tenuous connection to the Templars and religious articacts, whether they are important relics or items of gold and silver. The only object listed by Webb not attributed to the Royal Mints is '...a guilded trunk containing a rose of gold and emeralds two feet high' Where could this have come from unless pillaged? But as you know, I have shown that this could be a form of code. From the treatment above and in preceeding chapters, you can see that looking at it from a practical common sense point of view, the temple treasures have been consigned to history, certain to be scattered far and wide and as said, mostly melted down. It is this uncertainty about a religious treasure that means for me, a little cloud with 'Templar' on it, whilst almost dissolving, just won't blow away!

Was Ubilla in reality just a renegade Spanish Captain General who rather than let the Spanish Crown have his galleon full of silver, decide to hide it. Did he intend to go back for it one day? He drowned before he got back to Spain so someone was in on his secret and obviously his crew knew where it was buried. We are told that in the archives there is evidence that he admitted to his traitorship, who to? The location of his island was known by the Spanish Crown who passed this information to the English so where did they get it from? It would appear likely a secret letter was entrusted to the Crown by a survivor of the disaster (unlikely) or carried by an officer in a later convoy.

That Diego Alvarez (obviously not his real name) was of the Spanish officer class is certain, but how he came into the possession of unique codes and charts is uncertain. He knew where to go but was his mission to return the treasure to Spain? All we know is that he failed and by fair means or foul, Captain Brown made it his mission to secure the treasure for himself but ultimately ran out of time.

PART 9

CHAPTER 1

THE GATHERING OF CLUES
AND THE MONUMENT CIPHER SOLVED

The Shepherd's Monument, An Enigma Solved

As I believed the solution to the cipher on the monument produced numbers, then an alphanumerical code was employed and there had to be a key or encoding formula to solve it. Clues were found in a book where the author was similarly trying to decipher the code; he came close without realising it. That I happened to have this particular book emphasises the importance of having in your library anything remotely connected with your subject of research. This book was *The Knights Templar in the New World* by William F. Mann (Destiny Books, 2004). The book is a worthy companion to any on your bookshelves that talk about the 'Holy Grail'. William Mann claims to know where Prince Henry Sinclair established a secret settlement in Nova Scotia and hid the Holy Grail there. The location comes from extensive research and his eclectic knowledge of, amongst other things, geometry, history and surveying. His extensive knowledge of Freemasonry was also applied - his great uncle was at one time a Supreme Grand Master of the Knights Templar of Canada. The book is of particular interest to us because he applies his own mind and theories to the mysteries of Rennes-le-Château, Poussin's paintings, Oak Island and other subjects linked to our quest.

In his chapter on Anson and the Shepherd's Monument, he cites a code found in 1786. This was found in a raid by the Bavarian Government upon the house of a Reform Lawyer named Zwack who was a member of a new secret society known as 'The Illuminated Ones'. The raid revealed secret papers connected with the Order, and amongst them was a cipher. It is accepted by many though that the Illuminati were founded in ancient times. It is said they established the Cathars, the Knights Templar and the Alchemists as well as the Freemasons. Adam Weishaupt (1748-1830) is said to have formed this 'new' secret society. He joined the Freemasons in 1774, became disillusioned and founded the Illuminati in 1776. But maybe it should be said then that he revived the Order. It was formed as a secret society within the existing Masonic Lodges. As Freemasonry was then a secret society, the Illuminati was a secret society within a secret society. Weishaupt structured his Order on that of Freemasonry. The colours of this 'new' Order were red and white, the same as those of the Knights Templars, being a red cross on a white background. Red and white are the opposite colours for Alchemy; Red=Male and White=Female. This was identified in Star Codes, so the Illuminated Ones were close to Alchemy.

What is questionable is if Anson could have had any links with what was to become the Illuminati, as it is known this 'new' movement was not founded until 1776, some years after his death. But, the founder Adam Weishaupt had modelled his group to some extent on Freemasonry and some of their membership came from existing Masonic lodges. Quite probable then that Masonic codes and ciphers would have ended up with the Illuminati. That apart, Anson in his role as a naval officer would have been familiar with codes, the methodology being the same even if the codes he used were based on esoteric (secret) knowledge. Also, his high rank would have given him access to codes in circulation up to that time. But the question for me was, 'Would Anson have been familiar with a cipher used later by the Illuminati?' I.e. if *created* by the 'new' Illuminati, Anson could not, of course, have used it.

My research into Weishaupt and the Illuminati led to a book often referred to as *Memoirs Illustrating the History of Jacobinism* by the Abbé Augustin Barruel, a French Jusuit priest (1741-1820). This in fact was a sub-title to the book *Code of the Illuminati*. He cites the same code as used by William Mann in his book mentioned earlier. Talking about the Illuminati, Barruel states, 'For the Novice, the letters to his Superior are to be written in Cipher and he must make himself master of that cipher'. This still didn't answer my question but from further research it became clear this cipher was a variation on a code used in Elizabethan times by the 'Rosicrosse Literacy Society'. They used a number count to denote names and words. Two ciphers were used: the 'Simple Cypher' and the 'Kaye Cypher'. They are as follows:

Simple:

A	B	C	D	E	F	G	H	I	K	L	M
1	2	3	4	5	6	7	8	9	10	11	12

Kaye: 27 28 29 30 31 32 33 34 35 10 11 12

Simple:

N	O	P	Q	R	S	T	U	W	X	Y	Z
13	14	15	16	17	18	19	20	21	22	23	24

Kaye: 13 14 15 16 17 18 19 20 21 22 23 24

Francis Bacon was the Imperator of the Rosicrosse, The Order of the Rosy Cross, (the Rosicrucians). He used this cipher system to denote his own name, which was 100 in the Simple System and 282 in the Kaye System. So letter-numbers were summated to create that person's 'cipher signature' or footprint. Far beyond the 17th century, the descendants of Francis Bacon's school have left their imperishable footprints....all 'absolute in their numbers' attached to their works. Users of this cipher included John Dee and William Shakespeare. So did Anson leave a similar 'footprint' in number form?

The cipher cited by the Abbé Barruel::

A	B	C	D	E	F	G	H	I	K	L	M
12	11	10	9	8	7	6	5	4	3	2	1
N	O	P	Q	R	S	T	U	W	X	Y	Z
13	14	15	16	17	18	19	20	21	22	23	24

The 'Simple' system is exactly that, number substitution 1 to 24 for each letter in alphabetical order, except that I and J share the same number (4), as does U and V (20) (This is because in Elizabethan times, there were only 24 letters in the alphabet, I and J being the same and also U and V). The 'Kaye' system has a different set of numbers for the first 12 letters of the alphabet. You can see that to get their code, all the Illuminati did was to reverse the numbers in the Simple System for the first 12 letters.

'Zwack's' code then is a variation on the earlier Rosicrosse cipher. Here it is with its numerical key as reproduced by William Mann in his book:

A	B	C	D	E	F	G	H	(I	J)	K	L	M
12	13	10	9	8	7	6	5		4	3	2	1
N	O	P	Q	R	S	T	(U | V)		W	X	Y	Z
13	14	15	16	17	18	19		20		21	22	23	24

You can see this is not the same as the Barruel Cipher: B is shown as 13 instead of 11 and 13 is also N! One wonders why; maybe it was meant to be this way. For us, it does not matter. As you will see, it does not alter the end result.

A reminder of the Monument Cipher:

William Mann then went to apply the cipher the following way to the monument's inscription:

O.	U.	O.	S.		V.	A.	V.	V.
14	20	14	18		20	12	20	20

Summated to give: 66   and   72

The **D** and **M** become E and N, deciphered by taking one letter beyond as per Masonic principles. The solution therefore becomes:

REVEARSE 72-66 NE

According to Mr Mann, this meant, 'in order to find the mirror image or reflection of the Rennes-le-Château tomb, found in Poussin's painting, one must apply a diagram with 72 right angles on an axis of 66 degrees pointing northeast.' Although interesting in that NE and the important 72 comes out in his solution, I think we'll leave his theory there for now!

Intelligent guesswork and common sense told me that Anson had hidden the latitude and longitude (his footprint) within the Monuments cipher, so I was looking for two groups of figures comprising two figures for latitude (cannot be greater than 90) and no more than three for longitude (180 maximum). For me, simply applying the Barruel cipher numbers to the first row of letters and summating them gave us:

138

I was almost speechless when I saw that figure appear!

Similarly, D and M become 9 and 1. As they are on a different line from the other letters, this means they are to be used to form a separate value, not just adding to the rest. 9 and 1 then have to be reversed as per the sculpture (also you obviously cannot have a latitude with a figure greater than 90). So this becomes:

19

Now where have we seen those figures before, 19 and 138?

Anson has very cleverly hidden the location of the treasure island group in his monument. This was his cipher 'footprint'.

This is a very cunning use of the cipher as one would expect the 'U' and 'V' on the monument to have two different representations, but they don't; both alphanumerically are 20. Anson no doubt became aware of this variation of the early 'Simple Cipher' through his Masonic connections and used it to great effect on the monument. Besides that, Francis Bacon was Cipherist to the Government so maybe through those connections he became aware of it. He avoided the Kaye Cypher with its added complications and kept it 'simple'. Quite clear then that this is what the monument was for. This was Anson's way of hiding his secret 'chiseled in stone' forever. This is no mere chance or coincidence, the cipher does and *must* produce these figures. Taking everything into account, ***there is no other solution practically possible that makes absolute sense.***

No others have, in their attempts to solve this cipher, thought to apply the obvious (to me!) naval link of latitude and longitude as part of their encoding strategy. Having said that, how could anyone possibly know the 'key' to the cipher and so solve it? Besides that, how could anyone know that the answer was the location of a group of atolls? You would only know that if you knew about Ubilla and Anson's secret expedition. I was successful because I had a good idea what the answer was likely to be. With clues from Mr Mann's book, research and 'reverse engineering', I was able to achieve it. The other outstanding confirmation clue to the decoding is that Webb's report did in fact give a coded reference to latitude and longitude but you have to know of the monument's cipher to recognise it. The text of the Webb's report gives 'Arrived at position lat thirty **D** eight **M**'. Webb via his coded report was just secretly informing Anson that the treasure never left the location as **marked on the monument.**

The 'lat thirty D eight M' tends to get overlooked for what it really is; whilst Anson was probably meant to recognise that 'lat thirty eight' was confirmation of long 138 and 'DM' 19 lat, others took the latitude figure literally. We have seen from a previous chapter that the Salvage Islands are on the same latitude with a search by the Admiralty in 1813. Also searchers assumed the area around Coquimbo was where to look for something: horseshoe shaped bays at 30º 8' lat is an interesting coincidence, or is it? When you are 'in the know' as Anson was, the Webb statement 'Arrived at position lat thirty D eight M' is easily recognised as the location of the Pinaki group of atolls, so why the complicated star code? It is a vexed question or one of ambiguity. It is not something I am too concerned with. I know without doubt where our island is.

Without any of this prior knowledge and insight, however, you would have had to know the 'key' to solve the monument cipher. Did Anson and/or Webb leave any clues to what that key was? If they did, the only possibility I could see was via Webb, with his use of the word 'Rose' in the inventory of the treasure. He was using an agreed code word, confirming to Anson the use of the cipher used by the Rosicrosse Order i.e. a variation of the Simple Cipher. That theory apart, over the years of my research, 'rose', 'rose cross', 'Rosicrucians' and other seemingly obscure reference to the rose have cropped up. You may recall in the earlier Richard Latcham chapter where we talk about Castro's search on Guayacan, he found a copper plate which included, amongst other symbols, a rose. Maybe the 'rose' was a code clue lost and misplaced with time?

Let us stay with this enigmatic monument in an English country garden for a moment.

An Island Wreath?

I mentioned in an earlier chapter that I had a theory regarding the newly created ossuary on top of the tomb in the monument sculpture. Look at the wreath on the front of it. Does not the gap or opening normally appear at the top or bottom? (In Part 7, I showed you a wreath on a Roman tombstone, and the gap is on the bottom.) You can see in this instance, it appears facing east! Why would the sculptor do that? Now reverse it (as per sculpture), and what do we have? A pictorial representation of Pinaki where the pass into the lagoon is to the west. As well as knowing the coordinates of the island, this indicates Anson must have known what it looked like. This is backed up by earlier clues that said the map showed the 'contour' of the island. This therefore must have been part of the original information given by Ubilla. The ossuary then is to show another clue to the island i.e. its shape. The anomaly of the wreath's orientation would have normally been overlooked as visually one might expect to see a wreath on an ossuary without recognising the real intention. A subtle touch, as no one seems to have questioned this before.

You might have observed there is space for another row of letters below the cipher. I will suggest that as the latitude and longitude given did not pinpoint which atoll exactly[1], Anson, not wanting to name Pinaki, (it was named 'Whitsunday' in 1767 by the English explorer Samuel Wallis) decided to disguise a picture of it. As Pinaki Atoll is almost circular, a wreath does it perfectly, identifying this one uniquely shaped atoll in a group of four. Anson then abandoned a written coded descriptive clue (he probably intended it to be 'Horseshoe') of the atoll in favour of this subtle diagrammatic clue. The horseshoe/herradura clue then (with the latitude and longitude) must have originated from Ubilla and has come down from Anson. This clue must have been in the form of a pictorial representation or the atoll was described as 'tiena forma herradura'. If Brown was also aware of this clue then he kept it very much to himself as it is a bit of a giveaway.

[1]Because of the inaccuracies in measuring longitude in those days, Ubilla would not have been able to pinpoint any island/atoll amongst others on the longitude scale with any accuracy and certainly not within the vastness of the South Pacific Ocean, having only the stars to rely on. However, detailed surveying of the atolls in a group and relative to each other could be carried out, provided they were in line of sight. The existence and layout of the four 'blobs' on the Trinity Map suggests that somebody plotted the Pinaki group of atolls and recognised them as being close to the same layout as a Golden Section. We detailed the possible and probable layouts in Part 8.

The Bottom Line

The original cipher inscription then was probably intended to be as follows:

O·U·O·S·V·A·V·V

D·   M·

5 · 14 · 17 · 18 · 8 · 18 · 5 · 14 · 8 ·

The tablet 'blank' was obviously created originally with a three-line inscription in mind. Anson, for whatever reason, decided not to go ahead with the bottom line coded cipher for 'HORSESHOE' and created the wreath pictorial representation instead.

This may go some way to explaining why the letter **D** and **M** are so far apart; in order to use up the space. If they were shown together in the middle, just two lines of characters would have required a much shorter tablet. It is indicative that the third line contained a longer set of characters. The space between D and M adds to the mystery and maybe now it is not such a mystery after all.

The early name for Pinaki was 'Whitsunday'. You could suggest therefore that equally, Anson could have intended *that* name to be on the bottom line. Well no, because the code key does not allow specific numbers for I and U thereby adding unnecessary complications. Also, the atoll did not get that name until after Anson's death.

An enigma, which has baffled thousands for centuries, is now finally solved beyond doubt. **The decoding, with a solution that is obvious when you know what Lord Anson was secretly up to, is the final** proof that 'Treasure Island' does indeed exist, its location hidden in code on the Shepherdess Monument. *This is the missing link for all the stories.*

Take the point also, that this cipher appears nowhere else, only at Anson's ancestral home, defining the link.

Having decoded the monument cipher, it is time now to apply our knowledge to Wilkins' hidden clues.

CHAPTER 2

'FIGURING' OUT WILKINS AND THE CHARTS

The 1947 Book

Coded clues, some solved, some waiting for deciphering, appear throughout this book. The main one, the monument cipher, we have just covered in the last chapter, but there were numbers and letters given by Wilkins as part of the Kidd hoax/riddle which had not been solved. They must have had a meaning, otherwise he would not have given them and, when you know how his mind works, you know he is hiding clues everywhere.

The following is a prime example, but again to be recognised only by those 'who know'. He and his colleagues were having a bit of fun, something along the lines, 'We know and nobody else does! Hee hee!' It was the strange appearance of the series of letters in the 1947 book, *New Facts about Mysterious Captain Kidd and His Skeleton Island Chests* (I covered this book in Part 3) that caught my eye. I remind you of the letters:

EIE KIDD 1670

Using 'Reverse Engineering', it didn't take me long to work it out. The solution is a simple alphanumeric substitution. Employing numbers for the letters and summating them, the group becomes:

$$5\text{-}9\text{-}5 \quad 11\text{-}9\text{-}4\text{-}4 \quad 1670$$

Summate the revealed figures: **19**   28

167 is the key (o being zero to be ignored)
$$167 - 28 = \textbf{139}$$

Well fancy that, 19 and 139! Once again, **the latitude and longitude of the Pinaki group of islands.**

Key Chart and JF Code Revealed

The maps and Kidd/Palmer charts created by the Wilkins/Latcham group we now recognise as part of a fantastic deceptive hoax/riddle. It discloses to you, if you work, read, think and follow Wilkins' clues hard enough, that the correct island sought by all the searchers is actually Pinaki. We make a similar statement at the end of the 'Star Codes' chapter. The Kidd/Palmer charts were very clever and devious in their construction. You think they are leading you to 'Hei Ling Chau' Island off Hong Kong but no, it is JF Island, or is it Bahia Guayacan? Wrong again, it is Pinaki and has been all along. When you know how to apply the information, you can find the clues to Pinaki all over the place.

A methodology apparent so far is that some charts have to be used together. For example, the Kidd 'Skull' chart and 'Key' chart have to be used together to define the (false) location of the traditional spot 'X' (the middle 'T' in TURTLES). This is clever because the geometry and figures (72º NE from the 'ANCHORAGE', for example) taking you to the 'T' (for Treasure) make you believe you have cracked it; this is where the treasure is. But no, when you are aware of the real bigger picture, this geometric line is *pointing* to the word TURTLES, emphasising it i.e. turn the whole thing upside down. This is also why it appears in capital letters. Similarly, the 'Key' chart when inversed has to be seen to really be the old '25cent map' of JF Island. When you put them together, it is obvious. Now the neat trick is to put their latitudes and longitudes together, as follows:

Using the figures as whole numbers;

'Key' chart lat = 9, long = 31
JF chart lat = 33, long = 78
Add latitudes, 9 + 33 = 42, 180 - 42 = **138**
Add longitudes, 31 + 78 = 109, 90 - 109 = **19**
(Notice how '42' appears again).

You may ask, "How do you know to apply the figures this way?" Well in the early days of research, I knew all this was something to do with the lost treasure and knew all the stories were telling me something about Pinaki. As these stories were some riddle to do with Pinaki and we know the lat and long of that atoll, then applying 'reverse engineering' to bearings given in the riddle should create the formula for us. It makes sense to assume there is some formula involved that when 'solved' will give the position of Pinaki. Hence the obvious thing: add the (fake) bearings for the fake map of JF (Key chart), for that is what you are meant to take the hint and realise it is to the real bearings of JF. It was then easy to work out what was required to get the answer of 19 and 138. That and Wilkins' singular clue in his Kidd book about a Spanish Captain sighting the three (now missing) coral ringed 'isles'. (Doubters who say I am trying to make the figures fit should recognise the fact that *they do* fit!)

This riddle/hoax from Wilkins and Co was all so difficult, convoluted and intricate. The only way you could solve it was by 'knowing' things already. To solve it, you had to know it and to know it, you had it solved anyway. But that is how it has been all along in the stories, the little flags put in them by the authors as parts of clues to find the treasure that are signals that only others 'in the know' can identify. You need also to take note of the important instruction Wilkins is giving here, the need to work in and with opposites: North is added to South, Latitude becomes Longitude etc. as per the previous guidance and teachings of Alchemy. Back to the charts:

Charts W1 and W2 Code Revealed

When you know Wilkins is playing with figures, you can take a second look at some of them. In Part 3, we showed you two of his charts; we called them CHART W1 and CHART W2. They obviously depict the same island but contain contradictory information. We look in particular at W2, because as he shows North as South, he is suggesting it is upside down, as is the Kidd 'Key' chart depicting JF.

The directions on the bottom are:

18 W. and by 7 E. on Rock
30 SW. 14 N. Tree
7 by 8 by 4

Summate these to give us a total of 69 on the first and second line, and 19 on the third line. Similar directions on Chart W1 are:

18 NE by 7i W: on Rock.
26 ENE: by 18 SW: Palm
7 feet by 7 feet by 8

Summate these to again give us 69 first and second line with 22 on the third line

From all of this, we are meant to recognise that 69 + 69 = **138**, (from previous doctrine, maps are to be used together)and this together with the **19** once again gives us the ever repeating and recognisable coordinates close to the Pinaki group.

Note also on W1, the compass rose is showing North same as East! On both charts, the pictorial representation of his island is generally the same. You are meant to pick up on the information around the island that is not the same on both. You can now see the 'treasure directions' on both charts are not directions to a treasure on the island at all. Directions yes, but to an island group. Further misinformation on the caption to Chart W1 in Wilkins' book is, *'Found hidden in a sea-chest he gave, in Newgate, 1701, to his bos'n Ned Ward......'*

This we (I) know is complete rubbish! Both of these maps mention Laguna and Corall Bancks. On W2, he spells it Corral! No lagoon or coral on JF so he is drawing your attention to the South Seas where these *can* be found. Also via the spelling of 'Laguna', which is his spelling of Lagoon in French (Lagune). The clue is the spelling in French pointing to French Polynesia where lagoons', coral and Pinaki lies. Staying with 'Laguna' for a moment, on both charts Wilkins gives the clues: *'Landfall Heer'* and on W2; *'Boate Landeth Heer'.* On both charts, arrows point to the coast. Is this Wilkins letting on that perhaps he knows where the treasure burial party landed in the lagoon? This would place the spot somewhere in the south-east vicinity of Pinaki. Somewhere I have previously suggested as a possible location for the treasure.

Another one of Wilkins' map creations that appear in the same chapter as those above even tells us that a Spanish Grandee *'hid treasure in a cache at the back of this Bay in 1716'.* For Bay, you can read lagoon and for Spanish Grandee, you can read Ubilla. This date is very close to when Ubilla went on his clandestine trip. Underneath this appears the cryptic statement, *'It waits to be found by a modern treasure hunter'.* When written, these were 'modern' times for

Wilkins, so a strange statement to make, but not when you know something ulterior is happening. Applying alphanumeric again:

'modern treasure hunter' = MTH = 13, 20, 8.
The figures jump out at you again; **138 and 20.**
T(20) would have been the closest he could get to 19(S) which wouldn't fit into the statement.

Without coming out and actually saying so, through his games and codes, Wilkins is repeatedly pointing a big finger at a little group of islands in the South Pacific.

These two (Charts W1 and W2) groups of directions are obviously a form of code, obvious in that they do point to a specific location when you are familiar with Wilkins' games, but if not a code, what is their purpose? They are pretty useless. For example, 26ENE - what's that?! Shouldn't it be 64NE? The letters are there to confuse, which they do; it is the numbers that are important. And what rock? None shown. Palm! What Palm? There's going to be more than one, I would think! And so on. All this should be waking you up (again) to not believing everything that you see and read, especially if penned by Wilkins. It is a case of, as they say, 'Sorting out the wheat from the chaff', the chaff being nonsense. The mind of Wilkins was strange, cunning and mysterious. You, the reader, should be familiar with it now so did you spot another location clue in his W1 and W2 Charts not yet mentioned to you? I will point it out now if you didn't take note of it. This clue appears on both of these charts as **'Lat dmd'**. Immediately you should have suspected it, as three letters do not give you a latitude which cannot be greater than 90. This clue is, of course, alluding to the Webb letter report. As a reminder, it says (in part):

'Arrived at position lat thirty D eight M'

We know from the previous chapter that **D** and **M** gives us the 19º latitude. Just more confirmation, if you needed it, that Wilkins was familiar with the Webb letters. Not only that, Wilkins was familiar with the cipher Anson used on the monument as dmd i.e. 919 also adds up to 19! So he's making two statements in one and saying, "I know and if you can see it, so do you!"

If we digress slightly and go back to the chiselled boulder marks on Nova Scotia we can now say they should be treated with some suspicion – as with the marks EIEKIDD1670 which do not appear as straightforward as Wilkins makes out. Drawings of the marks are shown in my previous mentioned book on Kidd's charts. Two sets of marks, meaningless to most people, supposedly separate locations, drawn by two different people. I conclude in that book that they are differing interpretations of the same markings. But with the knowledge now possessed we can see that Wilkins could even have been familiar with the Spanish marks on Pinaki.

1671 is one date shown on the boulder, reverse this and 1761 is when Webb was recovering the treasure. An arrow is shown, also a 'L' shape. Just coincidence? I think Wilkins is up to his usual tricks of scattering clues around and showing that he knows all about Anson and his treasure.

Whilst we are talking about the Wilkins maps, let's go back to Part 3 and the chapter on Oak Island. You will recall 'halfe moon bay', This map is so typically Wilkins, full of his embellishments and information to deceive but! once again full of clues recognized only by those ' in the know' about Ubilla and Pinaki.

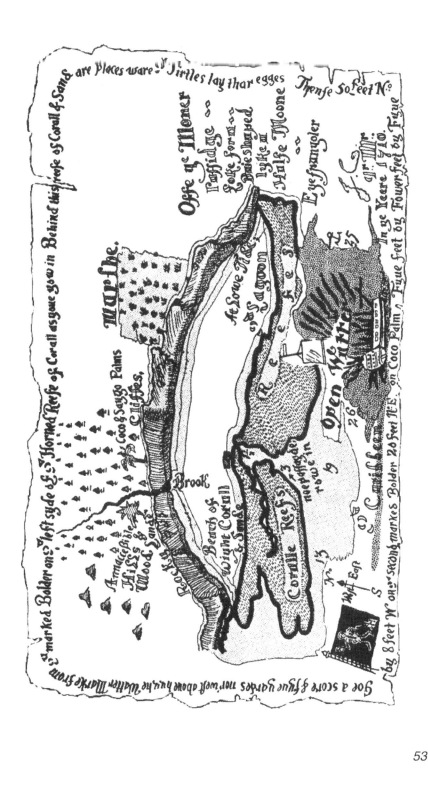

'...a Baie shaped lyke a Halfe Moone'. A clue to the shape of the lagoon on Pinaki.

On the bottom reference to 'markes Boulder 20feet NE''. (Similarly on bottom of 'Key' chart: 'Rocks 20 feet')

'Beach of Wight Corall & Sande'. Can only be Pinaki, not JFI.

'Score & five yards (25 yds. GE) Nor'weft above highe watter marks from marked boulder on left syde of Horned Reefe of corall as you gow in Behind this reefe of Corall & Sand are places ware Turtles lay thar egges Thenfe 50 feet N. (in olde English 's' looked like 'f'. GE). Important clues here, particularly 'marked boulder'. The word 'TURTLES' of course appears on the 'Key' chart.

'Eyefpanyoler' – A Spaniard.

Attempts at a signature 'j C'. Can only be Juan........Ubilla.

'Yr Mr in ye yeere 1710'. The Master in the year 1710. We don't know when Ubilla went on his clandestine trip but it has to be close to 1710.

The other main clue, impossible to miss is the drawing of a ship blowing up, alluding of course to Webb blowing his ship up.

Wilkins is again informing a select few that 'he knows'. The map appeared in 1940, many years before things started happening on JFI with Cousino and Co. Further proof that he had access to the Anson documents before WW2.

No one with any knowledge of maritime history, particularly charts would take Wilkins maps and charts seriously. (but I have to say, some still do!). They are a means to put on record enough information to lead you to Ubilla's treasure once you can decipher and 'read' them. I am not sure if he drew them convinced people would take them as genuine, or did he have a smile on his face when drawing them. The Kidd/Palmer charts were meant to be taken seriously but the others...?

A long standing point of argument has been the figures '?15 SE' on the Skull Chart. I have always maintained they are 515. Even the two different Scrimshaw carvings shown earlier show them as 515. Not a figure of degrees then but one would assume in context that they are paces. But is Wilkins up to his old tricks here again and this is a prompt to the Mar Del maps? Alphanumeric for Roman/Latin DMD is 5001000500!

Not only that, if you refer back to Part 5, chapter 1 and the picture of the stone slab, you will see bottom RH corner the letters LIXLIXL. Assuming these are Roman numerals/letters, they transpose to; 50 1 10 50 1 10 50. You have ask yourself why? Bit of a coincidence isn't it? Or is there in fact a Wilkins connection here!

A question easily raised at some point is if Wilkins and Latcham and co. knew the secret of Pinaki, why didn't they go there? It appears the intervention of WW2, a change in world politics and finally the age of those involved, defeated whatever plans they had. Finance may have also played a part. It would also have been a big undertaking travel-wise to get to Pinaki prior to WW2. After that, we know the entire Pacific was engulfed in the war. Although Hamilton did it, there was a lot of preparation and finance behind that group. We can only begin to speculate but a theory could be of perhaps Freemasons just wanting to continue to pass on clues about the lost treasure to ensure they were not lost but in a way that could only be recognised by other initiates of a certain degree or level or intellectual outlook. This further adds to the reasoning that Wilkins must have been a Freemason.

Another question you may ask is, as the Kidd/Palmer charts were, by their shape and coded clues, really deviously depicting JF Island, were they not planning to go there? This is not easy to answer as the participants all passed away a long time ago. But we can see, Wilkins knew all about Pinaki. JF Island then was for them the starting point, or stepping stone to Pinaki. This is where all the modern day clues originated so you had to go here or know all about the Webb letters and Anson's secret expedition.

On the Rio Grand

The words 'RIO GRANDE' (Big River) were for a long time a puzzle to us. They stand out on the Trinity Map in that they are the only words on it. Being modern English capital letters (and not ancient Spanish), it was obvious to us they were placed there by Wilkins or Latcham. If one accepts the previous assumption that Herradura Bay and Coquimbo Bay are being shown, then indeed a river does actually flow into the bay.

Immediately below the river name are five Hebrew letters. Translated, they are RIOGA. 'RIO GRANDE' is placed just above them to suggest a translated meaning.

Applying the alphanumeric code again, we get·

R=18, I=9, and O=15
G=7 and A=1
RIO summates to 42 and GA summates to 71.
Coniunctio: 42=**138** (longitude)
                    71=**19** (latitude)

This is the <u>only</u> example located for our lost treasure map where the number 71 is given as a cipher for 19º latitude.

Even with 4271 appearing nowhere else, there is ample corroborative evidence that a cipher group of numbers for latitude and longitude did appear on the face of the map. This in part can be explained by saying that if the original was that easy to solve and was known, you wouldn't be reading this book. The main reason though was that a number of factors were operating to cause the numbers to mutate during replication and transmission as time progressed. By identifying what was appearing on maps, you can follow the evolutionary mutations. The appearance of RIOGA immediately suggested an alphanumeric of some kind.

Another stage occurred when the number 42 was known and concentrated on to exclusion of the unworkable number 19. Being mixed in with the original reference to where the treasure was originally at 42º latitude (Compostella) did cause some more confusion because as there is 'no' longitude, this meant 4200, in other words 42º on the prime meridian. Hence Rennes-le-Château (on the Paris prime merididan) and its wayward story flourished.

You may recall from this (Rennes) chapter another positive permutation that showed itself:

180 - 42 = **138** anti (longitude)
42 + 67 = 109 - 90 = **19** agee (latitude)

Earlier on in this book, I mentioned the 'Nautical and Travellers Club' quoted by a lot of authors and researchers as holding documents and one in particular numbered 18,755. This document was supposedly left there by Keating. The problem with this document which they say *'can be found'* at the above premises is that it cannot be found! All that authors and the like are doing is copying the same statement; none of them have gone to these premises and looked at that document. They would have a problem if they tried to as the club and therefore the document doesn't exit. The numbers are in effect two groups: 18 and 755, and are a code. Divide one by the other and we get 41.944. It is easy to see that at some time in the past 755 was copied incorrectly and should have been 756. The answer to the division then becomes 42! I don't think any further comment is required.

You will see later on how 42 does indeed crop up again on the Trinity Map as a hidden clue to Pinaki.

At some stage also the Freemasons were supplied their own cipher group of four numbers. These came from the Anson line of codes because they were based on longitude and the Antares bearing. That cipher group had the numbers 4266 (or 4265). You will see permutations (because close enough was good enough) of it being used as latitude and longitude where the treasure was sought along the east coast of North America. Though they were told it was the key to the map, they weren't told the key to the cipher group itself. That key is the coniuncto, the knowledge that the opposite is required. But even if they didn't know the code key, they did know how to use the map. Remember Captain Allen? He was the Texan whose story we first raised in the chapter about Oak Island. He had used his map for his search in a unique way; each day he went to a position in the Atlantic Ocean of 44N 63W, then sailed on an undisclosed compass bearing towards where he expected to find the treasure island. This direction was described as being north-west of that starting position. You can recognise now that even though his starting position and directional heading seems wrong, he did understand how the map was to be used; possibly start at a point (the map centre) and sail in a particular direction. In this case, you can deduce that possibly his version of the lost treasure map had the Sheperdess' robe shape, which he understood to be an island with a triangle marked on it.

The reason Captain Allen sailed north-west from his starting point was due to the doctrine of Masonic maps being orientated so that east was at the top rather than north. When Captain Allen had aligned the top of his map to the east, the 246 bearing which normally produced a south-west heading from the starting point would then have been showing instead a north-west heading.

Another one of the reasons our friend Captain Kidd has been associated with Nova Scotia is due to the alphanumeric code. K, I, D, D, gives us 11, 9, 4, 4. With 180-119 giving 61, the result of 61W 44N is just another position in this area.

I will remind you of the degree of intellect going on here to side-track you to the real island of Hei Ling Chou (shown how in Part 3):

The latitude and longitude of JF Island is known, so knowing the same for the hidden island (group) a relatively simple subtraction gives the coded latitude and longitude to be used on the (Key) chart. And as we have seen, these coded coordinates somehow also give us the latitude and longitude of HLC Island which just happens to fit the Key chart almost perfectly.

Having found HLC, you are led to believe this island is the end of your search because not only is its size and shape right, its NS orientation[1] is also correct, brilliant! But it is just a dead-end for the unwary. Wilkins, as I have suggested is guiding you here to take you away from JF Island. By putting the give-away clue 'China Sea' on the charts, Wilkins is also suggesting to you that you've got it right. Or is he guiding you to JF to take you away from Pinaki? (You will see later that Wilkins is also giving another clue to Pinaki on the Key Chart.) As previously said, Wilkins was very devious.

Harold T. Wilkins passed away in 1962. Some critics have dismissed his books and writings as the rantings of an eccentric. There is no doubt he was a brilliant academic but a lot of what he has done is, as we have seen questionable and only as a result of subsequent extensive research and investigation. The majority of his readers would have had no reason to question his writings and it has to be said they would have thoroughly enjoyed his stories of mystery, pirates and treasure in far flung places. If you can read a book, put it down and say, "That was good," then you have satisfied the author and yourself. Wilkins was the prime source of the information about the Kidd/Palmer charts, and strange-related maps. In league with others, he created one of the world's best treasure chart mysteries that have fooled many for over 70 years. He could at any time have disclosed what he knew to silence his critics, but he chose not to. What strength of mind did it take for him to approach his end silent, choosing to put his trust in his plan that someone, someday might begin to see within the confusion of his stories the clues, hints and hidden directions leading to the map showing where Ubilla buried his treasure?

Back to related mysteries. Back in Part 3, I mentioned Wilkins' connection with Japan and a latitude figure that would be important. That figure was 139, which you are now very familiar with. It is the east latitude of Mount Akagi on Japan. In the 1880s, a mysterious American followed codes and a map to seek out a treasure on the slopes of Mt Akagi. Now known as the Tokugawa Treasure Legend, he never found anything because this was just another misinterpretation and application of our lost treasure clues.

In Part 1, I told you of a search on the Salvage Islands and how one expedition had found a copper coin with the four points of the compass and a letter 'N' at every point. Most would be completely baffled by this, unless you were familiar with the Spanish Code. Employing our knowledge of the code (if that is what is being used), the message it is giving could be, 'go NE 23 varas', from the following decoding:

N= 16, 4 x 16 = 64, plus 2 for the +, equals 66, nothing in the Spanish Code you can use utilizing 66 so must be something else;
N is constructed out of I+V (they often did this) i.e. 1 + 5 = 6, 6=E, so we have N+E i.e. NE.
Assuming the points of the compass are in the form of a cross +; The Spanish use the 'T' as a cross and sometimes the + as a 'T', and T is 23!
A vara is 30 American inches, 23 x 30 = 57.50 feet.

So they should have been looking 57/58 feet NE from where they were, or maybe 66 varas. But notice how NE rears its head again!

[1]Those searchers that think the charts are real tend to ignore this important aspect of island orientation.

CHAPTER 3

THE MAJOR CLUES AND MISSING MERIDIANS

All the clues revealed are just confirming what we believed at the beginning that Pinaki atoll is where a great treasure is buried. I don't know where exactly; that will depend on finding the 'great block of coral' with the Spanish signs and the correct interpretation of them. The clue 'NE', as you know, continually repeats itself so we know where on the atoll to start. My suspicions are, from previous doctrine suggested, that if nothing comes to light there, then the place to look is at the SE part of the atoll.

Some may say if you knew at the beginning it was Pinaki, why this book? Why all this work? Well besides being a fascinating research adventure, I had to confirm that Pinaki was the right atoll. You have seen so far how different expeditions went all over the archipelago as Pinaki was never actually identified as *the* island. All the numerical clues identified the Pinaki *group* of atolls but which atoll in that group is the right one? Answering this question is what a lot of the book is about. I also wanted to answer the questions why, who and when?

Major clues came only through diligent research. You can look on these clues as the scattered loose links of a broken chain (all of the scattered clues which were accumulated are far too numerous to recount here). Each individual link is seemingly solid on its own, as is the evidence and story it represents. For me, it was like exploring the rooms of an old house; you open one room to find others leading off, then you have to see where they go, only to be led off down other passages, and these all had to be examined. Some clues showed themselves as we opened doors; the Freemasons, the Templars and Solomon, for example, but for others I had to search. Only when linked back together could you see what the completed chain was representing; the completion of a literary research journey showing why and how, the way to a hidden treasure. Not only hidden physically by being buried, but also by being hidden behind the facade of ingenuity, deviousness, human greed and treasure stories, distorted and mutated by time.

Let us recap briefly on the **major** clues, first of all those that confirmed the group of atolls:

a) The most satisfying deciphering of all of the clues, that on the Shepherd's Monument at Lord Anson's ancestral home. This was the vital confirmation of the atoll's location and that the treasure was real. We were led here two ways, one via;

b) Westacott's Spanish book which told of the Cousino search on Juan Fernandez Island and the Webb letters. This is turn led us to;

c) Latcham's book, again in Spanish, which gave us diagrammatic clues and the 'Trinity Map' with its Golden Section triangle clue that showed the angular divergence between the atolls. This book also helped to confirm the shape of the atoll via;

d) Herradura Bay, Guayacan, the Spanish word 'herradura' we know means 'horseshoe', the geographical shape of the atoll.

e) The word 'horseshoe' linked us back to the Webb letters which spoke of the 'Horseshoe Expedition'.

f) The second way we were led to the 'Shepherd's Monument' was by way of Poussin's painting and the Rennes-le-Château mystery. I like to think *that* mystery has been cleared up as well!

g) The recognised collusion between Wilkins and Latcham produced wonderous clues. Whilst Latcham may or may not have been complicit in the Kidd/Palmer charts hoax, he more than likely kept things alive in Chile and South America between him, Wilkins and the Cousino group.

h) Wilkins' clues abound in his books, all leading by devious ways to the Pinaki group of atolls.

So which are the **major** clues that define Pinaki in particular as our treasure island? Very few, in fact probably no more than five:

a) Charles Howe. There must have been very convincing map clues given by Brown (Killorain) for him to spend 13 years on Pinaki. He was visited here by Nordhoff who provided the major clue;

b) The coral block, or rock (DNA) with the Spanish signs. Had Howe known what they were, he would have stayed here. We recognised them as markers to a treasure that could only have been on **this** atoll.

c) The 'horseshoe' DNA (herradura) clue that repeats itself. Only one atoll in the group has this unique shape - Pinaki!

d) The orientation of the wreath on the ossuary, duplicating that of Pinaki, also its shape, subtle subterfuge by Anson.

e) A descriptive view of the atoll: *'All that was visible was a long line of foam and the dark jungle of vegetation behind. The usual coral atoll, a narrow ring of land encircling a lagoon, barren of all but coconuts and scrub'.*

Howe cannot have known either of the 'horseshoe' clue or he wouldn't have gone to Hiti which is oval with no recognisable openings akin to that of a horseshoe. The only reason he would have gone there as discussed previously is because of the trinity DNA (three atolls in a compact group), an angular/bearing mix-up and/or the shape of the atoll at its NW corner, but by virtue of what they are, most atolls have this same shape. Very few have just **one** obvious opening/pass at WSW as on Pinaki.

The same can be said of the Hamilton Expedition. They started their search on Hiti (called 'Tatee' by them) before settling on Tuanaki. You may also recall that a descendant of Hamilton made an unsuccessful attempt to recover the treasure from Tepoto where he believed the treasure had been relocated. Tepoto is 10 nm SW of Hiti and part of that three-island group. What information did he have that decided this was the place to search?

The above raises a question about the map used by the searchers, which research tells us showed a 'contour'. The question is, 'part contour or full shape'? If using the same map that Anson was privy to, then obviously the map showed the full contour of the atoll.

The Irregularity of 139

The decoded location clues caused me something of a predicament. 138,19 or 139,19 which is what is decoded out from the various clues i.e. two sets of figures. MN's answer to that, as we have seen, was that 138/19 is representing a datum point for the centre of the Trinity Map. You then sail 246 to the Golden Section Triangle (a four atoll group with Pinaki offset below). If you find 139/19, this is for the Trinity (three atoll group including Pinaki). Whilst the latitude is constant at 19, the longitude has a 1 degree difference. Figuratively not a lot, but in practice, as we have seen in a previous chapter it represents 57 nautical miles. This throws a big question mark on the theory that from this position out (138, 19) a 246 or 244 bearing was taken to the atolls (240º actual to Pinaki). In practice you would just not be able to do this. For clear observation, you would have to be elevated and at the most, within about 15nm. maximum, particularly as these are low atolls.

The location clue that Anson and/or Ubilla left was as we know 138/19 and this, as we have seen on modern charts, pinpoints a location in open water 44nm from Pinaki. I would suggest it is evident then this can only be due to the inaccuracies in the measurement of longitude in those days. The decoded 19 always comes out at that because there was no problem with measuring latitude at that time. 139 appears because a lot of the decoding methods (star codes, for example) were not precise and 139 degrees is close enough because once we get there, we know where we are going. But, when they (Ubilla and Co) were on Pinaki taking sun and star measurements possibly with a backstaff (or Davis Quadrant as it was sometimes called), 138 is what they got and to be within 1 degree is quite good; inaccuracies of 2 degrees or more was the norm then. So if we take the above as being the case, of what use is the 246 or any other bearing? We don't need it, as once we are in the Pinaki group, as I have said before, we know which one of them is our atoll! I would suggest then maybe 246/244 was not part of the original (chart navigation) clues supplied by Ubilla but maybe something added at a later date or a misinterpretation by MN.

Latcham we know had a hand in the Trinity Map and if he also correctly and accurately plotted the Pinaki group using the 138 and 139 longitudes in the same manner I did in an earlier chapter, it could be that he thought a 244º30 bearing would help in identifying Pinaki. I don't know and we are, of course, assuming that the 116 line on the Trinity Map is important because it goes through the Golden Section Group. Perhaps it is meaningless as some other lines appear to be and has been taken out of context.

The above caused major unrest in the Edmunds/MN ranks because 246 was important to MN's theories (more on this later). This radial line is measured from the centre of the Trinity Map, MN in turn equates this centre point to 138 out in the ocean and also the centre (finger point) of the Shepherd's Monument. I am just trying to be practical regarding navigation of the time. What you have to keep clear in your mind is that Ubilla when on Pinaki by his own measurements thought he was at 138/19. He wasn't; he was at 139/19, or 138º40'/19, to be more precise using today's satellite technology.

Whilst on this subject, another interesting point is that Wilkins in his Kidd charts/JF Island hoax also gives us 138/19 when applying the key of adding opposites etc., but why didn't he fix it so that 139, 19 was the solution, 139 being closer to Pinaki as depicted on modern charts? It could only be that he knew 138, 19 was the required answer, so this is more proof that he must have been privy to the original Anson documents.

I am now going to open another can of worms regarding 138/139 and 246 that challenges some previous thinking.

The Missing Meridian

Those of you astute and with knowledge of 17th and 18th century navigation will have already been saying to yourself (and shouting at me), "It can't be 138º longitude because that is assuming Greenwich was used, when of course in those days the Spanish used Cadiz as their meridian!" You are right, of course. For Ubilla, Cadiz would have been at approximately 6º 30' West, so the real longitude that he arrived at was 138-6.5 = 131º30'. Bells should be ringing now; where have you seen that before? Well early on in this book, I showed you a Wilkins/Spanish clue; 'three coral-ringed and lofty isles' at 131º22'E. But more importantly on the Kidd/Palmer Key chart, these figures now jump out at you:

\ε   ' σ
                                    ϲ   ʟoɴɢ ÷3ıɴ0 ε
ʟᴀᴛ Ϩ.ℓ6 ɴ

Behind all the façade, Wilkins has all along deviously included the position of Pinaki (relative to Cadiz) on the Key chart. By putting '1' in front of the 9 and 3, we have 19.16 and 131.30 (remember his previous key of 100?), very close to today's GPS figures of 19º23' and 132º23'; discrepancies due to inaccuracies when taking measurements in the 17th and 18th centuries. If you want to play around with figures a bit more, use the quoted 139. Take today's Cadiz meridian of 6º17' off and we get 131º 43'. So whichever way you want to work it, Wilkins was in on it!

Those playing with and puzzling over the Kidd/Palmer chart figures and then associating them with JF Island (if you were clever) or any other island, would not have had a clue (excise the pun) that hidden within them were the coordinates of Pinaki. This is understandable because no one would have had any reason to suspect that a small atoll in the South Pacific Ocean would have had anything to do with Captain Kidd. You would only know of Wilkins' intent if you were aware that Pinaki was the final answer. Inject the key word 'Spanish' and therefore the Cadiz meridian, put two and two together, and the answer would be recognised by those in the know. To confuse things further, he has reversed N and E i.e. they should be S and W respectively (work in opposites). You may also recall in the chapter on the Key Chart solution that the code key was to add 100 to the figures shown which give us 131º30'. Very clever, for whilst sidetracking you to HLC Island, the longitude of Pinaki is there for those able to recognise it. (Nobody did!)

Alternatively, Wilkins was saying, 'The key is you put 1 in front of the 9 to get the correct latitude and also 1 in front of 31.30 to get the correct longitude.'

You would now be saying to yourself, 'If Ubilla supplied a longitude position of 131º30', why do all the clues provide 138/139?' The answer is quite logical and straight forward. Ubilla gave 131 or 131-30 to the Royal Society. Anson, when setting up his expedition, converted it to the meridian the English used at that time i.e. London, by adding the difference in meridians, hence 138.

The above is further evidence that Wilkins when utilising Cadiz in this particular code was aware of the Spanish connection and therefore aware of the Ubilla/Pinaki connection. In other words, as previously declared, further proof he must have seen the original Webb documents or a transcript of them.

The Trinity Map, another Look

Knowing the original figures for the location were arrived at using the Cadiz meridian now creates what has to be the real depiction of the radial lines on the Trinity Map. We orientate it so that east is now north as the Key chart clue (North same as E) and doctrine tells us. The radial lines on the derrotero (Spanish chart/waybill/map) now equate to (or represent) longitude lines i.e. the angular measurement from north is the longitude, the centre/north of the map equating to Cadiz.

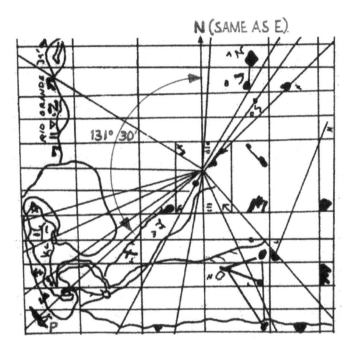

You can see from the above that 131º30′ west falls just about exactly on the line taking you through the ship, entry into what could be a lagoon and a (black) profile of Pinaki at sea level. Note how the pass into the lagoon is now orientated correctly i.e. SW.

If we now take the same map orientated with north at its diagrammatic top, there is another interesting revelation.

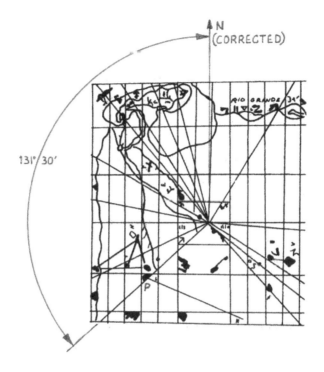

Again, 131º30′ just about falls exactly on the radial line with a 'blob' on it (P). I have previously identified this as probably representing Pinaki. What else can it be?

So here we have what has to be the correct interpretation of the Trinity Map, possibly 4 maps in one;

1) The angular (longitude) location of Pinaki can be measured.
2) A descriptive/diagrammatic clue of the atoll's shape.
3) The GR triangle showing the atoll group layout.
4) Maybe the grid lines some sort of clue to the treasure's location that is beyond me at the moment.

From the above, you can see what has to be the meaning of these two radial lines. Do not forget also in Part 8, I showed you how the right angle between them provided the setting for a G.R. Rectangle. I made a comment at that time; *'There has to be a reason for just two lines exactly at right angles'.* Those of you geometrically astute will be aware that if you turn the 131.30 arc 90º from E to N, the 'P' line separated by 90º on the same centre is bound to be 131º 30´ from N. You are just rotating the angular set-up. Even allowing for any possible draughtsmanship errors, time, distortion, reprinting and copying, the geometry is too precise to be coincidental.

So what are the others radial lines for? If the Spanish drew this, then utilising the Spanish Code may provide an answer as follows: There are 16 lines, the 16th letter of the Spanish alphabet is N, of these six extend outside the boundary of the map. The sixth letter of the Spanish alphabet is E. So again, the message is Northeast. Or are they just lines of confusion purposely included by Latcham?

One would suspect that as the Cadiz longitude (131.30) is shown on the Trinity Map as described above, then where is the latitude? What line is representing 19º(30')? Having measured them all with some accuracy, there is no 19º(30') angular relationship to a recognisable starting point i.e. one would assume at right angles to where longitude is measured from. The only possibility I could see was taking me back to the 'odd' line at the bottom, the only one that does not radiate from the centre. It does intersect the 'blob' that can be recognised as representing Pinaki (see also the GR Layout 2 in Part 7). This line is at approximately 21º to the horizontal. 1½º is a fine line of difference when you draw the two together. Maybe 19½º (a more precise position for Pinaki) when drawn or redrawn wasn't as accurate as it should have been. I can back up this theory as follows. Referring back to the previous Trinity Map diagram, this blob sits on a radial line which we have discovered is representing by angular measurement the distance from Cadiz to Pinaki. Now measure the angle of this radial line from the bottom horizontal baseline (the obtuse angle), and what do we get - 138º! Too precise to be other than what these lines are intended to be i.e. to give you the longitude of Pinaki and by rote the latitude. You may also recall this line is dual purpose in that it originally gave me the clue to a G.R. (nautical spiral) rectangle that pinpointed a possible landing place. Another possible clue that this line represents latitude is the small 'L' on it adjacent to the Pinaki 'blob'.

I mentioned earlier that 42 appears again as a clue on this map, the (acute) angle adjacent to 138 is, of course, 180-138=42! In other words, whenever 42 appears, via working in opposites, it is really giving you the longitude of Pinaki.

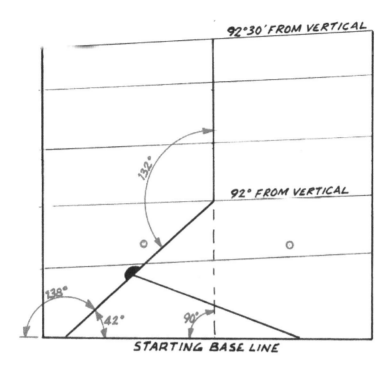

The above diagram defines these principle lines on the Trinity Map with the 'blob' obviously representing Pinaki. You could say they are a geometrical code, the key being 'measure the angles'. Two major clues defining Pinaki; 138 and 42 with that same radial line representing the angular distance from Cadiz. (131.30 can, due to the inaccuracies of measurement, be said to be 132.)

All of this proves that the Trinity Map is of Spanish origin and comes from the Ubilla line. Latcham more than likely had a hand in its current appearance. That the map, or a copy of it, was given to him by Wilkins is evident. Maybe with its publication in Latcham's book, Wilkins was hoping someone could sort out what it was all about. Whilst he knew the importance of 131 and Cadiz, did he relate that figure to the map? I somehow doubt it. Nowhere in his writings does Wilkins mention this map, he kept it pretty close to his chest. The only mention we have of it, outside Latcham's book, is amongst the 'Horseshoe' expedition papers sent by Webb to Anson; *'The map of a bay "Pascoy" with many lines, one indicating a point on the coast where the answer can be found.....'*

MN, Latcham, Wilkins and everyone else totally overlooked the above angular solution. If MN had stayed the course and stuck with me, he would have seen the real solution to the Trinity Map.

The previous diagram also demonstrates that when viewing the Trinity Map, the centre vertical line appears offset to the right. It is an allusion created by the horizontal lines not being at right angles to the vertical. The baseline is the correct starting point because we know this creates the required 138/42. The centre vertical line **is** at right angles to it.

You will notice in the previous diagram two small circles. These are replicating two small circles on the Trinity Map. They are the *only* two small circles. Again, you ask the question, "Why are they there?" By measurement, they are exactly parallel to the defined baseline. This rang a bell with me because it was a very similar pair of small circles on the Kidd 'Key' Chart that enabled me to solve the geometric clues on that chart. (See the Key Chart solution diagram at the end of this chapter.) If my suspicions are correct, then Wilkins and/or Latcham either copied these Trinity Map circles to define the correct lining up of the 'Key' chart, or he put them on the Trinity Map to do the same thing to that map. These two sets of circles are too similar in their application to be a coincidence. They do not do anything else other than that described. More evidence then that Wilkins was familiar with both charts. But, if I wanted to throw a spanner in the works, here I could say that in the Spanish Code, two circles represent two caves or hiding places.

246 as a Prime Number

Back to 246 as applied to the Trinity Map, and if it is important as MN implied. It appears numerically early on as Antares in the Webb coded report and later as a measured (inaccurately by MN) angle on the Trinity Map. You may need a reminder how Antares becomes 246. It is as follows.

You may recall Wilkins' 'PRISTARIUS' clue. This meant 'Prime Star Scorpius' and the Prime star in that constellation is Antares. Today's Star Charts give a RA (Right Ascension) value for Antares of just under 16 hours and 30 minutes. This, as a proportion of the total (24 hours), equates as the same proportion of 360º and is approximately 247º. It varies a couple of degrees depending when the observations were made. (We have seen via MN that it can also be read as 245/115.) 247 gives us a SHA of 113º which is the approximate value from the Star Almanac Table. Adding this figure to the declination (26º) gives the all important 139 figure for the Trinity group.

So is the radial line passing through the GR Triangle related to the Antares 246/7 as MN said? Fact is, you don't need both! It exists as a factor of Antares; you don't need the Trinity Map. Or is it on the Trinity Map because within a couple of degrees, it *is* a factor of Antares? Knowing now that the baseline of the Trinity Map is at right angles to the north line shown, an accurate measurement of the line passing through the GR Triangle Is closer to 116º than anything else. This, of course, equates to 244º, not 246 as a value or 247. Should not the line therefore measure 247º (or 113º) from north to conform to the star code? It doesn't, and a 3º angular difference is a lot. It could throw more doubt therefore (see previous *The Irregularity of 139* section) on the theory that the line is there as a pointer to Antares or as a measurement (or transit) from a point in the ocean (138) to Pinaki. But, it is a conundrum of numbers, the values vary with when, how they were taken, the interpretation of them, and rounding up or down. At the end of the day, it doesn't really matter, there's nothing to argue about; we know where our island/atoll is!

This treatise is here to cover the gaps for you, the reader, should you have raised the question yourselves. For example, if that line wasn't on the Trinity Map, would it make any difference? Only to the expounded theories that you must; 'from somewhere, measure an angle to somewhere'. You can look at it another way; if we didn't have the Antares star code clue, could we get the information from the Trinity Map? No, because there is no way *that* map is telling you that any of the lines represents a star and if it was, how would you know which one to use?

To the End of the Line (Map)

The symbols to the bottom right of the map are mystifying. What are they saying? Is that a 'Z' or is it a 'N', with the black diamond pointing to North? (North same as East.) In the Spanish Code, a filled-in diamond represents one league or 3 nautical miles (the early Spanish legua was equivalent to about 2.6 miles). The round blob linked to it is one of the symbols for a cave. But the message 'cave NE, 3 nautical miles' doesn't fit in with Pinaki. If a Spanish code, there is another possible interpretation: a blob attached to a line means 'feet'. A league symbol doesn't apply here so the 'N' could be saying '16' or if a 'Z' - 28. So 16 or 28 feet East. There are several strange shapes on this map, they remain a mystery, unless they are meant to confuse. I believe this map is a part-copy of an original Spanish map, so who knows if anything has been added or left off, and for what reasons?

So, 138/139/131/132, and seemingly meaningless strange shapes and lines. One can argue, postulate and theorise all day long, as previously declared. But it would have been good to tie in what is on the Trinity Map with what we know and confirm the author's/ creator's intentions. As you can see, we have already gone a long way to achieving this. There are maybe more discoveries to be made regarding this map but we have to stop somewhere, and anyway, I think I have more than demonstrated its purpose.

The same applies to the crazy drawings in Latcham's book. What information, if any, is hidden within them that can further our quest? Only the treasure location; I doubt if he knew it. If he did, then because of their collaboration, Wilkins would have known it. Brown knew it, of course, and gave misdirections to Howe. Keating, we suspect, was the only other person who knew the location. It brings us back to Wilkins. He was privy, as we have proved, to the original Anson documents found before WW2. If whoever buried the treasure followed the Spanish doctrine for retrieval, then that surely would be directions to the coral block, as the final directions were carved into that block. Any directions then on the original derrotero would have been known by Wilkins, but it is not obvious in any of his work that he is giving clues to a location on Pinaki, just the island itself. It could be then that there were no directions, just clues to the island/atoll location that contained, via the coral block, the treasure location. The atoll is small so shouldn't take anyone too long to find the all-important coral block. You know where to start the search; NE part of the atoll! This would have been the only location clue on the original map and is why it has repeated itself in many coded and disguised forms since. Ubilla was indicating where on the atoll to look for the coral block/rock.

Further confirmation the Trinity Map is a treasure map lies in the probable interpretation of the rectangle drawn in the centre of the map. The Spanish code has two meanings for this; a box and treasure. A black blob (as shown on the map) in a rectangle is saying 'gold buried in box or chest' or chamber. Out of interest, a heart in a rectangle means 'King's Treasure'.

A Summary of the Clues

This is as good a place as any to briefly group together the main clues documented over time, both in this book and elsewhere, that relate to our quest. At the same time, it helps to remind you of them and the fascinating stories they are part of:

- From early on, 'The Horseshoe' and 'Herradura' clues, and also various part-enclosed bays, islands and atolls.
- The Genesis event of Webb dying, leaving a map and clues. This spawned many other similar and traditional stories, notably the dying Killorain leaving a map to Howe.
- 138, 139, 19, 42, many times.
- Relocation (of treasure) and 're-buried' clue in various forms, notably from Cocos.
- A list of treasure in various guises as follows:
  - 14 tons of gold ingots, golden candlesticks, necklaces of diamonds etc.
  - 4 tons of gold, huge quantity of pearls, diamonds and amethysts, all in metal caskets.
  - 30 kilo ingots in seven chests. Inca gold, wedge-shaped ingots.
  - Church relics, coin, gold and silver ornaments.
  - Coins, bullion, church plate and jewellery.
- The Webb inventory of (real) treasure.
- Location and burial clues in various forms as follows:
  - Two days and 30 trips in longboats (Cocos). Four weeks to land treasure because of surf and shallow reefs.
  - No pass deep enough to admit schooner.
  - Lonely little atoll, coral, small, deserted, scant vegetation, in the Tuamoto group.
  - Located in a hollow not too far from the sea. Excavated a cave. Cave in cliff.

- Three or four steps made down to cave, two or three chambers constructed for diversion of treasure.
- Brown - Face of cliff blown down to hide location, no cliffs on Pinakil
- Sailing mark, Sugarloaf (Pan de Azucar), Church Rock, Coral Pinnacle/Column.
- White beach, Playa Blanca.
- Taken to Δ (Trinity) Land, Trinidada, Triangle, Golden Ratio.
- Three cairns, three peaks, three mountains, three dots, three islands, three circles, La Trinidad, Cerro tres Puntas.
- 84ft E by N and 75ft N by E (from? GE). NE recurring. NE by E ½ E.
- 'Keating looked at the chart and read how the treasure hunter should proceed to the north-east part of the island.'
- North same as East. NE, many times.
- 'Apparently he (Alvarez) had distorted the directions'.

- Several stories of old charts/papers/documents found in an old house in England - 'an epic written on ancient parchment - an heirloom of an old county family'. All alluding to Anson and the family home.
- A rock marked with hieroglyphics, Ebanin, Rock with strange markings. 'Mysterious marks would be found carved on one of the reefs'.
- 'Marks on the rock' - Admiral Robinson expedition.
- Angular clues: 36, 72, 42, 76, 246/7.
- 1.6183, 1681, 44106813, 681, 16081, all alluding to the Golden Ratio.
- The Holy Grail (Graal), Jerusalem, Solomon, Menorah, Templars.
- Poussin's painting and Rennes-le-Château.
- The stone slabs at Rennes-le-Château.
- The Rennes 'ANSION' emblem/symbol.
- The Shepherd's Monument.
- The continuing teachings, beliefs and practices of Freemasonry that hide the secret of/way to a (Templar) treasure.

- Hints to star constellations.
- The Kidd charts trail that ultimately leads to Pinaki.
- The Shepherd's Monument with its defining clue
- The final solution of the Trinity Map identifying the Pinaki group of atolls.

A précised selection of the major clues written, documented and passed down over the last 200 years. There are probably many more yet to be found.

I would guess also that possibly one of the original map clues was an indication of the atoll size. Besides its unique shape, Pinaki is small by comparison to most atolls; it would fit into a circle 1.25 miles in diameter. You would think then that this atoll is very inconspicuous, tiny when compared to the thousands of other atolls and islands on the planet. You couldn't name them all on something 59cm x 35cm, the size of a desk chart/atlas of the world, such as I have on my desk. I find it very strange then that a lot of these atlases and globes do just that; they show and name Pinaki! Why don't they name the other same-size atolls or islands that are bigger?

So our treasure island is very much in the public domain; it is there, **the** Treasure Island, pinpointed for all the world to see!

A lot of you will be asking "Why can't B Keiser the searcher on JFI 'see' it also?" A good question. Why does he keep pouring money into a bottomless pit? Maybe if he reads this book he will stop because he is not aware of the research and revelations in these pages prior to reading it. Well not strictly true, if you recall at the beginning of this book we did communicate with him suggesting he may have interpreted some information incorrectly. But it was ignored. He should be asking 'What evidence is there that Ubilla buried anything here and that Webb recovered it and reburied again here?' Because there is no hard factual evidence any of this happened. The only documents that tell of the venture – the Webb letters, make no mention of JFI. Because 'valley of Anson' is mentioned and this appears on later maps, Keiser has assumed it can only be JFI. If there was any evidence – and this huge treasure was really there, why hasn't he found any trace of it? He should really be asking himself that question after what, - at least 12 years of searching with no results.

According to Keiser, in 1761 Webb found Ubilla's gold hidden inside a tunnel of mountain rock. Webb carved the name 'ANSON' into the wall. Keiser points out an 'S' shaped design and 3 holes, all evidence he says that Webb was here. We know he had problems with his ship so returned and reburied the treasure at a location near the original cave. (known as Robinson Crusoe's cave).

None of the above is proof Webb was on JFI. I think Keiser is taking liberties with the story here; we know Anson was here in 1741 so he or any of his crew could have made the marks – or anybody else wanting to make their mark, as people do.

The 3 holes are interesting, - in the form of a triangle! Maybe Ubilla, after burying his gold on Pinaki called here and made these marks as a clue. Who knows and why are they there?

In an original version of one of the Webb letters is the (part) statement.....'new hiding place valley of Anson a cable length from the observation point....' So knowing what we now know this could mean that the treasure is 202 yards (cable) from the block of coral (observation point). 'valley of Anson' mentioned as a ruse, as why mention 'Valley of Anson' when Webb never went there?

The above directions *could* have been meant to be read slightly different. If you recal, Webb's letter was almost certainly in Latin. The copies that Wilkins came across may not have been original but already translated. Whatever version ended up in Coulsin's hands was itself translated again into Spanish, then English. Easy then to appreciate that the final accepted version commonly used reads differently to that on the original document penned by Webb. By including the location code in his letter it makes sense that Webb would include(confirm) the treasure location also. Look again at the (part) sentence in Webb's letter that says; '.....*a cable length from the observation point in direction great yellow stone depth fifteen feet.*'

Due to loss in several attempts in translation this could have been meant to read; '....*a cable length from the great yellow stone observation point depth 15 feet.*'

Makes more sense doesn't it? The 'great yellow stone' is of course our block of coral with the marks on it. Should the marks on the block be erased or worn off, it could be a sensible thing to do to start searching 202 yards away. The Spanish code after all will be telling you the place to dig is a certain distance from the block. To see if this figure could be representative of a Spanish code length I calculated it to be equal to 22 imperial inches, achieved as follows;

Cable=607.6ft ÷ 2.5(2.5ft=1Vara) = 243 Varas = 24.3 Spanish inches (1 Spanish inch represents 10 varas) x .914 = 22 inches imperial.

So you would be looking for a linear mark(s) 22 inches long if the above proposition were true.

(This exercise is included to also remind you how to convert a measured Spanish code length to a real measurable distance)

To believe another scenario, that Webb recovered the treasure from JFI and then reburied it on Pinaki requires you to believe the Spanish never noticed anything untoward going on on the island and never noticed an English ship anchored off there for a few days! So I must point out again, it is obvious that Keiser and the other believers are ignoring the fact that – as pointed out earlier in this book - when Webb supposedly visited JFI in 1761, the island was already occupied by the Spanish. I fail to see how two visits by Webb (as stated by Keiser) in an English ship would go unnoticed by the occupiers, his enemy!

Not only that, JFI has been the haunt of pirates and corsairs, especially the English and French for hundreds of years.

Something else that Mr Keiser and his followers are overlooking is that Webb's expedition was called the ' Expedicion Herradura'. Chosen for obvious reasons; the lagoon on Pinaki is roughly horseshoe shaped. Keiser doesn't appear to have put too much thought to that as there is nothing on JFI that can relate to that shape i.e. no connection there. As an intelligent man I am sure he must have questioned the title and probably assumed it related to the similarly shaped bays on the Chile coast close to Coquimbo. This where the untrue story takes place of Cousino finding a box containing Webb's letter. Let's face it, If you want to get an important letter to England's highest authority in the Navy, you are not going to put it in a box and bury it on a remote beach where it may never be found, are you?

I of course benefit from the knowledge that the treasure is buried on Pinaki and of those as yet unaware of my revelations there are many that are not convinced by Keiser's story. An example of one of these, and one with some 'clout' in this business is Robert Marx. He is

American and lives in Florida. Now in his eighties he is known as the world's most successful treasure hunter. Of Keiser's claims he says (sic) "I guarantee it's all bullshit. I know everything that's going on. The number of bona fida treasure projects in South America you can count on one hand. There's nothing on Robinson Crusoe Island. This shit has been going around for years"!

Another claim of Mr Marx is that he can put 'Sir' in front of his name. He was made a 'Knight-commander in the Order of Isabella the Catholic' by the Spanish government for his re-enactment in the Nina 11 of Christopher Columbus' first voyage of exploration. And with over 60 books to his name does one ignore the comments of someone with much respect, knowledge and experience?

The 'damning'(if that is the right word) evidence against Keiser are the latitude and longitude figures that repeatedly appear for the Pinaki group of atolls. Also in code in the Webb letters, the D and M is so obvious and proof when you see the link to the Shepherd's Monument at Anson's ancestral home and the defining clue here of course with the cipher containing the same letters and by deciphering, the same latitude and longitude figures.

I admire Bernard Keiser, a lot of his time and money has gone into his project. He blindly believes he's got it right and that one day he'll find it. He is the only one with a licence to search and with a treasure he estimates to be worth $10 billion, his 25% cut of that makes it all worthwhile.

As this chapter is about clues gathered, I can take you back to a subtle one you probably missed. Back in Part 1 we talked about Trinidad Island, the Salvage Islands and Christian Cruise. Those stories have a familiar 'feel' to them now – a Spanish ship making for the home port but prevented from doing so and buried the treasure it was carrying on a lonely island. How the one survivor (the dying sailor of similar stories) gave him the marks on the rock – and we all know now what marks he was referring to. But most intriguing, - the latitude of the Salvage Islands is 30° 8′N i.e. the same figures as the Webb letter figures (30D8M). So somehow those figures were infused into the story Cruise gave but the longitude figures lost. These figures must have come down from the Spanish line as the secret of them from the English/Admiralty line died with Anson and Webb.

As we know, Rear-Admiral Robinson searched on the Salvages in 1813 and as a private venture he looked again in 1856. He found nothing but fragments of a story. He himself said in later years, to quote (in part) '....but thus it is all in history, truth and falsehood are mingled together in one gorgeous and brittle mass.'

The Current Situation

Anyone with a computer can look up links to the Treasure of the Tuamotus/Lima/Peru and Cocos Island. It soon becomes evident that the traditional story is still believed, and even today there are variations. In an earlier chapter, we mentioned how one researcher discovered that there was no Father Matteo in the church records of Pisco, and also no 14 tons of gold hidden in the crypt. So why did he not question the story, as we have? In our Pacific Island stories, one or two authors suspected something was wrong with this tale, but did not follow up their insight.

Some current variations available:

'During the war of the Pacific (1879-83) our Australian mercenaries stole 14 tons of gold from a church in Pisco, Peru.'

'December 1859 they landed on a small atoll in the Tuamoto Group.'
(So they buried it 20 years before the stole it!!)

'In 1859 several chests of treasure were stolen. Alvarez and Barrett killed in a brawl after the arrived in Australia in about 1850.'
(So killed before they stole it!!)

'After about 14 years Howe abandoned his search and returned to Tahiti. He then discovered that some Polynesians pronounce 't' by placing the top of the tongue under the top lip so it sounds like a 'p'. So could Pinaki possibly have been Tinaki? Howe scanned charts of the area and found a small island called Tuanaki. He visited Tuanaki and its neighboring islands and discovered one which contained all the features on the treasure map.'

'They buried most of the treasure on Pinaki or Raraka atolls, he (Howe) finally located part of the treasure on an island near Raraka.'

'Howe went back to Tahiti, he asked some of the natives about the Bosun Bird, the ship that originally sailed from Pisco with four sailors. They told him the ship did not anchor near Pinaki but at a different atoll. Island is located near Katiu and Makemo, coral pinnacle on the eastern side of the atoll, there is a pass just to the left of the pinnacle. There is a pear-shaped pool about 3 miles from the pass with 7 coral blocks nearby.'

'In 1913 Howe began a 13-year search which finally located part of the treasure on an island near Raraka.'

'Studying a pile of aerial photographs with a powerfull magnifying glass I found myself staring at Killorain's treasure island. There, on the edge of the lagoon was a pear-shaped pool and at the entrance to the lagoon stood a large column of coral. Surveyors had used the column as a triangulation point and gave its latitude and longitude as 16º49´ S and 144º 16´ W. An adventurer and his family traveled here in search of the treasure. He said the pear-shaped pool has silted up but is still visible from the air. Close to the pass of the lagoon he used a metal detector to search the coral debris and picked up a strong signal. He uncovered a hoard of over 130 silver and copper religious medallions. Subsequent analysis confirmed they were of South American origin and dated around 1830.'

Maybe from a wrecked ship carrying missionaries to the islands?

The following map identifies the atolls mentioned above

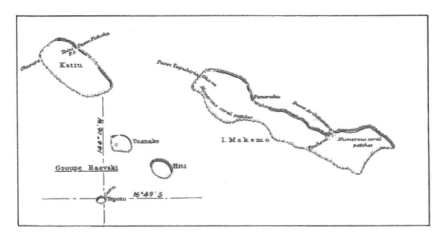

THE RAEVSKI GROUP OF ATOLLS WHERE A LOT OF THE ACTION TOOK PLACE

This group of atolls is approximately 360 nautical miles north-west of Pinaki and Raraka atoll is approximately 30 nm NW of Katiu. You can see the cairn (triangulation point) just NE on Tepoto

So the accepted treasure tale continues, and it is a good one. Maybe because it is now so ingrained in history *'and all the books say so, so it must be true'*, people cannot or will not accept it is not true. Well I have exposed the myth and shown the evidence, not only for the 'Loot of Lima' story but also Rennes-le-Château and the indisputable link to Anson. The Monument cipher has been solved confirming our findings and the Trinity Map is solved defining Pinaki as *the* treasure location. As a bonus, the Kidd/Palmer charts are finally shown for what they are; a gloriously deceptive hoax and cover-up. They never did, and never were, meant to be leading you to the hiding place of Captain Kidd's non-existent buried treasure. (I have previously mentioned that the only treasure ever found of Kidd's was the cache he buried on Gardiners Island and recovered soon after his capture.)

A Final Run-in with the Kidd Charts

This book originated because I had written a book about what were (pre-2000) believed to be Kidd's charts. Subsequent knowledge gleaned from a further 10 years' research for this book means that I can say, without any doubt whatsoever, by following these charts and newfound knowledge, you will ultimately be led (via JF and HLC islands) to Pinaki and Ubilla's treasure. We have seen also that Wilkins was privy to the Anson/Webb documents and hid part of that knowledge in the Key chart (the latitude and longitude relative to Cadiz). So it is fitting to end this chapter with the Kidd/Palmer charts, now that we know what the final goal was and see if anything else can be gleaned from them pertaining to Pinaki.

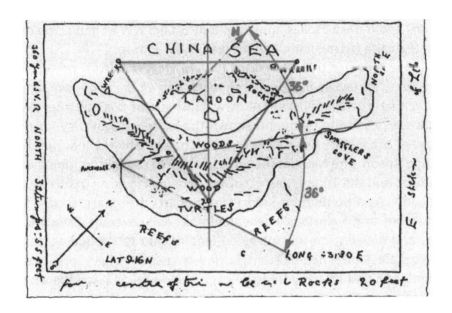

The previous image is part of the charts solution from my Kidd book. The dot at the 'Anchorage' and 'Smugglers Cove' suggests they should be joined. The fact that it immediately creates the all-important 36º angle from north confirms this. You need to go back to the 'Skull' chart in Part 3 to be reminded that '36NE 36NE' as it appears there has to be used on the Key chart (both charts have to be used together). The triangle was discovered when lining up the chart on my drawing board (the two circles mentioned previously having to be used). The wreck circles were exactly in line. I could quickly see that the centre of this line took you exactly through the odd shaped 'A' at the top, three circles and the 'T' in TURTLES. An almost perfect equilateral triangle can now be created. The point of the triangle is almost on the 'T' and you are meant to guess that this is where the Treasure is. To confirm this, there are three letters on the 'ridge' to the left; 'TA -- T'. i.e. 'Treasure at T'. Wilkins could even be saying, 'Treasure at Trinity!

The bottom boarder contains the words that more than likely originally read: *'fourth.......centre of triangle leads to Rocks 20 feet'*

'Fourth' could be queried because the 'f' is not how Wilkins shows it elsewhere. As a likely alternative, it could be a 'P' and the word more than likely 'Point'. So the bottom border message reads: *'Point of centre of triangle leads to rocks 20 feet'.* The triangle created then is that referred to in the border. It is important DNA, as you know, and is also pointing to the word 'TURTLES'. As declared back in the earlier chapter, it is highlighting the word as a hint that the chart must be turned upside down.

The wording in the right-hand border remains obscure; is the predominant word *'E.....Skeleton or Shelter'*? At the end of the day, it doesn't matter!

Both charts between them show sand, coral, reefs and lagoon. These are not features of JF (or HLC) Island so they must be for Pinaki, which has them all. The 'Skull' chart shows a smooth coastline, more akin to that of Pinaki. So could Wilkins, by virtue of the fact that it is banana-shaped, really be showing you the coastline and lagoon line of the main (centre) part of the atoll? Both charts are showing 'hatched lines running along the centre of the island; is he hinting here at the centre continuous higher rim of the atoll? If you refer back to the 'Skull' chart, you will notice an 'X' in the middle of the island, adjacent to where on the Key chart the point of the triangle is. Also *'........leads to Rocks..'.* in the margin. Could this mean the ebanin or coral block? A track is also shown leading to (or from) the 'X' going along the ridge. There are four conspicuous dots along it starting at the X. What are they for, unless indicating burial places? So maybe 'fourth' was the correct interpretation of that suspect word. On the other hand, Wilkins could have added them for fun... or confusion. Who knows, until we get there!

A final clue, and showing that Wilkins *does* have a sense of humour is his small drawing of a seahorse in the previous 'Key' chart. I have enlarged it below:

It is, of course, alluding to Anson via 'horse' and therefore 'herradura'. He couldn't resist putting something on that chart that related to Lord Anson, to be recognised only by those in the know.

Wilkins, as we know, is dropping hints to Pinaki, Anson and a Spanish Grandee all over the place. Here also then, within the charts is he giving more clues to a lonely atoll in the South Pacific Ocean? No one could ever have made the connection unless aware of the real and true story. This answers the question, 'If he is showing where 'treasure island' is through his clues, why would you need star codes?' You would need to know of the Anson/JF/Westcott connection. Wilkins knew a lot more than he let on. Well, not strictly true. He did 'let on' but only by following the trail and solving the clues did you find out what he did know. More importantly, you had to *know* there *was* a trail to be followed to start with.

If you could track Wilkins' articles down, you will come across a piece he wrote for *Modern Mechanix* in 1936. It tells of his planned expedition to find Kidd's treasure (it never happened!). When you sort out the misinformed familiar story of the charts and Palmer, you are left with a statement that again shows Wilkins knew all about our island in the South Pacific Ocean. I quote:

'Coral reefs abound...by day and night navigators must keep a sharp look-out and the lead going. It would be well to give this region a wide berth in foul weather, or in the dark. What better place for Kidd's lost treasure than this forbidden, mysterious sea of lone palm and coral islands?'

The previous chapters also answer the statement, 'having solved the Trinity Map, you don't need anything else!' Not quite true, of course. The map is giving the location of a group of islands, or atolls. The golden section triangle in relation to the Pinaki 'blob' helps to identify that group. Whilst our prior knowledge can identify Pinaki as 'the' island, the map doesn't pinpoint it. You need knowledge of the 'herradura' clue to identify which atoll.

The previous paragraph also helps to explain the statement I made earlier on in this book; *'It (Alchemy colour codes etc. GE) all 'thins' out later on in the book and becomes easier to understand even to the extent that some of it can be ignored.'*

So now, even coming towards the end of this book and thinking we've got it all down, things are still coming to light, mostly as a result of the progressive and ongoing research involved. It was never a case of I knew it all at the beginning, let's get it down in a book! Many important discoveries were made over a period of several years. For example, it wasn't until relatively recently that the Cadiz connection to the Key chart was made, and that only by thoroughly examining the nautical and navigational issues of the Trinity group. Although, you could say it was staring us in the face all along as I had previously mentioned it in my Kidd book!

Partway through this book (and research), I made another statement: *'The Kidd chart hoax, which when solved seemed to show how the Trinity Map was to be read and applied'.*

A surmise, you can now see, was very true

An Enigma Persists

For years, I have been baffled by, and greatly admired, what I can only call a 'convoluted conundrum'. Namely that one set of prime figures on the Key chart can be mathematically related to three different islands central to the quest.

These figures, as whole numbers, are 9 and 31. When combined with the latitude and longitude of JF Island (33 and 78), they produce the position of Pinaki. When employing the key code and meridian, they give us the position of HLC Island in the China Sea. On their own, when employing the key code and meridian, they again give us the position of Pinaki. Unbelievable! I still can't get my head around that. The creators of this enigma were quite brilliant, very lucky, or it's one hell of a coincidence these figures all worked to the same goal.

A final word on charts. A map with an 'X' marking a treasure location has been the traditional way of showing a 'treasure island' for hundreds of years, mainly due to books like *Treasure Island* and numerous films. The Kidd charts and others were created in a similar format because *that was the traditional depiction of them.* A fictional treasure map, created for whatever purpose, was expected to look like that. The Trinity Map you have seen is a **real** treasure map, looking nothing like what might be expected by the average reader. It is drawn in the form of a Spanish derrotero or waybill. It gives all you need to find our treasure island. There is no 'X' marks the spot because being Spanish, once on the island you know you have to look for a coded marker; in our case, a coral block.

When faced with the Trinity Map for the first time, it was a case of, 'How is anyone expected to sort that out? What do all those lines mean?' But the creator put it down to be read and followed by someone in the know. If not in the know, you are left floundering in the dark. Solving it first of all required a determination to do so, followed by logic, common sense, knowledge in the required field and a little luck. What I am getting at here is; nothing is insurmountable. It may take years, but the solutions and answers are there.

PART 10

ON TREASURE ISLAND

Here we are near the end of this remarkable story. All that is left is to work out where on our island lies Ubilla's treasure that *could* include items from the Jerusalem Temple. Whilst this story of the treasure makes a possible case for some of the Temple Treasure ending up on an atoll in the Pacific Ocean, I doubt it and can only base this book on what has been discovered and interpreted so far for that particular treasure.

Even though we are now at the outer edge of knowledge in regards to the history of the treasure, there are still some unique groups of what seem to be directional instructions that can be isolated in various writings that perhaps might lead to it. I am not saying these are right or wrong, just putting forth some observations. It is up to you if you want to use them. The author accepts no responsibility for blank holes in the sand if you choose to follow them! Before we start, there are some considerations that need to be kept in mind for the clues about to be given.

A semicircular coral atoll of the type suggested by the code word 'Horseshoe' has a profile where the island is thickest in depth of land mass towards the centre of the atoll's ring then tapers towards the beaches of the outer and inner lagoon. As suggested in an earlier chapter, it seems obvious that for maximum protection, any cached items would be buried towards the centre of the atoll's ring away from the erosive effects of tide and weather on the atoll's shoreline. The Spanish doctrine would have required the construction of a secure vault or crypt. This would have been easy to do in the limestone (the aged coral) which makes up the atoll's stable layer underneath the sand. Beneath that is basalt. The descriptions given in the linked stories. which talk of the treasure being in some type of rock vault or rock topped cave, seem to support this view. The doctrine also suggests that if started from a top surface rather than a slope or side, you have to dig down one Estado's depth to reach the entrance.

Other stories suggest there is more than one cache. Forbes' version for Cocos Island tells us the treasure was buried in the sand being placed on the underlying rock shelf (gold, because of its high density, will slowly sink through sand).

When you look at the list of treasure given in the Webb report, it talks about 864 bags of gold. These are probably made up of the Spanish gold Ubilla made off with. These bags were taken to the island in company with what *could* be items from Solomon's Temple. To fit all this together would then have required the construction of a vault of rather large dimensions. It is more likely that there are two (or even more) caches, but one at least is a small secure vault cut into the limestone to hold the most precious items from the Temple. As the ground surrounding the lagoon rises creating slopes each side, it is more likely a vault may have been constructed *into* the slope to avoid flooding. My only problem with this is there does not appear to be any steep slopes on Pinaki. The bulk Spanish gold may be buried as a separate cache (or caches) elsewhere in the sand or coral. This does raise an issue because the Spanish signs are indicative of just one location. There would have to be another set of signs if there is another vault. Maybe there are, or were! To add weight to this theory is the fact that the Spanish did not normally bury gold and silver together; they constructed separate vaults. There is also the strong evidence that Brown attacked the Australia to Britain gold specie ships (maybe three) and added this loot to the treasure already there. Another vault may have been required for this.

We also need to consider what happened when Webb recovered the treasure. After the storm, did he put it back in the exact same location he found it or somewhere else on the atoll? My guess is the same place; he wouldn't then have had to construct new vaults.

One of the interesting things to learn from the Japanese Tokugawa Treasure legend mentioned earlier is that the American identified the treasure had been moved from one mountain to another. This could be dismissed as being simply the mistranslation of Webb's report but mistranslating Webb's report this way goes on to infer the treasure was relocated to Juan Fernandez Island, completely outside the Trinity group. In the case of the Tokugawa Treasure, it was said to be moved to a new location but this new location was one of the mountains (islands) that made up a group of three. With all these considerations in mind, here are some clues and methods to find the treasure which were identified, that you might wish to try applying to the island:

1) Howe from Brown: We are able to deduce that Howe was following a special version of a lost treasure chart. It is unlikely this was original but a copy supplied by Brown, but did he leave any information off it? That the Trinity Map exists shows that two maps are probably required for this treasure. One, the Trinity Map that identifies where the group of atolls are and how many, and the second showing where on the atoll the treasure or coral block lies. Howe knew that the three or four dots on his map related to the layout of a group of atolls incorporating a triangular pattern but he also had some bearings to follow on the atoll. It appeared there were also markers in the form of trees or palms that had disappeared. This was also proof that there was more than one map. Though Howe was trying to obscure Captain Brown's directional instructions from others, we should be able to deduce what are original and what are Howe's later fabrications, to aid us in understanding how he was interpreting the map.

Another point to consider is that the original map, besides showing where the island is (the Trinity Map) would probably have included directions to the marked rock. These are the only directions required as the decoding of the signs shows where the treasure is buried. Brown then, knowing where the location was, maybe created a chart of his own based on that drawn by Alvarez, but with directions straight to the treasure. Howe thought he had all that was required off Brown to find the treasure, which is why he was confident enough to go off on his own. He never found anything so these directions were either altered in some way, contained misinformation or Brown deliberately left crucial information off. Alternatively, as stated, markers have been obliterated by time, maybe even by the natives unaware of what they were.

I have previously declared that I do not go along with previous theories that an island profile was depicted (or misinterpreted) on the Shepherd's Monument. In this case, another reason would be that if I was leaving a map with clues, it would have to include a profile of the atoll or part profile of the cachement area that could be recognised when on the atoll. With the exception of the wreath, there is nothing in the monument that can be obviously recognised as part of the profile of Pinaki.

I think it much more probable that *if* the sculpture was used, then it was because the robe outline shown in a previous chapter could depict an island and it was supposed to be JF Island. There is also the question brought up earlier in this book; who, 150/200 years ago, operating in the southern hemisphere, would have even been aware of the Shugborough estate and that it had a monument hiding a secret? How could anyone have known, outside The Royal Society, of Anson's involvement with a tiny atoll in the South Pacific Ocean? However, to continue:

As part of his story, Howe claimed he had located three caches on the island, a chest with jewellery, another chest with doubloons and the bulk gold in the lagoon. He claimed he reburied the jewellery from the 'pinacle' '84 feet E. by N., and 75 feet N. by E.' from the pinnacle. (Notice how similar this grouping of directions is to those on Wilkins charts W1 and W2?) Howe was possibly misinterpreting or expecting that on 'the island', there were separate caches buried at the points maybe marked by the smaller Masonic style three dot triangle that maybe made up the entire golden section triangle. The directions '84 feet E. by N., and 75 feet N. by E' are in the form of bearings found on other lost treasure maps but at these locations nothing was ever found by Hamilton. It could be, of course, that Howe subtlety changed his directions and 'E by N' and 'N by E' should have read NE. Surely they are one and the same? So both on the same line and nine feet apart!

Whilst Howe didn't find the two chests (that was a fabrication), he possibly did give the correct bearings to find the treasure to Hamilton, as far as he understood them. If Hamilton's group just happened to land on the right island, they then had the real bearings. The detail about the gold being in a pear-shaped pool was the truth as far as he knew it. Howe had probed around the area in the lagoon marked by this map. After eliminating any shallow areas of the lagoon he could access, a deep (pear-shaped) pool he could not access by default then became identified as the location for the gold.

The northwest sector, including the lagoon there, has been extensively excavated already, either by Howe or later searchers.

2) Spanish: Locate the marked rock on Pinaki atoll and follow the Spanish doctrinal instructions given by the symbols to locate the treasure (you will know from the *Spanish Signs and Symbols* chapter that the length of the vertical bar on the third symbol is very important as it equates to a distance). Here, they are again along with a picture of the Masonic Jewel for the 21st degree of the Scottish Rite. Strange, don't you think? An arrow in a triangle! Anyway, follow those signs:

We are, of course, relying on them having been accurately copied by Nordhoff. If not, then our previous interpretation of them may not be of much use but at least we know we are in the right area. At least with this book, you now have the knowledge to decode the signs, even if they are different to that depicted.

3) Masonic: Associate the horseshoe shape of Pinaki atoll with that of the Holy Royal Arch. If you do so, you will observe the keystone of the arch with its circle containing a dot (see above symbols) now equates to a position on the east side of the island. Try searching there about the centre of the atoll's ring.

3a) Masonic: Know that the east is an important direction for the Freemasons so head over to the east side of the atoll again and literally seek the Temple of Solomon. The Masonic lore is that the treasure is in Enoch's Vault over which the Temple of Solomon is built. Captain Brown supplied information to both Howe and the Gennessee expedition but where Howe searched the northwest sector of Pinaki, the Gennessee expedition, following Brown's instructions sought out a native temple on the east side of Tupai. This instruction was withheld from Howe and does conform with Masonic lore that the place to dig is under the Temple in the east. You will just have to determine the most eastern part of the island. There is no way to actually plot out the dimensions of the Temple to determine its central point because these are solar Temples taking their alignment from the sun in its annual travel through the seasons. For example, the position of the pillar known to Freemasons as Jachin on the northeast side of the entrance door is determined by the sun at its summer solstice, the southeast pillar Boaz, uses the winter solstice (in the northern hemisphere). East is determined by the sun when it reaches the middle of these two extremes. The positioning for a Temple in Jerusalem would be different for one plotted here. Go to the east anyway and then track back west to see if you can discover the top of the vault. The Freemasons suggest some sort of capstone is to be found with a ring in it. You could build a tripod like the Freemasons use with a block and tackle attached to pull up the capstone. There is a not well known variation on this which says the entrance way to the chamber with the treasure is to be found in the southwest corner of the Temple; again, search for the ringed stone that you pull up.

4) Alternatively, you have the option from a previous chapter that the Trinity Map is showing a profile of Pinaki and the landing place of the treasure. So if everything else fails, the southeast corner of the atoll is where to start looking. To back this up, look at the repeated NE and 'North Same as East'. If we assume north is east on the Pinaki chart, then NE is same as southeast This next clue group seems to be using a method so arcane it just sounds like it might be the right one. The author Robert Charroux, who you know was aware of the treasure, did provide a further set of directional instructions amongst the other details given in his book. These are again attributed to have come from Keating having been given to him along with a map by 'Thompson'.

Disembark in the Bay of Hope between islets, in water five fathoms deep. Walk 350 paces along the course of the stream then turn NNE for 850 yards, stake, setting sun stake draws the silhouette of an eagle with wings spread. At the extremity of sun and shadow: cave marked with a cross. Here lies the treasure.

Personally, I would treat these Thompson/Keating instructions with some suspicion and maybe even ridicule, as who is going to step out half a mile? (850 yards.) It is just not practical on an atoll this small (or anywhere else!). Instructions out of necessity would and should be kept simple. The same goes for star/Sun sighting and rods etc. Too complex, you just need a starting point, angular bearings in relation to North and distance(s). In other words; the Spanish signs! These directions are a fabrication and more than likely meant for Cocos Island. But, I have to show you, the reader, the options. Maybe by now you have some ideas of your own. All I can add to these dubious Keating instructions is, was he surreptitiously hiding the fact that he knew about the star and Bible code? Reference to an eagle should trigger the memory. I mentioned in an earlier chapter that the star Antares is represented by the symbol of an eagle. The Book of John in the Bible code is alluded to by an eagle or bird, usually represented by the carving of wings. It is more food for thought.

Some of the above theories you can see are treating the GS triangle as a clue to the location of separate caches, separated by the angles of this triangle but with no hint as to the scale of it or distances involved. More evidence then that as shown in a previous chapter, the GS triangle is there purely to show the layout of the atolls relative to Pinaki.

Alternatively, you might not worry about the above directions; just take appropriate detecting equipment. Not as straightforward as it sounds. A typical hand-held metal detector – even the expensive ones would be useless here. You have to have a machine capable of 10ft depth on a large mass and one that will work in a saline environment. You also have to work between palm trees! Having been a detectorist for many years I can tell you the equipment that will work satisfactorily here is very limited. A pulse machine is probably best. They are very expensive and look nothing like a conventional detector. They are usually found in use underwater looking for wrecks and artefacts but are easily adapted for land use. Your search would start in the vicinity of the coral block utilising the measurements already deciphered out of the signs. Search along the highest part then along the slopes down to the lagoon, away from the ravages of tempest, typhoon and tsunami. An amount of gold and/or silver that large should be quickly located with the right equipment. The block with the Spanish signs is the key; let us hope it is still there. Which brings me to the next point; is the treasure still there? Will this book start a stampede to the South Pacific? If you, dear reader, are one of those contemplating this, please read on.

First of all appreciate the treasure may have already been removed by an expedition or person(s) in total secret, unknown to me or anyone else. This book tells you where it is (or was) located. I can give no guarantee it is still there but I would be very surprised if it wasn't!

Nothing is straightforward for anyone contemplating a search here. Pinaki was very well chosen to hide this treasure. You cannot fly here. Even on the closest island (Nukutavake) there are no hotels, accommodation or restaurants. No internet or broadband, indeed communication with the outside world is still letter and steampacket! Although as I write this I believe broadband and mobile phones etc. are slowly creeping further out of Tahiti into the east Pacific.

Even if you can get to Nukutavake, unless you have your own boat you have to rely on one of the locals taking you to Pinaki. There is no guarantee on this. As with most small boat trips, you are at the mercy of the wind and weather, so it is important to go at the right time of year. It is not easy to land on Pinaki because of the reefs and people have in the past lost their lives here. Having arrived and again because of the unpredictable weather, there is no guarantee your local boatman can come back and take you off when requested. So you have to take enough food, maybe even tents, – just in case you get stuck there for an unpredictable time like Robinson Crusoe. Also be aware that the natives of Nukutavaki farm coconuts here and are therefore regular visitors, any treasure hunting expedition is not likely to go unnoticed by them.

A word of caution; when metal detecting, one must be aware that all land belongs to someone and permission must be sought. The same applies here. This is just metal detecting on a much bigger scale. These islands and atolls are in French Polynesia and so belong to them. Before embarking on any expedition, permission to search must be obtained from the French Government. Then a deal should be negotiated to determine how much the finder gets, before any digging is carried out. None of this is simple or straight forward; for example, should a treasure be found, who does it belong to: France, Spain, England or Chile? I have also been advised that Pinaki belongs to the people of Nukutavake, the atoll just to the north of Pinaki. So ownership could be something of a minefield! But also realise that after all your work, expedition planning, team gathering and costs involved, you may not obtain permission to search! In these circumstances, should you be unwise enough to go ahead anyway, be aware that everything, including anything found, is likely to be confiscated. If, on the other hand, permissions are sought that lead to a profitable conclusion, a gold bar or two would not go unappreciated for my little bit of input!

If you do go (See Postcript 1 below), most, if not all the research work has already been done for you in this book. The problems and hard work will begin when you find the treasure!

Good Luck

Postscript 1) During the many years of writing and research, I was often asked "Are you going to go and look for it?" My reply was I could never afford it and it needs more than one person, also, as with my Kidd book, this book was written specifically to tell the story and show the solutions to enduring mysteries. Ideally of course if I was going to go out there I needed a tv production company to fund an expedition and film it for a documentary, this in return for film rights. Many letters and calls to producers fell on deaf ears. They seem not able to look beyond their office window but when a story they rejected turns out big, they fall over themselves backwards trying to get it! Responses usually said "Have you found it?" or "We would want to see the book first." With the latter reply, of course it is then too late! Once the book is out, so is the secret. So any search for the treasure needed to be done prior to publication. You may (or may not) be pleased to know that by the time you are reading this I/we will have been to Pinaki. I was surprised by an offer I initially didn't' expect from a contact who, as it turned out, now knowing him as well as I do – I should have not been surprised by! He, as it happens, has a relative in the tv and film world and the rest as they say is........ So it's a case of 'watch this space' and maybe look out for a sequel to this book. The fact that there may not be any headline news about a discovery does not mean that nothing was found! Some things have to be kept quiet until the right time.

Postscript 2) I was asked, "What's next? Any other books?" I am already on to other things but during completing of this book, I came across some intriguing documents relating to John (Henry?), Avery, or 'Avery the Pirate'. If genuine, then Avery did indeed bury a treasure (he accumulated more than any other pirate during his brief career) and not amongst shaded palm trees on a distant shore, but here in the UK! So who knows....?

Also, recently another old (genuine) Spanish treasure map turned up. Sent by a collegue who couldn't get anywhere with it. I immediately recognised certain things, a tenuous link to Anson's gold and thought 'here we go again!' But, as with Avery, it will all have to wait. I have a plaque on my office door;

'Due to the current workload, the light at the end of the tunnel has been turned off.'

Says it all really!

PASS INTO THE LAGOON, PINAKI. THE PHOTOGRAPH SHOWS THAT THIS ATOLL HAS A LOW PROFILE

ADDENDUM

STAR CODES

The Star Code, Practical Calculations

From the table, we have a SHA for Antares of 112º 31'. 5 and 26º 27' Declination.

Using the alchemic code of adding the opposites we get 112º31' 5 + 26º27' = 138º58' 5. We can easily round this up to **139º**. You can see this figuratively is the longitudinal position for Pinaki. But this is achieved without any reference to the point of Aries.

At this stage, we have to look at real figures for the early 18th century and time of day for star fixing.

From data available, astronomical twilight on Pinaki is 20 hrs. UT (Universal Time) is -9hrs. For most purposes, UT is now identical to GMT, also known as Zulu Time.

Pinaki twilight time is therefore 20 - 9 = 11.00 hrs.

For Pinaki on 17th January, at this time Aries is approximately 281º .

For ballpark figures add 48' to 2008 Aries values for 1761, so it is now approx. 282º

For Antares a SHA of 116º18' and Declination of 25º52'.7S applies.

For Elnath a SHA of 282º11' .9 and Declination of 28º22'.9N applies. (Note, our star values have changed by approximately 4º in 250 years.)

Replicating the above formula for El Nath, i.e. Star GHA = RA (SHA) + Aries GHA

(Because star measurement accuracy at sea up to mid-18th century was only + or - 1º, we can use our figures as whole numbers).

So, 282 + 282 = 564, minus 360 = 204º GHA which equates to **156º E, Dec 28º 23N**.

Applying same for Antares: 116 + 282 = 398, minus 360 = 38º GHA which equates to **322º E, Dec 25º 52S**

Let us now decode the other phrase, 'Longitude for the observation point is direction Great Charioteer depth fifteen degrees'.

This phrase is referring to the prime star of the constellation Aurigae (Magnum Aurigae), which is the star Capella. You will note Webb is giving a 'depth', in other words a negative 'latitude' of 15 degrees in this code phrase.

Capella = Alpha Aurigae

Applying same previous principles:

For Capella, a SHA of 285º13'.8 and Declination of 46º'44' N applies.

Aries is same at 282

So, 285 + 282 = 567, minus 360 = 207 GHA which equates to **153º E, Dec 46º 44'N**

Applying the code which says to use opposites figures i.e. long. minus lat.

153-15=**138º**

For our latitude (declination), we use the declination values of Capella and Elnath: 46º 44'-28º 23'=17º21'

Add the 'hidden' coded figure of 2º from the Latin phrase and we get **19º 21, the latitude of Pinaki almost exactly.**

A clever code. You can see that without knowing the code key, although being designated certain stars, you could never arrive at the latitude and longitude of Pinaki.

The application of N, S, E or W doesn't come into it because Webb knew where he was going in terms of which part of the globe.

Regarding the 139 derived from Antares, you would have to know that the SHA and Dec figures (RA) were to be added together.

But we are still left with Antares and the 'impossible' value of 322º, so how to resolve this? You apply previous coded principles:

Add lat and long of Elnath i.e. 156º+28º 23' = 184º23'

Take this figure from long of Antares; 322-184=**138.**

From a practical navigating point of view we must also be aware that a navigator in the South Pacific i.e. in the Southern Hemisphere, would not necessarily be able to view our Prime stars.

The Star Codes and Their Cipher Calculations

Working with modern tables that assigns a value closer to 246 for Antares, in the 18th century the SHA value in ephemeral tables for Antares would be about 116º18.6', equivalent to the old RA of 244º41.4', (notice how close this is to the 244º30' angle going through the atolls in the GR. Layout 1, in an earlier chapter) we can say 245º. As 246 was the number which appeared in the 19th and 20th century stories studied, the persons who were giving this value were then using later tables. It was therefore necessary to use 246 when disassembling the code fragments in the stories to learn what the formula keys were. Any code therefore would have to take into account that the value for Aries and a stars position change as well as another factor not immediately apparent. Even though it looks like astronavigation is being used, these stars were not selected because a sailor quadranted their position from the deck of a ship in the South Seas in 1761. They were chosen because they had ulterior meanings. We therefore only need to use the ephemeral tables as a cipher clerk would use a code book; to take a code name (the star) then look up a number assigned to it and apply a key (the formula) to encode/decode it.

A quick calculation will reveal that using the value of 245 and subtracting this from 360 will give us 115 (equivalent to SHA). As this number appears as one of the bearing sets on the Alphamap and is the figure '?15SE' alluded to on the (Wilkins) Kidd/Palmer 'Skull' chart, then you should also be suspecting it has some other importance apart from just being the reciprocal of 245º. Whether then we are talking about 246/114 or 245/115, we are still talking about Antares.

The Mathematical 2nd Key

We are working on the phrase 'Altitude Schuba 1 Depth Aurigae 1' from one of Anson's documents which is 'Altitude Antares Depth El Nath'. Though 'altitude' and 'depth' may sound as if reference is being made to measurements in the single dimension of height, it is actually two dimensions being referred to. This misunderstanding may have been because the same word in Latin 'altitudo' can be used for both altitude and depth. You have to assign the meanings to the words as if quantifying a three-dimensional object in its height, width and depth. 'Altitude' is therefore referring to longitude and 'depth' is referring to latitude.

The key is a formula which uses the RA and Dec of each star as the factors in an overall computation modified by one of two sub-rules/calculations predicated on whether the star is being used to encode longitude or latitude.

The overall computation is that you need to add the stars 'opposites', that being its longitude (RA converted to degrees) to its latitude (Dec), but you must use either:

Sub-rule 1: For a star used to encode longitude, you must convert its RA to SHA (i.e. 360 minus RA) first, before adding the Dec.

Or Sub-rule 2: For a star used to encode longitude, you add the RA to the Dec and subtract 90 from the sum.

Consulting astronomical tables for the stars in each constellation for the 1950 equinox will produce the following data:

Antares = Alpha Scorpii
RA: 16h 26min. 20.206sec (246.5º). DEC: -26º19' 21.95

El Nath = Gamma Aurigae=Beta Tauri
RA: 5hr 23min 7.71sec (80.75º). DEC: +28º 34' 1.74"

For the star Antares if used to encode longitude (altitude): RA = 246.5º

Sub-rule 1, 360-246.5 = 113.5

Adding opposites of stars longitude and latitude is 113.5 + 26 = **139.5º longitude**.

For the star El Nath if used to encode latitude (depth): RA = 80.75º

Adding opposites of stars longitude and latitude is 80.75 + 28 = 108.75

Sub-rule 2, 108.75 - 90 = **18.75º latitude (19º).**

Because star measurement accuracy at sea at this time was no better than + or - 1, we can use our figures as whole numbers. Even so, the nomination of the position of 139º longitude 19º latitude is immediately recognisable as pertaining somehow to Pinaki Atoll. It is even achieved without any reference to the point Aries.

Of course, anyone without knowledge of astronavigation could accept this for Pinaki. But it is pretty close to that island and could be treated with some suspicion, implying that the documents were modern fakes, the creators not appreciating the implications of time, star movements and measuring datums. The pros and cons are as follows.

The encoding method of using a stars name, which is then converted into a numerical value via an encryption formula, cannot produce the exact value for your nominated location anyway. Only at best a position in the near vicinity. You have to use what stars you can, those that produce a value near to what you require. So far though, all that has been produced is the above rather involved explanations requiring the author's interpretations and claims of discovering the keys for formulas requiring intricate sub-rules to make them fit. To dispel any doubts in response to the above con, the same key (addition of opposites) and methodology will be used to decrypt any further codes we come across. These will consistently produce the same answers as to proof of the key's validity.

Let us now decode then the other phrase; 'Longitude for the observation point is direction Great Charioteer depth fifteen degrees'. This phrase is referring to the Prime star of the constellation Aurigae (Magnum Aurigae) which is the star Capella. The trouble is only one star has been nominated but we have the extra coded clue 'depth fifteen degrees'.

Capella = Alpha Aurigae

RA: 5h 12min 59.5sec. (78º). DEC: +45º 56' 58

Adding opposites of stars longitude and latitude is 78 + 45 = 123

Now add the coded 'latitude/depth' of 15º = 123 + 15 = **138º**

BIBLIOGRAPHY

Andrews, Richard & Schellenberger, Paul, *The Tomb of God*, Little Brown & Co., 1996

Anson, George, *A Voyage Around the World*, 1748

Baigent, Michael, Leigh, Richard & Lincoln, Henry, *The Holy Blood and the Holy Grail*, London: Arrow Books, 1996

Baigent, Michael, Leigh, Richard & Lincoln, Henry, *The Messianic Legacy*, Corgi Books, 1986.

Barruel, Abbé Augustin, *Memoirs Illustrating the History of Jacobism*, 18th Cent.

Bartram, John, *The Making of the Oak Island Mystery* .www

Beard, Charles, *The Romance of Treasure Trove*, London: Sampson Low Marston & Co., 1933

Becke, Louis, *Pacific Tales*, 1897

Borrow, George, *The Bible in Spain*, 1843

Boudet, Henrie, *La Vraie Langue Celtique*, 1886

Burstein, Dan, *Secrets of the Code*, London: Weidenfield & Nicholson, 2004

Brisay, Judge Mather Des, *History of Lunenburg County*, 1870

Brookesmith, Peter, *Incredible Phenomena*, London: Orbis, 984

Byrne, Patrick, *Templar Gold*, California: Blue Dolphin Publishing, 2001

Byron, Kenneth, *Lost Treasures in Australia & New Zealand*, Sydney: Ure Smith, 1964

Campbell, Malcom, *Searching for Pirate Treasure in Cocos Island*, New York: Frederick Stokes Company, 1932

Carson, Mary, *Handbook of Treasure Signs and Symbols*, Deming: Cache Press, 1980

Charroux, Robert, *Treasures of the World*, New York: Paul S Erickson Inc, 1966

Chastain, Dayne, *Follow the Signs*, Seminole: Twinke Publishing, 1997

Chetwood, John, *Our Search for the Missing Millions*, South Sea Publishing Co., 1904

Cleator, P.E., *Treasure for the Taking*, London: Robert Hale Ltd, 1960

Clifford, Barry, *Return to Treasure Island*, New York: HarperCollins, 2003

Cooper, James, *Sea Lions*, 1849

Cooper, Robert L.D., *Cracking the Freemason's Code*, Rider, 2006

Crooker, William, *Oak Island Gold*, Halifax: Nimbus Publishing, 1993

Crooker, William, *Tracking Treasure*, Halifax: Nimbus Publishing, 1998

Driscoll, Charles, *Doubloons*, New York: Farrar & Rhinehart, 1930

Edmunds, George, *Kidd the Search for His Treasure*, Pentland Press, 1996

Elms, Charles, *The Pirates Own Book*, Salem: Marine Research Society, 1924

Gardner, Laurence, *The Shadow of Solomon*, Harper Element, 2005

Gessler, Clifford, *Road My Body Goes*, New York: Reynal and Hitchcock, 1937

Goodwin, Malcom, *The Holy Grail*, UK: Penguin Books, 1994

Gosse, Philip, *The History of Piracy*, New York: Tudor Publishing Co., 1932

Gosse, Philip, *The Pirates' Who's Who*, Modern Reprint

Fanthorpe, Lionel & Patricia, *Secrets of Rennes-le-Château*, Maine: Samuel Weiser Inc., 1992

Farwell, George, *The Treasure of Tuamotu*, The Queenslander, 1937

Fitts, James Franklin, *Captain Kidd's Gold*, A.L. New York: Burt, 1888

Fredea, Josophene, *Collier's Magazine*, 1905

Furneaux, Robert, *On Buried and Sunken Treasure*, UK: Longman Young Books, 1973

Furneaux, Robert, T*he Money Pit Mystery*, New York: Dodd Mead & Co., 1972

Haggard, Rider H. *King Solomon's Mines*, 1885

Harris, Graham, *Treasure & Intrigue, The Legacy of Captain Kidd*, Dundurn, 2002

Harris, Graham & Macphie, Les, *Oak Island and its Lost Treasure*, Formac Distributing Ltd, 1999

Haagensen, Erling & Henry, Lincoln, *The Templars Secret Island*, New York: Barnes & Noble Books, 2004

Hamilton, George, *The Treasure of the Tuamotus*, New York: Stanley Paul & Co Ltd, 1939

Hancock, Ralph & Weston, Julian, *The Lost Treasure of Cocos Island*, New York: Thomas Nelson & Sons ,1960

Hayden, Kevin, *Port of Pirate Treasure*, A Marine History Publication, undated

Haydock, Tim, *Treasure Trove*, New York: Henry Holt & Co., 1986

Inman, Herbert, *Royal Arch Working Explained*, London: Spence & Co.,1933

Joltes, Richard E., *Critical Enquiry*, www

Kemp, Peter & Lloyd, Christopher, *Brethren of the Coast*, Heinemann, 1960

Kenworthy, Charles, *Treasure Signs Symbols Shadows and Sun Signs*, California: Quest Publishing,1991

Kenworthy, Charles, *Spanish Monuments & Trail Markers to Treasure*, California: Quest Publishing, 1993

Knight, Edward, *The Cruise of the Alerte*, London: Longmans Green & Co., 1904

Knight, Richard, *Treasure*, UK: Penguin Books, 1986

Lafond, Gabriel de Lurcy, *Voyages Autour du Monde*

Langdon, Robert, *Pacific Islands*, Monthly Magazine

Latcham, Richard, *El Tesore De Los Pirates De Guayacan*, 1935

Layton, Lou, *The Spanish Code to Treasure*, 2004

Lincoln, Henry, *The Holy Place*, Corgi Books, 1991

Mackenzie, Donald, *Myths and Traditions of the South Sea Islands*, London: The Gresham Publishing Co. Ltd, 1930

Mann, William, *The Knights Templar in the New World*, Destiny Books, 2004

Mann, William, *The Templar Meridians*

Nesmith, Robert, *Dig for Pirate Treasure*, New York: Bonanza Books, 1958

Nettleton, Stuart, *The Alchemy Key*, 2004

Nickel, Joe, *The Secrets of Oak Island*, Sceptical Enquirer Magazine, 2000

Nobili, Riccardo, *The Gentle Art of Faking*, Philadelphia: J B Lippincott Co., 1922

Nordhoff, Charles, *Faery Lands of the South Seas*, 1921

Oscar, Alan (William Boultbee Whall), *Captain Kid's Millions*, London: Chapman & Hall, 1897

Pacific Promotion, *L'ile au Tresor*, Tahiti, 1996

Paine, Ralph, *The Book of Pirate Treasure*, London: Heinemann, 1911

Phillips, Graham, *The Chalice of the Magdalene*, Vermont: Bear & Co., 2004

Phillips, Graham, *The Templars and the Ark of the Covenant*, Vermont: Bear & Co., 2004

Pickett, Mike, *Treasure Hunters Field Notebook*, California: THU Publishing, 2001

Platt, Cameron & Wright, John, *Treasure Islands*, Colorado: Fulcrum Publishing, 1993

Price, Jim, *Spanish Signs and Symbols Made Simple*, Arkansas: Shadow Publishing, 2000

Prodgers, Cecil, *Adventures in Peru*, New York: E P Dutton, 1925

Putnam, Bill & Wood, John Edward, *The Treasure of Rennes-Le-Château*, Sutton Publishing, 2003

Reiseburg, Harry Lieut., *My Compass Points to Treasure*, London: Collins, 1957

Reiseburg, Harry Lieut., *I Dive For Treasure*, New York: Frederick Fell Inc., 1970

Robinson, Hercules Rear-Admiral, *Sea Drift*, Portsea, 1858

Sede, Gerade De, *La Tresor Maudit de Rennes-le-Château*, 1967

Shaffer, Steven, *Of Men and Gold*, 1994

Snow, Edward Rowe, *True Tales of Pirates and their Gold*, 1953

Snow, Edward Rowe, *True Tales of Buried Treasure*, New York: Dodd Mead & Co., 1955

Spruce, Richard, *Notes on a Botanist on the Amazon and the Andes*, 1908

Sterndale, Handley Bathurst, *My Adventures and Researches in the Pacific*, Canberra: Mulini Press, 2001

Stevenson, Robert, *Treasure Island*, 1883

Stewart, Fred, *Interpretations of Treasure Signs and Symbols*, 1988

Verrill, Hyatt, *The Real Story of the Pirate*, London: D Appleton & Co., 1923

Verrill, Hyatt, *They Found Gold*, Rio Grande Press, 1936

Villard, Bernard, *Le Vieux 'Charley'*

Wagner, Kip, *Pieces of Eight*, New York: Dutton, 1967

Westcott, Anthony, *El Tesoro De Lord Anson*, Santiago: Sociedad Las Orcas Ltda., 1999

Wilkins, Harold T., *Hunting Hidden Treasures*, New York: E P Dutton, 1929

Wilkins, Harold T., *Modern Buried Treasure Hunters*, New York: E P Dutton, 1934

Wilkins, Harold T., *Modern Mechanix Hobbies and Inventions Magazine*, 1936

Wilkins, Harold T., *Pirate Treasure*, New York: E P Dutton, 1937

Wilkins. Harold T., *Captain Kidd and His Skeleton Island*, New York: Liveright Publishing, 1937

Wilkins, Harold T., *Treasure Hunting*, Boston: Bruce Humphries Inc., 1939

Wilkins, Harold T., *Panorama of Treasure Hunting*, New York: E P Dutton, 1940

Wilkins, Harold T., *New Facts About Mysterious Captain Kidd and His Skeleton Island Chests*, Kansas: Haelderman Julius Publications, 1947

Wilkins, Harold T., *Mysteries of Ancient South America*, 1945

Wilkins, Harold T., *A Modern Treasure Hunter*, Kansas: C & J Temple Ltd., 1948

Wright, Theon, *The Voyage of the Herman*, New York: Hawthorn Books, 1966

Young, John K, *Sacred Sights of the Templar Knights*

ACKNOWLEDGEMENTS

Not as many as one might expect as this was a new investigation on a new subject. Books that proved useful during research are listed in the Bibliography, on the previous pages.

I have gone to great lengths to establish copyright ownership of material it was necessary to use, in particular that contained in H.T. Wilkins' books. Whilst a lot of his material is suspect, I nevertheless acknowledge the source and inspiration. He told colourful stories in his own style and I am grateful he recorded a lot of the Kidd/Palmer history, even if some of it is questionable. Most of the photographic material used in his books relating to that subject was not owned by Wilkins but by Mrs Dick who passed on copyright and authority to Mr A. Howlett (instumental in publishing an account of the Kidd charts in the 1950s). He subsequently passed authority on to me for my Kidd book, published in 1996. As stated in that book, many attempts have been made to contact Maurice Taylor, last known owner of the Kidd charts, or chart. The charts' whereabouts are a complete mystery, not that it matters anymore, as you will see.

Owing to the upheaval and changes in the publishing world over the last 20 years or more (takeovers etc.), rights in some books have changed ownership sometimes several times. It is quite common for publishers not to be aware even of their rights in a particular book. To compound the problem, some of the books quoted from are in Spanish! All this has made it very difficult, sometimes impossible, to establish copyright ownership. Any copyright holders not contacted because of the aforementioned problems and the fact that most publications consulted are now long out of print, I thank in advance and ask that they contact the publishers so that proper acknowledgement can be made in any future editions.

One of the Spanish books, in particular *El Tesoro de Lord Anson* by Anthony Westcott is a fairly recent publication, even so and despite having an email contact address for a descendant of the author, no contact could be made with the family. The lot of the author is not an easy one!

Some people I would like to mention: Mike Neon, of course, already mentioned in the Introduction, for his early research and input; he started me out on this project but unfortunately abandoned it halfway through. Philip Masters (deceased) USA, instrumental in finding Blackbeard's wreck off North Carolina; a friend, always helpful, and remembered with great affection.

Blue Dolphin Publishing and Patrick Byrne for help regarding the Freemasons and also permission to quote from his *Templar Gold*. Mike O'Dougherty for help with astronavigation. Lou Layton (Spanish Signs) USA, and also Steve Schaefer USA. Geoff Bath of www.innertraditions.com for permission to quote from William Mann's *The Knights Templar in the New World*. Photograph of Ubilla's gold whistle courtesy of Sotheby's Inc. 1993. I have to mention Hawthorn Books Inc. of New York City; their work *The Voyage of the Herman* by Theon Wright contained a lot of crucial information but alas, efforts to contact them failed.

Thanks Ron and Alex Hill for help with proofreading and computer work, in particular with my Kidd and Anson website. My agent Susan Mears for her help, encouragement and endeavours in getting this book to print. Chris Day of Filament Publishing Ltd for believing in my work. Last but not least; my partner Julia for her unfailing encouragement and support.

Lightning Source UK Ltd.
Milton Keynes UK
UKOW06f0728120816

280535UK00001B/41/P